Some Descendants
of
Michael and
Sarah (Catlin)
MITCHELL

I0105266

of
Connecticut and Massachusetts

1694-1988

Compiled by
Marilyn Jordan-Solari

HERITAGE BOOKS
2008

HERITAGE BOOKS

AN IMPRINT OF HERITAGE BOOKS, INC.

Books, CDs, and more—Worldwide

For our listing of thousands of titles see our website
at
www.HeritageBooks.com

Published 2008 by
HERITAGE BOOKS, INC.
Publishing Division
100 Railroad Ave. #104
Westminster, Maryland 21157

Copyright © 1988 Marilyn Jordan-Solari

All rights reserved. No part of this book may be reproduced or
transmitted in any form or by any means, electronic or mechanical,
including photocopying, recording or by any information storage
and retrieval system without written permission from the author,
except for the inclusion of brief quotations in a review.

International Standard Book Numbers
Paperbound: 978-1-55613-141-7
Clothbound: 978-0-7884-7470-5

In loving memory
of my mother
Mabel Ruth (Redman) Jordan
1902 - 1970

§

And to my grandchildren
(in order of their birth)

Christopher Jordan Wahl
Anna Francesca Manta
Erik Ricardo Pasalagua
Jeri Lynne Wahl

§

"Let us, before we die, gather up our heritage,
and offer it to our children." - Will Durant.

TABLE OF CONTENTS

Table of Contents

PREFACE

On a rainy winter day early in 1976, I happened upon a bundle of family letters and postcards that had come to me at my mother's death. This correspondence, dating back to the early 1900's, was written by various Mitchell great-aunts and uncles, my Mitchell great-grandmother, and grandmother, and one by my grandfather detailing the death of my grandmother at a tragically early age.

To make sure I had properly identified all persons mentioned in this correspondence, I turned to a copy of a family history written and privately published in the 1960's by my mother's eldest sister, Clara Lue (Redman) Hopp. The more I read about the ancestors and descendants of my grandmother, Nettie Jane (Mitchell) Redman, the more fascinated I became. So it was that I entangled myself in the absorbing and relentless grip of genealogical research, a total redirection of my life.

Flawed though it may be in early ancestral lineages, the Nettie Jane (Mitchell) Redman book was the greatest legacy I could have received, an invaluable stepping stone to the past. Without its inspiration, I may never have begun my search.

Twelve years later I am prepared to present the story of this particular Mitchell family, certainly not in its entirety, but in as complete a form as I find possible at this point. This is primarily a male-line genealogy. Most female lines are not followed beyond the first generation of children under the new surname since there was far too little data to allow tracing those lines to the present day. However, female lines in several of the most recent generations have been continued up to the present day, allowing living descendants to trace their ancestry back to the first generation.

All male lines are traced as far as the extent of information available to me. In some cases, this proves extensive. Where little data is presented, I hope enough exists to allow today's descendants to connect with this lineage, or at least find their way pointed toward areas of research which will result in making that family connection.

The book begins in 1694 in a small Connecticut village. From there it moves to Massachusetts and then on to New York and Vermont before beginning the move westward. I have a great deal to say about some of these ancestors, very little to say about others, depending on what material I've been lucky enough to find. I hope to show you something of the conditions under which they lived, the problems they faced, and the stalwart sturdiness with which they coped with life as it was for them. I do not intend to give history lessons, but since history is inseparable from genealogy, historical facts must be introduced at times for a more thorough understanding of these ancestor's lives.

The compilation of this work has been made possible in a number of different ways. I have written literally thousands of letters, including a good many to relatives, asking for family data. I have spent hundreds of hours hunched over microfilm readers, viewing census and other filmed records, and have amassed a considerable collection of deed records, marriage, death, cemetery, church, probate, and civil court records. Where applicable, Revolutionary War, War of 1812, and Civil War records have been obtained from National and State Archives. Untold hours have been spent in libraries searching books of vital records, and early

Preface

genealogical compilations and histories. Membership in genealogical societies across the country has put me in touch with others interested in the same line, and I have traveled to as many areas of the country as I could to visit the places where some of these ancestors lived.

There are far too many people to be thanked for their help with this project to list them all, although credit has been given those generous people throughout the book. Special mention must be made of Jean McVicker Jackson of Zionsville, IN who for so many years was a most interested and zealous co-researcher. Special thanks must also be made to those of you who so patiently filled out and returned family data forms; and to the various county clerks and recorders, librarians and archivists who have answered my requests for information. Last, but not least, I thank my husband for painstakingly proofreading this manuscript, for his valued criticisms, and for silently bearing with such inconveniences as late and hasty dinners and delayed housework, the results of my persistent love affair with the history of this family.

I sincerely hope others will take up this search where I've left off, discover and correct my errors (for there will surely be errors, despite all caution), and fill in the gaps I have regrettably left.

Marilyn Jordan-Solari
64 E. Elkin St.
Sonora, CA 95370
1988

EXPLANATIONS AND ABBREVIATIONS

This genealogy uses a consecutive numbering system designed for easy determination of a person's ancestors or descendants. Arabic numbers flush with the left margin are individual paragraph numbers and are part of the parental column. Slightly indented numbers under each parental sketch are childrens' numbers which become paragraph/parental numbers only when they are carried on into the next generation. Thus paragraph #680 in Generation 11 becomes child #680 under paragraph #576 in Generation 10, #576 being the parent of #680. Continue back in this way or reverse the procedure to trace children forward.

All numbered children's names appear in boldface type. Only those children carried into the next generation also have numbers printed in boldface with a corresponding plus sign in boldface (+) located opposite their names at the right hand margin of the page.

Except for the last few generations, children of female Mitchells who are carried into the next generation are not given Arabic numbers but appear in paragraph form as part of their mother's sketch, and given small Roman numerals in boldface type to aid readability.

Dates written with a slash mark are those occuring prior to the calendar change in 1752 when the year ended on March 25th. Thus, a date written as 2 Feb 1731/2 means it was recorded as happening in 1731 but actually occured in 1732 by our modern day method of reckoning.

The Mitchell family chart following the list of abbreviations carries on only males. It can be used as a type of index since the number preceding each name is the one under which that person appears in the main text. Each indentation on the chart represents a new generation. When two given or surnames are separated by a slash mark such as Esther/Eunice or Royce/Rice, it means both names were used by or for that person. When a line appears in front of a surname or after a given name such as ___Bass or

Explanations and Abbreviations

Lucy___, it means no given or surname is known. The symbol (=) as used in the chart means married. This and all other abbreviations used in the chart and the main text are explained below.

****

adm=administrator/tion
admx=administrix
adpt=adopted
ae, aet=of age
aft=after
amt(s)=amount(s)
anc=ancestor/tress/try
ano=another
Arch=Archives
app't=appointed
b=born
bc=born about
bef=before
betw=between
Bk=book
b/l=brother-in-law
bpt=baptized
bur=buried
ca=about
cem=cemetery/ies
ch=child, children
Clk(s)=clerk(s)
Co=county
Coll=collection
cou=cousin(s)
d=died
dau=daughter
dc=died about
dec'd=deceased
desc=descendant(s)
div=divorced
d/o=daughter of
dsp=died without issue
dy=died young
ed=editor, edition
f, fem=female
gr.=great

grdn=guardian
grdnship=guardianship
grfa=grandfather
grmo=grandmother
grst=gravestone
Inf=Infantry
inf=infant(s), infancy
k=killed
kn=known
lvd, lvg=lived, living
m=married,month(s),male(s)
m1)=married first (etc.)
mc=married about
Mss,mss=manuscript
nr=near
p, pp=page, pages
par=parents
per=perhaps
prob=probably
rec=record(s)
rec'd=received
ref=reference(s)
res=resided, residence
sib(s)=sibling(s)
sic=copied as written
s/l=sister-in-law
s/o=son of
Twp=township
un=under
unmar=unmarried
V.,Vol=volume
V/R=vital records
w=wife
wid=widow, widower
w/o=wife of
y=year(s)
(=) married

The Mitchell Family Chart

Some Descendants of Michael & Sarah (Catlin) Mitchell

CHART 1

```
1)Michael-bc1670/5=Sarah Catlin lvd CT-MA
   2)John-b1695/6=Katherine Munson lvd MA-CT
      11)James-bc1721=Jane Strachen/Stracken lvd CT
         43)Mary-b1743/4
         44)Elizabeth-b1745/6 d1751
         45)Martha-b1747/8 d1751
         46)John-b1750
      12)Moses-bc1723=Mary Ives lvd CT
         47)Katherine-b1746 d1746
         48)Asaph-b1748=Susannah Cowles lvd CT-NY
            99)Asaph-b1787=Lucy____ lvd CT-NY
               167)Emeline=___Bass/Boss
               168)Alanson lvg 1852 NY
               169)Harvey-bc1820=Louisa____ lvd NY
               170)Henry W.
               171)Sylvania M.=___Bill
            100)Susannah-b1791
         49)Moses-b1750=(per) Lucy Warner
            101)Jotham-bc1772/5=1)Mary____ lvd NY
               172)Oliver M-bc1803=1)Eliza A.____
                  269)Orson bc1830
                  270)Thomas-bc1833
                  271)Horace-bc1836
                  272)Harrison-bc1840
                  273)Mary E.-bc1846=____ Drake
                  274)Orville O.-b aft 1850
               173)Mary/Polly=Samuel D. Booth
         50)Mary-b1752 d1756
         51)Jotham-b1754=Rebecca Royce/Rice lvd CT
            102)Betsey-b1783 d1784
            103)Betsey-b1785=Christopher Atwater
            104)Moses-bc1786 dsp1811
            105)Sally-lvg 1811 unmar
            106)Laura=Walter Booth lvg MA 1811
            107)Aaron-b1794 dsp1811
         52)Mary-b1757 d1806 unmar
         53)Esther-b1760=Moses Root lvd CT
         54)Zenas-b1762=Abigail Merriman lvd CT
            108)Silvana-b1785 d1805 unmar
            109)Abigail-b1787 d1805 unmar
```

The Mitchell Family Chart

```
            110)Harriet-b1793
            111)Zenas-b1795
            112)Theodita-b1798
            113)Titus-b1801=Maria Barnes
            114)Charles Henry-b1805
    13)John-bc1725?=Lydia Sperry lvd CT
        55)Lydia-b1750
        56)Damaris-b1754
3)William-b1697=Anna Wait lvd MA
    14)John-b1723
    15)Anna-b1724=(per)John Ball
    16)Ebenezer-b1726/7 dsp1748
    17)Abigail-b1728=Daniel McKENNEY lvd MA 2ch
    18)Elijah-b1730=Elizabeth Miller lvd MA
        57)Anna-b1761
        58)Moses Miller-b1763=3)Lydia Hale lvd MA
            115)Ebenezer-b1794 dsp1815
            116)Bathsheba-b1796
            117)Lucinda-b1798
            118)Moses Miller-b1800 d1802
            119)Elizabeth-b1803
            120)Alonzo-b1806=1)Fidelia ____ lvd MA
                174)Ellen-b1836
                175)Lydia P.-b1838 d1839
                176)Sarah M.-bc1845
            121)Lydia-b1810 d1824
            122)Eunice-b1812
            123)Mercy M.-b1815
            124)Isabella O.-b1818
            125)Lydia R.-b1824
        59)Sylvia-b1765
        60)Elizabeth-b1767
        61)Elijah-b1769=Cynth(i)a Taylor
        62)Eunice b1772 dy
        63)Eunice-b1774=Lemuel WETMORE lvd MA-VT 6ch
        64)Lydia-b1775 d1775
        65)William-b1776 dy
        66)William-b1777=Mercy Wise lvd MA
            126)Anson-bc1799=Melinda ____ lvd MA
                177)Porter=Persis Field lvd MA
                    275)Chester G.F.-b1845 d1846
                    276)Jennie-b1848=____ (Barlis?)
                    277)Edward b aft 1850
                    278)Mary-b aft 1850
```

The Mitchell Family Chart

       279)Cora-b aft 1850
    178)Maria=Lorenzo D. Kenney
    179)Anson F. lvg 1867
    180)Gilbert F.-bc1827/8=Margret Christie
    181)Charlotte-bc1829=James M. Cumins
    182)Abigail-bc1832=____Miller
    183)Asa H.-bc1837
    184)William W.-b1839 d1844
    185)Harriet-bc1842/3=____ Brown
    186)Willard G.-b1844
    187)William M.-b1844
    188)George E.
  127)Lyman
  128)Porter-bc1801 d1803
  129)Content-b1803 d aft 1864 unmar
  130)Miles-b1805=Martha D.____ lvd MA
    189)Edward Harrison-bc1840
    190)Martha Matilda-bc1842
    191)Emma Elizabeth bc1844 d1849
    192)Webster Clay-bc1846
    193)Content Antoinette-b1848 d bef 1852
  131)Mary-b1807=John Holden lvd MA
  132)William Miller-b1809
  133)Willard Morely-b1809
  134)Elijah-b1813=Catherine Prentice lvd MA
    194)James Catlin-b1846
    195)William Wise-b1848
19)Aaron-b1732/3
20)Sarah-b1734=Caleb WRIGHT lvd MA 7ch
21)Rhoda-b1736=Abraham Bass
22)Rachel-b1739/40
4)Sarah-b1698/9=1)James HOUGH lvd MA-CT 10ch
5)Michael-b1700/01=Mary____ lvd CT-MA
  23)Joel-b1721=Mary____ lvd CT
    67)Mary-b1743
    68)Clare/Clary-b1746
    69)Joel-b1748
    70)Michael-b1750
    71)Nash-b1753
    72)David-b1756
    73)Elisha-b1758
    74)Amasa-b1761=Mary Freymauer?
  24)Moses-b1723
  25)Katherine-b1725

6)Mary-b1703 dy
7)Joseph-b1705=Mary Allis lvd MA
   26)Joseph-b1726/7=Lydia Foster lvd MA-NY
      75)Lydia-b1752=Caleb HURLBUT, Jr. MA-NY-IN 8ch
      76)Experience-b1754=John Fuller
      77)Ensign-b1759=Lucy Hubbard (Chart 2)
      78)Thankful-b1762=Zadock KING, Jr. MA-NY 8ch
      79)Tryphena-b1765
      80)Joseph-b1768=Zipporah Brainard MA-NY-OH-IL
         146)Joseph-b1790=Irene Bigelow NY-OH-IL
            245)Irene-b1814 d1837 unmar
            246)Joseph K.-b1815 d1835 unmar
            247)Russell B.-b1817=1)Julia Ann Bay
               352)Amelia-b1847 d1848
               353)William H.-bc1849
               354)Brainerd-b1848=Belinda Smith
               355)Clymene-b1851=John H. Wright
               356)Irene-bc1853 dy
               357)Emma-bc1857
               358)Franklin-b1859=Arabella Parker
            248)Benjamin B.-b1820 d1844 unmar
            249)Lucy-b1823 d1823
            250)Thankful-b1824 d1825
            251)Electa V.-b1826=Andrew M. Hill
            252)Abigail A.-b1829 d1832
            253)John F.-b1832=Elizabeth A. Rossen
               359)Henry-bc1861
               360)Wilhemina-bc1864
            254)Joseph-b1834 d1834
         147)Newman-bc1790/1800=Nancy Mann lvd NY-OH
            255)Erastus W.-bc1817/18=Clarissa Smith
               361)Leonard-bc1841
               362)Lorenzo-bc1843
               363)Sylvester G.-b1846=Eliz. Shilling
                  415)William dy
                  416)Margaret-bc1876=H.E. Wilcox
                  417)Estella-bc1878=Wm. Crowther
                  418)James L.=____ Smith
                  419)Sylvester dy
                  420)John R.
                  421)Guy
                  422)Clara
             256)Sarah E.-b1820=Benj. TAYLOR 7ch
            257)Leonard-bc1827

The Mitchell Family Chart

    258)Seth W.-bc1832
  148)William-bc1790/1800?=Naomi James
    259)Daughter-bc1810/20
  149)Abner-bc1807/8=1)Louisa M.____
    260)William-bc1830
    261)Alanson-bc1833
    262)Joseph-bc1835
    263)George-bc1838
    264)Rebecca-bc1846
27)Mary-b1731/2=Samuel BELDING lvd MA 11ch
28)Hannah-b1732/3=1)Zadock KING lvd MA 4ch
29)Tabitha-b1736/7=Gershom TUTTLE lvd MA-VT-NY 9ch
30)Abner-b1738=Abigail Warren lvd MA-NY
  81)Abigail-b1763
  82)Consider-b1765=Esther Rawson lvd MA-NY
    150)Hardasah-b1787
    151)Abigail-b1789
    152)Electa-b1791
    153)Orra--b1793 d1873 unmar
    154)Consider-b1795
    155)Elizabeth-b1797
    156)Levi-b1801=1)Britannia Gould lvd NY
      265)Mary Jane-bc1825=Charles S. Anderson
      266) Dau=____ Hanchett
      267)Consider Gould-b1830=1)Ann E. Mixer
        364)Minnie-b1858 d1888 unmar
      268)Celestia A.-bc1844=William Bailey
  83)Cynthia-b1768=Ira HAWKS lvd MA-VT 9ch
  84)Mary-b1770=Israel HAWKS lvd MA 11ch
  85)Abner Warren-b1772 dy
  86)Asaph-b1773=Lucy Blodgett lvd MA
    157)Dolphin/Adolphus/Dolphus-b1794
    158)Edwin-b1796 d1797
    159)Edwin-b1798 dsp1817
    160)Lucy-b1800 d1891 unmar
    161)Louisa-b1801=____ Bishop
    162)Lucretia Billings
    163)Louanna-b1807=1)Jacob Smith
    164)Edmund Frederic
    165)Benjamin Franklin
    166)Maria/Myra-d unmar
  87)Martha-b1775=Joseph TRASK lvd MA-NY 9ch
  88)Aphalinda-b1782=Zebulon TUTTLE lvd MA-NY 8ch
  89)Abner-b1786

The Mitchell Family Chart

      31)Experience-b/d1746
   8)Jonathan-b1707/8=Lydia Howe lvd CT
      32)Sarah-b1735/6=(per) Abel Sizer
      33)Abner-b1738=1)Esther Johnson lvd CT-NY
          90)Mabel-b1764=Ezekiel Lyman
          91)Prudence-b1766
          92)Submit-b1768
          93)Lydia-b1771=_____ Wheeler
          94)Esther-b1774
          95)Hannah-b1779=_____ Lyman
      34)Camp-b1741
      35)Amasa-b1742
      36)Lydia-b1744
   9)Catherine/Catheron-b/d1710
   10)Samuel-b1712/13=Abigail Cook lvd CT
      37)Michael-b1739
      38)Oliver-b1741
      39)Samuel-b1743=Elizabeth Stark lvd CT
          96)Elizabeth-b1764
          97)Medad-b1765
          98)Samuel-b1767
      40)Abigail-b1746=Samuel Sizer lvd CT-NY
      41)Rebecca-b1748/9
      42)Medad-b1751

                    CHART 2

   77)Ensign-b1759=Lucy Hubbard lvd MA-NY-VT-PA-OH
      135)Ensign-b1787=Elizabeth Calvin lvd NY-VT-PA-OH-IL
          196)Calvin-b1816=Eliza Ann Allen (Chart 3)
          197)Joseph-b1818=Sarah Ann Hannah lvd OH-IL
              286)John H.-b1844=Lucinda Thompson
                  385)Charles Wesley-b1869= _____
                      i)Frederick
                  386)Laura A.-b1871 d1872
                  387)Frederick J.-bc1875=Dora Carson
                  388)Rosa Mary-b1879=Hiram SHEPHERD 2ch kn
                  389)Nora B.-b1884=Owen Ingram
                  390)Ora C.-b1884=Della M. Ballard
              287)Chandler-b1845=Marica Hartley (Chart 4)
              288)George H.-b1847=Mary E. Stewart
                  394)Laura E.-b1882
              289)Francis Marion-b1850 d1866 unmar
              290)Joseph Ensign-b1855=Anna_____

                    -xviii-

The Mitchell Family Chart

198)Chandler-bc1819/22=Jane E.____
199)Lucy-b1820=Maranda RALSTON lvd IL-IA-WI 2ch
200) Elizabeth-b1820/25?
201)Nancy-b1823=Wm. KIRKPATRICK lvd IL-MO-SD 5ch
202)Mary-b1825=William T. FULLER lvd OH-IL 7ch
203)Samuel-b1828=2)Harriet J. Calvin lvd OH-IL
   296)Sarah Emma-b1853 d1869 unmar
   297)John A.-b1859 d1860
   298)Gertrude-b1867 d1870
   299)Herman Calvin-b1871=Jesse Maude Tucker
      395)Helen Harriet-b1897=Walter T. KILE 1ch
      396)Catherine E.-b1907=1)James D. Savoye
204)John-b1831=Mary E. Smith lvd IL-WA
   300)Ida B.-bc1863=____ Dalton
   301)William T.-b1867
   302)Margaret E.-bc1868=Frank P. Jackson
   303)Ella Cyldie-b1869=Frank Houk
   304)Olive O.-b1871=James A. Darby
   305)Carrie E.-bc1874=George E. Edwards
   306)Agnes-b1881
   307)Mamie-b1883=Albert Birkes
136)Chandler-bc1788= _____ lvd NY-OH-IL
  205)Ensign-bc1810=Sarah/Sally____
   308)Silas-bc1834=S.I.____
   309)Chandler-b1835=Sarah Jane____
      397)John-bc1862
      398)Alvin/Alva-bc1865
      399)Jesse-bc1867? dy
   310)Moses-bc1839=Susan____
   311)Lucinda I.-bc1840
   312)Thomas-bc1842
   313)Sarah/Sally-bc1846
   314)David F.-bc1848
   315)J.W. (male)-bc1851
   316)M.A. (female)-bc1853
   317)G.W. (male)-bc1856
   318)Ensign-bc1858
   319)M.E. (female)-bc1860
  206)Jane-bc1824/5=William T. WATSON lvd OH-IL 6ch
137)Mary-b1792=Benjamin REYNOLDS lvd NY-OH-MI 6ch lvd
138)Claudius-b1794=Nancy Lambert lvd NY-VT-PA-OH
  207)Sarah-b1817=Remembrance WILLIAMS OH 9ch
  208)Lavina-b1819=Gabriel M. POTEE lvd OH 6ch
  209)Martha Ann-b1821=Rob't ELLISON lvd OH 4ch

The Mitchell Family Chart

210)Joshua-b1823=Elizabeth C. Rigdon
   320)Wesley F.-bc1842
   321)Mary Jane-bc1844
   322)Thomas J.-bc1846
   323)Claudius N.-bc1848
   324)Elizabeth-b1850
211)Lucy-b1825=John Moore
212)Chandler-b1828=Elizabeth A. McConkey Hendrix
   325)William Clinton-b1850 d1861 unmar
   326)Claudius Newton-b1852=Frances E. Hunter
      400)James C.-b1887=1)Belle Guy
      401)Juliet-b1890=Edw. N. JEWELL 1ch
      402)Robert-b1890 d1967 unmar
   327)Charles Lincoln-b1861=Lizzie B. Davidson
      403)Florence E.-b1894=Cloyd WHARTON 3ch
      404)Helen Jean-b1896=Raymond M^{c}VICKER 1ch
      405)Jane Taggart-b1899=Wilfred MARSH 1ch
213)Claudius-b1830 d1831
214)Nancy-b1832=____STANDLEY
215)Elmira-b1834=Isaac POTEE lvd OH 9ch
216)Newton B.-b1841 d1849
217)John Milton-b1844 d1847
139)Lavina-bc1796?=John Payne/Pain(e)
140)Roxanna-bc1798?=William MARRS lvd NY-PA-OH 7ch
141)Experience-bc1800/01?=Nath'l GRIFFIN PA-OH 6ch
142)Ira-b1803=Jane Rhodes lvd PA-OH-IN-IA
   218)Abigail E.-b1830=Welcome B. WALKER IN-IA 3ch
   219)Obed H.-b1833=Amanda R. Sutton lvd IN-IA-MO
      328)Guy S.-b1867
   220)Ira R.-b1835=Lydia Green
   221)Lucy M.-bc1838=Henry H. HESS lvd IN-IA-MO
   222)Elizabeth M.-b1840=Henry H. HESS lvd IN-IA
   223)John Ensign-b1842=Elma M. Henderson lvd IN-IA
      329)M. Merta-b1872 d1936 unmar
      330)D. Isa/Iza-b1881=1941 Lawrence Widdefield
   224)Francis M.-b1845=Anna E. Kittle lvd IN-IA
      331)Herman I.-b1886
   225)Leonard M.-b1848=Ellen M. Murphy lvd IN-IA
      332)Aura/Orrie-b1875
      333)Phebe/Cada-b1877=George W. Merrill, Jr.
      334)Dorothy/Dottie-b1880=Dow Roof
143)Lydia-b1805=Charles RIGDON lvd PA-OH 6ch
144)Abizer-b1807=Margaret Ann Stanley lvd PA-OH
   232)Roxanna Mary-bc1833 dy

```
233)Ira-b1835=Eliza Jane Bland
    340)Ida Mae-b1859=James H. McCLINTOCK 2ch
    341)Presta Ira-b1864 d1879 unmar
234)Jane-b1837=William BROWN 5ch
145)Newman-b1811=Cassandra/Cassie Bradley lvd OH
    235)Abigail-bc1838=John H. KENNEDY lvd OH 3ch
    236)Lydia Jane-b1840=David BALES lvd OH-TX 4ch
    237)Melissa-b1841 d1865 unmar
    238)Julia Ann-b1842 d1854 unmar
    239)Charles E.-bc1845=Mary Elizabeth Heffley
        346)Alice J.-b1869=Harry F. FAUVER lvd OH 3ch
        347)Harry H.-b1871 d1914 unmar
        348)Raleigh-b1873=Metta Rafferty
            411)Charles Nathaniel
            412)Dolly Elizabeth
        349)Noel-b1889=Blanche M. Rafferty
            413)Roger Lyman-b1915
    240)Isabel-b1847 d1854
    241)Male-b1849 d1849
    242)Lucinda-b1850 d1851
    243)Nancy Ella-b1854 d1863
    244)Electa-b1855=Lewis Harlen CREAMER lvd OH 2ch
```

CHART 3

```
196)Calvin-b1816=Eliza Ann Allen lvd OH-IN-IL
    280)Orlando Allen-b1846=Margaret Ellen Mesnard lvd IL
        365)Allen Calvin-b1873=2)Augusta Barbara Hartman
            423)Ora Allen-b1897=3)Lucy Jane Jolly dsp
            424)Oscar Calvin-b1901=1)Audrey Trippe
                488)Evelyn L.-b1927=Charles WOODS
            425)Edgar Samuel-b1903=1)Zola Hopper dsp
            426)Burl Kenneth-b1906=Gertrude Ruth Bjurstrom
                489)Patricia Joyce-b1937=Hugh A. McFARLAND
                490)Judith A.-b1940=James W. RHODES
                491)Lynda Diane-b1945=Donald L. SIKES
            427)Stella L.-b1908=1)W. HANSON=2)____ BALSLEY
            428)Velma Augusta-b1914=Russell W. HOOKER
            429)Vernon Hartman-b1919=Virginia J. Johnson
                497)Helen Louise-b1947=Charles E. Shaw
                498)David Allen-b1949=Dorothy F. Woodfall
                499)Arlan Charles-b1950=Retha A. Ruhnke
                    599)Alan Chad-b1979
                    600)Nicole Augusta-b1981
```

601)Jenna Louise-b1984
500)Michael Lee-b1952=2)Deanna J. Thompson
602)Christina Marie-b1980
366)Anna Christina-b1875=Cornelius REDMAN
367)Nettie Jane-b1877=Anthony REDMAN
368)Mary Eliza/Mollie-b1878=Albert Marion Taylor
369)Amanda Ellen-b1880=William Rollie JONES
370)Ensign Franklin-b1882=Essie Elsie Robertson
452)Eugene Franklin-b1905=Ethel E. Triplett
540)Barbra Jane-b1935=George W. GOODNITE
541)Lynda Gene-b1941=James D. Trotter
542)Evelyn Ann-b1944=2)Boyd Terrel SCHUCK
453)Harry Victor-b1907=Anna J. Mikulska
543)John Mikul-b1935=Virginia S. Tucker
669)John Mikul-b1960=Cindy Malice Eads
i)Peter Mikul-b1984
670)Steven Lee-b1961=Dana Marie Crowder
i)Karla Marie-b1986
671)Phillip Wayne-b1963=Alison Greenwood
672)Jeffrey Scott-b1965
673)Robert Mark-b1969
544)Mary Anne-b1940=Henry B. CUMMINGS
545)David Lee-b1943=Louise Gwen V. Hodo
674)David Lee-b1962=Lesha K. Zeigler
i)David Lee III-b1985
546)Frances Elaine-b1948=Gary Edward HAMNER
454)Raymond Allen-b/d1910
455)Daphna Irene-b1912=Newell Smith ESTESS
456)Joe Calvin-b1914=Elizabeth Hudson
549)Jerry C.=Thelma Becker
i)Jay
ii)Joe
457)Howard Leo-b1921 d1944 unmar
458)Russell Glen-b1922=Jean Chiles
550)Russell Glen-b1946=Wyona Smith
676)Dawn
677)Kelly
551)Sharon-b1950=James LONG
281)David Oscar-b1846=Carrie Belle Simonton
371)Walter H.-bc1879 dy
372)Victor Earl-b aft 1880 dy
373)Lulu B.-b1885=J.R. CALHOUN
374)Georgia/Kitty-b1887=Presley Louis NEVILLE
375)Winnie Maude-b1893=Raymond Elmer SMITH

376)David Ralph-b1899=Marguerite Robertson
  468)Beulah-b1921=Henry Ginder
  469)Marilyn-b1923=Henry RUSCH
  470)Freda Bernell-b1925=Robert Lee WALLACE
  471)Verneva-b1927=Jack Bernhard ANDERSON
  472)Helen Mayonne-b1929=Arthur Edward LUSTIG
  473)Myron Calvin-b1931=Patricia Joan Harris
    565)Calvin Wayne-b1953=Mary Beth Ludwig
      678)Melissa Ann-b1977
      679)Timothy Wayne-b1981
    566)Sharon Elaine-b1955=Steven Kent TARR
    567)Janean Kay-b1958=Steven Anthony Bushur
  474)Clayton Ralph-b1934=Joyce Marlene Pulliam
    568)David Clayton-b1956
    569)Cynthia Suzette-b1959=John Whitehead
    570)Lisa Kay-b1961=Mark Douglas Johnson
    571)Jodi Michelle-b1968
  475)Shirley-b1936=John Lynn Snyder
  476)Marthagene-b1939=Ross Eugene WOODY
282)Ensign Samuel-b1848=Lucretia Hart dsp
283)Elijah Chandler-b1850=Evelyn/Eveline Trexler
  377)Noble-b1875 d1941 unmar
284)Claudius Elias-b1856=Rhue Ethel Donaldson
  378)Mabel F.-b1887=John T. Scryples dsp
  379)Daniel Palmer-b1888=Lillace Montgomery
    477)Robert-b1921
  380)Nellie Pearl-b1891 dy
  381)Claudius Elias-b1895=Helen A. Claar
    478)Ruth C.-b1921 d1986 unmar
  382)Ruby Ethel-b1897=George H. Telger dsp
  383)Gladys M.-b1902=____ Plestina dsp
  384)Melba-b1906 dy
285)Joseph Calvin-b1859=Kate (Lidy) Gordan dsp

CHART 4

287)Chandler-b1845=Marica Hartley lvd IL
  391)Son-b/d1875
  392)George Alvin-b1877=Ida M. Stout dsp
  393)Claude Glen-b1879=2)Olive E. Blanchard lvd IL
    479)Chandler Orville-b1903=Leone Edwards
      576)Chandler Earl-b1926=Anna Maria Bogner
        680)David Chandler-b1951=Jennifer Winland
          i)Heather Renee-b1977

The Mitchell Family Chart

681)Rebecca Ann-b1953=Jerry Lee CUSICK
682)Thomas Earl-b1956=Regina (Wolfe) Hoult
  i)Dedra Marie-b1985
577)Eleanor Marica-b1928=James Monroe TAYLOR
578)James Edward-b1930=Martha Jane Parks
  686)Richard Allen-b1952=Cecelia D. Barrett
    i)Josie Dorthea-b1983
    ii)Betsy Jane-b1985
  687)Robert Lee-b1953=Debra Lynn Coan
  688)Donald Joe-b1956=Rita Joyce Switzer
    i)Chris Lynn-b1974
    ii)Andy Scott-b1976
    iii)Kelly Dawn-b1981
    iv)Wendy Jo-b1984
  689)Joanne Kay-b1957=Tony William RIGDON
  690)Gary Ray-b1958=Priscilla Ann Eyer
579)John Richard-b1932=Barbara Ann Martin
  691)John William-b1952=Janzetta D. Gossett
    i)Steven William-b1977
    ii)Tracy Lynn-b1981
  692)Deborah Ann-b1953=Timothy Leroy BOTNER
480)Dugan Bruce-b1904=Blanche Bratton dsp

INTRODUCTION

Origin of the Mitchell Name

Prior to the Battle of Hastings in 1066 A.D., people
of the British Isles did not bear surnames. After that
date William the Conqueror who led the victorious Norman
invasion of the Isles ordered all men to choose a surname
and be entered in his famous Domesday Book, devised as a
method of ensuring that every man paid his due taxes.

Mitchell, as a surname, may have been introduced into Great Britain by the Normans of France. It is thought
by some to have originated from the baptismal name of
Michael, meaning, in this case, "son of Michael," derived
from an ancient Hebrew word meaning "one who is like God."
As the palatal form of Michael, it is pronounced with the
blade of the tongue near the hard palate to form a "ch"
sound instead of a hard "k" sound.

Others surmise that Mitchell as a surname may have
come from the Anglo-Saxon word "muchel," meaning "mickle"
or great.

There is a tradition long handed down in this branch
of the Mitchells that the family came from Scotland. Indeed, there were many Mitchells in Scotland, the name
often written MacMichie, translated as "son of Michael."
Those of Midlothian, Scotland sometimes spelled the name
Mitchael. Many of that name settled in Lanarkshire in the
south of Scotland, and Angus and Aberdeen in the northeast
by the 15th century. Scots of that name moved to the north
of Ireland and to England during the perilous years of the
17th and 18th centuries.

In early English records, the name was often spelled
Micahel, Michel, Micael, Michilson, and Michell, the last
spelling being used often in the South of England, particularly Cornwall. In this country, the name was frequently
spelled Mitchel or even Mytchel. People who neither
read nor wrote could not control the spelling of their

Introduction

names by various recorders of statistics and legal
transactions who sometimes were barely more literate
than themselves.

The English Mitchell shield is silver, emblazoned
with seven tigers, each devouring a cross. In Scotland
the Mitchell shield is black with three gold diamonds on
it. This is not to suggest that this branch of the
Mitchells stemmed from an armorial family.

Speculations on the Ancestry
of Michael Mitchell

The first known Mitchell to these shores was Experience Mitchell who came from England on the ship "Anne" in
1622, later marrying Jane Cooke, daughter of a Mayflower
Compact signer. By the mid-1600's several by that name
had settled in the Province of Maine. Between 1635 and
1655 at least fifteen by that name had emigrated from England to Virginia. In 1651/2 the ship "John and Sarah"
brought Scots prisoners from the Battle of Dunbar, including a James Mickell and a James Michell, these prisoners being sent to New England and sold to the colonists as
"slaves" who treated them rather as indentured servants.

Andrew Mitchell was a resident of Charlestown, MA
before 1688. George Mitchell was in Boston, MA in 1644.
Matthew Mitchell arrived in Boston in 1635, bringing with
him a wife and two sons. John Mitchell died at Hartford,
CT in 1683, leaving a widow and six children. William
Mitchell of Newbury died in 1654, leaving two sons and two
daughters. In 1650 Thomas Mitchell of New Haven "complained of ye fence at plaines as naught generally..." He
died about 1660 having had no surviving male issue.

Another family "story" implies that Michael Mitchell
came to the Colonies from Barbados. Again, there were any
number of families by this surname living at an early date
on this island. John, age 20, was a passenger on the
"Dorset" to Barbados in 1635. William of Kingston-on-
Thames came to Barbados as a bonded passenger in 1668.
Another William, also a bonded passenger, arrived from
Middlesex, England in 1674. Records of Parish Registers
including births and deaths, lists of inhabitants, landed
proprietors and the like contain a number of Mitchell
names as do Barbados records of wills and administrations
in the Dept. of Archives at Black Rock, St. Michael.

Introduction

Colonial New Jersey had its share of Mitchells at an early date. In 1683 one James Mitchell, carpenter of Northumberland, England, came to New Jersey with his family to work as an indentured servant to Arant Sonmans. He died shortly after, leaving a widow, Mary, and sons John, Jacob, William and Nathaniel. Another who came as a servant was one Richard Mitchell. Early deeds mention Robert Michel, Charles Michel and Frances Michel, all merchants of London.

An exhaustive search has been made among these various Mitchell families who arrived between 1622 and 1700 for clues that might point to the ancestry of Michael Mitchell. To date he can not be connected to any of them.

Because naming their children was a matter of great importance to Michael and his wife (as is true of most parents of then and now), it must be equally important to us as a possible indication of Michael's origins. The July 1984 issue of the New England Historical & Genealogical Register carried an intriguing article by John J. Waters entitled "Naming and Kinship Patterns and Usage 1693-1759" which might apply in addressing the puzzle of Michael Mitchell's background. Mr. Waters cites four naming patterns among the English and English colonists of America, i.e., traditional (family names); Biblical (preferably Old Testament); virtue names such as Silence, Prudence, Discipline, etc.; and eclectic (no use of family names; prone to the usage of such names as Charles or James, made popular by the fashionable French court).

Of these four systems, six of the Mitchell children appear to bear traditional names that can easily be linked to the family of Sarah (Catlin) Mitchell. The remaining three - William, second son; Michael, third son; and Catherine, third daughter - are out of "sync" and do not appear in either the Catlin family or in the ancestral lines which connect with the Catlin family.

Theoretically, William, as the second son, should bear the name of Michael's father since John, the first son, was named after Sarah's father. William was one of four great names of the medieval Norman-Catholic past which were held by sixty percent of English males prior to the change in religion (i.e., before King Henry VIII's break with the Holy Roman Church). This name ranked third in usage in England in 1700, second in York Co., VA 1649-1699, and not at all in New England.

Introduction

Michael, the third son, was obviously named after his father. Traditionally, a family would only be free to name a son after his father if sons had already been named after the paternal and maternal grandfathers. It is an Old Testament name after the archangel Michael for whom Michaelmass is celebrated as a church holiday in England. It did not rank in popularity at all on Mr. Waters' lists in England, Virginia or New England.

Catherine, the third daughter, bore a name that held no ranking in New England but was tenth in popularity in England, eleventh on the list in Virginia. Since two older girls had been named Sarah for her mother and Mary for her mother's mother, Catherine might (traditionally) have been the name of Michael's mother.

In considering the names of their children, one is left with a haunting sense that Michael and Sarah sprang from different backgrounds in both a geographic and an idealogic sense. Michael's ties with the British Isles, whether it be Scotland, England or Ireland, seem to be stronger and more recent than Sarah's, she being of the second generation of her family born in the Colonies. The lack of success this researcher has had and many others before me in connecting Michael to any other of the known Mitchells who emigrated to the Colonies in the 1600's leads one to the inevitable conclusion that Michael himself was an emigrant. His apparent lack of ties to either parents or siblings suggests he may have arrived as an indentured servant, raising himself from that status by dint of hard work and marriage into the solidly founded Catlin family.

Notes on the Ancestral Lines
of Sarah (Catlin) Mitchell

The proven ancestral lines of Sarah (Catlin) Mitchell include the surnames Catlin, Baldwin, Ward, Whitlock and Harding.

Sarah's paternal grandmother was Isabelle Ward who made the arduous sea voyage to the Colonies at around seventeen years of age. It is only reasonable to believe that she made the journey under the protection of her two brothers, Lawrence and George Ward, who came from England on the ship "Hector," arriving in Boston on 26 June 1637. A search for a complete passenger list for the "Hector" was made without success. However, an excerpt from Isabel MacBeath Calder's "Passengers on the Hector, 1637-1638" ("Ship Passenger Lists, National & New England [1600-1825]," Carl Boyer 3rd) names Lawrence and George Ward among the inhabitants of St. Stephen's parish, Coleman St., London, who joined with John Davenport and Theophilus Eaton, organizers of a company to settle on the Connecticut River. Their arrival was recorded by John Winthrop.

If the sum total of erroneous material written about the Wards of New England, especially that dealing with the ancestry of Isabelle and her brothers, was thrown into a furnace and burned, it would heat a good sized house for at least a year. Worthy of investigation is data which has crossed my desk several times lately. This data states that Isabelle Ward was born about 1620 at Brafield, England (probably Brafield-on-the-Green, Northamptonshire), daughter of John and Elizabeth (Haselford) Ward. No proofs have accompanied this information. "The Visitation of Northamptonshire 1681," p. 224, does list Ward of Brafield, including John Ward, second son of Robert of Knoll in co. Warwick, but this visitation concerns only John's eldest son, William.

Unworthy of consideration is all unreferenced material variously calling the Ward siblings children of James Ward (Robert); first cousins of Stephen Ward (James, Robert); or grandchildren of James Ward (Robert) by an unnamed son. Equally to be ignored is the statement that Stephen Ward (James, Robert) was husband of Joyce Traford who was later the "Widow Ward" of Wethersfield, CT. The maiden name of Joyce Ward, widow of Wethersfield, is unknown, but that she was the second wife of Richard Ward of Stretton, co. Rutland, England has been amply proved in an article by J. R. Hutchinson, New York Genealogical & Biographical Record, Vol. 49, pp 262-4.

It is my own conjecture that a family connection may have existed between Isabelle Ward and the Widow Joyce Ward of Wethersfield. This is not based on the often printed "tradition" that the Widow Ward was conveyed to the Colonies by the brothers Lawrence and George Ward. True, Joyce was in London on 2 Oct 1635, proving her deceased husband's will, but since she seems to have been accompanied to the Colonies by her son-in-law and her daughter, John and Mary Fletcher, she was hardly in need of assistance from the Ward brothers. Rather, it is based

on my difficulty in not drawing an implication from the
fact that Lawrence and George Ward settled first in New
Haven, whereas Isabelle, a young, unmarried woman, was
clearly living in Wethersfield as is shown by her marriage
there about 1641 to John Catlin.

According to Virkus in his "Immigrant Ancestors,"
John Catlin was a trader, said to have gone from England
to Barbados, then to Virginia before arriving at Wethersfield about 1640. He was a juror at Hartford when he died
in 1644, leaving Isabelle with a young son, John Jr., born
about 1643. His probate record (under the name of John
Cattell) shows that the inventory of his estate, evaluated at 69 pounds, was taken 17 July 1644 by John Coleman
and Samuel Hales, and was admitted to court in September
by "Will' Gybbins & his widdowe, to administer."

Isabelle's second husband was James Northam who
died in 1661. His estate, inventoried at Wethersfield
on 27 Feb 1660/61 by John Lattimore and Thomas Hurlbut,
was evaluated at 278-10-00. By the terms of his will,
Isabelle would inherit the entire rather considerable
estate unless she should remarry, at which time two-
thirds of the estate would go to her and her children. A
later document states that "The Widow doth declare it to
be her minde that her eldest son by her first husband
should have a lesser share yn any of the rest of the children, and the Widow did declare yt it was her husband's
minde yt her eldest son by him should have a larger portion
yn the rest of the children, both wch the Court Judgeth
equall and ought to be attended." ("Early Connecticut
Probate Records," Vol. I, p. 139, Charles Manwaring.)

The wording of this declaration clearly indicates
that Isabelle had at least two sons by her marriage to
James Northam. One of these sons may have been Samuel
Northam who married Mary, daughter of John Dickenson of
Hadley, MA, in 1674. In 1686 Samuel Northam appeared at
Deerfield, MA, the residence at that time of Isabelle's
son, John Catlin, Jr. Called "carpenter" by George Sheldon in his history of the town, Samuel served on many of
the same committees with John Catlin, and in 1696 he sold
his home lot #26 in Deerfield to John, removing then with
his family to Colchester, CT.

According to Sylvester Judd's "History of Hadley,
MA," James Northam had signed an Agreement or Engagement
"At a meeting at Goodman Ward's house, in Hartford..." on

18 Apr 1659, thus declaring his intention to remove himself and his family "out of the jurisdiction of Connecticut into the jurisdiction of the Massachusetts..." to the new settlement of Hadley. In February, 1661, he was one of 46 east side proprietors but ceased to be so at his death in that year. The move to Hadley by Isabelle seems not to have been made until after James Northam's death. Certainly she was there when she married her third and last husband, Joseph Baldwin, who had come to Hadley from Milford, CT about 1662. When Isabelle's childless brother, Lawrence Ward, died in Newark, NJ in 1670, his widow relinquished administration of his estate to "Esebell Baldwyne, wife of Joseph Baldwyne of Hadley, Mass..." This duty Isabelle promptly turned over to her son, John Catlin, and her nephew, John Ward, son of her deceased brother George.

Isabelle (Ward) Catlin-Northam-Baldwin died at Hadley on 8 Dec 1676. She was probably no more than fifty-six years of age.

Sarah (Catlin) Mitchell's maternal grandfather was Joseph Baldwin, third husband of her paternal grandmother, Isabelle Ward. The Baldwin family can be positively traced back to Richard Baldwin, born about 1578 at Cholesbury, co. Bucks, England, and buried there on 2 Nov 1632. Richard married Isabel Harding on 31 May 1598 at Amersham, co. Bucks. Joseph, sixth child of Richard and Isabel, was born at Cholesbury about 1610/12. By terms in his father's will of 23 Dec 1630, Joseph inherited "one meadow platt, Hunt's Wicke, one-half acre more or less lying and adjoining my cottage that John Dorrell now dwells in, for him to possess at age twenty-one..." Brother Nathaniel inherited ten pounds and brother Timothy, the eldest, inherited the "rest" of his father's property.

On 10 Nov 1636 at High Wycomb, co. Bucks, Joseph Baldwin married Hannah Whitlock. Several years later, he and Hannah took ship for the Colonies, accompanied by his brothers Timothy and Nathaniel and their wives, his sister Sarah, and Sarah's husband, John Searles.

Lack of a sufficient amount of property and money, and the unsettled political conditions in the 1630's was probably the impetus behind this move to a raw, new world rather than religious persecution, although the Baldwin's first place of settlement, Milford, CT, was definitely a

Separatist stronghold. At a town meeting there in 1640, it was "Voted, that the earth is the Lord's, and the fullness thereof; voted, that the earth is given to the Saints; voted, that we are the Saints."

The quaint term "Saints" was a name given to themselves by the English Separatists - Congregationalists who wished to sever all ties to the English Mother Church; the same who later came to be known as the Pilgrim Fathers, but not the same as the Puritans who wished only to purify the Church of its sins, not leave it entirely. The above quoted resolution was also an expression by the Milford townspeople of their feelings toward the Indians who did not understand the philosophy of land ownership and thought the land, like the air, the waters of the earth, the sun and all beneath it, belonged to no one and to everyone. This conflict in attitude between the settlers of Milford and the Indians reflected beliefs generally held in common by the early colonists.

At the organization of the Milford church in 1644, Joseph and Hannah Baldwin and their first four children (Joseph, Benjamin, Hannah, Mary) were baptized together on the 23rd of June. Between that date and 1653, five more children, Elizabeth, Martha, Jonathan, David and Sarah, were born at Milford where the family remained until Joseph's removal to Hadley, MA about 1662. Hannah may have died at Milford before the family went to Hadley. A 1663 Hadley town plat shows a home lot for Joseph Baldwin but not for the Widow Northam which may indicate he was married to Isabelle (Ward) Catlin-Northam by that date.

After the death of Isabelle in 1676 but before 17 Sep 1678, Joseph Baldwin married a third time to the twice-widowed Elizabeth Gibbons, relict first of Luke Hitchcock of Wethersfield, and second of William Warriner who died in 1676. She also survived her third husband, Joseph, who died at Hadley on 2 Nov 1684. Joseph's will, dated 20 Dec 1680, left land in Hadley to the children of his deceased son, Joseph, Jr.; land in Milford to his sons Benjamin, Jonathan and David; and personal property to his daughters, Hannah, wife of Jeremiah Hull of New Haven, and Mary, wife of John Catlin of Arthur Kill, New Jersey (near Newark).

The parents of Sarah (Catlin) Mitchell were John Catlin, Jr., son of John and Isabelle (Ward) Catlin-Northam-Baldwin, and Mary Baldwin, daughter of Joseph and

Hannah (Whitlock) Baldwin. At their marriage on 23 Sep 1662, John's step-father became his father-in-law, and Mary's step-mother became her mother-in-law.

Early deaths of spouses and rapid remarriages of the survivors within the communities where they lived, led to very tangled relationships among the first settlers of this country, much more complicated that merely having one's step-parents become one's in-laws. For example, William Warriner, second husband of Elizabeth (Gibbons) Hitchcock-Warriner-Baldwin, had been married first to Joanna Searles, sister to John Searles who had married Sarah Baldwin, sister of Joseph Baldwin, the third husband of William Warriner's second wife. William and Joanna (Searles) Warriner were the parents of James Warriner who married Elizabeth Baldwin, daughter of Joseph. Joseph's daughter, Hannah Baldwin, married Jeremiah Hull whose son Jeremiah, Jr. married Mehitable Smead, sister of Ebenezer Smead who married Esther Catlin, daughter of John Catlin (son of Joseph Baldwin's second wife by her first marriage) and Mary Baldwin, Joseph's daughter. I could continue in like vein but this is enough to give you an idea of the incredible maze we must traverse to sort out the involved kinships of our pioneer ancestors.

Within a few years after their marriage, John and Mary Catlin moved to Branford, CT. John's maternal uncles, Lawrence and George Ward, had come from New Haven as early settlers of Branford when it was founded in the spring of 1644 as part of New Haven Colony. Branford became a haven for Wethersfield inhabitants who fled their town to escape quarreling between several Wethersfield ministers, each claiming the right to act as sole town minister. Soon after the Catlins arrived, a new threat to religious "freedom" arose. The Colony of Connecticut with its more relaxed religious policies, obtained a patent uniting themselves with the Colony of New Haven. Desiring to keep their Congregationalist religion "pure," the town of Branford sent agents to obtain new lands on the Passaic River in New Jersey.

In a Branford town meeting on 30 Oct 1666, a few ground rules for the new settlement in New Jersey were adopted. It was ruled that "none shall be admitted free men or free burgesses, within our town upon the Passaic river, in the province of New Jersey, but such planters as are members of some or other of the Congregational churches; nor shall any but such be chosen to magistracy, or to carry on civil judicature, or as deputies or assistants to have power to vote in establishing laws, and making or repealing them...we shall, with care and dilligence, provide for maintenance of the purity of religion as professed in Congregational churches."

Among those signing this document, so amazing to us now for its forthright denial of religious freedom but typical of the day, were Lawrence Ward, Josiah Ward, John Ward, John Ward Sr., and John Catlin.

Within a few months the Catlins embarked with those of their neighbors and Ward relatives who elected to leave Branford, moving by vessel down Long Island Sound to the site of their new settlement. First known as Milford, it was later called New-Work or New-Ark, and finally Newark. An early map of the town locates the Catlin's home lot lying next to that of Lawrence Ward. Just east of their adjoining property ran Mulberry St. with the river beyond that and Broad Street to the west. Most of the Catlin children were born here, including Sarah.

In the stimulating atmosphere of a new undertaking, John Catlin became an active citizen of Newark. In 1676 he was a "teacher." In 1678 he was "Town's Attorney," an "honest brother" empowered to "take care that all town orders be executed and if a breach occurs to punish the offender." From 1676 to 1681 he was a town selectman. By trade, he was a turner, "a man who shapes forms with a lathe," that is, a furniture maker.

The questing spirit of our pioneer ancestors is never more evident than in John Catlin's decision to leave Newark. For seventeen years he had been a respected, influential citizen of a town he helped found, had a growing, healthy family, and a trade. Yet he seems to have tired of the confinement of an area so rapidly increasing in population and perhaps yearned for the frontier. In 1683 he and Mary, their five daughters and two young sons left for Hartford, CT where his eldest daughter, Mary, married Thomas French on 18 Oct of that year.

Hartford was merely a stopping-off place for the Catlins. Their final destination was Deerfield, described by Richard I. Melvoin as "a frontier outpost, the northernmost Massachusetts settlement in the Connecticut River valley, the last of a thin chain of towns that stretched north from Springfield. The closest settlement was Hatfield, ten miles south; there were no towns in the region to the east or west of Deerfield." ("Communalism in Frontier Deerfield," from Early Settlement in the Connecticut Valley, Historic Deerfield, Inc. & Institute for MA Studies, Westfield State College, 1984)

Precisely because it was so isolated, Deerfield was a small community, independent for the most part of the dominance of the General Court in Boston. Mr. Melvoin describes life in Deerfield as communal, all citizens required to participate in town affairs, using largely a barter form of economics which created an interdependence among the inhabitants rather than dependence on the richest and therefore most powerful resident as in other Connecticut Valley towns. Even the Deerfield church practiced a form of open communion as preached and popularized by the Rev. Solomon Stoddard of Northampton.

Living in such a remote outpost as was Deerfield also meant living with the ever present and very real danger of Indian attack. But John Catlin, long since dignified by the title "Mister", found his niche here. As to be expected, he participated vigorously in town affairs, serving numerous times as moderator of town meetings, and on many town committees including one in 1690 to see to the town fortifications after Indians burned Schenectady, and Northfield was deserted by its people, leaving Deerfield once more the northernmost frontier outpost.

Between the years 1690 and 1697, the war known as King William's War, one of many French-Indian conflicts with the English, raged throughout the Colonies. During that time, no one was allowed to live outside the town fortifications. No man went to his fields alone but under armed guard. Some families removed temporarily from Deerfield to go to safer, more populated areas further down the Connecticut River such as Hadley who, not affected by this war, held out a welcoming hand to people fleeing such settlements as Northfield, Deerfield, Hatfield and Brookfield, all endangered towns.

At the start of King William's War in 1690, the Catlin family was composed of four daughters between the ages of six and twenty-two, and three sons aged three, eight and ten. I strongly suspect that the Catlins were among those families who left Deerfield due to the makeup of the family - the elder children all female and the sons quite young. During those years of war, the name of John

Catlin seems to drop from Deerfield town records, an unlikely occurrance unless he was no longer in that town. Perhaps the Catlins sought refuge in or near Northampton. John's daughter, Hannah, married Thomas Bascom about 1690 and her first child was born in 1692 at Northampton. James Corse who married John's daughter, Esther, about 1690, seems to have had Northampton connections. Esther Catlin, another daughter, married Ebenezer Smead about 1694, his father, William, originally of Northampton, also dropping from Deerfield town records between 1688 and 1697. Sarah, fifth of John's daughters, married about 1694 to Michael Mitchell. None of these marriages are recorded in Deerfield or in any other records of marriages in Connecticut or Massachusetts prior to 1700.

It is not proven that the Catlin family did leave Deerfield for those seven years of war, but the next public record of John Catlin in Deerfield does not occur until January 1695/6 when he was again town moderator, leaving an unexplained gap of six years.

With the treaty of 1697 ending King William's War, a welcome peace once again lay on the land. It would be short-lived. A space of only five years separated this war from the next. If the Catlins left Deerfield in 1690 for haven elsewhere, they merely averted momentarily the tragedy that would befall this family in the infamous attack on Deerfield in 1704. It has been said that no family in Deerfield suffered more. The following section on Michael and Sarah (Catlin) Mitchell will contain an accounting of the 1704 Deerfield attack and its effect on both families.

FIRST GENERATION

1. **MICHAEL MITCHELL,** the earliest known ancestor of this
branch of the Mitchells bearing that surname, was probably born between 1670 and 1675, assuming he was at least
twenty-one years old at marriage. As discussed in the
Introduction to this book, he was probably the emigrant to
the Colonies.

Michael's marriage to Sarah Catlin, born about 1675
in or near Newark, NJ, fifth daughter of John and Mary
(Baldwin) Catlin, probably took place about 1694. As no
marriage record has been found, this date is also based on
other dates - the birth of their eldest known child in
Jan 1695/6, and the date of 24 Apr 1694 when Michael was
granted 30 acres of land by the town of Wallingford, CT.
(Grants of land were not usually bestowed on bachelors.)

The first permanent settlement of Wallingford was in
1670, the first settlers coming mostly from New Haven although some were from Boston, MA. The town encompassed an
area 10 miles wide and 10 miles long, including the land
within the towns of Meriden, Cheshire and the eastern part
of Prospect. It was bounded north by Farmington (later
Southington) and Wolcott; west by Waterbury; south by New
Haven, and east by Branford and the Totoket Mountains.

On 30 Nov 1695 Michael added to his Wallingford property by buying five acres of land for seven pounds from
William and Sarah Cole. The deed specifically reserved
one-half of the fruit of the orchard on the property yearly until Cole should "have an orchard at my new house
which will afford a competent supply for my family."

This may seem an unusual condition to place on the
sale of a piece of land but it was soundly based. Undoubtedly the fruit in question was apples, a staple food for
colonists, who planted fruit trees early on with apples
becoming a favorite in New England. Apples could be stor-
ed for long periods of time in cool root cellars, or dried
on long strings hung in front of the fireplace and used at

leisure in wintertime. Apples were made into vinegar, cider, wines and cordials and were used in many desserts.

Michael and Sarah left Wallingford in 1697 for Deerfield, a remote frontier outpost in Massachusetts, the northernmost such town in the Connecticut River Valley. During King William's War between the English and the French (1689-1697), the risk of living in such a small, isolated community was so great that Deerfield had nearly stopped growing. Sarah's parents, brothers and sisters lived in Deerfield. At a time when families were tightly knit for both economic and emotional reasons, Sarah probably welcomed this move.

In 1698, Deerfield granted Michael thirty acres of land and a home lot at Green River. At a town meeting on 1 Mar 1699, his grant was confirmed, but since his original grant had not been laid out, he was given in lieu of it the acreage that had originally been laid out to Samuel Root who had forfeited his claim, provided Michael stayed on the land for another year to fullfill Root's term of time, and paid due "Rates." This land lay "...near Brooks Brook running from Green River west & swamp..." in an area north of Deerfield which later became Greenfield.

The Mitchell home, like those of their neighbors, would have been a simple cabin, built of logs and chinked with mud and moss, possibly snuggled partially into the side of a sheltering hill. Its few windows did not contain glass but were covered with heavy wooden shutters which admitted no light when closed but were more practical in case of Indian attack. The fireplace may have been built of logs and clay. It was not unusual for such a fireplace to catch on fire itself. A turkey wing made a satisfactory brush to keep the hearth clean of ashes. On cold winter nights, the fire heated no more than an area three feet distant. People went to bed early to keep warm as well as conserve precious fuel.

Light in the cabin came from a pitch pine knot kept burning in a corner of the fireplace on a flat stone, keeping smoke and tar drippings out of the room. Candle making was hard work so they were used sparingly. Perhaps rush lights were used, the outer bark of the common rush stripped off, exposing the inner pith which was then dipped in tallow and allowed to harden. A constant fire was kept going. When it had to be relit, flint and steel were used with an old scrap of linen serving as tinder.

First Generation

The furnishings were sparse – a crude bed in which the entire family slept excepting the newest infant who had its own wooden cradle; a board laid across two trestles for a table, some backless benches for seating, and perhaps another crude table for the preparation of food. A spinning wheel was not a piece of furniture; it was a necessity. A few rough shelves held household articles with other items hung from the rafters and walls of the cabin.

Clothing, all made by the women of the household from wool or home-grown flax, spun by them into thread, then woven into fabric, was minimal and worn constantly until no longer useable as garments. Any extra clothing or outer wear hung from pegs driven into the cabin walls. Bathing of the entire body was infrequent and sanitary products were unknown. Women used linen rags which were re-used after washing.

Food was cooked in the fireplace in front of which hung lines of drying apples and herbs. Most meals consisted of meat and vegetable stews which were easiest to prepare. Sometimes meat was spitted over the fire or baked in heavy iron pots set among the hot ashes. Sometimes the family hunting knife was the only utensil available to prepare food. Refrigeration was unknown. Food was smoked or pickled to preserve it. No one could afford to throw away any food, even that which was barely edible. Spices were used lavishly to disguise the taste of rotting food. Illness was not connected with the eating of tainted meat.

At meals food was served in wooden trenchers, shallow bowls often shared by two people. Likewise, drinking cups or noggins were fashioned from wood or gourds and shared. Forks were unknown so food was eaten with fingers or with spoons carved from wood or horn. Children did not sit at the table with adults but stood behind them and had food passed back to them. They were expected to maintain complete silence at mealtimes.

In these rude, uncomfortable conditions, Michael and Sarah lived a life of unrelenting hard work, tilling the land, tending whatever animals they owned, paying their taxes in the form of produce from the land, enduring sicknesses with only home made medications available to treat them, praying for Divine guidance and protection, and raising their family.

On 12 Nov 1702 Michael sold his five acres of land in Wallingford which he purchased from the Coles in 1696, the deed again specifying that the Coles would receive half the crop from the orchard. In this same year, Michael as a "newcomer" was appointed hayward by the town of Deerfield. His job was keeping the cattle, sheep, and hogs from breaking through from the town common or roadways into enclosed fields, and to impound strays. Unlike today, the settlers fenced their animals out, rather than in.

The peace of 1697 was brief. Upon ascending the throne, one of Queen Anne's first acts in May 1702 was the declaration of war against the French, instigating yet another of the various conflicts between the English and the French which spanned many decades. This war, known as Queen Anne's War, like the others, was not confined to the European continent. Once again the French in Canada would ally with several Indian tribes and begin plans to swoop down on English frontier towns in one murderous raid after another.

When the chilling news of resumed hostilities reached Deerfield in June, the town was galvanized into action. A town meeting was called to discuss the urgent business of the town fortifications which had fallen into disrepair since 1697. Every adult male was made responsible for an assigned portion of so many rods width of the walls and faced with a fine if he failed to make repairs by a certain date. A plea for help was sent to the Provincial Governor of Massachusetts who immediately sent a party of soldiers to protect and assist the settlers. Timber for firewood was cut and hauled into the fort in unusually large quantities. Every eye and ear strained for signs of danger from the surrounding hills. Nerves were not soothed by reports of attacks from Canada on the coastal towns of Maine. But as 1702 wore on into 1703 with no indication of trouble in the Connecticut Valley, the settlers began to relax their vigilance.

On the night of 8 Oct 1703, two young Deerfield men went out onto the commons (fields shared by all for grazing animals), looking for their milk cows. Open areas such as the commons had been avoided during the day as too unprotected from view of possible enemies in the hills. Darkness would prove no protection this night. To the bereavement of their families and the alarm of the town, the young men were carried off to Canada by Indians.

Doubt about the adequacy of Deerfield's fortifications was once more on everyone's lips. Again, the town petitioned the Governor for aid in strengthening town palisading. Fearing the worst, those living outside the fort were compelled to leave their homes and return to the comparative safety of the town. At this point there were nearly three hundred men, women, children and soldiers in Deerfield, most of them residing outside the town. Suddenly, the ten to fifteen houses inside town walls were forced to accommodate all.

Even the best of frontier homes was not large. Now each house was crowded far beyond its capacity. The women had trouble cooking and getting on with daily chores. The men were driven out into the chill weather to escape the confusion. Sleeping at night was difficult. If the Mitchells moved into the Catlin house, (as seems reasonable), it had to accommodate four adults and eight children ranging in age from infants to teenagers.

The settlers were also feeling a great deal of anger toward the French and their Indian allies for their "unfair" methods of warfare. Indians knew nothing and cared less about English ideas of fair play. They never openly advanced over the fields, announcing their hostile intentions blatantly like so-called civilized nations. They utilized the element of surprise, the cover of trees and bushes and darkness to rush forward in sudden, silent attack. The English colonists didn't understand this type of fighting although they learned well from it. Less than a hundred years later, their descendants would use Indian guerilla tactics to fight and win their own war for independence from the English monarchy.

The fall of 1703 faded into winter, an unusually severe winter for Deerfield. Snow piled high along the walls of the fort and lay deep in the woods so that every footprint, even that of an Indian moccassin, could easily be detected. Foul weather plus two hundred miles of wilderness lying between Deerfield and Canada seemed ample protection against attack. There had been many instances of "cry wolf," so many that the settlers no longer believed every report of impending peril. Gradually life in Deerfield resumed its normal pace as many began returning to their homes which lay outside the fort.

If Michael and Sarah had sought the comparative safety of Deerfield's protective walls in the late fall of 1703 (as had many others), it would be at this point that they would have returned to their home north of Deerfield.

Such a decision quite probably saved this family from
nearly certain death had they remained in town.

We are very much indebted to George Sheldon for his
bone-chilling, very complete account ("A History of Deerfield, MA") of the events leading up to the morning of
February 29, 1703/4. Through his eyes we learn that several nights before the 29th, strange noises were heard a-
round the walls of the fort, trampling sounds like the
footsteps of many men. Older settlers, veterans of Philip's War, recalled a similar occurrence in 1672 in which
sounds of beating drums, hoofbeats of horses, and the
booming of guns seemed to come from the clear air just a
few days before the outbreak of war. In an age of super-
stition, the unexplained footsteps around the walls of
the fort were dread omens, striking icy fingers of fear
into the hearts of all as they huddled in their beds on
those frigid winter nights.

By the night of the 28th, three feet of snow lay on
the ground, piled twice as high in places where the wind
had drifted it. All within the fort slept, unaware of the
creeping menace from the north.

About two hours before daylight on the 29th, a combined force of two hundred to two hundred fifty French
soldiers and Abenaki Indians converged on Deerfield, si-
multaneously attacking the homes to the north of town and
the town itself, climbing up the drifted piles of frozen
snow along the walls of the fort to gain easy access to the
homes inside. Within minutes, the town was in a pande-
monium, the bizarre scene lit by flaming pine torches carried by the Indians as they set fire to houses and barns
and herded captives toward the meeting house.

Some of the settlers defended their homes from behind
bolted doors until those doors were broken in or they were
driven out by fire. Some escaped to the Wells house, the
best defended outside the fort, or leapt out windows to
run barefoot through the snow toward Hatfield some ten
miles to the south. Everywhere the air was filled with
the screams of animals being slaughtered, groans of the
wounded, and the crying of frightened children. Some
settlers were murdered in their beds. Others were scalped
on their own doorsteps. A number were found huddled in
cellars, smothered by smoke from their burning houses.

The mayhem continued for several hours or more. By
the time the sun had been up for an hour, the captives were

hastily herded together for the long trek north to Canada before the fires from burning buildings could draw reinforcements from the lower towns. When help from Hatfield arrived, they were joined by Capt. Wells, a number of citizens from the Wells and Stebbins houses, and the garrison soldiers who chased the last of the invaders across the north home lots and the meadows beyond. It was a helterskelter sort of pursuit, tinged by the desire for revenge, unorganized and unsuccessful. The settlers and soldiers, with no snow shoes, could only follow the exact path left by the fleeing enemy in the deep and softening snow. The chase was soon given up.

A record of those slain, captured, wounded or remaining alive and well after the raid is available to us in "Fitz John Winthrop's Table of Losses," made on the spot and shortly after the fact. The Mitchells are listed as having no losses either to themselves or their property. Yet Sheldon tells us that "...two thirds of those who lost life, or liberty, are known to have been in the fort, or north of it..." Only eleven families are listed as having suffered no damage at all, some of whom lived south of the fort. How did the Mitchells, who lived north of the fort, escape unharmed? An old family story, impossible to verify, says Michael and Sarah lived over the side of a hill and had let the fire go out in the night. With no smoke rising from their chimney and blowing snow drifted over the house, they were well camouflaged. There may be a grain of truth to this story which is certainly plausible. Suffice it to say, the Mitchells were lucky, and so were all their descendants, for without their good fortune on that day, this story would end here.

At just what moment did the Mitchells become aware of the attack? Surely by daybreak! A trip outside for more firewood or to milk the cow and they would have seen the smoke from the burning town rising in the air. Realizing its ominous meaning, they would remain at home behind shuttered windows and barred door until it was safe to venture out and into Deerfield. When they finally learned full details of the raid, the shock to Sarah must have been brutal! She had lost nearly her entire family!

Sarah's father, John, and her brother, Jonathan, had stayed in their house, bravely defending it until they, along with house and barn, were consumed by flames. Her mother, Mary, and two younger children were driven out of

the house by the flames, captured, and taken to the meeting house. Sarah's sister, Mary French, her husband,
Thomas, and five of their six children were captured,
their four-week old son, John, killed. Mary would die
on the march to Canada. Her sister, Elizabeth, widow of
James Corse, was captured along with her daughter. She
also died on the march to Canada. Sarah's brother, Joseph
Catlin, was killed in the pursuit of the attackers across
the north meadows. His wife, Hannah (Sheldon) Catlin, was
wounded, but recovered and several months later gave
posthumous birth to a son, the couple's first child. The
two children captured with Sarah's mother, seventeen year
old John, and young Ruth, were taken to Canada and would
not return home until 1706 and 1707.

Sarah's mother, Mary, although a captive, was not
taken with the others to Canada. It is said that she was
saved by her "practical Christianity." Mrs. Lucy D.
Shearer, a Catlin descendant, wrote a letter to George
Sheldon in 1875 which tells of the following Catlin family
tradition. "A Frenchman was brought in (to the meeting
house) and laid on the floor; he was in great distress, and
called for water. Mrs. Catlin fed him with water. Someone said to her, 'How can you do that for your enemy?' She
replied, 'If thine enemy hunger, feed him; if he thirst,
give him water to drink.' The Frenchman was taken and
carried away, and the captives marched off. Mrs. Catlin
was left. After they were all gone, a little boy came that
was hid in the house. Mrs. Catlin said to the boy, 'go run
and hide.' The boy said, 'Mrs. Catlin, why don't you go
and hide?' She said, 'I am a captive; it is not my duty to
hide.'...some thought the kindness shown to the Frenchman
was the reason of Mrs. Catlin's being left."

Sheldon tells us that in 1704, of Deerfield's forty-
one houses, "...at least fifteen were within the line of
the stockades. About twelve were north, and fourteen
south of it. When the night of February 28th closed down,
two hundred ninety one souls were under their rooftrees.
Of these, twenty were garrison soldiers, two visitors
from Hatfield, and two hundred sixty eight inhabitants...
In a few hours all but one hundred and twenty-six of the
inhabitants were either killed or in the hands of a cruel
enemy, on a march over the snow to Canada, three hundred
miles away." Some did not survive the march. Some like
the daughter of Elizabeth (Catlin) Corse, remained in

Canada, professed to the Catholic faith, married and raised families there. Some were held captive for a few years and then allowed to return home. One survivor of the massacre, Mary (Baldwin) Catlin, simply lost the will to live. On 9 Apr 1704, just a few weeks after the raid on Deerfield, she died.

At first the surviving inhabitants wanted to abandon Deerfield, quite a natural reaction. They were prevented from this by Col. Samuel Partridge of Hatfield. The women and children were sent to the lower towns such as Northampton, Hadley and Hatfield. All surviving able-bodied men were impressed as soldiers in the Queen's service, serving alongside sixty Connecticut men who had been sent up on permanent duty to establish a military post at Deerfield.

The impressed men were allowed two days out of five to cultivate their fields, this being done under the guard of armed soldiers. With so few days to devote to their fields, crop size that year was diminished. But they were assured of enough food to stay alive, each man receiving a military sustenance per day consisting of a pound of bread, a bit more than half a pound of pork or beef, eight ounces of "pease," and two quarts of beer.

Deerfield was not directly attacked again although there were many incidents over the next several years in which Deerfield people were killed or captured by small bands of raiding Indians. The danger involved in cultivating their fields was very real. Making a decent living became difficult. Eventually, Michael and his family returned to his original thirty acre grant in Wallingford. But on 17 Feb 1706/7 Michael, "sometime of Deerfield" but now "residing in Wallingford," sold his land there to Francis Hendricks for fifteen pounds and came back to his home in Deerfield. (On previously cited deeds, he made his "mark." This mark varied only slightly from deed to deed. Roughly, it resembled a sprawling capital "M."

With the signing of the Treaty of Utrecht on 30 Mar 1713, Queen Anne's war ended and Deerfield was back to normal. Four more children had been born to Michael and Sarah, the last one in 1713. Then another tragedy befell this family. Certain explanations come to mind for what transpired but will not be delved into here. The documents speak for themselves. (Massachusetts Council Records, Vol. VI, p. 305, 621, MA State Archives, Boston)

"At a Council held at the Council Chamber in Boston upon Thursday the 27th of January 1714...A Petition preferred by Sarah Mitchel wife of Michael Mitchel of Informing That her Sd. husband was lately convicted by his own confession of comitting fornication with a Negro wench, Praying to be divorced & to have her estate in Lands which she brought with her in mariage setled on her & such part of her husbands estate as she is dowable with by the Common law. ¶Ordered That the Sd. Michael Mitchel be served with a copy of the Petition & be heard thereon before this Board on the tenth day of June next, if any thing he have to say why the prayer thereof should not be granted & that the Justices of the County take order to sequester & secure his estate that it may be for the support & benefit of his wife & family."

No document relating to an appearance before the Board by Michael is in Massachusetts State Archive records. Michael apparently had nothing to say in his own defense. The second document states:

"At a Council held at the Council Chamber in Boston on Wednesday November 19th 1718...It appearing to this Board that Michael Mitchel of Deerfield within the County of Hampshire has been convicted of Fornication with a Negro Woman. ¶Ordered That the Sd. Michael Mitchel and Sarah Mitchel his wife be divorced from each other and that the Bonds of Matrimony between them be from this time wholly broken & dissolved...¶Whereas the Sd. Sarah Mitchel at the time of her mariage to the Sd. Michael was seized of Lands in her own right which are not disposed of, It is further ordered That the Sd. Sarah Mitchel shall have hold and enjoy & dispose as she shall see meet all such Lands as she was so seized of in her own right at the time of her mariage to the Sd. Michael Mitchel & not yet disposed of by her consent."

Because of its unique circumstances, this divorce case was specifically mentioned in an article entitled "Divorce & the Changing Status of Women in Eighteenth-Century Massachusetts" by Nancy F. Cott. (The William & Mary Quarterly, 3rd Series, Vol. 33, No. 4, Oct 1976, p. 586.) Ms. Cott suggests that the interracial nature of the confessed adultery was the crucial factor in this case. Out of fourteen women presenting adultery-based divorce petitions to the Massachusetts Court prior to 1773, only two were granted divorces - Sarah Mitchell and

one other woman who petitioned in 1752 on combined grounds
of desertion, adultery, and cohabitation.

As an interesting comment on the double standards of
the day, Ms. Cott footnotes the Sarah Mitchell vs. Michael
Mitchell case thusly. "The older definition of adultery
...hinged on the involvement of a married woman. Thus a
married man's sexual transgression could still be called
fornication, if his partner was single."

Location of the property belonging to Sarah as mentioned in her divorce papers has not been discovered.
Certainly it did not include her portion of her father's
estate which came to her after marriage and by wording of
John Catlin's administration papers was given to Michael
"in right of his wife."

On 3 Mar 1718/19 "Michael Mitchel of Deerfield" sold
to Thomas French (probably his former brother-in-law),
also of Deerfield, "...in Consideration of a Valuable Sum
of Money..." his home lot "...Granted to me by the town of
Deerfield...upon the River Commonly known by the name of
Green River..." and his thirty acres of land "...Called
meadow lands..." This deed was signed by mark before two
witnesses, Ebenezer Brooks and John Catlin (Jr.).

There has been some confusion regarding the above
deed. Some believe it may refer to Michael's son by that
name. There are good arguments against that idea. Young
Michael was barely seventeen years old when the above
property was re-confirmed to Michael at a town meeting in
March 1717/18 which called Michael one of those to whom
"...there hath been formerly...grants of land..." And
clearly the property described in Michael's deed of sale
matches that of his granted land in town records. Note,
too, that Sarah was given by divorce decree only that
property of which she had been "seized" prior to her marriage, leaving Michael in possession of his Green River
lands, and free to dispose of them if he wished. But he
could not do this until the Court in Boston had made their
ruling on the case. Although the junior Michael Mitchell
did own property in the Green River area, that did not occur until a later date, after his marriage about 1720.

After the finalization of their divorce late in 1718
and Michael had disposed of his Green River property early
in 1719, Michael simply...disappeared. Sarah and her
children gravitated once more to the Wallingford, CT
area. Only three of her children would return to the

First Generation

Deerfield area - William, who settled in nearby Greenfield (once part of Deerfield); Michael, Jr.; and Joseph,
who eventually settled in Deerfield. Sarah also returned
and probably lived in the household of her son, Joseph.
She died in Deerfield on 30 Dec 1736. Children of Michael
and Sarah (Catlin) Mitchell were:

2. **John** b 22 Jan 1695/6   +
3. **William** b 21 Apr 1697   +
4. **Sarah** b 19 Feb 1698/9   +
5. **Michael** b 8 Mar 1700/01   +
6. **Mary** b 10 Jul 1703; d in infancy.
7. **Joseph** b 2 Sep 1705   +
8. **Jonathan** b 18 Jan 1707/8   +
9. **Catherine** (Catheron) b 1 Sep d 17 Dec 1710.
10. **Samuel** b 7 Mar 1712/13   +

SECOND GENERATION

The children of Michael and Sarah (Catlin) Mitchell belonged to that generation of children who never knew true peace in their lifetimes.

The year 1637 saw the beginning in this country of over a hundred years of conflict between England and France. By the time the first four Mitchell children had been born, English colonists had already endured three major conflicts. First was the Pequot War which began in 1637. Second in 1675 came King Phillip's War, named for Metacomet, sachem of the Wampanoag Indian tribe, but called Phillip by the English. At the end of this war in 1677, many towns in Massachusetts such as Northfield, Deerfield, Brookfield, Worcester, Lancaster, Groton, Mendon, Wrentham, Middleborough, Dartmouth, Warwick, Wickford and Simsbury had been abandoned, leaving "jumbles of blackened ruins and weed-choked gardens." Third came King William's War from 1689 to 1697.

This was followed by Queen Anne's War (1702-1713), King George's War (1743-1748), and the French-Indian War (1754-1763), called the Seven Years War by Europeans.

In the Deerfield area, there was a localized conflict in the early 1720's called Father Rasle's War. Other areas of New England had their conflicts in between these major wars that were given local names. As Donald Barr Chidsey comments ("The French and Indian War"), "In the century and a half that England and France had faced each other, snarling, in the New World, peace had never really broken out - except on paper."

As the last of the French-English wars wound to a close in 1763, conflicts between the English colonists and the Mother Country began to escalate. Not all of the colonists were Whigs (we would call them liberals today) who favored less stringent taxation, more home control, and ultimate separation from Britain. Many were Tories who approved of continued rule by the British Crown in spite of a good many inequities in its administration. The result was strife and bitter argumentation between townspeople, many of whom were related by blood or marriage. For example, the Mitchells of the Deerfield, MA area, who were Whigs, were at odds with some of their Catlin relatives who were Tories.

Eventually the day came in 1776 when "the shot heard 'round the world" was fired and war - the great war for American independence - began.

---

2. **JOHN MITCHELL** was born 22 Jan 1695/6 at Wallingford, CT but grew up in Deerfield, MA where his parents moved when he was quite young. Before 1720 John was again at Wallingford where he married 27 Oct 1720 Katherine Munson, born 3 June 1704 at Wallingford, daughter of Samuel & Martha (Farnes/Fern[e]s) Munson who were among the first settlers of that town. On 20 Jan 1721 John purchased land at Wallingford from Solomon Munson, the deed witnessed by Samuel Munson. John made his "mark" on this deed, a circle surrounded by five short strokes, rather like rays emanating from a miniature sun. Known children, probably born at or near Wallingford, were:

11. **James** bc (1721?) +
12. **Moses** bc 1723 +
13. **John** bc (1725?) +

3. **WILLIAM MITCHELL** was born 21 Apr 1697 at Deerfield, MA; he married 27 Oct 1721 to Ann(a)/Annah Wait, daughter of William & Ann(a) (Webb) Wait of Northampton, MA. Ann(a) died 11 Aug 1756 at Greenfield, MA and William died there in October 1775, not long after he had sold his thirty acre farm with buildings on the 16th of that month to his son Elijah for the sum of 80 pounds.

The "shire town" of Greenfield was incorporated in 1753. Prior to that it was part of Deerfield, called the Green River lands after the river that flowed north to south through the town. Up to the date of incorporation, births, deaths, and marriages of Green River residents appear in both Greenfield and Deerfield vital records. Although this makes it a bit difficult to tell if William and Anna always lived in Greenfield after their marriage, I believe they did. In 1723 Deerfield town records show William with two shares of Green River commons with no acreage noted, but in 1726 he is listed as owning lot #5 of one acre, his brother, Michael, Jr., owning one acre in the adjoining lot #6. At a Proprietor's meeting on 16 Mar 1737/8, William along with Benjamin Hastings and Jonah Holmes had their house lots "...at Green River formerly laid out to them..." confirmed.

Lot #5 lay in Green River Town Plot on the south side of the street "...joyning to ye street north and west on ye Country road that goeth to Green River South." This lot plus four others were sold to Aaron Denio between 1738 and 1743.

William also had two other lots laid out to him, one of 15 acres and one of 30 acres on the west side of Green River. The 15 acre lot must be the one described by Thompson ("History of Greenfield, MA") as "the little place by the brook." The 30 acre lot must have been William's own farm "on the opposite side of the Shelburne road" which he sold to Elijah. Thompson says this land was passed on to Elijah's son, William, and to William's son, Anson, who conveyed it to his sister, Content, who sold it in 1864. Unless Thompson refers to another piece of property, this can not be so, as Elijah sold the 30 acres he bought from his father to Daniel Field of Deerfield in 1784. Both the deed from William to Elijah in 1775 and the deed from Elijah to Daniel Field in 1784 describe the property as bounded north by Isaac Foster, east by David Smead, south by Caleb Wright & Jonathan Hoit, and west by Ebenezer Allen & Caleb Wright who was William's son-in-law.

Before 1753, the residents of Green River had no church of their own, attending the church in Deerfield. William was a member in good standing of the Deerfield church. In 1743 and again in 1748, he received money from a special church collection taken up from time to time to aid members in financial need. Life for frontier farmers of modest acreage was always a struggle.

Like his brother, Joseph of Deerfield, William was more concerned in church affairs than town office. At the incorporation of Greenfield in 1753, William was one of twelve men who proposed the formation of a new church in Greenfield. Late in the fall, a committee of five was appointed "...to wate on the Rev'd Mr. Billing..." regarding his acceptance of a ministerial post. Rev. Mr. Billing, as did these men, held to the old views that none but children of church members should receive baptism, and none but church members should vote in public affairs. This opinion was not shared by the Rev. Ashley and his Deerfield congregation. The Deerfield church refused letters of dismission to their removed Greenfield members and withheld a requested letter of recommendation for the new organization. The resentment which resulted led to years of friction and animosity between the two churches.

William and Anna's children put down deep roots in Greenfield, some descendants still in the Greenfield-Shelburne area in the late 1800's. Children of William and Anna (Wait) Mitchell (recorded at Deerfield) were:

14. **John** b 16 Apr 1723
15. **Anna** b 30 Oct 1724; prob m 14 Feb 1751 John Ball ("Early CT Marriages," Wallingford-Meriden V/R).
16. **Ebenezer** b 2 Jan 1726/7; dsp (unmarried) 26 June 1748, killed in "Hobb's Fight," King George's War (French-Indian).
17. **Abigail** b 24 Sep 1728   +
18. **Elijah** b 3 Oct 1730   +
19. **Aaron** b 29 Jan 1732/3
20. **Sarah** b 18 Dec 1734   +
21. **Rhoda** b 9 Dec 1736 m 28 Jan 1766 (Greenfield V/R) Abraham Bass of E. Hoosick, NY. (Deerfield, MA V/R also list marriage intentions for Rhoda to Samuel Catlin 7 Jan 1756.)
22. **Rachel** b 6 Mar 1739/40

4. **SARAH MITCHELL** was born 19 Feb 1698/9 at Deerfield, MA; married 1) 9 Jul 1718 at Wallingford, CT as his 2nd wife, James Hough, whose 1st wife, Hannah Clark, died 3/4 Mar 1718, leaving 4 children. James, son of Samuel & Mary (Bate) Hough, was born 15 Dec 1688 at Wallingford; died there 20 Oct 1740. At his death, Sarah was left with 8 children at home, 5 of them age 10 and under. Nonetheless, she did not remarry for 14 years when on 16 Jan 1754 (Wallingford, CT V/R) she became the third wife of Mathias Hitchcock of Meriden, CT. She had no children by this second marriage.

Sarah's children (HOUGH) were: **(i)** Ephraim b 9 Apr 1719 d 16 Feb 1781 m1) 12 Nov 1739 at Wallingford to Hannah Royce b 1 Jul 1716 d 16 Feb 1777, d/o Robert & Joanna (Gaylord) Royce; m2) 5 June 1777 Lydia Dennison, d/o James & Dorothy (Morris) Dennison, widow of Jacob Goodsell; 10 children by 1st marriage; **(ii)** Daniel b 6 Mar 1721 d 25

Jul 1768 m1) 20 Jan 1741 Mindwell Judd b 10 Apr 1719 d 21
Mar 1741/2; m2) 29 Nov 1743 at Wallingford to Violet Benton; 11 children by 2nd marriage; **(iii)** Abigail bc 1722-25
m 6 Nov 1740 Samuel Holt; **(iv)** Ebenezer b 22 Jan 1726 m1)
Lydia Buell who d 20/21 Jul 1756, age 35y; m2) 17 Nov 1757
Abigail (Bacon) Plumb; 4 children by 1st marriage;
(v) David b 28 Feb 1728 d 18 Oct 1729, age 1y 7m 20d;
(vi) Sarah b 18 Oct 1730 d 10 Nov 1741, age 11 years;
(vii) David b 28 Jan 1733 d 27 June 1752, age 19 years;
(viii) James b 24 Mar 1735 d 9 Nov 1754, age 19y (date of
death from 1st Congregational Church records, Meriden, CT
although Davis' "History of Wallingford, CT" says this
James m Lucy_____ who d 5 Oct 1775, age 51y); **(ix)** Barnabas
b 5 Sep 1737 m 29 Jan 1760 at Meriden, CT to Esther/Eunice
Weeks; 7 children, all b or bpt in Litchfield Co., CT;
(x) Mary b 25 Nov 1739.

5. **MICHAEL MITCHELL (JR.)** was born 8 Mar 1700/01 at Deerfield, MA. He served under Capt. Samuel Barnard in Father
Rasle's War, a local conflict between the English and the
French. He was granted property in the Green River lands
(later to become Greenfield) by the town of Deerfield
where his first two children were born. By 1725, although
still listed as a Green River property holder, he had moved to Wallingford, CT where his third child was born.
  He was a trader according to various cases in Hampshire Co., MA Inferior Court of Common Pleas records of
1729 and 1730. A sample case is the suit of Daniel Arms,
husbandman of Deerfield, who sued Michael, "trader of
Wallingford," for recovery of 100 gallons of "good mer-
chantable molasses," and 53 gallons of "good Barbados
Rhum," due by note of 10 May 1728 per writ of 20 May 1729.
Daniel was awarded the molasses and rum through Michael's
default by non-appearance. Another case dated 1730 concerned Nathaniel Bancroft, yeoman of Windsor, CT, who
sued Michael for recovery of money under Michael's bond
of 3 June 1729. Michael pleaded not guilty and asked
for abatement. Unlike most of the other cases, this
one went before a jury who found in Michael's favor and
charged him only for court costs of 16 shillings.
  Not long after 1730 Michael returned to Deerfield.
His name appears on a list of members "now in ye church" as
of 10 July 1733. He owned land at Deerfield (i.e., Green
River) but didn't seem to prosper. In 1740 he failed to

pay tax of 3 shillings 6 pence on two shares of undivided commons, necessitating sale of part of it in 1742 by the assessors. At his death in 1760, money he had borrowed 31 years before from John Catlin and James Kellogg was still owed to John and to the estate of James Kellogg, deceased.

Michael's estate inventory listed assets of "One Lot up Long Hill Iner Commons of ( ) acres...one Lot Iner Commons 6½ acres...two Lots on the North West Division...one Lot Country farmes one acre...two commons in the undivided Lands...one note of hand seventeen shillings two pence two farthings." Money from the sale of his estate was not sufficient to pay his debts. On 8 Dec 1761 the appointed Commissioners apportioned the proceeds of the sale of both real and personal property among Michael's creditors at the rate of "four pence three farthings to the pound & no more." In this way, debts totaling 60 pounds were "satisfied" with only a bit over 16 pounds.

Administrator of Michael's estate was his eldest son, Joel, who was then living at Wethersfield, CT. Joel's administration account of 1761 reflects a long list of out-of-pocket expenses totaling over 15 pounds for such items as "one gorney from Springfield to Hadly to see what was Due to the Estate...one gorney mour to Northamton Expenses & hors...to Major William for searching the Records and Riteing...", money paid to the "Lawer...Clark of the Cort," and so forth. No mention is made in these administration papers of a widow or other heirs, making it likely that Joel was Michael's only surviving heir at his death.

Michael married about 1720 to Mary____about whom we have no data. She may have died prior to 1733 as she is not mentioned with Michael on the list of Deerfield 1st Congregational Church members. Known children were:

23. **Joel** b 19 Jul 1721   +
24. **Moses** b 11 May 1723
25. **Katharine** b 22 Jan 1725

7. **JOSEPH MITCHELL (SR.)** was born 2 Sep 1705 at Deerfield, MA. He died 16 Sep 1794 at Deerfield. He married 2 Nov 1726 at Sunderland, MA to Mary Allis, daughter of William & Elizabeth (Davis) Allis. Mary was born 18 Feb 1705/6 at Hatfield, MA, and died 8 Nov 1783 at Deerfield. Both she and Joseph are buried in the Old Deerfield Cemetery.

Nearly four months to the day after Joseph and Mary were married, their first child was born. Four days after the birth, Joseph and his wife were fined 30 shillings each by the Court of General Sessions of the Peace for Hampshire Co., the charge obviously being fornication. The record shows that they paid their fines.

This sort of infraction was not uncommon in colonial times and not especially frowned upon from a moral point of view as long as the young couple married. Bundling, a custom carried over to the New World from England, Wales, and parts of Europe, was responsible for some of these "early" births. In winter, a young man who came courting, had often walked miles to the home of his young lady. He had worked hard all day and had only the evening in which to visit his sweetheart. The young couple had to share the room with her family. Often, the parents would retire early for the sake of keeping warm. In the same way, the young woman and her suitor lay on the floor in front of the fireplace near her parents' bed, covering themselves. In the presence of love, all things are possible. But in the case of Joseph Mitchell, we can not blame bundling for the "premature" birth of their first child who seems to have been conceived in the middle of the summer when there was little necessity for keeping warm. Accusing married couples of fornication and fining them was merely a legal formality, designed to satisfy the law of the land.

Joseph and Mary remained in Sunderland for only a few years, removing to Deerfield before 1732. His mother was probably living with them as "Sary Mitchel" is noted as among the members of the Deerfield church in 1733.

The first deed recorded in Hampshire Co., MA records for Joseph Mitchell is dated 22 Oct 1741 in which he sold property in Falls Fight Township, later Fallstown, and at the incorporation of the township in 1762, Bernardstown. This tract of land had been granted to the survivors and descendants of survivors of the Falls Fight. In 1738 Joseph had purchased the house lot and meadow lands of one Preserved Wright, heir of James Wright, who lived in New Hampshire. The property was merely an investment for Joseph who had been given the work of building a saw mill on Fall River near the meadow lands. For his work he was given entitlement to the exclusive mill privileges of that part of Fall River, but only if he also set up a grist mill near the saw mill for the benefit of the community. Joseph completed the saw mill but did not proceed with work on the grist mill, selling out in 1741 to Hezekiah

Newcomb of Lebanon, CT and Simon Gager of Norwich, CT for the sum of 30 pounds.

Although all frontier settlers had to farm to furnish their tables with food, many men had another occupation as well. Joseph was a weaver. He probably kept sheep for their wool, may have grown some hemp, and definitely grew flax, a delicate plant with dainty, drooping blue flowers that was so important to the Colonies, laws were passed requiring every family in Massachusetts and Connecticut to spin so many pounds of flax per year or pay a fine.

The process of growing and preparing flax before it was brought to the spinning wheel and then to the weaver's loom involved many steps and much hard work. Sowed broadcast in May, it was weeded by the women and children when the plants were 3 to 4 inches high. At the end of June or first of July, the men and boys pulled the ripe flax up by the roots and laid it in the sun to dry, turning it twice or more each day. It was then "rippled" to remove seed bolls which were saved for the next planting, tied in beats or bates (bundles), and stacked in stooks for a second drying in the fields. Night time accumulations of dew wet the flax. Heavy boards weighted with stones were then piled on, removed in a week or so, and the rotten leaves stripped off. Again, the flax was spread for drying and then bundled.

Now the flax had to be "broken," a job that took the muscles of a strong man. It was usually broken twice on a flax brake, then scutched or swingled to remove any small pieces of bark clinging to the stems. If he worked very hard, a man could swingle 40 pounds of flax in a day. After a second swingling, the flax was put into a wooden trough and pounded with a huge pestle shaped instrument to soften the fibers. Last, it was hackled with a hetchel comb several times, using combs of various fineness, the fibers sorted according to thickness, and finally wrapped around the spindle, ready for the spinning wheel.

During the long, tedious job of growing and preparing flax for the wheel, Joseph must often have wished for more and older sons. But when the flax was ready for spinning, he could be grateful for his three daughters who would help their mother with that job. Colonial women were expert and hard working spinners. One of the most important items a bride possessed when she left her parents' home was a spinning wheel. Women often carried small spinning wheels to a neighbor's house so they could spin and gossip at the same time. It was considered a healthy exercise for women, adding to their femininity and good spirits.

Once the flax was spun into thread, it was ready for Joseph who probably had a special room or outbuilding where he kept his looms. Here the woven cloth was fulled, washed, scratched and dressed with teazels, dyed or bleached, and tented before it was ready to be made into clothing and household articles. Sixteen months has elapsed between the planting of the flax seed and the finished product - bolts of linen cloth.

Linen was too valuable to make into clothing for every day wear. Tow (short flax fibers) was also spun and made into a rough cloth that stayed prickly until it had gone through many washings. Cloth from tow was the material used for everyday clothing. Having fine linen cloth on hand was as good or better than having money. What Joseph didn't sell, he would have traded in the village for salt, sugar, spices, tea and so forth.

In town affairs, Joseph was not an active participant, but in church affairs he took an interest. When the meeting house was renovated in the late 1760's, the new steeple was placed on a different part of the roof, leaving an ugly patch where the old one was removed. The town refused additional money for repairs, but townspeople could make contributions in wheat, rye or cash. Joseph contributed four pounds cash. His assigned seating in the meeting house was at the back of the church, two sections from the pulpit to the south which in 1777 he shared with Joseph Smead, John Amsden, Moses Nims, and two widows, Rhoda Childs and Sarah Shattuck.

At that time the town minister was Rev. Jonathan Ashley, an ardent Tory. He did nothing to hide his loyalty to the Crown, publicly praying from his pulpit for the King. In 1774 the town had voted to refuse Rev. Ashley both salary and firewood, hoping to persuade him to leave, but he did not. The Tory faction in town then came out in full force to reinstate Rev. Ashley's salary plus the raise he had been given in 1762. Joseph and his son, Abner, along with a large group of Whigs, signed a protest against the vote but, being in the minority, it did no good. This warring between the Whigs and their Tory minister continued until 1780 when Joseph and others in Deerfield shared the expense of convening a council to settle the matter.

This council sat for ten long days, but, being equally divided, resolved nothing. Rev. Ashley himself solved the argument by passing from this world to the next in August of that year.

Colonial courts were kept as busy as ours today. People sued other people for a variety of reasons but mostly over unpaid notes due them. There are many cases indexed to Joseph Mitchell in the Inferior Court of Common Pleas of which six only are for jury service. At times it is difficult to tell if a case involved the senior or the junior Joseph since it is not designated. Joseph, Sr. both sued and was sued, sometimes winning, sometimes not.

Obviously, Joseph was a successful man. He provided well for his family, paid his taxes, could contribute to the church in cash rather than kind, and had enough money left over to speculate in property. He and Joseph, Jr. bought and sold property between themselves more than once. Besides the property at Bernardstown which he sold in 1741, Joseph was also an early proprietor of Conway which was set off from Deerfield in the 1750's. At the 1763 division of land in Conway, he was granted lot 27 of 120 acres which he sold almost immediately to Isaac Amsden of Stamford, CT. (Isaac was married to Joseph's first cousin, Hannah Catlin.) Joseph also owned in common with others in the town two islands in Deerfield River. In 1773, the islands were sold to Jonas Locke. His final sale of property occurred less than six months before his death in 1794 when Joseph and his son, Abner, sold six acres of land they owned jointly in the "Beaver dam part of Deerfield."

Lest you believe Colonial husbands and wives lived together in a state of harmony and bliss, let us consider an intriguing item that appears in Deerfield 1st Congregational church records under date of 23 June 1762 which reads: "The church being met a case respecting the wife of Joseph Mitchell was laid before the church. She being accused of several unbecoming expressions relating to her husband particularly calling him a dog and saying he showed a devilish spirit and she justifying those expressions before the church. Voted that she be debarred from communion until she manifests a different temper & a sorrow for her sin."

The question is not only _why_ Mrs. Joseph Mitchell spoke in this manner about her husband, but _which_ Mrs.

Joseph Mitchell was involved? In 1762 both Joseph, Sr. who was married to Mary Allis, and Joseph, Jr., his son, husband of Lydia Foster, lived in Deerfield, although Joseph, Jr. would move to nearby Ashfield that year.

In June of 1762 the junior Mrs. Joseph had been married for eleven years, was the mother of three children, and about to deliver her fourth. She seems a less likely candidate than the senior Mrs. Joseph, known by record to be a member of the Deerfield church. In that year, Mary, wife of the senior Joseph, was fifty-six years old, and had been married nearly thirty-six years; her children were grown and married, and she had grandchildren. Her household may have been under some stress at that time. In 1760 Zadock King (Sr.) had been declared "a person non compos mentis" by the Court of Probate at Northampton, MA (Vol. IX, p. 184), and he was put under the guardianship of Joseph whose daughter Hannah was his wife. From an accounting made by Joseph to the Court of debts due from the estate of Zadock King, it is clear that Zadock not only owed his father-in-law and others a great deal of money (over 106 pounds), but was actually residing with the Mitchells as is apparent by Joseph's charge against the estate for thirteen weeks board. Presumably, Hannah and the four King children were also living with the Mitchells and may still have been in 1762.

Joseph was in his eighty-seventh year when he wrote his will. On a Saturday, 14 Apr 1792, his friends and neighbors, Phine(h)as Arms of nearby Wapping, Ithmar Burt, tailor, and "Lawyer Sam" Barnard, both of Deerfield, witnessed the document.

Calling himself yeoman of Deerfield, "...weak in Body but of sound Mind & Memory...", he directed that twelve pounds each be given "...to my Daughter Mary, Wife of Samuel Belding...to my Daughter Hannah Bigelow...to My Daughter Tabitha, Wife of Gershom Tuttle." Eight shillings apiece were to go to "...my Grandchildren Ensign, Joseph, Lydia, Thankful, & Trifena, Children of my late Son Joseph...", all legacies to be paid within two years after his death. To his youngest and only surviving son, Abner, whom he appointed co-executor with Samuel Childs, Joseph left "...All my Messuages, Lands & Tenements whatsoever, and wheresoever...all the Rest & Residue of my Goods, Chattels, & personal estate I give to my said Son Abner Mitchel..."

Joseph lived a little more than two years after writing his will, dying on a Tuesday, 16 Sep 1794, just past his eighty-ninth year, a far longer lifetime than many of his contemporaries. In the year of his death, "Yankee Doodle" was published; Eli Whitney was granted a patent on his cotton gin; President Washington, who had begun his second term of office the year before, celebrated his 35th wedding anniversary; and the United States Post Office was permanently established. Deerfield, MA had long since ceased to be a frontier town.   Children of Joseph and Mary (Allis) Mitchell were:

26. **Joseph** b 3 Mar 1726/7   +
27. **Mary** b 10 Mar 1731/2   +
28. **Hannah** b 9 Jan 1732/3   +
29. **Tabitha** b 9 Feb 1736/7   +
30. **Abner** b 28 Oct 1738   +
31. **Experience** b 10 June 1746; d 27 Oct 1746.

8.   **JONATHAN MITCHELL** was born 18 Jan 1707/8 at Deerfield, MA. He married 5 June 1733 at Guilford, CT to Lydia Howe of that town.   Lydia's ancestry is unknown, but the very unusual name given to her third child suggests that she may have borne some relationship to one of the Camp families who were early in the Hartford and Wethersfield, CT area. (Several by this name appear in Barbour's "Families of Early Hartford, CT.")

After living in Guilford for a few years, Jonathan and his family moved to Durham, CT in Middlesex Co. where Jonathan, Lydia, and their two eldest children were baptized on 13 Apr 1740. Regrettably, after the baptism of young Lydia in Durham in 1744, we lost sight of this family and attempts to trace them have not succeeded.

A Jonathan Mitchell is listed in the "Connecticut Probate Index 1641-1948" under File #3146 dated 1644, containing one "miscellaneous" item. Since this document comes from the records of Woodbury District in Litchfield Co., it is doubtful that it applies to the above Jonathan. Jonathan was a given name used by several other unrelated Mitchell families in New England. File #3146 might pertain to an ancestor of the Jonathan Mitchell who appeared in the 1790 CT Census as a resident of Southbury Twp. of Litchfield County.

A strong possibility exists that Jonathan and his family moved to Middletown, CT not far north of Durham, where two of Jonathan's children were married. He may have died there prior to 1790, leaving no probate records or none that exist today. An Amasa Mitchell served in the Revolutionary War from CT, perhaps the one who married at East Haddam, CT 8 June 1786 Hulda Stocking, and listed there in the 1790 census (1 male 16 & up, 1 male under 16, 2 females) along with a John, Joseph and Asa Mitchell. Although he appears to be in the correct age span, it is not known if this Amasa was the same as the one listed below as son of Jonathan. Known children of Jonathan and Lydia (Howe) Mitchell were:

32. **Sarah** b 12 Jan 1735/6   +
33. **Abner** b 23 Aug 1738   +
34. **Camp** b 8 Nov 1741
35. **Amasa** b 21 Nov 1742
36. **Lydia** b 20 Nov (Guilford V/R); bpt 25 Nov 1744 (Durham V/R).

10. **SAMUEL MITCHELL** was born 7 Mar 1712/13 at Deerfield, MA and married 5 Jan 1738 at Wallingford, CT to Abigail Cook, born 9 Oct 1711 at Wallingford, daughter of John and Abigail (Johnson) Cook.

There are a number of records in Connecticut and Massachusetts pertaining to Samuel Mitchell. Smith's "History of Sunderland, MA" says Samuel was there in 1734 and had land granted to him in 1737 (1737/38?) "...if he abide five years." Hampshire Co., MA deed records show that Samuel Mitchell purchased land on 20 Oct 1733 in Sunderland from Daniel Russell (Bk 1:133). On 8 Nov 1736, Samuel Mitchell "of Sunderland" bought land at Bernardston from Solomon Boltwood (Bk 1:157), and on 28 Aug 1738, Samuel Mitchell "of Lower Ashuwelot" (Ashuelot, a stream near Northfield's area) purchased a tract in Northfield from Tahan Grant of Hadley (Bk 1:157). In 1743 Samuel Mitchell "of Deerfield" was one of the original proprietors in Charlestown. Yet Samuel's first five children were born at Wallingford, CT between 1739 and 1749 according to Jacobus ("Families of Ancient New Haven") who cites Wallingford Vital Records. Noticeably, only the fifth child has a baptism record there at the 1st Congregational Church in nearby Meriden.

These facts seem to indicate that Samuel did not live at Wallingford after his marriage until a short time before the birth of Rebecca early in 1749 and that the births of his first four children were recorded at Wallingford long after the fact, a not unusual practice, particularly for families who moved around a bit. Samuel may have taken up his proprietorship in Township No. 4 in Charlestown in 1743 but decided to remove his family to the safety of Wallingford at the onset of King George's War (Old French-Indian War). In the spring and summer of 1746, Sheldon tells us that "...skulking parties of the enemy killed, wounded or captured sixteen persons at No. 4, Northfield, and on the Ashuelot above..." ("History of Deerfield, MA") It was a less than healthy place for anyone, especially a man with a young family.

Little is known of Samuel's children. Possibly his son, Michael, was the Michael Mitchell appearing on a list of "North Farmers" at the incorporation of Meriden, CT in May 1806 (town meeting of Sep 1805; "History of Wallingford, CT," by C. H. S. Davis, p144); an Oliver Mitchell served in the Revolutionary War from CT (widow, Anna, pension #W-1632); an Oliver Mitchell is also in the 1790 census of East Windsor, Hartford Co., CT, listed with a family of "5 other free persons." However, this sort of classification indicates that this was a family of free black persons.

Like his brother, Jonathan, Samuel "disappears" in the 1750's. By the birth record of his sixth child, he removed his family to Farmington in Hartford Co., CT by 1750 or 1751. His name is not listed in the "Connecticut Probate Index 1641-1948." Known children of Samuel and Abigail (Cook) Mitchell were:

37. **Michael** b 26 Feb 1739
38. **Oliver** b 14 Apr 1741
39. **Samuel** b 17 Aug 1743   +
40. **Abigail** b 26 Apr 1746   +
41. **Rebecca** b 3 Feb 1748/9
42. **Medad** b 18 Aug 1751

THIRD GENERATION

Soon after the end of the last French-Indian War in 1763, a general trend towards migration to more remote areas began to manifest itself among the members of this generation. These children had been born on the frontier, grown to adulthood there, and were now living in well settled communities. Opportunity for the average family lay not at home but over the horizon. They began to sell what property they owned, load up their families and household goods, and set off for new frontiers in sparsely populated areas of Vermont, New York, Pennsylvania, and on west where land was plentiful and cheap. Tracing their movements and detailing their personal lives becomes difficult as they moved into locations where record keeping was much less immaculate than in the older, settled towns which they had left.

Congress authorized the first census of the United States in 1790. This census is a useful but limited tool for the genealogist. It was intended as a military census to determine how many males were of eligible military age. Therefore, only two age classifications are used, one for all males in a household age sixteen and up, and one for all males under the age of sixteen. Females in a household were counted, but not put into an age grouping. Only the name of the head of household appears with no distinction made between his own wife and children and others who may have been living with the family at the time.

Like their fathers and mothers, this generation of Mitchells had grown up with war. Most had survived the various conflicts which had plagued the Colonies for over a hundred years. Now, looming into their lives was a much larger war, the revolt of the Colonies against their ancestral homeland. Thousands upon thousands of books have been written, minutely describing the uneasy relationship between the British Crown and her American Colony. But what **really** made these Colonials fight?

Sixty-seven years after the Battle of Lexington, Levi Preston, who had run sixteen miles to get into the fight, was asked his opinion of the oppressions that had led up to the war such as the Stamp Act and the tea tax. He exclaimed he had never seen one of those stamps and never had drunk a drop of tea. The questioner then supposed Levi had been reading Sidney or Locke about the "eternal principle of liberty." No, he had read "...only the Bible, the Catechism, Watt's Psalms and Hymns, and the Almanac." What then had made him get into the fight? "'Young man... what we meant in going for those redcoats was this: we always had governed ourselves, and we always meant to. They didn't mean we should.'" ("John Adams, the Statesman of the Revolution," by Mellen Chamberlain)

William Pitt, one of the few British defenders of America, said, "If I were an American as I am an Englishman, while a foreign troop was landed in my country I would never lay down my arms, - never! never! never!" And so they did not, these new Americans, until their country's independence was won.

---

11. **JAMES MITCHELL**, son of John and Katherine (Munson) Mitchell, was born about (1721?), probably in or near Wallingford, CT. He married there 7 Mar 1743 to Jane Strachen/Stracken. Birth records for their children are found in Wallingford Vital Records. A baptism record for the fourth child is also found at the 1st Congregational Church in Cheshire, CT. Known children of James and Jane (Strachen) Mitchell were:
  43. **Mary** b 10 Jan 1743/4
  44. **Elizabeth** b 25 Jan 1745/6; d 29 Aug 1751
  45. **Martha** b 15 Mar 1747/8; d 30 Aug 1751
  46. **John** b 6 June 1750; bpt June 1750

12. **MOSES MITCHELL**, son of John and Katherine (Munson) Mitchell, was born about 1723 at Wallingford, CT. He died 7/8 Nov 1797 (age 74 or 75) at nearby Meriden and is buried in the Old Graveyard there.

Moses married twice. His first wife and mother of all his children was Mary Ives, daughter of Gideon & Mary (Royce) Ives, whom he married on 11 Apr 1745 at Wallingford. Mary was born 16 Dec 1724 at Wallingford and died 14 May 1776 (age 52), buried in the Old Meriden Graveyard.

Moses married his 2nd wife 11 Dec 1777 at Wallingford, Patience Benham, daughter of Nathan & Mary ( ) Benham. She may be "The Widow Mitchel" whose death on 8 Oct 1803 is recorded by the 1st Congregational Society of Meriden.

Five years before his death, Moses made his will. From the will (CT Probate Index, File #1202) and other papers in his probate file, we can tell quite a bit about this man. For example, by trade Moses was a leather tanner and a shoe maker, a very successful one if we can judge by the extensive inventory of his estate.

He dressed soberly as befitted a man of his age in clothing of dark brown, reddish brown, or black; his great coat was for winter wear; his best coat, black silk handkerchief, and linen shirt presumably for special occasions such as Sunday church. He owned a "timepiece" which may refer to a pocket watch. He was a literate man. His "library" is mentioned along with such books as a "Great Bible," a "Maggazine Book, Lyrick Poems, Gospel Sonnets," and an "old Health Book."

He kept hogs and sheep, had an ox, a cow, a yearling steer, a calf and an old mare. His larder and barn were stocked with butter, cheese, barrels of beer and cider, barrels of beef, pork and salt beef, potatoes, soap, Indian corn, barley, flax and flax seed, rye, oats, and barley malt, as well as fodder for the animals.

There were six beds in the house and plenty of coverlets, blankets, "ticken," pillowcases, sheets and bolsters to furnish them all, plus a warming pan to ease the transition into bed on cold winter nights. One chamber pot served the household which was a small one at his death, consisting only of Moses himself, his second wife, Patience, and his spinster daughter, Mary. The kitchen was well equipped with utensils and crockery, including a pewter platter marked "P.B." which belonged to Patience. His house was comfortably furnished with a variety of chests of drawers, "Great" chairs, "black" chairs, and "red" chairs, a dressing table, other types of tables, and the usual candlestick holders.

By terms of his will, Moses was generous to his sons, stating that "...what I have heretofore given to or done for my sd Sons shall not be counted in the settlement of my estate nor any inference had thereunto..." His daughter, Esther, "wife of Moses Root," was to have her previous gifts included as "...so much in her share of my Estate."

This amounted to 38 pounds 19 shillings and 8 pence. Daughter Mary had no such restrictions placed upon her share of her father's estate.

After leaving his wife "...the improvement of one third part of my estate of her natural life...", Moses bequeathed his best suit of clothes to son Asaph; his shop-barn, the land it stood on, and all his tanning and shoe making tools to son Zenas. The remainder was to be divided between sons Asaph, Moses, Jotham and Zenas, and daughters Mary and Esther (with the above exception). The sons received one third part more than the daughters.

Moses Mitchell's estate distribution report contains a paragraph intriguing in its detail outlining the widow's share. "Set to the Widow...the Improvement of one half the front Room below in that part of the House belonging to the Deceased also one half of that part of the Kitchen room, fireplace & Oven belonging to the Deceased and one third part of that half the Cellar belonging to the Deceased, also one third part of the front Chamber and one half the Garret belonging to the Deceased. Together with a privaledge of the Water and Ten Rods of Land Adjoining East of the House at the Northeast part of the thirty Rods of Land Appraised with the House and one third of that half the Barn belonging to the Deceased to include the North Stable and the Benefit of passing on the floor and the Remainder in the Bay, the west side of the floor. Also one third of that part of the Hoghouse belonging to the Deceased." This was followed by a description of the fifteen and a half acres left to Patience which was bounded on land set off to Zenas Mitchell, the highway, and Joel Yale's land.

The distribution also set off land to the four sons and to daughter Mary whose share was six acres and sixty rods bounded on land set to the widow, land belonging to Zenas, land belonging to Dan Collins, and the highway. All received a share of the "moveables." It is gratifying that Patience was allowed to keep her own monogramed pewter platter as part of her "improvements."

A constant reference to "one half" of kitchen room, garret, front room, cellar, barn and hog house belonging to the deceased infers that Moses owned his house in joint tenancy with others, probably one or more of his sons. Asaph is mentioned in the distribution as inheriting a "right in House," the other sons as inheriting a "right in

Buildings." Zenas specifically had the "shop-barn" and the land upon which it stood.

Moses appointed sons Jotham and Zenas his executors; the will was witnessed by John Willard, Dan Collins, and Nathaniel Yale. His signature on the will is clear and strong, indicating he was in vigorous health as he neared his 70th birthday. Children of Moses and Mary (Ives) Mitchell were:

47. **Katherine** b 4 Apr, bpt 27 Apr 1746; d 12 May 1746.
48. **Asaph** b 24 June, bpt 24 Jul 1748   +
49. **Moses** bpt June 1750   +
50. **Mary** bpt 2 Aug 1752; d 5 Apr/June 1756.
51. **Jotham** b 1 Apr, bpt 7 Apr 1754   +
52. **Mary** b 26 Mar, bpt 8 May 1757   +
53. **Esther** b 4 Aug 1760   +
54. **Zenas** b 10 Apr 1762   +

13. **JOHN MITCHELL**, son of John and Katharine (Munson) Mitchell, was born about (1725?) in or near Wallingford, CT. On 8 Feb 1750 at Wallingford, he married Lydia Sperry, daughter of Joseph & Lydia (Munson) Sperry.

Like James, his eldest brother, John and his family drop out of sight in the 1750's. Of John's two known children, birth of the first is recorded in Wallingford, her baptism at the 1st Congregational Church in Cheshire, CT. The birth of the second child is in New Haven, CT vital records. John's other brother, Moses, is so well recorded in Wallingford and Meriden records simply because he remained in one area. This suggests that James and John did a fair amount of moving around, possibly leaving Connecticut to "go west" to a less settled area. Known children of John and Lydia (Sperry) Mitchell were:

55. **Lydia** b 24 Oct 1750
56. **Damaris** b 16 Dec 1754

17. **ABIGAIL MITCHELL**, daughter of William and Anna(h) (Wait) Mitchell, was born 24 Sep 1728 at Deerfield, MA (probably in the Green River district of Deerfield which later became Greenfield). She married 30 Nov 1748 at Deerfield to Daniel McKenney.

The ancestry of Daniel McKenney (McKanny/McKinne/ McKeny/Kenny/Keny/Kenne/Kenee) is unknown. In 1652 Capt. Jno. Greene of the ship "John & Sara" took a ship load of Scots prisoners to Massachusetts, by Order of the English

Government. His orders were "...as winde & weather shall permitt to sett sajle for Boston in New England & there deliver our Orders and Servants to Tho: Kemble of charles Toune..." On the passenger list were a number of men by the surname Mackhene and Mackajne, including a Dani-- Mackajne and a Dan. Mackajne. These Scots survivors of the Battle of Dunbar 3 Sep 1650 in which the victorious Cromwell took 10,000 prisoners, had been banished to this country. As Rev. John Cotton wrote to the Lord General Cromwell, they were to be sold "...not...for slaves to perpetual servitude, but for 6 or 7 or 8 yeares... he that bought the most of them (I heare) buildeth houses for them, for every four an house, layeth some acres of ground thereto, which he giveth them as their owne, requiring 3 dayes in the weeke to worke for him...and 4 dayes for them themselves, and promiseth, he will set them at liberty." ("Ships Passenger Lists, National & New England, 1600-1825," Carl M. Boyer 3rd, pp 154-157.)

Daniel McKenney was a soldier during King George's War (Old French-Indian). In 1746 he served under Capt. Stevens. On 26 June 1748 he was serving under Capt. Hobbs when he was wounded and severely disabled in the same action that took the life of Abigail's brother, Ebenezer. Note that Abigail married Daniel McKenney after he was so badly injured in the Hobbs' Fight. She wished to marry him despite his disablement.

Abigail was admitted to the church in Deerfield on 21 Oct 1750, the same day her second child was baptized. Her husband, Daniel, died shortly after that date. Where and when Abigail died and if she remarried after her husband's death are undiscovered.

Abigail's children (McKENNEY) were: **(i)** Daniel b 25 Sep 1749; **(ii)** Ebenezer bpt 21 Oct 1750; m "before" 1773 Lois Locke, d/o Jonas and Mary (Dwight) Locke. It was from Ebenezer's great-uncle, Joseph Mitchell (and other joint owners), that Jonas Locke bought the two acre island in Deerfield River that was later known as Locke's Island. Ebenezer McKenney and his family removed to Black River, NY (that part of Jefferson Co. formed from Oneida Co. in 1805). 3 children known.

18. **ELIJAH MITCHELL,** son of William and Annah(h) (Wait) Mitchell, was born 3 Oct 1730 at Deerfield, MA (Green River District, later Greenfield). He died 9 Nov 1812

(age "about 86" but actually 82) at Greenfield. His burial place was probably Lower Meadows Cemetery, the third burial place to be selected by Greenfield townspeople, in which "...hallowed soil rest the remains of the Smeads, Armses, Nimses, Mitchells and others of the old families who settled these rich meadows..."

On 1 Jan 1761 (Deerfield, MA V/R) Elijah married Elizabeth Miller, a fourth cousin of his through common Baldwin ancestry. Elizabeth, daughter of Moses & Elizabeth (Field) Miller, was born 16 Jan, bpt 21 Jan 1732/33 at West Springfield, MA. Elizabeth's maternal grandparents, Deacon Samuel & Mary Field, lived at Deerfield which is no doubt how she met Elijah Mitchell. She died 19 Sep 1802 at Greenfield, aged sixty-nine years.

Late in 1774 the First Continental Congress met in Philadelphia and adopted a "Declaration of Rights" in answer to "The Intolerable Acts" or "Coercive Acts", presented early in the year by Lord North. These were 1) The Boston Port bill, closing the port except for firewood and provision, until the tea dumped by Colonists in the infamous Boston Tea Party of 1773 was replaced; 2) British officials in Massachusetts accused of committing crimes "in the line of duty" could be tried in another Colony or in England; 3) The Massachusetts Charter was amended to greatly enhance the Crown's power and to limit town meetings to one a year; 4) The Quartering Act which held the Colonists responsible in part for the expense of quarters and provisions for British troops stationed in the Colonies, and also gave their British commanders a great deal of power.

These "Intolerable Acts" came on top of the Sugar Act of 1764 (tax act); the Currency Act of the same year (hampered Colonial business); and the Stamp Act of 1765 (another tax act). By the autumn and winter of 1774-1775, towns throughout New England began forming groups of armed volunteers called Minute Men because they could be ready for an emergency "at a minute's warning."

About sunrise on the morning of 19 Apr 1775, seven hundred red-coated troops sent by Governor Gage to seize the powder magazine at Concord, met with a group of about seventy Minute Men (who were warned the night before by William Dawes and Paul Revere of Boston) on the green at Lexington. The British gave the order to disperse, someone fired a shot, and the British fired a volley. The

Minute Men retreated, leaving eight of their number dead. After they reached Concord, the British found most of the gunpowder had been carried away, but "...a sharp action occured at a bridge north of town - 'the shot heard round the world'...(they) began their return to Boston...Minute Men and militia swarmed along the line of march, firing from behind fences and trees...the (British) regulars were saved from rout only by a relief column from Boston. Forty-nine Americans and seventy-three British were killed." ("The American Quest," Vol. I, Leland D. Baldwin & Erling A. Erickson, 1973.)

Greenfield's response was immediate. The day after the Concord fight, Capt. Agrippa "Grip" Wells formed a company of Greenfield men who joined Col. Samuel Williams' Regiment of Minute Men for a ten day period of service, leaving hastily for Concord. Descendants of Elijah Mitchell can be proud that his name appears on this company's payroll. He was nearly forty-five years old with six children at home, two others having died in infancy, one just the month before. Yet he never hesitated to take up arms in defense of the Colonies. His patriotism and courage are unquestionable.

This was not the first service Elijah had seen, having fought in the last of the French wars (1759), nor would it be his last. In September 1776 he joined Capt. Wells' Co. (Col. Sam'l Brewers'/Bowers' Reg't) for a three month period of service at Fort Ticonderoga. (One wonders if he happened across Ensign Mitchell, his young 1st cousin-once-removed, who was ending a nine month stint at Fort "Ti" just as Elijah arrived.) He was given a private's pay of five shillings four pence per day plus mileage which he calculated the following year at ninety-two miles.

Elijah's final enlistment was for a term of four days in Capt. Timothy Child's Co., Col. David Field's Reg't, who marched on 14 Aug 1777 to answer the alarm at Bennington. The company started for Bennington but were too late and were ordered to turn back.

The names of Elijah Mitchell and Miller Mitchell appear on the payroll of Capt. Moses Arms (Col. Joseph Stebbins' Reg't), commanded by Col. Hugh McClallan, to defend the arsenal at Springfield, MA during Shay's rebellion in 1787 (mustered in 17 Jan). Surely this Elijah was the son of Elijah, Sr., age eighteen in that year, who enlisted with his older brother, Moses Miller Mitchell.

Third Generation

Elijah (Sr.) appeared on the Greenfield Tax List of 1775, the year he purchased his father's thirty acre farm. This farm, adjacent to that of his brother-in-law, Caleb Wright, he sold on 7 Feb 1784 to David Field (Bk 4:80, Hampshire Co., MA Deeds). He supposedly owned other land which was passed down to his youngest son, William, but in 1798, the only Elijah Mitchell appearing on the Greenfield Tax List for that year is listed as the occupant of a house or lands owned by others.

The 1790 MA Census lists Elijah Mitchell in Greenfield with two males age 16 and up (himself and Elijah, Jr.), two males under age 16 (William, age 13, and ?), and five females (daughters Anna, Sylvia, Elizabeth, and Eunice; wife Elizabeth). Elijah's eldest son, Moses Miller, had married that year but does not appear in this census. He may have been living with his wife's relatives (see Moses Miller Mitchell, #58).

A seating chart of the Old Meeting House on Trapp's Plain at Greenfield, dated about 1800, places Elijah, Sr., son Moses Miller, and their families in pew box #27, located to the left of the door leading out to the porch on the west side of the church. Elijah's youngest son occupied pew box #23, just across from #27 to the right of the same door (when faced from inside the church). This meeting house was unheated until 1816 when a box stove was installed despite a great deal of protest from many who felt it would "vitiate" the air. Given the usual length of sermons then, it is hard to imagine a preference for an unheated church during a New England winter. Those were hardy souls who opposed the comfort of a stove!

Until 1811 Greenfield had been part of Hampshire Co., but in that year it became a town in the county of Franklin which was formed from Hampshire. Probate records for Elijah who died the year following should be in Franklin Co. Probate files, but an inquiry regarding such records proved fruitless. Possibly Elijah had dispersed any property he may have owned before that time. As a widower of ten years at the time of his death, he might have been living with one of his sons, whatever household goods he owned long since disposed of or blended into the son's household. It's a pity that probate records for Elijah are not available to us. Such records would allow us a much more detailed glimpse into the personality and daily life of this man and his family than can be offered without them.

Children of Elijah and Elizabeth (Miller) Mitchell -
the first two births recorded in Deerfield, MA V/R, the
rest in Greenfield, MA V/R - were:
57. **Anna** b 28 Aug 1761
58. **Moses Miller** b 28 Nov 1763   +
59. **Sylvia** b 27 Nov 1765
60. **Elizabeth** b 28 Nov 1767
61. **Elijah** b Oct 1769; m 20 Nov 1794 at Montague, MA to
    Cyntha Taylor of Montague. (Marriage intentions
    had been filed earlier at Greenfield, MA.)
62. **Eunice** bpt 9 Aug 1772; died young.
63. **Eunice** b 1 Jul 1774   +
64. **Lydia** bpt 9 Mar 1775; d 11 Mar 1775.
65. **William** bpt 10 Nov 1776; died young.
66. **William** b 16 Sep 1777   +

20. **SARAH MITCHELL**, daughter of William and Anna(h)
(Wait) Mitchell, was born 18 Dec 1734 at Deerfield, MA
(Green River district, later Greenfield). She married
Caleb Wright on 25 Mar 1763 at Greenfield, the marriage
performed by Rev. Roger Newton.

Caleb's ancestry is unknown. He is called simply "of
Greenfield" by Sheldon ("History of Deerfield, MA").
He was taxed at Greenfield in 1775 for his property which
abutted the south and west boundries of that owned by Sarah's father, William, and later her brother, Elijah, who
sold his land in 1784. In 1785 Caleb was taxed at Deerfield, and the 1790 census lists Caleb Wright in Charlemont, MA with one male age 16 and up and two females in the
household. Sarah's younger cousins once-removed were
neighbors - Consider Mitchell, and his 2 sisters, Mary
and Cynthia who were married to the brothers Israel and
Ira Hawks.

As plausible as the above paragraph seems, given
rather scanty information, I question its total veracity.
Greenfield Vital Records reports the death on 28 May 1777
of Caleb Wright. It has been assumed that this referred
to Caleb, Jr., eldest child of Caleb and Sarah. However,
Thompson's "History of Greenfield, MA" also contains
Greenfield deaths as recorded by the Rev. Roger Newton.
His record states simply "...May 28 - Caleb Wright..." He
does not add "son of Caleb" or "aet 13 years" as was usual
when he noted down the death of a child or young person.
Instead, his notation is made in the same manner he used

to record deaths of adults in his books. If, then, this is a record of Caleb, Sr.'s death, the Caleb Wright who was taxed in Deerfield in 1785 and appears in Charlemont in 1790 was certainly Caleb, Jr. who was contemporary in age with what would be his own second cousins in Charlemont. Again, if it was Caleb, Jr. in Charlemont in 1790, he didn't remain long. Vital records for that town list no births, marriages, or deaths for anyone by the surname Wright before the year 1830.

Sarah's children (WRIGHT), all baptized at Greenfield on 10 June 1776, were: **(i)** Caleb b 29 Dec 1763; **(ii)** Sarah b 11 Feb 1765; **(iii)** Dorothy b 15 Feb 1768; possibly the Dorothy Wright who m 5 Feb 1795 Dan Chapin at Greenfield; **(iv)** Daniel b 27 June 1769 (a Daniel Wright was on the payroll of Capt. Moses Arms' Co., mustered at Greenfield on 17 Jan 1787 for the defense of the Springfield arsenal during Shay's rebellion, the same company in which Moses Miller and Elijah Mitchell, Jr. served); **(v)** Samuel b 4 Apr 1772; **(vi)** Thomas b 30 Sep 1773; **(vii)** William bpt 10 June 1776.

23. **JOEL MITCHELL**, son of Michael and Mary ( ) Mitchell, was born 19 Jul 1721 at Deerfield, MA, and died 1 Jan 1763 at Wethersfield, CT. He married about 1742 Mary _____ who was living 22 Dec 1763.

Joel's death came a little over a year after he had settled his father's estate in Hampshire Co., MA. At his death he was in his forty-second year; he left 8 children, ranging in age from nineteen to one year, seven months.

He was a poor man. The inventory of his estate taken 16 Jan 1763 is short; nearly every item on it is described as "old." Although Mary had to make her "mark" on administration papers, Joel could read and write. He owned a psalm book, other "old books," and an ink horn. Being too poor to own a clock or pocketwatch, he told time by an "houer glass." He also owned two "old pair of compasses."

Joel was a joiner by trace (i.e., carpenter) as joiners "touls" are twice mentioned. He shaved since he had a "rasur" so, not surprisingly, he owned a looking glass. His wardrobe was small - a pair of britches, a coat and jacket, a great coat, two pairs of stockings, a hat, a pair of shoes and a pair of boots.

Household furnishings were so few they were lumped into one category as "bed and furniture," plus a few chairs, some without bottoms. Kitchen equipment and eating utensils were minimal. There were no luxuries on this list. Most of the items on the inventory were set to the widow, including the looking glass.

At the final settlement of the estate on 22 Dec 1763, Mary, as widow and administrix, presented a list of estate connected expenses to the court. Listed were "Sundry funeral charges, coffin, grave, etc.," court and appraisers fees, costs of trips to court, rental of a horse to get from Wethersfield to the court in Hartford, and an allowance for costs of "keeping my Infant Child" while she was away from home. Total expenses were a little over four pounds which the Court allowed her.

The Bond of Administration on Joel's estate was in the names of Mary Mitchel and Daniel Andrus of Wethersfield, witnessed by Zerah Kibbe and David Webster. A Mary Mitchell, possibly Joel's widow or his daughter, was married to Daniel Andrus on 2 Aug 1764 at Wethersfield.

The birth of Joel's first child is recorded in Farmington, CT, but the rest are recorded in Wethersfield. Baptism records for the three eldest children are in Meriden, CT. Children of Joel and Mary ( ) Mitchell were:

67. **Mary** b 2 Sep 1743; bpt 5 Oct 1746.
68. **Clare/Clary** (son) b 4 Feb 1746; bpt 5 Oct 1746.
69. **Joel** b 5 Jan 1748; bpt 10 Jan 1748.
70. **Michael** b 16 Dec 1750   +
71. **Nash** b 9 Apr 1753   +
72. **David** b 11 Mar 1756
73. **Elisha** b 7 Aug 1758
74. **Amasa** b 30 May 1761   +

26. **JOSEPH MITCHELL (JR.)**, son of Joseph and Mary (Allis) Mitchell, was born 3 Mar 1726/7 at Sunderland, MA. His parents moved to Deerfield, MA when he was a small boy.

In 1744 the Pocumtuck Valley in which Deerfield was so pleasantly situated had known peace for twenty years. No longer on the frontier, the town had long since torn down watchtowers and other defenses. When France and England declared war against each other in March of that year (King George's War or Old French-Indian War), Deerfield once again appealed to Boston for financial aid to rebuild fortifications. When they were ignored, Deerfield had to vote a tax raise and pay for it themselves. They lay uncomfortably near Crown Point, NY, a French fort on Lake Champlain. A request for soldiers was granted and Deerfield become a commissary town.

People living outside the town began flocking into Deerfield and the town had to find housing for them. Lack of space forced the town to allow keeping of hogs, pens and gardens in the town street. Rev. Ashley seized the chance to preach a violent sermon, painting lurid pictures of destruction, murder and ravished women, calling his parishoners unclean, intemporate, prideful, neglectful of the Sabbath, given to swearing and taking God's name in vain. Many in Deerfield remembered earlier wars and feared far more their earthly enemies who were unlikely to be deterred with the acts of repentance demanded by Rev. Ashley.

The Indians were anxious for scalps or prisoners, but especially prisoners who brought a higher price since the French could ransom them. Scouting parties in 1745 saw few signs of Indians, but 1746 was a different story. Members of the Smead and Hawks families, related to the Mitchells, were taken at the fall of Fort Massachusetts in that year, four of the Smeads dying in captivity. Depredations increased against townspeople, their crops and livestock. Those who were too imprudent or impatient to wait for guards to accompany them to their fields often paid with their lives or their freedom.

In 1748 a list of soldiers serving from Deerfield includes the name of young Joseph Mitchell. Many on this list were men related to Joseph by blood or marriage. In this year, Joseph's cousin, Ebenezer Mitchell of Greenfield, lost his life in a surprise attack on Capt. Hobbs' company. The same attack left Daniel McKenney, who would marry Ebenezer's sister, with crippling injuries.

The Treaty of Aix la Chapelle "ending" this war was signed on 7 Oct 1748. This treaty bought time for France but did nothing for England. The unsettled question of French-English boundaries was turned over to a commission and France continued to encroach on territory claimed by both countries. Anticipating renewed hostilities, England began upgrading their Colonial forts in 1751. Again Deerfield became a military depot for such supplies as powder, lead, clothing and rum, brought from Boston and destined for the northwest frontier. Governor Shirley set his standards for the "ideal" soldier, declaring they be not "under 18 or over 35, sound men, not under 5'4" in their stockings, and no Roman Catholics." The last stipulation is understandable since the French enemy was of that religious persuasion.

Threat of war did not deter young love. On 29 Jan 1751 Joseph Mitchell married Lydia Foster at Meriden, CT. Lydia was born 17 Feb 1732/33 at Wallingford, CT, daughter of Timothy and Thankful (Ackley) Foster. At her marriage, Lydia's father settled a dowery on her of 400 pounds (Old Tenor 47.10), just as he did on her sisters. The young couple took up residence in Deerfield where Joseph and his brother-in-law, Zadock King, were admitted to communion in special ordinance on 23 Feb 1752 in the Deerfield 1st Congregational Church.

As the last of the French wars progressed, Joseph appeared again on a list dated 1756 of Deerfield men who were impressed into His Majesties' Service, probably going to serve under Lord Loudon's command in the Albany, NY area. Sheldon states ("History of Deerfield, MA") that men taken in these impressments were "...the real bone and muscle of Deerfield and could not be well spared under her straitened circumstances." Greenfield and Northfield were similarly "drained of their best material."

Joseph's length of service is unknown but he was back in Deerfield by the fall of 1758 as his first son was born in June 1759. Joseph's first of many property investments was 10 acres in "that part of...Deerfield called Wapping" which he bought in 1761 from Ebenezer Wells. The next year he bought land at Huntstown from his father - Lot No. 15 of 50 acres and part of Lot No. 4. He lived on No. 4 (later seeming to own the entire 50 acre parcel) which bounded No. 15 to the south with an east-west highway running between the two lots.

The Huntstown Grant (changed to Ashfield in 1765) called for the settlement there of a learned, orthodox minister, and the erection of a meeting house. Orthodox meant Congregational, of course. Although the war and later disagreement over the final building site would delay its completion for almost thirty years, the church itself was organized on 22 Feb 1763. As one of the original members, Joseph Mitchell signed the Articles of faith and covenant.

Joseph's years in Ashfield were busy ones. At various times, he served as Town constable, on committees to keep roads repaired, and as town fence viewer. He is thought to be Ashfield's first innkeeper. He was issued a license in August 1763 as "innholder, retailer and common victualler in his dwelling house for a year..."; he was bonded to "keep good rule and order in his house (and) to keep and render accounts and pay the duties" required.

The public house or inn was an important community center. As early as 1656 the General Court of Massachusetts passed a law enforcing the opening of some kind of public house in every town. Only grave, responsible men were recommended by town officers for this "duty." The innkeeper saw that no games of chance were played in the house; that no one drank to excess or remained in his house after certain hours of the night. He maintained order, did not harbour unsavoury characters, did not allow his license to be used by others for selling "ale, beer, syder," did not sell wine or liquor to Indians or Negroes, and was careful to report the name of any stranger staying in his house more than a day or a night to a town officer who could "warn out of town" anyone they thought might be detrimental or become a town charge.

Besides a convenience for travelers and a place for locals to exchange news and opinions, the public house was often a meeting place. Until the Ashfield meeting house was completed, the Proprietor's meetings were held at the home of "Landlord Mitchel" and they continued to meet there until the meeting house was finished in 1770. The first legal town meeting in 1766 was held at Joseph's inn on the east side of Bellows Hill. (Incidentally, the "town" picked up the bar tab for these meetings.)

Hard cash was in short supply in Colonial days. Since Joseph had an inn to provision and was also dealing in land transactions, the number of court cases involving suits against him for unpaid, overdue notes is not surprising. He was sued two times in 1768, once by Moses Clark of Sunderland, and once by Timothy Dwight of Deerfield. In 1769 Thomas Williams of Deerfield sued and Jonathan Ashley took him to court in 1773. A different case was that of Israel Williams, Jr. of Hatfield, shopkeeper, who sued in 1772 for "divers Goods, Wares & Merchandizes" valued at over two pounds which had been delivered to Joseph in 1771 and not paid for. In all of these cases, the court found against Joseph who simply failed to appear.

Curiously, in 1765 Joseph, Jr. sold back to Joseph, Sr. Lot No. 4 containing "a Dwelling house and half a pot ash house" and No. 15 containing "a House and Barn" which he had originally purchased from his father, plus Lot No. 5 of fifty acres, adjoining No. 4 to the west. Then in 1768 Joseph, Sr. sold all three lots back to Joseph, Jr. These transactions were probably equivalent to our going to the bank for a loan.

The genealogy of the Mitchell family in Sheldon's "History of Deerfield, MA" states that Lydia, wife of Joseph, Jr., "...was a wid. Nov. 2, 1773." Sheldon's basis for that statement remains a mystery. Indeed, Joseph was very much alive in 1773 although no longer living in Massachusetts. By 1771 Joseph had divested himself of all property except a parcel in "Parsons town" (Hawley) which he had mortgaged in 1769 to Jonathan Arms, and his house-lot in Ashfield. On 6 June of that year, he sold No. 4 to Joseph Stebbins of Deerfield, and set out with his family for a new frontier - Skenesborough, NY (then in Charlotte Co., now in Washington Co.).

Major Philip Skene who modestly named the town after himself had been granted huge tracts of land in New York State from 1759 on. In July 1771 he received a "Little Patent" of nine thousand acres, most of it in the Skenes-borough (later Whitehall) area. He had advertised widely for new settlers, offering rent inducements and describing the good farming land thereabouts. That it was not! Lying at the south end of Lake Champlain with mountains to the west, the land was level and undulating to the center and east, but the soil was hard, stiff clay, best suited for grazing. The land directly around Skenesborough was marshy. Besides mosquitos which George Washington reportedly said were so bad they could bite through the heaviest boot, there were "punchins" or "punkies," tiny gnats that could not be heard, could barely be seen, but bit viciously. Furthermore, the entire eastern half of New York State was a "hot spot" during the Revolutionary War, wide open to British and Indians sweeping down via Lake Champlain from Canada.

In 1780 Skenesborough was burned to the ground. Only their first record book survived and from that we learn that Joseph Mitchell was chosen one of four fence viewers in 1784. (Fences had to be kept repaired to keep livestock out of fields.) His name is also on a petition dated 13 June 1781 addressed to the Vermont State Legislature. This petition stated that since Major Philip Skene (a

Tory) had joined the enemy, thereby forfeiting his land, the inhabitants of Skenesborough wished to form a new six mile square township named South Haven to be incorporated under the laws of Vermont. ("State Papers of Vermont," Vol. V, pp 259-60.)

At the heart of this petition were the activities of Ethan Allen and his brother, Ira, who were trying to negotiate a secret and separate armistice between Britain and Vermont. Petitions like this one came from townships all along the New York-Vermont border, especially after the General Assembly of Vermont flatly declared in 1781 that all land west of Vermont to the Hudson River was part of their state. These petitions alarmed the other States who felt, if carried out, they would give every county, even every township, the right to secede. New York was ready to go to war with Vermont over the situation. Finally, in 1782 the Vermont Legislature formally relinquished their claim and a month later, residents who had favored secession reaffirmed their allegiance to New York, delaring they had only hoped to avoid the horrors of a British invasion by annexing to Vermont.

Survival must have been extremely difficult for the Mitchells during the Revolutionary War years. There is no evidence that they removed to a safer spot; there is little evidence that they did not. Joseph's eldest son enlisted at Skenesborough in 1776; his eldest married daughter remained there; and Joseph can be pinpointed there in 1781 and 1784.

On 18 Mar 1786 (sworn the same day at Northampton, MA) "Joseph Mitchel of Skeensborough, N.Y. (sold) to Jonathan Arms of Deerfield Consideration of Forty pounds...one certain tract or parcel of land lying & being in the township called No. 7 or Persons town (Hawley) Containing 100 acres of land bounded northerly upon Moses Heightons land so called westerly upon Jonah Cooleys land which he purchased of Moses Parsons of Middlefield southerly upon Hezikiah Warriner & easterly upon a lot called No. 9 the aforesaid 100 acres of land lies in the County of Hampshire (MA)." The property described in this deed is identical to that in the 1769 mortgage by Joseph Mitchell of Ashfield to Jonathan Arms, except Heighton was called Harton in the earlier deed. (Bk 2:272 & Bk 4:346)

Joseph's death occured sometime between the date of the above deed and 14 Apr 1792 when he is called deceased in his father's will. Possibly he died before 1789. In December of that year, the estate distribution papers of Lydia's father, Timothy Foster (Sr.), left to Lydia "The Old House 3.5.0...set also to sd Lydia thirteen Acres of 139 Rods of Land at ye North East Corner of ye Land that lieth on ye West Side of ye County Rode sd Land being 31 Rods in Width North & South bounded East on Highway South and West on Timothy Fosters (Jr.) Land & North on Thomas Fosters Land Estimated at...37.5.0." (Wallingford, CT Probate Records) On a single sheet in these probate records, listing total amount to be distributed to Timothy, Sr.'s daughters, Lydia's name is written with "Mitchel" inscribed above it and a scrawled word after which appears to be "Wid."

In the 1790 Washington Co., NY census, a Joseph Mitchell is listed beside Caleb Hurlbut who had married Joseph and Lydia's eldest daughter. The family has one male age 16 and up, one male under age 16, and two females. This can not be Joseph and Lydia but probably their youngest son, Joseph, who had married about 1788 and had a son born in 1790. The extra female is probably the widowed Lydia.

Somewhere in an unknown, unmarked site lies the mortal remains of Joseph Mitchell, Jr., husband and father, yeoman, innkeeper and farmer, patriot and pioneer; the words on these pages are his sole monument. Children of Joseph and Lydia (Foster) Mitchell were:

75. Lydia bpt 22 Mar 1752   +
76. Experience bpt 4 May 1754   +
77. Ensign bpt 1 Jul 1759   +
78. Thankful bpt 12 Sep 1762   +
79. Tryphena bpt 17 Feb 1765 (lvg 1794)
80. Joseph b 22 Sep, bpt 23 Oct 1768   +

27. **MARY MITCHELL,** daughter of Joseph and Mary (Allis) Mitchell, was born 10 Mar 1731/32 at Deerfield, MA. She married 18 June 1753 at Deerfield to Samuel Belding, Jr., born 1 Apr 1729 at Deerfield, son of Samuel and Elizabeth (Ingraham/Ingram) Belding.

In 1761 Samuel Belding bought Lot. No. 49 at Ashfield (then Huntstown) from Richard Ellis, including "buildings and edifaces" on the property. The 1st Congregational Church at Ashfield was organized in 1763 at the home of Deacon Ebenezer Belding, "thought" to be Samuel's cousin. In 1765 Samuel served as first town clerk of Ashfield.

Samuel and Ebenezer Belding lived with their large families in an area of Ashfield known as "Beldingville." Four generations of Beldings lived on the Samuel Belding farm there. His great-grandsons founded Belding Bros., a silk firm with large mills in CT, MA, Belding, MI, San Francisco and Montreal. Two of his great-grandsons were still living in 1895, Alvah N. and Milo M. Belding.

Birth records for all of Samuel and Mary's children are in Ashfield, MA Vital Records. However, it is doubtful that they moved to Ashfield from Deerfield much before 1761. Samuel served in both the Old French-Indian War and the last French War, being impressed along with other Deerfield men in 1756 to serve under Lord Loudon. This is the same company in which Joseph Mitchell, Jr., Mary's brother served. Samuel's father, Samuel Belding, Sr., had owned both Lots 10 and 11 in Deerfield which his heirs sold in 1761 to Joseph Stebbins. This coincides with the year in which Samuel, Jr. bought his Ashfield property.

Samuel's will dated 18 Sep 1809 gives "my beloved wife Mary the use, rents, profits, and 1/3 part of my real estate as long as she remains a widow;" names son John executor, and daughters by their married names (Franklin Co., MA Probate V.3:126 dated 9 Jul 1816). He died at Ashfield 19 Dec 1815, age 86 years 8 months. Mary's death is not in Ashfield Vital Records, nor is she mentioned in Samuel's estate probate papers of 1816.

Mary's children (BELDING) were: **(i)** Daniel b 17 June 1754 m 10 Feb 1774 Ruth Sadler; **(ii)** Mercy b 9 Oct 1755 d 16 Nov 1755; **(iii)** John (Rev. sol.) b 17 Dec 1756 d 25 Mar 1839 Ashfield, MA m 15 Jul 1784 Priscilla Wait; 12 ch; **(iv)** Mary b 3 Mar 1758 m 28 Feb 1780 Daniel or David Rider (see "History of Deerfield, MA," Vol. II, p269; Errata, pp 398, 405); **(v)** Mercy b 29 Nov 1759; d 27 Jul 1831, age 71y m 6 Sep 1781 Azariah Cooley d 9 Mar 1829 Washington, D.C.; 18 ch; **(vi)** Esther b 18 Apr 1761 m Wait Broughton; **(vii)** Samuel b 26 Nov 1762 died young; **(viii)** Asenath b 29 Feb 1764 m Solomon Phillips; **(ix)** Lovissa b 6 June 1765 m Joseph Lillie; **(x)** Samuel b 10 Nov 1767 m 20 May 1790 Elizabeth Clark (at Buckland), b 5 Aug 1771 Ashfield, MA, d/o Robert & Mary ( ) Clark; fam to Pomfret, Chautauqua Co., NY where Samuel d 15 Nov 1833; Elizabeth lvg 1850 Census in Chautauqua Co. as "Betsy Belden" with son-in-law David Clark; 7 ch named in father's probate; **(xi)** Elizabeth b 7 Jan 1770 m Jonathan Gay; **(xii)** Aaron b 21 Jul 1774; not

named in father's 1809 will. (Additional Belding family
data is courtesy of descendant Sally A. Ryan, 302 W. El
Caminito, Phoenix, AZ 85021.)

28. **HANNAH MITCHELL,** daughter of Joseph and Mary (Allis)
Mitchell, was born 9 Jan 1732/3 at Deerfield, MA. She
married 3 Jul 1751 at Deerfield to Zadock King, son of
Thomas and Sarah (Mygatt) King. Zadock was baptized on
27 June 1725 at Hartford, CT, died 25 Aug 1769.

Zadock King is thought to have gone to Deerfield from
Northampton, MA where his great-grandfather, John King,
had been a pioneer settler. It is also believed that Zadock, who was a turner by trade, learned his craft from
someone who had acquired this skill in the Spencer workshop at Hartford and that Zadock introduced the Spencer
chair tradition to Northern Hampshire Co., MA.

Since his children were born or baptized in Deerfield
we assume this is where he plied his trade until the late
1750's when he became ill. By 8 July 1760, Zadock was under the guardianship of his father-in-law, Joseph Mitchell, Sr. On that date Joseph presented an accounting of
debts due from the estate of "Zadok King a person non compos mentis" which totaled over 106 pounds. Money was owed
to "Doctr. Bartlet," Doctr. Thomas Williams," and "Doctr.
Blogget," as well as Samuel "Belden," Abigail Hitchcock,
Samuel Wells, Mr. Mather, and Lt. David Field. In 1755
and 1758 Zadock had borrowed from Joseph Mitchell, Sr.,
owing him over 50 pounds (with interest) in 1760. He
and his wife, Hannah, and the four children, were living
with Joseph as is indicated by Joseph's charge against the
estate for thirteen weeks board at nine shillings a week.
(Hampshire Co., MA Probate Records, Vol. IX, p 184.)

Sheldon says ("History of Deerfield, MA," Vol. II)
that after Zadock's death in 1769, Hannah married second
on 20 Jan 1778 to Jotham Bugbee. I contend that Hannah's
second husband was Jotham Bigelow. In Howe's genealogy of
the family ("The Bigelow Family of America," p 55), he
states that Jotham Bigelow had married first Persis Temple who died about 1748. He then married Mary Richardson
in 1750. Soon after 1761 Jotham moved to Guilford, VT
where he was one of the first settlers. He died there on
8 Apr 1786. His will, written three days before, mentions
his wife, Hannah, which indicates he had married a third
time. The will of Joseph Mitchell, Sr., written in 1792,

leaves 12 pounds to his daughter, Hannah Bigelow. The husbands of Hannah's two sisters are named but no husband is given for Hannah, indicating she was a widow.

Hannah may have gone to live with son Jesse. The 1800 census of Florida, Berkshire Co., MA shows Jesse King's family with 2 females age 45 and up. One of these two females may have been Hannah, age 67, and the other Jesse's wife. (Thanks to Alice Holt, 2611 Liberty, North Bend, OR 97459 for King family data.)

Hannah's children (KING) were: **(i)** Hannah b 10 Apr 1752 m 15 Jan 1778 Gershom Hawks; **(ii)** Zadock, Jr. b 24 Jan 1754 m 2 May 1781 his cousin **Thankful Mitchell** (#78, 4th Gen.); **(iii)** Jesse bpt 2 Nov 1755 d 21 Oct 1833 (will dtd 22 Oct 1828) Berkshire Co., MA m 29 Apr 1779 Elizabeth Todd bc 1758 Londonderry, NH d 4 Sep 1827; both bur King Cem., nr Florida, Berkshire Co., MA; 10 ch per Sheldon's King genealogy; **(iv)** Abner bpt 22 Nov 1757.

29. **TABITHA MITCHELL,** daughter of Joseph and Mary (Allis) Mitchell, was born 9 Feb 1736/7 at Deerfield, MA. She married 22 Dec 1757 at Deerfield to Gershom Tuttle, Jr., born 22 Aug 1738 at Farmington, CT, son of Gershom and Lois (Allis) Tuttle. Gershom and Tabitha were first cousins. Their mothers were sisters, daughters of William and Elizabeth (Davis) Allis. Gershom's marriage record calls him "of New Cambridge," CT.

Records of "Revolutionary Men of Oneida Co., NY" (a D.A.R. publication) state that Gershom Tuttle was born in Cheshire or Bristol (near Farmington), CT and that he died at Watertown (Jefferson Co.), NY on 5 Jan 1818. He was a Captain in the Revolutionary War and a Colonel in the War of 1812. He first removed from Bristol, CT to New Hampshire, thence about 1790 to Clinton (Oneida Co.), NY where he joined the Congregational church in 1798.

A good deal of the information on the children of this family has come from "Tuttle-Tuthill Lines in America," by Alva M. Tuttle (1968, p 224). Mr. Tuttle lists the births of the first three living Tuttle children as Farmington, CT and the fourth in Bristol, CT. The family is found in the 1790 census in Claremont, Sullivan Co., NH with 1 male age 16 and up, 1 male under 16, and 3 females.

Independent research by a professional researcher in Oneida Co., NY revealed some further data on Gershom and Tabitha Tuttle. In 1797 Gershom belonged to the Hanover

Third Generation

Society, 2nd Congregational Church in Kirkland, NY. The
wife of Gershom Tuttle joined the 1st Congregational
Church of Clinton, NY on 3 Jul 1795, and Gershom joined on
19 Aug 1799. (This church later became the Stone Presbyterian Church.) Tabitha Tuttle is listed as a member
there in 1801 and on 13 May of the same year at a church
meeting, Gershom Tuttle and Timothy Barns were "appointed to make provision for the Lords Supper for the Two Communion Days next ensuing..." (This is the same church to
which Abigail, wife of Tabitha's brother, Abner Mitchell,
belonged in 1801.) The last trace we find of Tabitha is a
record of her membership in the Baptist Church of Whites-
boro (Oneida Co.), NY on 6 July 1819. (Source: Vols. 7,
11, 14 of D.A.R. Church, Bible and Cemetery Records of
Oneida Co., NY.)

Tabitha's children (TUTTLE) were: **(i)** child, d.y.;
(ii) Solomon b 31 Mar 1762 m1) Sarah Matthews; m2) Martha
Alexander; **(iii)** Theodore b 27 Nov 1763 (one of this name
is found in the 1850 Watertown, Jefferson Co., NY Census,
p 327); **(iv)** Joseph d 4 Sep 1848 Fairfield, MI; m Sarah
(Sharker) Hamlin who d 7 Dec 1852; **(v)** Gershom b 11 June
1769 d 5 Sep 1823 Vigo Co., IN m 8 Jul 1788 at Farmington,
CT to Pamela Strong Clark; **(vi)** Bertha m David Mills of
Rutland, NY; **(vii)** David; **(viii)** Zebulon m 25 Jan 1798 to
his 2nd cousin **Aphalinda Mitchell** (see #88, Fourth Generation); **(ix)** Sabra m Seth Heath of CT.

30. **ABNER MITCHELL,** youngest son of Joseph and Mary (Allis) Mitchell, was born 28 Oct 1738 at Deerfield, MA. He
married about 1761/62 Abigail Warren, born 28 Jan 1740 at
Marlboro, MA, daughter of Daniel and Martha (Coolidge)
Warren. (Bond's "Genealogy & History of Watertown, MA,"
2nd edition, p. 962, has a genealogy of the Warren family,
but see section on Some Allied Lines for corrections to
Bond's material.)

Sheldon has little to say about Abigail ("History of
Deerfield, MA," Vol. II) except that she was "sis. of Neverson Warren," and that she "drafted a bed quilt for Dr.
Williams' wife on 12 Aug 1774. Both Abner and Abigail were
members of the 1st Congregational Church at Deerfield,
she being admitted to communion on 3 Apr 1763. In 1777-78,
Capt. Mitchell (Abner) occupied the third pew removed
from the pulpit at the back of the church, next to his
father's pew. Abner shared his pew with Samuel Dwelley,

-60-

Simeon Harvey, Gideon Dickenson, Capt. Jonas Locke, and Samuel Tennant.

Too young to be in the French-Indian War of 1744-48, Abner was of age to serve during the last French War. In 1757 he was on the descriptive rolls of Lord Loudon; in 1758 he served under Capt. Elijah Smith. During the Revolutionary War, he was a Captain of Militia at Deerfield.

In 1779 and 1780, Abner was appointed to the Deerfield Committee of Safety along with four other Deerfield men. Theirs was not an easy task. These years were a low point in the American struggle for independence. Many Whigs or Patriots became discouraged. Tyrannical taxation by the British had started this war. Now the Whigs found themselves bearing a similar heavy yoke of taxation to support the war effort. So many able-bodied men had been drafted that agriculture was nearly at a standstill. Money had depreciated to the point of making business transactions almost impossible. The Committee of Safety had to combat a general feeling of "peace at any price" while the Tory faction in town, growing bold, tried once again to take over town affairs. Town meetings were "frequent and stormy..." as one can easily imagine.

In 1783 at the close of the war, Abner was among the Deerfield delegates attending a convention of representatives from No. Hampshire Co. towns, their job to discuss ways of alleviating various deplorable conditions existing in the area during those first post-war years. Only responsible, clear-thinking men would have been offered such a post.

Abner and Abigail lived in the area of Deerfield known as Wapping, their household containing not only their own large family but by 1790 Abner's widowed father, Joseph, as well. Abner and his father occasionally bought and sold property together, their last transaction occuring on 21 Apr 1794 when they sold six acres called Beaverdam in Deerfield to Asahel Wright, this property bounded south on Solomon Hawks land, east on Major Seth Catlin's land, north on Hannah Williams', and west on the brow of the Hill. At his father's death less than five months later, Abner, as sole surviving son, inherited all of his father's remaining property, both real and personal.

Sheldon says Abner died "abt. 1795." Instead, he began selling off his property, including some to his son,

Asaph, in Charlemont, MA. Early in 1800, Abner and his
family moved to Oneida Co., NY along with his married son,
Consider, and his married daughter, Aphalinda Tuttle.
Abner and Consider appear side by side in the 1800 Census
there, living in Paris Township. Although no deeds have
been found there in Abner's name, Abigail who is specifically called "...wife of Abner Mitchel, a member of the
Church in Deerfield, Mass..." joined the 1st Congregational Church of Clinton, NY on 8 May 1801 (later known as
Stone Presbyterian, Clinton Village, NY).

There is no record that Abner also joined the church
in Clinton, and neither he nor Abigail are listed as head
of household in the 1810 census. We can not presume a person is dead, however, simply because they are not in a
census index in an area where they appeared ten years before, although this may be the case. Consider and perhaps
another of Abner's sons did remain in Oneida Co., NY although they, too, are not there in the 1810 census index.

Children of Abner and Abigail (Warren) Mitchell, all
baptized at Deerfield, MA were:

81. **Abigail** bpt 24 Apr 1763
82. **Consider** bpt 26 May 1765   +
83. **Cynthia** bpt 24 Apr 1768   +
84. **Mary** bpt 29 Jul 1770   +
85. **Abner Warren** bpt 31 May 1772; died young.
86. **Asaph** bpt 5 Sep 1773   +
87. **Martha (Patty)** bpt 19 Nov 1775   +
88. **Aphalinda** bpt 3 Mar 1782   +
89. **Abner** bpt 25 May 1786   +

32. **SARAH MITCHELL**, daughter of Jonathan and Lydia
(How[e]) Mitchell, was born 12 Jan 1735/36 at Guilford, CT
(baptized 13 Apr 1740 at Durham, CT). She married 4 Jul
1753 at Middletown, CT to Abel Sizer, born 5 May 1732 at
Middletown, son of Anthony and Sarah (Tryon) Sizer. Abel
died 21 Mar 1814 at Middletown, CT, and Sarah died there
on 14 Feb 1825. (1790 Census Middletown, CT, 1 male 16 &
up, 1 male under 16, 2 females in the Abel Sizer family.)

Sarah's children (SIZER), all born at Middletown, CT,
were: **(i)** Lydia b 1 Sep 1754 d 21 Nov 1820 Elizabeth, NJ m
27 Apr 1775 Jedediah Johnson, Jr.; 10 ch; **(ii)** Sarah b 20
Jul 1756 m 2 June 1775 Joseph Pierson; 13 ch; **(iii)** Jonathan (Rev. sol.) b 17 Sep 1758 d 8 Dec 1835 m1) 29 Nov 1778
Elizabeth Pelton; m2) 3 Dec 1795 Mary Thompson; 6 ch;

(iv) Rosanna b 13 Aug 1760 m 15 June 1816 Stephen Ward; **(v)** Abel b 7 Nov 1762; **(vi)** Timothy b 8 Aug 1765 ml) 27 Dec 17__ Olive Pelton; m2) 21 June 1792 Molly Hamlin; m3) 10 Sep 1795 Rebecca Plumb; 3 ch kn; **(vii)** Lucretia m 8 Aug 1786 Isaac Pierson; **(viii)** Ruth m 1 Nov 1801 Isaac B. Doolittle; 9 ch; **(ix)** Hope; **(x)** Amasa m Annah B.___; d 23 Oct 1856 Meriden, CT; 4 ch kn.

33. **ABNER MITCHELL**, son of Jonathan and Lydia (How[e]) Mitchell, was born 23 Aug 1738 at Guilford, CT (baptized 13 Apr 1740 Durham, CT). He married 4 Sep 1763 at Middletown, CT to Esther Johnson, ancestry unknown. In the 1790 Census, Abner and family were in Middletown, CT with 2 males 16 and up, 1 male under 16, and 6 females listed. Living next door is Martha Johnson with 2 females in her family, such proximity suggesting that Martha may have been Esther's widowed mother.

By 1802 Abner and his family were in Turin, Oneida Co. (now Lewis), NY where on 5 Sep he bought land in Township No. 4 from Jeduthan Hughes and Adah his wife (Bk 9:515 Oneida Co. Deeds). In 1809 Abner donated land to the town of Turin for a burial ground, and in 1813 he bought land from his son-in-law, Ezekial Lyman, and Stephen Munger, of Paris, Oneida Co., NY. (Ezekial married Mabel Mitchell at Middletown; in the 1790 census, Ezekial was in Royaltown, Windsor Co., VT with 2 males age 16 and up, and 3 females in the houshold.)

After his wife's death, Abner married second Zerviah ____. He wrote his will in May 1816 at Turin, naming wife Zerviah, and daughters Mabel Lyman, Prudence, deceased (her heirs inherited), Submit, Lydia "Wheler," Esther, and Hannah Lyman. Still in Lewis Co., NY in the 1820 census, Abner died there between 1822-1825. In 1827, Zerviah Mitchell, "...late of Turin, now residing in Meriden, CT in New Haven Co...", sold land in Lewis Co., NY to the Baptist Convention of New York.

Children of Abner and Esther (Johnson) Mitchell, probably all born at Middletown, CT, were:

90. **Mabel** b 15 Jul 1764; m 22 Sep 1785 Ezekiel Lyman
91. **Prudence** b 15 Mar 1766; d before 1816.
92. **Submit** b 31 Jan 1768; living 1816.
93. **Lydia** b 12 Aug 1771; m before 1816 _____Wheeler.
94. **Esther** b 27 June 1774; living 1816.
95. **Hannah** b 27 Jul 1779; m before 1816 _____Lyman.

39. **SAMUEL MITCHELL (JR.)**, son of Samuel and Abigail
(Cook) Mitchell, was born 17 Aug 1743 at Wallingford, CT.
He married there 20 Oct 1763 Elizabeth Stark. Known children, births recorded at Wallingford, CT, were:
96. **Elizabeth** b 24 Jul 1764
97. **Medad** b 2 Dec 1765
98. **Samuel** b 9 Nov 1767

40. **ABIGAIL MITCHELL**, daughter of Samuel and Abigail
(Cook) Mitchell, was born 26 Apr 1746 at Wallingford, CT,
died 10 June 1823 at Steuben, Oneida Co., NY. She married
30 Apr 1767 at Cromwell, CT to Samuel Sizer, born 30 Nov
1744 Middletown, CT, son of Anthony and Sarah (Tryon) Sizer; he died 23 Sep 1823 at Steuben, NY, buried with Abigail
in the family cemetery on the Lewis farm. (A State Education Dept. monument placed in 1932 at the grave site calls
Abigail the daughter of Abigail <u>Tyler</u> Mitchell.)
      According to the "Sizer Genealogy" (Lillian Hubbard
Holch, 1941, p211-213), Samuel Sizer was a ship builder
at Derby, CT during the Revolution, building the barge in
which Arnold defended Lake Champlain. In 1787, he was
"associated with Baron Steuben, in the wilderness of...
Oneida Co., NY, being the first settler of the entire region...cleared the land now known as "Sixty Acres," and
built a house in 1787 for the Baron."
      (On 3 June 1817 Samuel & Joel Sizer & wives sold 210
acres on the west side of Black River for $1,000 to Asaph
Mitchell, Jr., all of Steuben. Asaph Mitchell, Jr. & Sr.
& wives sold to Joel Sizer for $1,000 half of Lot #6 in the
Holland Patent. Bk 29:400-3 Oneida Co., NY Deeds.)
      Abigail's children (SIZER) were: **(i)** Samuel b 10 Mar
1768 d 21 Apr 1769; **(ii)** Anne b 10 May 1770 m 1793 Barnabas
Brooks; no ch; **(iii)** Rebecca b 28 Feb 1773 d Feb 1824 Madison, NY m1) 1794 August Corey d 1805 (4 ch); m2) Levi Love
(2 ch); **(iv)** Samuel b 25 Jan 1775 d Feb 1776; **(v)** Joel b 16
Jan 1777 m 1801 Elizabeth Carey; no ch; **(vi)** Asa Bill b 5
June 1780 d 22 Nov 1829 Trenton, NY m1) 25 Dec 1801 Eliza-
beth Starr b 22 June 1782 Middletown, CT d/o Elihu & Mary
(Birdsey) Starr d 23 Jan 1817 (3 ch); m2) 6 Jul 1817 Mary
Walker Saltar b 31 Oct 1793 d 13 June 1882 Toledo, OH (4
ch); **(vii)** Samuel b 22 Jan 1783 m Lois Love at Madison, NY
(2 ch); **(viii)** Abigail b 20 Sep 1785 d ca 1864 OH age 78y m
Elihu Jones; no ch. (Sizer family data from descendant
Alice Pryor, 34 Logan Terr., Golf, IL 60029.)

FOURTH GENERATION

The children of this generation, like their forebear-
ers, were survivors. As formidable an enemy as any Indian
was the Spectre of Death which came often and in various
guises. There were deaths by accident, of course. People
drowned, were run over by and fell from carts, had trees
fall on them. Infants fell off of beds or were smothered
in the covers, or toddled into fireplaces or fell into
vats of boiling water. Women often died in childbirth
and their infants with them, twins seldom surviving for
long. Suicide was fairly rare but not unknown.

But disease in an age when there were few effective
medications was the most common cause of death. Surgery,
if at all possible, was crude, performed with unsterile
instruments under similar conditions. People succumbed
to throat distemper, typhus, spotted and putrid fevers,
the "rattles," the "gravel," pleurisy, canker rash, consumption, boils, "hooping" cough, jaundice, scurvey, can-
cer, nose bleeds, lung abcesses, and epidemics of dysentery. The death records of Rev. Roger Newton of Greenfield, MA tell us that fifty-seven died in that town of
dysentery alone between mid-July and the end of December
in the year 1802.

Doctors were helpless in the face of the more inex-
plicable disorders. What could they do for the woman who
died of dysentery, complicated by "...a Passage which extended from her Stomach to & through her back, out of
which issued a great part of her food for several years."
Some died of the treatment itself as in the case of an
amputated limb or the boy who died of "...mortification
in his arm by being blooded." Those who died of old age,
and there were many who lived into their 80's and 90's,
possessed hardy constitutions indeed!

For the most part, this generation of Mitchells continued the migration begun by those in the former generation. Although a few remained in the area where they were

-65-

born, there seemed to be an almost mass exodus to other locations, especially New York State. Some had gone as young children with their parents. Others removed after they were grown, married and had children of their own.

After a few years in New York, Vermont or New Hampshire, many began moving West into Pennsylvania, and from there into the Ohio Territory, lured by land that was fertile, cheap and plentiful. They faced frontier conditions with the same fortitude that had typified their ancestors, clearing land, breaking the virgin sod, wary of Indians, living in rude surroundings, depending solely on what equipment and supplies they managed to bring with them. They were armed with strong backs and considerable skills - men and women alike.

The children of this generation inherited a legacy of post-war depression which arrived at the end of an eight year long fight for the privilege of self-government. They were pioneers not only of new territory but of a new nation, their task the rebuilding of a war-torn country.

---

48. **ASAPH MITCHELL,** son of Moses and Mary (Ives) Mitchell, was born 24 June 1748 at Wallingford, CT, baptized 24 July at the 1st Congregational Church, Meriden, CT. He married first 30 Jan 1771 at Wallingford to Phebe Shailor and may have gone to Southwick, MA with his brother, Moses (#49), and various Hough and Ives relatives; an "Aspeth" Mitchell and wife Phoebe are on a list there of early church members dated 25 Sep 1773 ("Historical Facts & Stories About Southwick," 1951). If there were children of this marriage, none are known. Asaph married second on 7 Feb 1785 Wallingford to Susanna Cowles, born 1 May (bpt 18 May) 1748 at Wallingford, daughter of Joseph and Susanna (Cook) Cowles.

Asaph is mentioned at the establishment of the Baptist Church in Wallingford in 1786 and is there in 1790 with himself, a male under 16 and 2 females in his family. His father's will of 1792 calls him "my beloved Son" and leaves him his best suit of clothes plus an equal share of property and belongings and a "right" in the house.

In 1806 Asaph was named in the administration papers of his sister, Mary (#52), but his residence is not given and he is "lost" during the next two census periods. (He was not the Asaph of Deerfield, MA who was son of Abner.)

It is difficult to tell just when Asaph and Susanna moved their family to Oneida Co., NY but they were there by 1817. On 3 June of that year, Asaph Mitchell and Susanna his wife, Asaph Mitchell, Jr. and Lucy, his wife, sold for $1,000 half of Lot #6 in Holland Patent to Joel Sizer (see #40, 3rd Gen.) (Will Bk 29:400). This property had been purchased on 13 Jan 1817 for $370 from James and Mary Stuart of the City of New York and described as the north half of Lot #6 of 46 acres. (Bk 29:399)

On the same day that Asaph Sr. and Jr. sold the above described property, Asaph Mitchell, Jr. bought 210 acres on the west side of Black River for $1,000 from Samuel Sizer and Abigail, his wife, and Joel Sizer and Elizabeth, his wife. (Bk 29:403) Undoubtedly this was a joint purchase by Asaph Sr. and Jr. as the two seemed to be inseparable. The 1820 Census of Boonville (formerly Steuben), Oneida Co., NY shows Asaph Sr. and Jr. and their families living in the same household. They are still in this location in the 1830 census.

Quite probably Asaph Sr. died not long after 1830. A deed dated 20 May 1833 shows Asaph Mitchell and Lucy, his wife and Timothy Jackson and Lucy, his wife, and Daniel Benedict and Esther, his wife, all of Boonville, Oneida Co., NY, joining tenants to William G. Hubbard of the same place, selling Black River land in Boonville (Bk 66:133). Only two of Asaph Sr.'s children are positively identified but one can not rule out the fact that this deed looks very much like a sale of land by co-heirs of a deceased parent. Known children of Asaph and Susanna (Cowles) Mitchell, births recorded at Wallingford, CT, were:

   99. Asaph (Jr.) b 4 Nov 1787   +
  100. **Susannah** b 7 Aug 1791

49. MOSES MITCHELL (JR.), son of Moses and Mary (Ives) Mitchell, was baptized June 1750 at the 1st Congregational Church in Meriden, CT. He is probably the Moses Mitchell who married 27 Aug 1772 Lucy Warner ("Early CT Marriages," Wallingford-Meriden records).

His father's will, written in 1792, left Moses a one-third share in the remaining property and in "moveables," as well as a "Right" in the "Buildings." In 1806 Moses is mentioned in the estate administration papers of his sister, Mary (#52). His residence is not given in 1792, or 1797 at the probate of his father's estate, or in 1806.

Fourth Generation

The 1790 census lists two Moses Mitchells in CT, the first in New London Co. with 1 male over age 16 and 1 female in his family, indicating he was either a young, newly married man or a man whose fmaily had grown and gone, neither category fitting Moses, Jr. The second in Wallingford was Moses, Sr., father of Moses, Jr., with himself, his wife and his unmarried daughter in the family, proving that Moses, Jr. was not living with his father.

There were also two Moses Mitchells in Hampshire Co., MA in 1790. The first lived in Blandford and had 1 male age 16 and up, 3 males under age 16, and 3 females in his household. Living a few doors away was William Mitchell with 3 males age 16 and up, and 2 females in his family. Blandford Centre Cemetery has headstones for Elizabeth, wife of William Mitchell, 1758; Susannah, wife of Moses Mitchell 1785; Isobel, wife of William Mitchell, 1788; and William Mitchell, 1796. Moses of Blandford appears to be William's son, and not Moses, Jr., son of Moses, Sr.

The second Moses Mitchell lived in Southwick and was recorded there in Oct 1781 on a list of male inhabitants subject to Military Duty. He appears there in the 1790 census along with numerous Hough and Ives families to whom Moses, Jr. was related, including Elijah Hough, the father of Lemuel, an early Oneida Co., NY settler. On a list dated 25 Sep 1773 of early church members during Rev. Forward's pastorate is Aspeth Mitchell and wife Phoebe, undoubtedly the same as Asaph, brother of Moses, Jr., who had married Phoebe Shailor in 1771. The Roots of Southwick may also have been related to Moses, Jr. whose sister Esther had married Moses Root (see #53).

In the 1790 census, Moses (called Deacon) has 1 male age 16 and up, 3 males under age 16, and 4 females in his household. He does not appear in Southwick in the 1800 Census, but such a man does appear in the 1800 Census of Steuben Twp., Oneida Co., NY, his household containing in that year 1 male age 10 but under 16, 2 males age 16 but under 26, 1 male age 45 and up, 1 female age 10 but under 16, 2 females age 16 but under 26, and 1 female age 45 and up - a family composition that exactly matches that of Deacon Moses of Southwick in 1790. It is unfortunate indeed that Southwick Vital Records were destroyed by fire about 1840.

As slender as these facts may be, it is more than probable that Moses, Jr. was Deacon Moses of Southwick, MA in 1790 and Moses of Steuben, Oneida Co., NY in 1800. A history of Remsen, NY (Oneida Co.) states that the first religious service of the Baptist church there was held on 10 Jan 1803, Deacon Moses Mitchell presiding. (It seems that Moses "went over" to the Baptists as did his elder brother, Asaph.) On 12 May 1804, Moses witnessed the will of Isaac Staples of Steuben (Bk 1:155); and the account book of Brayton store at Westernville Village, Oneida Co. (the only store in the area at that time), names Moses, Eli, and William Mitchell in their records from 1796-1804.

Moses was still in Oneida Co. in the 1810 Census, and in 1814 he appeared in Steuben on an Oneida County Census of Land Owners (including those who leased) along with Jotham Mitchell and Asaph Mitchell, Jr. He is not found in the 1820 Census and perhaps died in Steuben between 1814 and 1820.

Who were Moses Jr.'s children? Our only real "facts" about them come from census records. He had two sons and two daughters born between 1774 and 1784, then another son and daughter born between 1784 and 1790. All were still unmarried in 1800.

Perhaps the most likely candidate as a son of Moses, Jr. is Jotham Mitchell. Moses, Jr. had a younger brother named Jotham who died in Meriden, CT in 1825. (Of his two sons, neither was named Jotham and both died unmarried in Meriden, CT in 1811.) So strong is the probability in my opinion that Jotham of Oneida Co., NY was a son of Moses, Jr., I will include him in the Fifth Generation and discuss him more fully there.

Eli Mitchell who is listed on the Brayton store account books 1796-1804 with Moses is a possibility. One might be a bit more sure except for the unknown William Mitchell also listed on that store account. Oneida Co. deeds record a William Mitchell of "Blanford," County of New Hampshire, Mass., buying property in the John Tyler Patent in 1803 from Jeptha and Jeptha Brainard, Jr. of Whitestown and Western, Oneida Co., NY (Bk 11:166). There seems to be no other record of this William except for the above deed and his appearance in the 1800 Census of Oneida Co. along with an Isaac Mitchell (p 204). Both are men age 45 and up.

Eli and Marinda Mitchell of Boonville (formerly Steuban), Oneida Co., NY bought property in Holland Patent in 1827 from Schuyler and Sally Bucek (Bk 43:12). Eli is in the 1820 Census of Oneida Co., NY in Boonville (p. 175) with 1 male under age 10, 1 male age 26 but under 45, 2 females under age 10, 2 females age 10 but under 16, and 1 female age 26 but under 45. Eli, age 70, born in Massachusetts, farmer, and Jerusha, age 67, born in Connecticut, are in the 1850 Census of Oneida Co., NY in Ada (formed from Boonville in 1846). Living with them is Henry Mitchell, age 21, and Elvira Hyde, age 32, both born in NY.

Another intriguing Mitchell in Oneida Co. during the same time period was Barnabas. A D.A.R. publication says that Barnabas was born in Meriden, CT; married Mary Tyler; died at Remsen, NY 14 Mar 1813; served in 8th Co. of 5th Regiment, CT; enlisted 1 July 1781 in Capt. Bingham's Co., 5th Regiment of the Line; came to Remsen from Meriden, CT in 1792. Jones' "History of Oneida Co., NY" adds that Barnabas came from Meriden, CT, settled in 1792, had a son Milo Mitchell, Esq., and a daughter Polly who was the first white child born in the area. Roberts' "History of Remsen, NY gives the names of his children as Clarissa, Olive and Tyler, born in CT; Polly, Milo, Melissa, Charlotte, and Amanda, born in NY. The D.A.R. Patriot Index says he was born in 1764.

From about 1757 to 1803, baptism records for the 1st Congregational Church in Meriden, CT are mostly missing. The baptism of Barnabas is not registered there, nor is his marriage. In the 1790 Census, he is probably the Barnabas Mitchell in Ballstown, Albany Co., NY with 1 male age 16 and up, 1 male under age 16, and 3 females. There is no other man listed by that name in that census year in CT, MA, VT or in another NY location. He is in Oneida Co., NY in the 1800 Census.

Fairfield Cemetery, Remsen, NY has a number of Mitchell burials. Milo d 31 Mar 1870 in the 74th year of his age; Katie Hinkly, wife (of Milo), d 11 Jan 1829, age 30y; Anna Price Humphry, wife of Milo, b 3 June 1800, d 13 Jan 1880; Eliza Ann, wife of Richard Jones, daughter of Milo, d 25 Mar 1859 at 24y 6m 21d; Catherine, daughter of Milo and Ann, d 20 Mar 1872, age 39y; Harriet, daughter of Milo and Ann, d Feb 1845, age 6y. Milo Mitchell's will (Oneida Co. Surrogate Court, Bk 20:425) names wife Ann and children Catherine, James, Caroline, Sarah, and Isabella. The Oneida Co., NY Census of Land Owners in 1814 lists "Molly" (Milo) and Tyler Mitchell in the town of Remsen. These two lived next to each other in the 1820 Census.

Other Mitchell heads of household in Oneida Co., NY in the 1820 Census were Hugh and Thomas S. in Utica; James in Western; Jared in Paris; Joseph, Levi, and Warner in Westmore; Mary in Rome; and Samuel in Lee.

A probable son of Moses and Lucy (Warner) Mitchell, Jr., undoubtedly born at Southwick, MA, was:

   101. Jotham bc 1772-1775   +

51. **JOTHAM MITCHELL**, son of Moses and Mary (Ives) Mitchell, was born 1 Apr 1754 (baptized 7 Apr) at Wallingford, CT. He married there 14 Mar 1782 to Rebecca Royce, born 16 Apr 1758 at Wallingford, daughter of Gideon and Rebecca (Johnson) Royce. Jotham died at Meriden, CT on 2 Nov 1825 (age 71y 7m 1d) and Rebecca died there 15 May 1811 (age 54y). Both are buried in the Old Meriden Graveyard.

Jotham would have been old enough to fight in the Revolutionary War. "Mitchell Family Records," by J. Montgomery Seaver, lists a Jotham Mitchell as having served in the Revolutionary War from Massachusetts. Whether or not he was the above Jotham is not known. One would expect the above Jotham to have joined a Connecticut company, provided he served at all.

Of Jotham's six children, the births of only the first two and the last are in Wallingford, CT records. This leads me to suspect that he and his family moved to Bristol, CT not far northwest of Meriden between 1785 and 1786, returning to Meriden between 1790 and 1794. He is in Bristol in the 1790 Census with 1 male age 16 and up, 1 male under age 16 and 3 females in his household. In the 1800 and 1810 Census, he is in Meriden, New Haven Co., CT.

At the death of his father in 1797, Jotham was a co-executor with his brother, Zenas. He received a share of his father's estate equal to that received by his brothers which amounted to 9 acres of land from the north end of his father's farm, a "Right" in the "Buildings," and a portion of the "moveables." He is also mentioned in the estate distribution papers of his sister, Mary (#52), who died in Meriden in 1806.

The year 1811 was a tragic one for Jotham. Within a month and a half's time, he lost Rebecca, his wife of nearly thirty years, and his only two sons, Moses and Aaron. Moses, although unmarried at age twenty-five, had amassed enough worldly goods to have an estate. An "Heirs Agreement" in his estate papers contains a clause

subjecting his sisters' inheritance to the maintenance
and support of his father "...at all times during his natural life..." It adds: "We...also for the further consideration of respect & affection which we have for our
father the said Jotham Mitchel do severally covenant &
agree with said Jotham Mitchel, that we will contribute to
his maintenance & support at all times during his natural
life; as his the said Jotham's circumstances may require,
to the full amount of our respective shares in the estate
of said Moses Mitchel deceased, and in proportion to our
respective shares in the estate, should...Jotham's circumstances require the same." This agreement was signed
by Jotham's three daughters and two sons-in-law.

Jotham died leaving no will or estate. Since he does
not appear in the 1820 Connecticut Census, he was undoubtedly living with one of his married daughters. Children
of Jotham and Rebecca (Royce) Mitchell were:

102. **Betsey** b 18 Oct 1783; d 26 Nov 1784, age 13m 8d.
103. **Betsey** b 18 Jan 1785; m (before 1811) Christopher
     Atwater.
104. **Moses** bc 1786   +
105. **Sally** - living but unmarried in 1811.
106. **Laura** - married Walter Booth (he was elected deacon
     at Wallingford on 1 Sep 1814; died 1870.)
107. **Aaron** b 4 Apr 1794; dsp (unmarried) 11 June 1811.

52. **MARY "POLLY" MITCHELL,** daughter of Moses and Mary
(Ives) Mitchell, was born 26 Mar 1757 (baptized 8 May) at
Wallingford. She died unmarried on 12 Mar 1806, age 49,
at Meriden, CT and is buried in the Old Meriden Graveyard.

Mary was still living in her father's household in
1790 and presumeably continued to do so even after his
death in 1797. At that time Mary inherited six acres and
sixty rods of her father's land, bounded "...South Part
on Land set to the widow of the Deceased and part on Zenas
Mitchels Land, East on Dan Collins, North on Land before
Set to Zenas...West on Highway..." She also shared ownership of the buildings on the land and had a portion of the
moveables set to her.

At Mary's death in 1806, her brother, Zenas, was appointed co-administrator with Asaph Merriam of her estate
which involved mostly clothes, bedding, a few household
items and a note of hand against her brother, Zenas. Everything she owned she left to her four brothers and her

sister. Brother Asaph received such items as a "best chest...Japan tea canister...4 pounds Hetcheled flax... 10 yards whitened cloth...1 poor bed blanket..." plus items of wearing apparel. Brother Moses was left 1 great coat (which had probably been his father's), 1 flannel gown, 2 flannel shirts, 1 petticoat, 1 broadcloth cloak, and 1 brass kettle. Brother Jotham seems to have received the most, inheriting a bed stand, feather bed and pillows, an old chest, a Dutch wheel, a tablecloth, pair of horn buttons, bed quilts, and such clothing as a pair of ear muffs, a bonnet, ribbons, and gowns. Brother Zenas received only a few items such as whitened cloth, a pair of white mitts, and a single sheet, the money he owed the estate being included as part of his share.

Sister Esther, "wife of Moses Root," received the bulk of her sister's belongings. Let us hope that Esther and Mary were about the same size or that Esther was a clever seamstress for she fell heir to most of Mary's clothes. Mary owned any number of gowns described as of silk and calico; striped, spotted and flannel. She also received the looking glass, large wheel, feather bed and bolster, Mary's white shawl, numerous pairs of stockings, pocket handkerchiefs, bedding, and Mary's "close" basket. (Wallingford, Ct Probate Records, File #1201)

As a spinster, Mary enjoyed rights which her married sisters did not possess. She could sue, administer her own estate, buy what she wished, sell or will inherited property, make business transactions, and keep any earnings from employment. She must have sold the land she inherited from her father as no land appears on the inventory of her own estate.

In an era when marrying and having children was considered the behaviour of a "normal" female, we wonder if Mary remained single out of choice, lack of opportunity, or, since she died at such an early age, because of general physical frailty. She was only nineteen when her mother died, but she did not remain single to care for her widowed father since he remarried the year following her mother's death. It is possible that she remained at home to care for her younger brother and sister while matrimonial opportunities slipped through her grasp.

53. **ESTHER MITCHELL,** daughter of Moses and Mary (Ives) Mitchell, was born 4 Aug 1760 at Wallingford, CT. She

married before 1790 Moses Root. Jacobus ("Families of Ancient New Haven") calls her Rother with a question mark. He was right to question this name. That she was Esther and that she married Moses Root is stated not only in her father's will and distribution but in her sister Mary's estate distribution papers as well. (See #52.)

Although there is a "Lieut." Moses Root living in Southwick, MA in the 1790 Census, Esther's husband was more likely the Moses Root living in nearby Cheshire in that year, his family composed of 1 male age 16 and up, 2 males under age 16, and 3 females. One can not help but notice the many surnames in Cheshire who were related to the Mitchells by marriage - Hough, Ives, Tuttle, Cook, Benham, Sperry, and How. There were also many Attwater families in Cheshire and it may be through her Aunt Esther that Betsey Mitchell, daughter of Jotham (#51) met her husband, Christopher Atwater.

54. **ZENAS MITCHELL,** son of Moses and Mary (Ives) Mitchell, was born 10 Apr 1762 at Wallingford, CT. He married 10 June 1784 at Wallingford (9 June per Cheshire, CT Congregational Society records) to Abigail Merriman, born 8 Nov 1762 at Wallingford, daughter of Titus and Dinah (Andrews) Merriman.

Zenas and Abigail joined the 1st Congregational Church at Meriden, CT in 1790. They are listed in the 1790 Census in Wallingford Twp., New Haven Co., CT with 2 males age 16 and up, 1 male under age 16, and 4 females in their family. (They may have had a son and daughter who died young, or another family with a son was living with them.)

At the death of his father in 1797, Zenas was left his father's tanning and shoe making tools, his shop and the land upon which it stood. Undoubtedly, he followed the same trade as his father before him. Zenas also became a deacon in the Meriden Congregational Church. Davis' "History of Wallingford, CT" says that his membership "ceased" about 1813 and that Zenas left the area in 1814.

From here on, the trail grows cold. Researchers of this line should be cautioned that while Zenas was a rather unusual given name, there were several of them in the unrelated line of Experience Mitchell, early emigrant to Plymouth, MA. In census records of 1800, indexes for the states of MA, CT, NH, VT, NY, PA, RI and ME were searched for Zenas Mitchell. The only man found by that name was living in Plymouth Co., MA with 1 male under age 10, 1 male and 1 female aged 16 but under 26 in the household. Clearly, this was not the above Zenas Mitchell, although we know he and Abigail were still living in that year.

Zenas is listed in New Haven Co., CT in the 1810 census but not in 1820. The 1820 New York census index revealed two by that name - Zenos in Olean Twp., Cattaraugus Co. (p 8), and Zenas in Milton Twp., Saratoga Co. (p 232).

Worthy of mention is a third Zenas Mitchell, named in a biography of John Sylvester Mitchell as his father. ("History of LaSalle Co., IL," Vol. I; records of Maggie Mitchell, 77 Homestead Lane, Attleboro, MA) According to John Sylvester Mitchell's obituary, he was born 4 Sep 1814 at Penn Yan, Ontario Co. (now Yates), NY, son of Zenas and Eleanor (Race) Mitchell, and died in 1890. The biography mentioned above says that Zenas Mitchell was in the Revolutionary War, joining at age sixteen, was in Ohio in 1816 and at Fort Harrison, IN in 1818 (another source says Fort Harrison, IN in 1814). He then moved to what is now Edgar Co., IL near the town of Paris. He was working as a carpenter on a house in Charleston, IL when he fell and was instantly killed (sometime before 1831).

Some problems arise in reconciling Zenas, son of Moses Mitchell, with Zenas, father of John Sylvester Mitchell. Although Zenas, father of John S., was between 50 and 60 years of age when John S. was born (indicating that Eleanor Race was a second wife), John S. was supposedly the second child born to Zenas and Eleanor. Proof is lacking that Zenas, son of Moses, was widowed in time to remarry and have two children by 1814. No death record has been found for Abigail (Merriman) Mitchell nor has a marriage record for Zenas Mitchell to Eleanor Race.

In "Families of Ancient New Haven," Jacobus shows only one child, Titus, for this family. But records of Wallingford (first 5 children) and Meriden (last 2 children) name a total of seven. Per these records, the children of Zenas and Abigail (Merriman) Mitchell were:

108. **Silvana** b 21 Mar 1785; d 24 Dec 1805 (Levina, 20y).
109. **Abigail** b 24 Jul 1787; d 1 Dec 1805 (Abigail, 19y).
110. **Harriet** b 6 Mar 1793
111. **Zenas** b 28 Nov 1795
112. **Theodita** b 3 Aug 1798
113. **Titus** b 16 Jul 1801; m Maria Barnes.
114. **Charles Henry** b 3 Apr 1805

58. **MOSES MILLER MITCHELL,** son of Elijah and Elizabeth (Miller) Mitchell, was born 28 Nov 1763 (Deerfield, MA Vital Records).

Sheldon's Mitchell genealogy in Vol. II of "History of Deerfield, MA" says Moses Miller married first an unknown wife who died 13 Oct 1790 "in travail with her infant." He gives Moses Miller's second wife as Bathsheba Smith and their marriage date as 16 June 1791; and his third wife as Lydia Hale "of Greenfield" whom he married 29 May 1793 at Bernardston, MA.

It is more likely that his "unknown" first wife (as given by Sheldon) and his wife, Bathsheba Smith, were one and the same. Greenfield, MA Vital Records have marriage intentions for Moses Miller to Bathsheba Smith on 16 June 1790. Records of Rev. Roger Newton of Greenfield show that he consecrated this marriage on 22 May 1790. (Thompson's "History of Greenfield, MA," Vol. II, p. 708) Although it is strange that the date of intentions is nearly four weeks after the marriage took place, one thing is clear. The correct year of marriage was 1790, not 1791. Undoubtedly, Bathsheba Smith was "the wife of Miller Mitchell" who died "in travail" with her infant some five months after their marriage.

Moses Miller seems to have preferred going by his middle name rather than his first. He is not listed in the 1790 Massachusetts Census under either name and may have been living with a relative of his wife, Bathsheba. This census does list as living in Greenfield, a Joel Smith with 2 males age 16 and up and 4 females in his household. Joel Smith had married Elizabeth Dickenson of Whately, MA in 1786. Members of his household in 1790 may have been Joel and Elizabeth Smith, two Smith daughters, Moses Miller and Bathsheba Mitchell. During Shay's rebellion in 1787, Joel had served in the same company as Moses Miller and his brother Elijah Mitchell at the defense of the arsenal in Springfield, MA.

Dates of death for Moses Miller and second wife Lydia are unknown. There are no probate records on file for him in Franklin Co., MA. Births of all of his children appear in Greenfield, MA records although the death in 1824 of his daughter, Lydia, is recorded both in Greenfield and Shelburne, MA records (Sheldon says she died in Shelburne.) He owned property in Greenfield which he sold between 1805 and 1810 but seems to have remained in that

town until at least 1824 when his youngest child's birth
was recorded there. Children of Moses Miller and Lydia
(Hale) Mitchell, all recorded at Greenfield, MA, were:
115. **Ebenezer** b 13 Nov 1794; d 22 Sep 1815 (Greenfield).
116. **Bathsheba** b 8 Jul 1796
117. **Lucinda** b 27 Sep 1798
118. **Moses Miller** b 19 Jan 1800; d 8 Sep 1802 at Greenfield of dysentery, age 18m.
119. **Elizabeth** b 2 Aug 1803
120. **Alonzo** b 6 Mar 1806   +
121. **Lydia** b 5 May 1810; d 24 Sep 1824 (Shelburne).
122. **Eunice** b 27 May 1812
123. **Mercy M.** b 19 June 1815
124. **Isabella O.** b 28 Apr 1818
125. **Lydia R.** b 1 Aug 1824

63. **EUNICE MITCHELL,** daughter of Elijah and Elizabeth
(Miller) Mitchell, was born 1 Jul 1774 at Greenfield, MA.
She married there (int.) 11 Jul 1800 Lemuel Wetmore (al-
ternate spelling, Whitmore), born 24 Feb 1778 at Greenfield, son of Beriah and Abigail (Dowd) Bacon-Wetmore.
After the birth of their second child, Eunice and Lemuel
removed to Pittsford, VT where both were still living in
1830. Eunice was probably the "Unice Whitmore" who was
allowed a debt on claim in 1833 from the estate of her
brother-in-law, Samuel Wetmore of Ira, VT. (Rutland Co.,
VT Probate Court District Records, #15, [1833-1836],
pp 18-19, on microfilm #028,786 at Salt Lake City.) Deed
records for Lemuel are also available in Pittsford, VT.
    Eunice's children (WETMORE), first two born at Green-
field, MA, all recorded at Pittsford, VT, were: **(i)** Ira
b 23 May 1801; **(ii)** Fanny b 17 Nov 1802; **(iii)** Betsey b 23
Mar 1805; m by 23 Apr 1827 Leonard Wheeler b 2 Mar 1804,
Langdon, NH, s/o Benjamin & Abigail (Colburn) Wheeler;
Betsey & Leonard left VT for Crawford Co., IL in 1843;
from Erie, NY via the Erie Canal to Buffalo, then by lake
to Cleveland, then by canal to LaFayette, then by steam
boat down the Wabash River to Bristol, they landed opposite Palestine, IL; Betsey was living 1850 in Crawford Co.
but dead bef 9 Mar 1858 when her husband m2) Crawford Co.,
to Amanda M. Scott; Leonard d there 19 Jan 1876, bur in
Palestine Cemetery, Lamotte Twp., Crawford Co., IL; 5
surviving children, all of whom lived and died in Crawford
Co., IL; **(iv)** Moses b 17 May 1807; **(v)** Eunice b 28 Mar

1809; **(vi)** Sophia b 17 June 1812. (Data on Eunice [Mitchell] Wetmore & family provided by Douglas Richardson, P.O. Box 1036, Bethany, OK 73008.)

66. **WILLIAM MITCHELL,** son of Elijah and Elizabeth (Miller) Mitchell, was born 16 Sep 1777 at Greenfield, MA. He died there before 10 Oct 1854 when his will (dated 1 Feb 1848) was probated. William married at Deerfield, MA on 23 Dec 1798 (int.) Mercy Wise, born about 1770 (probably in CT), daughter of Joseph and Judith ( ) Wise, who came from Lebanon, CT about 1777 and settled at Turnip Yard, a district in the Sugar Loaf range just south of Deerfield. Mercy was still living at Greenfield in 1860, aged 90, with her unmarried daughter, Content, aged 56. Both the 1850 and 1860 census show Mercy as being seven years older than her husband, William.

William was a joiner (carpenter) by trade. His will left his chest of joiner's tools to be equally divided between his five sons, Anson, Miles, Elijah, William, and Willard. His daughter, Mary, "wife of John Holden of Adams" (MA), was left her father's "small bible" and one-half of her mother's wearing apparel after Mercy's decease. The other half of his wife's clothing was left to his daughter, Content, who also received the rest of William's property, both real and personal, provided she supported and maintained her mother during her natural life. Anson, as eldest son, was appointed executor.

William's probate (File #3258, Franklin Co., MA) was not settled for three years. In 1856 Anson declared the estate unable to pay all its debts and declared insolvency. In 1857 the estate was declared deficient by the sum of $1,661.65 and William's real estate was ordered sold. An auction sale of his property was published on 20 Feb in the Greenfield "Franklin Democrat" and the sale held at noon on 19 Mar. William's land, situated about a mile west of Greenfield village, consisted of about four acres with a dwelling house, barn and out-building, all encumbered by the widow's dower. The highest bidder was his daughter, Content, who bought the premises for $125.00.

In October 1857 a surplus of $102.85 was distributed at the rate of 5 cents and 2 mills on each dollar of claim, excepting $20.20 of preferred debts which was paid in full. Anson received $2.98 on his claim of $57.43, and Content was allowed $72.57 on her claim of $1,400.00.

Married nearly 56 years at his death, William and Mercy had lived a simple and frugal life. William's personal estate was evaluated at only $31.49. It consisted mainly of tools of various sorts, including the joiner's tools he left his sons, a few articles of furniture and bedding, two hats, two pairs of boots, other wearing apparel, a set of tinware, and a "library" valued at fifty cents. Children of William and Mercy (Wise) Mitchell, all born at Greenfield, were:

- 126. **Anson** bc 1799   +
- 127. **Lyman** (probably died young)
- 128. **Porter** bc 1801; d 3 Aug 1803 at Greenfield of dysentery, aged 2y.
- 129. **Content** b 1 Oct 1803; d unmarried (after 1864 when she sold land at Greenfield to Dan'l D. Kellehar).
- 130. **Miles** b 21 Aug 1805   +
- 131. **Mary** b 4 Jul 1807; m 5 Jul 1832 John Holden (Greenfield church record calls both "of" Adams, MA).
- 132. **William Miller** b 26 Sep 1809 (twin)
- 133. **Willard Moreley** b 26 Sep 1809 (twin)
- 134. **Elijah** b 16 Nov 1813   +

70. **MICHAEL MITCHELL,** son of Joel and Mary ( ) Mitchell, was born 16 Dec 1750 at Wethersfield, CT. Only twelve years old at his father's death, neither Michael nor his siblings were mentioned in their father's probate papers.

The Administration Bond posted by Michael's mother, Mary, and Daniel Andrus, at Joel's death in 1763 was witnessed by David Webster. The probate file of Michael Mitchell of Wethersfield, dated 2 June 1777 (Hartford, CT Probate District, #3743) contains only one document, an Administration Bond filed by David Webster and Mabel "Mitchel," both of Wethersfield. The presence of David Webster's name on both Administration Bonds is a significant clue in proving that Michael Mitchell of the 1777 probate was the same as Michael, son of Joel.

Webster family genealogies in Barbour's "Families of Early Hartford, CT" includes just one David Webster. He was born 29 Jan 1721 (Glastonbury V/R), son of Jonathan and Esther (Judd) Webster. David married first Lydia Andrus, second Zerviah (Hart) Allen, and third Olive (Smith) Deming. Although Barbour does not carry David's line on, it is interesting to note that David's brother, Jonathan, who married Mabel Risley in Feb 1730, had a daughter named Mabel (but no data given). Only two of Jonathan's twelve children are given baptism dates. It is possible that his daughter, Mabel, was contemporary in age to Michael Mitchell.

David Webster who was definitely contemporary in age with Michael's father, Joel, may also have named a daughter Mabel. It would not be unusual for a father to post bond with a widowed daughter on the administration of her deceased husband's estate.

These observations are meant merely as interesting signposts for any researchers concerned with this particular family. They are not to be construed in any way as proof of relationships.

71. **NASH MITCHELL**, son of Joel and Mary (   ) Mitchell, was born 9 Apr 1753 (Wethersfield, CT V/R), baptized on 14 Oct 1753 at Meriden, CT. A Nash Mitchell appears in the 1790 Massachusetts Census in Sheffield Twp., Berkshire Co. with 1 male age 16 and up, 3 males under age 16, and 4 females in his family. (Note: The Town Clerk of Sheffield found no Mitchells listed in Sheffield, MA Town Records 1730-1810, but the "History of Berkshire Co., MA," p 206, listing Revolutionary soldiers serving from Sheffield, included the names of Amasa, Amos, and Nash Mitchell.)

74. **AMASA MITCHELL**, son of Joel and Mary (   ) Mitchell, was born 30 May 1761 at Wethersfield, CT (Barbour's Vital Records of Wethersfield, Vol. II, p. 119).

A query submitted by Mrs. Norman H. Terando of Indianapolis, IN stated that Amasa Mitchell was born in 1761 at Wethersfield, CT; died in Scott Co., IN in 1851, and married in 1788 at Schoharie Co., NY to Mary Freymaurer, daughter of Johanne, Jr. and Dorothea (Bouck?) Freymaurer. (Schoharie Co. was formed in 1795 from Albany and Otsego Cos., NY. Amasa Mitchell is not listed in the 1790 NY Census Index.) A letter to Mrs. Terando was returned to me marked undeliverable.

An Amasa Mitchell served in the American Revolution from the state of Connecticut. Amasa Mitchell is also listed in the D.A.R. Patriot Index as born 29 May 1761, died 11 Jan 1851, married Mary Frymier; fifer; Massachusetts service. See reference in #71 above to an Amasa Mitchell serving from Sheffield, MA. (Note: New Haven, CT V/R lists an Amasa Mitchell who d 12 Feb 1851.)

75. **LYDIA MITCHELL,** daughter of Joseph, Jr. and Lydia (Foster) Mitchell, was baptized 22 Mar 1752 at Deerfield, MA. She lived at Deerfield until the early 1760's when her parents moved to nearby Ashfield, MA. About 1771, the family moved to Skenesborough, Charlotte Co., NY (now Whitehall, Washington Co., NY). She married about 1778-1780 Caleb Hurlbut, Jr., born Aug 1753 in Litchfield Co., CT, son of Caleb and Mary (Bartholomew) Hurlbut. (The Hurlbut name has varied spellings in records such as Hurlbutt, Hurlburt, Hob(b)art, Hurlbat, Halberdt, etc.)

The Hurlbuts were in Skenesborough by 1775 as seen from a listing of Philip Skene's tenants up to that year. Included are the names of Caleb Hurlbut, Benoni Hobbert, Benjamin Hobbart, and Azul Hobart. Lemuel and Thazer Bartholomew are also listed. The D.A.R. Patriot Index, however, shows Caleb Hurlbut, Jr. to have served in the American Revolution from Connecticut. An interesting item from the "Whitehall Papers" (Vol. XV, p 319, Albany, NY Library) illustrates well the political divisions that occasionally occured in families during the Revolution, and may well explain why Caleb, Jr. did not serve from New York. "Caleb (Hurlbut, Sr.) was a Tory, but the Bartholomews were staunch Rebels. At the time of the Burgoyne invasion, the Hurlburts resided in a log house...Mary (wife of Caleb Hurlbut, Sr.) overheard a plot on the part of the Tories to capture the Bartholomews, and that night she climbed out of the attic window and ran across the woods and fields to Lemuel's (Bartholomew) house and warned him so when the Tories appeared in force the following day, the expected victims had escaped."

During the early years of settlement in Eastern New York, the "Yankees" (from such areas as MA and CT) were often at odds with their "Yorker" neighbors. "Yankees" favored town government. "Yorkers" believed in county government which smacked of aristocracy to the "Yankees" who were more attuned to Vermont's political idealogies. Vermont herself was trying to claim all territory as far west as the Hudson River. At the beginning of the 1780's, residents of New York counties bordering Vermont began sending a flurry of petitions to the Vermont Legislature, each one asking Vermont to establish new townships in areas claimed by New York, with the idea of settlement under Vermont's jurisdiction. Caleb, Jr., several of his brothers, and a number of Bartholomews, were signers of

Fourth Generation

two such petitions in 1781. These petitions failed since
New York steadfastly refused to relinquish any land they
considered their own.

Caleb, Jr. and Lydia appear in the 1790 Census of New
York in Whitehall Twp., Washington Co. (p 195) with 1 male
age 16 and up, 1 male under age 16, and 5 females in the
family. (Next door is Joseph Mitchell, assumed to be
Lydia's brother, but the presence here in 1800 of a Joseph
Mitchell, too old to be her brother, casts doubt on this
assumption.) Caleb and Lydia continued to live in Washington Co. until Feb 1819 when they moved to Jennings Co.,
IN at the request of their youngest son, Lewis, who was a
Methodist minister at Vernon. They are here in the 1820
Census (1 male, 1 female, both age 45 and up) along with
Lewis who shows a male age 26/45 and a female age 16/26 in
his household, indicating that he may have had a first
wife prior to his marriage in 1822 to Ann Wood (or
the female may have been a sister, not yet married.)

Caleb, Jr. died in Jennings Co., IN in Sep 1824 and is
buried in a cemetery at Paris Crossing. His name is on a
plaque erected at the courthouse in Vernon, naming Revolutionary War soldiers buried in Jennings Co., IN. Lydia
sold her Jennings Co., IN property and moved on with her
son, Lewis, to Madison, Jefferson Co., IN. In the 1830
Census, Jefferson Co., the family shows with 1 male age 5
but under 10, 1 male age 30 but under 40, 1 female age 10
but under 15, 1 female age 30 but under 40, and 1 female
age 70 but under 80 (Lydia, age 78). Lydia died in Nov
1831 at Lewis' home in Saluda Twp., Jefferson Co., IN.

Lydia's children (HURLBUT), probably all born in
Washington Co., NY, were: **(i)** Thankful m John M. Ballard;
(ii) Lydia m John McFerrin; **(iii)** Gerulia m Daniel Man-
well; **(iv)** Rachel m Abel Benjamin; **(v)** Mary ("Polly") m
Lemuel Hale; **(vi)** Caleb III b 1792 m Pamela/Permelia Mc-
Ferrin; res. at Madison, IN but d 21 Apr 1833/4 at Cincinnati, OH; Permelia (grst) was b 21 Sep 1795, d 31 Mar
1872, bur in Springdale Cem., Madison, IN; 7 children;
(vii) Cyrenia m James Chandler; d 1849; **(viii)** Lewis b 17
Oct 1794 m 28 Feb 1822 Ann(e) Wood(s) in Jennings Co., IN;
d 3 May 1876; Minister of the Gospel (Methodist); res.
1820 Jennings Co., IN; 1830 Jefferson Co., IN; 1840 Ripley
Co., IN; 1850 Franklin Co., IN. (Thanks to Carol R.
Austin, 9726 Mirage Cir., Garden Grove, CA 92644 for data
on Caleb, Jr., Caleb III, and Lewis Hurlbut.)

76.   **EXPERIENCE MITCHELL**, daughter of Joseph, Jr. and
Lydia (Foster) Mitchell, was baptized 4 May 1754 at Deerfield, MA. When she married John Fuller on 11 Jul 1774,
Deerfield V/R call her "of Ashfield." (John Fuller is also called "of Ashfield" by Sheldon in his Mitchell genealogy, "History of Deerfield, MA," Vol. II.)

The ancestry of John Fuller is unknown. John and
Thomas Fuller were original proprietors in the Dedham
Grant, drawing Lots No. 15 and 25 in Deerfield (or vice-
versa - Sheldon lists it both ways). Thomas died in Dedham, MA in 1690. It is possible that John never lived in
Deerfield. He (or Thomas) may be the ancestor of the John
Fuller who with his wife, Anna, had a son, John, baptized
in Dedham, MA on 17 Jan 1741/2, the parents entering the
church on the same day.

A John Fuller is found in the 1790 Census in Plainfield, MA (near Ashfield) with 1 male age 16 and up, 3
males under age 16, and 1 female. Fuller households in
Ashfield, MA at the 1850 Census were: Luke Fuller, age
70, b MA with Irene (54, MA) and Rosetti (12, MA); Joseph
Fuller, age 62, b MA with Lucretia (49, MA) and Lucretia W. (37, MA); William Fuller, age 42, b MA with Polly
(43, MA), William (17, MA), and Henry (7, MA).

77.   **ENSIGN MITCHELL**, son of Joseph, Jr. and Lydia (Foster) Mitchell, was baptized 1 Jul 1759 at Deerfield, MA.
He married about 1786 to Lucy Hubbard, probably born on
2 Feb 1762/4 in MA (possibly Berkshire County). Her parentage is unproven (see Some Allied Lines for more data.)

Ensign moved to Ashfield, MA with his parents when he
was about four years old, living there until the age of
twelve or thirteen when his parents left Ashfield to settle on land patented to Philip Skene in NY, locating about
three miles from Skenesborough in Charlotte Co. (now
Whitehall, Washington Co., NY). At that time, Vermont was
part of New York State and Charlotte/Washington Co. included the present day Vermont county of Rutland.

The site of Skenesborough (or Skenesborough Landing
as it was then known), was once called Kahchoquahna, meaning "fish dipping place," by the Indians. Incorporated by
patent in 1765, it lay at the southern extremity of Lake
Champlain on Wood Creek. It was marshy country, full of
mosquitoes and tiny gnats called "punchins" or "punkies."
Although they were smaller than the eye could see, they

were capable of biting viciously. The shores of Lake Champlain, of Lake George to the west, and the land for many miles around, was thickly wooded with trees of enormous size. The soil in the immediate area was hard, stiff clay, better suited to grazing stock than tilling.

The Mitchells were adamant Whigs, firmly opposed to the British Tory government. At the onset of the Revolutionary War, Ensign was not quite sixteen years old. In Oct 1775 he enlisted as a private in Capt. Daniel Mills' Co., Col. Van Schaik's NY Battalion of General Schuyler's Regiment for a term of 9 months. According to Ensign's pension application papers of 1832, he "...remained at Skeensborough landing from the time he entered the service untill the ensuing Winter when the troops were marched from thence on the Ice to Ticonderoga..." They were stationed there until the following spring when "...they were marched to Lake George and there remained to the expiration of the term for which he entered the service." Military papers state his enlistment as 26 Jan 1776 (not Oct 1775 as Ensign said), and his discharge date as 7 Sep 1776. Perhaps he enlisted in Oct 1775 but was not mustered in until the following January. In 1832 "...from age and infirmity...", he could not "distinctly recollect."

By mid-June 1777, General Burgoyne began his advance from Canada with 7,000 British regulars and German mercenaries, about 250 Canadians and Tories, and about 500 Indians, capturing Fort Ticonderoga in July after the Americans evacuated it and fled to Skenesborough. Gen'l Burgoyne pressed on and captured Skenesborough later that same month, then waited there for his Indians who were still plundering in the vicinity of Ticonderoga.

Popularly called "Gentleman Johnny," Burgoyne had previously instructed his Indians as to their expected conduct in war, warning that he positively forbade "...bloodshed when you are not opposed in arms...Aged men, women, children and prisoners must be held sacred from the knife or hatchet, even in the time of actual conflict. You shall receive compensation for the prisoners you take but you shall be called to account for scalps." He was applauded by the Indians ("Etow, Etow!") but the English laughed at this speech. Needless to say, the Indians did not obey Burgoyne's instructions.

Prior to its capture by the British in 1777, Skenesborough was a bustling harbor town. Lying at the head of lake navigation, it was an important crossroads and the port of shipping for supplies going to Fort Ticonderoga. ("Philip Skene of Skenesborough," Doris B. Morton, 1959) To defend the lakes in northern New York against the British who were busily constructing their own ships on Lake Champlain, Generals Gates, Arnold and Schuyler were ordered to provide vessels for an American Navy. Young, energetic Benedict Arnold was chosen to supervise the repair of existing ships and the construction of new ones at Skenesborough. Skenesborough's sawmill and bloomery (forge), formerly belonging to the Loyalist Philip Skene, hummed with activity. Blacksmiths, carpenters and shipwrights poured into the area. Ships were of two types, either galleys holding a crew of about 80 and 8 to 10 cannon, or gondolas, smaller in size, with a couple of swivel guns and two 12 pounders. Once built, the ships were taken up Wood Creek to the lake, floated up to Ticonderoga for outfitting, then on north to rendezvous at Crown Point.

At the approach of the British in 1777, the American garrison at Skenesborough blew up the fort and retreated to Fort Ann. Fire from burning ships in the harbor spread, destroying the sawmill and the forge. Many of the citizens fled while Loyalists (Tories) moved in to live in their abandoned houses. Philip Skene returned to British occupied Skenesborough. Many of the Skene tenants had remained although it is impossible to tell if Ensign's family remained or not. In his pension application papers he does not mention his place(s) of residence from the time his military service ended until the end of the war except that his discharge paper which was signed by General "Skyler" (Schyler) and his "...entire stock of property was destroyed by Fire at the town of Kingsborough by the Indians and Tories..." He probably meant Kingsbury which lay southwest of Fort Ann in Washington Co. In Oct 1780, Fort Ann was captured by the British. Immediately after, the Indians and Tories proceeded to Kingsbury, then occupied by only seventeen families, all of whom fled. When the burning and pillaging of Kingsbury was over, only two houses were left standing.

From 1783 until about 1788, Ensign lived at Whitehall (the name changed in 1786 from Skenesborough). He was the grantee there on 30 May 1785 of property which had belonged to Philip Skene but which Skene, as a Tory, had been forced to forfeit. This property, 162 acres bordered by

Wood Creek, was mortgaged to Dr. John Williams, a physician and surgeon from England who became one of the largest landholders in the county. By the terms of the mortgage, "...if the said Ensign...pay to the said John...the sum of forty three pounds seven shillings seven pence... on or before the first day of June 1792 with the lawful Interest Annually according to the Condition of a certain Bond or writing Obligatory...herewith executed by the said Ensign unto the said John as a Collateral security then these presents and the said Bond or writing Obligatory shall cease and be null and void...the foregoing record...a true copy of the original mortgage examined and compared this 24th June 1785."

At that time, rather than being considered a lien on property, a mortgage was a conditional transfer of legal title to the real property as security for payment of debt by the mortgagee. If the conditions of the mortgage were met, the mortgage became void. If not, the mortgager who not only still held actual title to the property but also had the right to possess the land from the date of the mortgage, again became full owner of the property. Postwar America suffered a depression from 1784 through 1789. Since no record exists showing that Ensign sold this land in Washington Co., we can not tell if he had to forfeit the land to Dr. Williams or not.

About 1788 Ensign and his family moved to Essex in Chittenden Co., VT. Essex, chartered in 1763 by Governor Benning Wentworth, had begun settlement in 1783 on lands that were the first speculation of Ethan Allen's Onion River Co. Ensign is on record there as having taken the Freeman's Oath prior to 1793. He appears there in the 1790 Census (not taken in Vermont until 1791 when Vermont joined the Union) with 1 male age 16 and up, 2 males under age 16, and 2 females.

After two poor crop years, Vermont was experiencing a famine in 1789. The area where Ensign settled, not far inland from the eastern shore of Lake Champlain, was good land, "...not very heavy timbered or stony or mountainous; well intersected with streams...moose plenty...people hunt them...eat them in lieu of beef and get their tallow. Bears and wolves plenty..." as noted by Nathan Perkins, a Congregational missionary who visited Vermont in 1789 and was appalled at conditions there, even in the northern part of the state which was better off than the southern.

Fourth Generation

In his diary Mr. Perkins described "...people with nothing to eat...to drink...to wear...all work, & yet the women quiet, serene, peaceable, contented, loving their husbands...their homes...wanting never to return...nor any dressy clothes...tough are they, brawny their limbs - their young girls unpolished & will bear work as well as mules. Woods make people love one another & kind & obliging and good natured...leave their doors unbarred. Sleep quietly amid fleas...bedbugs...dirt & rags. ("Outsiders Inside Vermont," compiled & edited by T.D. Seymour Bassett) By 1791, the year Vermont joined the Union, its rawness had begun to disappear. Settlers who had purchased a few acres for almost nothing could sell at a high price and re-establish themselves with much larger acreage in areas where land was cheaper.

In 1792 (coincidentally, the year payment on his mortgage in Washington Co., NY was due), Ensign had moved his growing family to "New Galloway" (original name of Galway) in Saratoga Co., NY. On the 25th of July, Ensign and his brother, Joseph, "...of the State of New York town of Galoway do acknowledge ourselves firmly bound...unto the town of Whitehall in the sum of five Hundred pounds... the condition...such that if the above Boundeds Ensign Mitchel and Joseph Michael (sic) do...truly maintain or cause to be maintained at their own expense their aged mother Widow Lydia Mithel (sic) and do indemnify the sd town that she shall never become chargeable to the town... during her life, then...the above Obligation to be void ...and other wise to remain in full force..." ("Whitehall Town Record Book 1, State Library Mss. Room, Albany, NY). The "Whitehall Papers" (Vol. XXI, p. 102, Albany, NY State Library, dated 2 Apr 1793) further explains that Joseph and Ensign Mitchell, "...two substantial and well to do citizens...", were required to enter an understanding with two sureties that their mother would not become a Whitehall town charge, before they were allowed to bring her to their home in Galway, NY.

Before 1800 Ensign and his family had moved on to Pennsylvania. His pension application papers name the county, but the handwriting is unclear. The 1800 census shows Ensign in Wysox Twp., Luzerne Co., PA with 1 male under age 10, 2 males age 10 but under 16, 2 males age 26 but under 45, 3 females under age 10, 1 female age 16 but under 26, 1 female age 26 but under 45, and 1 female age 45

and up (probably Ensign's mother, Lydia). All are identified but 1 male age 26/45 and the female age 16/26.

In 1800 Luzerne Co., PA encompassed its present day
boundaries as well as the counties of present day Lacka-
wanna, Susquehanna, Wyoming and the eastern portion of
Bradford. A query to The Historical Society of Pennsylvania in Philadelphia disclosed that Wysox (Wysock) Twp.
was located in present day Bradford Co., PA. The Mitchell
family did not remain here long. A biography of Ensign's
son, Ira, states that he was born in 1803 in Tioga Co.
(formed in 1804 from Lycoming), PA; that the family left
Tioga Co. when he was six years old (ca 1809), traveling
south to Pittsburg, then via the Ohio River to Cincinnati.
They may have lived a few years on the Kentucky side of the
river, but by the birth of their youngest child, Newman,
in 1811 they were in Ohio, his biography stating he was
born in that year "...on the banks of the Ohio River, forty
miles above (east) of Cincinnati."

Ensign's only brother, Joseph, an itinerant Methodist
minister, had moved to Madison Co., OH by about 1812.
Perhaps this was one reason why Ensign left Brown Co. in
1815 to settle in Goshen Twp. of Champaign Co. just west
of Madison Co. He lived here for "eight or ten years" before moving over to Monroe Twp., Madison Co. about 1824.
He is here in the 1830 Census, his two unmarried sons,
Abizer and Newman, still in his household.

There are no probate records filed for Ensign in Madison Co. (several early will books are "missing") nor in
any of the surrounding counties. A copy of Ensign's will
was obtained from a descendant, Carl M. Creamer of Mechanicsburg, OH who has several family documents in his
possession. Dated 27 June 1833 at Madison Co., Ensign
asked to be "...buryed in a plain Christian like manner."
He gave to "my beloved wife Lucy all the Household and
Kitchen furniture of every description." To his youngest
son, Newman, he left 220½ acres of land "...whereon I now
live lying on the waters of Treacle's creek...to be laid
off that part of my...land which ajoins Young Patrick and
John Wards lands...I reserve unto my self one hundred and
twenty two Acres and a half of said tract (for my) use...
so long as I live and also the power to sell and Convey
said...land if it should suit me so to do in which case I
give...unto my said son Newman an equivalent in Value
elsewhere in any lands I now own or may possess."

To his sons "Chandly, Ensign, Claudius, Iry," Ensign gave ten dollars each. To his daughters "Experience, Roxanna, Polly and Lydia," he gave five dollars each. He also bequeathed "unto John Pain who married my Daughter Lavina one Dollar." The rest of his "personal Estate goods and chattles" went to Newman. John Ward was appointed executor, witnessing the will along with Fletcher N. Pratt, and J. H. Daviess. Ensign signed in a legible but quite shaky hand.

Mr. Creamer also sent a copy of a memorandum dated the first of February, 1832 between Ensign and son Newman in which Ensign agreed to "procure for Newman Mitchel from James Galloway a general warranty deed of conveyance of one hundred acres of land off the Northwest part of Survey No. 7402 upon which I now live to be done as soon as the said James Galloway makes me a like deed for the whole of said tract. Likewise...Newman Mitchel is to have one-third of the livestock in my possession at the time the above mentioned land is paid for." (His signature on this unwitnessed memorandum is very firm. As on his will, he spells his name as Mitchel.)

On 2 Jul 1832 Ensign had purchased 204 acres from James Galloway of Green Co., OH for $306.00. This land lay on the waters of the spring fork of Treacles Creek in Madison Co., part of military surveys 7402, 12021, 12251, 12287, and 12283. However, he sold 102 acres of this land on 16 Jul 1832 to John Ward for $204.00 (Charles Guy witnessed), and on 13 Sep 1834 sold the other 102 acres for $204.00 to Matthew Y(oung) Patrick (John Ward witnessed). Besides a deed dated 1 June 1830 when Ensign sold 50 acres in Champaign Co., OH to Cyrus Taylor (Benjamin Griffin witnessed), no other deeds appear in Madison Co. records in his name.

Another document of interest, copied and sent by Mr. Creamer is an article of agreement dated 26 Dec 1838 between Abizer and Newman Mitchell and "Lucy Mitchell Their Mother" in which Abizer and Newman agreed "to support their Mother during her natural life in a comfortable manner to live with which she sees cause and when she chooses providing when she is living with one it shall be no expense to the other or if she lives with any of her other Children the (parties of the) first part will allow a reasonable compensation to be judged by three judicious persons this the (parties of the) first part agrees to in

Consideration of a former article which existed between them and their parents..."

Ensign's application (R.7271) for a Revolutionary War pension was refused by the Pension Bureau in Washington, D.C. on grounds of insufficient proof of his service. Several letters in his file prove he was still living in December 1838, but he does not appear in the 1840 Ohio Census. His date of death is given by various sources as 1839 and is probably correct.

Lucy's date of death is unknown. No proof exists that she died about 1845 as has been said by some. She is not in the 1840 Ohio Census under her name, nor is she found in the households of her children. Both Ensign and Lucy are buried in a family cemetery in Madison Co., OH on land they once owned. At one time the graves were marked, and the burial lot, located on a small knoll, was surrounded by a low picket fence. The site is about a tenth of a mile from the intersection of Ware Road and the Mechanicsburg-Sanford Road, the knoll in a corner of a fence which follows a creek. Children of Ensign and Lucy (Hubbard) Mitchell were:

135. **Ensign** b 3 Mar 1787   +
136. **Chandler** bc 1788/9   +
137. **Mary (Polly)** b 29 Sep 1792   +
138. **Claudius** b 6 Jan 1794   +
139. **Lavina** bc (1796?)   +
140. **Roxanna** bc (1798?)   +
141. **Experience** (bc 1801?)   +
142. **Ira** b 3 Jul 1803   +
143. **Lydia** bc 1805   +
144. **Abizer** b 27 Mar 1807   +
145. **Newman** b 29 Apr 1811   +

78. **THANKFUL MITCHELL**, daughter of Joseph, Jr. and Lydia (Foster) Mitchell, was baptized 12 Sep 1762 at Deerfield, MA. She married 2 May 1781 Zadock King, Jr. (Greenfield, MA V/R calls both "of Deerfield"). Zadock was born 24 Jan 1754 at Deerfield, son of Zadock and Hannah (Mitchell) King. Zadock, Jr. and Thankful were first cousins since Zadock's mother was a sister to Thankful's father. (The "Genealogical & Family History of Central New York," by William R. Cutter, pp 556/7, contains a biography of Zadock, Jr., but gives an erroneous King ancestry. See Allied Lines.)

Fourth Generation

Although born in Deerfield, Thankful spent her early childhood in nearby Ashfield, MA where her family moved in 1763. Since she was only about nine years old when her parents moved to Skenesborough, NY (now Whitehall, Washington Co.), it is assumed she went with them. The fact that her marriage record is in Greenfield, MA may indicate that her family temporarily left Skenesborough, an area of frequent Tory and Indian attack during the Revolutionary War years, and fled to the safety of Greenfield where her father had Mitchell relatives.

Zadock King is listed in the 1790 Census of Conway, Hampshire Co., MA with 1 male age 16 and up, 1 male under age 16, and 6 females in the family. By 1800 the family had moved to Ashfield, MA. On 17 May 1801 the Baptist church there voted "...after considerable labor with Brother Zadock King for his joining the Methodists..." that they could no longer "...commune with him in his present condition." Zadock requested that the church give him in writing the scriptural reasons for their decision, and a committee was chosen for that purpose. On 24 June the committee reported that they had complied with Zadock's request. ("History of Ashfield, MA," by Rev. Dr. Thomas Shepard, 1834, p 153) The Biblical passages chosen to substantiate the Baptists' reasons for their inability to "commune" with Zadock are unfortunately not revealed.

Before 1810 Zadock and Thankful had moved to Waterford in Saratoga Co., NY where they were still living in 1820. Nothing further is known of them although a history of Saratoga Co. mentions several of their sons. J. M. King & Co., a stock, dye and tool works, was founded in 1829 by Daniel B. King, brother of (John) Fuller King, the "projector of the hydraulic canal" in Waterford known as the King Canal. Called "an active business man and an inventor, with Mr. Livingston, of improved canal locks," John Fuller King had designed and constructed the canal in 1828. Joseph Mitchell King was a banker and establisher of the J. M. King Iron Works at Waterford (Ref: Cutter).

Thankful's children (KING) were: **(i)** Roxanna (perhaps the Roxana Maynard, age 68, b MA, living in 1850 with Foster King. See #6 below.); **(ii)** Villers/Villas b 1790-1800; **(iii)** Experience b 1790 d 10 Feb 1847 at Beekmantown, NY, bur in Clinton Co., NY; m Ebenezer Allen b 4 Mar 1776 MA d 20 Feb 1864 in OH; **(iv)** David Brainard; **(v)** Daniel Bromley – the 1850 Census of Waterford, Saratoga Co., NY, p 17, lists him as Daniel, age 52, a manufacturer of stocks and dyes, b CT (?), with Gertrude (49, NY); also in Daniel's houshold, listed as a separate family, is Minor King, 27, machinest, b NY, & Susan (24, NY); **(vi)** Foster - in the 1850 Census of Half Noon, Saratoga Co., NY, p 47, Foster King is listed as age 62, farmer, b MA, with Lucy (52, NY), Jane (23, NY), John (17, NY), Sarah (13, NY), & Wesley King (11, NY); also living with the family is Chester Hancok (2, NY), Roxanna Maynard (68, MA), James Murphy (26, Ire.), and Catherine Cody (35, Ire.); **(vii)** John Fuller, died ca 1835; **(viii)** Joseph Mitchell, b Waterford, NY d there 1871 m Jane Palmer; 2 ch., Mary E. & Catherine who d in infancy.

80. **JOSEPH MITCHELL (III)**, son of Joseph, Jr. and Lydia (Foster) Mitchell, was born 22 Sep 1768 (baptized 23 Oct) at Ashfield, MA. He married about 1788/89 (possibly at Spencertown, NY) to Zipporah Brainard, daughter of Nathaniel and Rebecca (Stoe) Brainerd/Brainard, originally from Middletown, CT. ("The Genealogy of the Brainerd/Brainard Family in America 1649-1908," by Lucy Abigail Brainard, Vol. II, pp 60/61, says Zipporah married Joseph Mitchell, a Methodist minister, but erroneously states that they had no children.)

At about age two, Joseph's parents moved to Skenesborough, NY (now Whitehall, Washington Co.) where the family settled as tenant land holders of Philip Skene. During the Revolutionary War years, this area was a "hotspot" of Tory and Indian activity. The family may have taken temporary refuge with relatives in more southern areas of New York or in Massachusetts.

Joseph was indeed a Methodist minister, one of the early intinerant circuit riders in Eastern New York, Vermont and parts of Massachusetts. He received his "call" to the ministry under the tutelege of Lemuel Smith and succeeding ministers to the Cambridge circuit which had been established in 1788 and included Granville and Whitehall Twps. in Washington Co., NY. By 1794 Joseph had been admitted "on trial" as an itinerant preacher under the supervision of Robert Green, and assigned to the Cambridge circuit, preaching at the Ashgrove Methodist Episcopal church in Granville, NY and other churches on the circuit.

In 1795, still "on trial," Joseph preached under the guidance of Jesse Stoneman on the Litchfield circuit, but by 1796 he had been admitted to "full connection" and assigned to the Granville Circuit with Ralph Williston under him. He was no doubt impressed with the rhetoric of the famed Methodist evangelist Lorenzo Dow, first minister in 1796 of the newly formed East Whitehall Methodist church. For several years Joseph traveled extensively with Lorenzo Dow who was often referred to as "Crazy Dow" and described in one unflattering sketch as having a "long flowing beard and hair, singularly wild demeanor and pungency of speech."

By 1797 Joseph had been elevated to Deacon and was preaching on the Dutchess circuit under Philip Wager. When the first Methodist Society in Vermont was formed in 1798, Joseph, now an Elder, rode the Vergennes circuit which included most of the counties in Western Vermont. A report from the "Vermont Historical Gazateer" of a stop in Essex, Chittenden Co., VT gives us insight into the opposition Joseph and his fellow preachers faced: "The first preacher of this persuasion (Methodist) was a Mr. Mitchell. The first and only sermon he delivered was in the house then owned by Deacon Kellogg. He was cordially received by the members of the Congregational church, as was every evangelical preacher; but his attack upon their characteristic doctrine did not please them, and they sent him forward on his journey..."

During the summer of 1799, "Rev. Mr. Mitchell of some other part of the State," appeared on the part of the Methodists at a "great public meeting for a doctrinal debate held at Montpelier," VT. In 1800 and 1801 Joseph continued his ministry on the Pittsfield and Whitingham circuits. In 1802 he seems to have received no appointment although by 1803 he was riding the Fletcher circuit in the Pittsfield District. This included churches in VT, NY and MA. He is listed as one of the early ministers of the Methodist Episcopal church (formed in 1800) at Rowe, MA, a Franklin Co. village near the VT border.

The early career of Rev. Joseph is recorded in the Troy Conference Records of the Methodist Episcopal Church which are extant up to the year 1813. The last entry in these records (and a puzzling one at that) for Joseph is dated 1804. He is listed as among those "who are under (i.e., junior in) a location through weakness of body or family concerns." I haven't even a good guess at the portent of that rather cryptic statement.

Fourth Generation

There were a number of Joseph Mitchells in New York State census records of 1790 through 1810. None can be positively identified as Rev. Joseph Mitchell. He was probably the Joseph living next door to his sister, Lydia, wife of Caleb Hurlbut, in the 1790 Census of Whitehall, Washington Co., NY with 1 male age 16 and up, 1 male under age 16 and 2 females in his family. He was a resident of Galway, Saratoga Co., NY in 1792 when he and his brother, Ensign, posted bond to the town of Whitehall that their aged mother, the Widow Lydia Mitchell, would not become a town charge. As a circuit rider, he was necessarily gone from home for long periods of time. Perhaps his family lived in the household of friends or relatives by unknown surnames for much of this time.

By or before 1812, Joseph and his family had followed his brother, Ensign, to Ohio. Beers' "History of Champaign Co., OH" mentions that shortly after the Presbyterian Society was formed (1807), the Methodists organized and itinerant Methodist ministers began making their rounds of the various circuits. Mitchell, Miller and Crume are named as being among the first of these circuit riders. Mitchell is described as being an uncompromising opponent of collegiate education. Both Mitchell and Miller are portrayed as being exceptionally vulgar in language, "vulgar," in this case, meaning as distinguished from the educated or cultivated. He was probably the Rev. Joseph Mitchell who preached the burial service of Mrs. Elisha Rodgers in June 1812 at Worthington, OH (in adjoining Franklin Co, OH).

Beers' also mentions Joseph in his "History of Madison Co., OH," stating that he came there in 1812/13, settled in the southwest part of Pike Twp., purchased 900 acres of land, and became an extensive farmer and stockraiser. He adds that Joseph was "a leading, active man in the Methodist Episcopal church...a minister during a greater part of his life...devoted to itinerant work..." Indeed, in 1817 and 1818 he paid $1,800.00 for a total of 950 acres, land which would eventually bring him a handsome profit, but he retained only 200 acres of it for his own farming and grazing purposes.

On 15 Dec 1818 Joseph and "Zeporah his wife" sold 185 acres to Levi Patrick for $925.00 (Joseph, Jr. witnessed). No connection is known to exist between the Patrick and Mitchell families, but it is worth noting that in 1834,

Fourth Generation

Joseph's brother, Ensign, sold part of his Madison Co. property to Matthew Y. Patrick who became his neighbor. Andrew Alden bought 254 acres from Joseph on 27 Jul 1819 for $762.00. Later, Joseph's son, Newman, was appointed co-administrator of Andrew's estate with Elizabeth Alden, wife of Andrew. They filed a petition in 1827 before the Madison Co. Court of Common Pleas, attesting to the estate's insolvency. The Alden property, purchased from Joseph Mitchell in 1819, was sold at public vendue to Ira Stacey, the highest bidder at $2.78 per acre. A final report was filed 21 Nov 1832 by "Newman Mitchell and Elizabeth Alden, Administrators of Andrew S. Alden, deceased." One suspects that Elizabeth Alden was nee Mitchell, daughter of Joseph and Zipporah, sister of Newman, although no proof yet exists of this relationship.

In what appears to be an attempt to establish his sons near him, Joseph sold each of them (except for Abner who was still a minor) 100 acres of his land for $200.00. These deeds are dated 4 Oct 1819 to Joseph, Jr. (witnessed by Newman Mitchell); 14 Oct 1819 to Newman (Joseph Mitchell, Jr. witnessed), and 7 Apr 1820 to William. Four days after the date of William's deed, William sold his land back to his father for $1,000.00 "...upon this express condition that if...William Mitchell...gives...Joseph Mitchell annually one equal half of all the produceries had on the...premises and one equal half of all the nut stock...now uppon said premises and continues to give him one equal half of the profits arising there from anualy during his natural life and after the said Joseph Death (sic) if he should die before him give his wife Zipphoriah Mitchel (sic) the annual stipend...every thing here in contained shall...be void...but in case default be made ...in complying (William) doeth agree...to sell and dispose of the said premises..." Inexplicably, "William Mitchel and Naoma Mitchel his wife" again sold this property to Joseph for $200.00 on 6 Oct 1824.

He appears in Madison Co., OH in the 1830 Census, although the sesquicentennial history of Pekin, Tazewell Co., IL states that "...fiery, plainspoken Joseph Mitchel was installed in 1829 as the (Methodist) congregation's first minister." Apparently he divided his time between his home in Madison Co., OH and his pastoral duties in Pekin, IL. He purchased public domain land in Tazewell Co. in 1830 and 1831 (80 acres Section 35; 80 acres Section

14, both in Twp 25 Range 5W near Pekin). Not until 25 Jan 1832 did Joseph and Zipporah (Zephy) "of Madison Co.," OH sell their remaining 200 acres "on the waters of Little Darby" to William Curl for $1,400.00. He then permanently settled in Tazewell Co. with sons Joseph Jr. and Abner.

The sesquicentennial history calls him "Father Mitchel" and describes him as a "...very strict leader of his flock...On one occasion some of the younger members of the congregation produced a bass viol to provide accompaniment for the singing. No sooner had they begun to tune up than Father Mitchel was on his feet, crying, 'What's this! What's this!' Informed of the young men's intentions, he replied, 'No such thing! No such thing! It's an ungodly great fiddle, take it out! Take it out!' Thus it would seem...that Pekin's first choir, consisting of seven male voices...sang without accompaniment. Father Mitchel was even less receptive to competition...He showed much consternation when a Reverend Carey...began to hold meetings across the street from Father Mitchel's services. Although many of the congregation felt compelled to hear this great speaker, they were so impressed by Mitchel's disapproval...they went to great lengths to sneak into the evangelist's meetings. Father Mitchel would pace the aisles...his eye on the entrance...across the street, and everytime another wayward soul crossed its threshold, he would interrupt whatever he was saying to remark, 'There's another one gone to hell.'"

Chapman's 1879 "History of Tazewell Co., IL" calls Rev. Joseph a man of "great power and eloquence, and eccentric to a great degree. His flights of oratory at times were truly sublime." Both Chapman and Bateman (1905 history) tell the story of Father Mitchell preaching one Sunday on the "pomp and vanities" of the world, hoping his congregation was not guilty of wearing "frippery." In walked a widow in her new clothes and a "startling" new bonnet. The sight was too much for him. Pointing a finger directly at her, he said, "Yes, and there comes a woman with her cow upon her back and her brass kettle on her head." (He apparently practiced what he preached. At his death, his inventory listed 1 hat, 1 coat, 1 overcoat, 5 vests, 2 "pare" drawers, 2 shirts, 1 horse, 1 saddle and saddlebags, 1 trunk, 1 chest, 1 gun, 2 traps, pigeon net, shoe punch, a mortar, and basket of "vials," the lot worth a total of $27.25.)

Fourth Generation

Under Rev. Joseph's leadership, Pekin's first church building was erected in 1839. Pekin's sesquicentennial history states: "The dream of Father Mitchell and church leaders was a structure of grandeur, with a lower level for Sunday School rooms and the upper area to be a beautiful auditorium to serve as a sanctuary for worship...Due to lack of funds, only the lower level was finished..." The congregation eventually outgrew this church and in 1847 it was sold and converted into a livery stable.

In 1833, Joseph sold half of his 160 acres in Pekin Twp. to "His Son Abner." (Zipporah, living in Jan 1832, was not named in this deed, leading to the conclusion that she was deceased by June 1833.) In 1835, Joseph sold his remaining 80 acres and moved in with Abner who had purchased 80 acres in Morton Twp., selling the 80 acres in Pekin Twp. adjoining his father's in 1836. Joseph remained active in real estate transactions during the final years of his life, buying and selling lots in Pekin, sometimes in co-ownership with Abner in whose household he appears in the 1840 census as a man aged 70 to 80 years. Perhaps his last business transaction is represented by a note signed on 26 Jul 1842 by himself and his sons, Joseph, Jr. and Abner, promising to pay E. S. and D. Mark $409.24 within a year at 12% interest "for value received." But if the interest was paid "promptly at the end of the year" they were to have 12 months longer to pay the principal. (Joseph, Sr. and Abner had done business with Elijah S. and David Mark in 1834, selling them lots in Pekin.)

Rev. Joseph died at his son Abner's home in Morton Twp., Tazewell Co., IL on 3 Sep 1844, leaving no will. His eldest son, Joseph, Jr., was appointed administrator. On 24 May 1847, Joseph, Jr. wrote from Bloomington, IL to Noel Johnston, Esq. (P.J.P.) in Pekin that his "...health has been and now is very poor which is my apology for addressing you at this time and in this manner. I have obtained those receipts required for a final Settlement of the Estate of Joseph Mitchell Dec'd, one from Abner Mitchell, the other from R. B. Mitchell (Joseph, Jr.'s son) as agreed upon between me and Mr. Mark at your office and for fear that I should not be able to attend at your office on the first Monday of June...I herein inclose Said receipts requesting you to pass them to my Credit...I think you can make final Settlement with them without my being present and discharge me from further Obligations in reference to

said Estate. If not write to me and I will come down when-
ever my health is Such that it will be prudent..."

Rev. Joseph lies buried in Hirstein Cemetery (originally Christian Cemetery) about 4 miles from Washington,
IL on the road to Pekin (near Morton). His grave is marked
with an undated stone reading simply "Rev. Mitchell." If
his wife, Zipporah, is also buried here, her grave is unmarked, although if Zipporah died in Tazewell Co., IL,
she is more likely buried in Pekin Twp. (My gratitude to
Loree Bergerhouse, Corr. Sec'y of the Tazewell Co., IL
Genealogical Society for her invaluable help in searching
county records, etc.) Known children of (Rev.) Joseph
and Zipporah (Brainard) Mitchell were:

   146. Joseph (Jr.) b 9 Aug 1790   +
   147. Newman bc 1790-1800   +
   148. William bc 1790-1800?   +
   149. Abner bc 1807/8   +

82. CONSIDER MITCHELL, son of Abner and Abigail (Warren)
Mitchell, was born 15 May 1765 at Deerfield, MA. He married Aug 1785 at Conway, MA to Esther Rawson, baptized
1 Nov 1764 (Conway V/R) or 26 May 1765 (Deerfield V/R),
daughter of Silas and Abigail (Chapin) Rawson. Silas Rawson, married to Abigail Chapin 5 Jan 1762 at Mendon, MA,
was an early settler of Conway, MA. He was chosen there at
the first town meeting in 1767 as "sealer of leather."

Although all of Consider's children except the youngest (Levi, born in Oneida Co., NY) are recorded as born in
Conway, MA, their births are also in Charlemont, MA Vital
Records. Consider and Esther were living in Charlemont in
1790 (Census - 1 m un 10, 1 m 26/45, 4 f un 10, 2 f 10/16, 1
f 26/45). By 1800 he had removed with his parents, Abner
and Abigail Mitchell, to Oneida Co., NY where he first
settled about two miles east of Clinton Village, Twp. of
Kirkland. Consider and Esther have not been found in the
1810 or 1820 New York Census records, but they did remain
in that state.

The Mitchell family burial plot at Clinton Village in
the Old Burying Ground (Old Clinton Cemetery, Water St.)
is dominated by a very large, four-sided family monument,
erected by Consider's son, Levi. The rear side of this
monument is inscribed "Consider Mitchell, father of Levi,
born May 15, 1765, died Aug. 2, 1828, interred at Bennetts
Corners" (township of Lenox, Madison Co., NY). Bennett's

Corners, once a thriving little community, is now barely more than a crossroads. An old church is the only building there. Behind it is an area of rough ground covered over with thick brush which may have been the church burial grounds, but if Consider's body rests in this deserted place, there are no stones visible or printed records to prove it. (Thanks for the competent research of Vivian Y. Brecknell, Holland Patent, NY, who has unearthed many primary sources on the Mitchells of Oneida Co., NY; and to Nan Card of Elmore, OH for sharing Vivian's research.)

Esther, wife of Consider, died 22 Feb 1847, age 82 years, probably at Clinton Village, NY where she is buried in the family plot. Children of Consider and Esther (Rawson) Mitchell were:

150. **Hardasah** b 8 Apr 1787
151. **Abigail** b 17 Jan 1789
152. **Electa** b 22 Feb 1791
153. **Orra** (female) b 10 Nov 1793; d 13 Sep 1873, age 79, unmarried, bur Old Burying Ground, Clinton Village, Kirkland Twp., NY.
154. **Consider** b 23 Aug 1795
155. **Elizabeth** b 15 Feb 1797
156. **Levi** b 27 Mar 1801   +

83. **CYNTHIA MITCHELL,** daughter of Abner and Abigail (Warren) Mitchell, was born 13 Apr 1768 (baptized 24 Apr) at Deerfield, MA. She married 9 Aug 1785 Ira Hawks, born 10 Sep 1766 at Charlemont, MA, son of Gershom, Sr. and Thankful (Corse) Hawks/Hawkes ("Haks" in early records).

The Hawks family dates back to John[2] (John) Hawks who was in Deerfield before 1676. Ira's father and grandfather left Deerfield to settle at Charlemont, MA about 1751. Ira's great-grandmother, Elizabeth (Catlin) Corse, wife of James, was a sister to Cynthia's great-grandmother, Sarah (Catlin) Mitchell, so Ira and Cynthia were third cousins. At the marriage of Cynthia's sister, Mary, to Ira's brother, Israel (see #84), ties between the Hawks and the Mitchell families became very strong indeed.

The record of Cynthia's marriage to Ira is not found in either Deerfield or Charlemont Vital Records. Ruth M. Strube of Port Orchard, WA, a descendant, very generously sent me a copy of a handwritten paper that had belonged to her grandmother. This paper lists the date of Cynthia's marriage to Ira (although not the place) as well as the

names and birthdates of their children. At the bottom of
the page, noted in the same handwriting, is "Mrs. Hawks
Name before Marriage was Cynthia Mytchel."

Comparison of the Hawks family record with the Vital
Records of Charlemont illustrates that town records are
not always accurate. Charlemont V/R gives daughter Cynthia's date of birth as 3 Apr 1792, whereas the family record says 3 Apr 1790. The family record lists daughter
Thankful, born 14 Apr 1792. Thankful's birth is omitted
from Charlemont records entirely. The family record also
names three more children, born after Ira and Cynthia left
Charlemont, MA.

Between 1797 and 1799, Ira and Cynthia moved to Middlesex Twp., Chittenden Co., VT where they appear in the
1800 Census (1 m un 10, 1 m 16/26, 1 m 26/45, 3 f un 10, 2
f 10/16, 1 f 26/45). By 1810 something very odd seems to
have occured in this family. The census for that year
shows Ira still in Middlesex with only himself (age 45 &
up) and a male under age 10 (Zimri, born 1801?) in the
family. In 1820 Ira and Ira, Jr. had moved to Moretown,
Washington Co., VT, a short distance south of Middlesex,
where Ira, Sr. is shown as living alone. At the 1830 Census, Ira, Sr. is still in Moretown, listed as age 60 to 70
with a male and a female, ages 15 to 20, living with him.

With the disappearance of Cynthia and her children
(except possibly her youngest son) from Ira's household
in 1810, one naturally suspects some great tragedy such
as a devastating illness had struck this family; but Cynthia was still living in 1850 (census), age 82, birthplace
MA, with her son Abner and his family in Clinton Co., NY
(Ellenburgh). Her son, Zimri, was living in that county
and township as well. That Cynthia and Ira were divorced
is a distinct possibility. Interested descendants should
contact VT county clerks of Chittenden and/or of Addison
and Orange (from which Washington, originally named Jefferson, was formed in 1810).

Cynthia's children (HAWKS) were: **(i)** Emily (Emilia)
b 9 Dec 1786; **(ii)** Ira b 23 Jul 1788 m Aug 1813 Betsey
Sprague, probably at Moreton, VT; births of 3 children recorded there; **(iii)** Cynthia b 3 Apr 1790; **(iv)** Thankful b
14 Apr 1792; **(v)** Clorinda b 16 Jul 1794; **(vi)** Abner b 27
Dec 1796 d bef 1870 m 27 May 1822 Ruth Van Duzen; she & at
least 1 son moved to Charlevoix Co., MI bef 1870 where she
was still living, age 74, in 1880; 9 children known;

(vii) Roana b 31 Aug 1799; **(viii)** Zimri b 9 Dec 1801 m Almira _____ bc 1805 VT; he was a wheelwright, res. Ellenburgh, Clinton Co., NY in 1850; **(ix)** Lyndia b 3 May 1804.

84. **MARY (POLLY) MITCHELL**, daughter of Abner and Abigail (Warren) Mitchell, was baptized 29 Jul 1770 at Deerfield, MA. She married (int.) 12 Feb 1793 at Deerfield her 3rd cousin Israel Hawks, baptized 12 Aug 1764 (recorded at Deerfield), son of Gershom, Sr. and Thankful (Corse) Hawks. Israel was a brother of Ira Hawks who married Cynthia Mitchell, sister of his wife, Mary. (See #83 for more details on the Hawks family.) Israel may have had a previous wife. Charlemont V/R lists the death on 9 Jul 1792 of "Mary, w. Israel" Hawks.

Israel and Mary probably left Charlemont after the birth of their youngest known child in 1812. Marriages of their children, and deaths of Israel and Mary are not in Charlemont Vital Records.

Mary's children (HAWKS), all recorded at Charlemont, MA, were: **(i)** Israel b 24 Feb 1794; **(ii)** Barnard b 19 Jul 1795 d 5 Jul 1796; **(iii)** Barnard b 17 Jan 1797; **(iv)** Lorin b 9 Oct 1798; **(v)** Lyman b 13 Mar 1800; **(vi)** Mary "Polly" b 29 Nov 1802 d 2 Dec 1802; **(vii)** Mary "Polly" b 20 Nov 1803; **(viii)** Philena b 21 Oct 1804; **(ix)** Sarah b 31 Aug 1806; **(x)** Abner M. b 16 Oct 1810; **(xi)** Caroline b 22 Aug 1812.

86. **ASAPH MITCHELL**, son of Abner and Abigail (Warren) Mitchell, was born 6 Aug 1773 (Charlemont MA V/R, "Asaph, h. of Lucy), baptized 5 Sep 1773 at Deerfield, MA. He married 19 Sep 1792 at Deerfield Lucy Blodgett, born 23 Jan 1773 (Charlemont, MA V/R, "Lucy, w. of Asaph"), the daughter of Timothy and Melicent (Perry) Blodgett.

Asaph and Lucy lived first at Charlemont, MA, probably on land belonging to Asaph's father which he eventually purchased from him. Births of his first five children are in Charlemont records. Birth or infant baptism records for his remaining five children have not been found. Five of his children (Louisa, Lucretia, Edmund F., Benjamin F. and Maria/Myra) were baptized in Deerfield at the 1st Congregational Church on 2 Aug 1818.

By 1800 Asaph's parents and two brothers had gone to New York State. Three married sisters had also left Massachusetts, leaving one sibling, his sister Mary, wife of Israel Hawks, in Charlemont. Shortly after 1802, Asaph

returned to Deerfield Twp., "living on the road then running from Turnip Yard over the hill to the Upper Sunderland Ferry." Sheldon tells us that as Asaph was "going
home from Bloody Brook about 10 p.m. on 13 Dec 1805, he was
fired upon, when near home." By Dec. 16th, $150.00 had
been "raised by subscription as a reward for the arrest of
the intended assassin." Sheldon does not tell us if an
arrest was made. ("History of Deerfield, MA," Vol. II)

Of Asaph's children, only two remained in the Deerfield area. An obituary in the "Greenfield (MA) Gazette &
Courier," issue of 4 Apr 1891, reads: "South Deerfield:
"A very unusual coincidence in this village was the deaths
on Monday of Mrs. Hilton, mother (sic) of Mr. J. D. Everett and on Tuesday of Miss Mitchell, sister of Mrs. Hilton
and (death) of Miss Dorothy Bartlett. Combined ages of
the three are 251 years." Mrs. Hilton was Asaph's daughter, Louanna, whose death record states she died 30 Mar
1891, of heart disease, age about 85 years; and "Miss"
Mitchell, her sister, was Asaph's daughter, Lucy, whose
death record says she died 31 Mar 1891, of old age, at
about 91 years.

Neither Asaph's or Lucy's deaths are in Deerfield, MA
Vital Records, although Sheldon says that Asaph died on
24 Nov 1827 (probably in Deerfield Twp.); Lucy, if still
living at that time, may have gone to one of her married
children's homes. Children of Asaph and Lucy (Blodgett)
Mitchell (first 5 born at Charlemont, MA; second five
probably in Deerfield Twp., MA) were:

157. **Dolphin** (Adolphus/Dolphus) b 7 Aug 1794; went to
     Canada (Ref: Sheldon's Deerfield history).
158. **Edwin** b 28 Sep 1796; d 10 Apr 1797.
159. **Edwin** b 28 June 1798; d 28 Nov 1817.
160. **Lucy** b 26 Jul 1800; d unmarried 31 Mar 1891, 91y.
161. **Louisa** b 14 May 1802; m ____ Bishop of (New) York.
162. **Lucretia Billings** - went to Canada (Sheldon).
163. **Louanna** bc 1807; d 30 Mar 1891, 85y; m1) Jacob
     Smith; m2) 7 June 1850 Daniel Hilton.
164. **Edmund Frederic** - went "West" (Sheldon).
165. **Benjamin Franklin** - went "West" (Sheldon).
166. **Maria/Myra** - d unmarried in Canada (Sheldon).

87. **MARTHA (PATTY) MITCHELL,** daughter of Abner and Abigail (Warren) Mitchell, was baptized 19 Nov 1775 at Deerfield, MA. She married 21 Jan 1796 at Deerfield to Joseph

Trask, born 10 Aug 1773 at Monson, MA, son of Isaac and Ruth (Colton) Trask. After serving in the American Revolution, Isaac Trask moved his family to Zoar, MA, a village in an unincorporated area within the township of Charlemont. The family lived here until 1796 on land inherited by Isaac's wife, Ruth, from her father, Deacon Joseph Colton (line of "Quartermaster" George Colton).

In the year 1796 Joseph and Martha along with his father and family settled in Waitsfield, VT, both Joseph and Isaac appearing on tax lists there. Joseph made several purchases of land in Waitsfield, but by 1804 he had sold his property and headed west. His residence is uncertain until 1820 when he is found living in York Twp., Genesee Co. (now Livingston), NY. Martha is presumed to be the adult female listed in his household. In 1822 Joseph left NY and was one of the first settlers at Melmore, Eden Twp. in Seneca Co., OH where he appears in the 1830 census without a wife, Martha presumeably having died either in Genesee Co., NY or after their arrival in Seneca Co., OH.

Joseph left Ohio in 1835, accompanying several of his children to Durand, Winnebago Co., IL, and living with them until his death there on 17 Sep 1841. He is buried in Oakland Cemetery near Durand. He left no will or real estate, but at his death, a son made the statement that Joseph had thirteen children, seven sons and six daughters. Only nine of these children have been identified.

The Trasks had a strong tradition of education and all could read and write. They helped form new schools in many areas where they lived. The patriotism of the family matched that of the Mitchells, extending from the American Revolution through all the American wars. Most of the Trask men in the Civil War served in cavalry units, continuing their heritage of blacksmithing and their love for horses that began with Samuel Trask in the 1700's. A Trask grandson (Alvah, Jr.) was stationed several times in the West with Gen'l George Custer and later became the first mining inspector in the Black Hills of South Dakota. Another Trask descendant of this line (Matt) was an Indian fighter and scout in the West; even as an aged man, he wore his hair long and flowing, sported an enormous mustache, and clothed himself in buckskins. The Trasks were consistant voters in all elections. (Data on the Trasks was graciously supplied by descendant Nan [James] Card, Rte. 105, Elmore, OH 43416.)

Martha's children (TRASK) were: **(i)** Joseph C., occ: blacksmith; b 1796-1800 Waitsfield, VT d Nov 1843 Harris Twp., Ottawa Co., OH bur Thompson Cem. (now destroyed); m1) ca 1818 Genesee Co., NY to Lydia Dickinson bc 1790 to 1800 dc 1830/31; 4 children; m2) ca 1836 Anna ( ) Stiles, wid of Solomon; m3) 3 Aug 1838 Sandusky Co., OH to Rosanna (Overmyer) Walters, d/o Philip & Rosanna (Bischoff) Overmyer; 2 children; **(ii)** Alvah b 1796-1800 Waitsfield, VT dc 1849 Sacramento, CA; left his home near Toronto, Clinton Co., OH to join the "gold rush;" m1) ca 1825-1830 Seneca Co., OH to Emily _____; m2) 5 Sep 1840 Sally Hamilton at Belvidere, Jo Daviess Co., IL; **(iii)** Ruth b 1802 Waitsfield, VT m _____ Calwell; lvg 1860 at Winnebago Co., IL; **(iv)** Olive b 1800-1810 m1) 12 May 1823 Sandusky Co., OH to Willard Knight (div 5 Aug 1837 Huron Co., OH); m2) 14 Nov 1837 Winnebago Co., IL to Thomas Armstrong; **(v)** Henry (Harry) b 1807 NY m Elizabeth _____ in Seneca Co., OH; res. 1880 Bronson, Branch Co., MI; **(vi)** Linus Lafayette b 31 May 1810 NY d 31 Dec 1855 Harris Twp., Ottawa Co., OH bur Thompson Cem. (now destroyed); m 2 Dec 1832 Geauga Co., OH to Nancy Thompson; **(vii)** Levi d 1836-1840 Winnebago Co., IL; m 28 Jan 1836 Sandusky Co., OH to Melese Wheeler; **(viii)** Julius J. (Elias) b 1815 NY dc 1858/59 Durand, Winnebago Co., IL; mc 1822 Seneca Co., OH to Maryette Wordsworth; **(ix)** Abigail m 13 Apr 1843 Winnebago Co., IL to Erastus Andrus.

88. **APHALINDA MITCHELL,** daughter of Abner and Abigail (Warren) Mitchell, was baptized 3 Mar 1782 in Deerfield, MA. She married (int.) 25 Jan 1798 at Deerfield to Zebulon Tuttle, bc 1770-1775, son of Gershom, Jr. and Tabitha (Mitchell) Tuttle (see 3rd Generation #29). The Tuttle family descends from William Tuttle of Ringstead, co. Northampton, England, who came to New England on "The Planter" in 1635.

Gershom Tuttle, Jr. and Tabitha Mitchell were first cousins; his mother, Lois (Allis) Tuttle was a sister to Tabitha's mother, Mary (Allis) Mitchell. Through this relationship, Aphalinda and Zebulon were second cousins; they were first cousins as well since Aphalinda's father, Abner Mitchell, was a brother to Tabitha Tuttle, mother of Zebulon. Today, such intermarriage would not only be considered shocking, it would be illegal in many states of this country, but then it was not thought unusual.

Fourth Generation

At his marriage to Aphalinda (Af[f]alinda), Zebulon
was called "of Paris, NY" (Deerfield, MA V/R) which is located in Oneida Co. (formed 1798 from Herkimer Co., NY).
On 9 Aug 1800 Zebulon Tuttle of the "Town of Paris" sold
land in the "Brothertown Tract" for $432.00 to Anseline S.
Howland of the same place (Bk 7:433). Immediately following this deed is another, dated 14 Dec 1797 but recorded
on the same date as the above, in which Gershom Tuttle,
Jr. of the Town of Paris (then Herkimer Co.) sold land in
Paris, Brothertown Tract, for $300 to Zebulon Tuttle of
the same place.

Although they are not found in the 1800 New York Census, Zebulon and Aphalinda probably left Massachusetts
shortly before or about the same time that Aphalinda's
parents moved to Oneida Co., NY (1800). Two "Z. Tuttle"
heads of household are listed in Oneida Co. in 1810 (no
townships given), but neither can be positively identified as Zebulon. Alva M. Tuttle ("Tuttle-Tuthill Lines
In America") says Zebulon was in Rutland, NY in 1810. No
county was named and no Rutland, NY can be located. (Did
he mean Rutland, VT?)

Before 1820 Zebulon and Aphalinda were definitely in
Westmoreland Twp., Oneida Co., NY (Census 2 m un 10, 1 m
45 & up, 1 f un 10, 3 f 10/16, 3 f 16/26, 1 f 26/45). They
were still there in 1830 (Census 2 m 10/15, 1 m 15/20, 1 m
50/60, 1 f 5/10, 1 f 10/15, 1 f 15/20, 1 f 20/30, 1 f 30/40
and 1 f 40/50). On 1 Mar 1834 (recorded 3 Sep) Zebulon
Tuttle and "Affalinda his wife" of the Town of Westmoreland, Oneida Co., NY sold for $1,500.00 land in Cox's Pat-
ent to Brewster Abel of the same place (Bk 66:323).

Since Zebulon does not appear in New York census records after 1830, one might think the family had moved to
another state. However, the 1840 Census, Town of Vienna,
Oneida Co., NY lists an "Epphia" Tuttle with 1 male under
5, 1 male 20 to 30, 1 female 40 to 50 and 1 female 50 to 60
in the household. The female age 50 to 60 might have been
Aphalinda, age 58 in that year, and the female age 40 to
50 her eldest daughter, Aphia, about age 42 in 1840.
Aphia appears in this township in the 1850 census as the
head of household, age 52, birthplace MA; living with her
is J. B. Graves, age 50, birthplace NY; Sarah Graves, age
46, birthplace NY; Weltha A. Graves, age 11, birthplace
NY; and Sally Gifford, age 80, birthplace Nova Scotia.
Cemetery or probate records for Zebulon Tuttle have not

been found, but it seems more reasonable to believe that he died in Oneida Co. ca 1834-1840, and that Aphalinda, his wife, died there between 1840-1850.

It has been estimated (from the 1820 Census) that Zebulon and Aphalinda had at least nine children. Most of the data (except my comments in parenthesis) on the children of Zebulon and Aphalinda comes from Alva M. Tuttle's "Tuttle-Tuthill Lines In America" (published by the compiler, 1968, Columbus, OH). This data is presented with many question marks, inserted by Mr. Tuttle. I am sure he would agree that it is to be viewed sceptically until further proof is found.

Aphalinda's children (TUTTLE) were: **(i)** Aphia bc 1798 (MA; unmar 1850 census); **(ii)** Sarah bc 1804 (NY; per m J. B. Graves; lvg 1850 census with Aphia); **(iii)** Sina? died young; **(iv)** Truman bc 1811; **(v)** Flora? bc 1810's; died young? **(vi)** Flora? bc 1810's; **(vii)** Zebulon bc 1819; **(viii)** Lucinda? bc 1820-1825.

89. **ABNER MITCHELL (JR.),** son of Abner and Abigail (Warren) Mitchell, was baptized 25 May 1786 at Deerfield, MA. Two males of his age (under 16), one unidentified, appear in his father's household in the 1790 Census of Deerfield, Hampshire Co., MA.

Abner (Jr.) was about age 14 when his family moved to Oneida Co., NY in 1800. He is in that county and state in that year as a male age 10 to 16 in his father's family. This is the last apparent trace of Abner (Jr.); neither he nor his father are listed in the 1810 or 1820 Census in NY.

Abner (Jr.) was the second of his father's sons to bear that name. The first was a son named Abner Warren who was baptized 31 May 1772 at Deerfield and obviously deceased before the birth of Abner (Jr.) in 1786. Even though Abner (Jr.) appears in no known records with a middle name or initial, it seems logical that his parents would have given him the middle name of Warren after his dead brother, especially since Warren was Abigail's maiden name.

These speculations are the fruit of a discovery in Oneida Co., NY records of a deed (Bk 23:532) in which a Warren Mitchell of that county bought land on 20 Oct 1813 from Montgomery Hunt of Utica, NY, in Cox's Patent, Westmoreland Twp., where Aphalinda (Mitchell) Tuttle, sister of Abner (Jr.), and her family lived (see #88).

The 1820 census of Westmoreland, Oneida Co., NY (p 210) shows living there a "Warner" Mitchell with 2 males age 10 to 16, 1 male age 26 to 45, 1 female under 10, 1 female age 26 to 45, and 1 female age 45 and up. The age classifications of this family are intriguing. Abner (Jr., b 1786) would have been age 34 in 1820. If married by 1806 (age 20), he could easily have had two sons born between 1806-1810. The female age 45 and up could be a mother-in-law, but it could also be Abner, Jr.'s widowed mother, Abigail (Warren) Mitchell, age 80 in 1820.

Also listed in Westmoreland Twp. in 1820 on the same page with "Warner" Mitchell is Levi Mitchell (not son of Consider #82), and Joseph Mitchell, both age 26 to 45, or born between 1775-1794. Neither are identified at this time. Note also that the Abner Mitchell who is listed in the Town of Turin, Lewis Co., NY in the 1820 Census was from the Wallingford-Meriden, CT branch of the family (see 3rd Generation #33).

More research is needed to enlarge upon, thereby proving or disproving, the above speculations. They are offered in hopes of aiding researchers with "lost" Mitchell ancestors in this area of New York.

FIFTH GENERATION

Some members of this generation were born, lived and died in the New England home towns of their ancestors, but more were the offspring of parents who had come either as adults or as children with their parents to the wilderness areas of New Hampshire, Vermont, and New York. Regretfully, it was this very move which has caused us to "lose" a good number of them. Record keeping was often spotty or non-existant during the crucial early years in these areas. New York State, in particular, lost many early records as Tories and Indians swept down from Canada to burn and pillage towns during the Revolutionary War.

The fifth generation was born during or after the Revolution and the economic depression that followed. They were raised in homes where the Old New England saying, "Eat it up, wear it out, make it do, do without," was practiced, not just out of habit, but out of dire need. As this generation of Mitchells grew toward adulthood, their fathers began to look West; leaving their childhood homes, they traveled with their parents to the frontiers of Pennsylvania, Kentucky and Ohio, often making several stops before permanently locating. Eventually, some of these children, now grown with families of their own, went further - into Michigan, Indiana, Illinois and Iowa.

Will Durant said, "The first form of culture is agriculture. It is when man settles down to till the soil and lay up provisions for the uncertain future that he finds time and reason to be civilized." ("The Story of Civilization," Part I) Although Mr. Durant refers to a much earlier era, his words apply to the civilization of the Americas. Spain wanted gold; France, the fur trade. The English recognized the wealth of the land itself. So came the English yeomen with their wives and children to cultivate, sow and reap, to build and civilize.

As this generation filtered into the vast Ohio River Valley where land was rich, plentiful and cheap, they were able to farm and graze stock on a larger scale than their parents had been able to do. Towns sprang up; some fell by the wayside; others, like Toledo which began with five log cabins in a clearing, grew into important centers of commerce. To make life better for the coming generation, these pioneer men and women of the new frontier founded schools, churches, hospitals, libraries, and other cultural and practical institutions.

This is the generation that raised the sons who fought in the Civil War, and the daughters who waited patiently at home for fathers, brothers and husbands to return. The women of this generation are the ones about whom Alexis de Tocqueville spoke in writing of his travels through early 19th Century America: "The singular prosperity and growing strength of America ought mainly to be attributed to the superiority of their women."

****

99.   **ASAPH MITCHELL (JR.),** son of Asaph and Susanna (Cowles) Mitchell, was born 4 Nov 1787 (Wallingford, CT V/R). He died in Feb 1854 at Boonville, Oneida Co., NY. Asaph married about 1805-1810 to Lucy _____.

Although the date when Asaph, Jr. came to Oneida Co., NY with his parents is not certain, he was there by 1814 when he appears on a list of Oneida Co. landowners (and lessees) in the Town of Steuben. On 3 June 1817 "Asaph Mitchell and Sussana his wife, Asaph Mitchell, Jr. and Lucy his wife of the Town of Steuben" sold half of Lot #6 in Holland Patent for $1,000.00 to Joel Sizer (Bk 29:400). This property was called the "north half of Lot #6" of 46 acres at purchase on 13 Jan 1817 for $370.00 (Bk 29:399). In a second deed, also dated 3 June 1817, Asaph Mitchell, Jr. "of the Town of Steuben" bought 210 acres on the west side of the Black River for $1,000.00 from "Samuel Sizer and Abigail his wife and Joel Sizer and Elizabeth his wife of the Town of Steuben" (Bk 29:403). Abigail Sizer of Wallingford-Meriden, CT was nee Mitchell, a 1st cousin once removed to Asaph, Jr.'s father. (See #40. 3rd Gen.)

Asaph appears in the 1820 Census of Oneida Co., NY (p 174) in Boonville Twp. (formerly Steuben) with 2 males under age 10, 1 male age 26 to 45, 1 male age 45 and up, 1 female age 10 to 15, 1 female age 26 to 45, and 1 female age 45 and up. Undoubtedly, this was the combined family of Asaph, Sr. and wife Susanna; Asaph, Jr. and wife Lucy, their two sons and one daughter.

An Oneida Co., NY deed of 20 May 1833 (Bk 66:133) names Asaph Mitchell and Lucy his wife, Timothy Jackson and Lucy his wife, Daniel Benedict and Esther his wife, all of Boonville, "joining tenants to William G. Hubbard of the same," selling land on Black River in Boonville Twp. Asaph is not called "Jr." here, indicating that his father was deceased. Possibly Lucy Jackson and Esther Benedict were sisters of Asaph, Jr. and they were all selling land inherited from their father.

The 1850 Census of Boonville, Oneida Co., NY (p 188) lists Asaph as age 63, a farmer, born in CT, real estate valued at $3,500; Lucy (wife), age 55, born in CT; Harvey (son) age 29, farmer, born in NY; and Louisa (wife of Harvey), age 27, born in England. Asaph's will, dated 13 Dec 1852 (probated 6 June 1854, Oneida Co. Surrogate Court Records Bk 12:456) names wife Lucy (executrix); daughters Emeline Bass (or Boss), and Sylvina Mitchell (later reference made to Sulvania M. Bill); and sons Alanson, Harvey and Henry W. Mitchell. Birthdates are estimated from census records for the known children, all born in Oneida Co., NY, of Asaph, Jr. and Lucy (   ) Mitchell:

167. **Emeline** (prob bc 1805-1810); m bef 1852 _____ Bass.
168. **Alanson** (prob bc 1810-1820); living 1852.
169. **Harvey** bc 1820 m by 1852 Louisa _____.
170. **Henry W.**
171. **Sylvania M.** - prob m (aft 1852) _____ Bill.

101. **JOTHAM MITCHELL**, (probably) son of Moses, Jr. and Lucy (Warner) Mitchell, was born about 1775-1776 in CT. He married first ca 1800-1803 Mary _____ who died at Steuben, Oneida Co., NY on 15 Dec 1824, age 55 years ("Baptist Register Magazine," Mary "wife of Jotham Mitchell"). He married second 2 Mar 1835 to Nancy (Post) Brainerd of Leyden, Lewis Co., NY, the widow and second wife of Joseph Brainerd who died in 1831.

Nancy (Post) Brainerd was born 26 Jul 1788 at Saybrook, CT, daughter of Josiah and Lydia (Platts) Post who came to Leyden, NY in 1803. In "The Genealogy of the Brainerd-Brainard Family in America" (Lucy Abigail Brainard, Vol. II, p 75), Nancy is called "a woman of decided conviction and of large executive ability;" her early life was devoted to teaching and at the age of sixteen, she made a "profession" of religion, living the life of a devoted Christian up to the time of her death.

No absolute proof exists that Jotham was the son of (Deacon) Moses Mitchell, Jr., but a good deal of circum- stanial evidence points to this relationship. Jotham was probably named for his father's brother, Jotham, who died at Meriden, CT in 1825, leaving no son named after him. Jotham was probably born at Meriden, CT but baptism re- cords of the 1st Congregational Church there are scanty for the years 1757 to 1803. By 1781 Jotham's family had moved to Southwick, MA. A male of the correct age classi- fication to be Jotham is in the household of "Dea." Moses Mitchell there in the 1790 Census, as well as in the 1800 Census of Steuben, Oneida Co., NY. He is not with Moses, Jr. in the 1810 census but may be living nearby. (The census taker used initials rather than full first names and did not indicate townships in most of this census.)

Like Moses, Jr.'s father, Jotham was a shoemaker by trade. And like Moses, Jr., Jotham was a deacon in the Baptist church, presiding at the Remsen, NY Baptist church on 11 Jan 1823. He appears on the 1814 county cen- sus of landowners and lessees in Steuben Twp. along with Moses. He is in Steuben Twp., Oneida Co., NY in the 1820 Census (1 male 16/26; 1 male 45 & up; 1 female under 10; 1 female 10/16; 1 female 45 & up).

On 23 Feb 1835 (a week before his 2nd marriage), Jotham along with Oliver M. Mitchell and Eliza A., his wife of Steuben, Samuel D. Booth and Polly, his wife, of Trenton, sold Lot #154 of 64 acres in Steuben for $1,332, reserving a 20 foot square burial ground (Bk 69:214/5). This appears to be land owned (or leased) by Jotham, per- haps once his father's, which he sold along with a married son and daughter.

According to the Brainerd-Brainard genealogy, Jotham and his second wife, Nancy, removed in 1839 to Randolph, Portage Co., OH. Although they aren't found in the 1840 Census there, they are there in 1850. Jotham is listed as "Jonathan," age 74, shoemaker, born in CT, with wife Nan- cy, age 61, born in CT, and John A. Brainard, age 20, born in NY. Next door is Chauncey O. Brainard, age 33, born in NY, with his wife and family. (In the Brainerd-Brainard genealogy, two of Nancy's sons by her first marriage are Chauncey Otis, born 16 Dec 1816, and John Arza, born 5 Sep 1829, both at Leyden, NY.)

Jotham is not in the 1860 census of Portage Co., OH and perhaps died there before that year. Neither is Nancy (Post) Brainerd-Mitchell found there in 1860 although she supposedly died there on 8 May 1865. Known children of Jotham Mitchell by his first marriage to Mary (   ), born in Oneida Co., NY, were:

172. Oliver M. bc 1803   +
173. **Mary (Polly)** - m bef 1835 Samuel D. Booth.

104. **MOSES MITCHELL**, son of Jotham and Rebecca (Royce) Mitchell, was born about 1786, probably in Bristol Twp., New Haven Co., CT where his father was living at the 1790 census. He died at Meriden, CT on 4 Jul 1811 at age 25 years. His only brother had died the month before and his mother the month before that.

Unmarried at his death, Moses left a fairly substantial estate for a young man. It totalled $2,798.52 and included notes against his brother-in-laws, Christopher Atwater and Walter Booth, notes against Elisha Wells and John Bacon, a 25-acre property co-owned with John Lam with the house, barn, jappan shop and other buildings, plus half the corn growing on 3 acres of land which he also owned with John Lam. His brother-in-law, Christopher Atwater, was appointed administrator with his uncle, Zenas Mitchell, acting as surety.

Inventory of Moses' estate was taken by Asaph Merriman and Benajah Andrews, "Freeholders and Appraisers." It consisted mostly of clothes. From it, we conclude that Moses was quite a fashion plate. He owned a castor hat (usually made of beaver), linen and cotton shirts, neck handerchiefs, silk handkerchiefs in black and yellow, pantaloons of striped cotton, of nankeen (twilled cotton), another pair in white, and a fourth of "carrimon" color plus vests of violet, white, purple, blue, and black silk. He wore suspenders and owned several coats plus a great coat. His inventory included a gun, bayonet, cartridge box, uniform coat for military service, leather flask, an umbrella, a 2-horse wagon, tin box and harness. From the fact that there was a "jappan" shop on his premises leads one to believe he was a craftsman who peddled his wares from town to town.

The nuncupative will of Moses declared his "will and intention in relation to his estate" and was probably made orally on his death bed. His sister Sally Mitchel "should hold and enjoy as her own property, the one equal undivided moiety or half part in quantity & quality thereof..." Betsey Atwater, wife of Christopher Atwater, and Laura Booth, wife of Walter Booth, his sisters, "should hold & enjoy as their own property, in equal shares the remaining moiety or half part of his said estate." Both of these inheritances were subject to their maintaining and supporting their father, Jotham Mitchel, "at all times during his natural life." This document was signed at Meriden, CT on 10 Jul 1811 by Moses' three sisters and two brothers-in-law. (Wallingford, CT Probate District File #1203)

120. **ALONZO MITCHELL,** son of Moses Miller and Lydia (Hale) Mitchell, was born 6 Mar 1806 at Greenfield, MA. He married first about 1834-1835 Fidelia (Phidelia) _____ who died 29 Nov 1838, age 35 (gravestone record, Village Cemetery, Charlemont, MA V/R). He married second before 1845 Clarissa _____, born about 1806 in New York (1860 Census, Greenfield, Franklin Co., MA).

In the 1860 Census, Alonzo is called a blacksmith. He left no probate records in Franklin Co., MA. Known children of Alonzo Mitchell (first two by first marriage to Fidelia; third by second marriage to Clarissa) were:
   174. **Ellen** b 14 Sep 1836 (Charlemont, MA V/R).
   175. **Lydia P.** b 26 Nov 1838 d 26 Jul 1839 age 8m (grst., Village Cemetery, Charlemont, MA V/R).
   176. **Sarah M.** bc 1845 MA.

126. **ANSON MITCHELL,** son of William and Mercy (Wise) Mitchell, was born about 1799, probably at Greenfield, MA. His year of birth is given by Sheldon ("History of Deerfield, MA," Vol. II) although it appears in neither Deerfield nor Greenfield, MA Vital Records. Anson states his age in census records as 51 in 1850 and 61 in 1860, born in MA. There is nothing to indicate that his parents lived anywhere but Greenfield.

Anson married 5/6 Mar 1823 at Winchester, Cheshire Co., NH to Melinda Hutchinson (Bureau of V/R, Concord, NH) who was born about 1803 in NH (1850/1860 Census of Greenfield, Franklin Co., MA). By will, Anson left property in Winchester, NH to son Asa H. This land had been "conveyed" to Anson from his son, Gilbert F., on 28 Aug 1867. Perhaps Anson and Melinda lived in or near Winchester, NH for the first years of their marriage. Although those children

living at home in 1850 state they were born in MA, only two
of Anson's children appear in Greenfield, MA V/R - William W. who died there in 1842, and Willard G., born in
1844. Both of these dates were taken from gravestone records. (An inquiry and search fee was sent to the Town
Clerk at Winchester, NH but there was no response.)

In 1837 Anson bought a home in Greenfield on Music
Hill from Lucius Nims, but sold it in 1842 to Rev. Amariah
Chandler. He may have rented a house until he built a home
in March 1854 on the north side of Main St. in Greenfield
where he probably lived until his death. (The property
passed down to him from his great-grandfather, William
Mitchell, Anson sold to his sister, Content, who sold it
to Daniel Kelleher, deed recorded 9 Mar 1864, Bk 241:314.)

Anson wrote his will on 7 Sep and died 28 Oct 1867 at
Greenfield, MA. His executor, John J. Graves of Greenfield, stated on 4 Nov 1867 that Anson "left no widow" and
Melinda is not named in his will. He left $50.00 to his
daughter Charlotte Cumins, the Cheshire Co., NH property
mentioned earlier to his son Asa H., and the "rest and
residue" to his daughter, Harriet Brown, "to be held in
trust for her by John J. Graves" whom he directed to "ex-
pend the income and any part or the whole of said sum for
the benefit" of his daughter "as he should deem proper."
If Harriet died before the entire sum was spent, the balance was to be shared by his surviving children.

Clause #7 of Anson's will states without explanation
that "I purposely omit to give anything to my children
Porter Mitchell, Gilbert F. Mitchell, Abigail Miller,
Anson F. Mitchell, Willard G. Mitchell, William M. Mitchell and George E. Mitchell and my grandchildren Isa-
dore H. Kenney and Abigail M. Jones."

Anson's house and lot were appraised at $1,200.00;
his personal goods at $111.80. He seems to have been
adept at several trades. The 1850 Census lists him as a
machinist. The 1860 Census calls him a miller. He may
also have been a carpenter as his inventory included saws,
squares, augers and planes. He wore spectacles and owned
books, including two Testaments, a Bible, one "lot" of
old books, and three whose titles were given as "New
World," "Shrinking Bayonet," and "Color Guard." He owned
the usual household furnishings and a meager wardrobe
which included galoshes, an umbrella, and a fur collar.
At his death he had $10.35 cash on hand.

In 1868 Anson's estate paid his Baptist Society pew
rent owing. In 1869 his estate received small sums due it
from the Republican Lodge, the F.R.A. Chapter, the Connecticut Volunteer Encampment, and the "Titus Strong
Council." Dr. Severance was paid for medical attendance,
a $30.00 bill for his gravestones was paid and his daugh-
ter, Harriet, drew sums of money from the estate regularly
from Mar 1868 until Nov 1871. His son, Porter, received a
settlement of $100.00 against his demand of $286.41 "for
services rendered said Anson Mitchell during sickness,"
and for money paid out by Porter on his father's behalf.

Children of Anson and Melinda (Hutchinson) Mitchell
(order uncertain; estimated birth dates from 1850 Census)
were:

177. **Porter**   +
178. **Maria** m (int.) 8 Oct 1845 Lorenzo D. Kenney (Green-
     field, MA V/R); per d bef 1867 as she is not men-
     tioned in her father's will.
179. **Anson F.** - living 1867.
180. **Gilbert F.** bc 1827-1828   +
181. **Charlotte** bc 1829 m 29 Nov 1849 James M. Cumins
     (Greenfield, MA V/R Charlotte, 20, d/o Anson, to
     James M. [Comins], 24, carpenter of Northfield,
     s/o Asa and Fidelia.)
182. **Abigail** bc 1832 MA m _____ Miller; (per m1] to _____
     Jones; Anson's will called Abigail Jones grdau.)
183. **Asa H.** bc 1837 MA
184. **William W.** b Feb 1839 d 12 Dec 1844, 3y 10m
     (Greenfield, MA V/R from gravestone).
185. **Harriet** bc 1842-1843 MA m _____ Brown.
186. **Willard G.** (twin) b 22 Feb 1844 (grst., Greenfield,
     MA V/R); Civil War 52nd Inf.; bur on N side of Fed-
     eral St. Cemetery; he and his twin are called "pep-
     pery and pugnacious" in Thompson's "History of
     Greenfield, MA".
187. **William M.** (twin) b 22 Feb 1844; called William U.
     in some records, but William M. in his father's
     will; Civil War 52nd Inf. as a musician.
188. **George E.** bc 1846   +

130. **MILES MITCHELL**, son of William and Mercy (Wise)
Mitchell, was born 21 Aug 1805, died 11 Oct 1848 (Greenfield, MA V/R). He married probably about 1839 Martha D.
_____, born in 1811 (Greenfield, MA V/R, gravestone).

Fifth Generation

At the time of his death, Miles and Martha were renting a house in Greenfield from Benjamin Jackson. Called variously "jeweler" and "goldsmith," Miles had a shop "about on the present site of the Franklin house." (Thompson's "History of Greenfield, MA," Vol. II, p 185) This shop was furnished with the expected bench and tables with drawers, bench vise and tools, heated with a wood stove, and made homey by the addition of a looking glass, several engravings, a copper kettle, a clock, a pair of candlesticks and a lamp. It is clear that Miles was also a watch maker with the listing in his inventory of ten boxes of watch tools and materials, watch glasses and oil, and watch signs.

He was evidently a successful man at his trade. At his death, Miles had $1,012.50 in his savings account, $118.00 in notes at Greenfield bank, and $70.00 worth of "Silver coine" in his possession. This speaks of a frugal nature although his house was comfortably furnished with such items as a Vermont parlor stove, five glass lamps, carpets, three chamber pots, a tea tray, a "tea sett" and crockery in the parlor closet, ample furniture and linens, as well as tin, wood, glass and crockery ware in the "Buttery." He possessed several maps but no books are mentioned in his inventory.

Miles wore spectacles and shaved ("1 pair razors & strops"), his last shave performed by Francis Green after Miles' death which the best efforts of Drs. Stearns, Hovey and Deane could not prevent. His "burying lot" was purchased from J. J. Pierce for $5.00, and $3.00 was paid to Daniel Corby for digging his grave.

On 6 June 1849, Miles' widow, Martha D., petitioned the Franklin Co., MA Judge of Probate to appoint Lucius Nims of Greenfield as guardian for her five children, all "minors under fourteen years of age," and stating the full given names of these children. This document was dated at "Winchester" which was probably the town of that name in Cheshire Co., NH, lying on the Ashuelot River just a few miles north of the MA-NH border. (A query and search fee to the Winchester, NH Town Clerk has had no response.) Martha D. may have been born in that area and possibly married to Miles there.

Lucius Nims' guardianship report to the court (Franklin Co., MA Probate Records File #3256) dated 9 Oct 1855 charges the estate with $624.00 of expenses over a period of six years for board, clothes, and schooling for Miles' children as well as doctors bills and funeral expenses for his daughters, Content and Emma. This accounting was examined and approved by Miles' widow who signed her name in a feminine, slightly flourishing handwriting.

It is impossible to read the statistics on this family without feeling a strong sense of sympathy for Miles' widow. Martha D. was far gone in pregnancy with their fifth child (Content A.) when Miles died at age 43; she gave birth less than two months later. The following year her third child died and she lost her fifth by 1852. Apparently, her eldest child did not live long after 1855. The burden of these losses in such a short span of years must have been a heavy one for Martha D. to bear.

Children of Miles and Martha D. ( ) Mitchell (dates of birth from Greenfield, MA V/R taken from gravestones, or estimated from order of children given in guardianship papers) were:
189. **Edward Harrison** bc 1840 (from grst).
190. **Martha Matilda** bc 1842; living 1855.
191. **Emma Elizabeth** bc 1844 d 1849 (grst).
192. **Webster Clay** bc 1846; living 1855.
193. **Content Antoinette** b (posthumously) 6 Dec 1848 (Greenfield, MA V/R); d bef 29 May 1852 (grdnship).

134. **ELIJAH MITCHELL,** son of William and Mercy (Wise) Mitchell, was born 16 Nov 1813 at Greenfield, MA (V/R); he married before 1846 Catherine Prentice, born about 1823 in MA (age 27 in 1850 Census, Greenfield, MA).

Elijah's occupation was given as printer in the 1850 Census. Thompson's "History of Greenfield, MA" (Vol. II, p 846) also calls him a printer, "one of the oldest of his craft" in the state of Massachusetts, stating also that Elijah died 23 Feb 1867 at Adams, MA in an "almshouse."

Perhaps Elijah and Catherine lived in Montague, MA for a few years after their marriage as the birth of their eldest son is recorded there. Birth of their second son is in Deerfield, MA Vital Records.

Going on the supposition that both sons remained in Massachusetts and both had children age 10 or under in 1880, the Census Index (Soundex) for that year was searched, even though both James and William are among the most popular male given names. Only two possibilities were uncovered. Living in Brookfield, Worcester Co., MA in

1880 (Vol. 33, E.D. 804, Sheet 13, Line 9) was a James Mitchell, age 38, born in MA, with Sarah (36, MA), Albert (14, MA); Arthur (7, MA); Annie (5, MA); George (4, MA). Nearby in the same town and county (Vol. 33, E.D. 804, Sheet 11, Line 30) was William Mitchell, age 34, born in MA, with Dellia (34, MA); Harry (6, MA); Walter (4, MA). Ages given for this James and William are not quite a match for the dates of birth of Elijah's sons, but they are close, and this James is a few years older than William as was James, son of Elijah, older than his brother. That they live in near proximity to each other is indicative to a certain degree.

Known children of Elijah and Catherine (Prentice) Mitchell were:

194. **James Catlin** b 25 Feb 1846 (Montague, MA V/R).

195. **William Wise** b 25 May 1848 (Deerfield, MA V/R).

135. **ENSIGN MITCHELL (JR.),** son of Ensign and Lucy (Hubbard) Mitchell, was born 3 Mar 1787 near Whitehall, Washington Co., NY. He died 14 Jan 1879 in Edgar Twp., Edgar Co., IL, "the oldest resident of the township" at age 91 years 10 months 11 days.

Ensign married first 11 Jan 1816 in Clermont Co. (now Brown), OH to Elizabeth Calvin, born 1794-1800 in Mason Co., KY, daughter of James and Nancy (Cartmill) Calvin (see Allied Lines for correction of her parentage as given in "The Calvin Families," by Claude W. Calvin). Elizabeth ("Betsey") died 28 Nov 1845 in Edgar Co., IL. Ensign married second 21 Feb 1850 in Edgar Co., IL to Mrs. Mary Ann Eliza (   ) Riley, born about 1800 in Fayette Co., KY and still living in 1877. (On 5 Aug 1850 Ensign and Mary Ann relinquished by deed in Edgar Co., IL her property which "James H. Riley [her husband] died seized in fee simple," to her son William W. Riley, and her son-in-law Nathan Tucker, provided they paid her $10.00 annually for her lifetime [Bk 11:217].)

Ensign's growing up years were spent in a variety of places, his parents moving from Washington Co., NY to Essex in Chittenden Co., VT; then Galway, Saratoga Co., NY; then before 1800 to Pennsylvania where they lived first in Luzerne Co. (now Bradford) near the Susquehanna River, then in Tioga Co. In 1809 the family traveled via the Ohio River to Cincinnati, perhaps living in Kentucky for a few years, but in Clermont Co., OH by 1811.

Fifth Generation

According to a biography of Ensign's son, Calvin, he was a "Captain" in the War of 1812. However, he is not listed in the Index to the Official Roster of the War of 1812 in the Ohio Adjutant General's Department. His service may have been as captain of a local militia.

When Ensign's parents left Clermont Co. for Champaign Co., OH in 1815, he and his younger brother, Chandler, remained behind. He and Elizabeth settled in Pleasant Twp. in the White Oak Creek Valley just a few miles north of the Ohio River, but south of Georgetown, the boyhood home of Ulysses S. Grant. On 20 June 1818 Ensign bought 126 acres of land "on the waters of White Oak Creek" for $490.00 from Phebe Curry, mother-in-law of Elizabeth's brother, Samuel Calvin, whose land neighbored the Mitchells. This land, part of Survey 350 entered in the name of James Curry and "pattented to and conveyed by the heirs of Robert Curry deceased" to Phebe, his widow, was covered with beech, ash, hickory, sugar maple and black walnut trees. Erroneously surveyed in 1818, the boundaries were corrected by deed dated 13 Jan 1826 between Ensign and the heirs of the "late Phebe Curry." (Bk A:130 & E-5:255) On 2 Mar 1821 in two separate deeds (Bk B-2:509 & 511) Ensign had added 35 more acres to his holdings in the "Curry patent" which he bought from Elijah Evans (brother-in-law of Samuel Calvin) and Lucinda "his wife."

Family "tradition" states that Ensign was "mainly" engaged in pork packing and shipping produce to New Orleans on flatboats following the Ohio to Mississippi River route. (In plain language, he was a hog and grain farmer.) Pat Donaldson of Georgetown, OH who researched records for me in this area confirmed that "the location of Ensign's land would work out...for his pork shipping activities...(taking) his product down Free Soil Road to Higginsport on the Ohio River." Family "tradition" also says that Ensign lost most of his property in Brown Co., OH by signing notes for friends who defaulted on them, but I have found no evidence to prove this. The amount of land that he sold in 1830 prior to his move to Edgar Co., IL seems to nearly equal the amount he had purchased in 1818 and 1821. (60 acres to John Woods, Bk C-3:144; 23 acres to Samuel Calvin, Bk H-8:387; 70 acres to James Dennis, Bk H-8:404, Brown Co., OH Deed Records.)

The Ordinance of 1787 which provided a three-step plan whereby unsettled territories could obtain statehood had encouraged migration by guaranteeing citizens ultimate enjoyment of all political rights they had left behind. Illinois, by virtue of having the required population of at least 60,000, had become a state in 1818. Yet, migration into the state, particularly in the mid to southern areas, was not brisk until after the Black Hawk War of 1832 completed the expulsion of the Indians. In 1830, the year that Ensign brought his family to Edgar Co., Andrew Jackson was President, and Abe Lincoln, age 21, was nearly ready to enter politics. The territorial capital was Kaskaskia, but a state capital was established in Vandalia to encourage sale of property in that area. Chicago was still Fort Dearborn with a population of 50.

The new settlers were drawn to the untouched prairies of Illinois "covered with tall prairie grass where bright wild flowers bloomed" as much by its beauty as its "promise of the richness of the soil that lay under the prairie's tough, untilled sod...nature's promise of ample wealth, there for the taking by willing and hardworking men and women." ("The Story of Illinois," by Theodore Calvin Pease, 3rd edition, revised by Marguerite Jenison Pease) This "wealth" was a double edged sword. The unbroken sod covered masses of decaying vegetable matter. Once disturbed and exposed to the sun, the rotted humas that made the soil so rich, combined with stagnant pools and swamps dotted around the prairie, throwing a miasma into the air that brought wasting diseases such as intermittant fevers and ague to the settlers. Many died in those early years of taming the prairie.

Despite the fact that Illinois, including Edgar Co., was not totally unsettled, Ensign and Elizabeth were pioneers in every sense of the word. Accompanied by Elizabeth's unmarried first cousin, David Calvin, they loaded their wagons, collected their eight children (a ninth was born in Illinois), herded their animals together, and headed west across Indiana, perhaps stopping briefly in Johnson Co., IN to visit Elizabeth's parents who had moved there from Brown Co., OH about 1825.

Once in Edgar Co., Ensign chose land in the part of Carroll Precinct that became Edgar Twp., lying just north of the town of Paris near the small village of Bloomfield. He would have constructed a temporary three-sided shelter with a fire burning in front to house his family until he could build a cabin (perhaps a double cabin, considering the size of his family). Built of round logs, the cracks chinked, the cabin would be roofed with clap boards or shakes laid upon "ribs" and held down with weight poles. It had the usual large fireplace and probably a split log floor and would contain only what household items they had been able to bring or had made after their arrival.

Certainly Ensign had brought a heavy iron shod wood plow plus other farm and building tools, and perhaps seed for the first planting. Elizabeth would have brought her spinning wheel and wool cards, her iron soap making kettle and iron cooking utensils, bedding, whatever furniture could be fit in, and the few clothes they owned which were probably packed together in a sturdy trunk. No doubt both Ensign and his older sons owned hunting guns to procure the wild meat they would live on for the first several years, and to kill predators. The area teemed with deer, wild turkey, prairie wolves, raccoons, golphers, foxes, oppossum and skunks. In the warm months, any necessary traveling (to the nearest smithy, for example) and often even plowing was done at night to avoid the swarms of "greenhead" flies whose vicious bites drove both man and beast to a state of frenzy.

Elizabeth was the granddaughter of Capt. Luther Calvin of Kentucky frontier fame. She would need the pioneer strength of her ancestors during her first years in Edgar Co. Besides the arduous work of housekeeping under crude conditions, she would spin, weave and make all the clothes for her family and see to her many children. Women like Elizabeth were often terribly homesick for relatives and friends left behind. Additionally, she had to endure the physical stress and danger of pregnancy and childbirth just a year after her arrival in Illinois. The physical toll exacted upon pioneer women like Elizabeth too often resulted in premature death. While Ensign lived for 91 years, Elizabeth was no more than 51 at her death.

Ensign was a strong abolitionist. This was not only a popular view in Illinois which had "gone" anti-slavery in 1824, but also of the Methodist church in which Ensign was a leading member. (His father had been a "local exhorter" in the Methodist church in Ohio, and his uncle, the Rev. Joseph Mitchell, one of the early Methodist Episcopal itinerant ministers.) Ensign helped organize the first Methodist Society in Edgar Twp., serving for years as a class leader. In that capacity he had no voice in church politics which was the domain of the bishops and circuit riders, but he helped sustain the faithful and strengthen the converts. Methodism then preached simplicity in all things, strongly opposing such frivolities as dancing, card playing and fancy dress. Drinking of alcohol and slaveholding were, of course, considered major sins.

On 24 July 1875 Ensign wrote his will. His youngest son, John, whom he appointed executor, was left "...all my property both real and personal...conditioned that he shall provide a comfortable support for my wife Mary Ann should she survive me and to save trouble and expense I have this day made and executed a deed to my said (son) John Mitchell for all my real estate - but said deed is not to be delivered to him until after my death." He left $5.00 each to his children "...Lucy Roston...Chandler Mitchell...Nancy Kirkpatrick...(and) Polly Fuller." His sons, Calvin and Samuel, both still living, were not mentioned, and his son, Joseph, had predeceased him.

In 1877, just two years before his death, an event of great moment occured in Ensign's life. His four brothers, Claudius, Abizer and Newman in Ohio, and Ira in Iowa, journeyed to Edgar Co. for a reunion. Quite by accident, the three brothers from Ohio met Ensign's eldest son, Calvin, who had never laid eyes on his uncles before, in the town of Paris and learned they were all headed to Calvin's brother John's house. There, A. J. Riley of the Paris, IL "Gazette" witnessed and reported on the meeting of the five. "Some of the brothers had not seen each other for more than forty years, and when they all met and embraced each other, throwing their arms about each other's necks and exclaiming, 'my brother, oh, my brother, is it you!'...the whole scene...presented one of such joy and gladness...it reminds one...of the meeting of Joseph and his brethern...seldom do five brothers, all so advanced in years as these, meet together in this world."

Mr. Riley described Ensign as "...feeble in health and stricken in years, the old man's heart ran over with joy to see all his brothers once more in this world; buoyed up and nerved by the occasion, the old man, although his children had assembled only twenty-four hours before to see him die (as they expected), was able to sit up, and walk. Ensign...is a farmer by occupation, a Methodist by profession and republican politically. No man, perhaps, in Edgar county has done more hard work, and attended nearer to his own business..." The day ended with Bible reading, singing some of "Zion's songs," and prayers of benediction for all.

Children of Ensign, Jr. and Elizabeth (Calvin) Mitchell, all born in Brown Co., OH except the youngest, born in Edgar Co., IL, were:

- **196. Calvin** b 2 Dec 1816 +
- **197. Joseph** b 16 Jan 1818 +
- **198. Chandler** (bc 1819 or 1821/2?) +
- **199. Lucy** b 5 Mar 1820 +
- **200. Elizabeth** (census lists only 3 daughters, but an extra <u>male</u>, b 1820-1825, appears in 1830 & 1840. This name is from family records without source.)
- **201. Nancy** b Aug 1823 +
- **202. Mary (Polly)** b 11 June 1825 +
- **203. Samuel** b 4 Mar 1828 +
- **204. John** b 1 Nov 1831 +

136. **CHANDLER MITCHELL,** son of Ensign, Sr. and Lucy (Hubbard) Mitchell, was born about 1788, either in Chittenden Co., VT or Washington Co., NY. The 1850 census (taken 9 Nov) says he is age 63, born in VT; the 1860 census (taken 25 Aug) says he is age 72, born in NY. It is doubtful that he was born in 1787 (per the 1850 census) as his older brother, Ensign, Jr., was born in March of that year. As to his place of birth, the residence "time table" given by his father in his Revolutionary War pension application papers indicates 1788 as the year the family moved to VT. Chandler's place of birth depends very much on whether his family moved before or after he was born.

Neither the date and place of Chandler's marriage nor the name of his wife have been found. According to census records, she was born between 1780-1790 and died between 1840-1850. Since Chandler's eldest known child was born about 1810, he was probably married by 1809, possibly in Tioga Co., PA just before his parents left there. (Tioga Co. has no marriage records earlier than 1885.)

The 1830 Census of Brown Co., OH lists Chandler in Sterling Twp. (1 m un 5, 2 m 5/10, 3 m 10/15, 1 m 15/20, 1 m 40/50; 1 f un 5, 1 f 5/10, 1 f 15/20, 1 f 40/50). He was still in Brown Co., OH in 1840, listed as "Chandley," but had moved over to Pike Twp. If all the younger persons listed in Chandler's household in 1830 were his children, he had at least 7 sons and 3 daughters.

Fifth Generation

Between 1840 and 1850, Chandler left Brown Co., OH and moved to Pike Co., IL with at least two of his married children, son Ensign, and daughter Jane who was married to William T. Watson in whose household Chandler lived. A possible son might be John W. Mitchell who lived next door to the Watsons in 1850. He is age 30, born in Ohio; with him is wife Sarah C. (22, birthplace not given); Samuel W. (3, IL); and Rebecca I. (1 month, IL). In 1860 this family is in Hardin Twp. (Time post office), initials only used for the family - J.W. (41, OH); N.E. (34, MO); S. A. (14, IL); R.I. (10, IL), and M.E. (female, 2, IL). In 1870 John is called "Wright," age 51, OH, with Nancy (45, OH), and Nelly (13, IL); living next door is son Samuel, age 23, with wife Jane (20, IL) and son Orin (1, IL).

Another possible son of Chandler's might be George Mitchell who lived not far from the Watsons in 1850. He is age 26, born in OH, with wife Martha A., 21, born in KY. William Brace, age 10, born in IL is in their household. In 1860, George and Martha are also in Hardin Twp. (Time post office) and they appear there again in 1870 as George (42, OH) and Martha (40, OH). No children by the surname Mitchell appear with them in these three census periods. (George Mitchell was a purchaser at the estate sale of Chandler Mitchell, grandson of the above Chandler, who died in Pike Co., IL in 1868.)

There were various other Mitchells listed in Pike Co. in 1860 and 1870 census records. However, the only Mitchell heads of household there in 1850 were Ensign, son of Chandler, and the above John W. and George. Both John W. and George are of the proper age and birthplace to have been sons of Chandler. They will not be listed as such here since evidence is too scanty to justify it.

By the 1870 census, both Ensign Mitchell and Jane (Mitchell) Watson had left Pike Co. There are no probate records for the elder Chandler in Pike Co. and he is not living with any other family, indicating he either died prior to 1870 or left for an unknown location with his son and daughter. Certainly he was dead before 1877 when he was conspicuously absent from a reunion held by his five living brothers in Edgar Co., IL.

Chandler is an occupational surname. As such it is distinctive as a given name. It has been used among the descendants of his brother, Claudius, and even to the present day by the descendants of his brother, Ensign.

Fifth Generation

Known children of Chandler Mitchell and an unknown wife, all born in Brown Co., OH, were:
   205. Ensign bc 1810   +
   206. Jane bc 1824-1825   +

137. **MARY (POLLY) MITCHELL,** daughter of Ensign, Sr. and Lucy (Hubbard) Mitchell, was born 29 Sep 1792, probably in Essex Twp., Chittenden Co., VT where her parents were thought to be until 1793. She married 9 Dec 1808 to Benjamin Reynolds, born about 1784 (place of birth thought to be in Vergennes, Addision Co., VT), died 12 Aug 1855 in Van Buren Co., MI.

Her date of marriage comes from "family records," source unknown. If correct, her place of marriage may have been Tioga Co., PA where her family lived until about 1809. (Tioga Co. does not have marriage records earlier than 1885.) If so, Mary and Benjamin seem to have followed or accompanied Mary's parents to Ohio as the marriage record of their son, Benjamin, Jr., is found in Madison Co., OH records (1838, Vol. A:249).

Before 1840 Mary and Benjamin and their family, including their married son, left Ohio for Van Buren Co., MI, appearing there in Decatur Twp. in the 1840 census, and in Porter Twp. in the 1850 census. In both census periods, their sons Benjamin and Buel are living adjacent to their parents.

Mary is thought to have died between 1850 and 1852, based on lack of mention of her in Benjamin's probate papers. Her tombstone in Porter Cemetery (Porter Twp., Van Buren Co., MI) gives her date of birth but not her date of death. Inexplicably, her tombstone reads that she was "formerly of Essex Co., Conn." Although there is a town of Essex in CT, there is no county by that name. We presume a confusion on the part of her family, or a misunderstanding on the part of the stone maker since Mary's parents were not in CT in 1792. Rather, they were in Essex, a town and a township of Chittenden Co., VT.

Certainly Mary and Benjamin must have had more children than we have listed here, possibly sons who did not go to MI with their parents, daughters whose married names are unknown, or children who did not live to adulthood. Mary's known children (REYNOLDS) were: **(i)** Buel bc 1814 OH m by 1840 Mary ____; 4 children by 1850; **(ii)** Benjamin b 19 Apr 1816 Madison Co., OH d 7 Jan 1871 Van Buren Co., MI m 26 Sep 1838 in Madison Co., OH to Druzilla Whitaker b Oct 1817 Madison Co., OH d 23 Jul 1858 Van Buren Co., OH; 5 children by 1850; **(iii)** Samuel bc 1825 OH; **(vi)** probably Lucinda bc 1827 OH m ____ Harrison bef 1850; living 1850 with Benjamin (Sr.) & Mary Reynolds; no spouse shown but 6 Harrison children listed; prob only the 3 younger ones were Lucinda's; **(v)** Experience bc 1831 OH; **(vi)** Charles bc 1834 OH.

138. CLAUDIUS MITCHELL, son of Ensign, Sr. and Lucy (Hubbard) Mitchell, was born 6 Jan 1794, probably in Saratoga Co., NY where his father resided by 1793. (In census records, Claudius could not make up his mind about it, saying he was born in NY in the 1850 and 1870 census, but in VT in the 1860 and 1880 census.)

Claudius married first 12 Oct 1815 in Clermont Co. (now Brown), OH to Nancy Lambert, born 25 Dec 1795 in KY, daughter of Joshua and Anna ( ) Lambert. She died 24 Oct 1839 in Champaign Co., OH, age 43 years. Claudius married second 4 Apr 1840 in Champaign Co., OH to Mary Ann Reed, born 10 Aug 1803 (in VA per 3 census records); died in Champaign Co., OH on 13 Mar 1888. Claudius died there 17 May 1886; he and both his wives are buried there in Maple Grove Cemetery.

Although it contains a few errors, Beers gives an interesting account of Claudius' life in his "History of Madison Co., OH" (Pike Twp. section). Claudius was born of "poor but respectable parents;" during his childhood, he enjoyed "...his favorite dog and unerring rifle...ever on the chase for, or in mortal combat with, the wounded bear or stolen cub, and often came 'hand to hand' in contest with the wild buck deer." As a result, Claudius had not even a "common school education" and did not learn to read or write.

His first pair of pants were made by his mother "out of hair combed from their own cow in the time of shedding in the spring, mixed and carded with common flax tow... spun...and knit into a pair of pants." He owned his first pair of shoes at age ten, paying for them with money earned cutting and hauling wood on a hand-sled for several miles. At age twelve, he was capable of doing a man's work.

In 1815 Claudius moved with his parents to Champaign Co., OH. The first camp meeting held there at Mechanicsburg in July 1815 took place "on the low grounds back of the log church, in what is now Orin Taylor's pasture." On the evening Samuel Hinkle preached, "Uncle" Claudius (as he became known) was converted. In later years, he reflected that "My conversion was the plainest and most satisfactory thing I ever experienced...have never doubted it since, and, while I have received many blessings since, confidence in the work of my conversion has never been shaken."

Claudius returned to Clermont Co. to marry Nancy in the fall of 1815, bringing his bride home to live with his parents until Feb. 1st of the following year when he "took leave of his home...and commenced life for himself. The first day's work for himself he took his ax and maul, and cut and split 350 rails, for which he received 25 cents per hundred...not in cash, but in corn at 25 cents per bushel...The second day he made 250 rails and took his pay in tallow and fat meat." (Beers)

Beers' continues that on 7 Feb Claudius took lease of land on Spring Fork, and "...commenced to build a cabin, with the snow then six inches deep. He soon had his cabin up and a roof on the same, and the next day he and his young wife moved into it, cleared away the snow and built a fire on the ground; then to work they went...to fit up the new home. At a late hour that night they laid down some loose clapboards on the snow, on which they spread their scanty bedding, and...before retiring...knelt down upon the icy-cold ground by two blocks, their only chairs, and there offered their songs and prayers..." to God. The only utensil they had for cooking was an old iron pot, and their table-ware consisted of two broken knives and forks and two old pewter spoons. He had "one two-year old heifer upon which the tax was 8 cents, and he had more difficulty to...pay that 8 cent tax than any tax he has ever paid." Since, he has "paid his $300 tax with...ease."

Claudius is not listed in Madison Co., OH deed records at all. Apparently he did not own property until he moved over to Goshen Twp., Champaign Co., OH where he bought land on 26 Apr 1828 from his brother-in-law and sister, William, Jr. and Roxanna Marrs. That he had no trouble paying his taxes in future years is evident from census record evaluations of his real and personal property. In 1850 his real estate was worth $15,000; in 1860 it was listed at $11,250 with $12,525 in personal property. By 1870, his real estate was valued at $20,000; his personal property at $10,700. Before 1880, Claudius had retired from the farm and moved into Mechanicsburg where he remained until his death in 1886.

In 1877 Claudius traveled with his brothers, Abizer and Newman, to Edgar Co., IL for a reunion with their eldest brother, Ensign, Jr., and another brother, Ira, who lived in Iowa. The Paris, IL "Gazette" sent A. J. Riley to cover the event. Eighty-four years old at the time, Claudius is described by Mr. Riley as "full of vitality, physically, mentally, and morally. Although quite jocular, he is sound in the Christian faith, ready to give everyone that asked him to give a reason of the hope that is in him. Being in the banking business...for years, he stands with hands full of means...he, as his elder brother (Ensign, Jr.), has been a Methodist for 62 years by profession and a staunch republican."

Children of Claudius Mitchell (first 9 by wife Nancy Lambert; last 2 by wife Mary Ann Reed), all born in Madison or Champaign Cos., OH, were:

- 207. **Sarah** b 15 Mar 1817 +
- 208. **Lavina** b 22 Jan 1819 +
- 209. **Martha Ann** b 24 May 1821 +
- 210. **Joshua** b 22 May 1823 +
- 211. **Lucy** b 13 Dec 1825, Madison Co., OH; m 18 May 1854 John Moore in Champaign Co., OH.
- 212. **Chandler** b 29 May 1828 +
- 213. **Claudius** b 23 Dec 1830 d 1831 Champaign Co., OH.
- 214. **Nancy** b 15 Oct 1832 Champaign Co., OH; d 21 Oct 1859; m ____ Standley; 1 child, Tobias.
- 215. **Elmira** b 6 Dec 1834 +
- 216. **Newton B.** b 25 Sep 1841 d 1849 bur Maple Grove Cemetery, Champaign Co., OH.
- 217. **John Milton** b 19 Dec 1844 d 26 Feb 1847 bur Maple Grove Cemetery, Champaign Co., OH.

139. **LAVINA MITCHELL**, daughter of Ensign, Sr. and Lucy (Hubbard) Mitchell, was probably born about 1796 in Saratoga Co., NY where her parents were then living. She married 7 Dec 1820 in Champaign Co., OH to John Payne (sometimes spelled Pain[e]).

Almost nothing is known about Lavina. She was surely one of the 3 daughters aged 16 to 26 living with her parents in the 1820 Census of Champaign Co., OH. Although her sisters are all left a small legacy in their father's will dated 1833, she was not. Instead, her father left "unto John Pain who married my Daughter Lavina one Dollar...," a good indication that Lavina was then deceased.

Lavina may have died prior to 1830 since she and John have not been found in the census for that period. Madison Co., OH Grantee-Grantor Deed Indexes list a number of indentures in the name of John "Payne" or "Pain", dating from 1834 through 1864. If there were any children born of Lavina's marriage to John Payne, none are yet known.

140. **ROXANNA (ROXY) MITCHELL**, daughter of Ensign, Sr. and Lucy (Hubbard) Mitchell, was probably born about 1798 in Saratoga Co., NY. (A Marrs genealogy, compiled and privately published by Mabel Marrs of Fowler, KS, gives her birth year as 1792, but this is hardly possible since her sister, Mary, was born in that year.)

To my knowledge, Roxanna has not been found in the 1830 Census, the only one which would have occured between her dates of marriage and death. In determining her year of birth, we are left with only the census of 1790 VT (2 females); of 1800 PA (3 females under 10); and of 1820 OH (3 females 16 to 26). The 1810 census of this family would be an enormous help, but they were in Ohio by then and there is no 1810 census for that state in that year.

These census records have been carefully analyzed in conjunction with known birthdates of her sister and her brothers, knowledge of marriage dates (recorded and estimated), census records of her sister Lydia for 1830, and 1850 through 1870. It seems most certain that she was born between 1784-1800, and probably about 1798. It is more sensible to suppose she was only several years older than her husband (born in 1800) than 8 to 10 years his senior. It is also more sensible to believe that she bore a child every two to three years between the ages of 24 and 39, rather than between the ages of 32 and 47.

Roxanna married William Marrs (Mar/Mars/Marr), Jr. on 27 Sep 1822 in Shelby Co., OH (license issued 15 Sep in Champaign Co., OH). William was born 20 May 1800 in Bourbon Co., KY, son of William and Jane (McClure) Marrs. After Roxanna's death in Aug 1839 (per the Marrs book), probably in Shelby Co., OH, her husband married second about 1840/41 Mrs. Mary Jane (Sunderland) Corns, eventually adding 9 more children to his family of 7 by Roxanna. By 1845 William had moved to Allen Co., IN and from there to Douglas Co., IL where he died 15 Jan 1880; his second wife died 21 Apr 1906.

According to Mabel Marrs (above cited), William Marrs was blind for several years, but in the last seven years of his life, he regained his sight, so as the food on the table was passed, he could see his (2nd) wife sneaking food to the children under the table. "He was what you call 'chinchey'...downright stingy." She tells an amusing story about the time William objected to the color his (2nd) wife used to dye a pair of pants. He made some blue dye, dug a pit in the ground, and used it as a dye vat. Afterwards, the sheep stumbled into the pit, and turned themselves blue. People would ask how they got blue sheep but William wouldn't tell them, preferring to let people think the sheep were born that way.

Roxanna and William are not in the 1830 Census, perhaps living with relatives and so not listed as a separate head of household. They were in Champaign Co., OH in 1828 when they sold property to Roxanna's brother, Claudius. Roxanna was mentioned in her father's will dated 1833, but no residence is given for her.

Roxanna's children (MARRS), all born in Ohio, were: **(i)** Lucy Sina b 27 June 1823; **(ii)** Ensign b 3 Jul 1826; **(iii)** William III b 19 June 1827 Sidney, OH d 14 Dec 1903 m Margaret G. Robinson b 22 Dec 1825 d 14 May 1882; 8 children known; **(iv)** Elenor Jane b 13 June 1830; **(v)** Roxanna Experience b 21 Sep 1832 m John Fuller (she is with her uncle, Newman Mitchell, in Madison Co., OH in the 1850 census); **(vi)** Lydia Elizabeth b 1 Apr 1835 m ____ Denver; **(vii)** Eunice Emelina Eliza b 23 Jul 1837 m Wm. R. Johnson.

141. **EXPERIENCE MITCHELL,** daughter of Ensign, Sr. and Lucy (Hubbard) Mitchell, was probably born about 1800-1801 in Wysox Twp., Luzerne Co. (now Bradford), PA where her parents were living in 1800.

We know very little about Experience and her life. It has been said and repeated often that she was married to Nathaniel Griffin and that she had at least four children, sons named Thomas, Andrew, John and James. This data has no known source. No marriage record is found for Experience in Clermont Co., OH (now Brown) where she and her parents lived for a few years before coming to Champaign and then Madison Cos., OH. No marriage record is found for her in Champaign Co., OH where her parents were living in 1820, nor in Madison Co., OH where her parents had moved before 1830. Apparently, no one has unearthed a marriage record for Experience to anyone in the entire area, including surrounding counties.

There seems to be but one Nathaniel Griffin in the Champaign-Madison Co., OH area. This man married in Madison Co. on 8 Jan 1826 to Mary Patrick, born 1808 in OH, daughter of Levi and Clarissa (Patrick) Patrick. In the 1830 Madison Co., OH census, Nathaniel and his family were listed next to Ensign Mitchell and family. This is understandable since Ensign Mitchell's land lay next to that of the Patrick's. Ensign's will specified land lying next to that of Young Patrick who was probably the same as Matthew Y. Patrick to whom Ensign sold land in 1834.

One might suppose that Experience was the first wife of Nathaniel Griffin and that she had died before his marriage in 1826 to Mary Patrick. However, Experience was living in 1833 when her father made his will in which he left her the sum of $5.00. Ensign did not give his daughters' surnames in his will, and named only one son-in-law, John Pain, who had married his daugher, Lavina.

In the 1830 Madison Co., OH census, Ensign's family included (besides his wife) a female between the ages of 10 and 15. This is far too young to be Experience, and can not be her unless this was an erroneous entry by the census taker. Experience does not seem to appear in the households of any of her married brothers or sisters in 1830 or in subsequent years.

Nathaniel and Mary (Patrick) Griffin moved to Van Wert Co., OH by 1840, returning to the Madison-Champaign Co. area by 1846 (deed/census records); Mary died 31 Aug 1864. Nathaniel sold his farm in 1865 to Newman Mitchell (son of Ensign), and per the biography of a son-in-law, Richard M. Johnson (Beers' Madison Co. history, p1095), he "subsequently went to Illinois..." where he died on 10 Aug 1880; he was buried in Maple Grove Cemetery, Mechanicsburg, OH (dates 1804-1881). If he was ever married to Experience Mitchell, it was after 1864, and certainly there could have been no children by such a union.

142. **IRA MITCHELL**, son of Ensign, Sr. and Lucy (Hubbard) Mitchell, was born 3 Jul 1803 in Tioga Co., PA. His parents, natives of MA, had lived in NY and VT before coming to Luzerne Co. (now Bradford), and then Tioga Co., PA.

Fifth Generation

The Mitchells left Tioga Co. when Ira was six years old (1809), traveling south to Pittsburg, then via the Ohio River to Cincinnati where they may have lived on the Kentucky side of the river before coming to Clermont Co. (now Brown), OH by 1811. In 1815 Ira's parents moved to Champaign Co., OH. There Ira was married on 12 Dec 1826 to Jane Rhodes, the ceremony performed by Ira's uncle, Elder Joseph Mitchell, a Methodist Episcopal minister.

Jane, born in 1806 Ross Co., OH, was the daughter of John and Sarah (Brittin) Rhodes, both of whom had settled with their parents in Ohio prior to its statehood. In Ira's biography, John Rhodes is credited with being the first man to invent a mowing machine, riding on horseback from Ohio to Washington, D.C. to obtain a patent on it. The Rhodes house in Champaign Co., OH is supposed to have been the first there to be covered with boards put on with iron nails, and painted by Jane's father. ("Portrait and Biographical Album of Henry Co., IA," 1888, p 313-314)

In 1830 Ira (as "Arra") and Jane lived in Pike Twp., Madison Co., OH, near neighbors of Ira's uncle, Rev. Joseph Mitchell and his sons, Joseph, Jr. and Newman. About 1834, Ira and his family, accompanied by Jane's parents, moved to Perry Twp., Miami Co., IN where he "entered" on a 500 acre tract of heavily timbered land in the Pottawatomie Reservation. Ira's biography continues that "...only those familiar with making homes in the dense woods can appreciate the labor incident to clearing and getting into successful cultivation...land of such character." Ira was also a "great lover of stock," dealing largely in cattle, "...his prosperity...greatly due to his enterprising habits and indefatigable labor."

Ira continued to add to and improve his property which by 1850 was evaluated at $5,000; but in 1853 he decided to move to Iowa which had achieved statehood only 7 years before. After a residence of nearly 20 years in Miami Co., IN, they said goodbye to much - friends, a married daughter and their first grandchild, the graves of two children and of Jane's father. Loading their wagons, they traveled west, possibly crossing the Mississippi at St. Louis, then following the river north to Henry Co., IA in the southeastern tip of the state and not far inland from the Mississippi. Here they settled on a little more than a half section of land a mile west of the town of Salem, where they remained until Ira's retirement in 1884.

Ira had not seen his brothers for over 40 years when Claudius, Abizer, Newman (in Ohio) and he agreed in 1877 to meet at the home of their eldest brother, Ensign, Jr., near Paris, Edgar Co., IL. We are indebted indeed to the Paris, IL "Gazette" for sending A. J. Riley to report on this joyfilled occasion for he gives us a glimpse into the characters of these brothers that we otherwise might not enjoy. Mr. Riley wrote that Ira "...shows the Mitchell stock, and manifests his attachment to the family equally if not more than any. He is quick both in wit and step. He once mowed with a scythe an acre of grass in one hour and forty minutes on a wager. He is...the father of ten children, seven of whom survives to cheer their father and mother who are now traveling speedily to the grave. Being a congregationalist, he is quite liberal in his religious views. Politically, he is a republican."

Ira was certainly a man of great energy. His son-in-law, Henry H. Hess, said in 1888, "...I often worked for (Ira) who owned and carried on a large farm...I never knew of a family who could accomplish more labor in the same length of time than this family of Mitchells." He was also a generous man as can be seen by his will. His "attachment" to his brothers is evident by the pictures of Ira's children in family albums owned today by descendants of his Ohio brothers. Mr. Riley was guilty of poetic excess in describing Ira and his wife as "traveling speedily" to the grave. Ira lived another thireen years and Jane for three years beyond that.

Ira and Jane sold the farm in 1884, buying 4 lots in Salem and moving into town. On 15 Jan 1891, aged 87 years 6 months 12 days, Ira died from a recurring attack of "La Grippe" after a 3-month illness. He was buried in the Methodist Church cemetery in Salem, IA.

Jane, whose widowed son, Ira R., continued to live with her after her husband's death, died on 17 Dec 1893, age 87 years, buried on 19 Dec in Salem Union Cemetery. She seems to have succumbed to "La Grippe" as well. Both she and Ira R. were sick for some days and had to hire help to bring in wood, do washing and housecleaning. Mrs. Rapelway and Mrs. Johnson alternated "seting up at night with Mother" between Dec. 4th and 17th. Messages were sent to relatives on Dec. 9th and Jane's grandson, Ira Walker, rode in to see her. On the day Jane died, Etta Brown came in to do kitchen work, and on the day of her funeral, Frank Louis was in charge of "drawing evergreens" to decorate her grave. Three carriages and teams were hired to take the mourners to the cemetery. On the 22nd, flowers were sent up from St. Louis.

Ira's will, made 30 Dec 1885, left Jane all his real property and household goods, and "for her maintenance and support" one-third of all his personal property, monies and credits. At her death, any real estate, personal property, monies and credits unused were to be divided between four of his children, i.e., Elizabeth Hess, Abigail E. Walker, Obed H. Mitchell, and John E. Mitchell.

Sons Ira R., Frank M., and Leonard M. Mitchell were left $5.00 each since Ira stated he had already made advances to each "equal to what would be a fair and equitable interest in my Estate." Having "at different times" advanced about $1,000 to daughter Elizabeth Hess, about $700 to daughter Abigail E. Walker, about $500 to son Obed H. Mitchell, and about $800 to son John E. Mitchell, Ira directed that the remainder of the estate (apart from previously made bequests) be divided among these four "in such proportion as will, with the advances above enumerated, make their shares equal in my estate."

The only grandchild mentioned in the will was Alice Hess, daughter of Lucy (Mitchell) Hess, deceased, to whom he left $500 and "the organ now in our home in Salem." Sons John E. "of Henry Co., IA" and Obed H. "of Springfield, MO" were appointed co-executors, but the offical appointment of executor went to John E. on 18 Mar 1891. A full list of heirs with ages and residences was listed, ten in number, including the three daughters of Ira's deceased son, Leonard.

Ira's probate file is voluminous. To shorten a long, long story, Ira, Jr., dissatisfied with the way his brother was handling their father's estate, let it be known that John E. had written him a letter stating that as a non-resident, he was no longer able to assume executorship responsibilities. (John E. had moved to St. Louis; he denied writing this letter later.) Joel Jones was appointed in his place. When the news reached John E., he fired off a long and furious letter to the Henry Co., IA Circuit Court in which he stated: "For three years Ira Mitchell Jr. opposed all efforts of his sisters coming and taking care of their fond mother whose kindness and gentle care she sadly needed...necessitating the hiring of female

help...throughout these three years Ira Mitchell Jr. lived from the table furnished by Mother and had his washing
& sewing done by this hired help...it would be just that
this three years of boarding and lodging should be collected from him sufficient to meet the small amount of
debts contracted by him for her maintenance after her
money was all used up, a large portion of which went in
sustaining him."

Judging from grocers' bills submitted to the estate,
dated during the last three months of Jane's life, John E.
had a good point. Jane's table was amply provisioned with
such items as salmon, oranges, lemons, grapes, oysters,
peaches, pears, tomatoes, green gages, cheese, and varied
sorts of meat as well as the usual staples. Ira, Jr. had
not only submitted a bill to the estate for $85.06 cover-
ing money he said he personally spent on his mother from
Oct 13 to Dec 16, 1893, he submitted a second bill amount-
ing to $531.50 for "personal services rendered in care of
his mother" from Jan. 17, 1891 (two days after his father
died) to Dec. 16, 1893, reckoned at 50¢ per day for a total of 1,063 days.

On the other hand, John E. claimed that there was no
need to appraise and sell "the old homestead of my beloved
parents...", that there was no indebtedness as claimed
against his father's estate since he had long since paid
all debts, etc. However, Ira's four Salem town lots (Nos.
1, 2, 3, 4 in Block 25) had been sold on 4 Dec 1893 to R. A.
Goar for $38.48, amount of back taxes due for 1892. Joel
Jones, the new administrator, redeemed the property by
refunding to the purchaser taxes paid for 1892 and 1893
plus penalty and interest. Two days later, the property
plus "a triangular strip of ground lying on west side of
and adjoining lot no. four" was appraised and evaluated at
the sum of $1,200.00. John E. also seems to have borrowed
money from the estate, finally mentioning "two unpaid
notes" which he agreed to turn over to his legal successor
upon due notice, but "...to meet them now...is an utter
impossibility but I hope to by spring." The amount of
these notes was $622.23 in excess of any distribution por-
tion due him. John E.'s non-residence (which he disclaim-
ed, stating that Salem was his permanent home, and St.
Louis only temporary) was a deciding factor against him.

This unhappy situation was finally settled on 12 Sep
1894 by the ruling of Judge W. D. Tisdale of the Henry Co.,

IA District Court who confirmed the appointment of Joel Jones. Several months later, Joel Jones made payments to Frank M. Mitchell of $5.00; Ella M. Kronskup (widow of Leonard Mitchell) of $5.00; and Ira Mitchell, Jr. of $5.00. Obed H. Mitchell received $377.71; Abigail Walker was paid $226.62. There are no records in the probate file to show that Elizabeth (Mitchell) Hess or John E. Mitchell received any money at the time of final settlement, nor that Ira, Jr. was paid for the two claims he had filed against the estate.

Children of Ira and Jane (Rhodes) Mitchell (except Sarah and Claudius who died young), first 2 born in Madison Co., OH, the rest in Miami Co., IN, were:

218. **Abigail E.** b Dec 1830   +
219. **Obed H.** b May 1833   +
220. **Ira R.** b 18 Oct 1835   +
221. **Lucy M.** bc 1838   +
222. **Elizabeth M.** b May 1840   +
223. **John Ensign** b 25 Aug 1842   +
224. **Francis M. (Frank)** b Aug 1845   +
225. **Leonard M.** bc 1848   +

143. **LYDIA MITCHELL**, daughter of Ensign, Sr. and Lucy (Hubbard) Mitchell, was born about 1805 in Tioga Co., PA. She married about 1824 (place unknown) Charles Rigdon, born about 1798 in (Lexington?), KY, son of Dr. John and Elizabeth (Lamb) Rigdon, who came to Mad River Twp., Champaign Co., OH about 1800. Lydia died 1 May 1879 in London, OH. Charles died 23 June 1885 (age 86y) in Indianapolis, IN at the home of his son-in-law J. F. Burt. Both are buried in Oak Hill Cemetery, Madison Co., OH.

Some confusion exists about Lydia's birthdate. Her tombstone says she died at age 72 or born in 1807 in direct conflict with the birth of her brother, Abizer, in that year. The 1850 census lists her age as 45 (bc 1805); the 1860 census says age 59 (bc 1801); the 1870 says age 68 (bc 1802). The same confusion occurs regarding dates of birth for Lydia's daughter, Miranda (May) who was age 10 in 1850, age 20 in 1860 but whose tombstone states she was age 37y at her death in 1887 (or born ca 1850). Lydia A.'s tombstone reads born 18 May 1852, died 28 June 1871 age 19y 1m 10d, clearly an impossibility since she appears in the 1850 census as age 2 and in the 1860 as age 13. Of the three census periods (1850 thru 1870), the 1850 is the

only census in which ages given agree with known birthdates of Lydia's two eldest daughters, so it becomes the
most acceptable record of the entire family's ages. (Too
often, tombstones are erected some years after a death
and thence errors are made in dates and ages given.)

No such confusion exists in census records concerning
Lydia's place of birth. She firmly states PA in 3 succes-
sive census records even though she was between 4 and 5
years old when her parents left there (1809) and took the
Ohio River route to Cicinnatti, living first in Clermont
Co. (now Brown) until they moved to Champaign Co., OH in
1815. Lydia and Charles lived there for a few years after
marriage, but moved to Deer Creek Twp., Madison Co., OH
by 1830, probably living in the western half of the township which became Somerford Twp. in that year. They remained there, evidently running a successful farm, owning
$22,260 worth of real estate and $2,500 of personal property in 1870 (census). Shortly after 1870, they retired
and moved into the nearby town of London. Children of
Charles and Lydia (Mitchell) RIGDON, all born in Champaign
or Madison Cos., OH, were:

226. **Julia Ann** b 26 Sep 1825   +
227. **Emeline** b 22 Jan 1828   +
228. **Margaret A.** bc 1833 m Daniel D. Davison lvg Spring-
     field, OH as late as 1904.
229. **Sarah Jane (Jennie)** bc 1835 d 1903/4 m J. Francis
     Burt who d Mar 1900; to Indianapolis 1885; no ch.
230. **Miranda (May)** bc 1840 d 20 June 1887 m 23 Apr 1883
     Dr. F.M. George; in IN 1885; bur Oak Hill Cemetery.
231. **Lydia Adaline (Addie)** bc 1848 d 28 June 1871 bur
     Oak Hill Cemetery.

144. **ABIZER MITCHELL**, son of Ensign, Sr. and Lucy (Hubbard) Mitchell, was born 27 Mar 1807 in Tioga Co., PA. At
the age of two, his parents left PA, traveling by the Ohio
River route to Cincinnati, then to Clermont Co. (now
Brown), OH where they lived until 1815. In that year,
Abizer moved with his parents to Champaign Co., OH and
then about 1826 to adjoining Madison Co. where his father
settled on a 600 acre farm just south of the town of Rosedale. On 3 Nov 1831 in Champaign Co., Abizer married Margaret Ann Stanley, born 6 Apr 1809 (1850 census says NC).

A year before his marriage Abizer and Newman, his
younger brother, purchased 450 acres from their father

(225 each). In 1845 Abizer bought 65 more acres from Thomas Morris. Between that date and 1863 he dealt in only a few minor purchases of land and one small sale. In 1863 he sold his farm of 301½ acres to his son, Ira, and the remaining 8 plus acres to John H. Burnham. Abizer is the only one of his father's children who is not mentioned in his father's will dated 1833. Perhaps the 225 acres he "bought" from his father was actually a gift with no real money exchanging hands.

At the reunion of the Mitchell brothers in Edgar Co., IL in 1877 at the home of the eldest brother, Ensign, Jr., Mr. A. J. Riley of the Paris, IL "Gazette" who covered the event, described Abizer as having "...the peculiarity of being quiet and retired, yet sensitive...very devoted to religion...strong in faith and good works; having recently been bereaved of the companion of his youth, he feels that heaven has much greater attractions for him than this world...he is, by occupation, a farmer, by profession a Methodist, and politically, a republican."

Abizer's wife, Margaret Ann, had died the year before this reunion on 16 Sep 1876. In 1880 Abizer was living in Pike Twp. with his married granddaughter, Ida (Mitchell) McClintock, next to the residence of Abizer's son, Ira. Abizer's wish to "give up his stewardship and rest with Jesus" was granted on 7 Feb 1891. He is buried beside his wife in Maple Grove Cemetery, Mechanicsburg, OH. Children of Abizer and Margaret Ann (Stanley) Mitchell, all born in Madison Co., OH, were:

   232. **Roxanna Mary** bc 1833 d bef 1840.
   233. **Ira** b 26 Sep 1835   +
   234. **Jane** bc 1837   *

145. **NEWMAN MITCHELL,** son of Ensign, Sr. and Lucy (Hubbard) Mitchell, was born 29 Apr 1811 "on the banks of the Ohio River, forty miles above Cincinnati." (In river terms, a location "above" another is in the direction from which the river flows, so 40 miles "above" Cinncinati would be east, or in the approximate area of White Oak Creek where it flows into the Ohio in Clermont [now Brown] Co., OH.)

On 1 Jan 1837 in Madison Co., OH, Newman was married (by William Guy, J.P.) to Cassandra "Cassie" Bradley, born in Madison Co. on 17 Mar 1818, daughter of David and Nancy A. (Lawson) Bradley, both of Virginia. Newman died near Rosedale in Madison Co. on 12 Jan 1884. Cassandra died there on 24 Feb 1885. Both are buried in the Guy Cemetery on the family farm near Rosedale.

In 1815 Newman had moved with his parents from Clermont Co. to a farm about four and a half miles south of Mechanicsburg in Champaign Co., OH. About 1826 the family moved to another farm of about 600 acres south of Rosedale in adjoining Madison Co. In 1830 Newman and his brother, Abizer, bought 450 acres from their father. Newman's half of the property is recorded by deed dated 1 Jan of that year between himself and James Galloway, Jr. A memorandum written by Newman's father in 1832 promised to procure for Newman "from James Galloway a general warranty deed of conveyance of one hundred acres of land off the Northwest part of Survey 7402 upon which I now live... as soon as the said James Galloway makes me a like deed for the whole of said tract." At the time that land was paid for, Newman was to have one-third of the livestock in his father's possession. He was also bequeathed the remainder of his father's property in his father's will of 1833.

Newman continued to buy property, paying taxes in 1852 on 477 acres of Madison Co. land. In 1853 he bought the "Tom Morris farm" near Tradersville in Somerford Twp. (Madison Co.) and moved to that location. Between that date and 1865 (when he bought the Nathaniel Griffin farm), he added more land to his holdings; after the Civil War, he purchased land in conjunction with his son, Charles E., as an equal partner. By 1883 Newman owned over 2,000 acres of "improved" farm land.

According to Beers' "History of Madison Co., OH," "Uncle" Newman was "diligent, industrious and honest... his word always passed at par value...," his money made in "legitimate enterprises," and never "indulging in any 'wild cat' speculations." He "dealt in cattle and other live stock...," farmed "extensively," employing hired help to quite an extent, and was a "good husband...father...neighbor...a peaceable and law-abiding citizen, and a good example for young and old alike."

A. J. Riley of the Paris, IL "Gazette" who reported on the reunion of the five Mitchell brothers in 1877 at the home of the eldest brother, Ensign, Jr., gives us a more humorous, even a slightly tongue-in-cheek view of Newman. Mr. Riley describes him as "...peculiar in many things; one is, that he has no neighbors, having bought them all

out for miles around him, and is only desirous for what
land now joins him. Like Jacob of old, he has herds of
cattle and herds of sheep, and not being a Jew, he also has
on his 'little' farm, a few hundred head of hogs, all of
which he regards himself only as steward for the Master,
and doubtless needs much grace to help in the discharge of
his duty to God and man. He is the father of ten children,
only four of whom are left to cheer the heart of their father and mother, and enjoy the good things of this life
gathered by their industry and economy. Being a Methodist
and of rather an excitable temperament, I should guess
him a little boisterous when his soul is filled with heavenly fire."

It goes without saying that Newman became a prosper-
ous farmer. That he engaged farm hands and a domestic as
well to help Cassandra in the house can be told by the
census records. From one hired hand in 1850, he jumped to
five in 1860 (including a 14 year old black boy by the
sole name of "Nigger Bill") plus a housegirl. In 1870 he
had three hired hands and a domestic, his property evaluation in that year $87,000 and personal property $12,000.
By 1880 he was down to just one full-time hired man, having no doubt turned over the operation of his farm to his
son, Charles E.

Newman made his will on 9 Oct 1882 while he had the
"strength and capacity so to do..." He left all of his
property, both real and personal, to his wife, Cassandra,
after empowering his executor, Dr. William Morrow Beach,
to "erect a family monument over my grave with the names
of my deceased children carved thereon, which is not to
cost more than one thousand dollars."

Cassandra wrote her will on 31 Dec 1884, also appoint-
ing Dr. William Morrow Beach as executor. Unlike Newman
who kept his will short and simple, Cassandra's will runs
on for many pages as she specifically described the enormous amount of real estate that she left to her children,
Charles E. Mitchell, Lydia Jane Bales, and Electa Creamer, and to her grandchildren, Florence Guy and Geneva Kennedy, daughters of her deceased daughter, Abigail.

Although well endowed with the material things of
life, Newman and Cassandra were not so lucky with the
things of life that money can not buy. Of the ten children
Cassandra bore, only five lived to adulthood, one of that
five dying at age 24. All are buried with their parents in

Guy Cemetery. Of the remaining four, only one lived to extreme old age, the other three dying at ages 37, 45, and 53. Children of Newman and Cassandra (Bradley) Mitchell, all born in Madison Co., OH (asterisk indicates date on gravestone when it varies from other records) were:

    235. Abigail 21 May 1838   +
    236. Lydia Jane (Jennie) b 16 Jan 1840   +
    237. Melissa b 22 Mar 1841 d 7 Jan 1865
    238. Julia Ann b 20 Aug 1842 d 10*/29 Feb 1854
    239. Charles E. 9 May 1845   +
    240. Isabel b 19 May 1847 d 1 Feb 1854
    241. (Male) b 1 Apr 1849 d 20*/23 Jul 1849
    242. Lucinda Virginia b 28 Dec 1850 d 20/22* Nov 1851
    243. Nancy Ellen b 25 Feb 1854 d 2 Oct 1863
    244. Electa (Lettie) b 25 Nov 1855   +

146. JOSEPH MITCHELL (JR.), son of (Rev.) Joseph and Zipporah (Brainard) Mitchell, waɔ the fourth consecutive male in this line to bear that given name, it also being his Mitchell grandfather and great-grandfather's name. Before them it was the given name of his Baldwin 4-times great-grandfather through the maternal lineage of his great-great-grandmother, Sarah (Catlin) Mitchell.

Joseph, Jr. was born 9 Aug 1790, probably not in Champlain, Essex Co., NY (per "The Bigelow Family of America," by G. H. Howe, 1890), but in Whitehall Twp., Washington Co., NY located at the southern tip of Lake Champlain. His father is listed there in the 1790 Census with 1 male under age 10 and living next door to Lydia Hurlbut (wife of Caleb, Jr.), his father's eldest sister. Joseph, Jr. married 18 May 1813 in Madison Co., OH 18 May 1813 to Irene Bigelow, born 2 Sep 1791 in Chesterfield, NH, daughter of Russell and Lucy (Sangor) Bigelow.

The Bigelows had moved to Pittsford, VT by 1796, then in 1800 to Franklin, VT (where Russell Bigelow is called "probably" the first Methodist there), and in 1802 to "St. Armands," Canada. At the beginning of the 1800's, "great inducements were made to the people of the States to settle in Canada East. Many people in VT went over the line and settled until 1812 when the difficulties between the United States and Great Britain terminated in war. These people, being Revolutionary soldiers or descendants of Revolutionary soldiers, resolved to leave the domain of George III." (Beers, "History of Union Co., OH") On

20 Sep 1812, Russell Bigelow and his family were among those who left, arriving after 6 weeks in Worthington, OH, and settling in the Darby Plains area of Madison Co., OH by 1813. The Mitchells and the Bigelows had much in common - their New England ancestry and their professed religion. Irene's brother, Rev. Russell Bigelow, Jr., was a very prominent, popular and eloquent minister of the Methodist Episcopal church.

After marriage, Joseph and Irene lived in Pike Twp., Madison Co. In 1819, his father sold him 100 acres of his own farm, doing the same for his brothers, Newman and William, their lands all bordering each others. They remained there until 1832 when Joseph and Irene, Joseph, Sr. and son, Abner, moved to Tazewell Co., IL. On 14 June 1832, Joseph and Irene sold their 100 acres in Madison Co., OH to his brother, Newman; both appeared personally at Pekin before J. C. Morgan, Clerk, who used his private seal on the document, there being "no official Seal yet provided..." (Bk 7:492 Madison Co., OH Deeds).

Joseph and Irene had already buried two children in Madison Co., OH. In Tazewell Co., IL between their arrival in 1832 and 1844, they buried 5 more children. On 16 Jan 1845, Irene died, probably in Tazewell Co. although Joseph was in McLean Co., IL before May 1847. (Joseph and Irene were among the original members of the Morton Methodist Episcopal church in Morton Twp., Tazewell Co., IL.)

By 1860 Joseph was living in Whitehall Twp., Greene Co., IL with his son, Russell, and family, and his unmarried son, John F. Joseph died "in Illinois," probably at the home of his son where he was residing in 1860. Children of Joseph, Jr. and Irene (Bigelow) Mitchell, first 8 born in Madison Co., OH, last two in Tazewell Co., IL, were:

245. **Irene** b 22 Feb 1814 d 25 Jul 1837 age 23y.
246. **Joseph K.** b 28 Sep 1815 d 15 Mar 1835 age 20y.
247. **Russell Bigelow** b 19 Dec 1817   +
248. **Benjamin Bigelow** b 17 Feb 1820 d 9 Mar 1844 age 24y.
249. **Lucy** b 20 Apr 1823 d 13 Oct 1823 age 5m 23d.
250. **Thankful** b 24 Dec 1824 d 3 Dec 1825 age 11½m.
251. **Electa V.** b 2 Oct 1826 d 20 Nov 1855 age 29y; m 9 Oct 1851 Andrew M. Hill.
252. **Abigail A.** b 13 May 1829 d 4 Oct 1832 age 3y 4m 21d.
253. **John Fuller** b 30 Jul 1832   +
254. **Joseph** b 3 June 1834 d 5 Sep 1834 age 3m 2d.

147. **NEWMAN MITCHELL**, son of (Rev.) Joseph and Zipporah (Brainard) Mitchell, was born between 1790-1794 (census records), probably in New York, either Washington or Saratoga Co. (His father, a resident of Galway, Saratoga Co. in 1793, was admitted "on trial" as an itinerant Methodist minister in 1794, riding the Cambridge Circuit which included Washington Co., NY in that year.) This Newman is not to be confused with his cousin, Newman, son of Ensign Mitchell, Sr., and nearly 20 years junior to the above Newman, son of Rev. Joseph Mitchell.

Newman came to Madison Co., OH about 1812 with his parents and family. There on 10 May 1815 he married Nancy Mann, the ceremony performed by his father. Nancy, born about 1796 in VT, was probably the daughter of Samuel and Sarah ( ) Mann (see further). In 1819, Newman's father sold him 100 acres of his farm as he also did to Newman's brothers, Joseph, Jr. and William. Since all of this land came from the property Joseph, Sr. had purchased in 1817 and 1818, all four farms adjoined as did the land he sold in 1819 to Andrew and Elizabeth Alden, possibly his son-in-law and daughter. The probability of this relationship is strengthened by the fact that Newman was administrator with Elizabeth Alden in 1827 on Andrew Alden's estate.

When Newman's father and brothers, Joseph, Jr. and Abner, decided to move to Tazewell Co., IL in 1832, Newman elected to remain in Madison Co. On 14 June 1832 he bought Joseph, Jr.'s 100 acres for $300.00. Later that year, he and Nancy sold half of this property to John Runyan for $275.00, making a tidy $125.00 profit.

Samuel and Sarah Mann, thought to be Nancy's parents, came to Madison Co., OH "about 1815" from Vermont. In the 1820 Madison Co., OH census, they lived in Pike Twp., "next-door" to Newman and Nancy. In the 1840 census, the Newman Mitchell household contained a male who was the age of Samuel, but no corresponding female. Sarah Mann had apparently died between 1830 and 1840. Samuel died on 28 Aug 1840, age 80 years 11 months 15 days. (His broken stone lies in the same cemetery where Newman's uncle, Ensign Mitchell, Sr. and his wife lie buried.) On 19 Sep 1840, Samuel D. Mann, Lorenzo D. Mann and Samantha his wife, Benjamin W. Mann and Jane (nee Guy) his wife, and Azro L. Mann and Mary his wife, sold for $2,250.00 to Newman Mitchell, John A. Mann, Orin F. Mann, and Rebecca P. Mann, all their "title, interest, estate" in Survey #6877 containing 235 acres. This property lay next to Survey #7230 where Newman and Nancy lived.

Not long after 1840 Newman and Nancy moved over to adjacent Goshen Twp., Champaign Co., OH where Newman died in 1844. On 7 June 1844 Benjamin Taylor, Erastus Mitchell, O. F. Mann and Cyrus Taylor of Champaign Co., OH signed a bond as joint administrators of Newman's estate. Benjamin Taylor was Newman's son-in-law; Cyrus Taylor was Benjamin's father; Erastus Mitchell was Newman's son, and Orin F. Mann was probably his wife's brother.

Newman's property in Survey #7230, Madison Co., was sold on 16 Jan 1846, "excepting the present Grave Yard" of one-quarter of an acre. Erastus W. Mitchell and Benjamin Taylor as administrators of Newman's estate, and Nancy Mitchell, Emaline Taylor, Leonard Mitchell and Seth Mitchell as respondents, sold the property to Newman Mitchell of Madison Co. (son of Ensign, Sr. and cousin to the above Newman, deceased in 1844) for $2,401.50 (Madison Co. Deeds, Bk 17:58/59). On 6 Oct 1847, Newman's property in Survey 6877 lying in Madison and Champaign Co. which he had purchased from the Manns in conjunction with other Manns in 1840 was sold to Jacob R. Ware - 264 acres "more or less" for $620.00. In this deed (Bk 21:266/67) "Nancy Mitchell, Benjamin Taylor and Sarah Emeline Taylor his wife, Erastus W. Mitchell and Clarissa Mitchel his wife and Leonard Mitchell" are called "widow and heirs of Newman Mitchel deceased." Seth W.'s name is omitted from this deed, but in a deed recorded in 1852, Seth W. as grantor "sells" the same amount of acreage to J. R. Ware (Bk 21:475). Possibly Mr. Ware wished to sell the property and needed Seth W. to legally relinquish claim to it.

As a point of interest, a good many years prior to the Civil War (1820's-1830's) there was a general influx of Quakers from slaveholding Southern states into non-slave states. The area around Brown Co., OH had a large Quaker settlement and many blacks escaping slavery crossed the Ohio at this point, receiving aid from the Quakers who passed them via the "underground railway" into Canada. As early as 1840 slaves came through Mechanicsburg in Champaign Co. on their way north and there were men there who helped them. In Beers' "History of Champaign Co., OH (published 1881), he says "East of Mechanicsburg three or four miles, were men who heard the story of the poor blacks with compassion." Among the men named was Newman

Mitchell "who died many years ago." Since Newman, son of Ensign, Sr., was still living in 1881, this can be no other than the above Newman, son of Joseph.

There had always been a law against harboring slaves, but the Fugitive Slave Act of 1850 made it a Federal offense for a free man to do so. This act failed because it roused the anger of many Northerners, turning them into Abolitionists. Strong Methodists like the Mitchells already despised slavery as a mortal sin. The fact that Newman Mitchell, son of Ensign, Sr., had a young black boy working for him in 1860 shows <u>his</u> involvement in the anti-slavery movement; and Azro L. Mann, probably Nancy's brother, and one of the Taylors were accused with others of interferring with and preventing the capture of just such a fugitive slave working for a farmer near Mechanicsburg; they spent a brief time in jail until the situation was resolved. (Ref: "Historical Collections of Ohio," Vol. I, Henry Howe, pp 384-386.)

Children of Newman and Nancy (Mann) Mitchell, all born in Madison Co., OH, were:

- **255. Erastus W.** bc 1817/1818   +
- **256. Sarah Emeline** b 1820   +
- **257. Leonard** bc 1827
- **258. Seth W.** bc 1832

148. **WILLIAM MITCHELL**, son of (Rev.) Joseph and Zipporah (Brainard) Mitchell, was born about 1794-1804 (1820 census, age 16 to 26) in NY or VT, his father riding the Methodist Episcopal church circuit in both states during this time. William married before 1820 to Naomi James, daughter of Obediah James of VT who settled in Union Co., OH in 1814 (Union Twp., Union Co. was part of Pike Twp., Madison Co. before Union Co. was formed in 1820). By 1820 Obediah James and his family were living on property adjacent to William and Naomi.

William bought 100 acres of his father's land on 7 Apr 1820 for $200.00. Four days later his father bought it back from William for $1,000, provided William give him one-half the produce of the land; should his father die, the same was to go to William's mother, Zipporah. Inexplicably, in 1824 William and "Naoma his wife" sold this identical piece of land to his father again for $200. William and Naomi then "removed to the Western Reserve." A census search was begun for William and Naomi, but it was given up as impractical as there are too many by the name of William Mitchell in the 1830 to 1850 census.

The only known child of William and Naomi (James) Mitchell (from the 1820 Madison Co., OH census) was:

259. **Daughter** b betw 1810 & 1820

149. **ABNER MITCHELL,** son of (Rev.) Joseph and Zipporah (Brainard) Mitchell, was born about 1807-1808 in New York (census records). He appears in his father's household in Pike Twp., Madison Co., OH in both the 1820 and 1830 census. His first wife is named as Louisa M. on Tazewell Co., IL deeds where Abner moved before 1833 with his father and brother, Joseph, Jr. Louisa's maiden name is unknown but per the 1840 Tazewell Co., IL census, she was born between 1810-1820, apparently marrying Abner just after the 1830 census as their first child was born about 1830 in OH.

On 11 June 1833 Joseph, Sr. sold "Abner Mitchell his son" the north half of his 80 acre farm in Section 35, Town 25 in Tazewell Co., IL, deed witnessed by Orson Craig and Joseph Mark (Bk 5:192). In 1834 Joseph, Sr., Abner and Louisa M. "his wife" sold several lots in the town of Pekin to Elijah S. and David Mark, and another lot in that town to four Roberts men named as John Montgomery, Ambrose Bryant, Darius Phillips and Walter Basset. These two sales a bit more than equalled the amount Abner paid later that year for 80 acres located in Section 8, Town 25. In 1836 Abner and Louisa sold his 40 acres in Section 35, his father already having sold the adjoining 40 acres the year before. James B. Campbell bought the entire 80 acres for the impressive sum of $1,800. Probably Joseph, Sr. moved in with Abner after selling his land in 1835 as he was living with Abner at the time of the 1840 census (2 males under 5, 1 male 5 to 10, 1 male 10 to 15, 1 male 30 to 40, 1 male 70 to 80, 1 female 20 to 30).

After the death of his father at Abner's home in 1844, he moved to Mercer Co., IL. In 1847 he wrote a note in regard to his father's estate, dated at Millersburg, Mercer Co. Shortly after the birth of their last child, Rebecca (born about 1846), Louisa died, probably either in Mercer or adjoining Rock Island Co. where Abner had moved before 1850. He married second there on 10 Aug 1850 to Cynthia Sayre (Rock Island Co., IL Mar. Records #633).

Cynthia Sayre was born about 1809 in Ohio, probably in that part of Champaign Co. becoming Logan in 1818, where

where her parents, John and Jane (Valentine) Sayre, settled. Four years after her father died (1836), Cynthia's brother, Alanson Sayre, with his wife and other married brothers and sisters, brought Cynthia and her mother to Rock Island Co., IL. She was about age 41 when she became Abner's wife and step-mother of his 5 children. In 1850 Abner and Cynthia lived next-door to her brother, Alanson, and her sister, Emily (Mrs. John M. Wilson). Abner's son, George, was double-counted in the census that year, appearing with Abner as well as in the household of his step-uncle, Alonzo C. Sayre. Abner and Cynthia do not appear in the 1860 Rock Island Co., IL census. ("Portrait & Biographical Album of Rock Island Co., IL," 1885, Chapman Bros., pp573/4; 1850 Census, pp261, 263.)

According to Beers' "History of Madison Co., OH," Abner served in the Civil War, despite the fact he was in his early 50's at the time. The Rock Island County War Record does list an Abner Mitchell, enlisted 23 Sep 1861 as a private in Co. H, 45th I.V.I., transferred to the Invalid Corp 15 Sep 1863. Also listed is a William Mitchell who enlisted 23 Jul 1861 as a private in Co. D., 12th I.V.I., mustered out 10 Jul 1865, and an R. B. Mitchell, enlisted 10 June 1861, deserted 16 days later. There is no file on R. B. Mitchell in the National Archives, but there are on Abner and William Mitchell, both widow's pension applications. Data in Abner Mitchell's file does not agree with known facts on Abner, son of Joseph; even though a copy of his marriage license states he was born in New York and that his father's name was Joseph, it also gives his mother's name as Elizabeth, his first wife as Violet Jones whom he married in Springfield, IL, and his second wife (and widow) as Margaret Sayer, widow of Thomas and daughter of John and Ann Heslap, whom Abner married 17 Apr 1875 in New Diggings, Lafayette Co., WI where he died 23 Dec 1877. Data in the file of William Mitchell states that he died in 1868 or 1869 in Cheyenne, WY, that his first wife was Margaret Harrington by whom he had several children, all dead, and Margaret dying about a year before William married second 9 May 1861 in Rock Island Co., IL to Mary Boyle or Boyd, daughter of James, by whom William had no children. It is unlikely that Abner Mitchell of the above record was this Abner or that William was this Abner's eldest son. Other Mitchells lived in Rock Island Co., some of them from NY per a county history.

Children of Abner and Louisa M. (   ) Mitchell (no known children by his 2nd marriage), 1st born in OH, the rest in IL, were:

260. **William** bc 1830
261. **Alanson** bc 1833
262. **Joseph** bc 1835
263. **George** bc 1838
264. **Rebecca** bc 1846

156. **LEVI MITCHELL**, son of Consider and Esther (Rawson) Mitchell, was born 27 Mar 1801 near the village of Clinton in Kirkland Twp., Oneida Co., NY. He died there 17 Feb 1881 and is buried in Clinton's Old Burying Ground with his first and second wives in the family plot which is graced by a large, four-sided stone monument that he himself had erected before his death.

Levi was married three times. He married first about 1824 Britannia Gould, mother of his first three children. She died 23 Mar 1842, age 37 years. Levi married second about 1843 to Maryette ____, mother of his fourth child. Maryette had a daughter, Elizabeth, born about 1840, from a previous marriage (she is called Elizabeth M. Miller in Consider G. Mitchell's will). Maryette died 10 Mar 1854, age 38 years. Levi's third wife was also a widow. She was Mrs. Lucinda (   ) Sumner, born about 1815, died 5 June 1886, age 71 years, interred at Stockbridge, NY, probably beside her first husband. She had two children, Eliza J. "Jennie" and Charles F. Sumner. Lucinda's will left all to her daughter, Eliza J., executrix, with no other stipulations (Bk 38:570, Box 167, Oneida Co., NY Probate).

Levi appears in Kirkland Twp., Oneida Co., NY census records from 1830 through 1880. In 1860, he calls himself a "gentleman farmer," owned real estate valued at $2,700 and personal property of $2,000. In his will, Levi left to Lucinda, his third wife, "furniture enough to furnish one room and $175.00 for life semi-annually." To his son, Consider G., named executor, he left one-third of the balance, another third to his daughter, Celestia A. Bailey, and the remaining third divided between his granddaughters, Mary E. and Alice B. Hanchett (Bk 31:265).

The "Clinton Courier" carried his obituary, stating that "After a painful illness of about two weeks originating in cholera morbus and followed by apoplexy, our estimable neighbor and venerable fellow citizen...ceased to live; although he had recorded up the full measure of four score years his previous good health had seemed to promise his many friends a much longer stay with them. Mr. Mitchell was one of the few aged citizens (if not the last) who had spent a whole life in the Town that gave him birth...born...about two miles east of Clinton Village, beginning life when the Country was new, and helped clear away the forest...A person of naturally strong constitution and robust health he had seldom known a sick day until recent years when a rheumatic attack resulted in compelling him to resort to the use of a cane to support his large sized frame and to assist him in getting about; except a serious attack of kidney trouble about a year ago, his physical and mental faculties have been remarkably preserved, which may perhaps be credited in part to his uniformly temperate and frugal habits...previous to his last illness he was as capable of attending to any matters of financial interest, as in his palmiest days...many... will miss his friendly ways...Mr. Mitchell's religious faith embraced the doctrine of universal salvation; his political creed, democracy. His funeral was largely attended from his late residence on Fountain St..."

Children of Levi Mitchell, all born in Kirkland Twp., Oneida Co., NY (first 3 by first marriage, last by second marriage), were:

265. **Mary Jane** bc 1825 d 26 Sep 1846 age 21y m Charles S. Anderson; she and her son, Levi Mitchell Anderson, who d 6 Sep 1850 age 4y, are bur in family plot in Clinton, NY.

266. _____ (Daughter) b bef 1830 m _____ Hanchett; 2 children known, Mary E. & Alice B. Hanchett.

267. **Consider Gould** b 5 May 1830   +

268. **Celestia A.** bc 1844 m William Bailey; of New Cambridge, MA in 1881.

SIXTH GENERATION

The children of this generation were called upon to endure one of the most desperate times in this country's history - Civil War. The shelling of Fort Sumter in 1861 had an emotional impact on the country that has since been equalled only by the bombing of Pearl Harbor some 80 years later. Both in the North and the South, volunteer enlistments ran at such a high level, imposed recruiting was unnecessary. The war touched every life - up to, during, and beyond its duration. The men who survived it often returned sick in body and soul to their anxious parents, sisters, wives or sweethearts who waited at home.

The real cause of the war between the industrial North and the agricultural South was rooted in economic issues such as the quarrel between high tariffs versus low. Until the Missouri Compromise of 1850, North and South vied eagerly over new states as they were formed, each desirous of more senators to share their particular economic view.

Slavery, on the other hand, was the emotional issue of the war. Most Northern farmers knew little about the tariff issue, but they cared very much when propagandists told them that Southerners would be moving North, buying large tracts of farm land, and running them with "free" (slave) labor in direct competition with the Northern farmer who had to hire his workhands. These stories were the result of the Dred Scott decision which defined a slave as property, giving the slaveowner the right to move his property anywhere he wished. Prior to then, a slaveowner could move anywhere in the country, but he could not bring his slaves into "free" states. When these propagandists painted graphic pictures of blacks walking side by side on the streets with Northern white women, the attitude of the Northern farmer became socially as well as economically hardened toward the South.

Lincoln was not an abolitionist as the South claimed. In November 1856, Mary Lincoln wrote her sister that "In principle he is far from it...all he desires is that slavery shall not be extended, let it remain where it is." Lincoln and his wife believed in "gradual emancipation with compensation to slaveowners." ("Mary Lincoln," by Ruth Painter Randall, pp149-50)

But the South believed its own propaganda, just as the North believed "Uncle Tom's Cabin" was a true picture of Southern slavery. Lincoln's purpose in declaring war was preservation of the Union, not the freeing of slaves. The Emancipation Proclamation, delivered 1 Jan 1863, was a master political stroke. Headlines in England as well as America screamed "Lincoln Frees Slaves." With an abolitionist majority in Parliament, England reversed its decision to aid the South and declared its neutrality. In reality, the Emancipation Proclamation "freed" only those slaves in the Confederate States over whom Lincoln had no control; it did nothing for those in the five strategically important Union slave states of Missouri, Kentucky, Tennessee, West Virginia, and Maryland.

Although only the Union side of the Civil War is dealt with here, it must be understood that both the Northern and Southern soldier suffered like hardships. Both had more to fear than the dangers of battle. They also fought fleas, lice, dirt, cold, heat, bad food, inadequate clothing, ague (malaria), measles, pneumonia, small pox, diarrhea, tetanus, and gangrene. Doctors of the day had never heard of germs. They used unsanitary instruments on unsanitary operating tables, dressing wounds with clean but unsanitary bandages. Even a minor wound could prove fatal. For every man who died in battle, four others died of illness. At the end of the war, figures were compiled that showed at least 57,265 men had died from diarrhea alone, as compared with 44,238 who had died in battle or from battle sustained wounds.

The Civil War was not inevitable. Economic quarrels and the question of slavery could have been peaceably resolved, but the smoldering spark of distrust between Northerner and Southerner was steadily fanned into flames by propagandists on both sides until this nation was plunged into one of its most tragic wars.

For the most part, the Yankee soldier came from the common walks of life - farmers, teachers, shopkeepers, mill workers and the like. To be sure, there were deserters and cowards, but the majority stood their ground with courage, fighting under impossible conditions. They weren't afraid of death although they didn't exactly relish the idea either. As one young soldier wrote, "The difference between dyeing today and tomorrow is not much, but we all prefer tomorrow."

****

172. **OLIVER M. MITCHELL**, son of Jotham and Mary (   ) Mitchell, was born about 1803 in Oneida Co., NY. He married first Eliza Ann ____ by or before 1830. She was born about 1799 and died 16 June 1840, age 41. She was mother of Oliver's first four children. Oliver's second wife whom he married between 1840-1846 was Eunice ____, born about 1827 in NY, by whom he had two more children.

On 23 Feb 1835, Oliver M. and Eliza A. "his wife" of Steuben, and Samuel D. Booth and Polly "his wife" from the Town of Trenton, together with Jotham Mitchell (also of Steuben), sold Lot #154 in Steuben to James Owens, Jr., receiving $1,332.00 for this 64 acre tract, excepting the reserve of 20 square feet designated as a burying ground. (Bk 69:214/215 Oneida Co., NY Deeds) This transaction took place very shortly before Jotham's second marriage to the widow Nancy (Post) Brainerd. The land sold may have been inherited property from some family member, possibly Jotham's father, Moses Mitchell, who died in Oneida Co. before 1820.

Oliver M. lived his entire life in Oneida Co., NY; he was a farmer, value of his real estate in 1850 given as $2,300.00. He died there on 24 Feb 1877, age 74 years. Both he and his first wife are buried in the local cemetery in Holland Patent, NY. Papers in his probate file call him of Trenton, NY, and names his wife, Eunice, his children, and his grandson, Adolph E. Mitchell, son of his deceased son, Horace. Thomas is not mentioned although he was in his father's household in the 1850 census. Children of Oliver M. Mitchell (first 4 by 1st marriage, last 2 by 2nd marriage), all born in Oneida Co., NY, were:

269. **Orson** bc 1830
270. **Thomas** bc 1833
271. **Horace** bc 1836 d bef 1877.
272. **Harrison** bc 1840
273. **Mary E.** bc 1846 m bef 1877 ____ Drake.
274. **Orville O.** b aft 1850

177. PORTER MITCHELL, son of Anson and Melinda (Hutchinson) Mitchell, is named in his father's will as one of the seven of his ten surviving children to whom he left no legacy. Porter's date and place of birth are unknown; his father's residence at the time of his birth may have been NH or MA. He was named after his father's brother who died at age 2 years. Porter may have been the maiden name of his father's maternal grandmother, Judith ( ) Wise.

In 1868 Porter submitted an account against his father's estate totalling $286.41 for services rendered during his father's "sickness" and for money paid out by Porter on his father's behalf. He was paid $100.00 by the estate on 13 Jan 1869.

Porter married (int.) 17 Mar 1844 at Deerfield, MA to Persis Field, born 24 Oct 1821, daughter of Chester and Sophia ( ) Field. He died 14 Jan 1870 at Greenfield, MA, his widow taking administration of his estate with D. O. Fisk of Shelburne, MA.

From the inventory of his estate, we learn that Porter was a tinsmith, leaving in his shop such items as a tinner's forge, roof tin, English iron, galvanized iron, copper, sheet lead and pipe, and tin tea kettle lids. He owned a horse, a buggy, several sleighs, an express wagon, and a bass drum which leads one to conclude that he traveled to various towns to sell his wares, using the bass drum to literally "drum up" the attention of customers.

Porter's house contained a northwest, a southwest, and a "kitchen" bedroom. Persis owned a sewing machine, perhaps earning extra household money as a seamstress. Furnishings were minimal with few frills, although they did own two clocks, a whatnot, a looking glass, five "comfortables" (comforters), and a parcel of "old" books that were later sold for $59.00.

Porter owned no real estate. His personal estate was appraised at $1,015.47 which was sold at public auction on 2 Aug 1870. The cash derived from the sale was not sufficient to pay his debts. In 1871, Edward E. Lyman and Lucius Nims were appointed commissioners to examine the claims of creditors, the estate being deficient by nearly $800.00, after Persis, who still had two minor children, was granted a widow's allowance of $212.95. Among debts paid was $1.00 for a "tolling bell" which was rung on the day of Porter's funeral. (File #3257, Franklin Co., MA Probate Records)

Children of Porter and Persis (Field) Mitchell, probably all born in Greenfield, MA (death of first child and
birth of second in Greenfield V/R to 1850) were:

275. **Chester G. F.** b Apr 1845 d 6 Aug 1846 age 1y 4m.
276. **Jennie** b 8 Nov 1848 m bef 1870 _____ (Barlis?)
277. **Edward** b aft 1850
278. **Mary** b aft 1850
279. **Cora** b aft 1850

180. **GILBERT F. MITCHELL**, son of Anson & Melinda (Hutchinson) Mitchell, was born about 1828 in MA (census). He
married (int) 13 Oct 1849 Margrett Christie of Heath, MA;
she was born about 1830. In 1850 Gilbert F. and Margrett
lived next door to Gilbert's parents, his occupation giv-
en as "firrer" (Greenfield, Franklin Co., MA census).

Of his father's ten surviving children, Gilbert F.
was one of the seven to be specifically excluded in his
father's 1867 will from receiving a legacy. He may have
lived for a time in Winchester, NH; his father left land
there to Gilbert's brother, Asa H., which was deeded by
Gilbert to his father on 28 Aug 1867.

The Grantor Index of Hampshire Co., MA (1787-1889,
p 88) lists many deeds in the name of Gilbert F. Mitchell,
all for land sold in Shelburne to Roburtus H. Farnsworth,
Ira Arms, A. G. Burton, George H. Farnsworth, Abel Good-
nough, Julia Wilson, James McLeach, Charles A. Gould, and
the Arms Academy. These deeds are all recorded between
June 1853 and March 1880. Any descendants of Gilbert F.
and Margrett (Christie) Mitchell should search Shelburne,
MA records for further data.

188. **GEORGE E. MITCHELL**, son of Anson & Melinda (Hutchinson) Mitchell, was born about 1846 in MA (census). In the
1860 Franklin Co., MA Census, he was living with his parents in Greenfield, age 15, attending school. George E.
served in the 27th Infantry during the Civil War, mustered
in 7 Aug 1862, mustered out 22 June 1864 as disabled.

Provided George E. married, had a family and remained
in Massachusetts, the 1880 MA Census Index (Soundex) was
searched for a man of his approximate age. A George E.
Mitchell, age 36, born in MA, was found living on Magnolia
Ave. in Gloucester, Essex Co. with wife Annie (36, MA);
children, Annie K. (13, MA); "Gorgia" B. (10, MA); Fannie A. (6, MA); and Charles E. (2, MA). Also living with

the family were Mellie E. Knowlton, sister-in-law (to the
head of household), age 28 (MA), and Jesse Knowlton,
brother-in-law, age 23 (MA). (Vol. 7, E.D. 181, Sheet 16,
Line 1) Immediately following this is another card for
George E. Mitchell, age 37, born in MA, living on Shurt-
leff St. in Chelsea, Suffolk Co., with wife Annie (38, MA)
and children, Annie K. (13, MA); Georgie B. (10, MA); Fannie A. (6, MA); and Charles E. (2, MA). Also in the household is Jesse Knowlton, brother-in-law (23, MA), and
Helen Knowlton, sister-in-law (25, MA). (Vol. 32, E.D.
787, Sheet 56, Line 14)

196. **CALVIN MITCHELL,** son of Ensign, Jr. and Elizabeth
(Calvin) Mitchell, was born 2 Dec 1816 in Pleasant Twp.,
Clermont Co. (now Brown), OH. He died 15 Nov 1887 in Jackson Twp., Effingham Co., IL. He spent his boyhood on the
family farm in Ohio which lay on White Oak Creek just a
few miles from the Ohio River. In his 14th year, his parents moved to Edgar Co., IL where he and his brothers helped his father establish a farm.

At age 21, Calvin began to "work for himself," spending four years as a State employee, building turnpike
roads in Clark Co., IL. From 1841 to 1844, he attended
college in Franklin, Johnson Co., IN where he graduated
with a "good practical education, together with civil en-
gineering." Calvin may have stayed with his mother's relatives while in Johnson Co. His grandfather, James Calvin, had died there in 1839, but his uncle, Hiram Calvin
(who named a son Ensign), lived there until 1856, residing
in Nineveh Twp. where Calvin's future wife lived. He married there (at the bride's home) on 13 Apr 1845 to Eliza
Ann Allen who came from a family of 11 sisters and 1 brother. Eliza Ann was born 10 Nov 1824 in Fayette Co., IN, the
daughter of Elijah and Christina (Banta) Allen. She died
4 Sep 1885 in Jackson Twp., Effingham Co., IL.

After marriage, Calvin taught school in Johnson Co.
until 1852 when he and Eliza Ann with Eliza's father went
to Clay Co., IL where Elijah Allen, a widower, bought a
total of 200 acres in Sections 3, 13, and 15, all of which
he sold later in 1853 to his daughter, Amanda M. Allen.
Calvin probably helped his father-in-law farm this property until 1854 when he bought his own 205 acre farm in
Section 7. In 1856, he bought 40 acres in Section 13 from
his sister-in-law, Amanda Malvina Allen, which was no

doubt the site of the steam mill he bought that year when he entered into the lumber business.

In 1857, Calvin sold his Clay Co., IL farm and moved his steam mill to Union Twp., Effingham Co., IL. The mill was not a success according to W. H. Perrin's biography of Calvin ("History of Effingham Co., IL," 1883) which adds that Calvin "traded the mill in 1858 for the 'old' Nelson farm of 160 acres." Calvin did not "trade" his mill which contained a steam engine, a circular saw mill, and a grist mill with furnishings and fixtures, both mills attached to each other and propelled by steam. Instead, he mortgaged it to his brother, John, in March of 1858. John was a resident of Edgar Co., IL. He gave power of attorney to John S. Kelly of Effingham Co. who recorded full payment of the mortgage of $1,500.00 in May 1858.

Meanwhile, Calvin bought the Nelson farm of 160 acres in adjoining Sections 22 and 27 (Jackson Twp.), paying $2,500.00 for it to George W. Nelson and wife, and Jesse Newman and wife. Obviously, he used the money John paid him for the mill, possibly borrowing the remaining amount from his brother-in-law and sister, William T. and Mary Fuller. In 1870 the Fullers quit claimed Calvin's 80 acre property in Section 22 for $300.00 to Calvin's sons, Orlando A. and David O. who then sold 40 acres of it to their brothers, Ensign S. and Elijah C., for $500.00. Perrin says that Calvin "by the most perservering industry and unswerving integrity...made up the losses and liquidated the debts incurred in the mill transaction." Calvin then settled down to full-time farming although he did serve several terms (1869-1871) as Effingham Co. Surveyor. The village of Montrose, laid out in 1870, was surveyed and platted by Calvin during his term of office.

In 1877, Calvin's father, Ensign, Jr., was fortunate to be reunited with his brothers, Claudius, Abizer, and Newman who lived in Ohio, and Ira from Iowa who met at his house in Edgar Co., IL. Calvin attended that reunion, meeting these now elderly uncles for the first time. It is hoped that neither politics nor religion was discussed at this reunion, Calvin being a staunch Democrat and a Baptist, while his father and uncles were strong Republicans and Methodists. When his father died less than two years later, his will left everything to his youngest son, John, with small cash bequests to his remaining children except for Calvin and Samuel who were not mentioned.

Perrin's 1883 Effingham Co., IL history contains a portrait of Calvin. He looks every inch what we imagine when we think of the Biblical prophet, Moses. He has a full mustache, hair falling just below his ear lobes, and side burns that extend down into a long, flowing beard. His expression is stern, yet wise. An informal picture of Calvin, taken with his son and daughter-in-law, David O. and Carrie, presents him with a more benevolent countenance. Even so, the strong planes of his face, a rather large but straight nose, wide brow and forthright gaze suggest the moral, mental and physical fiber of this man. Unfortunately, no portrait of Eliza Ann seems to exist.

After Eliza Ann's death in 1885, Calvin's eldest son moved his family into his father's house to care for him. On a crisp, sunny Tuesday in Nov 1887, Calvin started home from watching the field hands husk corn, taking a short cut through an orchard. Orlando went searching for him when he failed to arrive home at the expected time. He found his father near the orchard, still holding his hat in his hand which contained "nubbins" of corn he had picked up. He was kept several days, it not being sure if he was dead or alive, until a doctor could be found. Later, a cedar tree was planted to mark the spot where he fell.

Both Calvin and Eliza Ann are buried in Old Turner Cemetery, Jackson Twp., Effingham Co., IL. It is a small country burial ground, standing in the midst of peaceful fields dotted with grazing cows, shaded by trees on two sides. It lies not far from the old Mitchell home place. Children of Calvin and Eliza Ann (Allen) Mitchell, first four born in Indiana, last two in Illinois, were:

- **280. Orlando Allen** b 16 Jan 1846   +
- **281. David Oscar** b 30 Dec 1846   +
- **282. Ensign Samuel** b 17 Oct 1848   +
- **283. Elijah Chandler** b 24 Jul 1850   +
- **284. Claudius Elias** b 20 Oct 1856   +
- **285. Joseph Calvin** b 15 Dec 1859   +

197. **JOSEPH MITCHELL**, son of Ensign, Jr. and Elizabeth (Calvin) Mitchell, was born 10 Jan 1818 in Brown Co. (formerly Clermont), OH. Family bible records, generously shared by his descendants, state his year of birth as 1817 as does his tombstone. But that is unlikely as his brother, Calvin, was born Dec 1816. The 1850 census, taken after Joseph's birthday, gives his age as 32 (born 1818).

Joseph was 12 years old when his parents left Brown Co., OH for Edgar Co., IL. A great deal more was expected of children then than today. Even at that age, Joseph was capable of the hard work required in helping his father carve out a farm from the prairie. Indeed, children far younger than he were involved in many farm tasks. Since sons of farmers usually became farmers, and daughters grew up to marry farmers, it was thus that they learned the skills they would need as adults.

Joseph remained with his parents until his marriage in Edgar Co. on 3 Mar 1843 to Sarah Ann Hannah, born 17 Feb 1823 in Brown Co., OH, daughter of John M. and Charity (Mears) Hannah. (Descendants say Sarah Ann may have married second Samuel McCampbell and divorced him, but no substantiating records have been found; she was buried under the name of Mitchell.) The year after his marriage, Joseph bought 40 acres in Section 26 for $50.00 from his brother, Chandler. Subsequently, he bought more land from his father in 1851, his father-in-law in 1853, and Thomas D. Field in 1854. His last purchase was made in 1856 when he bought a little over 11 acres from Hamilton and Mary Dickey of Marion Co., IA. These continuing land purchases paint a picture of a successful man. Tragically, Joseph died on 6 Mar 1857 at age 39 years, leaving a young widow and 5 sons ranging in age from less than two years to thirteen years. He was buried in Wynn Cemetery (Old Bloomfield) near Bloomfield, Edgar Co., IL.

At Joseph's death, Sarah Ann was 34 years old. Most widows of that age with young children would hope for a speedy remarriage; barring that, they would eventually sell their deceased husband's property and move in with parents or other relatives. Sarah Ann did neither. A woman of strong character and independent spirit, she remained on the farm, running it and raising her boys. In 1864 she paid $2,500.00 to John Rice for land in Section 14; several months later she sold land for $3,200.00 in Sections 29, 30 and 31 to Zachariah Riley. Census records show her with no resident farm hands until 1880 when Sarah, then in her fifties and living alone, employed John Whitehead, age 25, on a full-time basis. Undoubtedly, she had been helped through the years by her Hannah and Mitchell relatives but seems mainly to have depended on her sons. Eventually, she moved into Chrisman where she was living alone in 1900.

Four years after Joseph's death, the Civil War erupt-
ed. Chandler, the second son, was the first of Sarah's
boys to go. He enlisted in Dec 1861 in a company commanded
by his cousin, John B. Hannah. He gave his age as 18 at
enlistment but in reality he was 4 months shy of his 17th
birthday. The following summer, Sarah signed a consent
form certifying that her eldest son, John H., was age 19
and free to volunteer as a soldier in the United States
Army. John H. was actually a half year short of age 18.
The company he joined included both his uncle, 2nd Lt.
John Mitchell, and his grandfather, John M. Hannah who
had enlisted as a sergeant despite his 62 years. Sarah
Ann was now left with George, age 15, Francis M., age 12,
and Joseph E., age 7, to help her run the farm. Unlike
many mothers, she was fortunate in that her soldier sons
survived the war, but her concern for their safety must
have weighed on her during the years they were gone.

Sarah Ann died 24 Feb 1905 at Chrisman, Ross Twp., Edgar Co., IL and is buried in Woodlawn Cemetery there. Her
obituary is dramatically titled "The Curtain Has Fallen."
"Grandma," as she was generally called, a member of the
Bloomfield Baptist church since 1859, had been "an invalid since Dec. 18, 1903..." but she "bore her sufferings
without a murmur..." which seems a fitting epitaph.
(Data on the Hannah family from Rachel H. Miller, 2752
Meadowbrook Dr. SE, Cedar Rapids, IA 52403, co-compiler
with Pauline Hannah of "The Hannah Family Record.")

Children of Joseph and Sarah Ann (Hannah) Mitchell
(plus twin girls who died in infancy ca 1853), all born in
Edgar Co., IL, were:

286. John Hannah b 12 Jan 1844   +
287. Chandler b 13 Apr 1845   +
288. George H. b 5 Apr 1847   +
289. **Francis Marion** b 6 Apr 1850 d 26 Jan 1866 bur Wynn
      Cemetery nr Bloomfield, IL beside his father.
290. **Joseph Ensign** b 10 Oct 1855 d 16 Oct 1894 at Normal,
      IL m Anna _____ who was lvg in 1894.

198. **CHANDLER MITCHELL,** son of Ensign, Jr. and Elizabeth
(Calvin) Mitchell, was born about (1819 or 1821/2?) in
Pleasant Twp., Brown Co., OH, moving with his parents to
Edgar Co., IL in 1830.

Chandler seems to have acquired property in Edgar Co.
at a fairly early age. In 1844 he sold his newly married

brother, Joseph, 40 acres in Section 26; and on 26 Apr 1850, he and Jane E. "his wife" of Burnett, Dodge Co., WI, sold 40 acres in Section 25 to his brother, Samuel.

Although his residence in 1850 is given in the above deed, Chandler is no where to be found in the 1850 census. However, his wife, Jane E., born about 1822 in IL, is living in Burnett Twp., Dodge Co., WI in that year with Chandler's brother-in-law and sister, Maranda and Lucy Ralston. Perhaps Chandler, like so many young and not-so-young men in 1849 and 1850, had gone "West" to find his fortune in the gold fields.

Chandler was still living in 1875 when his father left him a $5.00 cash legacy in his will. No other trace of him has been found. If he had children, their names are not known. But the 1880 Census of Mosquito Gulch, Park Co., CO (p 191) lists a Chandler Mitchell, age 29, single, miner, born in WI (about 1851), who might be a son of the above Chandler and Jane E. (   ) Mitchell.

199. **LUCY MITCHELL,** daughter of Ensign, Jr. and Elizabeth (Calvin) Mitchell, was born 5 Mar 1820 in Pleasant Twp., Brown Co., OH. She was named for her paternal grandmother, Lucy (Hubbard) Mitchell, a woman who seems to have been much admired and loved by her children.

Lucy moved with her parents to Edgar Co., IL in 1830 where she married 2 Mar 1842 Maranda Ralston, born about 1820 in OH (census). His parents are not known, but in McCaulley Cemetery (Brouillett Twp., Edgar Co., IL) there are numerous Ralstons buried, including James Ralston who died 17 Sep 1840 age 71 years 9 months; and Sally Manda Ralston, wife of James, who died 12 May 1873 at 91 years.

The Ralstons seemed to move around a good deal. In 1846 Maranda Ralston was living in Wapello Co., IA, a James Ralston also listed there in 1846 and 1847. By 1850 Maranda and Lucy were living in Burnett Twp., Dodge Co., WI. They have not been found in the 1860 or 1870 census, but in 1880 they were back in Edgar Co., IL. Living with them were their two children and a daughter-in-law. They were not in Edgar Co., IL in the 1900 Census, nor was their married son, but their daughter, Mary J., was living there alone, unmarried. She lists herself as a schoolteacher.

Lucy's children (RALSTON) were: **(i)** Mary J. b Oct 1846 Wapello Co., IA; **(ii)** James bc 1848 IL m by 1880 to Carrie _____, bc 1858 NY, parents both b in NY.

201. **NANCY MITCHELL,** daughter of Ensign, Jr. and Elizabeth (Calvin) Mitchell, was born Aug 1823 in Pleasant
Twp., Brown Co., OH. She was named for her maternal grandmother, Nancy (Cartmill) Calvin. In 1830 she moved with
her parents to Edgar Co., IL where she married 24 Jul 1843
William Kirkpatrick, born about 1819 in OH.

Between 1847 and 1850, William and Nancy moved to
Johnson Twp., Scotland Co., MO. They were still living
in that county in 1860 but in Green Twp. According to the
obituary of her eldest son, William and Nancy left MO in
1884, accompanied by Chandler and Elvis (sons) and families, to Pennington Co., SD. They patented 160 acres of
land in Sections 14 and 23, Township 1, near Rockerville
in the Black Hills and settled down to ranching. An Act
of Congress, approved 4 Jul 1897, made the area where
their land was situated part of the Black Hills Forest Reservation which forced William and Nancy to relinquish
their land four years later. Three separate deeds of relinquishment, all dated 31 Jul 1901, all signed by William and Nancy (who made her mark) and witnessed by their
son, Chandler, were required. The deeds specifically
state that in recompense they would be given an equal
amount of land in a location to be "hereafter selected."
(Bk 16:458,459,460 Pennington Co., SD Deed Records)

Nancy and her eldest son, Chandler, appear to have
had an extremely close relationship. Not only was she
living with him in 1900, but before his death in 1904, he
made specific provisions for Nancy in his will. He named
his brother, Elvis, executor and directed him to "furnish
and supply to my mother, Nancy Kirkpatrick, a home and
living, in the style and manner suitable to her age, manner of life and circumstances, and consistent with my estate, during her natural life; and shall...pay...all the
funeral expenses and the expenses of the last sickness of
my said mother..." He gave Elvis plenary authority to
sell his property if the income from his estate was not
sufficient to meet the expenses of caring for his mother,
the "intention of testator being to furnish his mother
with a home, living, clothing and all necessaries of life
and provide her with suitable burial..."

At a listing of Chandler's heirs in April 1904, Nancy
signed her name in an extremely shaky writing, her hand
perhaps being guided, as she also made her mark. The following month, Elvis made his executor's report, stating

that he had "secured a good home in the family of a daughter of Nancy Kirkpatrick...the same mother of deceased, at the price of ten dollars per month for her board and care while in good health; and clothes, medicines, doctor bills, extra; which the executor considers a very fair and moderate charge for the services rendered."

Although Nancy's husband, William, was alive in 1900, he was not with Nancy in the 1900 census. Per the obituary (1904) of son Chandler, William and "a brother" (Elvis) were among his survivors, the father and brother being of Rookins (St. Clair Co.), MO. Nancy does not call herself divorced or widowed in the 1900 census; possibly William wished to return to MO and Nancy, unwilling to leave her son, daughter and grandchildren in SD, refused to follow him. William and Nancy were both deceased before 1931 per the obituary of their daughter. William probably died in St. Clair Co., MO, and Nancy in Blackhawk, Meade Co., SD at the residence of her daughter. Children of William and Nancy (Mitchell) KIRKPATRICK, first two born in IL, next three in MO, were:

291. **Charles Chandler** b Sep 1844   +
292. **Mary Emily** bc 1847 Edgar Co., IL dy (aft 1860).
293. **Elvis** b May 1852   +
294. **Alfred** b Apr 1860 Scotland Co., MO d MO bef 1931.
295. **Sarah Olive (Ollie)** b 24 Oct 1861   +

202. **MARY (POLLY) MITCHELL**, daughter of Ensign, Jr. and Elizabeth (Calvin) Mitchell, was born 11 June 1825 in Pleasant Twp., Brown Co., OH. In 1830 she, "with her parents, and their rude moving outfit..." left Brown Co. and "ended their long and tedious journey at old Bloomfield, in Oct..." where Mary "lived and grew to womanhood, environed by all the disadvantages incident to frontier settlement, with few school and church privileges..." She married there 29 Dec 1846 to William T. Fuller, born 4 Dec 1821 (in Vanderburgh Co., IN per the 1850 census, but William's funeral remembrance card says he was born in VT and his eldest son also says his father's place of birth was VT in the 1900 census).

After their marriage, Mary and William lived for 8 years on a farm near Bloomfield, William calling himself a "farmer and plasterer" in the 1850 Edgar Co., IL census. About 1854 they moved into the Village of Bloomfield where William ran a grocery store. Mary joined the Baptist church in Bloomfield in 1858. Between 1849 and 1855, Mary and William lost 4 children. They lie buried in Franklin Cemetery, a small prairie burial ground, open to the sun, wind, rain and snow, located about 2 miles north of Paris on the highway.

In 1873, Mary and William moved to Newman in Douglas Co., IL where William ran a drug store. He became a member of the Masonic Lodge in Newman and Mary joined the Newman Christian Church, there being no Baptist church there. The Fullers always seemed to have a boarder living with them. In 1850, Mary's brother, Samuel, was with them; in 1860, they boarded Allen McClain (34, KY), a Justice of the Peace; in 1870, John Scott (23, IL), merchant, and Sarah McClure (23, IN), domestic servant, were in their household; and in 1880, John Bates (21, KY), store clerk, lived with Mary and William.

William T. died in Newman, IL on 29 Dec 1846, age 75 years 3 months 18 days, "gone but not forgotten." He was buried the following day in Newman City Cemetery, his grave marked with a large tree stump monument bearing the names of all his children, and the Masonic symbol.

After her husband's death, Mary lived with her children. She was in her son Ira T.'s household in 1900, but died 18 Aug 1905, age 80 years 2 months 7 days, in Newman at the home of her only daughter, Sarah (Fuller) McCown. Her obituary in the Aug. 25th edition of "The Newman Independant" calls her "one of the oldest pioneers of this part of the state...Mrs. Fuller's health for some time past owing to the infirmities incident to extreme old age had been feeble, and her mind often ran back to her childhood days, and lingered on the scenes of the past, but she remained ever patient, kind and cheerful...she received every possible attention that loving hands could give to smooth her pathway to the grave." Mary was buried on 20 Aug in Newman City Cemetery beside her husband. (Data on descendants from Mary's granddaughter, Luella [Fuller] Chandler, interviewed in 1977 in Newman, IL.)

Mary's children (FULLER), all born in Edgar Co., IL, were: **(i)** Ira T. b Oct 1847 mc 1878 Mary _____, bc 1852 IL d bef 1900 Douglas Co., IL; Ira T. & children moved to Norborne, Carroll Co., MO betw 1900-1905; 3 sons and 1 dau.; **(ii)** William B. (twin) b 2 Jan 1849 d bef 1850; **(iii)** Samuel B. (twin) b 2 Jan 1849 d 22 Nov 1852; **(iv)** Charles b aft 1850 dy; **(v)** Mary E. b aft 1850 dy; **(vi)** Sarah C. b Aug

1855 mc 1880 Jonathan C. McCown b Oct 1852 IL; res. Douglas Co., IL; 2 sons; **(vii)** Simon French b 9 Jul 1859 d 1937 at Newman, IL mc 1882 Ella Hooe b 30 Nov 1864 Newman, IL d 1942 Newman, IL d/o Benjamin & Johanna (Skinner) Hooe; 10 daus. & 1 son, all b Douglas Co., IL.

203. **SAMUEL MITCHELL,** son of Ensign, Jr. and Elizabeth (Calvin) Mitchell, was born 4 Mar 1828 in Pleasant Twp., Brown Co., OH. He was not yet three when his parents loaded their possessions into a wagon drawn by two yoke of cattle and began the trip overland to Edgar Co., IL, which became Samuel's lifelong home. He died there 10 May 1896 at his home in Horace and was buried on the 13th in Franklin Cemetery (remains moved in 1908 to Lot 783, Section F., Edgar Cemetery in Paris, IL).

Samuel was 17 years old when his mother died in Nov 1845. His grief over this loss may have been assuaged by a visit to his eldest brother, Calvin, in Johnson Co., IN where his Mexican War discharge papers erroneously stated he was born. At his brother's he would have met David B. Allen, brother of Calvin's wife. David, a man 20 years Samuel's senior, had served as sheriff of Johnson Co. and was a veteran of the 1832 Black Hawk War. No doubt Samuel heard talk here of the impending war with Mexico, of David's resolve to organize a company if hostilities broke out, and of government bounty land offered to soldiers, an exciting prospect for a young man. On 20 June 1846, two months after the war with Mexico began, Samuel was mustered in at Jefferson Barracks, MO as a private in Capt. John McConkey's Co. H, 4th Illinois Volunteer Infantry. (Two days before, David B. Allen was elected Captain at New Albany, IN of Co. C, 3rd IN Volunteer Infantry.) Samuel's soldier's discharge describes him as 5 feet 8 inches tall with light complexion, "black" eyes, and sandy hair.

After 2 weeks of training, the 4th joined Gen'l Zachary Taylor's command, moving to the border town of Matamoras, leaving there in Aug 1846 to move south along the San Juan valley through Mier and Cerralvo until they were in sight of Monterrey. On a foggy morning in September, the Americans attacked the city which surrendered 4 days later under a treaty of peace stipulating that the Americans make no further advance into Mexico for 8 weeks. In December, Samuel was back in Matamoras recovering from an illness, later rejoining his regiment and marching with them to Buena Vista in January 1847. Early in February, Gen'l Santa Anna attacked the city with 18,000 troops, but unable to budge the Americans after 2 days, he retreated.

Gen'l Taylor felt that the war could now be won without further bloodshed simply by holding his established line. President Polk and his advisors did not agree. Taylor was replaced by Gen'l Winfield Scott who had more daring plans. Moving down the Gulf of Mexico by sea, the Americans landed just south of Vera Cruz on 9 Mar 1847, laying siege to the fortress for 18 days. The surrender of Vera Cruz opened up the road to Mexico City, a rough road, upward through narrow canyons into the mountains. Santa Anna chose the steepest of all, the Cerro Gordo, to make his stand. But Gen'l Scott realized the futility of a straight forward attack. Instead, he picked New England men, familiar with mountains, to cut paths up the mountain to the east and west of Cerro Gordo over which the army could attack. By Apr 18th, the Mexicans were retreating in panic, leaving behind case after case of fireworks they had intended for a victory celebration. The Americans were hard on their heels, fighting skirmish after skirmish, steadily on the move over the rim of the mountains onto the high interior plateau.

If Samuel dreamed of entering Mexico City with the victorious American army, he was to be disappointed. His regiment and company got as far as Puebla just east of Mexico City when their 1-year enlistment expired, and they were ordered back to the States. Samuel paid for his "adventure" the rest of his life. During one of the battles, a cavalry charge had caught the foot soldiers of the 4th by surprise. Samuel had been trampled by some cavalry horses, permanently damaging his right leg, causing him to walk thereafter with a slight limp.

At New Orleans, a city so foreign in flavor that it was hard to think of it as an American city, Co. H was mustered out on 26 May 1847. Samuel paid a $5.58 clothing allowance debt, a bill of 13 cents he owed the sutler, collected 5 months back pay and headed home. (Capt. David B. Allen was not so fortunate, dying of "illness" the January before at Monterrey.)

Once home, Samuel wasted no time in applying to Washington, D.C. for his bounty land, requesting that a land warrant for 160 acres be forwarded to him at Paris, IL. The warrant was received in Nov 1847 but Samuel did not use it immediately. Early in 1850, Samuel's father remarried. His younger brother, John, was still at home to help their father on the farm, and would remain at home until 1852. Samuel waited until after the harvest, then drove a herd of horses overland to Milwaukee where he sold them. Moving on west to Baraboo, WI, he cashed in his land warrant, but soon traded his land in WI for 40 acres in Edgar Co., IL to add to the 40 acres he had purchased there in Apr 1850 from his older brother, Chandler.

With characteristic energy, Samuel began farming and improving his 80 acres. On 10 Dec 1852 in Edgar Co., IL the farmer took a wife, Martha Ann Long, born 13 Jan 1832 in Ross Co., OH, daughter of Andrew F. and Margaret (   ) Long. On 25 Sep 1859, six months after the birth of a son, Martha Ann died of typhoid fever. The following March, little John, not yet a year old, also died. Both are buried in Franklin Cemetery, Edgar Co., IL. Six year old Emma went to live with her Long grandparents.

As 1860 faded into 1861, Samuel and his neighbors became more and more preoccupied with the hotly debated issues between the North and the South. A supporter of the fledgling Republican Party, Samuel undoubtedly voted for Lincoln and, like him, believed that the preservation of the Union was of utmost importance. At the onset of the war in Apr 1861, Samuel began organizing Co. A which was attached to the 25th IL Volunteer Infantry, a regiment headed by Col. W. N. Coler of Urbana, Lt. Col. J. S. McClelland of Vermillion Co., and Major R. H. Nodine of Urbana. Samuel was elected ranking 2nd Lieutenant of Co. A which enrolled 1 June 1861 at Georgetown, IL, meeting on 2 Aug at the U. S. Arsenal Park in St. Louis, MO where they were mustered in for a three year period.

Late in August, the 25th left for training exercises in Jefferson City, MO. For the first few months, the regiment remained in MO, marching and counter-marching to various locations. On 6 Mar 1862, they participated in the victorious 3-day Battle of Pea Ridge, AR. Prior to the battle, Lt. Samuel had been sent to reconnoiter the Confederate position. Utilizing the skill and thoroughness that marked his entire military career, he was later granted a promotion on the success of this mission.

In May 1862 the regiment moved down the Mississippi to Pittsburgh Landing via the transport "Henry Clay." For the next five months they marched, foraged and skirmished in TN, MS, AL and KY. At the Battle of Corinth, MS early in October, Gen'l Rosecrans defeated the Confederate forces led by Gen'l Braxton Bragg who retreated into TN, ending the Confederate invasion of KY. Late in October, Gen'l William S. Rosecrans became the new Commander of the Army of the Cumberland of which the 25th was a part. Rosecrans was a large, hearty man, considered a top leader and well liked by his men who called him "Old Rosy," often singing as they marched "Old Rosy is our man, he'll show his deeds, where'ere he leads, Old Rosy is our man!"

On 30 Nov 1862, 2nd Lt. Samuel Mitchell was ordered to accompany the body of Charles A. Clark, late Captain of Co. A, 25th Reg't, back to IL. He was given exactly ten days to accomplish this unpleasant task. Several weeks later, he was promoted to Captain of Co. A, his certificate of promotion stamped "Promoted for Meritorious Service Rendered at Pea Ridge," retroactive to 28 Nov, the date of Capt. Clark's death.

Leaving Nashville, TN the day after Christmas, the 25th arrived at Murfreesboro to engage in the Battle of Stone's River which continued through 3 Jan 1863. Despite a tactical victory over the North, the Confederates withdrew. Each army had lost nearly a third of its men; almost 6 months were required to recuperate from this fearfully destructive encounter, during which time the 25th did picket duty, foraged and occasionally skirmished until the Battle of Champion's Hill, MI (Vicksburg Campaign). Here, Capt. Samuel, serving as staff officer, had his horse wounded. In a desperate attempt to escape Rebel gunfire, he threw both arms around his horse's head, holding it up until he had ridden out of danger.

After the fall of Vicksburg to the North in July 1863, Rosecrans began pushing Bragg's Confederates toward GA. By Sept. 4th, Rosecrans had crossed the Tennessee River and entered Chattanooga, believing he had Bragg in full retreat. Actually, Bragg was gathering his army around him at Lafayette, GA while the Confederate War Office frantically scoured the South for reinforcements. By the time Rosecrans realized that Bragg's reinforced army was about to mount a counter-offensive, he barely succeeded in regrouping his army at Chickamauga Creek, just south of Chattanooga. On Sept. 18, the 25th was sent to skirmish with the Rebels. Capt. Samuel's Co. A was beaten back six times, losing all but about 20 men under his command.

The Battle of Chickamauga (GA) was fought on Sept. 19 and 20, 1863. It was the story of Stone's River all over again with almost one-third of each army put out of action. Co. A was posted on the skirmish line in the heaviest part of the fighting. One by one, the men in Co. A fell until only 3 were left. A falling shell caught Capt. Samuel in the breast and shoulder, followed by a blow to the head from a gun butt. He dropped, unconscious and bleeding from the lungs, and was taken by person or persons unknown to a private home in Chattanooga where he lay recuperating until he was able to rejoin his company.

Gen'l Rosecrans had been replaced by Gen'l George H. "Pap" Thomas who was ordered to hold Chattanooga at all costs, vowing to do so "till we starve," a very real possibility as supply lines into Chattanooga had been cut, supplies on hand were down to 5 days, and only 2 days worth of rations were expected to get through in the near future. Slowly, the siege of the city was lifted, supply lines opened up, and the Northern position solidified. Gen'l Grant had just been appointed commander of the newly formed Military Division of the Mississippi (comprising the existing Departments of the Ohio, the Cumberland, and the Tennessee). Unsure of the veracity of a report that Bragg was removing his troops from Missionary Ridge and Lookout Mountain, Grant ordered an advance on the Rebel skirmish line, using just enough men to provoke a reaction from Bragg. Thus began the Battle of Chattanooga which lasted from Nov. 23rd through the 25th.

This battle would be one of the most visually spectacular of the war due to the nature of the terrain, a wide open plain of about 2 miles distance with a chain of low hills called Orchard Knob about halfway across. The Rebel outpost was positioned on Orchard Knob. From there to the rifle pits at the base of Missionary Ridge, it was a clear sweep, a gigantic stage on which each soldier could participate as well as observe the rest of the army, unlike the usual battle in which a soldier is involved only with the area directly in front of him. The Confederates on top of Missionary Ridge were equally able to view the entire battlefield.

By the end of the first day, Gen'l Thomas had taken Orchard Knob while Gen'l Sherman got into position north of the Ridge. At the end of the second day, Gen'l Hooker had captured Lookout Mountain; this battle, often called "the battle above the clouds," was actually fought far down the rugged, wooded slope of the mountain in a heavy, soaking mist.

At the start of the last day of the battle, the Rebels were concentrated in the rifle pits at the base of Missionary Ridge and on the crest of the ridge itself, thinly spread, but the extreme steepness of the hill seemed adequate protection. With orders passing between Grant and his generals with maddening slowness, it is not surprising that a misunderstanding arose. One of Thomas' divisions was commanded by Gen'l Wood who had 3 brigadiers under him, Gen'ls Willich, Beatty, and Hazen, positioned in the center of the field directly opposite the Ridge. Willich thought his orders were to take the rifle pits and then storm the crest. Beatty and Hazen thought (correctly) that they were to stop after capturing the rifle pits. The precipitous slope was considered so invulnerable, at least one of the generals had ordered his men to leave their horses behind.

Spread out in a line facing Missionary Ridge, Gen'l Thomas' men waited on Orchard Knob. Capt. Samuel, his arm still tied up from his injuries at Chickamauga, stood at the head of Co. A. The rains had let up and a weak afternoon sun shone on glittering bayonets and flags snapping in a chilly breeze. When the order came, a thundering wave of blue-coated soldiers charged across the plain, brushing aside Confederate skirmishers, until they came within rifle range of the Rebels. Men dropped like flies until the ground in front of the rifle pits was strewn with bodies, but still they advanced until the Rebels either ran away or surrendered. A pall of gunsmoke lay grey and acrid in the air.

To the amazement of the Confederates on top of the Ridge, Willich's men continued on up the slope. Beatty and Hazen soon realized that fire from the crest above made it too hazardous for their men to stay in the rifle pits. Officers were everywhere, urging their men to follow them to the top. Almost in unison, they swept up the impossible slope. About 30 feet from the Confederate guns, a shell exploded within inches of Capt. Samuel's face. He would not realize until later that the concussion from the exploding shell had permanently deafened his left ear. He sensed rather than heard himself yelling along with the rest as they saw Rebels, veterans and raw recruits alike, retreating in blind panic, and they knew the crest was won. For fully ten minutes, officers and their men cavorted in near hysteria among abandoned Rebel gun emplacements, waving their arms and clasping each other in brief embrace. Orders alone had not carried these men up that cliff. It was the most remarkable experience any of them had ever had.

After a few days of rest, the 25th marched for Knoxville. Between Dec 1863 and June 1864, the 25th marched and counter-marched all over East TN, returning to Cleveland, TN where they started for the front on 4 June with a supply train of 3,000 wagons and 1,000 ambulances. Three days later, they had joined their brigade and division and the Atlanta Campaign was underway. The 25th did not engage in the heavy battles fought in this campaign, but they were on the march daily, did picket duty, saw action at Noonday Creek, GA and were involved in skirmishes in GA at Pine Mountain, Kennesaw Mountain, Chattahoochie River, and Peachtree Creek.

Years later at Capt. Samuel's funeral, Chaplain Hiram Ashmore of the 25th related the following incident which probably happened during the Atlanta Campaign: "It was reported by a negro that the rebel soldiers were lodged in a confederate mansion close by. Mitchell was put in charge of a squad of men to get the 3 rebels. The house was searched thoroughly but no men found. Capt. Mitchell, on receiving the report...discredited that the search had been thorough, and sent the soldiers back, saying that they were told to fetch them. The men were finally discovered in a blind in the garrett. Their wives came forward and admitted that they had storied and begged the men's release. To their pathetic pleadings, Capt. Mitchell burst into tears, but did his duty and bore the confederates into camp."

This was the reaction of a disciplined, responsible officer in conflict with a sensitive, war-weary man. He had lost his mother, a brother, his wife and an infant son before the start of the war. He didn't know if his brother, John, who had been taken prisoner, was dead or alive. He had lost many of his men, some of them close friends, had himself been sick and injured, and his heart went out to these wives. But - he did his duty!

In 3 years time, the 25th had traveled 4,962 miles, 3,252 of them on foot and 1,710 by steamboat and railroad.

Now in sight of Atlanta, they received orders on 1 Aug 1864 to report to Camp Butler, IL, their 3-year enlistment expired. Mustered out on 5 Sep, Samuel left Camp Butler for home and a long awaited reunion with his family. He had grown several inches since his Mexican War days. He was undoubtedly gaunt but bore himself with the erect carriage of a natural horseman, despite his slight limp.

Recuperation over the next several months apparently included courtship. On 29 Nov 1864 in Edgar Co., IL, Samuel was married to Harriet Jane Calvin, born 29 Jul 1836 in Edgar Co., daughter of David and Jane (Mears) Stephenson Calvin. Harriet and Samuel were 2nd cousins, both of them being great-grandchildren of Capt. Luther Calvin, an early KY pioneer and Indian fighter. Until her marriage to Samuel, Harriet had taught school. That she was a woman of purpose, intelligence and energy can be seen in her portrait. She had a strong-boned face; wide, full-lipped mouth, strong chin and alert, deep set eyes. Her sense of taste and elegance is revealed in the home she and Samuel built in later years.

Although the war was drawing to a close and it was obvious that the North was winning, Samuel organized a new company early in 1865, re-entering as a 1st Lieutenant for a 1-year term. Co. B of the 154th I.V.I. Reg't was mustered in at Camp Butler, IL on 22 Feb. Assigned to headquarters at Nashville, TN, Samuel was promoted to Capt. of Co. C of the 154th on 10 June. The war had been over for several months but Samuel remained at Nashville, performing such chores as general court martial duties until his discharge on 18 Sep at Nashville. It has been said that Governor Oglesby of IL once remarked that Samuel was "a man who had seen more active service in the army than any other in the State of Illinois."

Over the years, Samuel's farm had grown to 220 acres. It was mainly devoted to raising full-blooded Shorthorns, and Poland-China and Berkshire hogs. He was also interested in draft horses and roadsters (horses used for driving or light work on ordinary roads). His war injuries continued to bother him and increasingly he had to hire help. In 1879, Samuel petitioned for a government pension of invalidism, based on both his Mexican and Civil War injuries. He was granted $17.00 per month in 1881.

Semi-retired in 1882, Samuel and Harriet built the beautiful home in Horace, IL, described as the "prettiest residence" in Edgar Twp. This home remained in the family until 1976. I had the good fortune to tour the home in 1977 through arrangements made with the present owners by Catherine (Mitchell) Savoye, Samuel's granddaughter. Although it was missing its front porch, decorated with gingerbread trim, the house was in excellent condition. Two and a half stories high, it is a period piece of spacious, high ceilinged rooms, many windows, beautiful wood doors, a graceful staircase with a highly polished walnut bannister, and dark wood floors. A large closet off the hired man's bedroom upstairs was still redolent with the aroma of smoked hams and bacon which once hung there. The house, approached down a long driveway, sits like an exquisite jewel in the midst of a large lawn surrounded by tall trees and flowering shrubs. Samuel had his picture taken sitting in a chair in front of the house, his full beard and mustache snow-white, his dog sitting by him.

Besides running his farm, Samuel was involved over the years with many local affairs, serving on the Central Committee and as delegate to county conventions of the Republican Party; as County Collector, Assessor, and School director; as a member of the Masonic Lodge, the G.A.R., and the Baptist church. But his physical condition continued to deteriorate. In 1887, he petitioned the government for an increase in his pension. In 1894, barely able to sign his name, he petitioned for another increase. One of the attestors to his disability was his kinsman, James W. Calvin who stated he had known Samuel since he was 9 years old, was and had lived at Samuel's house and worked for him for the past 5 years. He stated that Samuel "...is about blind in one eye and cannot hear with left ear...has complained of a numbness, helplessness in arms and hands...has a running sore on his right leg...I have had to help dress him and have seen Mrs. Mitchell...help to dress him...his hands are numb, and I think he has a...paralysis in hands and arms, that is the reason he can not dress and undress himself. In the morning his mind seems to be bewildered and he can't give directions as to what he wants done till toward the middle of the day...his memory is very poor."

By the date of Samuel's death in 1896, he was receiving a pension of $30.00 per month and had petitioned for yet another increase. There is no record that this final increase was granted. Harriet then asked for and was granted a widow's pension of $20.00 per month which she received until her death on 11 Apr 1911 at Horace, IL. She was buried in Edgar Cemetery in Paris, IL on the 13th. Her obituary in the Paris, IL "Gazette" called her "amiable and lovable, always a friend to the friendless...her home a model of hospitality...a woman of rare intelligence and education...a great reader...informed on current events..." and, besides a member of the Baptist church, she also was an early supporter of the W.C.T.U., and belonged to the W.R.C. of Paris and to Paris Chapter No. 7, O.E.S.

Nearly 1,000 people attended Samuel's funeral, including about 80 veterans who had served with him during the Civil War, and honorary pall bearers made up of Mexican War veterans. After the service at Horace, his body was taken to Franklin Cemetery where Samuel, age 68 years 2 months 6 days, was tenderly laid to rest. The funeral procession was more than a mile in length.

Children of Samuel Mitchell (first 2 by first marriage, second 2 by second marriage), all born in Edgar Co., IL, were:

296. **Sarah Emma** b 25 Aug 1853 d 22 Mar 1869.
297. **John A.** b 27 Mar 1859 d 10 Mar 1860 age 11m 3d.
298. **Gertrude** b 9 Jul 1867 d 11 Feb 1870.
299. Herman Calvin b 1 Aug 1871   +

204. **JOHN MITCHELL**, son of Ensign, Jr. and Elizabeth (Calvin) Mitchell, was born 1 Nov 1831 in Edgar Twp., Edgar Co., IL. He married there on 22 May 1860 Mary Elizabeth Smith, born 12 May 1841 in Edgar Co. She died of a paralytic stroke on 27 Nov 1906 in Pomeroy, Garfield Co., WA and was buried 2 Dec in the Pomeroy City Cemetery. John died 23 Jan 1918 at Walla Walla, WA where he was residing at 827 W. Alder St. His place of burial is unknown.

John's biography in "The History of Edgar Co., IL" (Wm. LeBaron, Jr. & Co., 1879) states that he lived with his parents until he was 18, when he went to Oregon and engaged in farming. Actually, John, like most young men of that era, probably didn't leave his father's household until he had reached age 21. He is in his father's household in the 1850 Edgar Co., IL census, taken in October.

In 1850, the Territorial Legislature of Oregon guaranteed settlers large tracts of land if they would live on and cultivate that land for 4 years. If John took up such a tract in Oregon, he didn't stay long enough to obtain ownership, remaining for only a year. From Oregon, he went to Yreka in Siskiyou Co., CA just across the OR-CA border where he worked in the gold mines. Yreka, whose "first and only industry in these mountains" was mining, had been established in Mar 1851 when gold was discovered in the nearby flats. It quickly became the commercial and transportation center for the surrounding communities and mining camps. The first log house in Yreka was built on North St. about 1853. On Miner St. is the old Yreka Hotel, no longer in use as such, and the Arcade Billiards Salon where Lotta Crabtree sang for the miners in the 1850's, and John C. Heenan, "The Benicia Boy," began his career as a fighter. ("History of Siskiyou Co., CA," H. L. Wells)

Trouble between the Indians and the white settlers in Northern CA, Southern and Eastern OR, and WA had been going on since 1851. Although 1853 and 1854 were fairly quiet, a federation had been formed of all the Indian tribes in these areas, led mainly by Tyee John and his brother, "Limpy," Rogue River Indians, and Pe-mox-mox, leader of the Cayouses and Columbias. In midsummer 1855, hostilities flared with sudden ferocity. Col. William Thompson describes the burning cabins, often immolating their occupants; waylaid travelers; murdered prospectors; women butchered under atrocious circumstances; and little children "seized by their heels and their brains dashed out against the corner of the cabin." ("Reminisences of a Pioneer," 1912) In Feb 1856, John became a 3rd Corporal in Co. B, captained by Abel George, of the 2nd Reg't Oregon Mounted Dragoons led by Col. R. L. Williams for a 4 month term of service, fighting in such battles as Hayes' Hill and Big Meadows. He was described at enlistment as 5 feet 10 inches tall with blue eyes, light hair and fair complexion. He would have furnished his own horse, arms, and ammunition although not blankets and provisions.

After John's discharge from service in the Rogue River Indian War in June 1856 at Jacksonville, OR, he returned to the gold mines near Yreka for another year. Yreka, although only 5 years in existence, had become a booming town, containing many substantial buildings and such commercial enterprises as bakeries, meat markets, a brewery, jewelers, barber shop, furniture store, a Masonic Hall, drug store, printing office, bookstore, clothing store and more. Yet, John elected to return to Edgar Co., IL, taking the overland route which took him from Yreka in the

Shasta Valley to Applegate's Cutoff in Utah Territory, up to Soda Springs in Oregon Territory (now Idaho), then to Chimney Rock in Nebraska Territory where he would cross through Iowa into Illinois. Once home, he returned to farming. Obviously, he was successful in the gold mines of Siskiyou Co. for in Mar 1858 he purchased a steam mill in Effingham Co., IL from his brother, Calvin, for $1,500. In no place does John ever state that he had lived in Effingham Co. so the purchase of this steam mill was probably for investment purposes only.

John and Mary Elizabeth had been married less than a year when the Civil War began. John's brother, Samuel, a recent widower, enlisted almost immediately. When it became clear that this war would not be the short-lived conflict people had first expected it to be, John enlisted on 28 Aug 1862, entering as a 2nd Lieutenant in Co. A, 79th Reg't I.V.I. Mary E. returned to her parent's for the duration of his service. John had fought in the battles of Stone River and Liberty Gap and been promoted to 1st Lt. when he was captured on 19 Sep 1863 during the first day of the Battle of Chickamauga (GA). He was taken by rail to Libby Prison in Richmond, VA via Atlanta, Augusta, Columbia and Raleigh. The journey of nearly 1,000 miles was "made in platform cars and with scant rations; a few crackers, a small piece of pork, and one or two pints of corn meal...made eatable by mixing with water, pasting this dough to a board and standing it near the fire until it was in some slight degree baked."

At every point on their journey, the local Rebels in authority examined the prisoners, confiscating their overcoats, knives, wool or rubber sheets, or any other desired equipment so by the time they reached Libby Prison they were "very destitute of blankets and clothing." Their first night at Libby was spent sleeping on a hard wood floor. This prison had been a tobacco warehouse located within a few feet of the Lynchburg canal and in view of the James River. It was 3 stories high in front, 4 in the back, built of brick and stone with the cellars (first story in the rear) on a level with the dock bordering the canal. The prisoners lived in seven rooms on the second and third stories.

John had been at Libby Prison for nearly 4 months when a fellow prisoner, Lt. W. G. Galloway of the 15th U.S. Regulars, wakeful during the night due to a fever, thought of digging an escape tunnel from some point in the east basement of the prison. The middle room on the first floor was accessible to the prisoners as it was where they cooked and ate. This room contained a massive brick and stone fireplace. In front of this stood three stoves on which they prepared food. Between the fireplace and the back of the stoves was a very small space. Someone had the idea of making an opening in the floor of the fireplace and by digging on an oblique angle, coming out in the cellar under the adjoining room which was seldom or never used. A secret work party was formed; they utilized knives, small hatchets, sharp pieces of wood, and a broken fire shovel, the stones which they removed being ingeniously replaced during the day and covered with a scattering of ashes. The excavated dirt was hauled out of the tunnel in shallow frying pans and distributed over the cellar floor, straw carelessly thrown over it, or put in boxes and barrels in small quantities.

The first tunnel failed. Their intention was to dig from the south end of the cellar, tapping into the sewer between the prison and the canal; but the odor was so terrible and the sewer so small, this excavation was abandoned. Several days before the final decision was made to give up on the first tunnel, there was a division in the working party and additional officers, including Lt. John Mitchell and Capt. Terrance Clark, his company commander, and 12 others were taken in on the secret and began digging a new tunnel at the east cellar wall. This work took nearly 3 weeks. On the night of 8 Feb, the tunnel was opened, but a mistake in measurement had been made and the opening was on the wrong side of the fence. It was hastily closed and another two feet were dug which now brought the tunnel out on the right side of the fence. On the next night, the exodus through the tunnel began, but Lt. John Mitchell was not one of the escapees. Suffering from pneumonia and pleurisy, he was too ill on that night to accompany his companions. He was still ill in May and was taken to the prison hospital where he was treated by a Rebel doctor from SC whose name John could not remember.

On 22 June 1864, John was sent from Libby Prison to Camp Oglethorpe about 1/4 mile east of Macon, GA. This camp was about 3 acres in size, surrounded by a high wooden stockade with sentries stationed around the outside edge on parapets. Fifteen feet inside the stockade ran a low picket fence called the "dead line." A man who stepped over this fence was immediately shot. Within the enclosure was a large building housing generals and other field officers. The remaining prisoners, mostly captains and lieutenants, fared as best they could in the open. Their daily rations here were 1 pint of corn meal and 2 ounces of rancid bacon packed in wood ashes. Occasionally, they got an ounce of rice or black-eyed peas and a half teaspoon of salt.

The following month (28 Jul), John was among 600 prisoners transferred from Macon to Charleston, GA to the fortress-like city jail, an 8-sided building of stuccoed masonry topped with a 40 foot tower. It was filthy. There were no cooking utensils and not enough wood to cook their small rations. Many suffered from scurvey and other diseases. There was almost no medicine and no room in the hospital for sick Union prisoners. The jail proper contained convicts, negro prisoners, military offenders and deserters from both sides; again, the Union officers were housed outside in the jail yard. This site was under constant Union bombardment. The Confederates had deliberately moved Union officers to this jail as hostages, hoping to force the Union into a general exchange of prisoners. Instead, the Union command confined 600 Confederate officers in a stockade on Morris Island in range of Confederate shore batteries.

From Charleston, John was sent to a camp in Columbia, SC until he was finally paroled at "N.E. Ferry, NC" in Mar 1865. He was granted a 30-day leave of absence, after which he reported to Benton Barracks, MO where he was on the sick list in Apr and May. He appears on a muster-out roll dated 12 June 1865 at Nashville, TN but was actually discharged under special order at St. Louis on 15 May. He brought home with him the knife he had used to help dig the escape tunnel at Libby Prison.

John returned home an ill man. Two years of bad and inadequate food and exposure to the elements had permanently damaged his health. The pneumonia and pleurisy he had contracted at Libby would reoccur in 1866 and 1875. He had chronic diarrhea, infected eyes, and scrofula, a tuberculous condition affecting the lymphatic glands, particularly those in the neck. For the first 2 years after the war, John was able to work at only half capacity, and after that at even less, unable to perform anything but light labor. At the time of his death, he was receiving a government pension of $30.00 per month. Perhaps his extreme physical disability after the war was the reason John's father directed by will that all his property, both real and personal, was to go to John.

After his father's death in 1879, John sold the farm and in the spring of 1880 took his family to Columbia Co., WA. In July 1880, they settled on land near the mountains just south of Pomeroy in Garfield Co., WA. They remained here until about 1894 when John sold the farm and moved into Pomeroy. In the 1900 census, John was renting a house in this city, his occupation listed as day laborer although he had been unemployed for 8 months out of that year. William T., his only son, and 2 unmarried daughters (Agnes and Mamie) were still at home; and they were keeping a boarder, 37-year old German born Otto R. Koenig, a mechanic who had been unemployed for 4 months.

Mary Elizabeth's obituary in 1906 lists as survivors (besides her husband), a son and daughter, "W. T. Mitchell and "Miss Agnes at home in Pomeroy;" daughters Mrs. Ida Dalton of Tacoma; Mrs. Maggie Jackson of Walla Walla; Mrs. Clyde Houk of Pomeroy; Mrs. Oatie Darby of Portland; and Mrs. Mamie Burks of Wallace, Idaho. She was preceeded in death by two children who had died infancy, and a daughter, Carrie Edwards, who "died on Puget Sound about five years ago." Mary E. was a Presbyterian, but her funeral services were conducted from the Methodist Episcopal church in Pomeroy.

In 1912, John moved to Yakima, WA where he worked as a gardener. By his death in 1818, he had moved to Walla Walla, WA, probably living there with his daughter, Margaret. Before the war, John had been an ambitious, hard working man with a bright future. He did not lay down his life for his country; he gave up the promise that future had held. Children of John and Mary E. (Smith) Mitchell (1st 6 b Edgar Co., IL; last 2 b Garfield Co., WA) were:

300. **Ida B.** bc 1863 m _____ Dalton.
301. **William T.** b Mar 1867 unmar 1906.
302. **Margaret E.** bc 1868 m 14 Nov 1886 Frank P. Jackson.
303. **Ella Clydie** b Nov 1869 m 9 Oct 1887 Frank Houk.
304. **Olive O.** b Sep 1871 m 17 June 1896 James A. Darby.
305. **Carrie E.** bc 1874 m 6 Oct 1897 George E. Edwards.
306. **Agnes** b May 1881 unmar 1906.
307. **Mamie** b Aug 1883 m 14 Dec 1902 Albert Birkes.

205. **ENSIGN MITCHELL,** son of Chandler Mitchell and an unknown wife, was born about 1810 in Clermont Co. (now Brown), OH. He married about 1833 in Ohio to Sarah (Sally) _____, born about 1820 in OH. Per census records, neither could read or write.

On 1 Oct 1842 Ensign and Sally sold 135-1/4 acres of land in Brown Co., OH to George M. Brown (Bk T-19:174). As this is their last recorded deed of sale in Brown Co. records, they probably left not long after for Pike Co., IL wehre they were living in 1850. Ensign's married sister Jane, and her husband, William T. Watson, and his father, Chandler, were also in Pike Co., IL in 1850.

In the 1860 Census of Pike Co., IL, Ensign (surname listed as Michael) and his family were living in Newburgh Twp. His real estate evaluation was zero, so he owned no land. Living next door to him is his eldest son, Silas, and his wife, listed only by her initials, S. I., age 24, born in OH, and their daughter, Mary, age 1 (IL). Ensign's sister, Jane Watson, and his father are in Hardin Twp. which adjoins Newburgh to the south.

By 1870, Ensign and Sally and most of their children had disappeared from Pike Co. Their son, Moses, may be the man by that name in the 1870 census living in Newburgh Twp. with wife Susan (24, IL) and children John (8, IL) and Flora (1, IL). In the same township not far away is Sarah Mitchell, widow of Ensign's son, Chandler.

Deed records can not be used to determine when Ensign and Sally left Pike Co., IL since Ensign owned no land there. The 1870 Census (unindexed for most states) has not been searched for them except in Pike Co., IL.

Children of Ensign and Sarah (   ) Mitchell, first 5 or 6 born in Brown Co., OH, last 6 in Pike Co., IL, were:

308. **Silas** bc 1834 mc 1857/58 S. I. _____.
309. **Chandler** b 17 Oct 1835   +
310. **Moses** bc 1839 prob mc 1861 Susan _____.
311. **Lucinda I.** bc 1840
312. **Thomas** bc 1842
313. **Sarah (Sally)** bc 1846
314. **David F.** bc 1848
315. **J. W.** (male) bc 1851
316. **M. A.** (female) bc 1853
317. **G. W.** (male) bc 1856
318. **Ensign** bc 1858
319. **M. E.** (female) b 1860 (age 5m on 14 Sep)

206. **JANE MITCHELL**, daughter of Chandler Mitchell and an unknown wife, was born about 1825 in Brown Co., OH. She married about 1847 William T. Watson, born about 1825 in IN. This marriage may have taken place just before Jane's father and married brother (#205 Ensign) left Brown Co., OH for Pike Co., IL. Although there is no Brown Co. marriage record for Jane and William, the 1840 census of that county shows a William Watson, Sr. and William Watson, Jr. on the same page as Jane's father, Chandler. The household of William Watson, Jr. contains a male age 15 to 20, or born between 1820-1825.

Jane and William are in Pike Co., IL in both the 1850 and 1860 census, her father living with them. William owned no real estate. Before 1870, Jane and William had left Pike Co., IL for an unknown location.

Jane's known children (WATSON), all born in Pike Co., IL (taken from the 1850/60 census), were: **(i)** Sarah E. bc 1848; **(ii)** Chandler b 1850 (age 5m in Nov); **(iii)** L. (female) bc 1853; **(iv)** M. (female) bc 1855; **(v)** William bc 1857; **(vi)** S. (male) bc 1859.

207. **SARAH MITCHELL**, daughter of Claudius and Nancy Ann (Lambert) Mitchell, was born 15 Mar 1817 in Madison Co., OH. She married 25 Sep 1834 in Champaign Co., OH to Remembrance Williams, Jr., born about 1813 in OH, son of Remembrance, Sr. and Jane ( ) Williams.

The files of Ken Potee (dec'd) included a letter from a Mary Skardon who said Remembrance was a soldier of the Revolution, born in Harrison Co., VA, going from there to Nelson Co., KY, then Zenia, OH, then Jefferson Co., IN, dying there 2 Feb 1843. Surely this refers to the <u>father</u> of Remembrance, Sr. who seems to be the man, age 73, born in MD, living with Robert and Elizabeth Williams in the 1860 census of Goshen Twp., Champaign Co., OH (p191). In the same county and township (1850 and 1860) lived Remembrance, Jr. and Sarah. His 1860 real estate evaluation was $4,080; personal property $800 (p187). Remembrance, Jr. died in 1880 and Sarah died 29 Jan 1905.

Sarah's children (WILLIAMS) were: **(i)** Claudius bc 1835; **(ii)** Mary bc 1837 m 13 Nov 1855 Eli Arbogast bc 1835 OH; lvg 1860 Pleasant Twp., Clark Co., OH, 2 doors from Otho & Dorothy Arbogast; 2 ch known; **(iii)** John bc 1839 d 2 Aug 1922; **(iv)** Lucy bc 1843; **(v)** Matilda bc 1848 d 4 May 1927 mc 1866 Robert Bayless bc 1830 OH d 21 Jan 1899 bur in

Maple Grove Cem., Champaign Co., OH; 6 ch; **(vi)** Lovena b
June 1850 d 7 Jan 1912 mc 1871 William Burnside bc 1841 OH
d 1928; 4 ch known; **(vii)** Jane bc 1851; **(viii)** Charley bc
1858; **(ix)** Pearl (son) bc 1862.

208. **LAVINA MITCHELL**, daughter of Claudius and Nancy Ann
(Lambert) Mitchell, was born 22 Jan 1819 Madison Co., OH,
married 4 Dec 1836 (Champaign Co., OH) Gabriel M. Potee,
born 21 Mar 1817 Frederick Co., MD, son of Sutton and Hannah (Markley) Potee. Lavina died 10 Dec 1882 at her home
in Somerford Twp., Madison Co. Gabriel sold his farm in
1885 and moved to Springfield, OH. He married 2) before
Mar 1886 Eusebia N.____, b 17 Jan 1836. He died 9 Oct
1894 at Bloomingburg, Fayette Co., OH. Gabriel and both
wifes are buried in Somerford Twp. Cemetery, Madison Co.
     After his marriage, Gabriel farmed rented land in
Pleasant Twp., Clark Co., OH for about 8 years; he then
bought land in Somerford Twp., Madison Co. He served as
township trustee for 3 terms. Both he and Lavina joined
the Methodist Church when they were age sixteen.
     Lavina's children (POTEE) were: **(i)** Sutton b 1 Oct
1838 d 3 May 1869 age 30y 7m 2d; **(ii)** Claudius bc 1841 d
Apr 1908 age "abt 68y" nr Mill City, Marion Co., OR (bur
there) m1) 26 Nov 1862 Clark Co., OH to Jane "Jennie" Eck-
les bc 1846 OH (moved to Dayton, OH bef Dec 1896 lvg 1905);
m2) Mrs. E. Merrill; 4 ch by 1st mar; **(iii)** Elizabeth A. bc
1844 m 12 Mar 1868 (Madison Co., OH) R.R. Ryan bc 1847 OH;
to NE ca1872; York Co., NE 1880C; to OR 1892; 3 ch known;
(iv) Newton bc 1847 d 1932 m 1882 Anna Roberts b 1853 d
1916; **(v)** John Milton b Oct 1849 d 1946 Bondville, IL at
home of dau Linnie Smith; m 30 Dec 1875 (Madison Co.) Ara-
belle Wilson b 20 Apr 1853 OH d 10 Feb 1912 Madison Co. d/o
Washington & Linnie (West) Wilson; 7 ch; **(vi)** Nancy A. b
10 Mar 1853 d 30 Mar 1889 Madison Co. age 36y 20d m 16 Mar
1876 (Madison Co., OH) Charles Gilbert b 1849 Clark Co.,
OH d 1932 s/o Sidney C. & Elizabeth (Clark) Gilbert; fam
lvg Cherokee Co., KS 1880C; Charles lvg Urbana, IL 1913;
both bur Somerford Twp. Cem., Madison Co., OH; 6 ch.

209. **MARTHA A. MITCHELL**, daughter of Claudius and Nancy
Ann (Lambert) Mitchell, was born 24 May 1821 in Madison
Co., OH. She married 23 Jan 1839 in Champaign Co., OH to
Robert Ellison, born about 1819/20 OH. In 1840, Martha A.
and Robert resided in Goshen Twp., Champaign Co., OH, but

by 1850 were living in Somerford Twp., Madison Co., OH (Robert marked "cannot read or write" in this census). It is possible that Martha A. and Robert left Madison Co. after 1850 since there seems to be no information on their dates and places of death, nor any children listed for them born after the 1850 census.

Martha A.'s known children (ELLISON), all born in Champaign or Madison Co., OH, were: **(i)** Claudius C. bc 1842; **(ii)** Mary Ann bc 1844; **(iii)** William A. bc 1846; **(iv)** Philander bc 1848.

210. **JOSHUA MITCHELL**, son of Claudius and Nancy Ann (Lambert) Mitchell, was born 22 May 1823 in Madison Co., OH. He married 2 Sep 1841 in Champaign Co., OH to Elizabeth C. Rigdon, born about 1822 in Ohio.

In 1848 Joshua bought 100 acres of land in Madison Co., OH from Jacob S. Adams (Bk 18:291), selling this same amount of acreage in 1850 to Charles Chappell (Bk 20:135). He then moved to Goshen Twp., Champaign Co., OH where he and Elizabeth C. are listed in the 1850 census. Joshua bought property there from Lewis C. Rigdon and wife.

Known children of Joshua and Elizabeth C. (Rigdon) Mitchell, probably all born in Madison Co., OH, were:

  320. **Wesley F.** bc 1842
  321. **Mary Jane** bc 1844
  322. **Thomas J.** bc 1846
  323. **Claudius N.** bc 1848
  324. **Elizabeth** b 1850 (age 4m at census)

212. **CHANDLER MITCHELL**, son of Claudius and Nancy Ann (Lambert) Mitchell, was born 29 June 1828 on the "old Mitchell farm" in Champaign Co., OH. He married there on 29 Mar 1849 to Elizabeth A. McConkey Hendrix, born 10 Oct 1828 in Clark or Champaign Co., OH, daughter of William S. and Elizabeth Thompson (McConkey) Hendrix.

Chandler was called "the greatest shipper of stock in this section...known all over central Ohio." He primarily raised sheep and eventually owned 3,000 acres of land. In 1860, Chandler's property adjoined that of his father which was adjacent to Chandler's brother-in-law and sister, Remembrance and Sarah Williams. His real estate was evaluated at $12,000.00; personal property at $3,500.00. By 1870, these figures had soared to $21,360.00 for real estate and $4,015 for personal property.

Chandler and Elizabeth A. had their portraits taken when they were probably in their early 40's. Chandler was a man of medium build with high cheekbones, a receding hairline, no mustache but side burns and a short, dark, trimmed beard. His expression is quite pleasant and he was quite nattily dressed with a black bow tie and checkered vest over a starched white shirt. He wore neither a ring nor a pocketwatch. Elizabeth was stylishly dressed as befitted the wife of a successful farmer. Her bonnet with flower decorated high raised brim was tied with an enormous bow, her dark hair parted in the middle and pulled back. She wore a cape that fell to about a foot or two above the hem of her voluminous floor length skirt. Black lace fingerless mitts adorned her hands.

Chandler died 24 Sep 1892 and Elizabeth A. died 4 Feb 1901, both in Champaign Co., OH, and both buried there in Maple Grove Cemetery. Children of Chandler and Elizabeth A. McConkey (Hendrix) Mitchell, all born in Champaign Co., OH, were:

325. **William Clinton** b 11 Jan 1850 d 7 Jan 1861.
326. **Claudius Newton** b 1 Jan 1852   +
327. **Charles Lincoln** b 22 May 1861   +

215. **ELMIRA/ALMIRA MITCHELL,** daughter of Claudius and Nancy (Lambert) Mitchell, was born 6 Dec 1834 Champaign Co., OH and married there 28 Apr 1853 Isaac Potee, born 16 Sep 1823 Madison Co., OH, son of Sutton and Hannah (Markley) Potee and brother to Gabriel who married Elmira's sister, Lavina. In 1880 Isaac retired from farming, moving into London where he died 25 Mar 1885 and Elmira died 1 Oct 1928, both buried in Somerford Twp. Cemetery, Madison Co. (Isaac had been married first 26 Sep 1850 Clark Co., OH to Rachel Marsh, daughter of Josiah L.; she died in 1852 leaving a daughter, Nancy J. Potee 1851-1923.)

As the youngest child, Beers' ("History of Madison Co., OH," Union Twp) says Isaac grew up with limited education and in pioneer surroundings, "often seeing a drove of twenty deer pass his father's door." At first, Isaac and Elmira lived in Somerford Twp. of Madison Co., then on Elmira's father's farm in Champaign Co., returning to Somerford Twp. in 1857 where they remained until 1880. Beers says Isaac was "connected with no organization whatever, except for the Methodist Episcopal Church, of which he has been an able member for over forty years."

In 1873 as an "able member," Isaac had the Somerford M.E. Church building erected at a total cost to himself of $2,500. He was church trustee, school board member, and a Republican. No doubt Elmira was also a staunch Methodist, her father as well as Isaac being of that persuasion.

Elmira's children (POTEE) were: **(i)** Claudius D. bc 1854 d 1917 mc 1876 per in Logan Co., OH Emma Brown; he was rec'd at Goshen Monthly Meeting (Quaker), Logan Co. 6th mo. 16, 1878; with wife & 4 ch he requested a certificate to Dale Monthly Meeting in Kansas 6th mo. 11, 1887; res in 1928 Hollandale, MI; 5 ch known; **(ii)** William Sutton b 9 June 1856 d 21 Sep 1863 age 7y 3m 12d; **(iii)** Amelia Rachel "Annie" bc 1859 d 1938 m1) 19 Dec 1878 (Madison Co., OH) Frank James Kiefer; she was Annie Taylor of Wellshire, OH in mother's obit 1928; **(iv)** Hannah b 1861 d 15 Sep 1863 age 2y 7m ___ d; **(v)** Idelia bc 1864 d 1925 m 22 Feb 1883 Madison Co., OH Alfred A. Lerew; to Dak Terr 1883; **(vi)** Della (also as Helena D. & Ellen) b 9 Sep 1867 d 1951 m 10 Nov 1886 (Madison Co., OH) Jonathan J. Bradley b 1864 d 1 Apr 1917 nr Lafayette, OH s/o Cornelius; 5 ch known; **(vii)** Gabriel "Rell" b 15 Feb 1870 d 1950 m 17 Sep 1891 (Madison Co., OH) Luella F. Bethards; lvg Bluffton, OH 1928; **(viii)** Isaac Milton bc 1872 d 1948 m Anna Lola Frost b 1870 d 1913; lvg Great Falls, MT 1928; 4 ch; **(ix)** Cordelia bc 1877 m 8 Sep 1897 (Madison Co.) Charles E Morrell; to Versailles, OH; Cordelia m2) ___ Stanley; lvg Columbus OH 1828; **(x)** Nora May b 1879 d bef 1883. (Thanks to Carol Sanford, 1191 Lincoln Rd., Columbus, OH 43212 for help with the Potee family and on other Mitchell descendants in Ohio.)

218. **ABIGAIL E. MITCHELL,** daughter of Ira and Jane (Rhodes) Mitchell, was born Dec 1830 in Pike Twp., Madison Co., OH. She grew up in Miami Co., IN where her parents moved in 1834. There she married 31 Jan 1850 to Welcome B. Walker, born about 1819 in "Canada West" (his parents both "foreign born" per census records). By 1858, Abigail E. and Welcome B. had followed Abigail's parents to Iowa where they had moved in 1853.

In the 1870 census, Abigail and her family were living in Mt. Pleasant, Salem Twp., Henry Co., IA. Welcome B. (erroneously listed as "Wm.") and his eldest son worked together as "painters," presumeably of houses. Welcome died before 1900, probably at Ottumwa, Wapello Co., IA where Abigail E. is listed in the 1900 census as a widow.

She was also living there in 1891 per the listing of heirs in her father's probate papers.

Abigail E.'s granddaughter, Nellie V. Walker, born about 1875 in IA, eldest daughter of Everett A. Walker, bears mentioning here. Nellie V. became a sculptor and worked at a studio at 6016 Ellis Ave. in Chicago, IL with the well-known Loredo Taft. In 1907, Nellie V. wrote a letter of inquiry to the Pension Bureau, Washington, D.C. about the Revolutionary War service records of her great-great-grandfather, Ensign Mitchell (Sr.); her address in Chicago at that time was 1038 Fine Arts Building.

Abigail E. must have been endowed with the same physical and mental energy ascribed to her father. In 1900, although 70 years old, she was caring for her grandson, Earl Paxton, born 1889 in Nebraska, son of Abigail's only daughter, Ella Jane. (Earl states his father was born in MD and his mother in IA. His father may have been Francis M. Paxton, bc 1854 MD, living in 1870 in Henry Co., IA with his parents, George W. and Edith B. Paxton.)

Abigail's exact date of death is not known but in 1914 she attested for her widowed sister, Elizabeth Hess, in Elizabeth's petition for a widow's pension, signing her affidavit with a very clear, strong hand which belied her 83 years. She was living at that time with her son, Ira, in Richland, Keokuk Co., IA.

Abigail's children (WALKER), first two born in Miami Co., IN, third in IA, were: **(i)** Everett A. b Dec 1850 mc 1873 Rebecca J. _____ b Apr 1848 OH; res 1900 Moulton, Appanoose Co., IA; real estate dealer; 6 children lvg 1900; **(ii)** Ira M. b Dec 1853 mc 1875 Martha R. _____ b June 1853 IA; res 1900 Oak St., Richland, Keokuk Co., IA; fire insurance agent; 5 children; **(iii)** Ella Jane bc 1858 IA d bef 1900 m _____ Paxton; lvd 1889 in NE; 1 son.

219. **OBED H. MITCHELL,** son of Ira and Jane (Rhodes) Mitchell, was born May 1833 in Pike Twp., Madison Co., OH. He married about 1866 Amanda Rebecca Sutton, born Dec 1844 in IL. In 1900 Obed H. and his wife were living in Campbell Twp., Greene Co., MO. Obed H. was a stockbroker and owned his own house. His wife (as Rebecca S.) states that her parents were both born in TN and that she was the mother of one child. Only child of Obed H. and Amanda Rebecca (Sutton) Mitchell, born in MO, was:

328. **Guy S.** b May 1867; bookkeeper; unmar 1900.

220. **IRA R. MITCHELL,** son of Ira and Jane (Rhodes) Mitchell, was born 18 Oct 1835 near Peru, Perry Twp., Miami
Co., IN. In his application for a Civil War pension, Ira
states that he married 15 Apr 1871 "Lida" (Lydia) Green
"in Missoura...down on the Thobes..." by a Mr. Hemenway,
"no license required." Lydia died "near Fort Hays, Kansas
at her sister's away out on a claim of sister in June
1885..." Ira and Lydia had no children.

Ira R. enlisted at Salem, IA on 3 Oct 1861 in Co. I,
14th Reg't, IA Volunteer Infantry. He is described as 5
feet 7½ inches tall with auburn hair, hazel eyes and light
complexion, a farmer by occupation. A corporal by rank,
he was later promoted to 5th Sergeant. Ira was discharged on 17 Feb 1863 at Keokuk, IA as unfit for duty for the
past 180 days, being "...afflicted ever since the Battle
of Fort Donaldson Feb. 13th, 14th, 15th, 1862, and was
taken prisoner at Shiloh April 6th, 1862, his unhealthy
diet increased his disease and has entirely reduced his
system. Disease Chronic Diarrhea in its worst form." The
examining surgeon at Benton Barracks, MO added that Ira
also suffered from "Chronic Opthalmia and...Rheumatism."

Seeking a government pension in 1888, Ira's brother-
in-law, Henry H. Hess, deposed that "...during my stay in
Salem (IA) prior to my enlistment...Ira was as stout,
healthy and as robust a young man as any in the country...
when I was in Salem spending leave of absence (1864) he
was very much reduced in flesh...suffering from a disease
of the kidney...brought on from the affects of exposure
and hardships...whilst he was a prisoner...in 1866, I
asked him what treatment he was persuing. He told me he
used no medicine, that he believed he was doing better by
the use of a Milk diet and coarse bread, no meats, nor coffee, nor tea. He said...he would not take medicine from
the best physician in Iowa...I know him to be strictly
temperate nor is he adicted to any bad habits."

Ira's claim to the Examining Board was for rheumatism
in every part of his body, shoulders, elbows, wrists, his
back, hips, knees and ankles; heart palpitations when
startled or exercising; and possible kidney disease. The
examining doctors indeed found rheumatism, "dynamic"
heart disease, and lumbago. Ira was awarded his pension
for disabilities equal to the "loss of a hand or foot."

After the death of his father in 1891, Ira remained in
Salem, IA with his mother until after her death in 1893.

By 1900 he was living in Richland, Keokuk Co., IA where he boarded with the Suliss family. Sometime after 1900, Ira made his way to CA. In 1915, Ira filled out a form to the Pension Bureau giving his address as 1846 Main St., San Diego, CA, stating in part that he was "...living alone in a cottage...will be 80 years old on Oct. 18, 1915. Never married but once nor was my wife...no children. I have done the best I can from memory - I can't remember anything. Memory gone - gone - "

Between 1915 and 1918, Ira moved to the Soldiers Home in Los Angeles, CA. A Declaration for Pension was filled out for him on 26 May 1922, stating that "old age renders him too feeble to walk..." Ira R. died at the Pacific Branch National Home for Disabled Volunteers on 4 Jan 1928 of chronic myocarditis and senile dementia. His brother, John E. Mitchell of Keokuk, IA, was named as his next-of-kin.

221. **LUCY M. MITCHELL,** daughter of Ira and Jane (Rhodes) Mitchell, was born about 1838 in Perry Twp., Miami Co., IN. She married in Henry Co., IA on 25 Jan 1864 to Henry Hyde Hess while he was home on veteran furlough. Henry H. was born 12 Sep 1837, son of D. C. and Lydia (Gaylord) Hess of NY and CT. In his Civil War reinlistment papers, Henry says he was born in Wayne Co., NY. In later years, his pension papers state his place of birth as Ionia Co., MI, and in all census records his place of birth is MI.

On 6 Jul 1861 at Mt. Pleasant, IA, Henry H. enlisted in Co. E, 1st Reg't, Iowa Volunteer Cavalry as a private. He was 5 feet 11½ inches tall with grey eyes, dark complexion and "light" hair, a farmer by occupation. In 1863, Henry began assisting the Regimental Veterinarian Surgeon and continued to do so for the remainder of his service. After he reinlisted as a veteran volunteer early in 1864, Henry did extra duty at Little Rock as a veterinarian surgeon. He was mustered out at Austin, TX on 15 Feb 1866. Throughout the war Henry furnished his own horse and horse equipment, occasionally his own forage and sustenance as well. He was periodically reimbursed by the paymaster for "use and risk" of his horse. At the end of his term of service, he received $400.00 bounty money, and retained one Spencer carbine and "accoutrements."

After the war, Henry and Lucy moved to Jasper Co., MO near Avilla, living about 20 miles from the homes of his brother and wife, Oliver and Zoe Hess, and his sister, Diantha "Dantie" (Hess) Hill. In the spring of 1870, Henry sent urgent word to his brother and sister that Lucy was desperately ill and not expected to live. Oliver, Zoe and Diantha came immediately, but Lucy died on 21 May 1870, three days after their arrival. She was buried in a cemetery near Avilla, Jasper Co., MO.

Henry moved to Elk Falls, KS after Lucy's death, probably leaving his daughter with her Mitchell grandparents. She was the only grandchild her Grandfather Ira Mitchell mentioned in his will, leaving Allie $500 and the organ from the family home in Salem, IA. During Henry's resi- dence in KS, he returned to Henry Co., IA and married his deceased wife's sister, Elizabeth M. Mitchell (see #221).

Lucy's only child (HESS) was: **(i)** Alice "Allie" Lee b 6 Dec 1867 nr Avilla, Jasper Co., MO; lvg unmar at Mystic, Appanoose Co., IA in 1891.

222. ELIZABETH M. (LIZZIE) MITCHELL, daughter of Ira and Jane (Rhodes) Mitchell, was born May 1840 in Perry Twp., Miami Co., IN. She married 19 Nov 1872 in Henry Co., IA to Henry Hyde Hess, her deceased sister's husband (see #220 for Hess data). Henry H. died of pneumonia on 19 Feb 1914 at Colorado Springs, CO, age 76 years 5 months 7 days, Elizabeth surviving him. He was buried there on 22 Feb.

In 1873 Elizabeth and Henry went to St. Louis, MO where they lived until just before 1880, returning then to Salem Twp., Henry Co., IA where they lived next-door to Elizabeth's parents. Although he still calls himself a farmer in the 1880 census, somewhere along the way Henry became a dentist, his occupation in 1900. By then, the family had moved to Marshalltown, Marshall Co., IA, living at 7 Grant St. with their married daughter, Diantha, her husband, Obed L. Burch, a "student and stenographer," and the two Burch children. Henry and Elizabeth's two unmarried daughters were also living with them in 1900, both of them stating their occupation as stenographer.

Just after 1900, Henry and Elizabeth retired and moved to Colorado Springs, CO, possibly for Henry's health. In 1912, Henry filed for an increase in his Civil War pension. A next-door neighbor, J. W. Pring, who described himself as "more like a brother than a neighbor," said that Henry H. "...is a great sufferer from rheumatism, so much so that he is frequently confined to the house for several days at a time and always walks with a cain...he also has a bad case of catarrh in his head and throat, complains of having kidney troubles...he is now totally disabled from performing any kind of manual labor."

After Henry's death, Elizabeth had to obtain depositions attesting to her marriage to Henry and her widowhood in order to obtain a government widow's pension. Filing affadavits on her behalf were Henry's brother, Oliver Gaylord Hess, a lawyer living in La Junta, CO, his wife, Zoe Hess, and Elizabeth's sister and nephew, Abigail E. and Ira M. Walker of Richland, IA.

Elizabeth's children (HESS) were: **(i)** Ionia Genevieve b 6 Oct 1874 at St. Louis, MO; lvg with parents, unmar 1900; **(ii)** Diantha "Danta" Gaylord b 28 Dec 1877 at St. Louis, MO mc 1896 Obed Leroy Burch b June 1873 in MO; res 1900 Marshalltown, IA; 2 children; **(iii)** Lydia H. b 8 Jan 1880 Salem Twp., Henry Co., IA; lvg with parents unmar in 1900.

223. **JOHN ENSIGN MITCHELL,** son of Ira and Jane (Rhodes) Mitchell, was named for his two grandfathers, John Rhodes and Ensign Mitchell. He was born 25 Aug 1842 near Gilead, Perry Twp, Miami Co., IN, and died 7 Jul 1930 at Keokuk, IA. He married 16 Aug 1868 in Henry Co., IA to Elma Marie Henderson, born about 1842 in IA, daughter of Duvall W. and Mary A. ( ) Henderson. Elma died 28 Jan 1899 at Columbia, Boone Co., MO.

John E. enlisted on 1 Oct 1861 as a private in Co. I, 14th Reg't, Iowa Volunteer Infantry, at Davenport, IA. He is described as being 5 feet 9 inches tall with light complexion, blue eyes and dark hair, a farmer by occupation. A picture of John E. in his Civil War uniform shows him to have been a very handsome young man, slender, clean shaven except for a trim mustache, and with a widow's peak which became more pronounced as he grew older.

John E.'s brother, Ira, enlisted in the same company as John. They were together in the Battle of Fort Donaldson in Feb 1862 and the Battle of Pittsburg (Shiloh, TN) where they were captured with the entire regiment about six o'clock on the evening of 6 Apr 1862. John E. was confined in rebel prisons at Memphis and Mobile, AL, then at Macon, GA until his parole on 28 May 1862 at Montgomery, AL. While in Confederate prison, he had his left arm tattooed with the Coat of Arms of America. After his parole,

John E. was sent to Benton Barracks, MO, then assigned to
guard duty at Cairo, IL with the Provost Marshall's office. In June 1864, he was sent to Memphis, TN on recommendation of Col. James J. Gilbert, commander of the 2nd
Brigade, 3rd Division 16th Army Corps, to serve as clerk
for Lt. J. B. Comstock, his rank now being 8th Corporal.
While in Memphis, he was treated in the hospital from Jul
22nd until Aug 5th for intermittent fever. He was discharged at Davenport, IA on 7 Nov 1864.

After his marriage, John E. moved around quite a bit
due to his chosen profession in sales. At his father's
death in 1891, he and Elma were living in Salem, IA but at
his mother's death in 1893, he and Elma were in St. Louis
where he was sales manager for Garretson, Cox & Co., publishers. His daughter, Merta, who graduated in 1894 from
the "Law School" at Greencastle, IN, was sharing her
father's offices in the fall of that year, working as a
bookkeeper and Attorney-at-law. (Descendants say that
the Indiana State Legislature held a special session to
allow Merta to practice law.) In June 1894, John E. received the disquieting news that he had been replaced as
executor of his father's estate, mostly based on the fact
that he was a non-resident of Iowa.

In a futile attempt to protest this removal, John E.
and Elma gave lengthy depositions in front of a Notary
Public in St. Louis, emphasizing that they were only temporary residents of St. Louis, that John was on a salary
and likely to be removed or sent elsewhere at anytime, and
that their permanent residence was Salem, IA where they
had property consisting of a house and outbuildings plus
parts of 2 lots owned by Elma. Their house in Salem, they
stated, was in such condition that "...within five minutes after unlocking the doors we can either commence
cooking or sleeping there." The house "contains chairs
and carpets, stoves and cooking utensils, books and book
shelves and book cases, bed clothes and wearing apparel,
mirrors and bric-a-brac, lounges and sofas, clocks and
wall ornaments, pictures and picture frames, table stands
and wardrobes and everything it takes to make up household
effects..." Elma had locked up the Salem house in the
fall of 1893 and gone to St. Louis with the family to be
with her husband as she had done once before when he had
been working in Chicago. Any return to Salem could be due
to "...sickness, from business necessity, for our health,

or because we have no other place to stay, and I don't know which will be cause first on our list."

Besides St. Louis and Chicago, John E. had lived at various times in Jefferson City and Columbia, MO, Winfield and Burden, KS, and Memphis, TN before he settled in Keokuk, IA where he lived on Pleasant Ave. He did not apply for a war pension until 1904 at age 62. He claimed no war-inflicted disabilities, simply citing his age as the qualifying factor. At that time, he was still working in sales. To prove his date of birth, he submitted a notarized copy of the birth records from his mother's family Bible (American Bible Society, NY, D. Fanshaw, Printer, 1840). He was granted $6.00 per month which was gradually raised to $30.00 per month by 1917. In 1915, John E.'s signature is firm and legible, the "t" in Mitchell crossed from the right edge of the "M" and extended well past the final "l" with the final "l" dropping down to double underline the last name. The "Portrait & Biographical Album of Henry Co., IA" credits John E. with being "the patentee of the washing machine bearing his name."

Children of John Ensign and Elma Marie (Henderson) Mitchell, 1st born in Salem, IA, 2nd perhaps in Burden, Cowley Co., KS, were:

329. **M. Merta** b 9 Nov 1872 d 1936 Salem, IA unmar.
330. **D. Isa (Iza)** b 28 Feb 1881 m 23 Nov 1941 Lawrence Widdefield who d 1956; Iza lvg 1957; no children.

224. **FRANCIS M. (FRANK) MITCHELL,** son of Ira and Jane (Rhodes) Mitchell, was born Aug 1845 in Perry Twp., Miami Co., IN. He married 1 Oct 1883 in Henry Co., IA to Anna E. Kittle, born Mar 1858 in IA, daughter of William and Minerva (Hannagan) Kittle. The Kittles arrived in IA in the early 1850's where William was first a carpenter and then a hotelkeeper in Salem.

In 1900 Francis M. and Anna were living at 1212 Bluff, Keokuk City, Lee Co., IA. His occupation at that time was travel agent and he was buying his own home. Only child of Francis M. and Anna E. (Kittle) Mitchell (born in IN per the 1900 census) was:

331. **Herman I.** b Jan 1886; lvg with parents 1900.

225. **LEONARD M. MITCHELL,** son of Ira and Jane (Rhodes) Mitchell, was born about 1848 in Perry Twp., Miami Co., IN. He married 16 Oct 1870 in Henry Co., IA to Ellen M.

Sixth Generation

"Ella" Murphy, born June 1851 in IN, daughter of William
J. and Ellender ( ) Murphy, both of VA. In the 1870 cen-
sus, taken before Ella's marriage, she was a dressmaker.
Leonard followed in the footsteps of his brother,
John E., and became a salesman. Presumably, he was on a
sales trip in 1880 when he was listed in the census with
R. R. and Lizzie A. Ryan of York Co., NE. Lizzie Ryan was
the daughter of Lavina (Mitchell) Potee (#208), and the
granddaughter of Claudius Mitchell of Ohio, an uncle to
Leonard who was Lizzie Ryan's 1st cousin once-removed.
In 1887, tragedy struck this family. For 32 days,
Leonard lay desperately ill with typhoid fever, succumb-
ing on 23 Oct 1887 at age 39 years. He lived in Salem, IA
at the time of his death and was buried in the Methodist
church burial grounds there. In 1893, his widow, Ella,
married William H. Kronscop, a grocery salesman with a 15
year old daughter, Mildred. In 1900 the Kronscop family
was living on W. Henry St., Mt. Pleasant City, Henry Co.,
IA. At this time, there were no children by Ella's second
marriage and her eldest daughter, Aura, was not living in
the household. Phebe was working as a sales lady in a dry
goods store. Dorothy listed no occupation. Ella stated
that she was the mother of 3 children, all 3 still living.
Children of Leonard M. and Ellen M. "Ella" (Murphy)
Mitchell, all born in Salem, Henry Co., IA, were:
332. **Aura (Orrie)** bc 1875; lvg 1900.
333. **Phebe (Cada)** b Dec 1877 m bef 1914 George W. Merrill, Jr.; res 1914 in Pueblo, CO.
334. **Dorothy (Dottie)** b Nov 1880 m Dow Roof.

226. **JULIA ANN RIGDON**, daughter of Charles and Lydia
(Mitchell) Rigdon, was born 26 Sep 1825 Champaign Co., OH
and married 19 Oct 1843 (Madison Co., OH) Calvin Fenton
Bales, born 30 Jan 1821 Frederick Co., VA, son of Moses &
Mary (Fish) Bales. (Calvin's brother, Thomas, married
Julia's sister, Emaline Rigdon [#227]; his half-brother,
David Bales, married Julia's cousin, Lydia Jane "Jennie"
Mitchell [#236], daughter of Newman.) Calvin died 3 Aug
1863 in Madison Co. and Julia died 25 Jul 1911 on the home
farm near Tradersville, Madison Co. Both are buried there
in Oak Hill Cemetery.
Bryan's "History of Madison Co., OH (1915) says that
Calvin (also called Colvin) and Julia moved to the home-
stead near Tradersville shortly after marriage. After he

cleared and drained part of his 400 acres of "wild land," Calvin put 75 acres into cultivation and sold part of the rest until 215 acres remained. He was primarily a stockman, owning many cattle and sheep. Shortly before he died Calvin bought 430 acres near London, OH, probably to use as grazing land for his stock.

Calvin's death in 1863 left Julia Ann with 5 children aged 5 to 18 years. She sold the property near London, had the Tradersville farm home remodeled and enlarged, and continued to live there with her children. Charles E., the eldest of her two sons, was not yet 15 when his father died but had worked with him since he was 10 years old. Bryan says Charles E. "carried" 300 sheep during the winter of 1863-1864. Eventually, he bought out his brother and sisters' share of the farm, enlarged it to 376 acres, and bought 5,000 acres of wheat and grass land in Kansas which he stocked with Herefords, a hardy beef cattle, red with white faces and markings. He never married.

Calvin and Julia were strong supporters of the Methodist Church at Tradersville, the Bales home known as "the home of the Methodist ministers..." which no doubt influenced their son, Milton M., who became first a Methodist minister and in later years a Baptist Doctor of Divinity.

Julia Ann's children (BALES) born in Madison Co., OH were: **(i)** Emeline b 20 Jan 1845 d 3 Oct 1887 (T.B.) Madison Co. m 1867 Daniel Hendrix b 9 Jul 1841 "nr Summerford, OH" d there 31 Jan 1919; C.W. vet; 3 ch; **(ii)** Mary Jane b 1 Mar 1846 d 19 Aug 1928 m 1 June 1871 William Laus Houston b 25 Dec 1843 So. Charleston, OH s/o Thomas Fisher & Rachel (Delashmut) Houston d 11 Mar 1900 London, OH; both bur there in Kirkwood Cem; 3 ch; **(iii)** Charles E. b 17 Nov 1848 d 12 May 1936 unmar; **(iv)** Milton McKindree b 14 Oct 1855 d 23 June 1944 m1) Stella E. Curtis b 1858 d 1909; m2) 3 Feb 1912 at Findlay, OH to Carrie Helen Bolton; grad of Garrett Biblical Institute; res 1912 Cleveland, OH; 1915 Homestead, FL; **(v)** Lydia Minerva bc 1858 m aft 1880 Dr. E. U. Wood, a physician and surgeon "of note"; res 1915 Columbus, IN.

227. **EMELINE RIGDON,** daughter of Charles and Lydia (Mitchell) Rigdon, was born 22 Jan 1828 (Champaign or Madison Co., OH) and married 6 Dec 1845 Madison Co. to Thomas Bales, born 9 Aug 1817 Frederick Co., VA, son of Moses and Mary (Fish) Bales. Emeline died 18 Jan 1897 in

Madison Co. and Thomas died 5 June 1902 in London, OH, both buried there in Oak Hill Cemetery.

Thomas owned much property in the Tradersville, OH area, value of his real estate in the 1860 census was $17,000. The 1875 Madison Co. Atlas shows his land next to that of his father-in-law and his brother Calvin, lying north of Tradersville, with other acreage south of town.

In 1853 the two eldest children of Thomas and Emeline died within a week's time and are buried in Nation Chapel Methodist Church cemetery just across the county line in Pleasant Twp., Clark Co., OH beside Thomas' sister.

Children of Thomas and Emeline (Rigdon) BALES, all born in Madison Co., OH, were:

335. **Laura** b 17 Sep 1848 d 2 Oct 1853.
336. **John Fletcher** b 14 Mar 1851 d 8 Oct 1853.
337. **Talitha** b 17 Jan 1855   +
338. **Alta Leora** b 31 Jul 1858 d 25 Jul 1914 nr Spring-
      field, OH in an auto accident; m 16 May 1883
      Charles W. Gray b 1852 d 1907; no children.
339. **Carrie** b 16 Nov 1868   +

233. **IRA MITCHELL,** son of Abizer and Margaret (Stanley) Mitchell, was born 26 Sep 1835 Madison Co., OH, married there 22 Oct 1858 Eliza Jane Bland, born 3 Feb 1837 in OH. Ira died 7 Apr 1883 and Eliza Jane died 23 Apr 1908, both buried in Maple Grove Cemetery, Champaign Co., OH.

In 1863 Ira bought $301\frac{1}{2}$ acres of land from his father in Madison Co. Per the 1875 Madison Co., OH Atlas, which calls Ira a farmer and stockraiser, this land lay in Surveys #12021 and 12583 near Rosedale.

Ira and Eliza Jane lost their only son in 1879 who died just about 3 months before his 15th birthday. Several months after his death, their only daughter married James H. McClintock, born in 1855 OH, died in 1931, probably the James McClintock, age 5 in 1860, living in the household of William and Eliza McClintock in Pleasant Twp., Clark Co., OH (p 24). After Ida Mae's death in 1889, Eliza Jane took her two McClintock granddaughters, Lella and Cora, to raise. In 1880 the McClintocks lived next to Ida Mae's father, Ira, whose widowed father, Abizer, is in the McClintock household. James H. McClintock married second Lydia _____, born 1860, died (1922?). (Data from granddaughter Sandra Fox Collins, 925 W. Fifth, Apt. 68, Marysville, OH 43040.)

Children of Ira and Eliza Jane (Bland) Mitchell, both born in Madison Co., OH, were:
340. **Ida Mae** b 23 Oct 1859 d 11 Apr 1889 m 6 Aug 1879 James H. McClintock.
341. **Presta Ira** b 17 Sep 1864 d 9 June 1879.

234. **JANE MITCHELL,** daughter of Abizer & Margaret (Stanley) Mitchell, was born about 1837 Madison Co., OH, and died there 4 May 1928, aged 91 years 3 months 15 days. She married 15 Oct 1857 William Brown, born 13 Nov 1829 in Madison Co., son of James and Mary Ann (Burnside) Brown. William died 12 Jul 1904 in Pleasant Twp., Clark Co., OH. Both he and Jane are buried in Maple Grove Cemetery in Mechanicsburg, OH. William was a farmer in the Nation Chapel area of Pleasant Twp. near the Champaign Co. line. About 1918, Jane and two children, Walter and Nella, moved from Clark Co. to Mechanicsburg.

Jane's children (BROWN) were: **(i)** Maude b 4 Oct 1862 d 1 Aug 1873 bur Maple Grove Cem; **(ii)** Son b/d 3 Feb 1868 bur Maple Grove Cem; **(iii)** Myrtle m John Adamson; lvg in Columbus, OH by 1905; still there 1956; **(iv)** Walter b 24 Aug 1875 d 23 Sep 1956 Champaign Co., OH bur Maple Grove Cem; unmar; **(v)** Nella b 1879 lvg 1956 unmar.

235. **ABIGAIL MITCHELL,** daughter of Newman and Cassandra (Bradley) Mitchell, was born 21 May 1838 Madison Co., OH, and married there 4 Sep 1855 John Henry Kennedy, born 24 Dec 1830 Madison Co., OH, son of John Henry and Jane (Teeters) Kennedy. He died there 2 Apr 1887. Abigail was deceased before 24 Dec 1884 per her mother's will.

Abigail's children (KENNEDY) were: **(i)** Florence bc 1857 m 15 Apr 1879 Charles Warren Guy, b 8 Nov 1843 Madison Co., s/o William & Adelaide (Fullington) Guy; lvg Mechanicsburg, OH 1894; 2 ch; **(ii)** Austin P. bc 1859 d 1880-1884 unmar; teacher; **(iii)** Geneva bc 1864 m 5 Oct 1887 Madison Co. Robert F. Chenoweth b 25 Feb 1861 Madison Co. d there 10 Feb 1913 s/o Francis Marion & Margaret (Rea) Chenoweth; div ca 1903/4; 2 ch.

236. **LYDIA JANE (JENNIE) MITCHELL,** daughter of Newman and Cassandra (Bradley) Mitchell, was born 16 Jan 1840 in Madison Co., OH, married there 6 Sep 1857 David Bales, born Sep 1836 Clark Co., OH, son of Moses and Catherine (Graves) Bales. David was age 13 when his father died.

He remained on the family farm until age 16, then "went West" for 2 years. After marriage, David and Jennie lived on his father's farm, buying an interest in it in 1862, then adding land until he owned 281 acres in Madison Co. He was a Republican and he and Jennie were members of the Christian Church (Beers' "History of Madison Co., OH").

About 1883, David (a Christian Church minister) and Jennie moved to Texas. They were in Abilene in 1884, in Jones Co., TX in 1900 living with their married daughter, Ida Goodyear and family, and at Buffalo Gap, TX in 1902, but then returned to Jones Co., TX. David died there at Truby 13 May 1916, and Jennie on 30 Jan 1931 (buried at Truby). (In 1885 Jennie inherited 180 acres of land and 1/4 of the "rest and residue" of the personal estate under the terms of her mother's will.)

Children of David and Lydia Jane (Mitchell) BALES, all born in Madison Co., OH, were:

342. Newman F. b 15 Oct 1858   +
343. Ida E. b 24 Sep 1861   +
344. Charles W. bc 1863/4 d 1883 unmarried.
345. Flora Mae bc 1866/7   +

239. CHARLES E. MITCHELL, son of Newman and Cassandra (Bradley) Mitchell, was born 9 May 1845 Madison Co., OH, married 9 Oct 1868 to Mary Elizabeth Heffley, born 14 Sep 1849 (per obit but not in 1850 census) Madison Co., daughter of Peter and Prudence (Mathes) Heffley. Charles E. died 9 Oct 1898. After his death, Mary Elizabeth (known as Lizzie) moved into Summerford where she died 4 Feb 1917. Both are buried in Somerford Twp. Cemetery.

Bryan describes Charles E. as "a man of great strength of character...strong mind, body and heart...one of the leading farmers in Madison County (who) pursued the even tenor of his way in a quiet, unostentatious manner, kept strictly to his own affairs and did the right as he understood it, keeping his conscience clear of offense toward God and man." His portrait shows him as possessing clean-cut good looks with hair, mustache and beard close trimmed ("History of Madison Co., OH," 1915).

After marriage, Charles E. bought a farm northwest of Tradersville; in 1869 or 1870 he moved to another 334 acre farm, also owning 442 acres near his father's old home which he inherited from his mother. He was an "extensive stock buyer and feeder," raising thousands of head of cattle, sheep and hogs. The home farm was later passed down to his sons by inheritance. (In the 1870 Madison Co., OH census, Charles E.'s household included Ann Hefley, age 10, and Mathias Hefley, age 21, both born in OH and probably related to Charles E.'s wife.)

Children of Charles E. and Mary Elizabeth (Heffley) Mitchell, all born in Madison Co., OH, were:

346. Alice J. b Dec 1869 +
347. Harry H. b 9 Aug 1871 d 22 Feb 1914 unmar.
348. Raleigh b 20 Nov 1873 +
349. Noel b 1889 +

244. **ELECTA (LETTIE) MITCHELL,** daughter of Newman and Cassandra (Bradley) Mitchell, was born 25 Nov 1855 Madison Co., OH, and married 27 Feb 1872 Fayette Co., OH to Lewis Harlen Creamer, born 18 Feb 1840 Jefferson Twp., Fayette Co., OH, son of Jacob and Elizabeth (Benson) Creamer. Lewis H. died 6 Apr 1920 at Mechanicsburg, OH, and Electa died there 9 May 1892. Both are buried in Maple Grove Cemetery, Mechanicsburg, Champaign Co., OH.

At the death of Electa's mother in 1885, she was left 400 acres of Madison Co. property adjoining that of her sister, Lydia Jane Bales, and of Mrs. D. W. C. Mann, Thomas Houston, heirs of Colvin Bales, Schuyler Lewis and the "agreement road line of R. G. Dun." She was also left one-fourth of the "rest" of her mother's personal estate.

Beers has nothing to say about Electa in his 1883 "History of Madison Co., OH" except to name her father and give her an erroneous date of marriage. He had nearly as little to say about Lewis H. except that he was a farmer of 200 acres of land near Tradersville in Madison Co., that he was a member of the Masonic order and "has been for sixteen years..." and that he was "...a young man of steady habits, and is much respected in the community..."

Children (born in Madison Co., OH) of Lewis Harlen and Electa (Mitchell) CREAMER, were:

350. **Iva Iona** b 17 June 1873 d 14 May 1946 unmar.
351. **Royalton Mitchell** b 1 Dec 1877 +

247. **RUSSELL BIGELOW MITCHELL,** son of Joseph and Irene (Bigelow) Mitchell, was born 19 Dec 1817 in Madison Co., OH. He was twice married, first on 16 Feb 1845 in McLean Co., IL (Bk B:97) to Julia Ann Bay who died in 1854; and second before 1857 Ursula R. Guin, born about 1820 in TN.

In the 1860 census, Russell and Ursula were living in Whitehall, Greene Co., IL (p 138). Russell's occupation was "editor of paper." He owned no real estate and lists personal property at only $75.00. Living with Russell was his younger brother, John F., a "printer," and Russell's widowed father, Joseph. Also in the household were Amelia D. Willson, age 57, and Napoleon Willson, age 8 months, both born in IL. Any relationship to Russell is unknown.

According to "The Bigelow Family of America" (pp 212/213), Russell and his family moved to Cedar Keys, FL. Known children of Russell Bigelow Mitchell (first 5 by 1st marriage, last 2 by 2nd marriage), born in IL, were:

352. **Amelia** b 12 Feb 1847 d 4 Mar 1848.
353. **William H.** bc 1849
354. **Brainerd** b 28 Nov 1848 m Belinda Smith.
355. **Clymene** b 9 Dec 1851 m John H. Wright.
356. **Irene** bc 1853; dy.
357. **Emma** bc 1857
358. **Franklin** b 25 Aug 1859 m Arabella Parker.

253. **JOHN FULLER MITCHELL**, son of Joseph and Irene (Bigelow) Mitchell, was born 30 Jul 1832 in Tazewell Co., IL, just a few months after his parents had come there from Madison Co., OH. He was living with his older brother, Russell B. (#247) in Whitehall, Greene Co., IL in the 1860 census, working as a printer, probably for Russell who was editor of a newspaper in Whitehall. John F. married Elizabeth A. Rossen and resided at Roodhouse, Greene Co., IL. Known children of John Fuller and Elizabeth A. (Rossen) Mitchell were:

359. **Henry** bc 1861
360. **Wilhemina** bc 1864

255. **ERASTUS W. MITCHELL**, son of Newman and Nancy (Mann) Mitchell was born about 1817/18 in Madison Co., OH. He married 2 Nov 1840 in Madison Co., OH to Clarissa "Clara" Smith, born about 1824 in NY (census). Dates and places of death for Erastus W. and Clarissa are unknown.

That Erastus W. was a son of Newman and Nancy (Mann) Mitchell is amply proved by Madison Co., OH deed records of the disposition of property in Madison Co. from his father's estate (see #147 Fifth Generation). Before 1850 Erastus W. and Clarissa had moved to Perry Twp., Logan Co., OH where they appear in the 1850 census (p 122).

They have not been found in later census records. A biography of their son, Sylvester G., says he enlisted in the Civil War at age 16 from Hardin Co., OH, and married there in 1872. This county should be searched by interested descendants for Erastus W. and Clarissa.

Known children of Erastus W. and Clarissa (Smith) Mitchell, born in Champaign Co., OH, were:

361. **Leonard** bc 1841
362. **Lorenzo** bc 1843
363. **Sylvester Greely** b 5 Jan 1846   +

256. **SARAH EMELINE MITCHELL,** daughter of Newman and Nancy (Mann) Mitchell, was born in Pike Twp., Madison Co., OH in 1820. She married there on 26 Jan 1837 (license issued 2 Nov 1836 Bk A:221) to Benjamin Taylor, born in ME about 1801 (1850 census), son of Cyrus and Abigail (Woodward) Taylor. Emeline, as she was usually called, died in 1853 in Champaign Co., OH and is buried there in Maple Grove Cemetery, Mechanicsburg. Benjamin married second Amelia Jane Baker. He died 7 May 1889.

In 1926, Emaline B. (Taylor) Beem, daughter of Benjamin and his second wife, wrote a family history in which she relates: "Benjamin and Orin (Taylor) were young men when they decided to come to Ohio; they (the family) sent the two young men on ahead and they selected Madison County. They stayed one year, then went back for the family; while in Ohio, they stopped with a Mr. Mitchel and family; while there, Benjamin fell in love with their daughter, Emeline, and later on they were married."

At the disposal of Emeline's deceased father's property in Madison Co. in 1845 and 1847, she is called Emeline Taylor in one deed and Sarah Emeline Taylor, wife of Benjamin, heir of Newman Mitchell deceased, in another as well as heir of Samuel Mann. (Madison Co., OH Deeds Bk 17: 58/59; Bk 21:266/67). These deeds also name her widowed mother, Nancy, her brother, Erastus and his wife, Clarissa, and her two unmarried brothers. (See #147 Fifth Gen.)

In the 1850 census, Benjamin and Emeline were living in Goshen Twp., Champaign Co., OH with a real estate evaluation of $4,100.00. Benjamin's parents and his brother, Orin, were also in that township and county. Living with Orin Taylor is Anna Taylor, age 88, born in ME. Although Benjamin's father, Cyrus, says he was born in NY, and his mother, Abigail, says she was born in NH, he and Orin both state they were born in ME. Living with Benjamin's parents in 1850 was Lydia Taylor, age 50, born in ME. (Data on the Taylor family courtesy of Carolyn Brooks, 2545 Hillsboro Ave., Dallas, TX 75228.)

Sarah Emeline's children (TAYLOR), first 2 born in Madison Co., OH, rest in either Madison or Champaign Co., were: **(i)** Nancy Abigail bc 1838; **(ii)** William Raper b 15 Jan 1839 d 11 Dec 1895 Franklin Co., KS m aft 10 Feb 1872 Mary Jane Robinson b 12 Apr 1852 Orange Co., NY d 2 May 1934 Franklin Co., KS; 1 dau known; **(iii)** Henry bc 1841; **(iv)** Leonard bc 1842; **(v)** Sidney bc 1845; **(vi)** Margaret bc 1847; **(vii)** Homer bc 1849.

267. **CONSIDER GOULD MITCHELL**, son of Levi and Britannia (Gould) Mitchell, was born 5 May 1830 in Kirkland Twp., Oneida Co., NY. He died 13 Feb 1907 at his home at 60 Rutgar St., Utica, Oneida Co., NY, and is buried in that county in the New Clinton Cemetery, Clinton, NY.

Consider G. married first in 1855 to Ann Eliza Mixer who died Aug 1862 in Jefferson Co., NY. She was probably buried in that county in Woodside Cemetery, Ellisburg in the Mixer family plot since Consider G. made provision in his will for maintence of the Grant Mixer lot in that cemetery. Consider G. married second in 1869 to Mary Robertson who died in 1903.

A lengthy obituary was printed in the 14 Feb 1907 issue of the "Utica Observer" (p 5) at Consider G.'s death which tells us a great deal about his life. In 1840 his parents moved from their farm "back in the country" to a farm on Utica St. in Clinton where Consider G. attended the district schools, completing his education at Clinton Liberal Institute. He then clerked at a store in Oriskany Falls and another in Deansboro, but the work "did not agree with his health." Shortly after his marriage to Ann Eliza in 1855, he returned to his father's farm in Clinton which he ran until 1862, renting the farm in that year "because of the illness of his wife" and moving to Jefferson Co., NY where Ann Eliza died, leaving Consider G. with a young daughter, Minnie. Consider G. then returned to Clinton, sold his farm, and moved to Utica, NY. For the next 20 years until his retirement in 1882, he was in the wholesale and retail mercantile business in Utica, first in partnership with D. P. Buckingham under the firm name of Buckingham & Mitchell; then in partnership with

Ellory and E. J. Stebbins as Mitchell, Stebbins & Co.;
and later in the same business alone at 33 John St.

His obituary described Consider G. as a man who had
enjoyed good health "until Tuesday last, when he was
slightly indisposed. He was able to be about...until Friday morning, when he was found in a semi-conscious condition, having suffered an attack of cerebral hemmorrhage."
He was a man of "sterling character...greatly attached to
his friends...ever solicitous of the welfare of all his
friends and one of his last acts while able to be about was
to extend aid to two former friends who were in need. He
was of a retiring disposition, but once formed, a friend-
ship with him was lasting. His long life was marked by
many acts of kindness, all accomplished in a most unosten-
tious manner." Consider G. was a Universalist and a
"staunch Republican...strong in his views upon public
matters (but) could never be induced to be a candidate for
public office...he was a great lover of his home, and
there spent the greater part of his spare moments."

Consider G.'s survivors were named as a half-sister,
Mrs. William Bailey, two nieces, Misses Mary and Alice
Hanchett of Deansboro, and Mrs. George H. Trickett of
Marlboro "whom he had brought up in his home since early
childhood."

Consider G.'s will was dated 10 May 1906 and probated
on 15 Apr 1907 (Oneida Co., NY Surrogate Court Records,
Bk 57:159). He was indeed a well-to-do and generous man.
After having his debts paid and funeral expenses taken
care of, he gave to the trustees of the Clinton Cemetery
Association $200.00 for the care of his father's lot in
the Old Burying Ground in Clinton, NY, including the
grave of Orra Mitchell (Consider G.'s aunt) and Edwin
Rice, adjoining on the northwest. Edwin Rice's relationship to the Mitchells is unknown but in the 1870 census of
Kirkland Twp., Oneida Co., NY, Orra Mitchell is listed
with an Edwin Mitchell, age 50, born in NY. Consider G.
also provided, as before mentioned, for the Grant Mixer
lot in Woodside Cemetery, Ellisburg, NY.

Consider G.'s will then bequeathed $10,000.00 each to
his nieces, Mary E. Hanchett and Alice B. Hanchett, plus
$1,000.00 each for them in trust. To his half-sister, Ce-
lestine A. Bailey, he left $500.00, and to Elizabeth M.
Miller, his step-sister, he left $500.00 plus $1,000.00
in trust. He gave $1,000.00 each to the House of Good

Shepherd, the Utica Orphan Asylum, and the Old Home for aged men and couples, plus $500.00 to the Church of Reconciliation and Rescue Mission. He bequeathed $500.00 to his nephew, Harley D. Mixer, and to his wife, Sarah Frances Mixer, $1,000.00. He left $1,000.00 in trust for his grandnephew, Charles Mitchell Mixer. His cousins, Adele Pearl and Jennie Pearl, were each left $500.00, and to Charles F. Sumner and Janette St. John, children of his step-mother, Lucinda Mitchell, he left $200.00 each.

The relationships described in Consider G.'s will are all explainable with one exception. The Hanchett girls, his nieces, were daughters of his full sister. They were called granddaughters in his father's will. Celestine A. Bailey was the daughter of Consider G.'s father by his second wife; Elizabeth M. Miller, step-sister, was the daughter of Consider G.'s father's second wife by a previous marriage of hers. Harley D. Mixer was a nephew by marriage, and Charles Mitchell Mixer was Harley's son. Charles F. Sumner and Janette St. John were children of Consider G.'s father's 3rd wife by her previous marriage. Adele and Jennie Pearl, whom Consider G. calls "cousins," can not be explained, nor is it sure whether they were blood cousins or cousins by marriage.

Only child of Consider Gould and Ann Eliza (Mixer) Mitchell (none by his 2nd marriage), born in Clinton, Kirkland Twp., Oneida Co., NY, was:

364. **Minnie** bc 1858 d 1888 unmar.

SEVENTH GENERATION

For the most part, the Civil War was fought not by the male children of this generation who were born too late to be of enlistment age, but by their fathers and uncles. Those of this generation who did enlist, did so while they were still in their teens.

The children of this generation were largely sons and daughters of farmers; of parents who had grown up in primitive pioneer conditions and had seen during their lifetimes enormous changes take place in agriculture. The invention of the McCormick harvester and reapers of other types which followed freed a man from the limitations of what he could reap by scythe in a harvest season. In the mid-1850's, the tedder and the steam plow came into being. Agricultural societies sprang up and dispersed information on scientific farming methods through their papers. The coming of the railroad speeded up the progress of the agricultural revolution.

The end result was a generation of children who were advantaged compared to their parents. They had better educations, lived in finer homes, and enjoyed heightened prospects. Some of this generation now began to leave the farm to become store keepers, realtors, writers, salesmen, teachers, or enter into other non-agricultural pursuits, as did a few in the latter part of the previous generation. Some of the daughters married men in these sorts of occupations, leaving the farm to move into the towns and cities. Family size slowly decreased as people began to relate family size to their ability to provide a better life for their children. On the farms, machinery made large families unnecessary although 6 to 8 children in a family was still not uncommon.

As enormous a transition as their parents had known, this generation would see the advent of such miracles as the automobile, the airplane, radio, electricity, and the telephone. They would experience the end of a Golden

Age in this country with the advent of World War I; some lived through the Great Depression of the 1930's. As in all previous generations, they enjoyed the good times, and coped with the bad with characteristic strength and native intelligence.

****

280. **ORLANDO ALLEN MITCHELL,** son of Calvin and Eliza Ann (Allen) Mitchell, was born 16 Jan 1846 in Johnson Co., IN. He married 14 Mar 1872 in Effingham Co. to Margaret Ellen Mesnard, born there 12 Sep 1856, daughter of Addison Emmit and Mary Ann (Mitchell*) Mesnard. Orlando died 19 Jan 1892 in Jackson Twp., Effingham Co., IL and Margaret E. died 16 May 1913 at Watson, Effingham Co., IL, both buried in Old Turner Cemetery in that county. (*Mary Ann's ancestors came from an unrelated Mitchell line from TN.)

After a few years spent in Clay Co., IL, Orlando's parents moved in 1857 to Effingham Co., IL. After his marriage, he and Margaret lived first in a small house on his father's land, moving then to another nearer a spring and, at his mother's death in 1885, moving his family into his father's house to look after him. They continued to live there after Orlando's father died in 1887. At a 1920 family reunion, the old home was visited and described as "improved, still very much the same, well preserved ..." (The house was still standing several years ago, but just barely.)

Orlando's wedding portrait shows us an attractive, slender-faced young man with high cheek bones and an almost frail build. He was dark haired with deep set eyes under heavy brows, hair slightly wavy, a dark mustache and short beard. Margaret had a full oval face, generous, well defined mouth, dark hair parted in the middle and drawn severely back behind her ears, a style she never varied. Her simple dress was set off by an elegant black lace collar, a jeweled brooch centered at the neck. She was not merely pretty, she was a handsome woman.

Orlando and Margaret prepared for their marriage by reading "Secrets of Love," a quaint book (1870) covering all facets (except those of an intimate nature), from the courtship to hints for happiness ("Make the most of everything and thank God you have so much."); short <u>and</u> long courtships, and early marriages were advised against.

Seventh Generation

In an interview with Orlando's daughter, Mary Eliza, by his granddaughter, Clara (Redman) Hopp, Orlando was described as "...a man of kind and loving disposition; no one was ever turned from his door; whatever was needed in the way of food or clothing was never denied. He loved to sing, and his children were taught the old familiar hymns, all standing by his chair looking on the same book as a rule. He loved good music and was a good Bible scholar and enjoyed discussing it with others." In fact, Orlando had been a minister of the Gospel in his younger days.

For the last several years of his life, Orlando was confined to his home with progressive tuberculosis (then called "consumption"), just barely able to oversee the farm. On 3 Jan 1892 (about 2 weeks before his death), Orlando wrote his will. He directed that 35½ acres of his property plus one mare, two colts, and one cow be sold to discharge his debts; that his wife, Margaret, be given the rest of his property in Section 27 plus an iron gray horse, an iron gray mare, and all the household goods. After her death, his eldest son, Allen C., was to have 2/3rds of the property and his youngest son, Ensign Franklin, the remaining 1/3rd after they had paid his 4 daughters, Annie C., Nettie J., Mary E., and Amanda E., $10.00 each. He appointed his wife, Margaret, and his brother, Elijah C. Mitchell, as executrix and executor. He signed with great difficulty.

Two days before his death, Orlando had a codicil to his will written, adding 8 &16/100 acres to be sold for payment of his debts, and he authorized his wife to sell or use the personal property bequeathed to her "as she saw fit." Of the property left to Margaret, 1/3rd was to be hers during her "natural life." The remaining 2/3rds was hers only during her widowhood. If she remarried, his son Allen would receive 2/3rds of it, the remaining 1/3rd being divided between his 5 remaining children. His signature on the codicil is nearly illegible. (Bk C:244/45 Effingham Co., Il Probate Records)

Orlando's estate inventory listed 1 old bay mare; 1 horse 5 years old; 1 mare 6 years old; a 2-year old colt and a yearling colt; 2 red cows and a calf; pigs, chickens, a spring wagon and a wagon, farm implements, lumber, and corn in the crib. Possessions in the house included an organ, a sewing machine, 3 beds and bedding, a carpet, heating and cook stoves, chairs, kitchen "furniture," a clock, family pictures, books, window blinds, a kettle, wearing apparel, and miscellaneous "possessions." The total value of these items was about $545.00. At a time when you could buy 22 pounds of the "finest" kidney beans for $1.00, the evaluation of the estate was not so small as it seems by today's standards.

After Orlando's death, Margaret continued to live on the farm, relying on her eldest son, Allen, to run it, but when he married in 1896, she moved into Dexter, IL and made her living by dressmaking. She was called on twice to help with grandchildren left motherless by death, also helping her mother nurse her father in his last illness. After 16 years of widowhood, Margaret married second on 20 Feb 1908 in Effingham Co. to A. B. Hood, moving to Gays, IL where Mr. Hood died in Dec 1911. For awhile, Margaret lived alone, but in Dec 1912, she moved back to Watson, IL where "sickness and pain came to torture her..."

A month before she died, Margaret wrote a last letter to her daughter, Mary Eliza. She complained briefly about feeling "...awefully bad..." and said she had been "...so hungry since I have been here...because I could not eat such things as Mother could eat. She could eat anything and lots of it." She added "Please do not mention what I said for most everybody is listing (sic) for something for a foundation to build on to make trouble." She was pleased that her mother, who was then living with her, had gone "...down in town this morning..." and had brought her "...muslin for a white skirt and embroiderie to trim it." All of Margaret's children were with her during part of her illness, but during the last week, her two surviving daughters, Annie and Mary E., never left her side. She was a member of the Christian church since age 16, then the Methodist church in Dexter, but was buried from the Watson Baptist church. She left 4 children, 21 grandchildren, her mother, 4 brothers and 3 sisters.

Children of Orlando Allen and Margaret Ellen (Mesnard) Mitchell (plus a son who died in infancy), all born in Jackson Twp., Effingham Co., IL, were:

365. **Allen Calvin** b 11 Aug 1873   +
366. **Anna Christina (Annie)** b 16 June 1875   +
367. **Nettie Jane** b 19 Mar 1877   +
368. **Mary Eliza (Mollie)** b 16 Nov 1878   +
369. **Amanda Ellen (Manda)** b 30 Aug 1880   +
370. **Ensign Franklin (Frank)** b 18 Oct 1882   +

281. **DAVID OSCAR MITCHELL,** son of Calvin and Eliza Ann (Allen) Mitchell, was born 30 Dec 1846 in Edinburgh, Johnson Co., IN. He died 25 Jan 1937 in Watson, Effingham Co., IL at the home of his daughter, "Kitty" Neville. David O. married 31 Oct 1878 in Effingham Co. to Carrie Belle Simonton, born 31 Jul 1858 in Vandalia, Fayette Co., IL, daughter of Hiram Powers and Amelia (Danbury) Simonton. She died 21 Sep 1902 near Perry, Noble Co., OK of heart disease. She and David O. are both buried in Old Turner Cemetery, Effingham Co., IL.

Several years before his marriage, David O. apparently went to NE for a time. An exerpt from "Sunday-School Advocate" in the possession of David's daughter, Kitty, is notated "received at Sunday School by David O. Mitchell in Glenville, NE on 8 Jul 1876."

David O. and Carrie posed for their portrait with David's father, Calvin, probably after David's mother died in 1885 (or surely she would have been in the picture, too), but before Calvin's death in 1887. David O. was short in stature, slender, but wide-shouldered. He was clean shaven although in later years he wore a mustache and chin whiskers. His hair, worn very short, looks of a medium shade. Carrie's dark hair was pulled back over her ears and plaited in a single braid which lay over her left shoulder. The brim of her ornate hat was upturned on one side with flowers on the high crown. Her outfit was very modish, the jacket and sleeves edged with ruching as well as the hem of her long skirt which had a matching band running diagonally across the front. She was a very pretty woman and wore here a pleasant, good-natured expression.

In 1880, David O. and Carrie lived in Jackson Twp. of Effingham Co., IL on property adjoining that of Carrie's parents. David's profession is given as farmer and Carrie's as "boarding" although there is no one else in the family except their infant son and 27-year old Isaac Beck, a workhand presumably employed by David.

A reunion of the 5 surviving Mitchell brothers took place in Effingham on Aug. 21, 22, and 23, 1920, the first time these brothers had all been together since the death of the eldest, Orlando, in 1892. The first day of the reunion, a Saturday, they met at the home of Claudius E. Mitchell (Sr.), "...having a social time, music both vocal and instrumental prevailing." After a "fine dinner to which all did ample justice," they spent the evening in a "reminiscent mood and the amusing stories they told on each other caused a continuous uproar of laughter."

On Monday, the brothers took an auto trip to the "old farm home, the scenes of their childhood and early manhood." They also visited Old Turner Cemetery where their parents, their eldest brother and his wife, and David's wife, Carrie, lay buried. Later, they met at David's home in Dexter, IL, had dinner prepared by his daughters and daughter-in-law, enjoyed "...singing, instrumental music, impromptu speeches by the brothers, and taking pictures." David O. was 74 years old at the time of this reunion. He was described as a man who "made a careful study of the soil, loved his horses, was a good neighbor, and always ready to help others. He had been first a schoolteacher, then a farmer and stockman. He was a Baptist and "politically a democrat."

Children of David Oscar and Carrie Belle (Simonton) Mitchell (except 2 unnamed who died as infants), all born in Effingham Co., IL, were:

371. **Walter H.** bc 1879 dy.
372. **Victor Earl** b aft 1880 d at age $3\frac{1}{2}$y.
373. **Lulu B.** b 9 Feb 1885 m J. R. Calhoun; only known child, a son, Clark.
374. **Georgia (Kitty)** b 18 Feb 1887   +
375. **Winnie Maude** b 6 Oct 1893   +
376. **David Ralph** b 24 Apr 1899   +

282. **ENSIGN SAMUEL MITCHELL,** son of Calvin and Eliza Ann (Allen) Mitchell, was born 17 Oct 1848 in Johnson or Brown Co., IN. (By 1850, his father had moved from Johnson to Jackson Twp., Brown Co., IN where the family appears in that census, surname misspelled in the census index as Mithcell.) Ensign S. married 14 June 1879 to Lucretia ("Lou") Hart in "Nealville," WI according to Clara (Redman) Hopp's family genealogy (1963). No Nealville is found in WI but there is a Neillsville there in Clark Co.

Although he was first a schoolteacher, Ensign S. worked most of his life for the Union Pacific railroad as a telegraph operator and station agent in various locations, the first being in WI. In 1892 when he attended the funeral of his brother, Orlando, in Effingham Co., he was living in Shelby, NE. By 1913, Ensign S. and Lou resided in Madison, NE where he sent a telegram in July to his brother, David O., stating that "Roy died at Los Angeles today. Funeral Shelby about Sunday. Tell the boys." The identity of the deceased Roy has not been determined.

Ensign S. and his wife came from Madison, NE to attend the Mitchell reunion in 1920, a biography of him at that time saying that although he was retired, "...he has investments that demand considerable attention. He is a dramatist and is the author of 'Mammon' and other fine plays. He is a member of the United Brethren Church...an Odd Fellow and a democrat politically." Ensign S. died on 6 Jul 1928 in Denver, CO. Lucretia's date and place of death is not known. They had no known children.

283. ELIJAH CHANDLER MITCHELL, son of Calvin and Eliza Ann (Allen) Mitchell, was born 24 Jul 1850 in Brown Co., IN. He married 21 Nov 1874 in Effingham Co., IL to Evelyn (Eveline) Trexler, born 31 May 1857 in Effingham Co., daughter of Jonathan and Drucilla (Foster) Trexler.

Although his death certificate and that of his son gives Elijah the middle name of Calvin, his niece, Winnie (Mitchell) Smith declares it was Chandler. This was later proved to be so. In 1874, Calvin and Eliza Ann Mitchell sold 100 acres of land in Section 27 to their sons "Orlando Allen Mitchell & Elijah Chandelar (sic) Mitchell." (Effingham Co., IL Deed Records, Bk 8:224)

As a young man, Elijah C. was a schoolteacher. When he celebrated his 64th wedding anniversary in 1938, an article commemorating the occasion stated that he and his wife lived on the "old Traxler farm, southwest of Effingham" for a few years after their marriage. Elijah was "engaged in an extensive timber business, buying many large tracts of timber in this and other states. He employed a large number of men to assist in making the timber into (railroad) ties. Many men say they got their 'start' working for E. C. Mitchell." Later they moved into Effingham where Elijah operated a men's clothing store, was a member of the Knights of Pythias and the Christian church, and was a "democrat politically."

In 1899, Elijah closed the store and moved to Shawnee, Pottawatomie Co., OK where they lived on Bell St. They were not at home when the census taker came calling in 1900. Data on the family was probably given by a next-door neighbor who knew only that "E. C." was a clothing merchant, and his wife had 1 child, a son Noble who was a "clothing laborer." A candid shot of Elijah C., Evelyn and Noble may have been taken here. They are seated on the grass in front of the steps of their house. Elijah C.'s hair, thinning a bit on top, had not yet turned grey. His face was deeply furrowed from his prominent cheekbones to below the corners of his mouth. Evelyn's hair was still dark. She wears a white cotton summer dress. Noble was also dark haired and very handsome, resembling his mother a great deal.

By 1920, Elijah, Evelyn and Noble had moved to Sulphur, OK where Elijah died at 5:45 on 17 May 1943 at his home at 1120 E. Second St. Cause of death was "congestive failure due to arterioschlerotic cardiovascular disease" of 10 years duration, complicated by senility. He was age 92 years 9 months and 24 days at his death. The informant on the death certificate was Mrs. James E. Sterner, 116 W. Arch, Nevada, MO, her relationship to the family unknown. Elijah C. was buried on 18 May in Shawnee, OK where his son, Noble, who had died 2 years earlier, was buried in the Shawnee Mausoleum. (At Noble's death, a Mr. Earl Masters was responsible for the account at the Frier Funeral Home in Sulphur, OK.) Evelyn was still alive at Elijah's death, her date and place of death not known.

Only child of Elijah Chandler and Evelyn (Trexler) Mitchell, born in Effingham Co., IL, was:

377. **Noble** b 10 Oct 1875 d 7 Oct 1941 unmar at Sulphur, OK; bur Shawnee, OK.

284. **CLAUDIUS ELIAS MITCHELL (SR.)**, son of Calvin and Eliza Ann (Allen) Mitchell, was born 20 Oct 1856 in Clay Co., IL. In 1857 his parents moved to Effingham Co., IL where he married 29 Aug 1886 Rhue Ethel Donaldson, born in Oct 1869 Fountain Co., IN, daughter of David M. & Matilda (Alford) Donaldson. Claudius E. died in Effingham Co. in 1937. Rhue E. died after 1920, exact date unknown.

Like his brothers, Claudius E. was a schoolteacher as a young man. Unlike his brothers, he remained in the field of education. After graduating from the "common schools" of Effingham Co., he attended State Normal at Carbondale, IL and Central Normal College at Danville, IN. After his marriage, Claudius E. and Rhue lived in Jackson Twp. (Effingham Co.) for 12 years, moving in 1898 to Mason Twp. where they lived on a farm there. On 9 Nov 1901, they moved into Effingham so that Claudius E. could take charge of the office of County Superintendent, an elective post which he had won on the Democratic ticket. He had been a Supervisor, Town Clerk and School Treasurer in Jackson Twp., and was re-elected to the Treasurer's position, but had resigned it when he moved to Mason Twp.

The 1910 "History of Effingham Co., IL (Bateman & Selby, p 824) carries a lengthy biography of Claudius E., citing the improvements Claudius E. had made since becoming County Superintendent, stating that there had never been a Superintendent in that county who was "...more on friendly terms with his teachers, for he possesses tact and good judgement as well as learning and skill in teaching, and makes friends everywhere...has displayed a keen insight in details...splendid executive ability...knows how to choose good teachers and to get satisfactory results from them...the grade of the pupils graduated from the county schools has been advancing each succeeding year." He was a man of "marked ability, scholarly in his tastes...(his) greatest training from the school of experience..." so that he was more "practical in his work and methods than others who have been taught what they know instead of wrestling it from a daily life."

In a picture taken of the 5 surviving Mitchell brothers at their reunion in August 1920, Claudius E. looks every inch the distinguished, scholarly gentleman; white haired with a mustache, slender faced, wearing rimless eyeglasses, he most resembled his brothers, David O. and Ensign S., all three of them looking a great deal like their maternal grandfather, Elijah Allen.

Claudius E. was also a Mason (Watson Lodge #602), member of the Watson M.W.A. #2705, Effingham K. of P. Lodge #168, and he and Rhue were both members of the Baptist church. "Their beautiful home in Effingham is supplied with modern conveniences, and is surrounded by an acre of ground, filled with shade and ornamental trees, that make it one of the most pleasant residences in the city." Children of Claudius Elias and Rhue Ethel (Donaldson) Mitchell, all born in Effingham Co., IL, were:

378. **Mabel F.** b Aug 1887 m John T. Scryples; no ch.
379. **Daniel Palmer** b 23 Nov 1888   +
380. **Nellie Pearl** b 26 Feb 1891 dy (bef 1900).
381. **Claudius Elias, Jr.** b 30 Mar 1895   +
382. **Ruby Ethel** b 6 Jul 1897 m George H. Telger; no ch.
383. **Gladys M.** b 4 Dec 1902 m ____ Plestina; no ch.
384. **Melba** b 26 Feb 1906 d in infancy.

285. **JOSEPH CALVIN MITCHELL**, son of Calvin and Eliza Ann (Allen) Mitchell, was born 15 Dec 1859 in Jackson Twp., Effingham Co., IL. He preferred going by his middle name, sometimes signing as J. Calvin Mitchell.

Joseph C. was a schoolteacher early in life. He then "...engaged in business, travelled considerably...wrote didactic stories (i.e., instructive), being the author of the 'Crater of Gold' series, 'The Struggle,' 'Future Government,' 'Cabin Dwellers,' etc." He was a Master Mason and an independent politically.

Joseph C. did indeed seem to get about quite a bit in the various businesses which he undertook. When he returned to Effingham Co., IL in 1892 for his eldest brother's funeral, he was living in Cherokee, IA. In 1900, he was living alone in Emington, IL, northeast of Pontiac (census). An old and undated business card of his reads: "Locating on Government Land a Specialty; Headquarters at the Merchants Hotel, Chamberlain, South Dak.; Bargains in Deeded Land." In 1906, a hand written postcard which he sent to his brother, David O., says: "One cent Amusement Hall for Ladies and Gentlemen; Agency for the Great Regina Concerto and Edison Phonographs & Records which are on exhibition; Machines bought & sold; 613 W. Holly St., Bellingham, WA; Calvin Mitchell, Prop."

Just before the turn of this century, America became embroiled in the Spanish-American War, a brief conflict lasting from April 21 to August 12, 1898. Cuba, a colony of Spain, wanted independent status and when this was denied her, she revolted. Americans sympathized with the plight of the Cubans, and when the U.S. warship, the "Maine," exploded in Havana harbor, Congress declared war to the cry of "Remember the Maine." After successfully blockading Havana harbor and several hard fought battles led by Col. Teddy Roosevelt and his Rough Riders, the U.S. was on the move against the Spanish in Puerto Rico when an armistice was signed. This treaty brought the end of Spanish influence in the Western Hemisphere and the Far East. Cuba gained her independence, and the U.S. gained Puerto Rico, Guam, and the Philippine Islands.

Joseph C. graduated from law school in 1898, immediately joining Co. F, 3rd IL Spanish-American War Volunteers and fought until the end of the war. Inexplicably, no record of his participation was found in the National Archives, nor is his name on an index of Spanish-American

War soldiers from IL in the State Archives, but the company number and regiment he served in is inscribed by him under his picture in the front of his book "Excerpts from the Crater of Gold," a Mysterious Manuscript by J. Calvin Mitchell, 1918 (in the possession of a descendant).

His experience with war seemed to affect Joseph C. a good deal. His "Crater of Gold" manuscript, written in rhyme, dwells on man's inhumanity to man and man's struggle to find the "truth." He expounds on man's inability to cope with "Infinity," and so accepting "Divinity as taught by some assumptive revelation old that claims to be the only truth that has been told; his onward progress to a new and higher plane is thus estopped...he stays a clog to universal peace of man." He eschewed blind faith in favor of intelligent behavior according to the proven laws of nature.

Although he would mature into a man with solidly built features, his hair thinning in his later years, at age 18 Joseph C. was a handsome boy with the face of a romantic. His dark hair, combed back, curled around his ears and on the nape of his neck. He had a deep cleft in his chin, a rather sensual mouth and a widow's peak above a broad forehead and fine eyes. Nevertheless, he did not marry until late in life to Mrs. Kate (Lidy) Gordan. According to his niece, Winnie (Mitchell) Smith, Kate was a childhood sweetheart; after her husband's death, Joseph C. and she were married, this marriage taking place after 1900 but before 1920 when "Calvin" and "Mrs. Calvin Mitchell," then living in Chicago, were counted among those attending the Mitchell family reunion in Effingham, IL. Although Kate had children from her previous marriage, she and Joseph C. had none. Joseph C. died 6 June 1944 at his home in Arlington Heights, IL and Kate died 2 Nov 1961.

286. **JOHN HANNAH MITCHELL,** son of Joseph and Sarah Ann (Hannah) Mitchell, was born 12 Jan 1844 in Edgar Twp. and Co., IL. In a "quiet home wedding" performed on 1 Mar 1868 by Rev. Weames, a Methodist minister, John H. was married to Lucinda Thompson at the bride's residence four miles northeast of Chrisman, Edgar Co., IL. Lucinda was born in Edgar Co., IL on 4 Mar 1848, daughter of Jesse and Arminta (Ingram) Thompson.

A biography of Lucinda's father states he was born 18 Feb 1818 in Washington Co., IN, coming to Edgar Co., IL

with his parents at age 12 and marrying there 8 Jan 1844
to Arminta Ingram, a native of Hawkins Co., TN. Jesse
Thompson "...began business for himself at the age of 19;
he had no assistance from his people; now, by hard work,
economy and good management, he has a property of nearly
four hundred acres of good land, well improved." ("The
History of Edgar Co., IL," Wm. LeBaron, Jr. & Co., Chicago, 1879, p 691)

After his father's death in 1856, much of the work on
the family farm probably fell on the sturdy shoulders of
12-year old John H. and his 11-year old brother, Chandler.
Despite being the younger of the two, Chandler was the
first to enlist at the onset of the Civil War in 1861. The
following summer, John H. enrolled on 12 Jul in the newly
formed Co. A, 79th Illinois Volunteer Infantry at Ridge
Farm in adjoining Vermilion Co., IL. On 19 Aug "S. A.
Mitchell" signed a "Consent In Case of Minors" form, stating that she was "...the mother of J. H. Mitchell, that
the said J. H. Mitchell is 19 years of age; and I do hereby
freely give my consent to his volunteering as a Soldier in
the Army of the United States for a period of Three Years."

Although the signature was Sarah Ann's, the blanks on
the form appear to have been filled out by another hand
which might account for the erroneous age given since
John H. was then actually 17½ years of age. The fact that
the consent form was not signed until over a month after
John H. enlisted implies that his mother was reluctant to
give her permission, perhaps finally being convinced by
her father, John M. Hannah, and her brother-in-law, John
Mitchell, both of whom had also enlisted in Co. A, 79th
I.V.I., the former as a Sgt., the latter as a 2nd Lt.

Promoted from Pvt. to 4th Corporal, John H. was first
sent to Camp Terry near Mattoon, IL. From there, the 79th
was ordered to Louisville, KY where they began marching
through KY, arriving at Perryville on 9 Oct 1862 after the
Confederate Gen'l Braxton Bragg had begun his retreat into TN. The 79th continued to march toward Crab Orchard,
then to Lebanon and Bowling Green, arriving in Nashville,
TN on 7 Nov. On 26 Dec, the 79th moved toward Murfreesboro
and engaged in the battle of Stone River. (John H. was
later promoted to 3rd Sgt. for "meritorious conduct" in
this battle.)

During the winter of 1863, the 79th remained at Murfreesboro, TN. At 3 a.m. on the morning of 24 June, they

began to move with Gen'l Rosecrans' Army of the Cumberland toward Tullahoma, TN where Gen'l Bragg was based. Between Rosecrans and Bragg lay a mountainous ridge, part of the Cumberland Mountains. Rosecrans had originally viewed the terrain as a hindrance but now saw it as advantageous in hiding his troops until he could launch a surprise attack against the Confederates. Four major passes crossed the ridge - Bellbuckle Gap in the center; Liberty Gap 1 mile to the east; Guy's Pass 6 miles to the west; and Hoover's Gap 5 miles east of Liberty Gap. "Just as the troops stepped out in the pre-dawn dark...one of the most extraordinary rains ever known in Tennessee at that period of the year..." began to fall and it continued for 15 days. ("The Civil War," Shelby Foote)

Rosecrans planned to send two of Thomas and McCook's corps through Hoover's Gap, Granger's corps through Guy's Gap, and Crittenden's corps east through Bridgeville toward McMinnville, this last move a feint intended to make Gen'l Bragg believe the main attack would come from the opposite direction. Meantime, one of McCook's three divisions of which the 79th was a part was to make a disconcerting attack on Liberty Gap. By the evening of the 25th amidst a steady, driving rain, Liberty Gap was taken, but not before a bullet had ended John H.'s active career as a soldier.

In 1887 John Mitchell of WA (an uncle) filed a "Proof of Disability" form for John H., stating that "On the 25th day of June 1863 he (John H.) was wounded - left thigh at Liberty Gap, Tennessee. In the last week of July, after leaving Hospital, was taken with Rheumatism...in his legs and hips which disability was incurred while in line of duty. He was with the command during the winter of 1862 and summer of 1863 and when the line of March was taken up in July 1863 to Talahoma, Tennessee, he was left behind on account of his Rheumatism. That the facts stated are personally known to the affiant by reason of his...being with the command and assisted in taking him to Hospital, and know...the Regimental Surgeon was treating him for Rheumatism at the time I assisted in taking him to hospital."

After a month long recovery from his gunshot wound, John H. briefly resumed active duty, but by September had returned to the hospital in Tullahoma, TN where he was treated for his rheumatism. From there he was transferred to Cumberland General Hospital in Nashville, TN where he

later developed gangrene in the middle fingers of both
hands, these fingers being surgically removed on 25 Jan
1864. In Feb 1864 John H. was transferred to the 40th Co.,
2nd Battalion Invalid Corps (later the 153rd Co., 2nd
Battalion Veteran Reserve Corps). At this time, he was
described as age 19, 5'8" tall, with blue eyes, dark hair
and dark complexion.

John H. remained at Nashville until he was mustered
out 30 June 1865. On 6 Jul before leaving TN, he filed a
Claim for Invalid Pension, citing the gunshot wound to
his left thigh and the loss of his fingers. This paper was
witnessed by Squire W. Mather of Dupont, IN and Lafayette
Gaston of Wilksville, OH who stated they had known John H.
for 1½ years. Despite the loss of his fingers, John H.
signed with a very legible and slightly flourishing hand.

After John H. returned to Edgar Co., IL, his principal
occupation was farming until the spring of 1873 when he
and his brother, George H., became partners under the
firm name of Mitchell Brothers, Chrisman, IL. The two
brothers mainly bought and shipped grain to Chicago and
Eastern markets and carried a full line of agricultural
implements. In 1874, John H. was elected as one of the
Trustees of the newly formed village of Chrisman; in 1879
he served as Supervisor of Ross Twp., and was on the Board
of Trustees as Treasurer. After 1880 but before 1900,
John H. and his family moved to Prairie Twp. where he owned 230 acres of land plus 13 acres of timber in an adjoining township.

His chronic rheumatism continued. In 1884, he was
examined by Dr. Samuel R. Gray, a practicing physician in
Chrisman, who declared in an affidavit for pension increase that "...John H. Mitchell has Sciatic Rheumatism,
which disables him from performing manual Labor one half
the time..." In subsequent affidavits, John H. signed
with a firm hand until 1912. By 1924 at age 80, he had
survived a slight paralytic stroke and had gangrene in
his left heel as well as suffering "general debility." He
could still sign his name but his hand was so shaky, his
daughter, Rose, had to fill out his paperwork for him.

John H. left no will. He had disposed of his property,
leaving a personal estate worth a maximum of $100.00.
His survivors were named as sons Fred J. (appointed administrator) and Ora Mitchell; daughter Rose Shepherd; and a
grandson, Frederick Mitchell, son of Charles W. who was

deceased. John H. died 12 June 1926 and Lucinda died on
15 Nov 1912, both at Chrisman, Edgar Co., IL. They are
buried in Prairie Twp Chapel Cemetery (Friends Chapel)
near Scotland, Edgar Co., IL. Children of John Hannah and
Lucinda (Thompson) Mitchell, born in Edgar Co., IL, were:

385. **Charles Wesley** b June 1869 d 1923 m aft 1900; 1 son
known, Frederick Mitchell, lvg 1926.

386. **Laura A.** b 3 Jul 1871 d 16 Sep 1872 age 1y 2m 13d.

387. **Frederick J.** bc 1875   *

388. **Rosa Mary ("Rose")** b May 1879   *

389. **Nora B.** (twin) b Feb 1884   *

390. **Ora C.** (twin) b Feb 1884   *

287. **CHANDLER MITCHELL,** son of Joseph and Sarah Ann (Hannah) Mitchell, was born 13 Apr 1845 in Ross Twp., Edgar
Co., IL. He married there on 13 Sep 1874 to Marica Hartley, born 26 Oct 1851 in Ross Twp., Edgar Co., IL, daughter
of Nathan and Elizabeth (Hoult) Hartley.

Chandler was not quite eleven when his father died in
1856, leaving Chandler and his elder brother, John H., to
help their widowed mother handle the work of the family
farm. Possessed of a more volatile temperament than his
brother, Chandler was the first of the two to enlist at
the beginning of the Civil War, enrolling at Paris, IL as
a coporal in Co. F, 54th Illinois Volunteer Infantry on 15
Dec 1861. Co. F was under the command of his uncle, Capt.
John B. Hannah. At enrollment, Chandler was described as
dark haired with brown eyes and light complexion, standing 5'7" tall, and 18 years of age. Actually, Chandler was
4 months short of his 17th birthday. (One wonders why no
"Consent in the Case of Minors" form was required of his
mother as was so with his brother, John H.)

In Feb 1862, Chandler was mustered in at Camp DuBois,
Anna, IL. The 54th was ordered first to Cairo, IL, then
on 14 Mar 1862 to Columbus, KY, a strategic point on the
Mississippi River well protected by a steep bluff. Union
forces had been unable to take this position until 3 Mar
when Confederate Gen'l Polk had evacuated, moving his
troops to Corinth, MS where Gen'l Bragg was consolidating
his command. Presumeably, the 54th was sent to fortify
Columbus which became a main Union supply post. Chandler
remained behind, hospitalized at Cairo with the measles
(a disease which caused the death of many a young soldier)
until he could rejoin the 54th in Columbus 3 weeks later.

On 18 Dec 1862, the 54th marched to Jackson, TN; three days earlier, Confederate Gen'l Nathan B. Forrest had crossed the Tennessee River at Clifton, heading toward Jackson. Forrest had been sent into TN by Gen'l Bragg at the request of Pemberton who commanded the Confederate forces at Vicksburg. Forrest's job was to take the pressure off Pemberton by destroying depots and railroads, capturing hospitals and guards, burning bridges, and generally harrassing Union troops in TN as much as possible. On the day the 54th reached Jackson, Forrest overwhelmed Union troops at Lexington, some of the Federals escaping and running the 25 miles back to Jackson with exaggerated stories of Forrest's strength. Forrest and his men followed, attacking Jackson on the 19th and cleverly manuevering so as to give the illusion of an enormous force of men. In reality, there were about 4 times as many Union soldiers inside Jackson as there were Confederates outside the city.

By the morning of the 20th, Forrest and his men had gone. Gen'l Sullivan, the commander at Jackson, set out after them. The 54th marched east to Lexington, returning to Jackson on the 22nd; then on the 24th south to Britton's Lane and Toon's Station, returning to Jackson on the 28th. But Forrest had gone neither east nor south, swinging northward instead to destroy the 60 mile long Mobile & Ohio railroad connecting Jackson to Union City near the TN/KY border. He then spent 2 days tearing up the Nashville & Northwestern railroad.

Forrest was now in a tight spot with Union forces converging from all sides. On 30 Dec, Gen'l Sullivan's 1st Brigade had passed Forrest without detecting him. Resuming his march towards Clarksburg, Forrest sent 4 companies to guard the road to the rear in case the lead Union brigade should retrace their steps. On the morning of 31 Dec, he met Sullivan's 2nd Brigade, battling with them until around 1 p.m. when white flags began showing along the Union line. As he was sending an unconditional surrender to the Federals, Forrest was attacked from the rear, his rear guard having gone up the wrong road which allowed Sullivan's 1st Brigade to catch the Confederates by surprise. The Confederates charged both to the fore and to the rear, then withdrew sideways, riding hard for the Tennessee River. They left behind not only the Union guns they had captured, but some of their own, as well as wagons full of ammunition and some 300 men who were taken while trying to catch their horses which had bolted at the first sound of gunfire.

Gen'l Sullivan came up behind with his 3rd Brigade on 1 Jan, and thought he'd broken Forrest's army. A cavalry regiment was needed to chase after Forrest, but before one could be mobilized, Forrest and his men, their mission of harrassment accomplished, had escaped over the Tennessee River. Gen'l Grant's lifeline, the railroads, had been cut from Jackson, TN all the way north to the KY border. During this period of time, Forrest had captured detachments of the 54th guarding the railroads and had destroyed nearly all regimental records. The balance of the records had been lost by the Quartermaster's Dept. in transit from Columbus, KY to Jackson.

In March 1863, Chandler was promoted from Corporal to 5th Sergeant, remaining with the 54th at Jackson, TN until 30 May 1863 when the 54th left Jackson for Vicksburg, MS as part of the 3rd Brigade, 2nd Division, 16th Army Corps, Brig. Gen'l Nathan Kimball, Division commander.

Seven months after the start of the war, President Lincoln had commented to a visitor, "See what a lot of land these fellows hold, of which Vicksburg is the key... Let us get Vicksburg and all that country is ours. The war can never be brought to a close until that key is in our pocket." By Oct 1862, the Federals held all but a 130 mile stretch of Mississippi River territory - that lying between Vicksburg, MS and Port Hudson, LA, effectively blocking Union use of the river. Down the Red, the Arkansas and the White Rivers which spilled into the Mississippi flowed cattle, corn and hogs which were taken to Vicksburg, then distributed by rail all over the South. Confederate troops as well were transported east from Vicksburg. The Union needed control of Vicksburg and the entire Mississippi to split the Confederacy and choke off the flow of supplies and men to the east, to provide them a highway for further operations and regain a vital trade route to the sea for Northern farmers.

Since Nov 1862, Gen'l Grant had been attempting to drive for Vicksburg. The combined harrassment in TN by the Confederates in that year plus the destruction of Grant's supply depot at Holly Springs, MS had halted this advance. An attempt to open a passage for gunboats on the Yazoo River which twisted tortuously south to the rear of

-221-

Vicksburg was blocked on 17 Feb 1863 by the Rebels at Fort Pemberton. Moving far south of Vicksburg, then swinging back north, Grant defeated the Confederates at Port Gibson, Raymond, Jackson, and Champion Hill, then routed Pemberton's rear guard at Big Black River, forcing Pemberton to withdraw into the protection of Vicksburg on 18 May. On the 19th, Grant's attack on Vicksburg was repulsed as was a second attack on the 22nd, after which Grant began his siege of the city.

The 54th had encamped at Satartia on the Yazoo River, but hearing that Confederate Gen'l Joe Johnston was moving toward them (a false alarm), Gen'l Kimball sent all of his supplies to Haynes Bluff, 25 miles down the Yazoo. This impenetrable position had been occupied by the Union only after Pemberton's forces had fled into Vicksburg. The 54th was now positioned on the extreme left of Gen'l Sherman's Union forces on the Big Black River, part of a huge semicircular rearward facing guard in case Gen'l Joe Johnston got up enough strength to attack from the east. A second inner semicircle of Union troops faced the city.

For the next six weeks, Union guns shelled Vicksburg both day and night. Although some residents had fled to the country, many had stayed to protect their property. Shells fell on soldiers and civilians impartially. Some fled to their cellars for protection. Others took to digging caves in the hillsides and were then half afraid to take refuge in them lest reverberations from exploding shells would cause them to crumble. Shelves in stores began emptying rapidly and soon hunger gripped the city. Rice and milk were staples although before the siege was lifted, Vicksburg citizens ate mule meat and rats, the latter having the flavor of fried squirrel "when properly fried." The heat and humidity of a Mississippi river town in summer was unbearable. Eating, sleeping and dodging shells became everyone's main preoccupation while Vicksburg took on the appearance of a ruined, deserted city.

Through it all, the women of Vicksburg behaved with admirable courage. To quote Emma Balfour, the wife of a Vicksburg physician, "The general impression is that they fire at the city...thinking they will wear out the women and the children and sick, and General Pemberton will be obliged to surrender the place on that account; but they little know the spirit of the Vicksburg women and children if they expect this..."

Seventh Generation

On 3 Jul 1863, Vicksburg surrendered. The next day, Union troops filed into the city to the courthouse for the ceremonial surrender. An early demonstration of jubulation by Union troops had béen squelched by Grant. Pemberton may have proved an inept commander, but Grant admired the bravery of the Confederate soldiers under Pemberton's command. The mood at the surrender was solemn as the Confederate soldiers lay down their arms. The war was far from over but the fate of the Confederacy had been decided with the surrender of this city. Union morale would hereafter be high.

The majority of the troops from eastward facing divisions posted outside Vicksburg were sent to chase Gen'l Joe Johnston out of Mississippi, but the 54th was attached to Gen'l Frederick Steele's Arkansas expedition and ordered to Helena, AR on 24 Jul, preparatory to an attack on Little Rock. At Helena on 5 Aug, Sgt. Chandler fell ill and was left there by his regiment when they marched out on the 13th. Suffering from chronic diarrhea, he remained hospitalized in Helena until 26 Aug when he was moved up river to the hospital at Memphis. Here he lay ill through the steaming hot month of September and part of October, an apparent mixup occuring when he left Memphis that month. A hospital muster roll reports that Chandler deserted on 18 Oct, but muster rolls for Co. F of the 54th show that Sgt. Chandler Mitchell had returned by 12 Nov. No punitive action was reported against him, leaving one with the impression that records of his departure from Memphis to rejoin his regiment at Little Rock were either misplaced or misfiled.

The 3-year enlistment of the 54th ended on 1 Jan 1864. A good 3/4ths of the regiment, including Chandler who was promoted at this time to Acting Sgt. Major, re-enlisted for a 1-year term and mustered in on 25 Jan at Little Rock. Despite a diet often consisting of nothing more than hard tack and meat, Chandler had grown 2 inches since 1861. He was shown as age 19 although his 19th birthday would not occur for another 2½ months.

The re-enlisted regiment was given a 1 month furlough with instructions to meet on 28 Mar at Mattoon, IL for the return trip. On that day an organized gang of Copperheads (Southern sympathizers) led by Sheriff O'Hair, attacked some of the men of the 54th at Charleston, IL, killing Maj. Shubal York, surgeon, and 4 privates, and wounding Col.

Greenville M. Mitchell, regiment commander. An hour later, the 54th arrived from Mattoon, occupied Charleston and captured 15 members of the gang. Taken to Fort Delaware under the authority of the War Dept., the prisoners chose Dennis Hanks, cousin to President Lincoln, as their intermediary. At a meeting in Lincoln's office, Sec'y of War Stanton was determined the Copperheads should hang, but Lincoln felt no harm would be done by releasing the prisoners, provided they promised to behave like good citizens. Eventually the prisoners were taken out of the hands of the War Dept. By Presidential direction, those who had already been indicted were handed over to local authorities and the rest let go.

After returning from veteran leave, the 54th engaged in a series of marches to various locations, fighting Gen'l Shelby on 26 June and returning to Little Rock on the 29th where Sgt. Chandler was admitted to the hospital a few days later for treatment of a boil. On 5 Aug, the 54th was assigned to guard 16 miles of Memphis & Little Rock railroad with 2 companies posted at each of its 5 stations. On 24 Aug 1864, Shelby attacked with 4,000 men and 4 pieces of artillery. Six companies, concentrated at one station by Col. Mitchell of the 54th, fought for 5 hours but were driven out and captured. Co. F and Co. H were at a distant station and were not involved.

The day book containing the morning reports of Co. F, 54th Illinois Veteran Volunteer Infantry for the period of 1 Jan through 15 Oct 1865 has been preserved by Eleanor (Mitchell) Taylor of Indianapolis, IN, great-granddaughter of Chandler Mitchell. This book, approximately 11x15 inches in size, is covered with a double thickness of a heavy, coarse, tobacco-brown paper. The book pages were once bound to the cover by means of sewing through the center fold with a medium weight thread. Kept by the company commander, the book reports in terse style the various activities of the company, naming those reduced in rank, exchanged prisoners received, promotions, desertions, deaths, returns from detached service, furloughs, and hospitalizations, discharges, and so forth. On 1 Jan 1865, Co. F. was stationed at Ft. Miner, AR and still under the command of Chandler's uncle, Capt. John B. Hannah. Remarks for the month of February include on the 4th "Sergt. C. Mitchell returned to the Company for Duty;" and on the 17th "Capt. J. B. Hannah mustered out by reason of

Expiration of term of service." On the 18th, Lt. John Sherman took temporary command of the company until 1 Apr when Chandler who had been promoted to 1st Lt. on 28 Mar assumed command of Co. F. Except for a brief hospitalization from 28 July to 9 Aug 1865 for acute diarrhea, and again from 2 to 7 Sep, Lt. Chandler remained in this position at Ft. Miner until he was mustered out with the company on 15 Oct of that year.

At his discharge, Chandler returned to Edgar Co. to his mother's house, appearing there with her in the 1870 census. Except for about 8 years when he lived in Newman Twp., Douglas Co., IL (listed there in the 1880 census), Chandler was a life-long resident of Edgar Co., IL. At one time he was a director of Mitchell School No. 17, a small Ross Twp. school located on land furnished by the Mitchell family. After the death of their son, Claude G., in 1906, Chandler and Marica took their two small grandsons, Dugan B. and Chandler O. Mitchell, into their household to raise.

Descendants have graciously shared photos with me of Chandler and Marica, both as young people and in later years. Marica was a slender young woman with expressive eyes below finely arched brows. She wore her hair parted in the middle with short, curled bangs, the sides upswept and falling loosely down her back from the crown. Chandler wore his Civil War uniform in his picture. His neck length dark hair is combed back over his ears. He sports a mustache and accent whiskers just below his lower lip but is otherwise clean shaven. His high forehead accentuated a straight forward, clear eyed gaze. In a word, he presented a dashing figure and must have turned many a young girl's head, but it was Marica he wanted. His satisfaction with that choice was expressed some 40 years later when in answer to a request for information from the Bureau of Pensions, he stated that "One marriage is all I have and (I) hope this may last until God Seperates us."

Throughout the years, Chandler's handwriting remained bold and clear; he used no unnecessary flourishes when signing his name. The chronic diarrhea he contracted during his war years continued to bother him. In 1888 it was attended by rheumatism and heart disease.

On 9 Sep 1914 Chandler wrote his last will and testament. To his "beloved wife, Marica..." he left all real and personal effects of every sort for her use during her natural life. After her decease, his son, George A., was to have 79½ acres in Prairie Twp., Edgar Co., IL; his grandson, Dugan B., was left an equal amount of land in the same township; his grandson, Chandler O., was left 97½ acres in Ross Twp., Edgar Co., IL. Both grandsons were to receive their property only after Marica's decease, the land to revert to his son, George A., should either or both grandsons predecease George. All three were given equal shares of any remaining personal property after his wife's death. George A. was appointed executor. A 7th stipulation directed Marica with looking after "...the welfare, maintenance and necessary education of my grand-sons Chandler O. and Dugan B. Mitchell, until they have attained the age of twenty-one." (Edgar Co., IL Probate Records, p 394)

Chandler died 11 Nov 1919 in Ross Twp., Edgar Co., IL and Marica died there 11 Apr 1929. Both are buried there in Hoult Cemetery. Children of Chandler and Marica (Hartley) Mitchell, were:

> 391. Son (unnamed) b & d 26 Sep 1875 Edgar Co., IL.
> 392. **George Alvin** b 11 Mar 1877 Douglas Co., IL dsp 24 Apr 1949 Edgar Co., IL m 16 Mar 1898 Edgar Co., IL Ida M. Stout d/o Samuel & Margaret (Hanna) Stout.
> **393. Claude Glen** b 3 Jul 1879   *

288. **GEORGE H. MITCHELL,** son of Joseph and Sarah Ann (Hannah) Mitchell, was born 5 Apr 1847 in Ross Twp., Edgar Co., IL. He married at Chrisman, Edgar Co., IL on 29 Dec 1880 to Mary E. Stewart, born Aug 1860 at Charleston, Coles Co., IL, daughter of Robert and Jennett (Brown) Stewart, both natives of Scotland. George H. died 24 Dec 1911 at Birmingham, AL. Mary E.'s date and place of death are unknown.

While his older brothers, John H. and Chandler, went off to war in 1861 and 1862, George H. remained at home to help his widowed mother run the family farm. He remained at home until after 1870. In 1880 he is listed in the Edgar Co., IL census living in Chrisman with the family of William and Sarah E. Stickel, "restaurant keepers." In this census, George H. calls himself a "grain dealer," having entered into partnership in 1873 with his brother, John H., as a dealer in grain, seeds and agricultural implements under the firm name of Mitchell Brothers, located in the village of Chrisman, IL.

Before 1900, George H. moved his family to Birmingham, AL, where his occupation was listed simply as "merchandise broker" in the 1900 census, renting a house in that city at 2130 - 8th Avenue. Only child of George H. and Mary E. (Stewart) Mitchell, born in Edgar Co., IL, was:

394. **Laura E.** b Sep 1882 lvg 1900 (no further data).

291. **CHARLES CHANDLER KIRKPATRICK**, son of William and Nancy (Mitchell) Kirkpatrick, was born Sep 1844 in Edgar Co., IL. He is listed as Charles in Scotland Co., MO census records of 1850 (Johnson Twp., p 142) and 1860 (Green Twp., p 184) although he customarily went by his middle name of Chandler in land and probate records and in later census enumerations.

Chandler married about 1870/71 in MO to Sarah Jane Coleman, born Sep 1851 in IA (1900 census), daughter of Cyrus Coleman. No marriage record was found for them in Henry Co., MO where they were living in Fields Creek Twp. at the 1880 Census (Vol 14 ED 172 Sheet 9 Line 1). Inexplicably, this census lists Sarah Jane as "Mary" Kirkpatrick, age 30, born in IL. Also listed with the family were Chandler's two eldest sons, Albert and (Elvis) Walter, and his brother, Elvis Kirkpatrick, who was still an unmarried man.

In 1884, Chandler and his family, along with Elvis (now married) and family, and Chandler's parents and single sister, removed to the Black Hills area of Pennington Co., SD where Chandler patented land in Sections 27 and 28 of Township #2. He later sold this property and patented another parcel in Section 12, Township #1 where he was living at his death. He apparently was primarily a raiser of stock as his 160 acre property was described in 1904 as producing "no income..." although his estate included cattle, horses and "stock."

In 1887 when the youngest of their four children was just a month old, Sarah Jane sued Chandler for divorce, notice being served to him in Pennington Co. on 25 May. The divorce was granted on 26 Jan 1888 "...in open court, at Deadwood, Lawrence Co., Dakota." The grounds, against which Chandler failed to defend himself, were "...willful neglect and cruel and inhuman treatment..." The decree further states that Sarah J. should be "...restored to all the rights of a single woman, and that the plaintiff be awarded the custody and control of the children of said marriage, towit: Albert, Walter, Burton and Hugh."(p 167 County Clerk's Office, Pennington Co., SD)

Three of these children were still living with their mother in Rapid City, SD in the 1900 Census, i.e., Albert, Burton and Hugh. The fourth son, Walter, was enumerated in 1900 as a hired hand on the ranch of William G. Strong in Pennington Co. (William Strong was married to Lillie Hayes, step-daughter of Chandler's sister, Sarah Olive.)

An interesting reflection of the moral climate at the turn of the century was Sarah Jane's refusal to admit her divorced status to the census taker. Besides confirming that she was the mother of 4 children, all living in 1900, she says she was widowed. Chandler, whose mother was the only other person listed in his household in 1900, had no such reservations, plainly stating that he was divorced.

Chandler wrote his will on 10 Feb 1904, stating first that he resided in Rapid City, Pennington Co., SD; that he was 59 years old, of sound mind and memory, and "not acting under duress, menace, fraud or undue influence of any person whatsoever." He requested that he be "...decently buried with proper regard to my station and condition in life, and the circumstances of my estate." Naming his brother, Elvis Kirkpatrick of Rookins, St. Clair Co., MO, as his executor, Chandler went to great lengths to provide for his mother after his death, even directing that his estate be sold if income from it was insufficient to pay for his mother during her life and at her death. Only after his mother was provided for was the remainder of his estate to be divided among his sons. To Hugh he left only one dollar with Albert, Elvis Walter and Burton receiving an equal 1/3rd. Thoughtfully, Chandler requested that all legal fees as well as his brother's expenses of travel or "any other unusual expense incidental" to the settlement of his estate be paid from that estate.

At Chandler's death in Rapid City on 22 Mar 1904, he owned "a farm of 160 acres, with suitable dwelling house, barn, buildings and improvements; also farm utensils, tools, etc., and horses, cattle and stock..." and personal property worth about $600.00. Unfortunately, there was no actual cash on hand for payment of doctor's bills, funeral expenses, or to provide for his mother. On 5 May 1904 after having Chandler's eldest son, Albert, named as guardian of his youngest son, Hugh, a minor, Elvis Kirkpatrick asked the court for permission to sell Chandler's

160 acre farm. He stated that he already had an offer of $650.00 for the property from Corbin Morse which topped the appraised value by $50.00.

On 9 May 1904, Elvis Kirkpatrick submitted his final report to the Pennington Co., SD court. Sale of real and personal property had brought $1,195.00. Expenses for Chandler's last illness, funeral, tombstone, and legal fees totaled $267.28. Executor's expenses included a commission for handling funds, round-trip railroad fares between MO and Rapid City and MO and Blackhawk, SD and for meals and "time lost from home" in the amount of $185.60, leaving a balance of $742.12 for distribution.

Chandler's obituary appears in the "Journal," Rapid City, SD. It mentions his arrival in SD from MO in 1884. At his bedside when he died were his four sons, Albert, Walter, Bert, and Hugh; his sister, Mrs. Hayes of Black Hawk, and her daughter, Cora; and his mother. Other survivers were his father and brother of Rookins, MO. Pennington Co., SD deed indices list the purchase in 1904 of Lot #726 in Mountain View Cemetery, Rapid City, by Elvis Kirkpatrick. Cemetery records list the burial there of Chandler Kirkpatrick in Lot #726 on 24 Mar 1956. Probably Chandler was initially buried in an unknown location, then moved to that lot in 1956, possibly by his youngest son, Hugh, who was his only surviving son at that date.

Of Chandler's sons, the first two did not long survive him. Elvis Walter's obituary (Rapid City "Journal") says he died there 18 Oct 1915; son of Chandler; born in Henry Co., MO on 26 Mar 1875; came to the Black Hills 24 June 1884; married 1908 to Mrs. Georgia Miles; survived by his mother, Mrs. Sarah J. Kirkpatrick, and two brothers, Albert and Bert, all of Rapid City; and one brother, Hugh, of Ekalaka, Montana. He was buried 20 Oct 1915 in Mountain View Cemetery (Lot #491, Site 5). Albert, the eldest son, followed soon after, being buried in Mountain View Cemetery on 12 Dec 1918 (Lot #491, Site 6).

A sketch on Chandler's son, Burton (Bert). appearing in "Black Hills People" states that he died June 1943; son of Chandler; brother of Hugh; an early pioneer who came with his family in 1884. Burton was buried 10 June 1943 in Mountain View Cemetery (Lot #491, Site 1). Hugh, the youngest son, was buried in Mountain View Cemetery on 24 May 1956 (Lot #491, Site 11-12), and his wife, Dola, was buried there 4 Dec 1935 (Lot #491, Site 10-11).

A query to the postmaster at Ekalaka, MT about Hugh
Kirkpatrick was answered by Mr. H. B. Albert of that town
who wrote on 12 Jul 1978: "I was employed in the bank here
at Ekalaka from 1913 until about 9 years ago...and was
acquainted with Hugh Kirkpatrick who, with his brother
Bert, homesteaded here, about 6 or 7 miles southwest of
town. Earlier in Montana history people generally did
not inquire as to where folks came from...They remained in
this area long enough to make final proof on their land
...they were both unmarried when they left here..."

Sarah Jane outlived all but her two younger sons, her
death record in Pennington Co., SD (#4465) giving a death
date of 13 Feb 1934 at 216 Quincy St., Rapid City, from
"hypostatic pneumonia due to senility." She was buried
beside her sons in Mountain View Cemetery on 15 Feb 1934
(Lot #491, Site 3-4). Children of Charles Chandler and
Sarah Jane (Coleman) KIRKPATRICK (1st 3 born in MO, 4th in
SD) were: **(i)** Albert b Oct 1871 d 1918; **(ii)** Elvis Walter
b 26 Mar 1875 d 18 Oct 1915 m 1908 Mrs. Georgia Miles;
(iii) Burton ("Bert") b Jul 1880 d 1943; **(iv)** Hugh b Apr
1887 d 1956 m Dola _____ d 1935.

293. **ELVIS KIRKPATRICK,** son of William and Nancy (Mitchell) Kirkpatrick, was born May 1852 in Scotland Co., MO.
In 1880 he was living (unmarried) with his brother, Chandler Kirkpatrick, in Henry Co., MO but married not long
after that to Mary _____, born Dec 1857 in PA (census).

In 1884, Elvis, his wife and small daughter left for
the Black Hills area of Pennington Co., SD. Making the
move with him were his parents, his brother Chandler and
family, and an unmarried younger sister. Here he patented
land in Sections 11 and 33 of Town #1. He remained in SD
until at least 1895 but before 1900 had returned to MO
where he was living at the 1900 census in Washington Twp.,
St. Clair Co. Evidentally, Elvis stayed in MO, possibly
in or near the small crossroads town of Rookins (now non-
existent) in St. Clair Co., southwest of Collins, where
he resided at the time of his brother Chandler's death in
1904. According to the obituary of his sister, Sarah
Olive (Kirkpatrick) Hayes, Elvis was deceased by 1931.

Known children of Elvis KIRKPATRICK (per 1900 Census)
were: **(i)** Minnie b Oct 1883 MO; **(ii)** Grace b Sep 1886 SD;
(iii) William E. b Aug 1888 SD; **(iv)** Mary N. b June 1892
SD; **(v)** Maggie J. b June 1895 SD.

295. **SARAH OLIVE (OLLIE) KIRKPATRICK,** daughter of William and Nancy (Mitchell) Kirkpatrick, was born 24 Oct 1861 near Rookins, St. Clair Co., MO. She came with her parents to the Black Hills area of Pennington Co., SD in 1884 where she married Alexander Porter Hayes/Hays in 1885. Alexander P. was born Jul 1849 (census) or 1845 (death cert# 272, age 63 in 1908) in Ohio, son of Robert Hayes. Alexander P. had 3 daughters, Emma, Lilly, and Alice, from a previous marriage.

Alexander P. died of "carcinoma of the stomach" on 20 Jul 1908 "at the ranch of William Strong...about six miles southeast of Rapid City..." but at the time was a resident of Blackhawk, Meade Co., SD. He left an estate in Pennington Co. "...consisting of personal property and effects...of uncertain value not to exceed $20.00;" an estate in Meade Co. "...consisting of an acre of land and a house thereon...in Blackhawk of the value of $200.00;" and a pension voucher dated 11 Jul 1908 for $36.00 in the possession of his widow, "Ollie" Hayes who petitioned for administration of his estate. His other surviving heirs were his daughters Emma Taylor of Farmingdale, SD; Lilly Strong of Rapid City, SD (wife of William Strong on whose ranch Alexander P. died); and Alice Blair of Rapid City, SD, all over 21 years of age and children of his 1st marriage. Heirs from his second marriage were his daughter Cora and son Carl, both under age 21 and both of Blackhawk.

Sarah Olive's mother, Nancy, was living with her in Blackhawk at the time Alexander P. died. By the terms of her brother's will who died in 1904, she was to receive $10.00 per month from his estate to pay for their mother's board and room plus extra for clothes, medicine, doctor's bills, etc. Since Chandler's estate ended up with a surplus of only $742.12, this money had long since run out. Undoubtedly she was forced to sell her property in Blackhawk and move back to Rapid City with her mother.

Sarah Olive died 30 Jan 1931, age 69y 3m 6d. Funeral services were held at the Congregational Church in Rapid City, SD and she was buried there in Mountain View Cemetery with her husband. Her obituary in the Rapid City "Journal" states that she was preceded in death by her father, mother, 2 brothers in Missouri, a brother, Chandler of Rapid City; and survived by her daughter, Mrs. Cora Leas of Lusk, WY; son Carl Hayes of Gordon, NE; step-daughters Mrs. Wm. Strong, Rapid City, Mrs. Emma Taylor,

Farmingdale; Mrs. Alice Blair, Caputa; and sister-in-law
Mrs. Sarah J. Kirkpatrick of Rapid City. A former neighbor of Sarah Olive's stated that "Mrs. Hayes was a local
character. Neighborhood children were afraid of her.
She wore long skirts and men's shoes tied on with twine."

Children of Sarah Olive (HAYES), born in Pennington
or Meade Co., SD, were: **(i)** Cora b Mar 1888 m ____ Leas;
of Lusk, WY 1931; **(ii)** Carl b Nov 1891; of Gordon, NE 1931.

299. HERMAN CALVIN MITCHELL, son of Samuel and Harriet
Jane (Calvin) Mitchell, was born 1 Aug 1871 at Horace, Edgar Co., IL. He was raised and lived all his life in the
lovely, spacious home which his parents built in Horace.
In his father's very brief will written 6 June 1895, Herman C. was left this home and all other property belonging
to his father to become his after the decease of his mother which occured in 1911.

Herman C. married Jessie Maude Tucker 24 Dec 1895 in
Edgar Co., IL (she detested her first name and never used
it). Maude was born 12 Dec 1877 at Cherry Point, Edgar
Co., IL, daughter of James A. and Catherine Elizabeth
(Bush) Tucker. James A. was born 16 Nov 1843 in Edgar Co.,
attended school there, did some farming as a young man,
taught school for 4 winters, and worked in a saw mill. In
1870 he went into the grocery business, operating as sole
owner at times and in partnership at others. In 1874 he
entered into partnership with S. D. Jenness under the
firm name of Tucker & Jenness in Cherry Point. The Business Directory in the 1879 "History of Edgar Co., IL"
lists this firm as "Dealers in Dry Goods, Hats, Caps,
Boots & Shoes, Hardware, Glass and Queensware, Choice
Staple & Family Groceries, and all Goods kept in a Retail
Store, at Lowest Cash Prices. All wishing articles in our
line will do well to call before purchasing elsewhere.
Country Produce taken in Exchange for Goods."

Catherine Elizabeth (Bush) Tucker was born 2 May 1847
in Ohio and died in Edgar Co. on 16 Nov 1899. James A.
Tucker died there 20 Feb 1891. Both are buried in Edgar
Cemetery in Paris, IL.

His mother having taught school in the years before
she married, was a woman of culture. Herman C. was raised
in a home where education was important. His teacher in
the arts of practicality would have been his father, Capt.
Samuel, a man much loved, respected and admired by his

family and community. As the only son and surviving child
of his parents, Herman C. was his father's valuable right
hand man in running the farm, especially in Capt. Samuel's
last years when he became extremely disabled from injuries he had suffered during his Civil War service.

The beautiful Mitchell homestead in Horace was eventually sold in 1976. At that time, it had been in the family for over 100 years.

Herman C. died 19 Nov 1957 at the homestead in Horace,
IL.   Jessie Maude died there 16 Apr 1974, age 96y.   Both
are buried in Edgar Cemetery, Paris, IL.   Children of Herman Calvin and Jessie Maude (Tucker) Mitchell, born at
Horace, Edgar Co., IL, were:

> 395. **Helen Harriet** b 31 Aug 1897   *
> 396. **Catherine Elizabeth** b 5 Aug 1907 lvg 1987 m1) 28
> June 1946 James Dodd Savoye (1911-1962); m2) 24
> Jan 1976 Wilford Harrison Crichfield (1905-1985);
> div 1984; no children by either marriage.

309. **CHANDLER MITCHELL,** son of Ensign and Sarah (   )
Mitchell, was born 17 Oct 1835 (based on age at death),
probably in Brown Co., OH. He came to Pike Co., IL with
his parents before 1850 and died there 24 Mar 1868, leaving a widow and 3 small children.

Little is known of Chandler's wife, Sarah Jane.   At
Chandler's death, Henry C. Foreman petitioned on 30 Mar
1868 for administration of Chandler's estate, stating
that the deceased had no real estate, possessed personal
property estimated to be worth about $600.00, and left a
widow, Jane, and 3 children, John, Alvin and Jesse Mitchell. Foreman called himself "Nephew & Requested by widow
of said deceased" to administer the estate. (It is more
likely that Foreman was Sarah Jane's nephew rather than
Chandler's nephew.)

Administration was granted to Mr. Foreman; his Administrator's Notice appeared in the "Pike County Democrat"
weekly from 2 Apr through 7 May. George A. Shriver, Shep-
pard E. Howland and John H. Dunham were appointed to appraise the estate.   Under law, Sarah Jane was allowed to
keep certain articles already in her possession - beds
and bedding, household and kitchen furniture, spinning
wheel, stove and pipe, wearing apparel for her and her
family, a "milch" cow and calf, provisions for a year and
food for stock for 6 months. Each item was given a dollar

evaluation and she was given credit for those items she did not own but were due her under the law - a loom and appendages, a pair of cards, a horse, a woman's saddle and bridle, sheep and fleeces, fuel for 3 months, and "other property." Total allowed the widow was $612.00 which represented her "dower." (Her name was signed to receipts as "Jane" or "Sarah J." to which she adds her "mark.")

The estate sale of "Chanley Michell" was held 20 Apr 1868. It was mainly farm equipment - a single and a double shovel plow, a 1-horse and a 2-horse plow, set of double harness, a 2-horse wagon, scythes and a snath, a meat tub, hay and stable forks, 29 acres of wheat in the west, east and northeast fields, 15 bushes of corn, 12 bushels of oats, sheep, a sow and 6 pigs, a white heifer and calf, a speckled cow and calf, a bay and a brown horse. Buyers were John Dunham, George Mills, S. E. Howland, Joseph Ruble, J. R. Davidson, D. N. Barngrover, Nancy Boyd, Jarred Long, Nicholas and H. C. Foreman, George Kesterson, Luke Alexander, A. Murphy, Albert Fidler, Reuben Sanderson, Isaac Porter, George "Michell," A. Moler, and Sarah Jane "Michell," the widow, who "purchased" a red cow, hogs and some bushels of corn.

On 22 May 1869, Sarah Jane contracted with a Mr. James (Lonny?) for "one set of Marble grave stones head Three feet incribed as follows Chandler Mitchell died March 24, 1868 aged 32 yrs 5 mo 7 ds to be set in blew river grain Soon as convinent..." for which she agreed to pay $22.00.

H. C. Foreman reported to the court 18 Aug 1869 that all estate debts had been discharged, including $65.00 to Dr. G. C. Pitzer for medical attendance for Chandler Mitchell "and family," and $12.00 to Dr. W. Hicks for 4 visits in March 1868. A balance of $386.00 on the widow's dower remained to be paid and was on that date. In May 1870, Mr. Foreman reported a balance of $306.45 in funds remaining and asked to distribute 1/3rd to the widow and the remaining 2/3rds to the guardian of John and Alvin Mitchell, heirs of the deceased. Since she was guardian of her children, Sarah Jane received the entire amount.

Sarah J. appeared in the 1870 census of Newburgh Twp., Pittsfield P.O., Pike Co., IL (p 16) as age 29, born in Ohio, possessing $1,000.00 in personal property. She was living in the household of Ellen Foreman, age 67, born in KY, real estate worth $8,000.00 and personal property of $200.00. In the same household was another Ellen Foreman, age 32, born in Ohio; Sarah's sons, John, age 8, and Alv<u>a</u>, age 5, both born in Ohio; and A. Mohler, age 51, a farmhand from Ohio. It seems probable that Sarah Jane was a daughter of the elder Ellen Foreman and perhaps nee Foreman herself. (Moses Mitchell, brother of Chandler, was living in the same township in 1870 and George Mitchell lived in adjoining Hardin Twp., Pike Co., IL.)

Chandler Mitchell appeared in the 1850 Pike Co., IL census with his parents but was not with them or in the county in 1860. If the 1870 census can be believed, he perhaps returned to Ohio before 1860, married Sarah Jane there, and had at least 2 children there before returning to Pike Co., IL. Jesse Mitchell, named as Chandler's child in the administration petition of 30 Mar 1868 probably died before 1870 since he did not receive a share of the estate balance in 1870 and is not listed with Sarah Jane in that census. No further trace of this family has been found to date in Pike Co., IL records.

Known children of Chandler and Sarah Jane (Foreman?) Mitchell (per census and probate records) were:

397. **John** bc 1862 OH; lvg 1870 Pike Co., IL.
398. **Alvin (Alva)** bc 1865 OH; lvg 1870 Pike Co., IL.
399. **Jesse** - prob d 1868-1870 Pike Co., IL.

326. **CLAUDIUS NEWTON MITCHELL,** son of Chandler and Elizabeth A. McConkey (Hendrix) Mitchell, was born 1 Jan 1852 on the family farm in Champaign Co., OH where he grew up, the eldest surviving son of a well-to-do farmer. His father primarily ran sheep and was known all over Central OH as a great shipper of stock. Claudius N. married 30 Oct 1878 Frances Ellen Hunter, born 24 June 1857 (per age at death) in OH. He died in Champaign Co. 29 Jan 1925, age 73y; she died there 14 Apr 1945, age 87y 9m 21d, both buried in Maple Grove Cemetery, Mechanicsburg, Goshen Twp., Champaign Co., OH.

Claudius N. and his wife appear in the 1880 census of Goshen Twp., Champaign Co., OH as Newton C. and Fanny E.; he was a farmer. Children of Claudius Newton and Frances Ellen (Hunter) Mitchell, born in Champaign Co., OH, were:

400. **James C.** b 7 Oct 1887 d 14 Jul 1954 age 66y bur Maple Grove Cem; W.W.-I vet.; m1) Belle Guy (div 1926); m2) Ruth Padget; no children.
401. **Juliet** (twin) b 27 May 1890   *
402. **Robert** (twin) b 27 May 1890 d 1967 unmar.

327. CHARLES LINCOLN MITCHELL, son of Chandler and Elizabeth A. McConkey (Hendrix) Mitchell, was born on the family farm 22 May 1861 near Mechanicsburg, Champaign Co., OH. He was the youngest of 3 children, all sons, the eldest of whom died just before his 11th birthday about 4 months before Charles L. was born. His father was a well known, very successful stockman, specializing in raising sheep for the market, a family business which Charles L. and his brother, Claudius N., would learn as they grew up.

Charles L. married 27 Mar 1889 at London, Madison Co., OH to Lizzie Belle Davidson, born 3 Aug 1868 at London, OH, daughter of Robert and Jane (Taggart) Davidson. Robert Davidson was born in Ireland in 1826, died at London, OH in 1899; his mother's maiden name was Mulholland. Jane (Taggart) Davidson was born in Ireland in 1844, died at London, OH in 1927, daughter of Thomas Taggart, Sr. and Martha Kingsbury of Ireland; she died at Xenia, OH.

Charles L. died 21 Feb 1906 on the family farm near Mechanicsburg and is buried in Maple Grove Cemetery in that town. After his death, Lizzie Belle married second 22 Apr 1916 in Covington, KY to Edward Armstrong, a widower. There were no children by this marriage. Lizzie Belle died 9 May 1949 at Jacksonville, Morgan Co., IL. She is buried in Maple Grove Cemetery under the name of Mitchell.

Children of Charles Lincoln and Lizzie Belle (Davidson) Mitchell, all born in Champaign Co., OH, were:

    403. Florence Elizabeth b 28 Jan 1894   *
    404. Helen Jean b 19 Mar 1896   *
    405. Jane Taggart b 15 Jul 1899   *

337. TALITHA BALES, daughter of Thomas and Emaline (Rigdon) Bales, was born 17 Jan 1855 in Madison Co., OH. She married 28 Nov 1876 Dr. Timothy Downing Beach, born 17 Jan 1848 in Brown Twp., Franklin Co., OH, son of Uri Beach II 1826-1909, and Eleanor (Downing) Beach 1825-1904. Talitha and Timothy lived in Catawba, OH for some years.

Talitha died 20 Nov 1942 and Timothy died 28 Dec 1922 at London, OH, buried there in Oak Hill Cemetery. Children of Dr. Timothy D. and Talitha (Bales) BEACH were:

    406. Leroy b 20 Apr 1878   *
    407. Alta b 29 Dec 1879   *
    408. Ada Gertrude b 9 Apr 1886   *
    409. Downing b 7 Oct 1888   *
    410. Darwin b 3 Jan 1894   *

339. CARRIE BALES, daughter of Thomas and Emaline (Rigdon) Bales, was born 16 Nov 1868 Madison Co., OH, died on 4 Apr 1945 Champaign Co., OH. She married 1st) 3 Sep 1884 John Fitzgiven, born 9 Sep 1860 at Mechanicsburg, OH, and died 23 Jan 1898 near Tradersville, OH, son of John and Mary (Powell) Fitzgiven. Carried married 2nd about 1899 Edward Mathew Fitzgibbon, born Jan 1870, died 12 Jan 1919 (reputedly a cousin of John Fitzgiven but using the Irish spelling). She married 3rd on 14 June 1920 Champaign Co., OH Francis Wilbur Hendrix, son of John and Mary (Davison) Hendrix; he died 31 Mar 1933 aged 70. All are buried in Maple Grove Cemetery, Mechanicsburg, OH (Carrie and her 2nd husband are both buried under the name Fitzgiven).

Carrie's children (FITZGIVEN), born in Champaign Co., OH, were: **(i)** Clarence b Oct 1885 d 24 Oct 1941 bur Maple Grove Cem; **(ii)** Laura B. b Oct 1887; **(iii)** Harry E. b Aug 1890; **(iv)** Mary E. b 18 Jul 1896 d 8 Jul 1901 bur Maple Grove Cemetery.

342. NEWMAN F. BALES, son of David and Lydia Jane (Mitchell) Bales, was born 15 Oct 1858 in Madison Co., OH. He married 7 Oct 1880 to Mary Lizabeth Everett (1860-1929). Between 1880 and 1883, Newman F. and his family moved to Texas, possibly to or near Jones Co. where his parents and his sister, Ida (Bales) Goodyear, had moved about 1883. Newman F. died 1 Sep 1926, place of death unknown, but his residence in 1916 was Mena, AR.

Children of Newman F. and Mary Lizabeth (Everett) BALES were: **(i)** Maude Lillian b 21 Dec 1881 d 7 Aug 1882 London, OH, 7½m; **(ii)** Royalton Everett b 1883 TX d 1958 m 1909 Lillian Ray; 6 children; **(iii)** William Arthur b 1886 TX d 1965 m 1907 Lula Owens; 6 children; **(iv)** Della Mae b 1888 TX d 1975 m 1910 Walter Lee Owens (1888-1965); 3 children; **(v)** Albert Merton b 1891 TX d 1967 AR m1) 1912 Amanda Miller; m2) 1950 Mrs. Rose Wright; 3 children from 1st mar; **(vi)** Ida Ella b 31 May 1898 TX d 14 Feb 1907 AR.

343. IDA E. BALES, daughter of David and Lydia Jane (Mitchell) Bales, was born 24 Sep 1861 in Madison Co., OH; died in 1926. She married in 1883 Charles A. Goodyear who was born about 1859 in Madison Co., OH, son of Monmorth P. and Mary Elizabeth (McCorkle) Goodyear. A biography of Monmorth P. Goodyear in Beers' 1883 "History of Madison Co., OH" (Somerford Twp., p 1111) mentions that "...Mr.

Goodyear's son, Charles, is a young man of industry and energy...much respected in the community..." Charles and Ida E. moved to Texas in 1891 where they are found in the 1900 census in Jones Co., Ida's parents living with them. Their third and fourth child were born in Texas.

Known children of Charles A. and Ida E. (Bales) GOODYEAR were: **(i)** Morrel b June 1884 d 1942 m Ethel Washburn; **(ii)** Francis "Frank" b Jul 1886 d 1963 m 1909 Norma Russell; **(iii)** Mary E. b Oct 1899 d 1919 m 1916 Emmett Woodard; **(iv)** Jewell b 1902 d 1951 m Allen Eason.

345. **FLORA MAE BALES,** daughter of David and Lydia Jane (Mitchell) Bales, was born in 1865; died in 1927. She married in 1890 Henry Cyrus Hall. Children of Henry Cyrus and Flora Mae (Bales) HALL were: **(i)** Willie C. b 1891 d 1976 m 1908 Fannie C. Rae; **(ii)** David L. b 1893 d 1929 unmarried; **(iii)** Annie May b 1900 m 1916 A. A. McDuff; **(iv)** Henry Cyrus, Jr. b 1908 m 1927 Vada Bell.

346. **ALICE J. MITCHELL,** daughter of Charles E. and Mary Elizabeth (Heffley) Mitchell, was born Dec 1869 in Somerford Twp., Madison Co., OH; she died in 1932. On 13 May 1890 Madison Co., she married Harry F. Fauver, born 30 Oct 1864 Union Twp., Madison Co., OH, son of Matthew J. and Maria Jane (Prugh) Fauver. He died in 1938 and is buried with Alice in Somerford Twp. Cemetery, Madison Co. (A biography of Matthew J. Fauver [as Fanver] appears in Beers' 1883 "History of Madison Co., OH"; also see Bryan's 1915 "History of Madison Co., OH" [p872/3] for an extensive biography of Matthew J. and Harry F. Fauver, including details on the Prugh family.)

Bryan's county history (cited above) contains a portrait of Harry F. who looks every inch the successful businessman he was. On the portly side and balding when this picture was taken, Harry F. was somberly dressed in a 3-piece suit and solid color bow tie. Nevertheless, the beginning of a smile and the crinkles at the corners of his eyes give the impression of a man who liked to laugh.

According to Bryan, Alice J. and Harry F. lived on a "...fine farm of 325 acres in Somerford Twp." Harry F. had opened a real estate and insurance office in the county seat of London in 1894. If the timetable in Bryan's history is correct, Harry F. began life in the business world as a very young lad indeed, working in his father's grocery store for a "few years." He then worked for about 10 years in the "carriage and vehicle business," for another 5 years as a traveling salesman, and 5 years in Mechanicsburg, Champaign ·Co., OH, all prior to 1894.

Harry F. was a Democrat, member of the Masons and Odd Fellows, and served 2 terms as Somerford Twp. treasurer. He and Alice belonged to the Somerford Twp. Christian Church, Harry serving as trustee. Bryan adds that Harry enjoyed "a very high degree of popular favor" throughout the area and was known far beyond his home county.

Alice J.'s children (FAUVER) were: (i) Gwynneth (Jo) b 1892; mar but dsp 1930; (ii) Matthew Mitchell b 13 Jan 1895 d Sep 1974 Somerford Twp, Madison Co., OH; m Nov 1933 (or 1932?) Irene Willard b May 1898 Somerford Twp., d/o Edwin E. & Alice (Evans) Willard d 19 Nov 1971; no ch; (iii) Harry Ordell b 1898 d 1957 m Lillian Morehart d/o Robert & Lily (Stewart) Morehart; lvg 1988; 3 ch. (All above bur Somerford Twp. Cem., Madison Co., OH.)

348. **RALEIGH MITCHELL**, son of Charles E. and Mary Elizabeth (Heffley) Mitchell, was born 20 Nov 1873 Somerford Twp., Madison Co., OH, and married there Nov 1907 Metta Rafferty, born 1882, daughter of Nathaniel S. and Elizabeth (Geer) Rafferty. Raleigh died in 1936. Both are buried in Somerford Twp. Cemetery.

In Bryan's "History of Madison Co., OH" (pp 711/12), published in 1915, Raleigh is termed a "...prosperous young farmer of Somerford township..." At his father's death, Raleigh inherited part of the "old homestead" and about 172 acres of his father's home farm. He sold his portion of the "old homestead" and spent his time developing the second farm where he "...erected good buildings... and...continued the drainage of the land which was begun by his father." The farm is described as having soil of exceptionally fertile "very fine black loam." Raleigh raised horses and Duroc-Jersey hogs. The 6-room family home, the barn, "a commodius, up-to-date structure," and the outbuildings were all painted in a "pleasing, harmonious color scheme." Raleigh apparently had little interest in public affairs, Bryan specifically stating that he devoted himself "almost altogether" to farming and had "little time for outside interests."

Raleigh's elder brother, Harry, is described as living "near" the "old home farm" by Bryan. Raleigh, as the second son and some 16 years older than his younger brother, Noel, remained on his father's farm, he and Noel apparently both living there even after they married. At their father's death in 1898, they undoubtedly both inherited a considerable amount of property since their father is said to have owned over 2,000 acres of land.

Children of Raleigh and Metta (Rafferty) Mitchell, born in Madison Co., OH, were:

411. **Charles Nathaniel** b 1909 d 1956
412. **Dollie Elizabeth**

349. **NOEL MITCHELL,** son of Charles E. and Mary Elizabeth (Heffley) Mitchell, was born in 1889 in Somerford Twp., Madison Co., OH; he died in 1938. On 1 June 1911 in Madison Co., OH, Noel married Blanche M. Rafferty, born 15 Aug 1890 in Somerford Twp., daughter of M. C. and Ora (Seeds) Rafferty. After Noel's death, Blanche married 2nd Benjamin Moore as his 2nd wife. Both are now deceased.

Bryan's 1915 "History of Madison Co., OH" (p 753) has a good deal more to say about the Rafferty family than it does about Noel except that he owned 173 acres of the "old farm, including the old homestead...a fine tract of land ...well improved and highly productive." We conclude that Noel stuck to the business of farming and had no time for public matters. (See #348 Raleigh Mitchell.)

Only known child of Noel and Blanche M. (Rafferty) Mitchell, born in Madison Co., OH, was:

413. **Roger Lyman** b 27 May 1915

351. **ROYALTON MITCHELL CREAMER,** son of Lewis Harlen and Electa (Mitchell) Creamer, was born 1 Dec 1877 on the family farm in Somerford Twp., Madison Co., OH. He married on 4 Mar 1903 to Leila Lenore Hendrickson, born 11 Jan 1881 at Milford Center, Union Co., OH, daughter of Albert and Adra (Needham) Hendrickson. Royalton died 5 Dec 1954 and Leila Lenore died 7 June 1950 at Mechanicsburg, OH. Only child of Royalton Mitchell and Leila Lenore (Hendrickson) CREAMER was:

414. **Carlton Mitchell** b 19 Apr 1904   *

363. **SYLVESTER GREELY MITCHELL,** son of Erastus W. and Clarissa (Smith) Mitchell, was born 5 Jan 1846 at Mechanicsburg, Champaign Co., OH. Before 1850, his parents had moved to Logan Co. just north of Champaign Co. where they

were living in Perry Twp. at the 1850 census. Sylvester G.
married 15 Nov 1872 in Hardin Co. (just north of Logan) to
Elizabeth Shilling, born 2 Mar 1855 in Hardin Co., OH,
daughter of John and Catherine (Stake) Shilling. (Per
Bateman & Selby's 1910 "History of Effingham Co., IL,"
p 825, John Shilling was born in Germany, settling first
at Strasburg, OH, then moving to Hardin Co., OH, and later
to Indiana where he died.)

Sylvester G.'s biography appears in the above cited
Effingham Co., Il history, stating that as a youth he went
to school in the winters and in the summers worked in the
"brick yard." At age 16 he enlisted from Hardin Co., OH
in Co. I, 45th Ohio Volunteer Infantry on 19 June 1862,
and was the second youngest in the regiment. The 45th was
assigned to the Army of the Tennessee and "...participated
in all the battles of the Atlanta campaign, being discharged at Camp Hooker, TN..." on 19 June 1865.

After returning home, Sylvester worked on the family
farm for a few years until his marriage, remaining in Hardin Co., OH after marriage until 1895 when he and his family moved to Effingham Co., IL. Here he owned 122 acres of
farm land in Sections #1 and #12, Mound Twp. Politically,
Sylvester G. was a Republican "but has never been very
active in public matters, his farm demanding all of his
attention."

Sylvester G. wrote his will 8 Jan 1910. He bequeathed
all of his personal property to his wife Elizabeth "...to
have absolute controll of and the right to dispose and use
the same for and during her natural life." He also left to
Elizabeth all of his real estate, described as the SE 1/4
of the SE 1/4 and the NE 1/4 of the SE 1/4 in Section #1;
the NE 1/4 of the NE 1/4 and that portion of the SE 1/4 of
the NE 1/4 "laying North of the National Road" in Section
#12. After Elizabeth's death, all remaining personal
property and the described real estate was to be divided
equally among his children, named as Margaret, Estella,
James L., John R., Guy and Clara. John and Fred Dickman
of Altamont, IL (Mound Twp., Effingham Co.) witnessed the
document. (Will Record Bk F:206/7 Effingham Co., IL Probate Records)

The will was admitted to probate 6 Jan 1913. On the
same date, a Bond of Administration found in Administrator's Records Bk C:97 named Sylvester G.'s wife, Elizabeth, as administratrix with her bondsmen being John and

Fred Dickman. Since Sylvester G. did not die intestate
(without a will), it is a puzzle why Elizabeth was made
administratrix rather than executrix. The Dickmans do
not seem to bear any relationship with the Mitchells except as good friends and neighbors, having in common with
Elizabeth a German ancestry.

Children of Sylvester Greely and Elizabeth (Shilling)
Mitchell, probably all born in Hardin Co., OH, were:
415. **William** d in infancy.
416. **Margaret** bc 1876 m H. E. Wilcox; in Omaha, NE 1910.
417. **Estella** bc 1878 m William Crowther; lvg NE 1910.
418. **James L.** m _____ Smith; lvg MT 1910.
419. **Sylvester** d in infancy.
420. **John R.** lvg NE 1910.
421. **Guy** lvg Effingham Co., IL 1910 (at home).
422. **Clara** lvg Effingham Co., IL 1910 (at home).

Approximately 200 years have elapsed since we first began our journey through time. We are entering a generation containing people who are living today, were living and personally known to us during our lifetime, or were known by and spoken of by our parents or other relatives.

In fleshing out the bare bones of pure data, always a primary goal in this genealogy (when possible), a number of sources have been consulted and utilized. Pertinent excerpts from letters written by or to some members of this generation have been used; excerpts from letters written to me about some members of this generation are quoted; portraits of some family members which are in my possession are described when applicable; and portions of Clara L. Hopp's personal reminiscenses from her book, "Nettie Jane (Mitchell) Redman - Her Ancestors and Descendants," have been cited.

Succeeding generations will not carry an introductory preface, being more devoted to the compilation of vital statistics, allowing today's descendants to connect with their ancestors of yesterday and a heritage of which they can be proud. To these descendants of the final generations, it seems appropriate to quote from Kahlil Gibran's "The Prophet" (Alfred A. Knopf, NY, 1966): "You are the bows from which your children as living arrows are sent forth...He bends you with His might that His arrows may go swift and far. Let your bending in the archer's hand be for gladness. For even as He loves the arrow that flies, so He loves also the bow that is stable."

****

365. **ALLEN CALVIN MITCHELL,** son of Orlando and Margaret Ellen (Mesnard) Mitchell, was born 11 Aug 1873 in Jackson Twp., Effingham Co., IL. Originally, he was named Calvin Allen Emmit after his Mitchell grandfather (Calvin), his

-243-

father and paternal grandmother (Allen), and his maternal grandfather (Addison Emmit Mesnard). As a young man, he changed his name to Allen Calvin, dropping the Emmit.

Allen grew up on the Jackson Twp. farm that his grandfather, Calvin Mitchell, had purchased in 1858. His father, Orlando, terminally ill with tuberculosis, was unable to do more than oversee the farm for some years before his death in 1892, depending on Allen a great deal. After his father died, Allen remained on the farm until he married. His mother then moved into Dexter, IL with her two youngest unmarried children, earning her living by dressmaking. The family farm with its rich bottom land, wooded hills and sparkling stream was eventually sold.

Allen's first wife whom he married 30 Sep 1896 was Margaret Jane Moffett, born 30 Nov 1874 in Macon Co., IL, daughter of John McDowell and Elizabeth J. (McDonald) Moffett. On the back of their wedding portrait, taken at Haws Studio, Decatur, IL, is written "Mr. & Mrs. A. C. Mitchell, Boody, Ill." (Boody lay 6 miles southwest of Decatur in Macon Co. on Route 48.)

The newly wedded couple stood on an opulent fur rug in front of a Grecian style studio backdrop. Allen, a slim young man, greatly resembling his mother, wore a 3-piece suit with a 2-button cutaway jacket, white shirt, white bow tie, and a watch chain from which hung a small, round medallion. Margaret was as elaborately gowned as she was plain of feature. Her dress was tightly cinched at her tiny waist, the floor length skirt topped by a jacket sporting triangular epaulettes over very full sleeves that were tight fitted from elbow to wrist. Beading trimmed the jacket's wide cuffs, front, collar edge and epaulettes. Margaret's hair style nearly defies description. Short with a middle part, it lay tightly curled on her head and was crowned with a spiral topknot that extended at least 6 inches above her head, held steady by a comb or barrette at the base. She clasped her left hand with her right, showing off her wedding ring.

On 18 Aug 1898, Margaret Jane died at age 28 years 8 months 19 days, leaving Allen with a year old son. She was buried with her Moffett relatives in Brown Cemetery (then Blue Mound) in Macon Co., IL.

Allen probably moved back to the Jackson Twp. farm in Effingham Co. after his wife's death, his mother moving in with him to care for his young son. In the 1900 census of Effingham Co., IL, he was living there with his son, his mother, his unmarried brother, Frank, and his second wife, Augusta Barbara "Gusta" Hartman whom he had married on 14 Feb of that year. Gusta was born 20 Apr 1882 in Macon Co., IL. (Her parents' names are unknown but in the 1900 census, she said both were born in Germany.)

Gusta's picture shows us a striking young woman with almost a heart shaped face, high cheekbones, rather sensual eyes below well delineated brows. Her simply dressed hair was middle parted and drawn softly back from her face, displaying a slight widow's peak. Her dress was plain except for vertical stitching on the bodice front, puffed sleeves and a stickpin at the throat.

Within a few years after his second marriage, Allen moved his family to a farm near Gays in Moultrie Co., IL, then just across the Moultrie Co. border to another farm in adjoining Shelby Co., IL where the last 4 of their 6 children were born.

Allen died 31 Aug 1963 in Effingham Co., IL and Gusta died there 30 Dec 1966. Children of Allen Calvin Mitchell, first one by his first wife, Margaret Jane (Moffett) Mitchell, remaining 6 by his second wife, Augusta Barbara (Hartman) Mitchell, were:

423. **Ora Allen** b 8 Aug 1897   *
424. **Oscar Calvin** b 10 Aug 1901   *
425. **Edgar Samuel** b 7 Feb 1903   *
426. **Burl Kenneth** b 26 Aug 1906   *
427. **Stella L.** b 12 June 1908   *
428. **Velma Augusta** b 11 June 1914   *
429. **Vernon Hartman** b 15 Jan 1919   *

366. **ANNA CHRISTINA (ANNIE) MITCHELL,** daughter of Orlando Allen and Margaret Ellen (Mesnard) Mitchell, was born 16 Jul 1875 in Jackson Twp., Effingham Co., IL. She married there on 26 Apr 1891 to Cornelius "Neil" Redman, born 3 Sep 1867 in Vincennes, IN, son of Henry Sinclair and Mary Jane (Garlinghouse) Redman. The wedding was held at Annie's parents' home, her father witnessing the ceremony and her brother and sister, Allen and Mary Eliza, serving as their attendants.

After marriage, Annie moved from the life of a farmer's daughter to that of a farmer's wife. She possessed a fragile blond beauty, closely resembling her younger sister, Mary Eliza (Mollie), whom she affectionately called

"Diza." In an era without the household conveniences we enjoy today, Annie's responsibilities as a farmer's wife entailed plenty of hard work - there were chickens to be tended, eggs to be gathered, butter to be churned. Bread was homemade and washing was done the hard way, on a scrub board. The vegetables from her garden had to be preserved, three square meals a day prepared on a wood cook stove, the children to be tended in sickness and in health without benefit of modern day aids and medicines. Yet the urge to express her thoughts in the form of poetry which seemed to be a natural heritage of the Mitchell children was so strong in Annie that she found time for her writing.

Annie was a news reporter for the "Altamont News" for years and had her poems printed by local newspapers from time to time. In 1938 she had a collection of her poetry published in a small booklet entitled "Echoes of the Heart" which she dedicated to her husband. In a letter to sister "Diza" written in 1939, Annie spoke of her failing eyesight, then of the programs where her "pieces" had been spoken as well as the various papers in which they had been copied. She added that "I don't take any credit - only just for using the gift that He gave. It has took hard work tho' many times." Her poetry in which she "... sought only to express the happenings of an every-day life in simple, every-day language..." covered a wide range of subjects. Many had religious themes and dealt with the loss through death of relatives and children. One concerned a favorite puppy named Dewey who had an unfortunate encounter with a rattlesnake, and in another unpublished poem written in the summer of 1908, she whimsically begged one of her sisters for a piece of her "fresh light bread dough," explaining that she had "...bought fresh yeast and I can't get it to raise; so if you're baking please oblige your Sister."

During these busy years, Annie had to cope with the stress of bearing 11 children, only 5 of whom survived to adulthood. Once she copied the following from a paper: "Those who have lost a baby are, so to speak, never without an infant child. The others may grow to womanhood and manhood, but this one is rendered an immortal child, for death has blessed it in an eternal image of youth and innocence." Her thoughts upon reading this were to ask God for the patience and grace to face such sorrows.

Eighth Generation

On 26 Apr 1941, Annie and Neil celebrated their Golden Wedding anniversary, again attended by Annie's brother and sister, Allen and Mary Eliza. Standing in front of a special table, they renewed their vows, the "groom" placing a new golden wedding ring on the "bride's" finger, saying, "I hope our love like this ring may have no end, but last 'til death us part." She answered, "Thank you, I, too, hope our love may last, not only 'til death us part but 'til death us join, and in a better home bye and bye, may we again together be, throughout all eternity." An open house for 120 friends and neighbors was held in the afternoon with singing, recitation of a special poem entitled "Golden Wedding" which was written by their son, Clinton, and serving of the many cakes that were brought, highlighted by a golden wedding cake presented by their son, Cecil, and his wife. It was several tiers high, the base of each tier surrounded by golden roses and white swans, topped by a large heart bearing a gold "50."

In several letters written to me by Annie and Neil's youngest son, Cecil, he reminisced about his parents. "I think they were unusual. They seemed to know much more than their formal education would indicate they should know. We sure didn't have money, so how did we always have the newspaper, farm magazines and other rather good class magazines come in our mail? Also, how many homes even way back then had daily devotions. My parents lived the part without being preachy about it. Dad, too, was easy going and laughed a lot, especially when out among people...Dad would do his shadow act sometimes (on) winter evenings. Other times Mom played the organ and we all sang...My brother (Clinton) and I got into the usual kid stuff - country hockey, running races, swimming, hunting...Maybe we had many things that others didn't have. We had fun evenings with popcorn, taffy and games.

One time a dog that I claimed started to eat the eggs. The dog had to be destroyed. Mom said that it was my dog and my job to take care of it. I took the dog on a rope, took my rifle, went back into the woods, tied the dog, sat in front of that dog...that dog looked me right in the eye and didn't move. Three shots and I'd missed every time. Went home expecting trouble but Mom turned away and I can still see the smile that she couldn't completely hide. I found out later that I couldn't even shoot a rabbit that sat still and just looked at me. Frank was the same way.

The year 1917 was a very tough, difficult one at our house. Everyone was sick including Dad and Mom that year, and all at the same time. I was about 5½ years old but no one (was) able to fix my meals. They kept me in one bedroom with permission to go to the kitchen for cold oatmeal. I know that about that time...the doctor said Frank couldn't live, and Ruth did die. I can't remember when Ruth was taken from the house...may be...neighbors had to do it because of so much sickness at our house...Rosie died the year after Ruth. Mom and Dad were more shaken up over that than anytime I can remember. I was outside the house...and remember Dad coming out and saying "she's gone." Later he made a remark that it was so unnecessary. Things were different around home for awhile."

Neil died in Effingham Co., IL on 14 Jul 1946, age 78 years, 10 months, 11 days, of arteriosclerotic heart disease (Adam-Stoke syndrome). Annie died there on 11 Oct 1946, age 71 years 3 months 25 days, of hypertensive cardiac disease, complicated by chronic gall bladder disease and a cerebral hemorrhage suffered 5 months prior to her death. Both are buried in Little Prairie Cemetery of the Jackson Twp. Baptist Church in Effingham Co., IL. Children of Cornelius and Anna Christina (Mitchell) REDMAN, all born in Effingham Co., IL, were:

430. **Clarence** b 4 Jan 1892 "bef time;" d 14 Jan 1892.
431. **Ernest** b 11 Feb 1893 d 18 Jul 1893.
432. **Bessie** b 2 Aug 1894 *
433. **Rosa Pearl** b 4 Feb 1897 *
434. **Paul** b 6 June 1899 "bef time;" d same day.
435. **David Franklin ("Frank")** b 29 Jul 1900 *
436. **Ruth Amelia** b 31 Jul 1903 d unmar 28 Feb 1917.
437. Son - b 6 Dec 1905 "bef time;" d same day.
438. **Clinton Cornelius** b 8 Jul 1907 *
439. **Cecil Howard** b 28 June 1911 *
440. **Ethel May** b 30 May 1916 "bef time;" d 13 Oct 1916.

367. **NETTIE JANE MITCHELL**, daughter of Orlando Allen and Margaret Ellen (Mesnard) Mitchell, was born 19 Mar 1877 in Jackson Twp., Effingham Co., IL. On 31 Dec 1895 at a home wedding there, witnessed by Cornelius Redman, Nettie Jane was married to Anthony Redman, born 7 Sep 1873 in Hillsboro, IL, son of Henry Sinclair and Mary Jane (Garlinghouse) Redman. (Anthony was a brother of Cornelius Redman who married Nettie Jane's sister, Annie, in 1891.)

Anthony, called "Ank" or "Hank" or sometimes "Jack," worked as a farm laborer, living for the first 7 years of his marriage to Nettie Jane in DeWitt Co., IL. Nettie Jane was described by her eldest daughter, Clara, as having "...inherited much of her father's sunny disposition, and appearance, but she was short as was her mother. She was slender, slightly under five feet in height, with light brown hair, bright blue eyes, and fair skin. She was a beautiful woman with a beautiful character...I never remember seeing her angry or hearing her gossip or criticize others. Her speech was pure and clean; free of slang or rough words. I believe she was a true Christian. I did hear her lovely voice singing when about her housework, although we lived on a farm, far from neighbors, and farther from her relatives...with a family of small children, she seldom got to leave her home and no doubt was very lonely at times, as my father worked from daylight till dark and often later. There was only a horse and buggy for transportation. Her mother (my grandmother Mitchell) would visit us for a few weeks now and then."

The summer after the birth of her 4th child in 1902, Nettie Jane's health failed. The family moved first to Effingham Co., Il to be near Nettie Jane's mother and family; thereafter, they moved often to be near a doctor they would hear of that might possibly be able to help her. Although a ladies' aid group from a nearby church helped out by sewing for her children, much of the household work fell on the shoulders of her two eldest daughters, Clara and Opal. Clara was often kept home from school, once missing an entire term. She was instructed to signal her father in the fields by hanging a white tablecloth on the line if Nettie Jane fell ill while he was away from the house. The youngest child, Mabel, spent much of her time living with Nettie Jane's married sister, Mollie Taylor.

By 1907, Nettie Jane's health seemed to improve; the family moved to a farm near Bement, IL in Piatt Co. Clara described the move as being by train, "...our furniture being in a box car, and we rode in a passenger coach at the rear of the freight train. We arrived about dark in the evening and, it being too late to get a teamster to move the furniture, we slept all night in the coach which was sidetracked every night to wait for the return trip south the next day. We ate in a small restaurant which was we children's first experience eating in a public place."

The next day the furniture was moved into the new home and the family settled in. Nettie Jane's health problems, complicated by the births of two more daughters who died in infancy, was not as improved as was originally thought. In the winter of 1908, Nettie Jane's sister, Mollie, wrote to their mother in Watson, IL that she had seen Nettie the Friday before. "She has had the gripp nerely every since you was here and has an awful cough. Poor thing she looks so pitiful. She got to talking of her troubles...and it is awful the way she talked...They have not got anybody to do the work yet and she says Ank won't try to get any one. They have been told of three different girls here in town and he won't see them. I guess he thinks when it comes to the Pinch I'll wait on him but I don't see how I can. Al (Mollie's husband) wouldent let me if I wanted to."

On 27 Dec 1909, Nettie Jane, in her 8th month of pregnancy, wrote her sister, Mollie, and her daughter, Mabel, who was again staying with the Taylor's. "We have an awful deep snow and had such a nice white Christmass...I got two nice big gingham aprons ready made...We live 1½ miles out in the country now. We moved two weeks ago I like it better out here. We will soon have a fresh cow. The man Ank is working for is going to furnish us a cow. We will get 7 doz hens and raise some chickens of our own. We had a rooster for dinner yesterday. Ank and Hubert have gone Rabbit hunting today...do you hear from Ma very often I wrote to her last week. The last time I heard from her she said she was talking of coming up and see me and stay two or three days...I do wish she would happen in about the right time. I did have neighbors before we moved who said they would help me when I needed them but I don't know anyone out here yet. Well Opal is making so much noise I can't write so I will quit...We are all as well as common except bad colds..." Enclosed in her letter were notes from the children to their little sister, Mabel. Clara and Opal had gotten "a little lamp" apiece and plenty of candy and nuts for Christmas. Opal promised to send her a paper doll, and Hubert complained that he was "not doing nothing" and "did not get nothing" for Christmas.

Nettie's son, Harry Allen Redman, was born the next month (29 Jan). On the "nice bright morning" of Feb. 8th, Nettie wrote her mother that she was "feeling lots stronger...I have a big boy...I got up yesterday for the first (time)...2 weeks ago I was so down in my back I could not write...I could not walk across the room or get up when down for four weeks before the baby was born...Clara is in the Kitchen at work, she has not went to school any since Christmass she had to stay at home with me and do the work. She can just make awful nice bread and atends to the milk and butter and does all the other work after dinner. We have 1/2 doz hens now. We get 4 and 5 eggs a day they are 25 cts per doz now...We give the baby the bottle and cows milk. Our old cow was fresh just long enough before the baby was born, for the milk to be good...I will close hoping to hear from you soon. I must rest awhile before the baby wakes...goodby..."

Two days after writing this letter (10 Feb 1910), she was dead. On 23 Feb, Nettie's husband wrote the following letter to her sister, Mollie: "I received your letter today and was more than glad to hear from you...you wasent worried eney more than I...I was afraid you or Mabel was sick. I was so sorry you did not get here (for the funeral) for I sent your message the first one and directed them to deliver it at once...I sent it at 7 oclock in the morning. I dident tel you when the funeral would be because I dident no when it would be myself...I thot if I wated to find out you wouldent get here. Nettie took with sick headache friday morning about nine oclock and died twenty minutes til nine in the evening. She was only sick about twelve hours and in vomiting bursted a blud vessel in her brain and died in a very few minutes...We are going to stay here where we are we have got a nice place here to liv. We hav got a woman in town to take care of baby til school is out we take milk to him every day. The girls are going to start to school in the morning again. Mollie... Mabel is yours now. Take care of her and make a woman out of her I will do the best I can for the rest of them. I will haf to close the girls are wateing on me to go to church...A. Redman."

At this time, the Redmans lived in the tenant house on John Morey's farm south of Bement, IL. Nettie's infant son, Harry Allen, was cared for after her death by Mrs. John Murphy in town but the arrangement was only temporary. He was later taken to an orphanage in St. Louis where he died that summer of measles. The remaining children at home, Clara, Opal and Hubert, ages 13, 11 and 9 at their mother's death, kept house for their father until Anthony married second on 11 Jan 1911 to Margaret Booker, born 26

Feb 1882 in Long Creek, Macon Co., IL, daughter of William Nelson and Mary Jane Elizabeth (Cox) Booker. Five children were born of Anthony's second marriage.

His eldest daughter, Clara, described Anthony as "a hard working man...a farmer most of his life. He loved us children. I have pleasant memories of sitting on his lap in a big old rocking chair and of running to meet him when coming from his work. He would catch in his arms the first one that got to him. I remember how sad I felt when I got too heavy to be carried and the younger ones still had that privelege. His complete confidence in me and the praise he always had for me have greatly influenced my life." Anthony's youngest child (by his 2nd marriage), Mary Jane (Redman) Root, remembered her father as a person whom "...everyone liked and he liked people. He had coal black hair, with just a touch of gray at the temples when he died. He combed it back with a 'roach.' His eyes were green, gray, blue, changing colors. When he felt bad, they were very blue. He had a big nose and very dark complexion. He was so dark when he was a baby, his mother was ashamed of him and wouldn't take him out. He had high cheek bones. There must have been some Indian blood somewhere along the line. He didn't smoke or drink but he did chew tobacco. He had perfect health except for his heart. When I was a year old (1923), he was greasing a wagon, getting it ready to start husking corn. When he lifted the wagon to put the wheel back on, he broke a valve in his heart. When he and Mom were married (1911), he weighed 150 pounds and I don't think he weighed any more than that when he died. I was proud of him..."

An account of Anthony's death taken from the "Bement Register" states that he died at his home in Bement at 9:30 p.m. Wednesday, Sept. 21, 1938 of a heart attack, age 65 years 2 weeks. He had suffered with "leakage of the heart for 16 years, but had been in his usual health until a short time before his death. He had retired from farming, moved to Bement and was working for the city, worked all day the last day of his life. Shortly after coming home, he complained of a smothered feeling, went to the porch and sat down, where his death occurred instantly."

Funeral services for Anthony were held on 24 Sep from the Christian Church in Bement, IL and he was buried in the Bement Cemetery where Nettie Jane, who had been a member of the Methodist Church in Dexter, IL, had been buried

at her death in 1910 (her grave is unmarked). Children of
Anthony and Nettie Jane (Mitchell) REDMAN were:

   441. Clara Lue b 21 Oct 1896   *

   442. Opal May b 6 Jul 1898   *

   443. Hubert Paul b 5 Oct 1900   *

   444. Mabel Ruth b 5 Oct 1902   *

   445. Ethel May d in infancy.

   446. Lottie Rue d in infancy.

   447. Harry Allen b 29 Jan 1910 d 25 Aug 1910.

368. MARY ELIZA (MOLLIE) MITCHELL, daughter of Orlando
Allen and Margaret Ellen (Mesnard) Mitchell, was born 16
Nov 1878 in Jackson Twp., Effingham Co., IL. She was married at the "bride's home" there on 24 Dec 1896 to Albert
Marion Taylor, born 20 Dec 1876 in Bethel, OH, son of William Sydney and Nancy Jane (Ingles) Taylor; he came to Effingham Co., IL with his parents in 1880.

Mollie and Al were never able to have their own children, but they deserve a place in this genealogy as surely
as do those who were able to produce offspring. After
their marriage in 1896, Mollie and Al lived with his parents in Effingham for a time, later moving to their own
home near Altamont, IL where Al farmed, also working as a
licensed realtor as a sideline for a few years. Because
of the failing health of Mollie's sister, Nettie Jane
Redman, Mollie and Al began taking Nettie's youngest
daughter, Mabel, to stay with them periodically when the
child was between 3 and 4 years of age. After Nettie's
death in 1910, Mabel was "given" by her father to Mollie
and Al to raise which they did with love and tenderness until she reached adulthood and married. There was no formal adoption but one was not needed for a child who had
already become as a daughter to them.

In 1911 the Taylors spent a year near Fox, AR where Al
was engaged in cutting timber for railroad ties. Returning to Illinois, they settled in Piatt Co. near Bement
where Al farmed until 1938 when ill health forced him to
retire. Moving into the small village of Milmine in Piatt
Co., Al operated a grocery store for 3 years until his
health deteriorated even more and he retired completely.
He died there on 22 Aug 1943, age 66 years 8 months 2 days.
His funeral services were held at home, conducted by Rev.
Raymond R. Brewer of the Methodist Church, burial in Bement Cemetery (Lot 143) on 24 Aug.

As a young woman, Mollie had the beauty of the typical Gibson girl. She was tall for a woman of that era, nearly 5'6", fair complected and blue eyed with a heart-shaped mouth in an oval face and masses of blond hair which she piled in swirls and puffs on top of her head. She retained a sweet faced beauty even into her elder years and was always slender. Many are the memories of the huge dinners she cooked for thrashers in her large farm kitchen - the table groaning under platters of fried chicken, home grown sliced tomatoes, dishes heaped with mashed potatoes and green beans from the garden, bowls of gravy, side dishes of home canned pickles, beets, jellies, preserves and crab apples, trays of biscuits accompanied by sweet cream butter, and fruit pies of various sorts, all washed down with quantities of coffee, iced tea or lemonade.

She was as good a seamstress as her mother had been before her. Pillowcases made of plain flour sacking were not used until they had been "fancied up" with delicately crocheted edging or daintily embroidered flowers. She pieced quilts as a matter of course, her favorite pattern being the Double Wedding Ring design. Even kitchen towels were given edgings of crochet. Her kitchen cabinet always contained peppermint candies and sugar cookies for young visitors and children were allowed to play dress-up with the old-fashioned clothes found in several trunks upstairs. She read her Bible faithfully every night by the light of a kerosene lamp, and kept her front parlor always ready for guests.

As a widow, she was not afraid to live alone. She became deaf in one ear and was fond of saying that if she heard any strange noises outside at night, she simply turned her good ear into the pillow and ignored them. But she was lonely. No one could have missed a husband more than she did after his death. In her Bible was a piece of paper written in her handwriting which said: "Senior years are sometimes lonely years and sometimes they are sad years; we find ourselves in the stillness of autumn time; sometimes we are hurt that those hurrying past do not notice that we are leaves about to fall. I believe in Prayer. We are Human and sometimes shed tears of loneliness." Finally, she could live alone no longer and moved to the Bement Resthaven Nursing Home where she died on 3 Jul 1963 at 2 p.m. She was buried on 5 Jul beside her husband in Bement Cemetery, Piatt Co., IL.

369. AMANDA ELLEN (MANDA) MITCHELL, daughter of Orlando Allen and Margaret Ellen (Mesnard) Mitchell, was born 30 Aug 1880 in Jackson Twp., Effingham Co., IL. She married on 24 Aug 1899 to William Rollie ("Will") Jones, born on 26 Nov 1873 near Greenville in Bond Co., IL, son of Henry Clay and Sarah Ann (Colgrove) Jones.

Despite his ill health, Manda's father was a cheerful man who loved music and singing and enjoyed teaching his children new hymns. In later years, the entire family would gather to sing around the pump organ which Manda's sister, Annie, played while Manda and her sister, Nettie, accompanied on the mandolin. On the inside cover of her father's hymn book ("The Sabbath School Harp," 1854), she wrote her name twice, once while living in Watson, and in a more mature hand while living in Dexter, IL. The last inscription is in colored pencil, each word done in a different hue. Under her first name, Manda drew a bouquet of flowers in red and yellow.

Like all girls of that era, Manda and her sisters were well versed in the arts of housekeeping. Her considerable artistic talent, however, was a gift. Large charcoal portraits that she sketched of her mother, her sister, Nettie Jane, and of herself are detailed, accurate and lifelike. It seems a shameful waste that the opportunity to receive professional training to develop her natural abilities was not available to her. Had she been born several generations later, her story might have had a different ending.

Manda was just 6 days short of her 19th birthday and Will was 26 years old when they married. In their wedding picture, a bust portrait, Manda was simply dressed in a white blouse with a high, round collar, bare of jewelry, lace or other adornment. The front edge of her jacket was sculptured and trimmed in braid of a matching color, the jacket sleeves only slightly puffed. She had luxuriant dark hair, softly full on the sides and drawn back from her face to cover the tops of her ears. Her mouth, slightly petulant in expression, had a small, full underlip, the thinner upper lip curving down at the corners. Like her mother, she was a handsome young woman. Will had the look of an outdoor man. His large oval eyes under thick, dark brows topped a short, sturdy nose and sharply delineated lips that matched his strong, square-jawed face. His hair was combed over from a side part, slightly waved in front. He wore a dark, vested suit, white shirt with a wide starched collar, and a diamond and star patterned four-in-hand tie, the only article of clothing in the picture that was not perfectly plain.

After marriage, Manda and Will moved to a farm in Shelby Co., IL near Windsor. By 1905, they were the parents of two children. Between January and July of that year, Manda wrote 5 letters to her sister, Mollie Taylor. In her first letter which she wrote while waiting for the "clothes to boil," she remarked on the cold weather, the cost for coal since "this is the first winter we haven't had wood to burn," and their new heating stove which they had bought for $19.00. She was pleased with her new sewing machine they had bought the fall before at Gays for $28.00, saying it "does fine work." She had to end this letter abruptly since her 3½ year old, Lela, "has taken charge of the washing and is doing it to suit herself."

In March, Manda wrote that she had been "having that stomach trouble again. I was sick yesterday evening and last night and my face looks like a green cucumber today ...you are ahead of me, I only have one hen setting I have lettuce radishes and onions up and peas planted. I am eating popcorn balls as I write. Lela pop(p)ed the corn ...she says she is a great big girl and she is. I wish you could see the kids, you wouldn't believe how fast they grow. I will close as we are scarce of paper. I have got 4 turkey eggs and would have some more if I could find the nest." The following day, she wrote again "as Ma is writing." She had "churned and ironed and done a little of every thing this morning and I am tired...My garden is looking nice...I have a good deal of garden put out...Will has 22 acres of corn ground plowed."

On the date of her May 11th letter, Manda was 1 to 2 months pregnant. She wrote that "we have washed today and I am awfull tired. I have been feeling pretty blue for the last few days my garden has been all under water untill this morning...We intended to come down there next Sat. and go to church at Little Prairie Sunday but the roads will be too bad." She reports she has over 70 baby chicks, 15 turkeys, and 7 more hens setting, then closes to go bring in her laundry as "it is so windy and looks like it might rain."

The proposed trip to Effingham Co. apparently took place as soon as the weather cleared, but Manda did not write again until July, complaining that the only time she had gotten to write was when she was too tired to do so. She had been working hard, again doing the washing, and commenting that the "weeds are about to take my garden. They got the start of me while I was down there." She had just gotten a letter from her mother who was now helping out Manda's ailing sister, Nettie, and she mentioned briefly that her brother and sister-in-law, Allen and Gusta, had been there on Monday and spent the night.

On 2 Dec 1905, Manda gave birth to twins, a boy and a girl. Eight days later, she was dead, probably a victim of postnatal hemorrhaging. Miraculously, the twins survived. Again, Manda's mother, Margaret Ellen, came to help care for her 4 motherless grandchildren until Will remarried on 23 Oct 1907 to Laura Helpingstine. (The twins were not given second names at birth, choosing their own when they were old enough to do so. Lucian took Henry after his Grandfather Jones, and Lucile picked Amanda for the mother she never knew.)

Manda died 10 Dec 1905 in Shelby Co., IL near Windsor and was buried there in the Ash Grove Christian Church Cemetery. Will died there on 4 Mar 1946 and is buried in the same cemetery. Children of William Rollie and Amanda Ellen (Mitchell) JONES, all born in Shelby Co., IL, were:

448. **Lela Blanche** b 10 June 1901   *

449. **Ira William** b 29 Mar 1903   *

450. **Lucian Henry** (twin) b 2 Dec 1905   *

451. **Amanda Lucile** (twin) b 2 Dec 1905 lvg 1987 m 28 Nov 1928 Mason Dewey Wade b 7 Feb 1898 Franklin Co., OH d Dec 1984; no children.

370. **ENSIGN FRANKLIN MITCHELL,** son of Orlando Allen and Margaret Ellen (Mesnard) Mitchell, was born 18 Oct 1882 in Jackson Twp., Effingham Co., IL. He married there at Mason to Essie Elsie Robertson, born 29 Jul 1886 in Mason, Effingham Co., IL, daughter of John David and Emma (Ballard) Robertson. (Perhaps the most ancient of all Scottish surnames, Robertsons were firmly established there before the coming of William the Conqueror in the 11th century. The name was derived from two Saxon words, "Rod" and "Bert," meaning famous in Council.)

A portrait of Frank (as he was called), taken when he was a young man, shows him with a most serious expression, giving no hint of his gregarious nature. He had the long nose inherited from both his parents, looked most like his mother in the shape of his lower face, chin and mouth, but more resembled his father in the eyes and forehead. He wore the traditional 3-piece suit with white shirt and starched collar, and sported a handsome striped cravat. He can not be called other than a good looking young man. One can only suppose, lacking photographic evidence, that Essie was the same "cute as a button" young woman that she was when she and Frank posed for their 60th wedding anniversary picture in 1964. She had a genuinely happy face that clearly revealed her congenial spirit.

In 1961, Frank wrote an autobiography to include in Clara L. Hopp's genealogy ("Nettie Jane [Mitchell] Redman - Her Ancestors and Descendants"). He states: "My life has been somewhat a wandering one: Graduate of a Teacher's college in Illinois, a Bachelor of Arts degree from the University in New Orleans, Master of Arts degree from the University of Alabama, Tuscaloosa, Alabama. My teaching career began in a one room school in Illinois, then principal of a school in Edgewood, Illinois for 3 years, principal at Ashmore, Illinois for 4 years, and then principal at Brighton, Illinois for 4 years."

Frank then went to Grand Bay, AL where he was a school principal for 6 years. He had visited Grand Bay in May of 1911 where he wrote to his mother: "I am a good ways from home and alone so I will write you and you will know I am alive...I was bathing in the Gulf day before yesterday. I think this is good country. I am going to build a little house here...I would like so much to have you all down here and see some of the things I see, the flowers are so pretty. I will be here for about 10 days yet, then I will go back to Ashmore. I don't kno(w) yet whither we will move down here this year or not, but we want to get away from the winters on account of the babies have croup so bad and there catarrh is unknown, and there is no lung trouble...Hundreds of people from north are coming in here and building beautiful homes, this will be a lovely country...E. F. Mitchell."

From Grand Bay, Frank and Essie went to Mississippi "...where I have been since 1922. I was principal of Macon for 4 years and Superintendent of Schools at Carthage for 4 years. After this I was at Gallman for 4 years, then Superintendent of Schools at Tylertown for 4 years. (Here is where I was badly injured in a car wreck and had to give up my work there.)...I became Superintendent of

Schools at Chubuta where I stayed for 7 years...then accepted a position as Director of the Mississippi School
of Refrigeration (A.G.I. School) for 4 years."
     At the end of this time, Frank retired. This compiler
remembers well a visit to the Mitchell home at 717 Winter
St. in Jackson, MS in 1950, the visit made in company with
Frank's sister, Mollie Taylor, and his niece, Mabel (Redman) Jordan. We were greeted with warmth and affection
and soundly hugged and kissed by Uncle Frank. Aunt Essie
fixed a sumptious meal, including tender yellow summer
squash, fresh picked from her garden, and sauteed with
bacon and onions. We came away with her recipe for Fool-
ish Pie, so-called because the meringue is on the bottom,
rather than the top of the pie. I have made it often since
and it bears sharing. "Make a pie shell and bake it until
it has started to brown, about 5 minutes. Mix together 1/2
cup sugar, 1 teasp. white vinegar, and 2 egg whites. Beat
until a meringue has formed. Put it in the pie shell and
bake until browned, about 15 minutes. Remove and cool.
Put fruit, such as diced sugared strawberries, on top,
cover with whipped cream, and serve. Oven temp. 350°."
     Given the poetic bent of the Mitchell family, it is
not surprising that Frank also wrote poetry, but apparently only as an amusement. Noted on the back of one of
his poems, written in 1908, is his assessment of his abilities: "This was written, when as a young man I thought I
could write poetry." Actually, the poem, entitled "A
Little Child to a Star," is lighthearted and pleasant.
     Frank died in Nov 1970 at Jackson, MS; Essie died 17
Oct 1978 in the Rankin General Hospital at Brandon, MS.
Her obituary states that she was preceded in death by her
husband, two sons, parents, brother, Victor Robertson;
sisters, Minnie Koss and Lillian Ruffner, and several
nieces and nephews in Illinois. Both she and Frank are
buried in Lakewood Cemetery, Jackson, MS. Children of
Ensign Franklin and Essie Elsie (Robertson) Mitchell,
first 5 born in IL, last 2 in AL, were:
     452. Eugene Franklin b 19 May 1905   *
     453. Harry Victor b 11 Sep 1907   *
     454. Raymond Allen b 8 Jan 1910 d same day.
     455. Daphna Irene b 24 May 1912   *
     456. Joe Calvin b 3 Jul 1914   *
     457. Howard Leo b 1 Feb 1921   *
     458. Russell Glen b 4 Nov 1922   *

374. **GEORGIA (KITTY) MITCHELL,** daughter of David Oscar and Carrie Belle (Simonton) Mitchell, was born 18 Feb 1887 in Jackson Twp., Effingham Co., IL. She married at Watson, Effingham Co., IL on 4 Nov 1906 Presley Louis Neville, born 19 Apr 1882 at Watson, IL, son of George W. and Harriet (Martin) Neville. Presley L. died 19 May 1951 at Watson, IL, and Kitty died 4 June 1968 at Elgin, IL. Both are buried in Altamont, IL. Children of Presley Louis and Georgia "Kitty" (Mitchell) NEVILLE, all born at Watson, Effingham Co., IL, were:

    459. **Oren Presley** b 10 Sep 1907   *
    460. **Aubrey Mitchell** b 27 June 1909 m 15 Dec 1931 to Helen Schlosser.
    461. **Geneva Ruth** b 2 Jul 1912   *
    462. **Harriett Loraine** b 4 Apr 1916   *

375. **WINNIE MAUDE MITCHELL,** daughter of David Oscar and Carrie Belle (Simonton) Mitchell, was born 6 Oct 1893 in Effingham Co., IL. She married Raymond Elmer Smith, born in Effingham Co., IL, son of Elmer & Laura (Alvis) Smith. (Raymond E. was still living in 1980.)

At age 6 or 7 years, Winnie had her photo taken, a curley haired, carrot topped, impish faced little girl wearing a ruffle trimmed cotton dress, long black stockings, and high topped shoes. She is still living today (1987); although her reddish curls have long since turned grey, she has retained her puckish personality. She spends her winters with her daughter, Verda, in Southern California. When I last visited her several years ago, her eyesight was failing badly but her mind was as keen as a new razor blade. She was quick to correct my mispronunciation of the family given name Ensign (En-sign, with a long 'i') as well as the middle name of a Mitchell relative which had been listed incorrectly on a death certificate. Her joy in talking "family" was evident - she apparently enjoyed her childhood - but she remains a person who very definitely lives in and enjoys the present.

Children of Raymond Elmer and Winnie Maude (Mitchell) SMITH, all born in Effingham Co., IL, were:

    463. **Vera Evelyn** b 16 Sep 1913   *
    464. **Nadine Frances** b 16 Nov 1916   *
    465. **Verda Eileen** b 29 Sep 1918   *
    466. **Robert Alden** b 2 Oct 1921   *
    467. **Betty Louise** b 30 Nov 1923

376. **DAVID RALPH MITCHELL,** son of David Oscar and Carrie Belle (Simonton) Mitchell, was born 24 Apr 1899 in Effingham Co., IL. He married there on 6 Jul 1919 to Marguerite Robertson, born 13 Feb 1900 in Jackson Twp., Effingham Co., IL, daughter of Alexander and Martha Jane (Davis) Robertson. (Per a descendant, Alexander Robertson was the son of William Robertson and Margaret Harrell; Martha Jane Davis was the daughter of Major Davis and Margaret E. Melender.)

As well as farming, Ralph (who preferred using his middle name) served for many years as a Supervisor in Watson Twp., Effingham Co. and was a member of the Watson Masonic Lodge. In 1969, Ralph and Marguerite celebrated their golden wedding anniversary with a dinner given in their honor by their children at the Ramada Inn in Effingham. A tall slender man with silver hair, Ralph very much resembled several of his Mitchell uncles in the portrait taken for that occasion. Marguerite, a pleasant looking woman whose hair was still dark, was diminutive in comparison to her husband.

Marguerite died 27 May 1979 at Pleasant Acres Nursing Home in Altamont, IL. Ralph died 9 Jan 1980 at St. Anthony Memorial Hospital in Effingham, IL. Both are buried there in Arborcrest Memorial Park. Children of David Ralph and Marguerite (Robertson) Mitchell, all born in Effingham Co., IL, were:

468. **Beulah** b 3 Mar 1921 m Henry Ginder.
469. **Marilyn** b 7 Feb 1923   *
470. **Freda Bernell** b 26 Jul 1925   *
471. **Verneva** b 16 Apr 1927   *
472. **Helen Mayonne** b 5 Jul 1929   *
473. **Myron Calvin** b 22 Nov 1931   *
474. **Clayton Ralph** b 23 Apr 1934   *
475. **Shirley** b 12 May 1936 m John Lynn Snyder; div.
476. **Marthagene** b 1 Feb 1939   *

379. **DANIEL PALMER MITCHELL,** son of Claudius Elias and Rhue Ethel (Donaldson) Mitchell, was born 23 Nov 1888 in Jackson Twp., Effingham Co., IL. He married Lillace Montgomery. In 1920 at a Mitchell family reunion held in Effingham, IL, Daniel P. is listed as attending, his residence at that time being Chicago, IL. Daniel P. was a teacher. At the death of his brother, Claudius E., Jr., in 1978, Daniel P. was not listed as one of his brother's

surviving kin. Only known child of Daniel Palmer and Lillace (Montgomery) Mitchell was:
477. **Robert** b 1921; last known lvg in CA.

381. **CLAUDIUS ELIAS (CLAUDE) MITCHELL (JR.),** son of
Claudius Elias and Rhue Ethel (Donaldson) Mitchell, was
born 30 Mar 1895 in Jackson Twp., Effingham Co., IL. He
married there on 21 Aug 1917 Helen A. Claar, daughter of
Walker B. and Clara (Lecrone) Claar.

Claude was a veteran of World War I; a 1924 graduate
of the University of Illinois; manager of Business Men's
Assurance in Springfield, IL; and a 50-year member of the
Masonic Lodge. He died 24 Nov 1978 at St. Anthony Memorial
Hospital in Effingham, IL and was buried there on 27 Nov
in Oakridge Cemetery. Helen A. was living in Effingham,
IL in 1980 but was deceased before 1986. Only child of
Claudius Elias and Helen A. (Claar) Mitchell, Jr., born
in Effingham Co., IL, was:
478. **Ruth C.** b 1921 d unmar 5 May 1986 Effingham Co., IL.

387. **FREDERICK J. (FRED) MITCHELL,** son of John Hannah and
Lucinda (Thompson) Mitchell, was born about 1875 in Ross
Twp., Edgar Co., IL. At his marriage there on 28 Apr 1897
to Dora Carson, he calls himself a merchant. His wife,
Dora, was born about 1875 in Henry, IL, daughter of Joel
and Elmira (Greenlee) Carson, her residence given as Mor-
timer, IL. Witnesses to the marriage were Fred's brother
and sister, Charles and Rosa Mitchell. Fred was still
living in 1926 when he was named administrator in Edgar
Co., IL of his father's estate. Children of Frederick J.
and Dora (Carson) Mitchell, if any, are unknown.

388. **ROSA MARY MITCHELL,** daughter of John Hannah and Lu-
cinda (Thompson) Mitchell, was born May 1879 (census) in
Ross Twp., Edgar Co., IL. She married at Chrisman, Edgar
Co., IL on 20 Sep 1905 to Hiram Shepherd, born in 1882 in
Dana, IN, son of J. P. and Ellen (Warren) Shepherd. (This
was Hiram's second marriage.) Rosa Mary died in 1944 and
Hiram died 17 Nov 1969 in Edgar Co., IL; both are buried in
Prairie Twp. Chapel Cemetery near Scotland, IL.

Rosa Mary's children (SHEPHERD) were: **(i)** Elizabeth
m _____ Vickory; bur in FL; **(ii)** Margaret m1) Arthur Wheat;
m2) Roy E. Payton; ch from 1st mar, Charles Edward Wheat,
d 1 Apr 1925, bur in Prairie Twp. Chapel Cemetery.

389. NORA B. MITCHELL, daughter of John Hannah and Lucinda (Thompson) Mitchell, was born Feb 1884 (census) in Ross Twp., Edgar Co., IL. She had a twin brother. She married 28 May 1911 at Chrisman, Edgar Co., IL to Owen Ingram, born in Edgar Co., IL about 1882, son of Sylvester and Caroline (Wallace) Ingram. Nora B. was probably deceased before 1926 as she is not mentioned as a surviving heir in her father's estate administration papers of that date. Children of Owen and Nora B. (Mitchell) Ingram, if any, are unknown.

390. ORA C. MITCHELL, son of John Hannah and Lucinda (Thompson) Mitchell, was born Feb 1884 (census) in Ross Twp., Edgar Co., IL. He was a twin to Nora B. above. He married on 26 Aug 1903 in Vermilion Co., IL to Della M. Ballard. He was named as one of the surviving heirs at the administration of his father's estate in Edgar Co., IL in 1926. Children of Ora C. and Della M. (Ballard) Mitchell, if any, are unknown.

393. CLAUDE GLEN MITCHELL, son of Chandler and Marica (Hartley) Mitchell, was born 3 Jul 1879 in Ross Twp., Edgar Co., IL. He was married first to Laura Taylor. They were divorced (no children). His second wife was Olive E. Blanchard whom he married on 10 Sep 1902 at Danville, IL. Olive E. was born 7 Feb 1881 in Edgar Co., IL, daughter of Bruce B. and Mary Elizabeth (Holler) Blanchard.

Claude Glen had his portrait taken in Danville, IL, possibly at the time of his second marriage. His hair, parted in the middle, was slicked down on top but tightly curled on the sides. He wore a full mustache. He was square faced with a tendancy toward an extra chin. His tie was tucked under his left jacket lapel, presumeably to show the tassel hanging on a cord around his neck, the significance of which is unknown.

In 1978, Anna Mitchell, wife of Claude G.'s grandson, Chandler E., wrote that Claude Glen was "...quite a character and had spent quite a lot of money for his folks. When they didn't hand over any more, he took out a bottle of carbolic acid and poured it in a tin cup (hanging) on the well, pumped it full of water and drank it. He then walked to the cornfield and died. She (his wife) left the children with his parents since they were more able to provide for them and returned to Ohio. But she came to visit them on occasion and her cousin wrote to us and said she loved her boys and she didn't forget them..."

Claude Glen's death certificate, dated 16 Jul 1906, states that he died in Ross Twp., Edgar Co., IL, age 27 years 13 days, at 7 p.m., of self-administered carbonic acid, 1/4 hour. He was buried in Hoult Cemetery, Edgar Co., IL near Chrisman. Olive E. eventually remarried to Stewart Dailey and had another son, Stewart, Jr. Her date and place of death are not known. Children of Claude Glen and Olive E. (Blanchard) Mitchell, born in Ross Twp., Edgar Co., IL, were:

479. **Chandler Orville** b 16 Jun 1903   ✱

480. **Dugan Bruce** b 28 Oct 1904 dsp 27 May 1971 m 26 Apr 1926 Blanche Bratton b 25 Mar 1904 Edgar Co., IL, d/o Thomas & Etta Alice (Lewis) Bratton; she d 19 Nov 1977 Edgar Co., IL.

395. **HELEN HARRIET MITCHELL,** daughter of Herman Calvin and Jessie Maude (Tucker) Mitchell, was born 31 Aug 1897 at the family home in Horace, Edgar Co., IL. She married there on 9 Sep 1915 to Walter Terrence Kile, born 12 Apr 1892 in Paris, Edgar Co., IL, son of Robert H. and Lula (Rogers) Kile. They were divorced in 1928 at Detroit, MI. Walter died 7 Jan 1950 at the Veterans Hospital in Ann Arbor, MI and Helen H. died 24 Oct 1971 at the Community Hospital in Paris, Edgar Co., IL. Only child of Walter Terrance and Helen Harriet (Mitchell) KILE was:

481. **Carolyn Mitchell** b 5 May 1916   ✱

401. **JULIET MITCHELL,** daughter of Claudius Newton and Frances Ellen (Hunter) Mitchell, was born 27 May 1890 in Champaign Co., OH. She had a twin brother, Robert. Juliet married Edward W. Jewell. They were later divorced.

Juliet's only child (JEWELL) was: **(i)** Marian b 21 Jul 1917 m Harold W. Shirey; div in 1970; 1 dau Rebecca b 21 Aug 1949.

403. **FLORENCE ELIZABETH MITCHELL,** daughter of Charles Lincoln and Lizzie Belle (Davidson) Mitchell, was born 28 Jan 1894 on the family farm near Mechanicsburg, Champaign Co., OH. She married at London, Madison Co., OH on 16 Aug 1916 to (Dr.) Cloyd Franklin Wharton. Florence E. died 17 Sep 1930 at Akron, Summit Co., OH and is buried in Ashland, Ashland Co., OH. A niece of Florence E.'s believes

Cloyd F. may have been born in Ashland, OH where he is also buried. She had no data on his date of birth or death
or his parent's names.
   Children of (Dr.) Cloyd Franklin and Florence Elizabeth (Mitchell) WHARTON, born in Akron, OH, were:
   482. **Elizabeth Jane** b 2 Jul 1918 m 19 Jan 1938 in Angola,
      IN Richard Mitten; div; no children.
   483. **Marjorie** b 20 Aug 1921   *
   484. **Cloyd Franklin (Jr.)** b 21 Dec 1924 d 1979.

404. **HELEN JEAN MITCHELL,** daughter of Charles Lincoln and
Lizzie Belle (Davidson) Mitchell, was born 19 Mar 1896 on
the family farm (in the same room as her father was born)
near Mechanicsburg, Champaign Co., OH. This house has
since burned down. She married 3 Oct 1917 at London, Madison Co., OH to Raymond Russell McVicker, born 18 Apr 1883
near Brownsville, Union Co., IN, son of Augustus and Ella
(Cross) McVicker. Raymond R. died 6 May 1970 at Indianapolis, Marion Co., IN; Helen J. died 13 Jan 1967 at
Franklin, Johnson Co., IN. Both are buried in Crown Hill
Cemetery, Indianapolis, IN.
   Only child of Raymond Russell and Helen Jean (Mitchell) McVICKER, was:
   485. **Jean Mitchell** b 20 May 1920   *

405. **JANE TAGGART MITCHELL,** daughter of Charles Lincoln
and Lizzie Belle (Davidson) Mitchell, was born 15 Jul
1899 on the family farm near Mechanicsburg, Champaign
Co., OH. She married 19 May 1924 at London, Madison Co.,
OH to Wilfred Marsh, born 14 Mar 1896 in Clark Co., OH, son
of Walter and Lizzie (Yeazel) Marsh. Wilfred died 17 Feb
1962 at Fort Wayne, Allen Co., IN; Jane T. died 8 Jul 1977
at London, Madison Co., OH. Both are buried at London, OH
in Maple Grove Cemetery.
   Only child of Wilfred and Jane Taggart (Mitchell)
MARSH was:
   486. **Mary Ellen** b 31 Mar 1929   *

406. **LEROY BEACH,** son of Timothy Downing and Talitha
(Bales) Beach, was born 20 Apr 1878 at Tradersville, Madison Co., OH and died 25 Feb 1953. He married 24 Oct 1900
to Nellie B. Funk.
   Children of Leroy and Nellie B. (Funk) BEACH were:
(i) William Eugene b & d 1903; **(ii)** Herbert Joel b 28 Feb

1905 d 6 Apr 1971 m 6 June 1936 Hildreth Tullis; ch Carolyn Kay b 1939; David Lee b 1940; Roger Gene b 1942; Martha Deanna b 1945.

407. **ALTA BEACH,** daughter of Timothy Downing and Talitha (Bales) Beach, was born 29 Dec 1879 at Catawba, OH, died 6 Dec 1962; she married 15 Feb 1899 Edward Fitzgiven, born in 1868 OH, died 16 Sep 1937, son of John and Mary (Powell) Fitzgiven (see #399 Carrie Bales whose 1st husband, John Fitzgiven, was said to be brother of Edward). Both are buried in Maple Grove Cemetery, Mechanicsburg, OH.

Children of Edward and Alta (Beach) FITZGIVEN were: **(i)** Grace b 8 Mar 1900 m 1927 William Carbill; **(ii)** Richard b 10 Sep 1905 d 1974 m 1935 Dorothy Steckney.

408. **ADA GERTRUDE BEACH,** daughter of Timothy Downing and Talitha (Bales) Beach, was born 9 Apr 1886 at Catawba, Clark Co., OH, died 8 Jan 1973. She married 5 May 1908 to Jesse Ellsworth Chance, born 12 Apr 1884, son of Dr. Joseph W. and Alpharetta (Snyder) Chance. Only child of Jesse and Ada Gertrude (Beach) CHANCE was: **(i)** Margaret Beach b 1912 d 1974 unmarried.

409. **DOWNING BEACH,** son of Timothy Downing and Talitha (Bales) Beach, was born 7 Oct 1888 at Catawba, Clark Co., OH and died 12 Jan 1944 in Deer Creek Twp., Madison Co., OH. He married 27 Sep 1916 in Peabody, Marion Co., KS to Hazel Elizabeth Hamilton, born at Cadiz, Harrison Co., OH, daughter of Samuel Rankin and Georgeanna (Dickerson) Hamilton. She died 16 June 1968 in the hospital at Columbus, OH. Both Downing and Hazel E. are buried in Oak Hill Cemetery, Madison Co., OH.

Children of Downing and Hazel (Hamilton) BEACH were: **(i)** Rebecca Jane b 8 Mar 1928 Columbus, OH m 12 June 1953 Wilbur Leslie France; no children; **(ii)** Elizabeth Ann b 24 June 1933 nr London, OH m there 23 Feb 1952 to Robert Dwight Sommers b 2 Oct 1922 Bourneville, Ross Co., OH, s/o Nelson Dwight & Laura Catherine (Hill) Sommers; ch Robert Downing Sommers b 6 Aug 1955 Columbus, OH m 7 Aug 1977 Roxann Lorraine Gill b 17 Feb 1955 Clarksburg, WVA, d/o James Edward & Dorothy Lorraine (Pitser) Gill; and Jane Ann Sommers b 25 Mar 1958 Columbus, OH m 11 Aug 1979 Stephen Edward Brock b 15 Mar 1951 Columbus, OH, s/o Elden James & Helen (Conway) Brock.

410. **DARWIN BEACH,** son of Timothy Downing and Talitha (Bales) Beach, was born 3 Jan 1894 at Catawba, Clark Co., OH and died 22 Aug 1936. He married 8 June 1916 Nellie Edna Lucas, born 1894, died 1952; both are buried in Oak Hill Cemetery, Madison Co., OH. Children of Darwin and Nellie Edna (Lucas) BEACH were: **(i)** Forrest Lucas b 13 Jul 1917; supposed to have changed his name to Frederick Barck, married, adopted a son & lvg in Portland, ME; **(ii)** John Downing b 25 Dec 1919 d 9 Sep 1944 (WW-II) unmar.

414. **CARLTON MITCHELL CREAMER,** son of Royalton Mitchell and Leila Lenore (Hendrickson) Creamer, was born on the family farm 19 Apr 1904 in Somerford Twp., Madison Co., OH. He married 30 Sep 1926 at Urbana, Champaign Co., OH Mary Elizabeth "Betty" Smith, born 21 Aug 1908 at Marysville, Union Co., OH, daughter of James O. and Dollie (Sarver) Smith. Carlton M. lives in Mechanicsburg, OH.
   Only child of Carlton Mitchell and Mary Elizabeth (Smith) CREAMER was:
   487. Robert Carlton b 18 Jul 1928   *

NINTH GENERATION

423. ORA ALLEN MITCHELL, son of Allen Calvin and Margaret Jane (Moffett) Mitchell, was born 8 Aug 1897 in Macon Co., IL. Ora's mother died when he was a year old. He was then raised by his grandmother, Margaret E. (Mesnard) Mitchell who was widowed, until his father remarried in 1900.

Ora was an exceptionally beautiful child, very blond with the face of a cherub. An informal photograph, taken before Ora's first birthday, shows his father holding him on the seat of a bicycle. A group of people are standing in the background against the wall of a large 2-story frame house, among whom were Ora's Mitchell grandmother and his uncle, Frank Mitchell. In another informal pose taken when Ora was about 2 years old, he is sitting on his grandmother Mitchell's lap. It is clear from the expression on her face that she adored this grandchild.

Ora was married three times. His first wife was Alice Steel whom he married 1 Jan 1923. He second wife was May ____. He married third 29 Jul 1939 in Washington D.C. to Lucy Jane Jolly, born 23 Sep 1897 in Breckenridge Co., KY. He retired in 1961 from the Fruit Growers Express Co. in Washington D.C. where he was head clerk in their general office, and moved to Silver Spring, MD. Ora died childless on 25 Jan 1979.

424. OSCAR CALVIN MITCHELL, son of Allen Calvin and Augusta Barbara (Hartman) Mitchell, was born 10 Aug 1901 in Jackson Twp., Effingham Co., IL, but grew up in Shelby Co., Il where his parents had moved by 1906. He died on 25 Sep 1974. Oscar C. married first 31 Jul 1925 to Audrey Trippe. He married second 6 May 1933 Melva Grimm, and third on 26 Jan 1956 to Helene Megarry (no children from these last two marriages).

Only child of Oscar Calvin and Audrey (Trippe) Mitchell was:

    488. Evelyn L. b 23 Feb 1927   *

425. **EDGAR SAMUEL MITCHELL,** son of Allen Calvin and Augusta Barbara (Hartman) Mitchell, was born 7 Feb 1903 near Gays, Moultrie Co., IL but grew up on his father's farm in adjoining Shelby Co., IL where the family moved by 1906. He was married first 6 May 1923 to Zola Hopper, and second on 26 Oct 1963 at Greenville, SC to Ruth A. (Young) Gilliland. There were no children by either marriage.

Edgar S. died 7 Feb 1985 at Sarah Bush Lincoln Health Center in Mattoon, IL. His obituary in a CMEC trade publication called him "...a gentleman of outstanding character and ability. First elected to the Coles-Moultrie Electric Cooperative Board of Directors in 1954, he served for the next 29½ years, holding the office of vice-president from 1973 until his retirement in October 1983. Mr. Mitchell was a true pioneer in rural electrification, operating a dairy and grain farm for many years near Gays. He was one of the first persons in the CMEC service area to employ electric ceiling cable heat in his home, when he built a new house in 1956. He was also one of the first persons (if not the first) to install on his farm a low-temperature grain drying system using electricity as the heat source...Mr. Mitchell was a retired farmer of 65 years, a member of the First Baptist Church in Mattoon and a member of Miles Hart Lodge 595 AF & AM. In the final analysis of the service and contribution Edgar Mitchell gave to the growth and stability of Coles-Moultrie Electric Cooperative over the years, there are...no words which can adequately express the value of his efforts and assistance to the benefit of the cooperative."

Edgar S. Mitchell was buried 10 Feb 1985 in Branchside Cemetery, Gays, IL. His widow, Ruth, is living (1987).

426. **BURL KENNETH MITCHELL,** son of Allen Calvin and Augusta Barbara (Hartman) Mitchell, was born 26 Aug 1906 in Shelby Co., IL (near Gays). He married 30 June 1936 to Gertrude Ruth Bjurstrom, born 22 Feb 1906 at Gays, IL, daughter of Charles Theodore and Selma S. (Peterson) Bjurstrom. She died 31 Mar 1974 at Arlington, VA and Burl Kenneth died there on 14 Jan 1986.

Children of Burl Kenneth and Gertrude Ruth (Bjurstrom) Mitchell were:
489. Patricia Joyce b 17 Mar 1937   *
490. Judith A. b 26 Aug 1940   *
491. Linda Diane b 24 Nov 1945   *

427. STELLA L. MITCHELL, daughter of Allen Calvin and Augusta Barbara (Hartman) Mitchell, was born 12 June 1908 in Shelby Co., IL. Children by Stella's first marriage to Walter HANSON were: **(i)** Betty Lucile dy; **(ii)** Thelma Jeanne m _____ Bolinger; 3 daus, Vicki, Bobye, Terri.

Child by Stella's 2nd marriage to _____ BALSLEY was: **(iii)** Sandra m _____ Ramsey; ch Paul Lee & Steven Douglas.

428. VELMA AUGUSTA MITCHELL, daughter of Allen Calvin and Augusta Barbara (Hartman) Mitchell, was born 11 June 1914 in Shelby Co., IL. She married 10 Jan 1934 to Russell William Hooker at Charleston, Coles Co., IL. "Russ" was born 9 Aug 1912 in Jasper Co., IL, son of David Franklin and Iva Bell (Stainbrook) Hooker. Velma A. died 26 Nov 1966 at Mattoon, Coles Co., IL and was buried on 29 Nov in Branchside Cemetery, Gays, IL. Russell W. (lvg 1987) married second Lillian Howes.

Children of Russell William and Velma Augusta (Mitchell) HOOKER were:

- **492. Jerry Allen** b 11 Sep 1934   *
- **493. Barbara Nancy** b 5 Dec 1936   *
- **494. Shirley Jean** b 12 Feb 1938   *
- **495. James William** b 22 Mar 1944 d same day.
- **496. Ronald David** b 12 Nov 1945   *

429. VERNON HARTMAN MITCHELL, son of Allen Calvin and Augusta Barbara (Hartman) Mitchell, was born 15 Jan 1919 in Shelby Co., IL. He married 9 Dec 1941 at Coeur D'Alene, ID to Virginia Josephine Johnson, born 22 June 1924 at Spokane, WA, daughter of Nelmer Daniel and Arva Victoria (Hubbard) Johnson. Nelmer D. was of Swedish ancestry and Arva V. from a Norwegian-Russian background.

Vernon H. died 8 Jan 1978 at Sarah Bush Lincoln Health Care Center in Mattoon, IL and was buried in Branchside Cemetery, Gays, IL. (Virginia J. married second _____ Kendrick.) Children of Vernon Hartman and Virginia Josephine (Johnson) Mitchell, 1st 3 born in Coles Co., IL, 4th born at Spokane, WA, were:

- **497. Helen Louise** b 17 Feb 1947 m 23 Aug 1972 at Denver, CO to Charles Emett Shaw b 15 Dec 1935 Trenton, TN s/o Alex & Ama Marie (Mullins) Shaw; no children.
- **498. David Allen** b 8 Feb 1949 m Dorothy Faye Woodfall.
- **499. Arlan Charles** b 26 Sep 1950   *
- **500. Michael Lee** b 7 Aug 1952   *

432. **BESSIE REDMAN,** daughter of Cornelius and Anna Christina (Mitchell) Redman, was born 2 Aug 1894 in Effingham Co., IL. She married in Effingham Co. on 23 June 1915 to Walter Pendlay, born 10 Nov 1890 in Summit Twp., Effingham Co., IL, son of Robert Newton and Martha Jane (Adams) Pendlay. Walter was a farmer.

On 6 Mar 1916 Bessie wrote to her aunt, Mollie (Mitchell) Taylor, to reassure her that her mother, who had been very sick, "...is better now. I was up there four days last week that is how I got such a cold. The storms were pretty bad but I came back home every day. Papa's almost lost a cow last week. They have to sit up with her yet I guess or did yet Sunday. The cow has a young calf." At this time, Bessie was a bride of less than 9 months and several months pregnant with her first child, but she seems full of energy, happily planning to "...get dirt this evening to plant tomatoes, cabbage and pansys in." In a postscript written the following day, Bessie divulged that her sister, Ruth, "...is staying at home now. Walter said she is a dandy little worker. She does about all the cooking and can bake light bread now. I think that is fine." She noted that her mother was still feeling better and so was the ailing cow.

Bessie and Walter lost their first born child that following February during the terrible winter sickness that also took the life of Bessie's sister, Ruth.

Bessie died 2 May 1951 in the hospital at Springfield, IL. Walter died 8 Sep 1972 in Effingham Co., IL. Both are buried in Funkhouser Cemetery, Effingham Co., IL. Children of Walter and Bessie (Redman) PENDLAY, all born in Effingham Co., IL, were:

501. **Russell Lyle** b 10 Sep 1916 d Feb 1917.
502. **Ethel Maude** b 5 Jul 1920   *
503. **Lorna Lucille** b 9 May 1926   *

433. **ROSA PEARL REDMAN,** daughter of Cornelius and Anna Christina (Mitchell) Redman, was born 4 Feb 1898 in Effingham Co., IL. She married there 22 Apr 1917 to Alva N. Dowds, born 1 Dec 1895 in Effingham Co., son of W. N. Dowds. To announce the marriage, handwritten cards were sent which read "Mr. and Mrs. C. Redman announce the marriage of their daughter, Rosa, to Alva N. Dowds Sunday, April 22, 1917 - At home on a farm near Altamont after May 1." Rosa's mother sent swatches of material used to make

her wedding gown and trousseau to Rosa's aunt, Mollie (Mitchell) Taylor - delicate bits of white lace and silk, eyelet, pale blue netting, satin ribbon, fine cotton, and a darker blue silk crepe. Written on one piece of material was "Nainsook like gown, skirt & corset-cover."

Rosa P. died 1 Mar 1918 near Altamont, Efingham Co., IL, leaving a week-old son. After her death, Alva remarried. According to the obituary of his son, Edwin A., Alva and his second wife had 4 sons and 2 daughters and in 1978 were living in rural Effingham Co., IL.

Only child of Rosa Pearl (Redman) DOWDS was: (i) Edwin Alva b 21 Feb 1918 nr Altamont, IL d 22 Apr 1978 bur Sidney, IL m Delphine Campton; ch Dorsey lvg Philo, IL 1978; Wanda m ____ Page lvg New Philadelphia, OH 1978; Alberta m ____ Rogers lvg St. Joseph IL 1978.

435. DAVID FRANKLIN (FRANK) REDMAN, son of Cornelius and Anna Christina (Mitchell) Redman, was born 29 Jul 1900 in Effingham Co., IL. He married in Effingham Co. on 27 Jan 1924 to Charlotte Icle "Lottie" Poynter, born 1 Jul 1901 in Lucas Twp., Effingham Co., IL, daughter of Thomas Z. and Van Dana (Stroud) Poynter.

Frank was employed by the United States Postal Service. After retirement, he worked for the Majeska & Wilson Real Estate office in Downers Grove, IL. He was a member of the Downers Grove Masonic Lodge, having resided in that city for 30 years prior to his death on 21 Oct 1983 in Westmont, Du Page Co., IL. He was buried on 24 Oct in Chapel Hill Gardens (W) Cemetery, Elmhurst, IL, survived by his wife (living 1987), his children, a brother, Cecil, 7 grand and 6 great-grandchildren.

Children of David Franklin and Charlotte Icle (Poynter) REDMAN were:
- **504. Glenden David** b 4 Mar 1925   *
- **505. Gernon Eldin** b 25 Jul 1926   *
- **506. Rita Leila** b 27 Sep 1933   *

438. CLINTON CORNELIUS REDMAN, son of Cornelius and Anna Christina (Mitchell) Redman, was born 8 Jul 1907 near Altamont, Effingham Co., IL. He married first 16 Aug 1931 Hazel Bingaman. (They were divorced; no children.) He married second 9 Jan 1934 Maybelle Finnerty. Clinton was a veteran of W.W.-II, serving in the United States Navy with the rank of Storekeeper 3rd Class.

Clinton died 13 Sep 1946 in Chicago, IL. A newspaper item reads: "Smoking in bed resulted in the death yesterday of Clinton Redmond, 39, of 3121 W. Washington, who suffered third degree burns when he fell asleep with a cigaret in his mouth. Redmond, according to his landlady, was a manager of a restaurant at 737 W. Madison..." He is buried in Little Prairie Cemetery (Jackson Twp. Baptist Church) in Effingham Co., IL where his father who had died 2 months before him, and his mother who died a month after him are buried. (Clinton's youngest two children were later adopted.)

Children of Clinton Cornelius and Maybelle (Finnerty) REDMAN were: **(i)** Howard Leroy b 8 June 1934 Effingham Co., IL; **(ii)** Donald Paul b 20 Oct 1935 Effingham Co., IL; **(iii)** Sandra Ann b 5 Nov 1938 Chicago, IL; **(iv)** Norman Dean b 9 Dec 1940 Chicago, IL.

439. **CECIL HOWARD REDMAN,** son of Cornelius and Anna Christina (Mitchell) Redman, was born 28 June 1911 in Jackson Twp., Effingham Co., IL. He married 7 Jan 1939 in Winnetka, Cook Co., IL to Pauline Naomi Tucker, born 27 Oct 1911 in Effingham Co., IL, daughter of James Otis and Hattie May (Perring) Tucker.

Four days after his wedding, Cecil's mother wrote to his aunt, Mollie (Mitchell) Taylor: "Well now, Diza, here comes a surprise. Cecil and Pauline Tucker were married Sat. evening at the home of Rev. Hermanson, are keeping house at 4737 Malden St., Chicago, Ills., Apt. 104. So now we are truly alone - last child married. Cecil & Pauline have always known each other. She, you know, is Jim Tucker's oldest daughter - just about Cecil's age. We couldn't have been better pleased if we'd made the match ourselves...Pauline has been a member of the church here, faithful in every way, several years. She's been working in Chicago about 3 years. She is a good dress maker, does all kinds of fancy work, makes quilts & has knitted several dresses besides sweaters while she's been employed up there...Cecil...is true blue, honest & hard working & he was our only dependance. But we are glad he has now a home, instead of just a room & eating restaurant food all the time."

It has been my pleasure to correspond with Cecil since 1980. His letters reflect the personality of a quiet, intelligent man, introspective at times and humorous at others, who hates idle gossip and is always ready and able to see the other side of the story. After his retirement, he and Pauline remained in Chicago until 1984 when they returned to Effingham, IL where they live in a tidy and attractively furnished home.

Only child of Cecil Howard and Pauline Naomi (Tucker) REDMAN was:

507. Steven Ray b 6 Mar 1943

441. **CLARA LUE REDMAN**, daughter of Anthony and Nettie Jane (Mitchell) Redman, was born 21 Oct 1896 in DeWitt Co., IL near Maroa. She married 17 Oct 1914 at Lincoln, Logan Co., IL to John Henry Hopp, born there 20 Oct 1891, the son of Jacob and Susan Agnes (Shade) Hopp, natives of Reading, PA and Maiden Creek, PA respectively.

Clara tells her own story best in her autobiography as excerpted from her family genealogy, "Nettie Jane (Mitchell) Redman, Her Ancestors & Descendants." Named for a local country schoolteacher, Clara Pharis, one of her earliest memories was her first day at school when she was 6 years 11 months old. "At noon my father came over to see if I was all right. I remember seeing my father ride up on horseback...I was sitting on the lap of a large red headed girl on the grass under the shade of a tree."

The next summer when Clara was nearly 8 years old, her sisters and brother all younger, her mother became ill. During this period of time, Clara recalled "...riding a gentle old driving horse named 'Old Fan.' We would get in the manger, climb on her neck, holding to her mane, and somehow manage to get on her back. Two of us and sometimes three would ride at once. She would walk around the barn lot with us, and what a thrill! We somehow escaped being killed while we were temporarily without a mother.

We soon moved to Effingham Co., Ill. to be near her (mother's) family...I again attended a country school...A great part of the land where we lived was timber. The farmers cleared off some each year and got the land ready for the planting of crops, using the wood for fuel and cutting some into cordwood for sale. We went to school through a woods pasture, along a footpath, crawled under a barbed wire fence and crossed a creek on a footlog which had been placed there for the purpose, with a wire at each side the right height for us to hold for support. The school was one-room with a large iron stove in the middle.

Eight grades were taught by one teacher. The seats and desks were long, at least two children to each seat. In front were two long seats where each class would sit to recite their lessons while the other classes studied. My schooling was sketchy, however, as my mother was sick most of the time and I, being the oldest, was kept home to help her...One year I missed the entire term...but I read everything I could get my hands on. I loved to read and still do. I also learned to crochet and sew quilt blocks and doll clothes. I would try to do everything I saw my mother doing, only on a smaller scale.

One summer my father drove a 'hack,' as it was called, to the Effingham County Fair. It was something like a spring wagon only with a longer bed with a long seat on each side the full length. He decorated it with red, white and blue bunting. It was pulled by a team of horses. He would drive along and call out, 'Hack to the fair grounds," until he had a load to take to the fair.

In spring and summer we had great fun gathering wild flowers in the woods around our house. Wild berries and fruit and wild grapes were plentiful also. Several kinds of nuts could be gathered in the fall. We always had our cellar full of apples and nuts and canned fruit in the fall. My father used to bury cabbage and carrots in the ground. He would dig a hole and line it with straw, put the vegetables on top, and cover with straw, then earth. They would be nice and fresh in the winter...

My father usually went to town for a supply of groceries every two weeks. It was an all day trip...when he returned, he always brought us a sack of sugar candy which was a great treat. We didn't have many boughten toys, but we used the things at hand; for instance, we girls would cut a piece of wild grape vine and use it for a jumping rope. We made our own checkerboard from the side of a cardboard box, making the squares with crayons and for the men, we went to the corn crib and got two different colors of corn. In the fall when the leaves fell, they were so deep, we had great fun playing with them.

A very pleasant memory is of riding on the water wagon with the older children at threshing time, taking drinking water to the men at work in the field, and then those wonderful dinners that were served to the threshers. The threshing machine was taken to a farm and all the neighbors helped one man, then moved and threshed the grain of the next farm on the line with all helping him...at each place, they had to feed all the men their dinner and supper. Of course, the wives went to help get the meal and with them were the children. We children had to wait until all the others were fed and they usually had to wash dishes and re-set the table. By that time, we were really hungry. I have a vivid memory of peeking through a partly open door, watching. I was just sure there wouldn't be any left of some food that I especially liked. Farmers in those days had none of the conveniences of town people, no electricity, no central heating system, water was pumped by hand from a well or cistern, all cooking was done on a coal or wood stove. Most of them, however, had a summer kitchen where they could cook and avoid heating the house...such a thing as an electric fan was unknown..."

When Clara was about 11 years old, the family moved to a farm near Bement, IL where Clara attended grade school. She was behind others her age, having missed so much time staying home with her ailing mother, but she was also small for her age so "didn't feel out of place." She and her sisters and brother were "called Indians by the children at school because of our name, Redman. We would get mad (I don't know why) and chase them...they would say 'Now I know they are Indians, they are on the warpath.'"

After the death of her mother when Clara was 13 years old, she was able to attend school regularly. "We lived one-half mile from Bement and walked to school and church and the weekly band concert in the park in summer. It was a custom then for people to go to town on Saturday night and stand around in the stores and visit and catch up on all the news of the week. When I was in my early teens, a Nickel-o-dian was started in Bement. It was moving pictures, black and white, no sound, and the picture was changed once a week. The charge was a nickel, hence the name. It was there I went on my first date. It was the first time I had attended.

I loved to read and was hungry for knowledge. I was ...a good student with top grades, having lacked 1/10th of 1% of having the highest grade in the county one year which grieved me. Some scholars were happy because they passed, and I was sad because I didn't have the highest grade. When I finished 8th grade, it was a question...if we would go on to high school. Nine students out of a class of thirty continued...I was one of the nine but quit before graduating. I planned to be a school teacher, but my father had married again and was raising another family so it wasn't possible for me to continue. My last year in school, I lived with a family in Decatur and attended Decatur High School. The next summer, I met my future husband (who) was working in Decatur and living with his sister...In the fall, he came back to Lincoln where he had employment...We were married soon after...

My children grew up during the 'depression days' that older folks will remember. Many were the economies we practiced. Most of us baked our own bread and worked all summer canning fruit and vegetables for the winter. I cut my children's hair and also that of several of the neighbor's children. I made...coats from old coats that some of the aunts, uncles and cousins had outgrown or partly worn out. I would salvage the good parts, often using the wrong side of the material for the new garment. Necessity taught me many things about remodeling and restyling clothes which I have put to good use ever since."

Clara was a cheerful, uncomplaining woman despite the many burdens she would bear throughout life. In 1917, her second child died of cerebral meningitis at age 5 weeks. In 1924, her eldest child died of a ruptured appendix at age 9 years, one week after her 5th child was born. Her second daughter, Nettie Jane, died in 1939 of a ruptured appendix, six weeks after she had been married. Her husband, John, died in Lincoln on 1 Jan 1944. She had 2 sons who served in W.W.-II. In 1945, she spent 9 months in the Palmer Sanitorium in Springfield, IL, suffering from tuberculosis, returning there for 18 months from Feb. 1952 to July 1953 where she underwent chest surgery (thoracoplasty). After recovery, she returned to her old job at Gossett's Department store doing clothing alterations and repair work. After retiring about 1960, she continued to alter and restyle clothes and do other dressmaking in her home, and began compiling material for a family history, typed partly by her son, Jim, and partly by herself after she took a typing course at age 66. Her son's help with her book which was published in 1963 was typical of the love, care and support she enjoyed from all her children.

Clara had been a Bible student since her early teens. In July 1933, she was converted, experiencing "the joy of salvation..." She was a charter member of Lincoln Hill Free Methodist Church, teaching Sunday School there for many years and held offices of Sunday School Superintendent, recording secretary and church librarian. She was a member of the Women's Missionary Society and the Women's Christian Temperance Union, and held several offices in both organizations.

Mentally and physically active until the very end, Clara died at her home in Lincoln, IL on 28 Oct 1976, age 80 years 1 week. She is buried with her husband in Union Cemetery, Lincoln, IL. Children of John Henry and Clara Lue (Redman) HOPP, all born in Lincoln, IL, were:

508. **Paul Raymond** b 27 Oct 1915 d 31 Aug 1924.
509. **Harold John** b 23 June 1917 d 4 Aug 1917.
510. **Geraldine May** b 23 June 1918　　　　　　　*
511. **Nettie Jane** b 20 Jan 1921 d 14 Aug 1939 m 7 Jul 1939 Ralph Worden, s/o Lester Worden.
512. **Donald Eugene** b 24 Aug 1924　　　　　　　*
513. **Robert Dean** b 25 Dec 1925　　　　　　　*
514. **James Wilbur** b 22 Apr 1935　　　　　　　*

442. **OPAL MAY REDMAN**, daughter of Anthony and Nettie Jane (Mitchell) Redman, was born 6 Jul 1898 in DeWitt Co., IL (near Maroa). Named Myrtle Opal at birth, appearing under that name in the 1900 census of Texas Twp., DeWitt Co., IL, she changed her name to Opal May as a young girl. She married 13 Jan 1915 in Bement, IL to George Edward Musson, born 16 Oct 1897 at Shumway, Effingham Co., IL, son of William Wilburforce and Mary Camilla (Bricker) Musson. Given the name of two English monarchs, George Edward was early nicknamed "King," and was called that all of his life. His grandparents, Daniel and Anna (Shelborn) Musson, were both born in England, coming to this country in 1850, living first in Ohio before settling in Effingham Co. about 1867.

Opal was 11 years old when her mother died and age 12 when her father remarried and began raising a second family. Living space in their small house became even more cramped when her ailing, widowed grandmother, Mary Jane (Garlinghouse) Redman, came to live with them. Opal and her older sister, Clara, were hired out as live-in house girls for local farm families. Even after the death of their grandmother in Apr 1911, Opal and Clara remained out of their father's house.

Temperamentally, Opal was as different from her sisters and brother as the day is different from the night.

Quick to anger, she is equally quick to forgive. She was always outspoken, her bluntness softened by her good sense of humor. She is never at a loss for a sharp comment or a quick retort, but she met her match in King who was an easy going man with an endless stock of goodnatured replies at his command.

Opal and King lived in Bement, IL for some years after they married, staying at first with King's parents. In 1918, King enlisted in the Army (33rd Infantry) with the rank of Pvt. 1st/Class, serving for about a year which "...wasn't long enough to get to be a General." He was sent to Eagle Pass, TX, a dry, dusty, remote town on the Mexican border where, according to King, "it hadn't rained for 20 years." In Oct 1918, Opal left her 2-year old son, Chester, with King's parents, and took her 1-year old daughter, Juanita, to Eagle Pass to join her husband. She started her trip armed with plenty of advice from her mother-in-law: "She said, 'don't talk to anyone, don't do this, don't do that, hide your money in your clothes somewhere, pin it in,' so naturally I did going down." The train from San Antonio to Eagle Pass had no sleeping accommodations, only seats. Opal "...went to sleep and Juanita went to sleep and fell out of the seat, and when I woke up, this man was setting there with her asleep in his arms. He had a gun on each side, and I said OH! What will I do! He happened to be the sheriff at Eagle Pass and he helped me with Juanita. But it sure scared me!"

In Eagle Pass, Opal and Juanita lived in a converted hotel where they had two rented rooms, a kitchen and living-room-bedroom combination, staying there until the following Feb 1919 when they returned home. In King's words, "She had to hurry home and tell'em she was starving to death so they'd let me out to come home and feed her." Opal admits she filled out the request forms, but says she didn't do it because she had to. It was her mother-in-law who insisted on it.

When she got back to Bement, Opal found her small son, Chester, "...so onery he wouldn't mind anything. They (his grandparents) couldn't get his hair cut because he wouldn't set in the chair. No matter what they told him, he just went and done as he pleased. I started in on that kid and I straightened him out in about a week. I took him to get his hair cut and Grandpa said, 'There's no need to take him because he won't set it that chair!' Well, I thought, I bet he will! And he did! The first time he got a licking with a yardstick after I come home, they thought I was just the most horrible person that ever lived!"

In the 1920's, Opal and King moved from Bement to Chicago, IL where King worked for Swift's, first as a meat grader for a year, then as foreman of various departments for 29 years. He was also maintenance supervisor for Minnesota Mining & Mfg. for 4 years before he retired. They were then living in Palos Hills near Chicago. Eventually, they returned to live in Bement, bringing with them their grandson, Billy Musson, whom they took to raise when he was about 5 years old

Some years ago, Opal began losing her eyesight, the result of degeneration of the retina, an inherited and inoperable condition. She continued to manage her household without help until a few years ago, but misses being able to read. She once complained that King wouldn't read the papers to her but that was just as well since "he is a terrible reader, everything just one continual sentence, no commas or periods or anything." King's mild reply was, "You get there quicker when you jump from one hill to another." This was typical of their many verbal exchanges and masked a deep affection for each other that lasted through 69 years of marriage until King's death on 28 Feb 1984 at Veteran's Hospital, Danville, IL. He was buried 1 Mar in Bement Cemetery near Bement, IL.

Opal is now (1987) living alone in a neat, comfortable apartment in Bement, IL near her eldest son. Despite her 89 years (in July), her sharp wit and affectionate good humor have remained intact. Children of George Edward ("King") and Opal May (Redman) MUSSON were:

515. **Chester Earl** b 13 May 1916   *
516. **Juanita May** b 24 Jul 1917   *
517. **George Edward (Jr.)** b 7 Jan 1920   *
518. **Jerry Robert** b 19 Sep 1929   *
519. **Jimmie Dale** b 4 Feb 1932   *

443. **HUBERT PAUL REDMAN**, son of Anthony and Nettie Jane (Mitchell) Redman, was born 5 Oct 1900. His family gives his place of birth as Altamont, Effingham Co., IL, but this is questionable since his parents were in Texas Twp., DeWitt Co., IL (near Maroa) in the 1900 census (taken on 19 June) and his baby picture was made at a studio in the town of Maroa nearby.

Ninth Generation

By Christmas 1909, the family, excepting 7-year old Mabel, Hubert's younger sister, was living in a tenant farmhouse just south of Bement, IL. Due to his mother's poor health and in that month her advanced state of pregnancy, Mabel had been sent to stay with her mother's sister, Mollie Taylor. On 27 Dec, Hubert and his sisters wrote short notes to Mabel to enclose in their mother's letter to her sister. Despite his mother's letter mentioning that Hubert and his father had gone rabbit hunting that day, Hubert wrote that he was "not doing nothing" and that he "did not get nothing" for Christmas, adding that "papa has went to town to get some chickens..." His dispirited tone leads one to believe Hubert had wanted to go to town with his father and had been told he could not.

Of all the children, Hubert most resembled his father, being of a slender build with a dark complexion. He was only 9 years old when his mother died, and just 10 when his father remarried. He did not seem to get along well with his stepmother, often walking miles to the Taylor's farm to see his sister and to get table scraps to feed his dog. Although Mabel was 2 years younger, she and Hubert were very close, perhaps in part because they shared the same day of birth. Mabel's first photo album is filled with pictures of her brother taken at the Taylor's farm.

On 18 Jul 1920, Hubert enlisted at Chicago, IL in the Army Air Corp as a Pvt. 1st/Class and was stationed at Fort Sill near the Witchita Mountains northwest of Lawton, OK, not far from the Texas border. He sent pictures back to Mabel, one taken beside a patch of cactus, another with the camp dog, and a third in which he pretended to be shooting a pistol that was taken "on top of a mountain 10 miles from camp."

Hubert was discharged on 19 Jul 1921 at Fort Sill, returning to Piatt Co., Il where he married on 28 Oct 1922 in Monticello to pretty, dark haired Ethel Marie Mellinger, born 5 Feb 1906 at Cerro Gordo, Piatt Co., IL, daughter of Franklin Roy and Katheryn (Wrightsman) Mellinger. Hubert and Ethel lived in various places in IL before moving to Indiana between 1933 and 1937, settling first in Jamestown. Ethel was the mother of Hubert's first 7 children. She died 25 Oct 1950 at Decatur, Macon Co., IL (of drowning) and was buried at Cerro Gordo, IL.

Hubert's second wife whom he married in June 1952 at New Ross, Montgomery Co., IN was Martha Belle Kinkead,

born 17 Aug 1923 at New Ross, IN, daughter of Martin L. and
Julia Elizabeth (Walters) Kinkead. They were divorced in
1953. (She was the mother of Hubert's 8th and last child.)
He married third on 9 Oct 1960 at Mace, Montgomery Co., IN
to Mary Evela (Royce) Manning, born 1 Jan 1900 in Fleming
Co., KY (no children by this marriage).

Hubert was diabetic most of his adult life, this con-
tion being an underlying cause of his death on 13 Dec 1961
at Rochester, Fulton Co., IN where he had lived for "a
number of years." His obituary in the Crawfordsville, IN
"Journal Review," gave his time of death as 11:45 a.m.
while "...in the office of a physician here. He became
ill while at work at McMahan Construction Co. He had been
employed by the firm as a mechanic for nearly 40 years."
The obituary added that Hubert was a member there of the
Grace Methodist Church, but he was not, as it stated, a
veteran of W.W.-I, that war having ended before Hubert
enlisted in the service. He was buried 16 Dec at the K. of
P. Cemetery in Mace, Montgomery Co., IN.

Children of Hubert Paul REDMAN (1st 7 by his marriage
to Ethel Marie Mellinger; last by his marriage to Martha
Belle Kinkead) were:

520. **Paul Allen** b 20 June 1923   *
521. **Aimee Marie** b 22 Jan 1925   *
522. **Katherine Ann** b 27 May 1927 d 5 Nov 1927 Bement, IL.
523. **Juanita Louise** b 2 Sep 1931   *
524. **Mary Ellen** b 31 Oct 1933   *
525. **Ruby Ethel** b 19 Jan 1937   *
526. **Franklin David** b 29 Jul 1942   *
527. **Dennis Wayne** b 23 Mar 1953   *

444. **MABEL RUTH REDMAN,** daughter of Anthony and Nettie
Jane (Mitchell) Redman, was born 5 Oct 1902 in Wapella
Twp., DeWitt Co., IL (near Clinton). She married 1 June
1926 at Springfield, IL to James Roy Jordan, born 30 Apr
1904 in Goosecreek Twp., Piatt Co., IL (near Deland), son
of Charles Alonzo and Rozella (Chamberlain) Jordan.

At about age 4 years, her mother's health deteriorated to the point where Mabel was often sent to stay with her
mother's sister and husband, Mollie and Al Taylor. At
her mother's death in 1910, Mabel's father gave permission to the Taylor's, who had no children of their own, to
keep Mabel and raise her and "make a woman out of her."
Although she adored her mother, Mabel remembered very

little about her except a game her mother played with her to get her to hurry in hooking up her shoe buttons, and her mother's singing as she worked around the house. She was told that her mother had been sitting on her father's lap, singing, when the angels came to take her to heaven, a story with no truth in it but one that she chose to believe all of her life.

In 1911, the Taylor's moved to Arkansas near the town of Fox where Al cut timber for railroad ties. It was a more primitive life than Mabel had known before with wild hogs ranging free in the woods to graze on acorns and an ever present danger from rattlers and copperhead snakes. In the rude log cabin where Mabel attended school, the snakes sometimes lay curled up on the rafters where it was warm. Once, coming home from the spring at dusk with a bucket of water, Mabel nearly stepped barefoot on a copperhead on the path. Luckily, the Taylor's dog, Benny, was with her, jumped out in front of her and killed the snake but not before he had been bitten. They were up all that night applying a drawing poultice of egg whites, alum and gunpowder to the bite and by morning, brave dog Benny was on the road to recovery.

Another time, Mabel was chased down a narrow mountain path by a herd of wild hogs. She escaped them by shinnying up a tree well used by the hogs as a scratching post. With the bark rubbed off, the tree was slippery. Mabel had tried to climb it before without success but being chased by a pack of hogs gave her the proper inspiration. She waited there an hour before the hogs meandered away and she could climb down and go home.

In 1913, the Taylors, having returned from Arkansas, moved to a farm near Bement, IL where Mabel spent the rest of her growing up years. The "Bement Register," issue of 22 Dec 1949, carried a print of Mabel's baby picture under the heading "Who Is This Little Christmas Doll?" She was 9 months old in this picture, a beautiful dark haired baby wearing a frilly white dress, her left hand reaching for a silver dollar "being jingled to attract her attention. A few years later, money was still attracting her, at least she saved all her Indian head pennies...she'd take them to town in her little green purse but not one would she spend, even tho no one else bought her the candy she so much wanted...She was very fond of cats, especially yellow cats, and dolls, and had a name for every one of them.

She really loved dolls but one day she got mad at one of them and spanked it so hard she broke its head."

The article continued: "She had two exciting adventures when she was a little girl. A boy cousin dared her to get in a nest of bees; she took the dare and so many bees got in her hair that in getting them out, said cousin pulled most of her hair out, too. When she was around 7, she scared a gander in the barnyard and he started at her, hissing and flapping his wings, but she grabbed his neck and held on till rescued...She loves music and was one of Miss (Nellie) Alvord's violin pupils and played in the Sunday School orchestra. She is a nature lover, very fond of flowers...She likes interior decorating and would have followed that line of work if she hadn't begun her other profession. She has often said to her children, 'The things that make my world go round are beauty and harmony,' which someway doesn't tie in with her earlier interest in dissecting turtles, etc. to see what they looked like on the inside."

Mabel's father often said she looked just like her grandmother, Mary Jane (Garlinghouse) Redman, and, indeed, the resemblance is striking when their photographs are compared. She inherited her olive complexion and her hair, thick and so dark brown it often looked black, from her father, but her bright blue eyes were a heritage from her mother. She retained a slender figure and youthful appearance well into middle age. She had a great deal of energy and determination and a hot temper when aroused. Barely over 5 feet tall, she was often referred to as the proverbial dynamite that comes in small packages. She was a skilled seamstress, making all of her own clothes and even her hats. She had many beaus but her first true serious love married another.

When Mabel graduated from Bement High School in 1922, the only qualifications necessary to teach in elementary schools was a high school diploma. She went on to complete a 6-week summer training course at State Normal Teacher's College in Normal, IL. She then began teaching in Piatt Co., IL rural schools, riding horseback between home and school in all sorts of weather. In 1923, her Uncle Al's mother wrote that "it dident seem reasonable for Mabel to be an old maid School Teacher but if she dident hurry up she would bee before long." This dire prediction proved untrue. It was while Mabel was teaching that she met her future husband, Roy. Among her students that year were a younger brother and sister of Roy's who one day forgot to take their lunches to school. Roy was sent to remedy the oversight, met the teacher and, obviously, liked what he saw. After they were married, Mabel stopped teaching to raise a family until her youngest child was ready for first grade. She then resumed a teaching career in the Piatt Co. School System that spanned 33 years.

It wasn't easy being a country schoolmarm in those days. The successful country schoolteacher had to be a self-starter, organized, self-reliant, creative, calm and in control during emergency situations, sole adminis- trator of discipline, and in possession of a passion for education that no circumstances would discourage. She had to stoke up the coal furnace on cold winter mornings and bank it down at night, see that the floors were swept, the blackboards cleaned, and other required housekeeping tasks were done. She was a nurse when the occasion demand- ed one, and she often taught when she herself was sick, as there were no substitutes to take her place. She was the arranger of school functions for parents, plays and reci- tations that she staged and directed. She spent her week- days teaching school, her nights and weekends grading papers and outlining study courses. If she was married and had children of her own, she also had to fit in all the duties of a wife and mother.

In the spring of 1941, Mabel and Roy moved to Bement, IL from Milmine, a distance of about 6 miles. That fall, Mabel began teaching at Elwood school, about 22 miles from Bement. In December of that year, Pearl Harbor was bombed and the United States was at war. When gasoline rationing was implemented, it was impossible to make the 22 mile drive to school and return home again every day of the week so Mabel moved a day bed into the school and spent 2 nights a week there. Fortunately, Elwood was one of the few country schools that had indoor plumbing. She cooked her dinner on the same electric plate that she used to provide her 20 students with daily hot lunches under a government school lunch program. In the spring, she took her students on field trips, packing her LaSalle with the younger boys and the girls, letting the older boys ride outside on the running boards, hanging on for dear life. It must have been a startling sight as she hurlted down the highway like the Old Woman in a Shoe on wheels.

Mabel was a good student as well as a good teacher. When she entered school in Piatt Co., IL in 1913, she was held back a grade due to inadequate instruction in Arkansas, but she soon made up for that. In 1917, she ranked 2nd in a class of 175 with an average of 95-2/9th, just 3/9ths of a point below 1st ranking Helen McPherson. Her Certificate of Final Examination shows grades ranging between 95 and 99 for all subjects except arithmetic on which she scored an 85. At the bottom of this certificate, she wrote, "Miss Blondella Clover, later Mrs. Paul Hawver, one of the very best teachers possible."

At the consolidation of country schools into town systems, Mabel began teaching 6th grade at Washington School in Monticello, IL where she spent 19 of her 33 years in elementary education. During 20 of these years, she continued her own education, taking correspondence courses, attending summer school, and later going to night classes in the winter. In 1952, she received a long coveted Bachelor of Science in Education degree from the University of Illinois in Champaign. This was followed by a Master of Education degree in 1954, and an Advanced Certificate in Education degree in 1960. For many years, she was a member of the Teacher's Reading Circle, and was an active life member of the National Education Association, a member of Lamba Chapter, Delta Kappa Gamma, and Alpha Chapter, Kappa Delta Pi.

During these years, Roy had worked at many jobs. The son of a farmer, he had grown up in the country, but the life of a farmer was not for him. When he graduated from 8th grade, his father could not spare a horse for him to ride into town to go to highschool, so he repeated the 7th and 8th grades until he was old enough to quit. For a few years, he worked as a farm laborer, then in the steel mills in Joliet, IL. He drove an ice delivery wagon, had a Watkins Products route, ran his own grocery store for a number of years, went to Texas and worked on the pipeline, then drove for various trucking companies. After the move to Bement in 1941, he began working for the local Marathon Oil Co. distributor. He was finally able to buy the distributorship for himself and ran this business very successfully until he decided to retire in 1967. He urged Mabel to retire at the same time. She was torn between her love of teaching and a desire to spend more time in the home she had purchased and remodeled in Bement in

1958. Reluctantly, she decided on retirement. After a few months of it, she began working part time in a small dress shop in Monticello, and teaching again part time as a private tutor.

Her retirement years were cut short. On 31 Dec 1970, Mabel died at St. Mary's Hospital in Decatur, IL of a "disecting aortic aneurysm." Her visitation at the Roux Funeral Home in Bement was attended by many of her former students, teachers with whom she had worked during her career, as well as friends and relatives. Funeral services were held at the Bement Methodist Church where both she and Roy were members. She was buried in Bement Cemetery near Bement, IL.

Roy remained in the home in Bement until the spring of 1987 when he moved to a nursing home near his son's residence in Mountain Home, AR. He is 83 years old. Children of James Roy and Mabel Ruth (Redman) JORDAN are:

   528. Keith Redman b 22 Aug 1926   *
   529. Shirlee Ann b 10 Sep 1929   *
   530. Marilyn Ruth b 23 May 1933   *

448. LELA BLANCHE JONES, daughter of William Rollie and Amanda Ellen (Mitchell) Jones, was born 10 June 1901 in Shelby Co., IL. She married 22 Feb 1922 to Bryan Franklin Peadro, born 8 Sep 1896 in Moultrie Co., IL, son of Edward Charles and Emma Frances (Wright) Peadro. Bryan died 22 Jan 1983 less than a year after he and Lela celebrated their 60th wedding anniversary. Lela is still living (1987) in the family home near Gays, IL.

At age 4½, Lela's mother died after giving birth to twins. Lela and her brothers and sister were fortunate to be raised by a warm, loving step-mother, but nevertheless, Lela never stopped missing her own mother. In 1977, Lela wrote about her childhood and her mother's death: "Mabel (her cousin) was one year younger that I was. When we were little girls and would go to Aunt Annie's and Aunt Mollie's...we would hide out and play with the kittens. Aunt Mollie never liked us to play with the kittens but we had lots of fun. We lived in Shelby County, 7 miles north and east of Windsor and always went to Ash Grove Christian Church which was about 2 miles from our home northwest.

I always thought my mother's birthday was March 19th. One time I was at Uncle Allen's and I said today was my mother's birthday. He said, no, this is Aunt Nettie's birthday. Your mother's birthday was August 30th. So you see, when one loses their mother when only 4 years old, you can't begin to know how much you have missed in life. I'll never forget the day my mother went to her heavenly home. She kissed all of us goodbye. Uncle Frank told me in later years that he was there, too. We were all around her bed, Uncle Allen, Aunt Gusta, Cal Henson, a neighbor. My mother closed her eyes, then she opened her eyes, looked up and smiled. Since I grew up, I know that's when God took my mother home, for she couldn't have smiled leaving babies 8 days old, Ira, 2, and I was 4. One time I told Uncle Allen and he said he thought he was the only one who saw my mother smile. Uncle Frank was two years younger than my mother and he always called me Manda; said I was just like her.

Well, anyway, I crawled under Mother's bed and they had a time getting me out. I expect it was the next day when I wanted to go in the bedroom where my mother was and Grandma wouldn't let me go. Well, you know, I went out doors and came in the bedroom door and I kissed my mother. She was so cold. I went to Grandma and asked her to cover her up. The day my mother was laid to rest, little Ira said, 'Why are you putting Mamma in that hole?' You know how sad that was! My mother, I know, was a wonderful person. I can remember how she would set in a rocking chair and play her mandolin and sing, but I can't remember her voice. I can just see her singing there. Oh, so much you miss when your mother's taken away so young. She was 25 years old.

I have my baby dress that my mother made all by hand. I often wonder how they kept them...first, Grandma, then my second mother...When I was married, Mamma (her step-mother) gave Ira's and Lucian's and Lucile's and my dresses to me and said, 'I've kept them, now you can...' Ira's was made like mine only no lace. Lucian's and Lucile's were made on machine so I always thought Aunt Gusta might have made them for being alike and on machine (I know my mother did have a machine before she died for Mamma always said that was dear mother's machine). Three of our great grandkids have had their pictures taken with my one-yard long dress on."

In 1986, Lela received a glowing tribute from her church: "This morning we are happy to present a special award to a special person...entitled the MA award. The person receiving this award taught Sunday School for 58 years. Each of her students were looked upon as her very own children. I visit in her house and I see pictures of so many different kids, some who are older that I am who were Bible students of this Christian lady. Each Sunday morning, 19 of her family grace our auditorium...one elder and two deacons (2 deaconesses), Sunday School Superintendent, organist, three Sunday School teachers are all products of her family. Our young ladies need to look to Lela Peadro as a person to pattern their lives after. Because of her outstanding contributions to the Kingdom of God, we present to MA PEADRO this Golden Cross."

Children of Bryan Franklin and Lela Blanche (Jones) PEADRO are:

- **531. William Edward** b 21 June 1924   *
- **532. Dallas Franklin** b 18 Sep 1926   *
- **533. Davadia Lela** b 6 Apr 1930   *

449. **IRA WILLIAM JONES,** son of William Rollie and Amanda Ellen (Mitchell) Jones, was born 29 Mar 1903 in Shelby Co., IL. He married 10 Aug 1929 to Ursle Azalee Hogsten, born 9 Aug 1910 in Cheboygan Co., MI, daughter of Burton Martin and Jemima Caroline (Conway) Hogsten. Ira died on 5 Aug 1962 at Flint, MI and was buried 8 Aug in Flint Memorial Park, Mt. Morris, MI. Ursle died 23 Mar 1985.

In 1977, Ira's sister, Lela Peadro, wrote about her brother: "Ira and Ursle are parents of Burton (Bud) Ira and Patricia (Patsy) Ann. Burton is a Baptist minister. He graduated from Northern Baptist Seminary, Chicago, and has been the minister of Birch Run Church since 1962. He is also principal of the highschool there at Mount Morris, MI. Patsy graduated from Wheaton College and the University of Michigan and is a teacher and (junior high) counsellor. At Ira's service, the minister said in his sermon, Bud (Burton), if you're the preacher that your dad was a man, you'll be a fine preacher. The minister had come to Ursle and asked for Ira's Bible...in his service, he had Ira's Bible and turned to pages that Ira had written in and marked. He said, 'I never preached his funeral. Ira did it for himself.'"

Children of Ira William and Ursle Azalee (Hogsten) JONES are: **(i)** Burton Ira ("Bud") b 2 Apr 1934 at Flint, Genesee Co., MI; unmar 1980; **(ii)** Patricia Ann "Patsy" b 26 Dec 1935 at Flushing, Genessee Co., MI; unmar 1980.

450. LUCIAN HENRY JONES, son of William Rollie and Amanda Ellen (Mitchell) Jones, was born 2 Dec 1905 in Shelby Co., IL. He married 19 Mar 1927 at Charleston, Coles Co., IL to Vera Dorthula Scoles, born 4 June 1907 in Shelby Co., IL, the daughter of Ezra Reuben and Cora Alice (Dowell) Scoles. Lucian died 3 Oct 1982 in Florida. Vera is living there (1987) in Gainesville.

Lucian and his twin sister, Lucile, were only 8 days old when their mother died. They were not given second names. Some years after their father remarried (1907), their step-mother suggested to Lucian that he should have a middle name. Lucian picked Henry after his Jones grandfather, and at their step-mother's suggestion, Lucile took Amanda after her deceased mother. Children of Lucian Henry and Vera Dorthula (Scoles) JONES are:

534. **William Ezra** b 17 Nov d 20 Nov 1927 Neoga, IL.
535. **Billy Joe** b 4 Jan 1929   *
536. **Vera Louise** b 29 Dec 1930   *
537. **Robert Lucian** b 17 Aug 1933   *
538. **Anita Lucile** b 3 Aug 1935   *
539. **Charles Ira** b 5 Aug 1937   *

452. EUGENE FRANKLIN MITCHELL, son of Ensign Franklin and Essie Elsie (Robertson) Mitchell, was born 19 May 1905 at Mason, Effingham Co., IL. He married 30 June 1930 Ethel Evelyn Triplett, born 23 Oct 1908 in Carthage, MS, daughter of Charner William and Bera ( ) Triplett. Eugene and Ethel are living (1987) in State College, MS.

Children of Eugene Franklin and Ethel Evelyn (Triplett) Mitchell, all born in Greenville, MS, are:
540. **Barbra Jane** b 28 June 1935   *
541. **Lynda Gene** b 14 June 1941 m 1 Sep 1963 (Dr.) James
     Donald Trotter.
542. **Evelyn Ann** b 9 Feb 1944   *

453. HARRY VICTOR MITCHELL, son of Ensign Franklin and Essie Elsie (Robertson) Mitchell, was born 11 Sep 1907 at Edgewood, Effingham Co., IL. He married 21 June 1932 in Birmingham, AL to Anna Jenina Mikulska, born 27 Dec 1909 in New York City, NY, daughter of Boleslaus and Staniska (Szczotkowski) Mikulski. Harry and Anna are living today (1987) in Tuscaloosa, AL. In 1963, Harry was chief accountant for the Gulf States Paper Corporation in Tuscaloosa, AL but, undoubtedly, is now retired.

Ninth Generation

Children of Harry Victor and Anna Jenina (Mikulska) Mitchell, all born in Tuscaloosa, AL, were:
543. **John Mikul** b 31 May 1935 *
544. **Mary Anne** b 15 Oct 1940 *
545. **David Lee** b 23 Sep 1943 *
546. **Frances Elaine** b 13 Nov 1948 *

455. **DAPHNA IRENE MITCHELL,** daughter of Ensign Franklin and Essie Elsie (Robertson) Mitchell, was born 24 May 1912 at Brighton, Macoupin Co., IL. She married 31 Nov 1909 at Shubuta, Clarke Co., MS to Newell Smith ("Sam") Estess, born 22 Nov 1909 in Pike Co., MS. Daphna is a retired high school teacher. Daphna and Sam live in Canton, MS (1987).
Children of Newell Smith and Daphna Irene (Mitchell) ESTESS, born in Canton, MS, are:
547. **Penelope Daphna ("Penny")** b 23 Jan 1943 *
548. **Newell Smith, Jr. ("Sam")** b 25 Sep 1950 *

456. **JOE CALVIN MITCHELL,** son of Ensign Franklin and Essie Elsie (Robertson) Mitchell, was born 3 Jul 1914 at Brighton, Macoupin Co., IL. He married Elizabeth Hudson. Only known child is:
549. **Jerry C.** m Thelma Becker; 2 ch Jay and Joe.

457. **HOWARD LEO MITCHELL,** son of Ensign Franklin and Essie Elsie (Robertson) Mitchell, was born 1 Feb 1921 at Grand Bay, Mobile Co., AL. He died unmarried on 5 Jan 1944 over Germany while serving as an Air Force pilot during World War II. An account written by the survivors of that flight appears in Clara L. Hopp's family genealogy, "Nettie Jane (Mitchell) Redman, Her Ancestors & Descendants," as follows: Howard was "with a crew of 8 men on a mission over Berlin, when they had a direct hit from the defense batteries. This hit knocked out two engines and injured the controls in the waist of the plane. He turned back, after two hours, having lost altitude down to 14,000 feet, ran into a terrible storm cloud, tried to go below it, the controls gave way, and the plane went into a spin. He ordered the men to bail out; 5 of them bailed out and 3 men stayed in. He fought the controls all the way down trying to save the plane and boys; all four were killed in the crash." Howard L. left 4 brothers, 1 sister and his parents to mourn the loss of this brave young man.

-292-

458. **RUSSELL GLEN MITCHELL,** son of Ensign Franklin and Essie Elsie (Robertson) Mitchell, was born 4 Nov 1922 at Grand Bay, Mobile Co., AL. He married in MS on 23 Jan 1943 to Jean Chiles, born 15 Jul 1925 in Wahalak, MS, daughter of Dr. _____ and Gertrude ( ) Chiles. (Gertrude married second E. C. Farr.) Russell G. married second Verdia Parsons and Jean married second John Smallenberger of Centerville, OH. Children of Russell Glen and Jean (Chiles) Mitchell are:

    550. Russell Glen (Jr.) b 10 Sep 1946   *
    551. Sharon b 14 Feb 1950   *

459. **OREN PRESLEY NEVILLE,** son of Presley Louis and Georgia "Kitty" (Mitchell) Neville, was born 10 Sep 1907 at Watson, Effingham Co., IL. He married 22 Dec 1934 in Arlington Heights, IL to Catherine Tena Brodin, born 24 Dec 1910 at Manistee, MI, daughter of Peter and Betty (Benson) Brodin. Only child of Oren Presley and Catherine Tena (Brodin) NEVILLE is:

    552. Duane Oren b 24 June 1938   *

461. **GENEVA RUTH NEVILLE,** daughter of Presley Louis and Georgia "Kitty" (Mitchell) Neville, was born 2 Jul 1912 at Watson, Effingham Co., IL. She married 29 May 1937 in Chicago, IL to Frank Victor Lindgren, born 2 Nov 1912 in Chicago, IL, son of Victor E. and Sigrid (Holmberg) Lindgren. Children of Frank Victor and Geneva Ruth (Neville) LINDGREN are:

    553. Gail Ruth b 5 Sep 1944   *
    554. Kenneth Frank b 11 June 1946   *

462. **HARRIETT LORAINE NEVILLE,** daughter of Presley Louis and Georgia "Kitty" (Mitchell) Neville, was born 4 Apr 1916 at Watson, Effingham Co., IL. She married 22 Nov 1939 in Chicago, IL to Edmund Walter Mears, born 29 Aug 1912 in Chicago, IL, son of William and Anna Patricia (Peterson) Mears. Children of Edmund Walter and Harriett Loraine (Neville) MEARS are:

    555. David Edmund b 22 Dec 1942   *
    556. Carol Ann b 20 Feb 1949   *

463. **VERA EVELYN SMITH,** daughter of Raymond Elmer and Winnie Maude (Mitchell) Smith, was born 16 Sep 1913 in Effingham Co., IL. She married 24 May 1935 at Half-Day, IL

Edward H. Lemm, born 16 May 1912 at Half-Day, IL, died on 26 Apr 1980 in Christ Hospital, Burbank, IL, buried there on 30 Apr in Chapel Hill Gardens. Only child of Edward H. and Vera Evelyn (Smith) LEMM is: **(i)** Sally Ann b 16 Feb 1936 Terre Haute, IN m 7 Nov 1970 Charles Wilbur; no ch.

464. **NADINE FRANCES SMITH,** daughter of Raymond Elmer and Winnie Maude (Mitchell) Smith, was born 16 Nov 1916 in Effingham Co., IL. She married 26 May 1936 in Highwood, IL to James Patrick Hickey, Jr., born 13 June 1913 in Highwood, IL, son of James Patrick and Victoria Ann (   ) Hickey, Sr. Children of James Patrick and Nadine Frances (Smith) Hickey, Jr., 1st two born in Lake Forest, IL, next three in Highland Park, IL, are: **(i)** Mary b 26 Aug 1937 m1) John Gustafson; m2) William Janis; **(ii)** James b 7 May 1940 m Nora Ori; **(iii)** Daniel b 12 Jul 1943 unmar 1980; **(iv)** Kathleen b 4 May 1948 m Larry Garrett; **(v)** Patricia b 16 Nov 1955 m Earl Jones.

465. **VERDA EILEEN SMITH,** daughter of Raymond Elmer and Winnie Maude (Mitchell) Smith, was born 29 Sep 1918 in Effingham Co., IL. She married first 5 May 1939 in Melrose Park, IL to Eugene C. Grinnell, born 21 Jan 1910 in Glen Ellyn, IL, son of Gilbert R. and Katherine (Giersback) Grinnell. Verda and Eugene divorced. Eugene married 2nd Ethel Secker. He died 17 Aug 1979 in Long Beach, CA, buried in Veterans Cemetery, Riverside, CA. Verda married 2nd 28 Dec 1962 Robert S. Phelps. Only child of Eugene C. and Verda Eileen (Smith) GRINNELL is: **(i)** Susan Gail b 7 Mar 1942 Elmhurst, IL m 28 May 1960 Tom Osborn.

466. **ROBERT ALDEN SMITH,** son of Raymond Elmer and Winnie Maude (Mitchell) Smith, was born 2 Oct 1921 in Effingham Co., IL. He married 10 Jul 1947 in Maywood, IL Ella Lydia Bonacker, born 10 Feb 1922 in Bellwood, IL, daughter of Gottlieb and Amelia (Erfurth) Bonacker. Children of Robert Alden and Ella Lydia (Bonacker) SMITH, born in Oak Park, IL, are: **(i)** Nancy Diane b 4 Oct 1948 m 17 Oct 1970 Andrew Dennis Borkowski; **(ii)** Gary Lee b 27 Aug 1950; **(iii)** Joyce Ann b 11 Nov 1953 m 23 Mar 1985 David Prahl.

469. **MARILYN MITCHELL,** daughter of David Ralph and Marguerite (Robertson) Mitchell, was born 7 Feb 1923 at Elliotstown, Effingham Co., IL. She married 26 Sep 1942

at the Zion Lutheran Church in Bellwood, IL to Henry Rusch who was born 9 Jul 1921 at Maywood, IL, son of David and Christina (Miller/Mueller) Rusch. Marilyn is a director for the Mary Kay Cosmetics firm. Children of Henry and Marilyn (Mitchell) RUSCH are:
  557. Dianne Joyce b 28 Jan 1948   *
  558. Gary Ralph b 30 Dec 1952   *

470. **FREDA BERNELL MITCHELL**, daughter of David Ralph and Marguerite (Robertson) Mitchell, was born 26 Jul 1925 in Effingham Co., IL. She married 12 Sep 1947 in Elmhurst, IL to Robert Lee Wallace, born 10 June 1924 in Oak Park, IL, son of Leon R. (Lee) and Helen Edith (Froemming) Wallace. Children of Robert Lee and Freda B. (Mitchell) WALLACE, born in Elmhurst, IL, are:
  559. Patricia Lynn b 24 May 1953   *
  560. **James Robert** b 16 Dec 1955
  561. **Scott Mitchell** b 24 Feb 1958

471. **VERNEVA MITCHELL**, daughter of David Ralph and Marguerite (Robertson) Mitchell, was born 16 Apr 1927 in Jackson Twp., Effingham Co., IL. She married 18 June 1949 in Elmhurst, IL to Jack Bernhard Anderson, born 4 Aug 1928 at Laurel, Jones Co., MS, son of Ben Otto and Inez Marie (Lindbergh) Anderson. Jack B. died 28 Dec 1979 at St. Petersburg, FL. Only child of Jack Bernhard and Verneva (Mitchell) ANDERSON is:
  562. Kenneth Lee b 23 Jul 1950   *

472. **HELEN MAYONNE MITCHELL**, daughter of David Ralph and Marguerite (Robertson) Mitchell, was born 5 Jul 1929 in Effingham Co., IL. She married 25 Nov 1948 in Sacred Heart Church, Effingham, IL to Arthur Edward Lustig, born on 18 Mar 1929 in Effingham, IL, son of Lawrence John and Arnieta Laura (Hutmacher) Lustig. Arthur died 19 Feb 1985. Children of Arthur Edward and Helen Mayonne (Mitchell) LUSTIG are:
  563. Cheryl Elaine b 17 Aug 1950   *
  564. Donna Rae b 1 Mar 1954   *

473. **MYRON CALVIN MITCHELL**, son of David Ralph and Marguerite (Robertson) Mitchell, was born 22 Nov 1931 in Jackson Twp., Effingham Co., IL. He married 24 June 1951 in Centenary Methodist Church, Effingham, IL to Patricia

Joan Harris, born 24 Jul 1932 at Newton, Jasper Co., IL, daughter of Dewey Wayne and Zola Magdalena (Allen) Harris. Patricia's great-grandfather was Dr. Zachariah Allen who practiced in Effingham and Jasper Cos., IL and was the first postmaster at Eberle and Winterrowd, IL.

The 1984 Effingham Co., IL history carries a sketch of Calvin and Patricia, stating that: "Calvin attended country schools in Jackson and Watson Townships. He graduated from Effingham H.S. in 1950. When a small boy, Calvin moved to Watson Twp., known as Loy Prairie, with his family. His father was supervisor of Watson Twp. for several terms...In 1952, Calvin served in the U.S. Army and served 14 months in Korea. After the service, he farmed with his father on the farm where they now live in Watson Twp. Since the deaths of his parents, Calvin has continued to farm the dairy and grain farm (now retired from farming). His great-grandfather, Calvin Mitchell, was the first surveyor of Effingham County."

Although Patricia was christened at the Christian Church in Newton, IL, both she and Calvin were baptized at the Centenary Methodist Church in Effingham on 18 May 1952 where they are still members.

Children of Myron Calvin and Patricia Joan (Harris) Mitchell are:

565. **Calvin Wayne** b 3 Sep 1953   *

566. **Sharon Elaine** b 21 Aug 1955   *

567. **Janean Kay** b 12 Apr 1958 m 31 Oct 1981 Steven Anthony Bushur; she holds a Bachelor of Science degree in Home Economics from Eastern IL Univ.; no ch.

474. **CLAYTON RALPH MITCHELL**, son of David Ralph and Marguerite (Robertson) Mitchell, was born 23 Apr 1934 in Jackson Twp., Effingham Co., IL. He married 12 June 1955 in Effingham, IL to Joyce Marlene Pulliam, born 30 Jul 1936 in Jasper Co., IL, daughter of Russell and Clara Joan (Pagel) Pulliam. Children of Clayton Ralph and Joyce Marlene (Pulliam) Mitchell, 1st 3 born in Effingham, IL, last one born in Springfield, IL, are:

568. **David Clayton** b 25 June 1956

569. **Cynthia Suzette** b 28 Mar 1959 m 22 Sep 1983 to John Whitehead.

570. **Lisa Kay** b 10 Apr 1961 m 29 May 1982 Mark Douglas Johnson.

571. **Jodi Michelle** b 26 Oct 1968

476. **MARTHAGENE MITCHELL**, daughter of David Ralph and Marguerite (Robertson) Mitchell, was born 1 Feb 1939 in Effingham Co., IL. She married 24 Jul 1957 in Corinth, MS to Ross Eugene Woody, born 5 Mar 1937 in Effingham Co., IL, son of Ross Granville and Eva Pauline (McGee) Woody. Children of Ross E. and Marthagene (Mitchell) WOODY are:
    572. **Gina Lynn** b 20 Jul 1958   *
    573. **Susan Shawn** b 5 Mar 1961   *
    574. **Shauna Dianne** b 16 Aug 1964 Kansas City, MO
    575. **Timothy Ross** b 9 Feb 1966 Kansas City, MO

479. **CHANDLER ORVILLE MITCHELL**, son of Claude Glen and Olive (Blanchard) Mitchell, was born 16 June 1903 in Ross Twp., Edgar Co., IL. He married 1 Sep 1925 at Watseka, IL to Leone Edwards, born 21 Feb 1903 in Greenup, Cumberland Co., IL, daughter of Elijah and Nellie (Roberts) Edwards.

Chandler O. was just 3 years old when his father took his own life. Chandler's mother, unable to properly take care of Chandler O. and his younger brother, Dugan B., left the boys to be raised by their grandparents, Chandler and Marica (Hartley) Mitchell. At their grandfather's death in 1919, they were left part of his property to be given them after the decease of their grandmother.

Chandler O. died 16 Jul 1966 in Ross Twp., Edgar Co., IL on the farm where he was born near Chrisman; Leone died in Edgar Co., IL on 27 May 1979. Both are buried there in Hoult Cemetery. Children of Chandler Orville and Leone (Edwards) Mitchell are:
    576. **Chandler Earl** b 22 Nov 1926   *
    577. **Eleanor Marica** b 23 May 1928   *
    578. **James Edward** b 19 Feb 1930   *
    579. **John Richard** b 22 Dec 1932   *

481. **CAROLYN MITCHELL KILE**, daughter of Walter Terrence and Helen Harriet (Mitchell) Kile, was born 5 May 1916 at Horace, Edgar Co., IL. She married there on 12 Sep 1940 to Paul Ernest Heche, born 13 Sep 1911 at Bluffton, IN.

Carolyn M. died quite suddenly on 29 Nov 1986 (in or near Skokie, IL where she and her husband lived). She was a particular favorite of her aunt, Catherine (Mitchell) Savoye who wrote early in December that "...my dear niece, Carolyn, died of a massive heart attack...it was such a horrible shock to all the members of her family...we were always more like sisters than aunt and niece. For the first time in five years, her two older girls were home (for Thanksgiving) with their families...the (twins) made up the complete family circle...they had such a lovely Thanksgiving...and the Friday following had been full of fun with Carolyn feeling especially gay and talkative everyone told me." In a later letter, Catherine wrote that Carolyn "...was a very systematized person...you'll be interested to know that she had had all their Xmas cards addressed a couple of months early; all Xmas gifts had been purchased, wrapped, tied with bows and all waiting in her old toy chest which Paul had refinished for her several years ago...after being stabilized at the hospital and seemingly getting along very well, she admonished Paul to be sure and dig out all of the Barnes' family gifts (for daughter, Melody) so they could take them home when leaving the next morning...Her wake and funeral services were attended by scores of friends and relatives, attesting to the fact that she had lived a beautifully full life."

After cremation, it was planned to take Carolyn's ashes for burial in May 1987 at Gravel Lawn Cemetery in Fortville, IN where her husband had grown up. Children of Paul Ernest and Carolyn Mitchell (Kile) HECHE are:

- **580. Melody** b 13 Oct 1946   *
- **581. Paulette** b 19 Aug 1948   *
- 582. **Barbara** (twin) b 21 Aug 1957 unmar 1987.
- 583. **William** (twin) b 21 Aug 1957 m 14 Sep 1985 Kimberly Wiese; no ch.

483. **MARJORIE WHARTON,** daughter of (Dr.) Cloyd F. and Florence (Mitchell) Wharton was born 20 Aug 1921; she married 13 Aug 1943 A. Wells Pettibone. Marjorie's children (PETTIBONE) are: **(i)** Susan b 2 Apr 1944; **(ii)** Ann b 29 Aug 1947; **(iii)** Laura; **(iv)** Meg.

485. **JEAN MITCHELL McVICKER,** daughter of Raymond Russell and Helen Jean (Mitchell) McVicker, was born 20 May 1920 in Pittsburgh, Alleghany Co., PA. She married 28 June 1947 to Robert Francis Jackson, born 6 Jul 1920 in Indianapolis, IN, son of Jefferson Robinson and Elsie Ann (Ramp) Jackson, natives of Paducah, KY and Bloomfield, IN respectively. Jean M. is a retired high school history teacher. Only child of Robert Francis and Jean Mitchell (McVicker) JACKSON is: **(i)** Robert Raymond b 13 Dec 1951 in Indianapolis, Marion Co., IN; unmar 1987.

486. **MARY ELLEN MARSH,** daughter of Wilfred and Jane Taggart (Mitchell) Marsh, was born 31 Mar 1929 at Evanston, Cook Co., IL. She married 30 Jul 1955 at Fort Wayne, Allen Co., IN to James Mason Givens, Jr., born 26 Dec 1928 at Gary, Lake Co., IN, son of James Mason and Elizabeth Jane (Banta) Givens, Sr. Mary Ellen's children (GIVENS) are: **(i)** Jane Ann b 20 Mar 1959 Indianapolis, IN; unmar in 1980; **(ii)** Mary Ellen b 4 Dec (1963?) Evanston, Cook Co., IL; unmar 1980.

487. **ROBERT CARLTON CREAMER,** son of Carlton Mitchell and Mary Elizabeth (Smith) Creamer, was born 18 Jul 1928 at Mechanicsburg, Champaign Co., OH. He married 2 Nov 1951 to Alice Andrea Fassos, born 11 Feb 1930 at Springfield, Clark Co., OH, daughter of Chris and Mary Maud (Houck) Fassos. (Chris Fassos was born in Greece.) Children of Robert Carlton and Alice Andrea (Fassos) CREAMER, all born in Mercy Hospital, Urbana, OH, are: **(i)** James Robert b 13 Sep 1953; **(ii)** Kimberly Diane b 17 Jan 1956 m 24 Aug 1976 Clyde Dennis Travis, s/o Elmer and Mildred (Cordell) Travis; **(iii)** John Drew b 19 Jul 1961.

488.   EVELYN L. MITCHELL, daughter of Oscar Calvin and Audrey (Trippe) Mitchell, was born 23 Feb 1927. She married Charles Woods. When last heard of by the family, she was in South America doing missionary work. Evelyn's known children (WOODS) are: **(i)** Alona Barbara b 10 Apr 1946 Kittery, ME; **(ii)** Marsha Helen b 16 Aug 1947 Miami, FL; **(iii)** Laura Lynn b 19 Sep 1948 Miami, FL; **(iv)** Judith Gail b 17 Aug 1949 Miami, FL.

489.   PATRICIA JOYCE MITCHELL, daughter of Burl Kenneth and Gertrude Ruth (Bjurstrom) Mitchell, was born 17 Mar 1937 in Washington, D.C. She married there on 27 Dec 1956 to Hugh Austin McFarland, born 20 June 1937 at Sanford, NC, son of Mutra H. and Flossie (Knight) McFarland. (Hugh and Patty were divorced Mar 1980.) In Patty's words, she is a "mother and homemaker first" and, second, a secretary in Tucson, AZ. Her daughter, Cynthia, and son-in-law, Aaron, live and work on a jersey dairy farm near Martinsville, OH. Her son, Hugh, Jr., is a junior at the University of Arizona; and her son, Kenneth, is a sophmore at Sabino High School in Tucson.

Patricia's children (McFARLAND) are: **(i)** Cynthia Diana b 26 June 1960 Marion, IN m 30 May 1981 Aaron Lee Farquhar; **(ii)** Hugh Austin, Jr. b 30 Apr 1963 Tucson, AZ; **(iii)** Kenneth John b 5 Sep 1970 Tucson, AZ.

490.   JUDITH A. MITCHELL, daughter of Burl Kenneth and Gertrude Ruth (Bjurstrom) Mitchell, was born 26 Aug 1940 at Baltimore, MD. She married 28 Mar 1964 at Arlington, VA to James W. Rhodes, born 28 Nov 1939 at Canton, OH, son of Daniel William and Ardeth E. (Lane) Rhodes. Judith A.'s children (RHODES), all b at Fairfax, VA and all lvg at home, are: **(i)** Jonathan Alan b 4 Feb 1966; **(ii)** Christina Ann b 6 Aug 1968; **(iii)** Jason Wesley b 22 Feb 1972; **(iv)** Jeffrey Lynn b 12 Aug 1974.

491. **LINDA DIANE MITCHELL,** daughter of Burl Kenneth and Gertrude Ruth (Bjurstrom) Mitchell, was born 24 Nov 1945 at Washington, D.C. She married 19 Aug 1967 at Arlington, VA to Donald Lemont Sikes, born 19 Mar 1945 at Washington, D.C., son of Walter Wingate and Jessie Lemont (Matthews) Sikes. Linda Diane's children (SIKES), born in Dunedin, FL, are: **(i)** Carmen Ruth (twin) b 29 Mar 1979; **(ii)** Eric Walter (twin) b 29 Mar 1979.

492. **JERRY ALLEN HOOKER,** son of Russell William and Velma Augusta (Mitchell) Hooker, was born 11 Sep 1934 near Gays in Shelby Co., IL. He married 13 Sep 1963 at the 1st Baptist Church in Mattoon, IL to Mary Jane Parker, born on 29 Aug 1935 at Carrizozo, Lincoln Co., NM, daughter of Aruel Everett and Eva (Olmstead) Parker. Jerry A. died 20 Nov 1984 in Olympia Fields Hospital at Mattoon, IL and is buried in Resthaven Cemetery in Mattoon. After his death, Mary Jane married second Philip Contant.

Children of Jerry Allen and Mary Jane (Parker) HOOKER (all b in Mattoon, IL except last 2 b in Charleston) are:
584. **Deborah Lynn** b 27 Mar 1954   *
585. **Jacalynn Ann** b 17 Feb 1955   *
586. **Jerry Glen** b 16 Aug 1956 unmar 1987 (in the army).
587. **Bradley Carl** b 4 Oct 1957   *
588. **William Eric** b 27 June 1959
589. **Laura Gay** b 8 Dec 1961 m 22 June 1980 Daniel Joe Smith; div; no ch.

500. **BARBARA NANCY HOOKER,** daughter of Russell William and Velma Augusta (Mitchell) Hooker, was born 5 Dec 1936 near Gays, Shelby Co., IL. She married first 6 Nov 1954 at Keokuk, Lee Co., IA to Robert James Jordan, born 11 Mar 1937 in Mattoon, IL, son of Howard James and Josie Elizabeth (Pruitt) Jordan. Barbara and Robert were divorced. Barbara married second 7 May 1970 at Charleston, IL to Robert Dwane Farris, born 3 Nov 1941 at Charleston, IL, son of Wayne Wesley and Phyllis Amelia (Stewart) Farris.

Barbara's children by her 1st marriage (JORDAN), born in Mattoon, Coles Co., IL, are:
590. **Dena Gayl** b 7 Dec 1955   *
591. **Christine Denise** b 23 Jan 1957   *
592. **Sali Elizabeth** b 22 May 1959   *
593. **Russell James** b 19 Jul 1962
594. **Teresa Dawn** b 15 Feb 1964

Barbara's child by her second marriage (FARRIS), born in Mattoon, Coles Co., IL, is:
595. **Michael Robert** b 1 Jul 1971

494. **SHIRLEY JEAN HOOKER,** daughter of Russell William and Velma Augusta (Mitchell) Hooker, was born 12 Feb 1938 at Mattoon, Coles Co., IL. She married there on 27 Jan 1957 to Paul Anthony Rippey, born 9 Jul 1938 at Arcola, Douglas Co., IL, son of Albert Francis and Louella (Pullen) Rippey. Children of Paul Anthony and Shirley Jean (Hooker) RIPPEY, all born at Mattoon, Coles Co., IL, are:
596. **Jodi Lynn** b 5 Sep 1957   *
597. **Lisa Annette** b 20 Oct 1960 m 26 Apr 1980 Donald L.
     Mast, s/o John Henry & Sharon Sue (Bird) Mast.
598. **Scott Anthony** b 30 Apr 1962

496. **RONALD DAVID HOOKER,** son of Russell William and Velma Augusta (Mitchell) Hooker, was born 12 Nov 1945 at Mattoon, Coles Co., IL. He married there on 16 Oct 1964 to Toni Fay Gullion, born 10 June 1947 at Mattoon, IL, daughter of Raymond Eugene and Hazel Louise (Icenogle) Gullion. Children of Ronald David and Toni Fay (Gullion) HOOKER, all born at Mattoon, IL, are: **(i)** Troy Allan b 13 June 1965; **(ii)** Michael Todd b & d 27 Jan 1967; **(iii)** Wendy Ellen b 3 Oct 1968; **(iv)** Jennifer Lee b 30 Oct 1972.

499. **ARLAN CHARLES MITCHELL,** son of Vernon Hartman and Virginia Josephine (Johnson) Mitchell, was born 26 Sep 1950 at Mattoon, Coles Co., IL. He married 6 Sep 1975 at Wathena, Doniphan Co., KS to Retha Arlene Ruhnke, born on 3 Aug 1952 at St. Joseph, Buchanan Co., MO, daughter of Paul Emil and Elsie Louise (Dombrowe) Ruhnke. Children of Arlan Charles and Retha Arlene (Ruhnke) Mitchell, (1st 2 b Denver, CO; 3rd at Hiawatha, KS), are:
599. **Alan Chad** b 30 Jul 1979
600. **Nicole Augusta** b 16 Jan 1981
601. **Jenna Louise** b 1 Jul 1984

500. **MICHAEL LEE MITCHELL,** son of Vernon Hartman and Virginia Josephine (Johnson) Mitchell, was born 7 Aug 1952 at Spokane, WA. He married first at Spokane on 7 Aug 1975 to Constance Susan Barnes. They were divorced in 1976 (no children). Michael married second 19 Sep 1978 at Spokane, WA to Deanna Jane Thompson, born 2 Jan 1957, daughter of

Ernest Lee and Margaret Ann (Parater) Thompson. Only child of Michael Lee and Deanna Jane (Thompson) Mitchell, born at Spokane, WA, is:
    602. **Christina Marie** b 13 Feb 1980

502. **ETHEL MAUD PENDLAY,** daughter of Walter and Bessie (Redman) Pendlay, was born 5 Jul 1920 at Funkhouser, Summit Twp., Effingham Co., IL. She married 2 Oct 1940 at Jasper, Newton Co., AR to James Harley Myers, born 11 June 1919 at Jasper, AR, son of Alfred and Rosetta (Plumlee) Myers. Children of James Harley and Ethel Maud (Pendlay) MYERS, born in Effingham Co., IL, are:
    603. **Richard Harley** b 10 Jul 1941 m 12 Oct 1962 Hilda Combs.
    604. **Thomas Lyle** b 15 Jul 1942   *
    605. **Ferne Marie** b 30 Jul 1944   *

503. **LORNA LUCILLE PENDLAY,** daughter of Walter and Bessie (Redman) Pendlay, was born 9 May 1926 at Funkhouser, Summitt Twp., Effingham Co., IL. She married first 5 Feb 1941 at Jasper, AR to Veilus Plumlee. She married second 2 Sep 1943 at Urbana, Champaign Co., IL to Frank Lawrence DeMar, born 30 Jan 1910 at Escanaba, Delta Co., MI, son of Zane and Corinne (Blanchet) DeMar. Lorna L.'s children (DeMAR) are: **(i)** Donald b 31 Oct 1954 Trenton, Mercer Co., NY; **(ii)** Michael b 27 Nov 1957 Iola, Waupaca Co., WI; **(iii)** Anita b 21 Feb 1962 Waupaca, Waupaca Co., WI.

504. **GLENDEN DAVID REDMAN,** son of David Franklin and Charlotte Icle (Poynter) Redman, was born 4 Mar 1925 in Effingham, IL. He married Oct 1944 at North Andover, MA to Frances Latham Bamford, born 14 Aug 1917 at Lawrence, MA, daughter of John Thomas and Alice Faxon (Horne) Bamford. Only child of Glenden David and Frances Latham (Bamford) REDMAN is: **(i)** Glenna Dee b 17 Feb 1954 Lafayette, IN m 6 Mar 1979 James Cumming; div.

505. **GERNON ELDIN REDMAN,** son of David Franklin and Charlotte Icle (Poynter) Redman, was born 25 Jul 1926 in Effingham, IL. He married 7 May 1949 in Downers Grove, IL to June Annette Reideler, born 17 June 1928 in Hinsdale, IL, daughter of William F. and Clara L. (Pelling) Reideler. Children of Gernon Eldin and June Annette (Reideler) REDMAN are: **(i)** Gary Lawrence b 1 Jan 1950 Hinsdale, IL m

29 Nov 1968 Mary Pscherer; **(ii)** Paul Gregg b 4 Oct 1952
Aurora, IL; **(iii)** Wendi Louise b 16 Feb 1954 Aurora, IL m
10 Nov 1979 Glenn Almen; **(iv)** Dean Andrew b 18 June 1955
Hinsdale, IL m 25 Aug 1973 Jeanne Locherco; **(v)** Keith Leslie b 16 Dec 1956 Elmhurst, IL m 27 Aug 1977 Crystal Bader.

506. **RITA LEILA REDMAN,** daughter of David Franklin and
Charlotte Icle (Poynter) Redman, was born 27 Sep 1933 in
Chicago, IL. She married 25 Oct 1952 to Charles George
Novak. Rita's children (NOVAK) are: **(i)** Diane Sherill b
26 Apr 1960; **(ii)** Lawrence Charles b 27 Nov 1963.

507. **STEVEN RAY REDMAN,** son of Cecil Howard and Pauline
Naomi (Tucker) Redman, was born 6 Mar 1943 in Chicago, IL.
He married there on 14 Mar 1964 to Phyllis Irene Jennings,
born 31 Jan 1941 in Chicago, IL, daughter of Jack and Lor-
etta Mae (Suter) Jennings. The Jennings and the Redmans
were friends when they were newly married couples, but
the Jennings moved to Springfield, IL when Phyllis was
young. After Phyllis was out of school, she went to work
in Chicago and renewed her acquaintenceship with Steve.
Children of Steven Ray and Phyllis I. (Jennings) REDMAN
are: **(i)** Steven Phillip b 15 Feb 1965 Edmonton, Alberta,
Canada; **(ii)** Chantelle Elizabeth b 3 Sep 1968 Halifax,
Nova Scotia, Canada.

510. **GERALDINE MAY HOPP,** daughter of John Henry and Clara
Lue (Redman) Hopp, was born 23 Jul 1918 at Lincoln, Logan
Co., IL. She married there 13 Jan 1939 to Carl William
Heinzel, born 19 Apr 1913 at Lincoln, IL, son of William
Paul and Hannah Louise (Hoffert) Heinzel. (William P.
was born 31 Dec 1884 in Lincoln, IL; Hannah L. was born 6
Apr 1886 in Germany.) Children of Carl William and Geraldine May (Hopp) HEINZEL are:
  606. Donald Carl b 3 June 1942   *
  607. Sandra Kay b 30 Mar 1947   *
  608. Shirlee Jean b 9 Nov 1948   *

512. **DONALD EUGENE HOPP,** son of John Henry and Clara Lue
(Redman) Hopp, was born 24 Aug 1924 at Lincoln, Logan Co.,
IL. He married there 25 Nov 1953 to Anneta Madge Willmert,
born 22 Apr 1927 at Beason, Logan Co., IL, daughter of
Jacob and Cora Lee (Camper) Willmert. (Jacob's parents,
Louis Willmert and Christianna Frederika Groenwald, were

born in Germany in 1835 and 1840; Cora Lee's parents, Joseph Henry Camper and Sarah Elizabeth Wood, were born in
VA.) Donald E. was in the Maritime Service from July 1943
to March 1953. Children of Donald Eugene and Anneta Madge
(Willmert) HOPP, born in Lincoln, IL, are:
> **609. Phillip Michael** b 23 Aug 1947   *
> **610. Jon William** b 2 Mar 1954
> **611. Donna Lee** b 21 Sep 1956   *
> **612. Donald Eugene (Jr.)** b 7 May 1958

513. ROBERT DEAN HOPP, son of John Henry and Clara Lue
(Redman) Hopp, was born 25 Dec 1925 at Lincoln, Logan Co.,
IL. He married first 15 Aug 1948 at Lincoln, IL to Kathlene Mae Birk, born 21 Nov 1930, daughter of George C. and
Nellie C. (Stanley) Birk. Robert and Kathlene were divorced. Robert married second 14 June 1974 at Poway, CA
to Dorothy Louise Williams (no children by this marriage).
Bob was in the Air Force from Jan 1944 to May 1946. He
worked as a machinery maintenance man in Lincoln for a
few years, then went to Chula Vista, CA where he was employed by the Solar Aircraft Corp. as a turbine motor
specialist. He is now retired and living in Pennsylvania.
Children of Robert Dean and Kathlene Mae (Birk) HOPP are:
(i) Randal Birk b 12 Aug 1951 Lincoln, IL; **(ii)** Tina Marie
b 5 Nov 1957 Decatur, IL m1) Robert Stevens; div; m2) 10
Aug 1985 James Bassett at Escondido, CA; 1 ch from 1st
marriage, Jamie Rene.

514. JAMES WILBUR HOPP, son of John Henry and Clara Lue
(Redman) Hopp, was born 22 Apr 1935 at Lincoln, Logan Co.,
IL. He married 18 Dec 1966 at Greeley, CO to Diana Faye
Poe, born 24 Nov 1946 at Fort Morgan, CO, the daughter of
Pearl Allen and Fay Ola (Meyer) Poe. Jim and his wife run
a State Farm Insurance Co. office in Laramie, WY. He does
a lot of hunting and fishing in his spare time. Children
of James Wilbur and Diana Faye (Poe) HOPP, both born in
Greeley, Weld Co., CO, are: **(i)** Rockwell Darin b 14 Jan
1969; **(ii)** Heather Renae b 16 Feb 1971.

515. CHESTER EARL MUSSON, son of George Edward and Opal
May (Redman) Musson, was born 13 May 1916 in Bement, Piatt
Co., IL. He married 12 Nov 1938 in Cicero, IL to Jose-
phine Celia Albano, born 24 Apr 1920 in Cicero, Cook Co.,
IL. Chester's career was with the U. S. Army, rising to

the rank of Warrant Officer, and working in various mis-
sile programs. After retirement, Chester and Josie moved
to Arkansas but eventually returned to Bement, IL to be
near Chester's aging parents. Chester runs a lawn service
business in Bement. Children of Chester E. and Josephine
Celia (Albano) MUSSON, born in Chicago, IL, are:

613. Judith Ann b 31 Dec 1939   *

614. Cheryl Ann b 30 Jul 1955 m 24 Nov 1973 _____ Mucci-
anti; div. 1975 Chicago, IL.

615. Chester William b 10 Jan 1961

516. JUANITA MAY MUSSON, daughter of George Edward and
Opal May (Redman) Musson, was born 24 Jul 1917 in Bement,
Piatt Co., IL. She married 12 Dec 1934 in Chicago, IL to
Joseph Phillip Scara, born 28 Nov 1915 (under the name
"Scro") in Chicago, IL, son of Peter and Cira (Montelbano)
Scro, both natives of Palermo, Italy. Joseph P. was a
supervisor for the Campbell Soup Co. He died in May 1982
in Chicago, IL. Juanita is a talented handicrafter. One
of her pet projects is making doll houses and their fur-
nishings. Children of Joseph Phillip and Juanita May
(Musson) SCARA, born in Chicago, IL, are:

616. Joseph Phillip (Jr.) b 14 Jul 1936   *

617. James Robert b 10 June 1938   *

618. Donald William b 21 Apr 1945   *

517. GEORGE EDWARD MUSSON (JR.), son of George Edward and
Opal May (Redman) Musson, was born 7 Jan 1920 in Bement,
Piatt Co., IL. He married 10 Oct 1942 in Chicago, IL to
Donna L. Staples, born 8 May 1923 in Waukegan, IL, daugh-
ter of Donald L. and Mary A. (Pink) Staples. George E.,
Jr. was a pilot in the U. S. Air Force for 4 years and held
the rank of 1st Lt. at his discharge. He operated a truck-
ing business in Chicago. Children of George Edward and
Donna L. (Staples) MUSSON, born in Chicago, IL, are:

619. George Edward (III) b 30 Jul 1943 m 23 Jul 1965 to
Gertrude Drucker.

620. Richard Donald b 3 Sep 1947   *

621. Laura Gayle b 24 June 1953 m 30 May 1977 Thomas
Michael Wheeler.

622. Robert Alan b 27 Aug 1958

518. JERRY ROBERT MUSSON, son of George Edward and Opal
May (Redman) Musson, was born 19 Sep 1929 in Chicago, Cook

Co., IL. He married 3 Sep 1964 in Indiana to Virginia Nykiel, born 19 Jul 1940 in Berwyn, IL. Jerry and Virginia were divorced in 1971 at Chicago, IL. Jerry was in the Army from Oct 1945 until Jul 1959 when he retired. He served in Korea and Alaska and at Hanford, WA as a military policeman, holding the rank of sergeant at his discharge. Jerry is an accountant residing in Champaign, IL. Only child of Jerry Robert and Virginia (Nykiel) MUSSON is: **(i)** William Allen b 11 Oct 1965 Berwyn, Cook Co., IL.

519. **JIMMIE DALE MUSSON,** son of George Edward and Opal May (Redman) Musson, was born 4 Feb 1932 in Chicago, Cook Co., IL. He married 4 Sep 1954 in Corinth, MS to Barbara Joan Jacobsen, born 7 June 1937 in Cook Co., IL, daughter of Earl Nels and Bessie Virginia (Smith) Jacobsen. Jimmie was in the Army for 4 years, serving in Korea and Germany, a sergeant at his discharge. He is in the trucking business and lives in Bolingbrook, IL. Children of Jimmie Dale and Barbara Joan (Jacobsen) MUSSON, born in Chicago, IL, are:

623. **Debra Lynn** b 23 Jul 1955
624. **Jacqueline Joy** b 22 Sep 1956   *
625. **Jimmie Dale (Jr.)** b 15 Oct 1957
626. **Thomas Edward** b 30 Aug 1959
627. **Gary Robert** b 10 Aug 1960
628. **April Mae** b 22 Mar 1962

520. **PAUL ALLEN REDMAN,** son of Hubert Paul and Ethel Marie (Mellinger) Redman, was born 20 June 1923 at Ashkum, Iroquois Co., IL. He married 10 Nov 1945 at Waynetown, Montgomery Co., IN to Bette Louise Demorat, born 22 Dec 1926 at Crawfordsville, IN, daughter of Forrest Clarence and Gladys L. (Douglas) Demorat. Paul A. died 1 Mar 1977 at his home in Jamestown, IN, age 53 years. He was a truck driver; graduate of Jamestown, IN H.S.; member of the Jamestown Methodist Church and American Legion Post #395. He served in W.W.-II. Burial was in Old Union Cemetery in Jamestown, IN. Bette L. married 2nd L. Eugene Reynolds. Children of Paul A. and Bette L. (Demorat) REDMAN are:

629. **Phillip Allen** b 22 Jul 1946   *
630. **Mark Lowell** b 7 Mar 1949   *
631. **Julia Marie** b 31 Jan 1952   *
632. **James Forrest** b 20 Mar 1954   *
633. **Jane Gayle** b 12 May 1958   *

521. AIMEE MARIE REDMAN, daughter of Hubert Paul and Ethel Marie (Mellinger) Redman, was born 22 Jan 1925 at Cerro Gordo, Piatt Co., IL. She married 27 Apr 1944 in Jamestown, IN to Harold Richard ("Slim") Bligan, born 25 Dec 1921 in Pine Grove, Schuylkill Co., PA, son of James Visit and Mary Alice (Reinhart) Bligan. Children of Harold Richard and Aimee Marie (Redman) BLIGAN are:

    634. Roger Eugene b 20 Jan 1950   *
    635. Beverly Joan b 9 Apr 1952   *

523. JUANITA LOUISE REDMAN, daughter of Hubert Paul and Ethel Marie (Mellinger) Redman, was born 2 Sep 1931 at Roberts, Ford Co., IL. She married 14 Jul 1951 in Indianapolis, IN to Edward Leo Howe, born 14 Apr 1929 in Indianapolis, IN, son of Cornelius Edward and Marie (Flynn) Howe. Children of Edward Leo and Juanita Louise (Redman) HOWE, all born in Beech Grove, IN, are:

    636. Kathleen Marie b 8 Jan 1952   *
    637. Edward Leo (Jr.) b 19 May 1953   *
    638. Timothy Paul b 31 Oct 1954   *
    639. Cynthia Ann b 5 Dec 1955   *
    640. **Joan Elizabeth** b 27 Jul 1958 m 23 Jul 1977 Terry Dale Tillett div 1985;
    641. John Brian b 14 Jul 1959   *
    642. **Nancy Leigh** b 3 June 1961 m1) 23 Aug 1980 Michael William Sahm div 1982; m2) 28 June 1986 Anthony Dwayne Davis.
    643. **Jill Lynn** b 20 Oct 1963
    644. **David Wendell** b 4 Jan 1970

524. MARY ELLEN REDMAN, daughter of Hubert Paul and Ethel Marie (Mellinger) Redman, was born 31 Oct 1933 at Delavan, Tazewell Co., IL. She married 28 Jul 1951 at Brazil, Clay Co., IN to Donald Eugene Manning, born 9 Apr 1932 at Mace, Montgomery Co., IN, son of Russie Vencil and Mary Ivela (Royce) Manning, natives of Menifee and Fleming Cos., KY respectively. Children of Donald Eugene and Mary Ellen (Redman) MANNING (first 3 born in Marion Co., IN; last 2 born in Howard Co., IN) are:

    645. Brenda Joyce b 9 Mar 1952   *
    646. Terry Ann b 29 Mar 1953   *
    647. Russell Gene b 13 Mar 1954   *
    648. Pamela Sue b 10 Jul 1957   *
    649. **Keith Alan** b 8 Dec 1960

525. RUBY ETHEL REDMAN, daughter of Hubert Paul and Ethel Marie (Mellinger) Redman, was born 19 Jan 1937 at Jamestown, Boone Co., IN. She married 28 Jan 1953 at Speedway, Marion Co., IN to David Howard Little, born 20 Oct 1934 at Rockville, Parke Co., IN, son of Robert David and Mildred Louise (Runyan) Little. Ruby and David were divorced in 1984. Ruby married second 31 Dec 1985 at Okeechobee, FL to Carl Willan Hankins. Children of David Howard and Ruby Ethel (Redman) LITTLE, born in Indianapolis, IN, are:

  650. Bruce Howard b 18 Sep 1953   *
  651. Robert David b 19 Feb 1955 m 7 Mar 1986 Brenda Sue Wilson at Dallas, TX.
  652. Paul David b 28 May 1960

526. FRANKLIN DAVID REDMAN, son of Hubert Paul and Ethel Marie (Mellinger) Redman, was born 29 Jul 1942 at Lebanon, Boone Co., IN. He married 31 Dec 1960 at Indianapolis, IN to Mary Alice Mason, born 23 Nov 1942 at Charleston, Kanawha Co., WVA, daughter of Arnold McCoy and Lillian Imogene (Lloyd) Mason. David and Mary Alice were divorced in 1971. Children of Franklin David and Mary Alice (Mason) REDMAN are: **(i)** Debra Lee b 8 Feb 1962 Biloxi, Harrison Co., MS; **(ii)** Dana Marie b 21 May 1964 Fukuoka, Japan; **(iii)** Lisa Diana b 23 May 1965 Tachikawa, Japan; **(iv)** D'Andrea Lynn b 23 Apr 1967 Indianapolis, IN.

527. DENNIS WAYNE REDMAN, son of Hubert Paul and Martha Belle (Kinkead) Redman, was born 23 Mar 1953 at Crawfordsville, Montgomery Co., IN. He married first 19 Jul 1971 to Patricia Anne McCandless, born 22 Oct 1952 at Crawfordsville, IN, daughter of Bud Herman and Earlina Margaret (Wilson) McCandless. Dennis and Patricia were divorced in 1977. He married second 4 Jul 1979 at New Ross, Montgomery Co., IN to Rosalie Diane Howard, born 31 Aug 1954 at Crawfordsville, IN, daughter of Rex Lavone and Rosemary (Rhoads) Howard. Children of Dennis Wayne REDMAN (1st by 1st mar; 2nd by 2nd mar) are: **(i)** Michelle Ann b 1 Oct 1972 Crawfordsville, IN; **(ii)** Paul Allen b 13 Jan 1982 Lafayette, IN.

528. KEITH REDMAN JORDAN, son of James Roy and Mabel Ruth (Redman) Jordan, was born 22 Aug 1926 at Decatur, Macon Co., IL. He married first 3 Aug 1951 at Houston, TX to Dorothy Nell (Temple) Littlejohn, born 21 May 1926 at

Blox, TX, daughter of John David and Sarah Marie (Hudson) Temple. (Dorothy had a son, Joseph Littlejohn, Jr., from a previous marriage.) Keith and Dorothy were divorced in 1968. Keith married second 24 Dec 1968 at Elkton, Cecil Co., MD to Gloria Elaine Miller, born 23 Jul 1939 at South Canaan, Wayne Co., PA, daughter of Harvey Elmer and Antoinette (Hanas) Miller (no children by this marriage).

Keith enlisted in the Navy shortly before the end of W.W.-II, serving on an L.S.T. mainly involved in transporting prisoners of war between Japan, China and Korea. He is a graduate of the University of Illinois with a B.S. in Chemistry. For 6 years he worked for Stauffer Chemical Co. in Freeport, TX, then joined the J. T. Baker Chemical Co., Phillipsburg, NJ, in 1956 as Production Supervisor. He was promoted to Assistant Manager H & F in 1966, and to Packaging Manager in 1968. In 1970, he was promoted to Manager of Production and Inventory Control. A cerebral aneurysm in 1980 forced his early retirement. Keith also suffers from a type of arthritis called ankylosing spondylitis (Marie-Strumpell disease), a painful and inflammatory disease of the spine, causing eventual rigidity and curvature if not treated in its early stages. The cause is unknown, but hereditary predisposition involving genetic marker B-27 which can be detected by a simple blood test, is known to play a major role. Keith and his second wife live in Mountain Home, AR.

Children of Keith Redman and Dorothy Nell (Temple) JORDAN are:
   653. Janice Anita b 25 Sep 1952   *
   654. Jeri Lynn b 10 Jul 1954   *

529. SHIRLEE ANN JORDAN, daughter of James Roy and Mabel Ruth (Redman) Jordan, was born 10 Sep 1929 at Lincoln, Logan Co., IL. She is a 1948 graduate of William Woods College, Fulton, MO, with an Associate in Arts degree. She married first 10 Sep 1948 in Fulton, MO to Arthur Wellington ("Art") Greene, Jr., born 29 Nov 1925 at Richmond, VA, son of Arthur Wellington and Madeline (Fitzgerald-Blake) Greene. (Madeline's father, Robert Fitzgerald, deserted from the Army and changed the family name to Blake to prevent detection by the authorities.) Art served in the Air Force from 1943 to 1945 and is a graduate of Westminster College for Men in Fulton, MO. He worked in sales until his retirement. Shirlee and Art were divorced in 1968 in Houston. Shirlee m2) 31 May 1968 David McMimm Harris, born 9 May 1940 in Houston, son of Edwin McMimm & Harriet Elizabeth (Calvert) Harris. David is a Research Specialist for Exxon Production Research in Houston, TX.

Children of Arthur Wellington and Shirlee Ann (Jordan) GREENE are: **(i)** Deborah Kay b 19 Nov 1951 Monticello, IL m 28 Apr 1979 Franklin Wayne ("Robert") Filla b 11 May 1954 Hallettsville, TX s/o Alfred Frank & Jessie Joyce (Judd) Filla; 1 dau Lexey Maree b 24 Jan 1987 Houston, TX; **(ii)** Madeline Dale b 26 Oct 1953 Houston, TX m1) 29 Sep 1972 James Warren Hanssard div 1973; m2) 29 Jul 1974 James Harold Mills; **(iii)** Stephen Patrick b 20 Aug 1958 Houston, TX m1) 17 Nov 1984 Dawn Marie Frazier (div 1986); m2) 22 Oct 1987 Leslie Giesen; **(iv)** Mark Christian b 12 Feb 1960 Houston, TX unmar 1987.

Child of David McMimm and Shirlee Ann (Jordan) HARRIS is: **(v)** Christopher David b 22 May 1970 Houston, TX.

530. MARILYN RUTH JORDAN, daughter of James Roy and Mabel Ruth (Redman) Jordan, was born 23 May 1933 at Milmine, Piatt Co., IL. She is a 1950 graduate of William Woods College in Fulton, MO with an Associate in Arts degree, majoring in Radio-Journalism. She married Donald William Smith at Houston, TX in 1950 (divorced 1951; no children). She married second 31 Oct 1953 at Hernando, MS to John Warren ("Jack") Sundene, born 12 Jul 1932 at Oak Park, IL, son of John and Agnes Sophia (Jorgensen) Sundene. Jack graduated in Jan 1955 from the University of Illinois with a degree in Architecture. He was in the Army Corps of Engineers for 2 years, stationed at Ft. Belvoir, VA, then Karlsruhe, Germany; discharged as 1st/Lt. Marilyn was at WDWS radio station, Champaign, IL (chief copywriter) from Nov 1953 until leaving in Oct 1955 to join her husband in Germany. Marilyn and Jack were divorced in 1969 in DuPage, IL. (Jack owned and operated Sundene Construction Co. in Glen Ellyn, IL until his death 21 June 1982 in Glen Ellyn, IL, burial there in Forest Hill Cemetery.) Marilyn married third 9 May 1969 in Wheaton, IL to Jack Bruce Solari, born 8 Nov 1924 at Sonora, Tuolumne Co., CA, son of John Baptiste and Amy Eudora (Jones) Solari. He was in the Army during W.W.-II (Pacific zone); and was a 30-year employee in sales with Van Waters & Rogers, promoted in 1978 to V.P. and manager of Cerritos, CA branch office, retiring in 1985. (No children by this marriage.)

Children of John Warren and Marilyn Ruth (Jordan) SUNDENE (1st born in Germany, rest in Chicago, IL) are:
655. Dawn Michelle b 25 Aug 1956   *
656. Jana Lynn b 21 Mar 1958; grad Wheaton College (IL) & N.I.U., Dekalb, IL (M.A.); teacher; unmar 1987.
657. Dana Anne b 27 Mar 1959   *

531. WILLIAM EDWARD PEADRO, son of Bryan Franklin and Lela Blanche (Jones) Peadro, was born 21 June 1924 in Whitely Twp., Moultrie Co., IL near Windsor. He married 18 Apr 1948 at the 1st Christian Church in Sullivan, IL to Pearl Leona Hawkins, born 14 Dec 1922 at Newman, Douglas Co., IL, daughter of Frank Wilson and Sarah Elizabeth (Walton) Hawkins. Children of William Edward and Pearl Leona (Hawkins) PEADRO, born at Mattoon, Coles Co., IL, are:
658. **Janice Lynn** b 12 Mar 1949 unmar 1986.
659. Gary Edward b 10 Dec 1951   *
660. Dennis Leon b 12 Jul 1953   *
661. Lora Leona b 21 Jul 1961   *

532. DALLAS FRANKLIN PEADRO, son of Bryan Franklin and Lela Blanche (Jones) Peadro, was born 18 Sep 1926 at Gays, Moultrie Co., IL. He married 20 Nov 1949 at Mattoon, IL to Elsie Irene Smith, born 11 Jul 1925 at Windsor, Shelby Co., IL, daughter of Rolla Vance and Edna Hazel (Carroll) Smith. Children of Dallas Franklin and Elsie Irene (Smith) PEADRO, born at Mattoon, IL, are:
662. Ronald Dallas b 14 May 1954   *
663. **Randall Vance** b 25 May 1958

533. DAVADIA LELA PEADRO, daughter of Bryan Franklin and Lela Blanche (Jones) Peadro, was born 6 Apr 1930 in Whitely Twp., Moultrie Co., IL. She married 27 Aug 1950 at St. Paul Lutheran Church, Strasburg, Shelby Co., IL to Leland Curtis Rincker, born 21 Sep 1924 at Strasburg, IL, son of Edwin A. and Rosetta Dorothea (Mueller) Rincker. Children of Leland Curtis and Davadia Lela (Peadro) RINCKER, born at Shelbyville, IL, are:
664. Eric Lee b 8 June 1951   *
665. Karlie Davadia b 2 Nov 1953   *
666. Curtis Dee b 1 June 1955   *
667. Lyndal Gay b 16 Oct 1956   *
668. **Irl Daryl** b 30 May 1958 m 24 Aug 1980 Eunice Anne Mason at Coldwater, Ontario, Canada.

535. BILLY JOE JONES, son of Lucian Henry and Vera Dorthula (Scoles) Jones, was born 4 Jan 1929 at Gays, Shelby Co., IL. He married 6 June 1953 in Chicago, IL to Juanita Willard. Only known child of Billy Joe and Juanita (Willard) JONES is: **(i)** Tommy Joe b 28 Apr 1954.

536. VERA LOUISE JONES, daughter of Lucian Henry and Vera Dorthula (Scoles) Jones, was born 29 Dec 1930 at Neoga, Cumberland Co., IL. She married 7 Jan 1950 to David James Beals. Children of David James and Vera Louise (Jones) BEALS are: **(i)** Barbara Jeannine b 18 Aug 1950 m 12 June 1970 Eugene Mark; ch Tiffany Rainee b 10 Oct 1971, Cecil Eugene b 12 Jul 1974; **(ii)** Marie Louise b 17 Dec 1952 m 10 Jan 1970 Anthony Walton; ch Tina Marie b 29 Jul 1970, Paul David b 21 Jul 1975; **(iii)** James Raymond b 27 Mar 1954 m 30 Dec 1978 Rudi Marila Dogoli; **(iv)** Teri Leigh b 24 Mar 1956 m 22 Mar 1975 Leonard Rudolph Renfroe; ch Russell Lee b 28 Oct 1975, Leonard Rudolph b 31 Dec 1976, Kathy Elaine b 26 Aug 1978; **(v)** Jeffrey Lucian b 9 Mar 1960.

537. ROBERT LUCIAN JONES, son of Lucian Henry and Vera Dorthula (Scoles) Jones, was born 17 Aug 1933 at Windsor, Shelby Co., IL. He married 1953 in KS to Carolyn Tabbert. Children of Robert Lucian and Carolyn (Tabbert) JONES are: **(i)** Roberta Carol b 8 Jan 1954 m Christopher Hoxie; **(ii)** Jacqueline June b 20 Jan 1956 m William Henry Wisham; ch William Henry, Jr. b Dec 1974, Shannon Michelle b 19 Jul 1978; **(iii)** Peggy Sue b 24 Jul 1957 m John Libby; ch Jason Robert b 12 Sep 1978.

538. ANITA LUCILE JONES, daughter of Lucian Henry and Vera Dorthula (Scoles) Jones, was born 3 Aug 1935 at Windsor, Shelby Co., IL. She married 7 Dec 1953 at Neoga, Cumberland Co., IL to William Walter Thompson. Children of William Walter and Anita Lucile (Jones) THOMPSON are: **(i)** William Kent b 27 Dec 1955 m 12 June 1976 Charlotte Susan Rigg; ch Jonathan Thomas b 20 Mar 1977, Bridgette Christine b 23 Nov 1978; **(ii)** James Andrew b 28 June 1957; **(iii)** Steven Lynn b 9 Apr 1959; **(iv)** Susan Leigh b 26 Apr 1964.

539. CHARLES IRA JONES, son of Lucian Henry and Vera Dorthula (Scoles) Jones, was born 5 Aug 1937 at Flint, Genesee Co., MI. He married 20 Oct 1956 Joyce Smith. Children of Charles Ira and Joyce (Smith) JONES are: **(i)** Gary Wayne b 7 Apr 1958 m Sheila Ard; ch Phillip Wayne b 11 Sep 1979; **(ii)** Sheryl Lynn b 2 June 1959; **(iii)** Lisa Lavone b 4 Nov 1967.

540. **BARBRA JANE MITCHELL,** daughter of Eugene Franklin and Ethel Evelyn (Triplett) Mitchell, was born 28 June 1935 at Greenville, Washington Co., MS. She married on 2 June 1957 at Starkville, Oktibbeha Co., MS to George Wendell Goodnite, born 25 Jul 1930 at Sardis, Panola Co., MS, son of John Felix and Bertha Estelle (Marshall) Goodnite. Children of George Wendell and Barbra Jane (Mitchell) GOODNITE, born at Starkville, MS, are: **(i)** Barbra Gay b 12 Mar 1960; **(ii)** George Mitchell b 8 Jan 1965.

542. **EVELYN ANN MITCHELL,** daughter of Eugene Franklin and Ethel Evelyn (Triplett) Mitchell, was born 9 Feb 1944 at Greenville, Washington Co., MS. She married first 14 Jan 1967 Harold McLaurin Crosby. They were divorced in 1970 (no children). She married second 3 Nov 1973 at Memphis, Shelby Co., TN to Boyd Terrel Schuck, born 8 Apr 1948 at Marion, Grant Co., IN, son of Boyd Lavon and Betty Alleen (Davis) Schuck. Only child of Boyd Terrel and Evelyn Ann (Mitchell) SCHUCK is: **(i)** Justin Mitchell b 8 Oct 1977 at Paragould, Greene Co., AR.

543. **JOHN MIKUL MITCHELL,** son of Harry Victor and Anna Janina (Mikulska) Mitchell, was born 31 May 1935 at Tuscaloosa, AL. He married there on 27 June 1958 to Virginia Sherwood Tucker, born 21 Oct 1936 at Mansfield, Richland Co., OH, daughter of Warren Robert and Kathryn (Sherwood) Tucker. John Mikul is a dentist in Tuscaloosa. Children of John Mikul and Virginia Sherwood (Tucker) Mitchell (last 3 born at Tuscaloosa, AL) are:
  669. John Mikul (Jr.) b 16 Mar 1960   *
  670. Steven Lee b 19 Jul 1961   *
  671. **Phillip Wayne** b 15 Oct 1963 m 18 Dec 1982 Alison Greenwood at Tuscaloosa, AL.
  672. **Jeffrey Scott** b 21 Feb 1965
  673. **Robert Mark** b 11 Sep 1969

544. **MARY ANNE MITCHELL,** daughter of Harry Victor and Anna Janina (Mikulska) Mitchell, was born 15 Oct 1940 at Tuscaloosa, AL. She married there 11 Jul 1959 to Henry

Boone Cummings, born 26 Nov 1938 at Tuscaloosa, AL, son of Oswill McGee and Katherine Elizabeth (Boone) Cummings, Jr. Children of Henry B. and Mary A. (Mitchell) CUMMINGS, born at Tuscaloosa, AL, are: **(i)** Henry Boone, Jr. b 11 June 1961 m 26 Apr 1986 Rena June Pearson in Tuscaloosa; **(ii)** Christopher Allen b 24 Apr 1962; **(iii)** Elizabeth Anne b 26 Oct 1966.

545. **DAVID LEE MITCHELL,** son of Harry Victor and Anna Janina (Mikulska) Mitchell, was born 23 Sep 1943 at Tuscaloosa, AL. He married there 3 Feb 1962 to Louise Gwen Veronica Hodo, born 13 Aug 1944 at Tuscaloosa, AL, daughter of Gerald Manly and Georgia May (Allen) Hodo. David Lee died 28 Mar 1976 at Tuscaloosa, AL. He was buried there at Tuscaloosa Memorial Park. Louise married second Dr. Richard D. Reynolds. Children of David Lee and Louise Gwen Veronica (Hodo) Mitchell, born at Tuscaloosa, are:
  674. David Lee (Jr.) b 15 Sep 1962   *
  675. **Victor Gerald** b 3 Jul 1968

546. **FRANCES ELAINE MITCHELL,** daughter of Harry Victor and Anna Janina (Mikulska) Mitchell, was born 13 Nov 1948 at Tuscaloosa, AL. She married there 15 Nov 1968 at Holy Spirit Catholic Church to Gary Edward Hamner, born 25 Jan 1945 at Tuscaloosa, AL, son of Edward Cullen and Notie Evelyn (Swindal) Hamner. Only child of Gary Edward and Frances Elaine (Mitchell) HAMNER is: **(i)** Chad Edward b 8 June 1973 at Tuscaloosa, AL.

547. **PENELOPE DAPHNA (PENNY) ESTESS,** daughter of Newell Smith and Daphna Irene (Mitchell) Estess, was born 23 Jan 1943 at Canton, Madison Co., MS. She married there 6 May 1967 to Leslie Franklin ("Frank") Adams, born 28 Nov 1936 at Charleston, MS, son of Herbert Leslie and Berta Mae (Roberson) Adams. Children of Leslie Franklin and Penelope Daphna (Estess) ADAMS, all born at Huntsville, Madison Co., MS, are: **(i)** Gregory Franklin b 10 June 1968; **(ii)** Sharon Denise b 6 Feb 1972; **(iii)** Debora Ann b 2 Oct 1973.

548. **NEWELL SMITH (SAM) ESTESS, JR.,** son of Newell Smith and Daphna Irene (Mitchell) Estess, Sr., was born 25 Sep 1950 at Canton, Madison Co., MS. He married first June Faye Thrash (they were divorced). He married second on

24 May 1975 in Dallas Co., TX to Kay Thompson, born 6 Nov 1950 at Corsicana, Navarro Co., TX, daughter of Charles Alton and Lucy Geraldine (Smith) Thompson. (Kay was previously married to and divorced from David Clingan. Neither Kay nor Sam had children from their first marriages.) Sam and Kay were divorced in Dallas Co., TX on 1 Oct 1984. They were remarried (to each other) in Dallas Co., TX on 24 Feb 1986.

Children of Newell Smith and Kay (Thompson) ESTESS, Jr., all born in Dallas, TX, are: **(i)** Charise b 10 Aug 1979; **(ii)** Lindsay b 16 May 1983; **(iii)** Newell Smith III ("Trace") b 9 Jan 1987.

550. **RUSSELL GLEN MITCHELL, JR.,** son of Russell Glen and Jean (Chiles) Mitchell, Sr., was born 10 Sep 1946 at Greenville, Washington Co., MS. He married Wyona Smith. Children, born at Dayton, Montgomery Co., OH, are:
676. **Dawn**
677. **Kelly**

551. **SHARON MITCHELL,** daughter of Russell Glen and Jean (Chiles) Mitchell, Sr., was born 14 Feb 1950 at Yazoo City and Co., MS. She married James Long. Known child of James and Sharon (Mitchell) LONG, born at Dayton, Montgomery Co., OH, is: **(i)** Jodi (dau).

552. **DUANE OREN NEVILLE,** son of Oren Presley and Catherine Tena (Brodin) Neville, was born 24 June 1938 at Des Plaines, Cook Co., IL. He married 31 Dec 1966 to Mary Ann Drewek, born 11 Oct 1936 at Milwaukee, WI, daughter of Thomas and Mary (Malgewski) Drewek. Children of Duane Oren and Mary Ann (Drewek) NEVILLE, born at Milwaukee, WI, are: **(i)** Christopher Calvin b 11 Jan 1970; **(ii)** Thomas Oren b 1 Aug 1974.

553. **GAIL RUTH LINDGREN,** daughter of Frank Victor and Geneva Ruth (Neville) Lindgren, was born 5 Sep 1944 at Evergreen Park, Cook Co., IL. She married 6 Jul 1968 at Chicago, IL to James William Powell, Jr., born 12 Mar 1944 at Chicago, IL, son of James William and Mary Elizabeth (Butkovich) Powell, Sr. Children of James William and Gail Ruth (Lindgren) POWELL, born at Omaha, Douglas Co., NE, are: **(i)** James William III b 8 Mar 1973; **(ii)** Kristin Ruth b 23 May 1975.

554. KENNETH FRANK LINDGREN, son of Frank Victor and Geneva Ruth (Neville) Lindgren, was born 11 June 1946 at Evergreen Park, Cook Co., IL. He married 17 Aug 1970 at Chicago, IL to Diane Elaine Lazar, born 9 May 1943 at Chicago, IL, daughter of John Joseph and Maryanna Eva (Gill) Lazar. Children of Kenneth Frank and Diane Elaine (Lazar) LINDGREN, born at Park Ridge, IL, are: **(i)** Mary Geneva b 11 Jul 1977; **(ii)** Kenneth Frank, Jr. b 19 May 1979.

555. DAVID EDMUND MEARS, son of Edmund Walter and Harriette Lorraine (Neville) Mears, was born 22 Dec 1942 at Chicago, IL. He married 25 Jan 1969 Darlene Hind. They live in Crown Point, IN. Child of David Edmund and Darlene (Hind) MEARS is: **(i)** Dax Evan b 25 Dec 1980.

556. CAROL ANN MEARS, daughter of Edmund Walter and Harriett Lorraine (Neville) Mears, was born 20 Feb 1949 at Evanston, IL. She married 31 Jul 1976 Walter Woron. They live in Marietta, GA. Child of Walter and Carol Ann (Mears) WORON is: **(i)** Christopher Mitchell b 15 June 1983 at Marietta, GA.

557. DIANNE JOYCE RUSCH, daughter of Henry and Marilyn (Mitchell) Rusch, was born 28 Jan 1948 at Hinsdale, DuPage Co., IL. She married 27 June 1970 Dallas, TX to William C. White III, born 29 Jan 1948 at Orange, Orange Co., TX, son of William C. and Laura Louise (Skinner) White, Jr. Children of William C. and Dianne Joyce (Rusch) WHITE III (born at Dallas, TX) are: **(i)** Tracy Lynn b 3 Mar 1973; **(ii)** William Brian b 29 Sep 1976.

558. GARY RALPH RUSCH, son of Henry and Marilyn (Mitchell) Rusch, was born 30 Dec 1952 at Elmurst, DuPage Co., IL. He married first 27 Nov 1971 to Barbara Ramler. They were divorced (no children). Gary married second 6 Sep 1980 at Messiah Lutheran Church in Richardson, TX to Mary Margaret Baugh, born 26 June 1957 at Dallas, TX, daughter of John Edward and Kathleen Mary (Bittel) Baugh. (Kathleen Mary Bittel's birth certificate says Elizabeth Jane. This was changed on her certificate of baptism to Kathleen Mary.) Gary and Mary Margaret live in Garland, TX. Children of Gary Ralph and Mary Margaret (Baugh) RUSCH, born in Baylor Hospital, Dallas, TX, are: **(i)** Michael Jordan b 2 Sep 1981; **(ii)** Michelle Dianne b 29 Jan 1985.

Tenth Generation

559. PATRICIA LYNN WALLACE, daughter of Robert Lee and Freda Bernell (Mitchell) Wallace, was born 24 May 1953 at Elmhurst, DuPage Co., IL. She married there 7 June 1975 to Eric Fred Fess, born 12 Jan 1953 at Highland Park, Lake Co., IL, son of Frederick Edwin and Julia Lorraine (Moulton) Fess. Child of Eric Fred and Patricia Lynn (Wallace) FESS is: **(i)** Andrew Wallace b 25 Jul 1979 Hinsdale, IL.

562. KENNETH LEE ANDERSON, son of Jack Bernhard and Verneva (Mitchell) Anderson, was born 23 Jul 1950 at New Orleans, Orleans Co., LA. He married 9 Mar 1979 at Seminole, Pinellas Co., FL to Donna Kaye Manning, born 14 June 1956 at Waycross, Ware Co., GA, daughter of John Francis and Dorothy Anne (Ruark) Manning. Children of Kenneth Lee and Donna Kaye (Manning) ANDERSON, born at St. Petersburg, Pinellas Co., FL, are: **(i)** Lauren Francis b 14 Sep 1979; **(ii)** Cara Lee b 14 May 1981.

563. CHERYL ELAINE LUSTIG, daughter of Arthur Edward and Helen Mayonne (Mitchell) Lustig, was born 17 Aug 1950 at Effingham, Effingham Co., IL. She married 15 Mar 1969 at Shumway, Effingham Co., IL to Donald Eugene Tipsword, born 19 Dec 1950 at Champaign, IL, son of Wayne Eugene and Mary Arlene (Rhodes) Tipsword. Cheryl and Donald were divorced in 1978. Children of Donald Eugene and Cheryl Elaine (Lustig) TIPSWORD are: **(i)** Troy James b 25 Sep 1969 Effingham, IL; **(ii)** Jennifer Ann b 14 Mar 1974 Arlington Heights, Cook Co., IL.

564. DONNA RAE LUSTIG, daughter of Arthur Edward and Helen Mayonne (Mitchell) Lustig, was born 1 Mar 1954 at Effingham, Effingham Co., IL. She married there 25 May 1974 to Wood Loy Stortzum, born 16 Jul 1954 at Effingham, IL, son of Herbert Wayne and Mineana (Loy) Stortzum. Children of Wood Loy and Donna Rae (Lustig) STORTZUM, born at Mattoon, Coles Co., IL, are: **(i)** Christopher Damian b 8 June 1976; **(ii)** Jamia Rae (dau) b 11 June 1977.

565. CALVIN WAYNE MITCHELL, son of Myron Calvin and Patricia Joan (Harris) Mitchell, was born 3 Sep 1953 at Paducah, McCracken Co., KY. He married 18 Jan 1975 at Effingham Co., IL to Mary Beth Ludwig, born 13 Nov 1956 at Effingham, IL, daughter of Harry and Mildred (Gruel) Ludwig, both natives of Effingham Co. Children of Calvin

Wayne and Mary Beth (Ludwig) Mitchell (1st b in Effingham Co., IL, second at Springfield, IL) are:
  678. **Melissa Ann** b 8 Apr 1977
  679. **Timothy Wayne** b 25 Aug 1981

566. **SHARON ELAINE MITCHELL**, daughter of Myron Calvin and Patricia Joan (Harris) Mitchell, was born 21 Aug 1955 at Effingham, Effingham Co., IL. She married there 3 Jul 1977 to Steven Kent Tarr, born 21 Jan 1954 in Jasper Co., IL, son of Arlin and Lanore (Matson) Tarr of Jasper Co. Children of Steven Kent and Sharon Elaine (Mitchell) TARR are: **(i)** Joshua Arlin b 4 Jan 1980 Cadillac, MI; **(ii)** Ashley Rebecca b 7 Aug 1983 Greenville, PA.

572. **GINA LYNN WOODY**, daughter of Ross Eugene and Marthagene (Mitchell) Woody, was born 20 Jul 1958 at Effingham, Effingham Co., IL. She married 7 Jul 1978 at Salt Lake City, Utah to Scott David Baird, born 16 Sep 1957 at Kalamazoo, MI, son of Charles William and Nova Jean (Hurt) Baird. Gina and Scott live in Aurora, CO. Children of Scott David and Gina Lynn (Woody) BAIRD are: **(i)** Christiana b 17 Oct 1980 Provo, UT; **(ii)** Andrew Scott b 29 Apr 1982 Provo, UT; **(iii)** Megan Marguerite b 8 Aug 1986 Wheat Ridge, CO.

573. **SUSAN SHAWN WOODY**, daughter of Ross Eugene and Marthagene (Mitchell) Woody, was born 5 Mar 1961 at Hannibal, MO. She married 15 Jan 1980 at Manti, UT to Robert Wayne Zenk, born 5 Apr 1957 at Walnut Creek, CA, son of William Robert and Carla (Polson) Zenk. Susan and Robert live in Liberty, MO. Children of Robert Wayne and Susan Shawn (Woody) ZENK are: **(i)** Robert Wayne II b 6 Oct 1982 Provo, UT; **(ii)** William Ross b 13 Jan 1985 No. Kansas City, MO.

576. **CHANDLER EARL MITCHELL**, son of Chandler Orville and Leone (Edwards) Mitchell, was born 22 Nov 1926 in Ross Twp., Edgar Co., IL. He served in W.W.-II. He married 26 Jan 1949 at Danville, IL to Anna Maria Bogner, born 19 May 1925 at Munich, Germany, daughter of Johann and Theresia (Baumer) Bogner. Children of Chandler Earl and Anna Maria (Bogner) Mitchell (b Danville, IL - hospital) are:
  680. **David Chandler** b 24 Nov 1951   *
  681. **Rebecca Ann** b 7 Feb 1953   *
  682. **Thomas Earl** b 8 Jan 1956   *

577. ELEANOR MARICA MITCHELL, daughter of Chandler Orville and Leone (Edwards) Mitchell, was born 23 May 1928 in Ross Twp., Edgar Co., IL. She married 24 Dec 1949 at Charleston, Coles Co., IL to James Monroe Taylor, born 23 Feb 1928 at Limedale, Putnam Co., IN, son of Roy John and Zelda B. (Diel) Taylor, natives of Putnam Co. Eleanor and James live in Indianapolis, IN where she teaches handicapped children. Children of James Monroe and Eleanor Marica (Mitchell) TAYLOR (born Danville, IL, Wabash, IN and Indianapolis, IN respectively) are:

  683. Michael James b 25 Nov 1951   *****

  684. Jane Marie b 2 Nov 1955 m 29 Aug 1981 Christopher Richard Holmes at Connersville, IN; no ch.

  685. Janet Kay b 8 Oct 1964

578. JAMES EDWARD MITCHELL, son of Chandler Orville and Leone (Edwards) Mitchell, was born 19 Feb 1930 in Ross Twp., Edgar Co., IL. He married there at Chrisman 17 Nov 1950 to Martha Jane Parks, born 23 Dec 1929 at Chrisman, Edgar Co., IL, daughter of John Kelly and Cecile Elizabeth (Rhyan) Parks. Children of James Edward and Martha Jane (Parks) Mitchell (1st born at Lompoc, CA, rest in Edgar Co., IL) are:

  686. Richard Allen b 8 Apr 1952   *****

  687. Robert Lee b 21 Jul 1953 m 1 May 1982 Debra Lynn Coan at Chrisman, IL; div; no ch.

  688. Donald Joe b 29 Mar 1956   *****

  689. Joanne Kay b 26 Apr 1957   *****

  690. **Gary Ray** b 13 Jul 1958 m 6 Sep 1980 Priscilla Ann Eyer at Gibson City, IL (expecting their 1st child in May or June 1987).

579. JOHN RICHARD MITCHELL, son of Chandler Orville and Leone (Edwards) Mitchell, was born 22 Dec 1932 in Ross Twp., Edgar Co., IL. He married there at Chrisman 2 Feb 1951 to Barbara Ann Martin, born 9 Nov 1934 at Marshall, Clark Co., IL, daughter of William Franklin and Esther Ethel (Nichols) Martin. Barbara Ann died 3 May 1980 in Paris Community Hospital, Edgar Co., IL, and was buried on 5 May in Hoult Cemetery near Chrisman, Edgar Co., IL. Children of John Richard and Barbara Ann (Martin) Mitchell (1st b in GA, 2nd in Edgar Co., IL) are:

  691. John William ("Bill") b 28 Jan 1952   *****

  692. Deborah Ann b 3 Oct 1953   *****

580. **MELODY HECHE,** daughter of Paul Ernest and Carolyn Mitchell (Kile) Heche, was born 13 Oct 1946. She married 12 Oct 1968 at Skokie, Cook Co., IL to Ronald Charles Barnes, born 20 June 1942 at Chicago, IL, son of Eugene Elmo and Irene (Soltesy) Barnes. Melody and Ron live in Jefferson City, MO. Children of Ronald Charles and Melody (Heche) BARNES are: **(i)** Amanda Kyle b 28 Jul 1972 Broadview, Cook Co., IL; **(ii)** Adam Kyle b 1 Sep 1975 Rolla, MO; **(iii)** Andrew Kyle b 15 Mar 1980 Rolla, MO.

581. **PAULETTE HECHE,** daughter of Paul Ernest and Carolyn Mitchell (Kile) Heche, was born 19 Aug 1948. She married 9 Aug 1969 at Skokie, Cook Co., IL to Gary Allan Frank, born 9 Nov 1943 at Chicago, IL, son of Melvin L. and Clare (Leske) Frank. Gary and Paulette were divorced in 1979. Paulette married second 18 Apr 1981 to John W. Proffitt, born 21 Oct 1944 at Carrier's Mills, IL, son of Charles and Wanda (McDermott) Proffitt. (No children by this marriage.) Children of Gary Allan and Paulette (Heche) FRANK, born at Bolingbrook, IL, are: **(i)** Jason Kile b 16 Feb 1970; **(ii)** Angela Mitchell b 25 Sep 1973.

584.   DEBORAH LYNN HOOKER, daughter of Jerry Allen and Mary Jane (Parker) Hooker, was born 27 Mar 1954 at Mattoon in Coles Co., IL. She married 18 June 1972 at the 1st Baptist Church in Charleston, IL to Larry Gene Marshall, born 10 Jul 1952 at Mattoon, IL, son of Delmar Edwin and Edna Bernice (Dixon) Marshall. Deborah's children (MARSHALL), all born at Mattoon, IL, are: **(i)** Mathew David b 3 Apr 1973; **(ii)** Melisa Dawn b 4 June 1974; **(iii)** Andrew Dale and **(iv)** Aaron Daniel, twins, b 25 Sep 1975.

585.   JACALYNN ANN HOOKER, daughter of Jerry Allen and Mary Jane (Parker) Hooker, was born 17 Feb 1955 at Mattoon in Coles Co., IL. She married first 4 May 1973 at the 1st Baptist Church, Charleston, IL to Charles Jeffrey Shafer, born 10 Jan 1955, son of Charles C. and Lila Mae (Newby) Shafer. Jacalynn and Charles were divorced in 1974.   Jacalynn married second 11 Aug 1978 John H. Nance (divorced 1980; no children). Jacalynn's child from her 1st marriage (SHAFER) is: **(i)** Jonathon Issaac Allen b 6 May 1973 at Mattoon, Coles Co., IL.

587.   BRADLEY CARL HOOKER, son of Jerry Allen and Mary Jane (Parker) Hooker, was born 4 Oct 1957 at Mattoon, Coles Co., IL.   He married first 26 Aug 1977 in Denver, CO to Alice Louise Porter. They were divorced and Bradley married second 20 Jul 1986 at the 1st Baptist Church in Denver, CO to Kimberly Ann Kraft. Bradley's child from his 1st marriage (HOOKER) is: **(i)** Jessica Michelle b 23 June 1981 at Denver, CO.

590.   DENA GAYL JORDAN, daughter of Robert James and Barbara Nancy (Hooker) Jordan, was born 7 Dec 1955 at Mattoon in Coles Co., IL. She married there 28 Jul 1972 to Wendell Raymond Hawn, born 25 Jul 1952 at Mattoon, IL, son of Robert Enfer and Helen Lucille (McCleary) Hawn. Dena Gayl's children (HAWN), born at Mattoon, IL, are: **(i)** Danielle Lynn b 1 Apr 1975; **(ii)** Wendell Raymond, Jr. b 1 May 1977.

591. CHRISTINE DENISE JORDAN, daughter of Robert James and Barbara Nancy (Hooker) Jordan, was born 23 Jan 1957 at Mattoon, Coles Co., IL. She married 6 Nov 1973 at the 1st Baptist Church in Cowden, Shelby Co., IL to James Melvin Turner, born 24 Dec 1949 at Mattoon, IL, son of James William and Eleanor Jane (Lockhart) Turner. Christine's children (TURNER), born at Mattoon, IL, are: **(i)** Ryan Eugene b 1 Jul 1974; **(ii)** James William b 20 Nov 1977.

592. SALI ELIZABETH JORDAN, daughter of Robert James and Barbara Nancy (Hooker) Jordan, was born 22 May 1959 at Mattoon, Coles Co., IL. She married there 10 Oct 1976 to Robert Elmer Young, Jr., born 10 Oct 1956 at Decatur, Macon Co., IL, son of Robert Elmer and Janis Darlene (Oliver) Young, Sr. Sali's children (YOUNG), born at Mattoon, IL, are: **(i)** Barbara Darlene b 29 Mar 1977; **(ii)** Terri Jo b 28 Oct 1978; **(iii)** Kimberly Ann b 7 Oct 1980.

596. JODI LYNN RIPPEY, daughter of Paul Anthony and Shirley Jean (Hooker) Rippey, was born 5 Sep 1957 at Mattoon, Coles Co., IL. She married 12 Oct 1974 at Arcola, Douglas Co., IL to Jerry Allen Livingston, born 5 Aug 1956 at Mattoon, IL, son of Gerald Eugene and Rushie Evelyn (Clark) Livingston. Jodi's children (LIVINGSTON), born at Mattoon, IL, are: **(i)** Toby Allen b 7 Feb 1975; **(ii)** Joshua Anthony b 20 Mar 1978.

604. THOMAS LYLE MYERS, son of James Harley and Ethel Maud (Pendlay) Myers, was born 15 Jul 1942 at Effingham, Effingham Co., IL. He married 6 Sep 1969 at Hammond, Lake Co., IN to Cheri Lynn Furticella, born 29 Mar 1947 at East Chicago, Lake Co., IN, daughter of Charles and Mary Lee (Webster) Furticella. Children of Thomas MYERS are: **(i)** Michelle Lynn b 18 Jan 1972 Hammond, Lake Co., IN; **(ii)** Richard Lyle b 5 Jul 1974 Hobart, Lake Co., IN.

605. FERNE MARIE MYERS, daughter of James Harley and Ethel Maud (Pendlay) Myers, was born 30 Jul 1944 at Effingham, Effingham Co., IL. She married 25 June 1962 at Gary, Lake Co., IN to James Edward Mason, born 7 Jan 1943 at Gary, IN, son of James Clinton & Phyllis Patricia (Archer)

Mason. Ferne Marie's children (MASON), born at Gary, IN, are: **(i)** Thomas James b 1 Apr 1963 m 23 June 1982 Northside Baptist Church, Princeton, KY Jennifer Lynn Ray b 1 May 1962 Princeton, Caldwell Co., KY d/o Clinton Johnson & Ira Louise (Menser) Ray; 1 ch Phillip Edward b 7 Sep 1984 Paducah, McCracken Co., KY; **(ii)** Timothy Edward b 24 Mar 1966 m 16 Aug 1986 United Methodist Church, Chesterton, IN to Michelle Renee Perdue b 21 Aug 1966 LaPorte, IN d/o Jerry Steven & Mary Louise (Fosdick) Perdue; **(iii)** Erica Hope b 1 Sep 1970.

606. **DONALD CARL HEINZEL,** son of Carl William and Geraldine May (Hopp) Heinzel, was born 3 Jun 1942 at Lincoln, Logan Co., IL; married 1st 24 June 1961 Lincoln, IL to Sandra Lee Clark, born at Lincoln, daughter of Warren and Judy Chandler (Plunkett) Clark. He married 2nd 7 Jul 1972 Lincoln, IL to Lucretia Maye (Webb) Parker, born at Lincoln, daughter of Truman & Phyllis (Edwards) Webb.
Donald's children (HEINZEL) by his 1st marriage, born at Lincoln, IL, are: **(i)** Laurie Ann b 2 Feb 1963 m 2 Feb 1981 Lincoln, IL to Dennis Ray Oliver b 27 Apr 1961 Princeton, KY s/o Donald Edward & Myrtle Lucille ( ) Oliver; 2 ch Jesse Ray b 9 Nov 1981 Peoria, IL; Amanda Lee Ann b 22 Sep 1983 Peoria, IL; **(ii)** Christopher Clark b 4 Feb 1967. Donald's children by his 2nd marriage are: **(iii)** Dustin Carl b 30 Dec 1974; **(iv)** Heather Lynn b 30 June 1980.

607. **SANDRA KAY HEINZEL,** daughter of Carl William and Geraldine May (Hopp) Heinzel, was born 30 Mar 1947 at Lincoln, Logan Co., IL. She married there 25 Nov 1966 Michael Alan Crews, born 17 Sep 1943 at Lincoln, IL, son of Estelle Stallings and Cecelia Gertrude (Rieman) Crews. Sandra Kay's children (CREWS), born at Lincoln, IL, are: **(i)** Ericha Lenore b 29 June 1967; **(ii)** Marta Christine b 3 May 1971.

608. **SHIRLEE JEAN HEINZEL,** daughter of Carl William and Geraldine May (Hopp) Heinzel, was born 9 Nov 1948 at Lincoln, Logan Co., IL; married there 24 Feb 1977 Gordon Kenton Johnson born 14 Feb 1948 at McLeansboro, IL, son of Wilford & Versa (Hall) Johnson. Her children (JOHNSON), born at Lincoln, are: **(i)** Matthew Robert b 15 Mar 1978; **(ii)** Mark Wilford b 29 May 1981; **(iii)** Aaron William b 7 Jan 1984.

609. **PHILLIP MICHAEL HOPP**, son of Donald Eugene and Annetta Madge (Willmert) Hopp, was born 23 Aug 1947 at Lincoln, Logan Co., IL. He married there 12 June 1976 to Karen Sue (Cobb) Swigart, born 20 Jan 1951 at Lincoln, IL, daughter of Everett L. and Martha Louise (Emmons) Cobb. (Karen's two sons by her previous marriage, Duane Craig Swigart, born 14 Jan 1968, and Harry Lee Swigart, born 23 June 1969, both at Lincoln, IL, were adopted by Phillip.) Phillip's child (HOPP) is: **(i)** Derek Michael b 24 Dec 1978 at Lincoln, IL.

611. **DONNA LEE HOPP**, daughter of Donald Eugene and Anneta Madge (Willmert) Hopp, was born 21 Sep 1956 at Lincoln, Logan Co., IL. She married there 23 Jul 1978 to Hank Barr, born 18 June 1956 at Lincoln, IL, son of Hubert and Mary Lucy (Ball) Barr. Donna's children (BARR), born at Lincoln, IL, are: **(i)** Brandy Nicole b 6 Aug 1979; **(ii)** Allecia Michelle b 16 Sep 1983; **(iii)** Kara Raye b 1 Dec 1984.

613. **JUDITH ANN MUSSON**, daughter of Chester Earl and Josephine Celia (Albano) Musson, was born 31 Dec 1939 at Chicago, Cook Co., IL. She married 10 Aug 1957 at Cicero, Cook Co., IL to John Fred Eads, born 29 Jan 1937 at Chicago, IL, son of John James and Edith (Barleman) Eads. John and Judith were divorced in 1976 at Chicago, IL. Judith's children (EADS) are: **(i)** James Patrick b 2 Nov 1959; **(ii)** John William b 11 Aug 1963; **(iii)** Jeffery Allan and **(iv)** Jerry Michael, twins, b 21 Sep 1967.

616. **JOSEPH PHILLIP SCARA, JR.**, son of Joseph Phillip and Juanita May (Musson) Scara, Sr., was born 14 Jul 1936 at Chicago, Cook Co., IL. He married there 23 Aug 1958 to Sandra Caroline Ordakowski, born 3 Dec 1939 at Chicago, IL, daughter of Walter Adam and Mary (Kobylarczk) Ordakowski. Joseph's children (SCARA), born at Chicago, IL, are: **(i)** Joseph Martin b 3 June 1959; **(ii)** John Michael b 8 June 1961; **(iii)** Diana Lynn b 17 Mar 1964; **(iv)** Jennifer Joanne b 12 Sep 1970.

617. **JAMES ROBERT SCARA**, son of Joseph Phillip and Juanita May (Musson) Scara, Sr., was born 10 June 1938 at Chicago, Cook Co., IL. He married there 25 Oct 1958 to Cynthia Lucia Kandalec, born 14 Aug 1939 at Chicago, IL, daughter of Charles Ambrose and Sarah Theresa (Brzycki)

Kandalec. James and Cynthia were divorced (1977). Children of James (SCARA) are: **(i)** James Robert b 24 Oct 1959 Chicago, IL; **(ii)** Tina Marie b 26 Oct 1960 Chicago, IL; **(iii)** Thomas Michael b 10 Oct 1962 Oak Lawn, IL.

618. **DONALD WILLIAM SCARA**, son of Joseph Phillip and Juanita May (Musson) Scara, Sr., was born 21 Apr 1945 at Chicago, Cook Co., IL. He married there 3 Sep 1967 to Ruth Ann Finnigan, born 20 Nov 1944 at Chicago, IL, daughter of Lewis and Ruth Louise (Hawerbier) Finnegan, Jr. Donald and Ruth were divorced (1974) at Chicago, IL. Donald's children (SCARA), born at Chicago, IL, are: **(i)** Michelle Lee b 25 Dec 1968; **(ii)** Cynthia Ann b 2 Jul 1970.

620. **RICHARD DONALD MUSSON**, son of George Edward and Donna L. (Staples) Musson, Jr., was born 3 Sep 1947 at Chicago, Cook Co., IL. He married there 29 Dec 1970 Jean Vocat, born 3 Nov 1947 at Chicago, IL, daughter of Joseph and Mary Jane (Graves) Vocat. Richard's children (MUSSON), born at Highland Park, IL, are: **(i)** George Joseph b 10 Dec 1974; **(ii)** Kristin Laura b 5 Sep 1976.

624. **JACQUELINE JOY MUSSON**, daughter of Jimmie Dale and Barbara Joan (Jacobsen) Musson, was born 22 Sep 1956 at Chicago, Cook Co., IL. She married there 7 Dec 1974 Gary Lee Cardona, born 15 Sep 1954 at Chicago, IL, son of Joseph Lawrence and Elizabeth Dorothy (Blackman) Cardona. Jacqueline's children (CARDONA), born at Naperville, DuPage Co., IL, are: **(i)** Melinda Lee and **(ii)** Amanda Lee, twins, b 17 Oct 1975; **(iii)** Jennifer Lee b 12 Aug 1977.

629. **PHILLIP ALLEN REDMAN**, son of Paul Allen and Bette Louise (Demorat) Redman, was born 22 Jul 1946 at Crawfordsville, Montgomery Co., IN. He married Kathy _____. Phillip's children (REDMAN) are: **(i)** Ross Michael b 9 Apr 1975; **(ii)** Adam Patrick b 14 Jul 1979.

630. **MARK LOWELL REDMAN**, son of Paul Allen and Bette Louise (Demorat) Redman, was born 7 Mar 1949 at Crawfordsville, Montgomery Co., IN. He married first 13 Nov 1972 at Lafayette, Tippecanoe Co., IN to Patricia Ann _____. They were divorced and Mark married second 20 June 1978 at Indianapolis, Marion Co., IN to Patricia Ann Memmer, born 19 Feb 1955 at Indianapolis, IN, daughter of James Albert

and Bonnie Jean (Combs) Memmer. Mark's children (REDMAN) (1st by his 1st mar, rest by his 2nd mar), born at Indianapolis, IN, are: **(i)** Holly Ann b 13 Dec 1972; **(ii)** Natalie Rae b 14 Mar 1983; **(iii)** Todd Allen b 8 Apr 1985.

631. **JULIA MARIE REDMAN,** daughter of Paul Allen and Bette Louise (Demorat) Redman, was born 31 Jan 1952 at Crawfordsville, Montgomery Co., IN. She married 11 Sep 1971 at Jamestown, Boone Co., IN to David Dane Heath, born 25 Feb 1951 at Crawfordsville, IN. Julia's children (HEATH) are: **(i)** Melanie Marie b 4 Mar 1972 Lebanon, Boone Co., IN; **(ii)** Erika Renee b 9 Mar 1981 Lafayette, Tippecanoe Co., IN.

632. **JAMES FORREST REDMAN,** son of Paul Allen and Bette Louise (Demorat) Redman, was born 20 Mar 1954 at Crawfordsville, Montgomery Co., IN. He married 21 Jul 1978 at Indianapolis, Marion Co., IN to Barbara Sue Scott, born 21 Dec 1953 at Indianapolis, IN, daughter of John Elmer and Mary Elizabeth (Saver) Scott. James Forrest's children (REDMAN) are: **(i)** Scott Paul b 1 May 1981 Indianapolis, IN; **(ii)** Jill Christine b 12 Apr 1984 Ft. Wayne, Allen Co., IN; **(iii)** Child b Apr 1987 Ft. Wayne, IN.

633. **JANE GAYLE REDMAN,** daughter of Paul Allen and Bette Louise (Demorat) Redman, was born 12 May 1958 at Crawfordsville, Montgomery Co., IN. She married 14 Jul 1979 at Indianapolis, Marion Co., IN to Robert Joseph Scott, born 1 Jan 1951 at Indianapolis, IN. Jane's children (SCOTT), born at Lafayette, IN, are: **(i)** Marcus Neil b 29 Dec 1983; **(ii)** Trevor Dane b 12 Sep 1986.

634. **ROGER EUGENE BLIGAN,** son of Harold Richard and Aimee Marie (Redman) Bligan, was born 20 Jan 1950 at Indianapolis, Marion Co., IN. He married there first on 10 Nov 1966 to Linda Diane Mead, born 18 Oct 1949 at Indianapolis, IN, daughter of William Edward and Melda Vlanche (Younger) Mead. Roger and Linda were divorced in 1980. He married second 22 Nov 1980 at Indianapolis, IN to Gina Marie Collins, born 17 Sep 1958 at Indianapolis, IN, daughter of Norman Eugene and Marie Josephine (Jardina) Collins.

Roger's children (BLIGAN) by his 1st marriage, born at Indianapolis, IN, are: **(i)** Aimee Jo b 24 May 1967; **(ii)** Roger Eugene, Jr. b 17 June 1971.

Eleventh Generation

Roger's children (BLIGAN) by his 2nd marriage, born at Indianapolis, IN, are: **(iii)** Carrie Renee b 30 Aug 1981; **(iv)** Ashley Marie b 30 Sep 1985.

635. BEVERLY JOAN BLIGAN, daughter of Harold Richard and Aimee Marie (Redman) Bligan, was born 9 Apr 1952 at Indianapolis, Marion Co., IN. She married there first 26 Dec 1969 to Michael Dale Bledsoe, born 19 Sep 1951 at Waverly, Pike Co., OH, son of Robert Elmer and Ocie Louise (Campbell) Bledsoe. Beverly and Michael were divorced in 1982 and she married second 18 Nov 1982 at Indianapolis, IN to Ronnie Ercel Barker, born 21 Nov 1949 at Thomasville, AL, son of Ercel W. and Josephine (Harvel) Barker. Child of Beverly's 1st marriage (BLEDSOE) is: **(i)** Lillian Dee b 24 May 1971 Fayetteville, Cumberland Co., NC.

636. KATHLEEN MARIE HOWE, daughter of Edward Leo and Juanita Louise (Redman) Howe, was born 8 Jan 1952 at Beech Grove, Marion Co., IN. She married there 15 Aug 1970 to Michael George Waugh, born 8 Oct 1951 at Indianapolis, IN. Kathleen's children (WAUGH) are: **(i)** Michelle Jung b 21 Nov 1975 Korea; **(ii)** Michael George, Jr. b 24 Jan 1978 Franklin, Johnson Co., IN; **(iii)** Anna Kathleen b 31 Aug 1981 Franklin, Johnson Co., IN.

637. EDWARD LEO HOWE, JR., son of Edward Leo and Juanita Louise (Redman) Howe, Sr., was born 18 May 1953 at Beech Grove, Marion Co., IN. He married there 29 Dec 1978 to Denise Ann Lohman, born 10 Sep 1956, daughter of Joseph Samuel and Margaret Ruth (Swartz) Lohman. Edward's children (HOWE) are: **(i)** Sarah Marie b 16 June 1979 Marietta, Cobb Co., GA; **(ii)** Benjamin Joseph b 22 May 1982 Acworth, Cobb Co., GA; **(iii)** Rebekah Howe b 21 Oct 1984 Acworth, Cobb Co., GA.

638. TIMOTHY PAUL HOWE, son of Edward Leo and Juanita Louise (Redman) Howe, was born 31 Oct 1954 at Beech Grove, Marion Co., IN. He married 5 Aug 1978 at San Diego, San Diego Co., CA to Barbara Ellen Gehrke, born 11 Feb 1957 in Illinois, daughter of Donald Edward and Marilyn Yvonne (Bergeron) Gehrke. Timothy Paul's children (HOWE) are: **(i)** Brian Edward b 5 Nov 1979 San Diego, San Diego Co., CA; **(ii)** Jennifer Elizabeth b 19 Oct 1983 Beech Grove, Marion Co., IN.

639. **CYNTHIA ANN HOWE,** daughter of Edward Leo and Juanita Louise (Redman) Howe, was born 5 Dec 1955 at Beech Grove, Marion Co., IN. She married there 8 Feb 1975 to James Allen Miller, born 14 Dec 1954 in Indiana. Cynthia's children (MILLER), born at Indianapolis, IN, are: **(i)** Corey James b 23 Sep 1976; **(ii)** Margaret Ellen b 22 May 1980.

641. **JOHN BRIAN HOWE,** son of Edward Leo and Juanita Louise (Redman) Howe, was born 14 Jul 1959 at Beech Grove, Marion Co., IN. He married in Oct 1980 at Smyrna, GA to Heidi Marie Clark, born 11 May 1962, daughter of John Joseph and Gisela Dorthea (Levinsky) Clark. John's children (HOWE) are: **(i)** John Joseph b 7 May 1981 Marietta, GA; **(ii)** Jacob William b 4 Jul 1985 Woodstock, GA.

645. **BRENDA JOYCE MANNING,** daughter of Donald Eugene and Mary Ellen (Redman) Manning, was born 9 Mar 1952 at Indianapolis, Marion Co., IN. She married 12 Oct 1970 at Tazewell, Claibourne Co., TN, to Danny Lloyd Roe, born 11 Dec 1951 at Knoxville, Knox Co., TN, son of Vibert Lloyd and Lula Gertrude (Williams) Roe. Brenda's children (ROE) are: **(i)** Lori Ann b 22 Jul 1972 Rantoul, Champaign Co., IL; **(ii)** Angela Michelle b 6 June 1974 Urbana, Champaign Co., IL; **(iii)** Jennifer Renee b 27 Oct 1976 Lafayette, Tippecanoe Co., IN.

646. **TERRY ANN MANNING,** daughter of Donald Eugene and Mary Ellen (Redman) Manning, was born 29 Mar 1953 at Beech Grove, Marion Co., IN. She married first 16 Sep 1972 at Kokomo, IN to Larry James Mayes. Terry and Larry were divorced in 1976 (no children). She married second 11 Mar 1976 at Cassville, Howard Co., IN to John Francis Chapin, Jr., born 6 Mar 1947 at Kokomo, IN, son of John Francis and Vivian Rose (Hatfield) Chapin, Sr. Terry's child by her 2nd marriage (CHAPIN) is: **(i)** Heather Dawn b 12 May 1977 Kokomo, Howard Co., IN.

647. **RUSSELL GENE MANNING,** son of Donald Eugene and Mary Ellen (Redman) Manning, was born 13 Mar 1954 at Beech Grove, Marion Co., IN. He married first 14 Jan 1974 at Kokomo, Howard Co., IN to Hedy VaLane Allen, born 9 Mar 1957 at Kokomo, IN, daughter of Kenneth Alton and Jaley Sexton (Shelton) Allen. Russell and Hedy were divorced in 1980. He married second 26 Jul 1986 at Kokomo, IN to

Rhonda G. (Campbell) Dickey, born 13 Apr 1958 at Louisville, KY, daughter of Benjamin W. and Bessie L. (   ) Campbell. Russell's children (MANNING) by his 1st marriage are: **(i)** Cara Nicole b 14 Jul 1975 Kokomo, IN; **(ii)** Matthew Tyler b 23 Mar 1977 Kokomo, IN; **(iii)** John Daniel b 5 Apr 1979 Paoli, Orange Co., IN.

648. PAMELA SUE MANNING, daughter of Donald Eugene and Mary Ellen (Redman) Manning, was born 10 Jul 1957 at Kokomo, Howard Co., IN. She married 29 Aug 1981 at Baltimore, MD to Ronnie James Georgieff, born 5 June 1955 at Baltimore, MD (now divorced). Pamela's child (GEORGIEFF) is: **(i)** Amber Marie b 4 Feb 1982 Baltimore, MD.

650. BRUCE HOWARD LITTLE, son of David Howard and Ruby Ethel (Redman) Little, was born 18 Sep 1953 at Indianapolis, Marion Co., IN. He married first there 16 June 1973 to Victoria Lynn Millikan, born 23 May 1955 at Indianapolis, IN, daughter of Charles Richard and Judith Ann (Shellhouse) Millikan. Bruce and Victoria were divorced in 1978. He married second 31 Oct 1981 at Indianapolis, IN to Beth Ann Braniff, born 4 Jul 1959 at South Bend, St. Joseph Co., IN, daughter of Donald Howard and Barbara Ruth (Smith) Braniff. Bruce's children (LITTLE), 1st by his 1st marriage, 2nd by his 2nd marriage, both born in Indianapolis, IN, are: **(i)** Bruce Jeremiah b 30 Jan 1976; **(ii)** Branden Lyndsey b 5 Oct 1982.

653. JANICE ANITA JORDAN, daughter of Keith Redman and Dorothy Nell (Temple) Jordan, was born 25 Sep 1952 at Weslaco, Hidalgo Co., TX. She married first 9 Nov 1968 at El Paso, El Paso Co., TX to Terry Ronald Vantreese, born 16 Jul 1948 at Abilene, Taylor Co., TX, son of Lawrence Valentine and Verna Mai (Billeaud) Vantreese, Jr. Janice and Terry were divorced in 1974 at Houston, TX. She married second 18 Dec 1975 at Houston, TX to Richard Wayne Turner (divorced; no children). Janice's children by her 1st marriage (VANTREESE) are: **(i)** Terry Ronald, Jr. b 19 Jan 1969 Newport News, Independent Co., VA; **(ii)** Kevin Ray b 14 Jul 1971 Houston, Harris Co., TX.

654. JERI LYNN JORDAN, daughter of Keith Redman and Dorothy Nell (Temple) Jordan, was born 10 Jul 1954 at Freeport, Brazoria Co., TX. She married first 10 Aug 1971 at

Houston, Harris Co., TX to Carlos Garcia, Jr., born 2 Sep 1949 at Corpus Christi, Nueces Co., TX, son of Carlos and Catarina (Barrera) Garcia, Sr. Jeri and Carlos were divorced and Jeri married second 3 Jul 1982 at Houston, TX to Jack James Chublakian. Jeri's children by her 1st marriage (GARCIA), born at Houston, TX, are: **(i)** Monica Lynn b 21 Aug 1972; **(ii)** Carlos III b 18 May 1976.

655. **DAWN MICHELLE SUNDENE**, daughter of John Warren and Marilyn Ruth (Jordan) Sundene, was born 25 Aug 1956 at the U.S. Army Hospital in Heidelberg, Germany. She married 16 May 1979 at Coupeville, Island Co., WA to Tracy Lee Wahl, born 29 Jul 1955 at Minneapolis, MN, son of Delton and Joanne (Anderson) Wahl. Dawn's children (WAHL) are: **(i)** Christopher Jordan b 11 Aug 1981 Naval Clinic, Cherry Point, Craven Co., NC; **(ii)** Jeri Lynne b 12 Feb 1986 Morehead City, Carteret Co., NC.

657. **DANA ANNE SUNDENE**, daughter of John Warren and Marilyn Ruth (Jordan) Sundene, was born 27 Mar 1959 at Resurrection Hospital, Chicago, IL. She married first 14 May 1982 at Orange Co., CA to Biagio Orlando Manta, born 9 Sep 1960 at Sannicola, Puglia, Italy, son of Pasquale and Anna Purificata (Esposito) Manta. They were divorced and she married second 29 Mar 1985 at Orange Co., CA Ricardo Pasalagua Castaneda, born 6 June 1963 at Mexico City, Mexico D.F., son of Jorge Pasalagua Diaz and Lidia Castaneda Cardenas. Child by Dana's 1st marriage (MANTA) is: **(i)** Anna Francesca ("Chessie") b 19 Apr 1983 Fullerton, Orange Co., CA. Child by Dana's 2nd marriage (PASALAGUA) is: **(ii)** Erik Ricardo Pasalagua b 12 Jan 1986 Yorba Linda, Orange Co., CA.

659. **GARY EDWARD PEADRO**, son of William Edward and Pearl Leona (Hawkins) Peadro, was born 10 Dec 1951 at Mattoon, Coles Co., IL. He married 18 Dec 1971 at Smyser Church, Moultrie Co., IL to Shirley Anne St. John, born 31 Dec 1952 at Mattoon, IL, daughter of Alvin Ralph and Edna Christine (Pickering) St. John. Gary's children (PEADRO) born at Mattoon, IL are: **(i)** Michelle Lee b 1 Aug 1972; **(ii)** Michael Edward b 13 Apr 1977.

660. **DENNIS LEON PEADRO**, son of William Edward and Pearl Leona (Hawkins) Peadro, was born 12 Jul 1953 at Mattoon,

Coles Co., IL. He married first 28 Nov 1971 at Windsor, Shelby Co., IL to Jessie Ellen Baker, born 17 Dec 1954 at Shelbyville, Shelby Co., IL, daughter of Harold Edward and Edith Ellen (Bolin) Baker. Dennis and Jessie were divorced (1976) and he married second 25 June 1978 at St. Louis, IL to Beverly Naomi Driskell, born 6 Jan 1953 at Mattoon, IL, daughter of Warren Elsworth and Irene Josephine (Bushue) Driskell. Children of Dennis (PEADRO) by his 1st marriage, born at Mattoon, IL, are: **(i)** David Leon b 19 June 1972; **(ii)** Dawn Ellen b 3 Oct 1974. Children of Dennis (PEADRO) by his 2nd marriage, born at Mattoon, IL, are: **(iii)** Andrew Dennis b 23 Oct 1982; **(iv)** Blake Warren b 16 Jan 1986.

661. **LORA LEONA PEADRO,** daughter of William Edward and Pearl Leona (Hawkins) Peadro, was born 21 Jul 1961 at Mattoon, Coles Co., IL. She married 24 Jan 1981 at Gays, Moultrie Co., IL (Christian Church) to John Kenneth Tipton, born 22 Nov 1960 at Charleston, Coles Co., IL, son of Charles Joseph and Marilyn Maxine (Stewart) Tipton. Lora's children (TIPTON) are: **(i)** Steven Kenneth b 14 Dec 1981 Wurtsmith A.F.B., MI; **(ii)** Rachel Marie b 24 Jul 1983 Mattoon, Coles Co., IL.

662. **RONALD DALLAS PEADRO,** son of Dallas Franklin and Elsie Irene (Smith) Peadro, was born 14 May 1954 at Mattoon, Coles Co., IL. He married 4 June 1977 at Neoga, Cumberland Co., IL to Susan Diane Maas, born 11 Apr 1954 at Chicago, Cook Co., IL, daughter of Rudolph W. and Sandra L. (Ohrn) Maas. Ronald's children (PEADRO), born at Mattoon, IL, are: **(i)** Jeffrey Ronald b 24 Aug 1980; **(ii)** Rebecca Lynn b 3 Mar 1982.

664. **ERIC LEE RINCKER,** son of Leland Curtis and Davadia Lela (Peadro) Rincker, was born 8 June 1951 at Shelbyville, Shelby Co., IL. He married 24 Jul 1986 at Toronto, Ontario, Canada to Jane Reid Williamson, born 22 June 1953 in Scotland, daughter of Adam and Alice (   ) Williamson. Eric's child (RINCKER) is: **(i)** Katherine Jean b 6 Jan 1987 Toronto, Ontario, Canada.

665. **KARLIE DAVADIA RINCKER,** daughter of Leland Curtis and Davadia Lela (Peadro) Rincker, was born 2 Nov 1953 at Shelbyville, Shelby Co., IL. She married 21 Nov 1971 in

Smyser Christian Church, Gays, Moultrie Co., IL to Harold Theodore ("Ted") Richardson, born 19 Aug 1947 at Centralia, Marion Co., IL, son of Harold Evert and Virginia Iris (Sigrist) Richardson. Karlie's children (RICHARDSON), born at Effingham, Effingham Co., IL, are: **(i)** Shawn Theodore b 17 Apr 1976; **(ii)** Yolanda Noelle b 24 Jul 1979.

666. **CURTIS DEE RINCKER**, son of Leland Curtis and Davadia Lela (Peadro) Rincker, was born 1 June 1955 at Shelbyville, Shelby Co., IL. He married 1 June 1975 at Windsor, Moultrie Co., IL (Christian Church) to Pamela Marie (Kelly) Peters, born 15 Feb 1957 at Lynwood, Los Angeles Co., CA, daughter of William Mitchell and Sophie (Yaworski) Kelly. Children of Curtis (RINCKER), born at Decatur, Macon Co., IL, are: **(i)** Cari Brett (dau) b 19 Feb 1980; **(ii)** Brenton Curtis b 8 Jul 1983.

667. **LYNDAL GAY RINCKER**, son of Leland Curtis and Davadia Lela (Peadro) Rincker, was born 16 Oct 1956 at Shelbyville, Shelby Co., IL. He married 22 June 1980 at Decatur, Macon Co., IL to Jennifer Spring Fenner. Leland's children (RINCKER) are: **(i)** Peter Hans b 1 Dec 1983 Springfield, IL; **(ii)** Timothy Cole b 30 Dec 1985 Mattoon, Coles Co., IL.

669. **JOHN MIKUL MITCHELL, JR.**, son of John Mikul and Virginia Sherwood (Tucker) Mitchell, Sr., was born 16 Mar 1960 at Birmingham, Jefferson Co., AL. He married 20 Jul 1979 at Tuscaloosa, Tuscaloosa Co., AL to Cindy Malice Eads. John, Jr.'s child is: **(i)** Peter Mikul b 20 Jan 1984 Birmingham, Jefferson Co., AL.

670. **STEVEN LEE MITCHELL**, son of John Mikul and Virginia Sherwood (Tucker) Mitchell, Sr., was born 19 Jul 1961 at Orlando, Orange Co., FL. He married 1 Aug 1981 at Tuscaloosa, Tuscaloosa Co., AL to Dana Marie Crowder. Only child of Steven is: **(i)** Karla Marie b 25 Sep 1986 Tuscaloosa, Tuscaloosa Co., AL.

674. **DAVID LEE MITCHELL, JR.**, son of David Lee and Louise Gwen Veronica (Hodo) Mitchell, Sr., was born 15 Sep 1962 at Tuscaloosa, Tuscaloosa Co., AL. He married there on 23 Dec 1983 to Lesha Kathryn Zeigler. David's child is: **(i)** David Lee III b 7 Mar 1985 Idaho Falls, ID.

680. DAVID CHANDLER MITCHELL, son of Chandler Earl and Anna Maria (Bogner) Mitchell, was born 24 Nov 1951 at Danville, Vermilion Co., IL (hospital). He married 11 Jul 1976 at Ridge Farm, Vermilion Co., IL to Jennifer Renee Winland, born 7 Feb 1956 at Danville, IL, daughter of Gerald Wayne and Lois Lorene (Cline) Winland. David and Jennifer were divorced in 1978. (David and his daughter live with his parents.) David's child is: **(i)** Heather Renee b 31 Mar 1977 at Urbana, Champaign Co., IL.

681. REBECCA ANN MITCHELL, daughter of Chandler Earl and Anna Maria (Bogner) Mitchell, was born 7 Feb 1953 at Danville, Vermilion Co., IL (hospital). She married 8 Aug 1975 at Paris, Edgar Co., IL to Jerry Lee Cusick, born 5 Oct 1953 at Paris, IL, son of Jerry Lee and Mary Louise (Campbell) Cusick, Sr. Rebecca's children (CUSICK), born at Paris, Edgar Co., IL, are: **(i)** Carrie Ann b 19 Nov 1975; **(ii)** Connie Louise b 10 May 1977; **(iii)** Candi Lee b 28 Aug 1982.

682. THOMAS EARL MITCHELL, son of Chandler Earl and Anna Maria (Bogner) Mitchell, was born 8 Jan 1956 at Danville, Vermilion Co., IL (hospital). He married 4 Sep 1976 to Regina Rae (Wolfe) Hoult, born 13 Aug 1958, daughter of Charles and Connie Sue (Thomas) Wolfe. Child of Thomas is: **(i)** Dedra Marie b 17 Jul 1985.

683. MICHAEL JAMES TAYLOR, son of James Monroe and Eleanor Marica (Mitchell) Taylor, was born 25 Nov 1951 at Danville, Vermilion Co., IL. He married first 25 June 1971 to Linda Kay Freeman (divorced 1974; no children). He married second 23 Aug 1975 at Indianapolis, Marion Co., IN to Teresa Joan Glass, born 21 Mar 1954 at San Diego, CA, daughter of Richard Lawrence and Dorothy Mae (Herald) Glass. Michael's children (TAYLOR) are: **(i)** Laren Jo b 7 Mar 1972 Danville, Hendricks Co., IN (she was adopted by Michael and Teresa in 1978); **(ii)** Melissa Kay b 12 Feb 1977 Indianapolis, IN; **(iii)** James Michael b 10 Jan 1979 Indianapolis, IN; **(iv)** Richard Chandler b 16 Nov 1980 in Indianapolis, IN.

686. RICHARD ALLEN MITCHELL, son of James Edward and Martha Jane (Parks) Mitchell, was born 8 Apr 1952 at Camp Cooke, Lompoc, Santa Barbara Co., CA. He married 13 Aug

1977 to Cecelia Diane Barrett, born 25 Apr 1954 at Danville, Vermilion Co., IL, daughter of Joseph Edward and Dorothy Maxine (Quick) Barrett. Richard's children, born at Paris, Edgar Co., IL, are: **(i)** Josie Dorthea b 3 Feb 1983; **(ii)** Betsy Jane b 7 Dec 1985.

688. **DONALD JOE MITCHELL**, son of James Edward and Martha Jane (Parks) Mitchell, was born 29 Mar 1956 at Paris, Edgar Co., IL. He married 29 Mar 1974 at Chrisman, Edgar Co., IL to Rita Joyce Switzer, born 21 Nov 1955 at Paris, IL, daughter of Clarence Raymond and Betty Joyce (Snedeker) Switzer. Donald Joe's children, born at Paris, Edgar Co., IL, are: **(i)** Chris Lynn (dau) b 3 Oct 1974; **(ii)** Andy Scott b 14 Apr 1976; **(iii)** Kelly Dawn b 14 May 1981; **(iv)** Wendy Jo b 30 Aug 1984.

689. **JOANNE KAY MITCHELL**, daughter of James Edward and Martha Jane (Parks) Mitchell, was born 26 Apr 1957 at Paris, Edgar Co., IL. She married 14 Jul 1979 at Missouri City, Harris Co., TX to Tony William Rigdon, born 5 Dec 1954 at Dayton, Montgomery Co., OH, son of Harry Brown and Alpha Billie (Reels) Rigdon. Joanne's children (RIGDON) are: **(i)** Anthony William b 3 Nov 1979 Anderson, Madison Co., IN; **(ii)** Chrystal Elizabeth b 27 Dec 1985 Cookeville, Putnam Co., TN.

691. **JOHN WILLIAM (BILL) MITCHELL**, son of John Richard and Barbara Ann (Martin) Mitchell, was born 28 Jan 1952 at Atlanta, Fulton Co., GA. He married 3 June 1973 in Edgar Co., IL to Janzetta Denise Gossett, born 27 Feb 1956 at Paris, Edgar Co., IL, daughter of Bobby Richard and Doris Lorena (Baugh) Gossett. Bill and Janzetta were divorced in 1985. Bill's children, both born at Paris, IL, are: **(i)** Steven William b 10 Jan 1977; **(ii)** Tracy Lynn (dau) b 25 Sep 1981.

692. **DEBORAH ANN MITCHELL**, daughter of John Richard and Barbara Ann (Martin) Mitchell, was born 3 Oct 1953 at Paris, Edgar Co., IL. She married 15 Mar 1975 in Edgar Co., IL to Timothy Leroy Botner, born 30 Dec 1954 at Terre Haute, Vigo Co., IN, son of James LeRoy and Shirley Ann (Eslinger) Botner. Deborah's children (BOTNER), born at Terre Haute, IN, are: **(i)** Kimberly Lynn b 14 Jul 1977; **(ii)** Benjamin Andrew b 2 Dec 1980.

SOME ALLIED LINES

Following is a compilation of surnames representing some of the lines which married into the Mitchell line. References are given for further information on the ancestry of these incoming lines. In certain cases, comments are made amending or enlarging on that information.

This listing is not included in the general index since it is already in alphabetical order. All surnames mentioned in the text are included in the alphabetical listing with reference(s) to the main surname under which they appear. Numbers after names of Mitchell spouses are paragraph numbers as assigned to them in the main text.

Reference page numbers are given as p=page(s); p187 is page 187; p187/88 is page 187 <u>and</u> 188; p187-194 is page 187 <u>through</u> page 194. TAG is "The American Genealogist." NEHGR/NEHGS are the New England Historical & Genealogical Register/Society. All other abbreviations are listed under "Explanations and Abbreviations."

****

ACKLEY: See Foster.

ALLEN: Eliza Ann=Calvin Mitchell-#196; allied lines Banta/Brower/Demarest/Monfort/Terhune; ref "History of Effingham Co., IL," Wm Henry Perrin, 1883, p185/6; "The Banta Genealogy," Theodore M. Banta, 1893, p10,15,28,49, 88,89; "The Demarest Family," Demarest Family Ass'n, V.II, 1964, Hackensack, NJ.

ALLIS: Mary (Wm, Sam'l, Wm)=Joseph Mitchell-#7; allied lines Davis/Edwards; ref "History of Hadley, MA," Sylvester Judd, p5/6; "History of Deerfield, MA," George Sheldon, V.II, p25/6; "History of Sunderland, MA," John M. Smith, p250/1; "Genealogy of William Allis of Hatfield & Descendants 1630/1919," Horatio D. Allis, p1-17; Savage;

-337-

Banks; Virkus; "1st Century of Springfield, MA," Henry M. Burts, 1899 (Edwards); "CT Nutmegger," V.10:#2 Sep 1977 (Edwards). Note: Horatio D. Allis says Mary, w/o Wm-1 Allis, was k at the Hatfield massacre 19 Sep 1677; this is refuted by Sheldon, Judd & Smith who say she d 10 Aug 1677. "History of the Ct Valley in MA," V.I, p399, lists those k in that attack. Mary Allis is not named; per Allis confused her with Mary, w/o Samuel Belding, who <u>was</u> on the list.

ATKINSON: See Miller; ref also the article "Richard Platt of Ware, Eng. & Milford, CT," pub in TAG, V.30:232-42; V.31:155-170.

BALDWIN: See Miller; allied line Harding; ref also "The Ancestry of Samuel, Freda & John Warner," Frederick C. Warner, 1949 (Baldwin/Edwards p33-35); "The Baldwin Genealogy from 1500 to 1881," Charles Candee Baldwin, 1881, p479-485; 1099-1101; "Families of Early Milford, CT," Susan Woodruff Abbott, 1979, p27-29,43,60,61; "The Victoria History of the County of Buckingham," Wm Page, V.II, p315/16; "Report of the Investigations Concerning the Family of Baldwin of Aston Clinton, Co. Bucks," Joseph L. Chester, NEHGR, Apr 1884, p160-165.

BANTA: See Allen.
BASSETT: See Wait(e).
BEAMAN/BEAMON: See Miller.

BELDING: Samuel (Sam'l, Dan'l, Wm)=Mary Mitchell-#27; allied lines Foote/Ingram/Smith; ref "History of Deerfield, MA," George Sheldon, V.II, p80/81; "History of Ashfield, MA," Frederick G. Howes, p311/12; "Our Yeoman Ancestors," Carol Clark Johnson, p388,393,407.

BIDWELL: See Brainard.

BIGELOW: Irene (Russell, Isaac, Isaac, Isaac, Samuel, John)=Joseph Mitchell IV-#146; allied lines Briscoe/Bond/Chamberlain/Flagg/Hyde/Sangor/Skinner/Warren/Woolson---ref "The Bigelow Family of America," Gilman B. Howe, 1890, p212/13; "Genealogies & History of Watertown, MA," Henry Bond, 2nd ed., reprint (Bigelow p29,31,682; Biscoe p42/43; Bond p46-48; Flagg p219/20; Hyde p304/05; Warren p620; Woolson p668/69).

Some Allied Lines

BIRDSALE: See Cowles.
BISCOE: See Bigelow.
BOND: See Bigelow.

BRAINARD: Zipporah (Nath'l, Obadiah, Caleb, Dan'l)=Joseph Mitchell III-#80; allied lines Bidwell/Johnson/Miller/ Spencer/Stoe/Stow; ref "The Genealogy of the Brainerd-Brainard Family in America 1649-1908," Lucy A. Brainard, V.II, p41,43,48,60; TAG V.27:164/65; the Brainard genealogy states that Zipporah & Joseph had no ch which was not the case; they were 4th cou tracing back to Ens. Gerard Spencer, the emigrant, their 3xgr.grfa. See also Foster.

BROWER: See Allen.
BURT: See Hawks.

CALVIN: Elizabeth=Ensign Mitchell, Jr.-#135; allied line Cartmill/LeFarge; ref "The Calvin Families," Claude W. Calvin, Pasadena, CA, 1945, p268/69,271/72; altho Calvin shows Elizabeth as d/o Vincent & Christina (Ruth) Calvin, it is more likely she was d/o Vincent's brother, James, & Nancy (Cartmill) Calvin. James, after "living many years in Brown Co., OH, removed about 1825 to Johnson Co., IN where he resided until his death." Calvin names James' ch as Luther, John, James, Samuel, Thomas, Joseph, Hiram, Nancy=___Titus, Mary=___Phillips, dau=___Lawrence, dau =___Wright, & dau___(no data); Johnson Co., IN Adm BK-AA contains Letters of Adm issued 5 Mar 1838 to George Titus on the James Calvin estate, Jacob Walker & Robert Moore, securities. Wid is Eliza Ann (prob a 2nd w); heirs are Luther Calvin; Ensign Mitchell & wife Betsey, late Calvin; Nancy w/o George Titus, late Calvin; Hiram & Joseph Calvin; Jacob Walker & wife Mary, late Calvin; Henry Woodward & wife Sarah, late Calvin, all adults; Moses & Lovina Calvin, under age 21. Samuel & John Calvin & the Mitchells are called non-residents of IN. Taken with the land dealings the Mitchells had in Brown Co., OH with Samuel Calvin and his in-laws, the Currys, it seems good proof that Elizabeth (Betsey) belonged to James rather than to his brother, Vincent Calvin (whose place as son of Luther Calvin is not yet secure).

CALVIN: Harriet J.=Samuel Mitchell-#203; allied lines Mears/Rollison/LeFarge; ref "The Calvin Families," Claude

W. Calvin, Pasadena, CA, 1945, p267/68,272/73; (Samuel's
mother & Harriet's father were 1st cou; see Calvin above).

CATLIN: Sarah=Michael Mitchell-#1; allied lines Baldwin
(see)/Harding/Ward/Whitlock; ref "History of Deerfield,
MA," George Sheldon, V.II, p104/05; "The Catlin Genealogy," Louise Catlin Cleaver Roloson, So. Brevard Historical Soc., Melbourne, FL, 1981; "A History of the Willis
Family," Chas. E. & Frances C. Willis, 1916 (Ward p109-
119); "Ships Passenger Lists, Nat'l & New England 1600-
1825," Carl Boyer III, p201/02; "History of Essex Co.,
NJ," Wm H Shaw, 1884, V.I (Catlin p360; Ward p20-23); "Papers of the New Haven Colony Historical Soc.," V.III, 1882
(Catlin/Ward p249-270); "Documents Relating to the Colonial History of the State of NJ," Wm Nelson, V.XXI, 1889.

CARTMILL: See Calvin, Elizabeth.
CHAMBERLAIN: See Bigelow.
CHAPIN: See Miller.
CHURCH: See Warren, Abigail.
CHURCHILL: See Cowles.
COOK: See Cowles.
COOLIDGE: See Warren, Abigail.
CORSE: See Hawks.

COWLES: Susanna=Asaph Mitchell-#48; allied lines Bird-
sale/Churchill/Cook/Ives/Parker/Royce/Sims; ref "Genealogy of the Cowles Family in America," Col. Calvin D.
Cowles, V.I, p1-75; (D. L. Jacobus calls her "Cole" in his
"Families of Ancient New Haven.")

CRANE: See Sayre.
CUNLIFFE: See Wait(e).
DAVIS: See Allis.
DEMAREST: See Allen.
DICKENSHEETS: See Potee.
DOOLITTLE: See Tuttle.

EDWARDS: See Baldwin; see Miller; ref also Walter C. Corbin Mss. Collection on file at NEGHS, SG COR-5-85 (Edwards
& Field p426); see also Allis.

FLAGG: See Bigelow.
FIELD: See Edwards; see Miller.

Some Allied Lines

FOSTER: Lydia (Timothy, Bartholomew, Bartholomew)=Joseph Mitchell, Jr.-#26; allied lines Ackley/Giles/Spencer/Verry; ref Wallingford, CT Probate Dist. File #562, 1788, CT State Lib. (Timothy Foster); "Families of Ancient New Haven," Donald L. Jacobus, p621; "Record of the Posterity of Reginald Foster," F. C. Pierce, 1899, p1015-1017; "The Giles Memorial," J. A. Vinton, 1864, p4-7 (Giles/Verry); Gloucester, MA V/R (Verry/Giles); Barbour Coll., E. Haddam, CT V/R, V.5:51 (Ackley/Foster); "Bosworth Genealogy," Mrs. Mary B. Clarke, 1926, V.I, Appendix p4 (Ackley/Foster); "Dawes-Gates Ancestral Lines," Mary W. Ferris, 1931, V.II, p41/42 (Ackley/Foster); TAG V.27:161-169 (Spencer/Ackley).

FRENCH: See Hawks.
GAYLORD: See Hess.
GILBERT: See Miller.
GILES: See Foster.
HARDING: See Baldwin; see Miller.

HAWKS: Ira (Gershom, Eliezer, Eliezer, John)=Cynthia Mitchell-#83; allied lines Burt/Catlin/Corse/French/Lawrence/Munn/Nims/Parsons/Smead/Wells; ref "Hist. of Deerfield, MA," George Sheldon, V.II (all but French/Lawrence & Wells); "History of the CT Valley in MA," Louis H. Everts, 1879, V.II, p709; altho neither Sheldon nor Everts lists Ira as s/o Gershom & Thankful (Corse) Hawks, Ira is in Charlemont, MA V/R as b 1766, s/o Gershom & Thankful; Everts adds to Sheldon's list of ch 3 more sons of Gershom & Thankful, i.e., Rufus, Ephraim & Reuben, altho they do not appear in Charlemont b rec. (Also see Catlin.)

HAWKS: Israel=Mary/Polly Mitchell-#84; see above Ira Hawks, brother of Israel.

HESS: Henry Hyde=1)Lucy M. Mitchell-#221;=2)Elizabeth M. Mitchell-#222; allied line Gaylord; ref Civil War pension papers of Henry H., Nat'l Arch., Washington, D.C. (giving data on sibs, par from bible rec, letters, affidavits).

HOLTON: See King.

HOUGH: James=Sarah Mitchell-#4; ref "Families of Ancient New Haven," D. L. Jacobus, p846 (also anc & desc).

HUBBARD: Lucy=Ensign Mitchell-#77. The anc of Lucy is shrouded; a query in TAG, V.XVII:59, 1940/41, submitted by a desc of her son, Ira, states she was b 2 Feb 176<u>2</u>, by fam tradition both b & m in Berkshire Co., MA; census rec from 1790 thru 1830 confirm she was b betw 1760-1770. Of her 4 sons who lvd past 1880, 3 state their mother was b in MA; the 4th says both mother & father b in VT, but he himself was b in VT. Aft a fruitless search thru a huge amt of Hubbard mat'l in CT, MA, VT, NY, all town clks in Berkshire Co. were queried for rec of b & m for a Lucy Hubbard; no m rec was found, & only the town clk of Sheffield, MA had a b rec for a Lucy H. as follows: "Hubbard, Lucy, reputed dau of John Hubbard which Susannah Highstead bore to him Feb. 2, 176<u>4</u>." In "Records of the Court of Gen'l Sessions of the Peace," Berkshire Co. (Great Barrington), 24 Apr 1764, p45/46, John Hubbard was ordered to pay support for the child, Lucy, & Susanna Highstead, as a single woman, was convicted of fornication & fined. No further connection has been made betw John Hubbard & the ch, Lucy, nor has further trace of Susannah Highstead been found. If Lucy who m Ensign Mitchell was d/o John Hubbard & Susannah Highstead, her illegitimacy is surely the reason why discovering her anc has eluded the best efforts of so many for so long.

HYDE: See Bigelow.
IVES: See Cowles
JOHNSON: See Brainard.

KING: Zadock, Sr. (Thos., Thos., John)=Hannah Mitchell-#28; allied lines Holton/Mygatt/Webster; ref "Families of Early Hartford, CT," Lucius B. Barbour, p310,347,675/6; "History of the CT Valley in MA," Louis H. Everts, V.I, p174,195,219; "The Spencer Family Workshop," Peter Miller (article ment. Zadock in <u>LeDespencer</u>, Journal of the Spencer Family Ass'n, V.10/#2, Jul 1986, p36).

KING: Zadock, Jr.=Thankful Mitchell-#78 (see Zadock, Sr. above, father of Zadock, Jr).

LAWRENCE: See Hawks.
LE FARGE: See Calvin.
MARKLE(Y): See Potee.
MARSHFIELD: See Miller.

Some Allied Lines

MEARS: See Calvin, Harriet.
MILLER: See Brainard.

MILLER: Elizabeth=Elijah Mitchell-#18; allied lines At-
kinson/Baldwin(see)/Beaman-Beamon/Chapin/Edwards/Field/
Gilbert/Harding/Marshfield/Platt/Wood/Young; ref "Families of Early Guilford, CT," Alvan Talcott, 1984, p422-
25; "History of Deerfield, MA," George Sheldon, V.II
(Baldwin p55-57; Field p155-163); "Field Genealogy,"
Frederick C. Pierce, 1901, p96-101, 114-119, 138-141,
152/53, 160/61, 211; "Springfield Families," Thomas B.
Warren, V.2 (F-O), 1934/5 (Miller p463-467); "Hale, House
& Related Families," D.L. Jacobus & E.F. Waterman, 1952
(Miller p715/16; Marshfield p710-712); "Dawes-Gates An-
cestral Lines," Mary Walton Ferris, V.II, 1931 (Beaman
p105-108); "Transcripts of Extracts of Devonshire Pro-
bates," Olive Moger, Salt Lake City Call # British Q Area,
942.35 S2m, V.4 (Chapin p1008, subpages a,b,c,f,g,h);
"The Gilbert Family," H.W. Brainerd, H.S. Gilbert, C.A.
Torrey & D.L. Jacobus, 1953 (Chapin & Gilbert p24, 50-53);
"The Ancestry of Samuel, Freda & John Warner," Frederick
Chester Warner, 1949 (Field p203/4; Atkinson p20; Chapin
p107/08; Edwards p186/7); "John Keep of Longmeadow, MA
1660-1676," Frank E. Best, 1899 (Miller p7-18).

MONFORT: See Allen.
MUNN: See Hawks.
MYGATT: See King.
NIMS: See Hawks.
PARKER: See Cowles.
PARSONS: See Hawks.
PECK: See Tuttle.
PLATT: See Atkinson.

POTEE: Gabriel M.=Lavina Mitchell-#208; allied lines Mar-
kle(y)/Dickensheets; ref TAG, V.46/#1, Jan 1970, p102/03,
anc chart of Frank Van Rensselaer Phelps.

ROLLISON: See Calvin.
ROYCE: See Cowles.
SANGOR: See Bigelow.

SAYRE: Cynthia=Abner Mitchell-#149; allied lines Valen-
tine/Crane; ref "Portrait & Biographical Album of Rock

Island Co., IL," Chapman Bros., 1885, p573 (biography of Cynthia's brother, Alanson Sayre).

SIMS: See Cowles.
SKINNER: See Bigelow.
SMEAD: See Hawks.
SPENCER: See Foster; see Brainard.
SPRAGUE: See Warren, Abigail.
STOE/STOW: See Brainard.
TERHUNE: See Allen.

TUTTLE: Gershom (Gershom, Timothy, Simon, Wm)=Tabitha Mitchell-#29; allied lines Allis (see)/Doolittle/Peck; ref "Tuttle-Tuthill Lines in America," Alva M. Tuttle, 1968, p224; "Families of Ancient New Haven," Donald L. Jacobus, V.VIII, p1881-1884, 1902-1904.

TUTTLE: Zebulon=Aphalinda Mitchell-#88 (see above Gershom Tuttle, father of Zebulon).

VALENTINE: See Sayre.
VERRY: See Foster.

WAIT(E): Anna=William Mitchell-#3; allied lines Bassett/ Cunliffe/Webb; ref Walter C. Corbin Mss. Coll. on file at NEHGS, SG COR-5-85 (Waite/Webb p1190); "The Ancestry of Samuel, Freda & John Warner," Frederick Chester Warner, 1949 (Bassett p49; Cunliffe p158/59; Wait p688; Webb p731-736); "Genealogical Dictionary of the First Settlers of New England," James Savage, V.IV, 1977 (Waite/Webb).

WARD: See Catlin.
WARREN: See Bigelow

WARREN: Abigail=Abner Mitchell-#30; allied lines Coolidge/Church/Sprague; "History of Deerfield, MA," George Sheldon, V.2, p211, 334/35; "Genealogies & History of Watertown, MA," Henry Bond, 2nd ed., reprint (Church p158; Warren p620/21,962); Sheldon calls Abigail "sis. of Neverson" who was bc 1749; Bond lists Abigail, b 1740 & Neverson, bpt 1749, among the ch of Dan'l & Martha (Coolidge) Warren, but says Dan'l d 9 Oct 1795, prob s/o John Warren & his 1st wife Abigail Hastings, yet no Dan'l is listed as ch of John nor when he was app't grdn in 1720 of the ch of his 1st wife. Rather, Dan'l was s/o Joshua (Dan'l, John) & Rebecca (Church) Warren as proved in his estate papers (Westborough, Worcester Co., MA Probates 1758-1765) that state assets of the estate included cash rec'd from the estate of "Joshua Warren, father of the dec'd;" wife Martha, admx; payments made to b/l Jed How; Phineas Hardy ment., prob ano b/l; youngest ch, Daniel (b Mar 1758) "was but four months old when the dec'd died." Listed were "cloaths and utensils left by Daniel Warren of Capt. Stephen Maynard's Compy., Col. Wm Williams Reg." left at Lake George Aug. 28, 1758. Either Daniel, father of Abigail & Neverson (and others) was k at the battle of Fort Ticonderoga in July 1758, or d later from wounds or disease. In 1766, Jonas Locke was app't grdn of Neverson Warren, called "heir of Daniel Warren, dec'd, of Westborough." (Hampshire Co., MA Probate Rec.)

WEBB: See Wait(e).
WEBSTER: See King.
WELLS: See Hawks.
WHITLOCK: See Baldwin; see Catlin.
WOOD: See Atkinson; see Platt.
WOOLSON: See Bigelow.
YOUNG: See Miller.

MISCELLANEOUS MITCHELL DATA

This chapter offers a potpourri of data collected over the years on Mitchells other than those who are the subject of this book. No data appearing in the main text is repeated in this chapter. My object in presenting this material is to expand the scope of the book by sharing all Mitchell information in my possession in hopes that some- one may profit from it.

Arrangement of material is by 1) state headings (in- cludes material from such sources as birth, marriage, death, probate and deed records, county publications, census records, etc.); 2) material from various publica- tions; 3) data in the form of queries either personally received or abstracted from genealogical quarterlies. Names and addresses of the submitters are given.

Data on the Mitchells of White Co., IN and Smith Co., TN comes from personal research as both represent ances- tral lines of mine. Neither line is related to the other or to the Mitchells in this book except by marriage. Ad- dress letters regarding either of these two lines to me. In the case of queries, address correspondence to the submitter of the query.

Abbreviations used in this chapter are either defin- ed in the front of the book or are understandable without further explanation. Although this section is indexed, I have alphabetized where possible or used bold face so as to ease its use by the researcher. I can not take respon- sibility for data sent to me by others in the form of transcribed statistics, queries, biographical material, census records, etc., all of which are often erroneous even when copied correctly.

Note: I have avoided material from MA since there is much easily accessible material in that state on early Mitchell families (such as the lines of Matthew Mitchell and Experience Mitchell), preferring to concentrate on transition states such as NY, PA, OH, IN, IL, KY, TN, etc.

Miscellaneous Mitchell Data

BARBADOS (WEST INDIES)

"The Original Lists of Persons of Quality," V.II, ed. by
John Camden Hotten, 1874:

Tickets Granted to Emigrants from Barbados to New Eng-
land, Carolina, Virginia, New York, Antiqua, Jamaica,
Newfoundland, and Other Places: (p388) 25 Apr 1679 **John
Michell** and **Richard Mitchell** in the ship "Nathaniel" for
Boston. (p368) 29 Apr 1679 **Richard Mitchell's** servant,
Mary Fitz Nichols, sent to Boston on the "Nathaniel."

Barbados Parish Registers, Births & Deaths, Lists of Inhabitants, Landed Proprietors, Servants, etc., 1678-1679:
(p473) Mr. **David Mitchell**, Parish of St. Michaells, 10
acres, no hired or bought servants or slaves. (p481)
Thomas Mitchell, Parish of Christ Church 22 Dec 1679, 1
acre, no hired or bought servants or slaves. (p438)
Anthony Michell & wife, 5 children, 2 negro slaves, 1680
inhabitants of town of St. Michaels. (p456) **Anthony Michell**, 5 acres, 1 hired servant, 4 negroes, Parish Register of St. Michaells 1678-9.

"Omitted Chapters from Hotten's Original Lists of Persons
of Quality...1600-1700," ed. by James C. Brandow, 1982:

(p115/6) **Thomas & William Mitchell** on list of soldiers
"with defaults for nonappearance" 9 Jan 1679. (p149)
Matthew Micall in Maj. Tho. Helmes command. (p31) **Mary
Michaell** buryed 7ber ye 29th 1678 in churchyard of St.
Josephs. (p158) **David Michell**, householder, 1 servant 6
Jan 1679 (Col. John Standfast's Co.). (p100) **Hen. Michell**
in Col. Lyne's Reg't of Foot 6 Jan 1679. (p11) Capt.
Richard Michell, 80 acres, 20 negroes, St. Phillips Par-
ish 1680. (p207) Capt. **Richard Michell** under command of
Capt. John Dempster. (p105) Capt. **Richd. Michell**, 4 men
on list of "P'sons that did not appeare in armes", Capt.
Vincent Dent's command 6 Jan 1679.

"Barbados Records, Wills, Administrations 1639-1680,"
V.I, ed. by Joanne McRee Sanders, 1979:

(p389) **John Michael** ment. as servant, Rice William's will
8 Jan 1667 St. Michaels Parish. (p263) **Charls Michaell**

-348-

Miscellaneous Mitchell Data

wit. to Cornell O'Haire's will 27 Nov 1650 All Saints and
St. Lucy's Parish. (p317) Capt. **Rich. Michell** wit. John
Sargeant's will 29 June 1680. (p3) **Samuel Michaell** wit.
Nicholas Alford's will 20 Sep 1649 St. Peter's Parish.
(p214) **Anthony Michell** ment. in Nathaniell Lane's will 28
Dec 1678. (p286) **Anthony Michell** wit. George Potter's
will 7 Sep 1652. (p257) **Edward & Katherine Michell** ment.
as "brother and sister" in Edward Nightingale's will 6
Jan 1668 St. Philips Parish. (p241) **James Michaell's** will
dated 4 Dec 1676, proved 5 Jan 1676, ment. Thomas Read
(friend, executor & legatee); Wm. Davies, James Calhus,
Capt. Thomas Kendall, Capt. Sam: South; wit. Robert Hill,
Saml: Sedgewick. (p157) **Margaret Michell** ment. as sister
in James Hacet's will 23 Jul 1657. (p8) **Richard Michell**
wit. John Arnett's will 4 June 1659. (p233) **Thomas Michell** ment. as son in Margaret Mapletopp's will 9 Feb
1669. (p243) **Atheriatius Mitchell's** will dated 23 Aug
1663, proved 14 Dec 1663, names **Anne Mitchell** (wife), Simon Mackler Sr. (friend); wit. Nicholas Simonds, Robert
Anson, Daniell Kennedy, Jacob Melckebeke. (p343) **Anthony
Mitchell** (friend & overseer), Thomas Summers' will dated
11 June 1652. (p168) **Stephen Mitchell** ment. in Rebecca
Harrison's will 20 June 1670 (widow of London). (p203)
Thomas Mitchell ment. as brother in Randolph Jones' will
25 Mar 1659. (V.II 1681-1700, p241) **Richard Michell, Sr.,**
St. Phillips Parish, will dated 17 Dec 1688, proved May
1689, ment. **Richard & John** (sons), Elizabeth Fauntleroy,
Lucy Beamont ("my sister"), Capt. James Fauntleroy, Capt.
Ira Welse, Richard Townsend (friends & executors).

(For information on Barbados records and research, write
Dept. of Archives, Black Rock, St. Michael, Barbados,
West Indies. Request price of copying and mailing.)

CONNECTICUT

Hartford Probate District, Hartford, #3742 **John Mitchell**
estate ("Deceased for Barbadoes June the first 1695");
inventory 10 Aug 1696 men. "Widdow Micholl"; debts owed
John Ladd's estate, Elloxland? Duggos' estate, Capt.
Stanly, Tho: Hancoxs; Deacon Wilson, Tho: Gilbert, Capt.
Bull, Mr. Sam: Harvard, Mr. Gibbon, Mr. Lord, Mr. Mackman,
_____ "Skinor". (This probate file contains no will, no
mention of children or widow's first name.)

Miscellaneous Mitchell Data

(Connecticut con't)

Hartford Probate District, Wethersfield, #3739 estate of
James Mitchell, will dated 19 Dec 1775 proved 26 Mar 1776;
codicil 5 Feb 1776; ment. wife **Arminel**, sons **James, David,
Stephen Mix Mitchell**; land in Wethersfield, Newington,
Middletown, South Hadley, Hampshire Co., MA, Glastonbury;
final property dist. Mar 1783, wit. **Mabel Mitchell**.

Samuel Mitchell m 10 Nov 1762 E. Haddam to Rebecca Cook
d/o Ebenezer; ch b E. Haddam: **(i)** James 15 Mar 1764; **(ii)**
Anna 17 Apr 1766; **(iii)** Ruth 4 Mar 1768; **(iv)** Lydia 11 Mar
1770; **(v)** Rebecca 26 Jan 1772; **(vi)** Samuel 24 Jan 1774;
(vii) Seldon 3 Nov 1776; **(viii)** Joseph 1782; **(ix)** Abigail
20 Dec 1784; **(x)** Mary 3 Mar 1786; **(xi)** Gilston 7 Apr 1788.
(Ref: N.E.H.G.R., Vol. 126:84)

"Families of Early Hartford, CT," Lucius Barnes Barbour,
1982 reprint (Key: Hfd = Hartford; Weth = Wethersfield):

(p94) Daniel Buck, Jr. (Hfd) m 14 Oct 1805 **Julia Mitchell**
(Weth); Notice in N.E. Palladium 29 Oct 1805, Julia d/o
Hon. **S. M. Mitchell**. (p253/404) Mary Freeman (Colchester)
m **Lot Mitchel** (Hfd) 8 Dec 1819. (p283) Elizabeth Graves,
d/o George, Jr. m ____ **Mitchell**. (p334) Giles Hurlburt
m2) **Abigail Mitchell** who d 5 June 1834 age 56y (Old North).
(p343) Daniel Judd m 4 Dec 1705 **Mercy Mitchell** (Woodbury).
(p403/4) **Elizabeth Mitchell**, d/o **John** bpt 4 Mar 1687/8 m
John Kilbourn as 2nd wife. **Sarah Mitchell** m 5 June 1712
Abiel Kilbourn. **Sarah Mitchell** d/o **John** m 5 June 1712
Abraham Kilbourn & d 3 Oct 1719. **John Mitchell** owned the
covenant (1st church) 4 Mar 1687-8 m Elizabeth Graves, d/o
Marshall. **John Mitchell** d 28 Jul 1683 m Mary ____; of Hfd
1655 freeman 1667; ch Mary bc1655; John bc1658 m Elizabeth
Graves; Sarah bc1662; Margaret bc1664; Mabel bc1666; Mir-
iam bc1668. (p428) Thomas Olcott m2) **Lucy Mitchell**.
(p591) Augustus Thatcher (Hfd) m **Eliza May Mitchell** 19
Oct 1819 (Weth. church).

"History of Wallingford, CT," C. H. S. Davis:

New Haven Vital Records:
(p7) **Elizabeth Mitchell**, d/o **Thomas**, b 6 Feb 1651.
(p31) **Elisabeth Mitchell** m 5 Dec 1672 Phillip Alcott.

Miscellaneous Mitchell Data

(Connecticut con't)

"CT Revolutionary Pensioners," comp. by CT D.A.R., 1982,
p103 (Key: Cont.= man paid by U.S. Gov't but enlisted
from State of CT; Cont. & Conn = service Cont., also in
state reg't; S = Survivor's file; W = widow's file; R =
rejected file; BlWt = bounty land warrant):

MITCHELL:
Daniel, widow Ruth, R7282 (soldier never applied).
David, Cont. (Conn.) S42981
Elisha, Cont. serv., lvd CT, wid. Mary, BlWt S12-100.
George, widow Lucy, BlWt 38534-100-55, W21807.
Ichabod S41007.
John Benjamin, widow Jemima, W15693.
Joseph, Conn. Sea Service R7278.
Joseph, Conn. & NY, R20404.
Margaret, former widow of Samuel Abbey.
Oliver, widow Anne, W1632.
William S13928.
Zephaniah, Conn. & Cont., S36155.

1850 Federal Census of Middlesex Co., CT:
(Key: H/H = in household of)
East Haddam:
p194 285/344 MITCHELL, Amasa 25 CT; H/H of Mary Perkins,
82 CT; 286/345 MITCHELL, Amy 50 CT, STARK, John 45, Hannah 43, W. Henry 20, Justus 16, Francis 13 (male), Ralph
10, all b CT.
p195 304/363 MITCHEL, David 38, Elisa 37, Harriet E. 15,
John 13, Martha 11, Julia A. 9, Warren 6, Charles 4,
Mary 2, all b. CT.
p198 349/410 MITCHELL, Mary 64 CT in H/H of CLARK, Oliver
C. 43, Cynthia 40, Oliver C. 18, all b CT.
p189 196/237 MITCHELL, Samuel 31, Cynthia E. 29, Ellen V.
5, CHAPMAN, Ann 66, all b CT.
p182 96/117 MITCHELL, Sophia 39 CT, BROWN, Harriet 16 CT.
p182 101/122 MITCHELL, Lorenzo D. 17 CT, H/H of SILLIMAN,
Huntington 55, Statira C. 52, Horace B. 20, Betsy Ann
18, William 19, Jared B. 27, Sarah D. 24, all b CT.
p180 71/85 MITCHELL, Warren 22 CT, H/H of JOHNSON, Emory
32, Elisa A. 29, Emory E. 9, all b CT.
Saybrook:
p253 504/554 MITCHELL, John 73, Sarah 70, Sarah 47,
Edward 19, all b CT.

(Connecticut con't)

1850 Federal Census of New Haven Co., CT:
(Key: H/H = in household of)
Menden:
p42 MITCHELL, W., 17 CT, H/H of Wockhoff? family.
p42/3 107/149 MITCHELL, Chauncey 30, Jerusha 25, Stephen
    Amos 3, Mary 6, Warren 10, all b CT.
p70 428/570-1 MITCHELL, Sylvester 47 CT, H/H of THORP,
    Joel 71, Laura 66, Gideon 45, Abigail 43, Mary 14, Lewis
    G. 8, Elvira L. 3, all b CT.
p73 469/621 MITCHELL, Sylvester 45 CT, H/H of DARELY? &
    CONKLIN families b Ireland.

Barbour Collection (L.D.S. film #002,983):
Winchester, New Haven Co., CT V/R:
V.3:329 **Lorenzo Mitchell** (Collinsville) m 3 Sep 1835 Mary
    Ann Blake (Winchester).
V.3:364 **Lorenzo Mitchell** d 17 Sep 1838.

Windham, New Haven Co., CT V/R:
V3:51 **Katurah Michael** (Windham) m 25 Sep 1792 Job Primus
    (Canterbury).
A-8 **Abraham Mitchel/Michell** m 27 Apr 1699 Mary Abbe.
A-29 **Daniel Mitchel** s/o Abraham & Mary, b/d 10 Dec 1700.

Windsor, New Haven Co., CT V/R:
V2:256 **Oliver Mitchell/Mitchel** d 10 Mar 1840 bur 13 Mar.
V2:252 **William Mitchell** d 18 May 1725.

Woodbury, New Haven Co., CT V/R:
V.1:78 Aaron Mitchell s/o David & Sarah b 18 Jan 1779.
LR2-203 Abijah Mitchell s/o David & Sarah b 24 Jan 1718.
V1:81 Abijah Mitchell m 15 May 1759 Anna Berry.
V1:45/108 Abijah Mitchell s/o Timothy & Elizabeth b 24
    Feb 1761 d 9 Mar 1761.
V1:45/84 Abijah Mitchell s/o Timothy & Elizabeth b 29 Mar
    1764 m 28 Jan 1784 Ruthann Roots.

Note: "Dawes-Gates Ancestral Lines," Vol. II, Mary W.
Ferris, pp589-592, discusses two theories regarding the
ancestry of **Hannah Mitchell** who married Robert Coe. One
theory is that she was daughter of Matthew Mitchell, and
the second that she was daughter of Thomas Mitchell.

ILLINOIS

CLAY COUNTY:

"Footprints Past & Present," V.5:4, Richland Co. Gen. &
Historical Society, Olney, IL:
Marriages:
. Alvina Mitchell to Nathanial Read 7 Dec 1854 BkA:82
Ison Mitchell to Dianna Ingraham 21 Mar 1844 Bk1:119
Martha A. Mitchell to William H. Holman 18 Oct 1855 BkA:89
Rosannah Mitchell to John Tadlock 15 Aug 1850 BkA:38
Samuel Mitchell to Sarah J. Spurlin 15 Jul 1855 BkA:86
Sarah Michel to John D. Christman 28 May 1849 BkA:28
Solomon Mitchell to Rebecca Bassett 18 Nov 1850 BkA:40
Thomas Mitchell to Rosanah Ingraham 20 Mar 1851 BkA:43

COLES COUNTY:

Richard Robert Mitchell, att'y of Charleston; editor of
the "Charleston Plaindealer-Herald"; born 21 Oct 1876 at
Charleston, s/o **Isaac B. Mitchell** & Florida A. Miles;
Isaac b Charleston; Florida A. b Franklin Co., KY; paternal grpar were **James A. Mitchell** & Margaret Esther Collum,
b at Jonesboro, TN; great-grpar **Robert Mitchell** (b Scotland) & Elizabeth A. Allison (b Jonesboro, TN). Maternal
grpar John A. & Julia A. (Trotter) Miles of KY; great-
grpar John & Maria Asabel (Tarleton) Miles of SC & KY.
Last date ment 1903; Richard R. unmarried. ("The History
of Coles Co., IL," p838)

DEWITT COUNTY:

Marriage Records:
1846 Feb 5 Benjamin Mitchell to Electa M. Brown A:53
1846 Sep 29 Malinda Michael to Orin A. Cody A:55
1849 Jan 1 John P. Mitchell to Elizabeth Gideon A:68
1850 Nov 28 Deborah P. Mitchell to Theodore M. Broun A:82
1854 Aug 30 Amanda Michael to William L. Todd A:123
1855 Jan 1 William T. Mitchell to Lovina M. Hull A:129
1856 Oct 30 Mary E. Mitchell to Austin J. Richey B:4
1857 Jan 15 Jas./John D. Mitchell to Josaphine Weaver B:20
1857 Jan 22 John H. Mitchell to Mary A. Hammond B:22
1861 Jan 24 Mrs. Esther Mitchell to John P. Clemons B:248
1861 Feb 12 John J. Mitchell to Charlott English B:251

Miscellaneous Mitchell Data

(Marriages - DeWitt Co., Illinois con't)

1866 Jan 1 Lander F.S. Mitchel to Mary E. Baldrick C:12
1869 Jan 6 Grace H. Mitchell to Joseph H. Merrell C:26
1869 Feb 18 Lewis Mitchell to Missouri Dickson C:27
1869 Apr 25 Henry Mitchell to Louisa A. Jackson C:28
1870 Aug 4 Florence Mitchell to Orin T. Colwell C:33
1871 Jun 8 A. Bartley Mitchell to Harriet Clapperton C:36
1872 Sep 10 William H. Mitchell to Harriett McMurry C:41
1872 Dec 4 William H. Mitchell to Ella Slover C:42
1873 Jun 8 Ella M. Mitchell to Simon B. Ewing C:44
1873 Aug 4 Daniel W. Mitchell to Rebecca Bushell C:45
1873 Sep 4 Selwyn D. Mitchell to Phebe A. Campbell C:46
1873 Sep 3 Leander S. Mitchell to Charlotte Phillips C:--
1875 Apr 15 George E. Mitchell to Maggie Johnston C:53
1876 May 3 John Mitchell, age 30 of Lorain, OH to Ida M.
    Norris, age 25 of DeWitt Co., IL C:57
1876 Dec 25 Laura F. Mitchell, age 19, to Emerson Hart-
    sock, age 23, both of DeWitt Co., IL C:60
1874 Mar 15 Carrie Mitchell of Princeton, IN to H. W. Web-
    ster of Clinton, IL (newspaper).

"DeWitt Co. Genealogical Society Quarterlies":
Newspaper abstracts:
    Mentioned in the Administration papers of Isaac W.
Coppenbarger, dec'd, 2 May 1900, rec'd from **E.B. Mitchell**
for pasture rent, sale of clover hay, oats and wheat...
    E.B. Mitchell, guardian for Walter Davis, minor heir of
Roxanna Davis, dec'd, 16 Nov 1900. **E.B. Mitchell**, guard-
ian for Ellsworth & Onie Doss, minor heirs of Samuel H.
Doss, 16 Nov 1900.
    Memoirs of Mrs. **Frances (Mitchell)** Peddicord, b 11 Dec
1800 near Lexington, KY; m 3 May 1821 Milzor Peddicord; to
Champaign Co., OH soon after mar; Mr. Peddicord d 1842,
leaving widow & 10 ch; Mrs. Peddicord to DeWitt Co., IL in
1854 where she d 20 Jan 1868 age 67y 1m 10d; funeral at the
Clinton M.E. Church 22 Jan. (V.6:2 Summer 1980 p48)
    W. T. Mitchell, administrator of the estate of William
Hull, dec'd; administration notice dated 17 Feb 1874.
    DeWitt Co., IL G.A.R. Members - **L. Mitchell**, Co. H,
30th Illinois Infantry.
    Centenary Church neighborhood 1875: "Mr. **Ross Mitchel**
owns a farm of 120 acres. Last winter he met with a sad
loss in getting burnt out..."

Miscellaneous Mitchell Data

Died in Texas Twp. at the residence of **R. B. Mitchell** on Monday, July 14, 1873 Mrs. Nancy Brown, mother of Mrs. J. C. Stokes of this city.

DeWitt Co., IL Militia Rolls 1861-1862 (males between the ages of 18-45) - **John H. Mitchell.** Listing of DeWitt Co., IL Revolutionary War ancestors - **Abraham Mitchell.**

In Chancery for Divorce: **Mary A. Mitchell** vs **John H. Mitchell** 5 Feb 1865.

Estate Sale, Philip Davis, 1 Dec 1843 - **Wm. Mitchell.**

Old Settlers Journal: **B. T. Mitchell,** Clinton, IL, was born 9 July 1823 in "Hershire," VA; to DeWitt Co. 1835.

Johnson-Bracken Family Records: Levi Rathburn Murphey, born 28 Dec 1847 Pughtown, Frederick Co., VA, s/o Hiram R. Murphey b 1797 d 1881 & **Grace F. Mitchell** b 20 May 1806 d 17 Dec 1880. Also listed, **Thomas Mitchell** b 18 Sep 1758. (Contributed by Mrs. Malinda Evans, Vol. III, #4, p113)

DeWitt Co. Abstracts of Wills, Vol. I, p92: **James H. Mitchell,** execr for George Gideon, will dtd 18 Sep 1879.

John P. Mitchell, one of the oldest settlers of the co. d yesterday (<u>The Clinton Public</u>, 25 Dec 1874 issue).

1850 Federal Census of DeWitt Co., IL:
(Key: H/H = in household of)
372/377 MITCHELL, J.P. 29 VA, Elizabeth 20 OH, MOORE, Blish 25 OH.
529/534 MICHELL, Benjamine P. 27 VA, Electa M. 24 NY, Augustus W. 2 IL, DESPANE, Mary 18 IL.
534/539 MICHELL, Frances L. (male) 52 VA, Deborah P. 18 OH, Wm. T. 16 OH, Mary E. 10 IL.
535/540 MITCHELL, James D. 22 VA, H/H of LINVERT, Henry.

1860 Federal Census of DeWitt Co., IL:
(Key: H/H = in household of)
16/16 MITCHELL, Frances L. (fem.) 3 mos. IL, H/H of MAYALL, James 45 MA, Mary Ann 39 OH, and children b IN.
22/22 MITCHEL, James D. 31 VA, Josephine 22 OH, Mary Jane 2, IL, John W. 1 IL, ROUZE, Jos 28 NJ, DUNCAN, Jas 19 IL.
145/139 MITCHEL, Wm. T. 26 OH, Lavina 26 OH, Laura Francis 2 IL, Jno. Mitchell 3 mos IL, STONER, Jno. 76 PA.
179/172 MITCHEL, B. L. (male) 37 VA, Electa M. 34 NY, Augustus W. 13 IL, Grace H. 9? IL, James F. 5 IL, CUNDIFF, Jane 19 OH.

Miscellaneous Mitchell Data

268/260 MITCHEL, Frances L. (fem.) 63 VA, Leander S. 24
  IL, PHILIPS, Charlotte 28 IN, DELAY, Coleman 17 IL.
423/417 MITCHELL, Geo. W. 36 KY, Maria 32 KY, Mary J. 8
  IN, Anna 5 IL, William 3 IL.
478/469 MITCHELL, Jno. P. 39 VA, Elisabeth 28 OH, James H.
  8 IL, Lillice 9 IL, CROSS, Delilia 19 IL, SMITH, Jno. A.
  25 OH.
644/628 MITCHELL, John 32 VA, Ann 20 OH, Adolphus 3 IL,
  infant (female) ? IL.
1914/1883 MITCHEL, Hester H. 27 OH, Rosetta 4 IL, H/H of
  JONES, V.A. (male) 39 VA, Lucy B. 31 OH.

<u>DeWitt Co., IL Cemetery Inscriptions</u>, printed by the
Decatur Genealogical Society, Decatur, IL (V.I-V):
<u>Woodlawn Cemetery</u> (Clinton, IL, V.III, Part 1 & 2):
Missouri Mitchell w/o Lewis 28 May 1848-6 Sep 1886
Earnest D. Mitchell 12 Oct 1868-14 Sep 1892 (gr dug 16Sep)
Benjamin T. Mitchell 1823-14 Dec 1909 age 86y
Electa M. Mitchell w/o Benjamin 1826-1877
Clara M. Mitchell 1863-10 Apr 1928 age 64y 5m 9d
Selwyn Delmar Mitchell 1850-17 Dec 1925 age 75y 11m 22d
S. D. Mitchell - grave dug 4 June 1883
Phebe A. Mitchell w/o S.D. 21 Apr 1856-3 Aug 1882
Fannie Mitchell w/o P.R. 1818-31 Jan 1903 age 85y
Frank W. Mitchell 1874-1940
N. Helen Mitchell 1887-24 Apr 1915 age 28y
Edmond G. Mitchell 1879-1933
Grace Costley Mitchell 1880-1963
Ross Mitchell 1823-11 Apr 1895
Hannah Mitchell w/o Ross 1831-13 Sep 1907 age 78y
John Payton Mitchell 25 Apr 1821 Frederick, VA-24 Dec
  1874 Clinton, IL age 53y 8m 3d
Laura Mitchell d/o J.P. & E. 7 Sep 1854 age 10m 17d
Cynthia Mitchell 15 Jul 1826-12 June 1900 (may be same as
  Mrs. B.F., 8 June 1900; stone matches a Mrs. Hickman's)
Caroline M. Mitchell 3 Mar 1844-14 Feb 1875 (on Mitchell-
  Brown stone)
William G. Mitchell 15 Aug 1901 age 38y
Mrs. Lewis Mitchell 24 June 1905 age 60y
Marry Louise Mitchell Sep 1920 age 67y 9m 18d
James H. Mitchell 6 Mar 1921 age 70y 5m 29d
Reba Alice Mitchell 27 Dec 1924 age 30y 8m 24d

Miscellaneous Mitchell Data

(Woodlawn Cemetery con't):
Edward B. Mitchell 5 Dec 1925 age 58y 2m 25d
Wm. C. Mitchell 22 Mar 1927 age 42y 10m 7d
Josephine Mitchell 2 Feb 1910 age 71y 8m 15d
Cecil E. Mitchell 5 May 1913
Mrs. E. P. Mitchell 4 Jan 1917 age 83y 3m 14d
Mrs. Carrie Mitchell 25 Apr 1900 (removed from Old Union)
Mrs. J. P. Mitchell 18 Nov 1903 age 72y
Lewis Mitchell 28 Feb 1904 age 67y
(also stones for Willie and Mary and for several unnamed
infants - no dates)

Texas Christian Cemetery (Texas Twp., V.IV):
Samuel A. Mitchell s/o George & Maria 4 Aug 1857

Maple Grove Cemetery (Santa Anna Twp, Farmer City, V.V):
Charles Franklin Mitchell 21 Apr 1893-3 Sep 1945 (on
    Vance lot)
Ruth Mitchell 16 Feb 1904-17 Nov 1904
Marcella Evans Mitchell 1846-1871
Peter Wiles Mitchell 1835-1903
Nancy J. Mitchell 1867-1951
Thomas S. Mitchell 1866-1933
Samuel Reed Mitchell 1863-1939
Eva White Mitchell 1863-1928
Bernice Mitchell 5 Jul 1916 - 29 Aug 1959
Hilda V. Mitchell 1903-1922
David Mitchell 23 Nov 1877-19 Nov 1914
J. E. Mitchell 1871-1917
Mary O. Mitchell "Mother" 1858-1922
Joseph H. Mitchell "Father" 1858-1939
Nancy Mitchell 1891-1930
Clarence D. Mitchell 1888-1962

City Cemetery (Santa Anna Twp., Farmer City, V.V):
Lydia Mitchell w/o H. 21 Jan 1868 in 32nd year
William D. Mitchell s/o H. & ___ 11 Oct 1870 age 6m 19d
Melsena Mitchell w/o P.W. d/o A. & E.E. Evans 14 May 1871
    age 27y 1m 27d
Frances Mitchell 2 Jul 1884-2 Jan 1908
Harry Mitchell 12 Aug 1875-16 Jan 1905
Frank ----- (Mitchell?)

Miscellaneous Mitchell Data

(DeWitt Co., Illinois con't)

Will Abstracts (Vol. I):

Will of Andrew S. Norris dtd 28 Apr 1880 (at age 58) d 12 May 1889 Farmer City; names wife Mary A.; youngest daughter **Ida M. Mitchell**; ch Amos L. Norris, Ivis J. Staley.

Will of Eliza Evans dtd 18 Apr 1889 Farmer City d there 7 Aug 1893; names ch of **Melcina Mitchell**, dec'd: **Thomas S. Mitchell, Iola Jane Mitchell, Eva Eliza Mitchell**; also ch of Sarah S. Evans, dec'd: Mary O. Evans, Wilbur W. S. Evans, Hannah Davidson; ch of Amos Evans, dec'd: Malinda A. Evans, Ora E. E. Evans, Hugh D. Evans; other heir, Mary A. Sidwell.

Will of William Fuller dtd 25 Apr 1893 (made at age 70y) d 10 Oct 1894 Clinton; names wife Rebecca; sons Thomas, John, Smith Fuller; grson Samuel Fuller; daughters Rebecca J. Vance, **Josephine Mitchell.**

Will of Joshua J. Miles of Clinton dtd 17 Jul 1896 (d 22 Jul 1896); wit by A. J. Richey & **E. B. Mitchell**, both of Clinton.

Will of Mary Alice Spink dtd 12 Aug 1896 d 11 Sep 1896 at Clinton; wit by James M. Kirk & **E. B. Mitchell**, both of Clinton.

Abstracts from "The Clinton Register":

Austin J. Richey, administrator of the estate of **Francis S. Mitchell**, dec'd; notice dated 15 Jan 1875.

Elizabeth Mitchell & James H. Mitchell, administrators of the estate of **John P. Mitchell**, dec'd; notice dated 20 Mar 1875.

Reunion Proceedings of the Yates Phalanx 1882-1903:

16th Annual Reunion, Blue Island, IL 1896: Co., H, **William C. Mitchell**, Independence, O.T. (sic)

(Note: "DeWitt Co. Genealogical Society Quarterly" abstractions cover all Mitchell references from Vol. 1 #1 Winter 1975 through Vol. XIII #4 Winter 1987, excepting land/personal property tax listings.)

The Clintonia '20, pub. by the Clinton High School Senior

Class of 1920, ment. **Muriel Mitchell**, sophomore; Alumni List 1872-1919: **Edwin B. Mitchell**, attorney, Clinton, Class of 1887. ("Dead" written after in longhand.)

Miscellaneous Mitchell Data

EDGAR COUNTY, ILLINOIS:

Marriage Records:
Abraham Mitchell to Emily A. Clarke 17 Mar 1861
Alexander C. Mitchell to Rachel Hardy 18 Sep 1873
Benjamin F. Mitchell to Mahala J. Long 25 Sep 1870
Charles H. Mitchell to Harriett Gordon 3 Jul 1870
H. H. Mitchell to Nancy Stanley 23 Dec 1851
James Mitchell to Cynthia J. Dairs 13 Mar 1856
James W. Mitchell to Mary Dollarhide 19 May 1864
John Mitchell to Aereatla F. Daniel 19 Jan 1871
John Mitchell to Sarah S. Hill 2 Apr 1868
Margaret Mitchell to Mathias Chrisman 7 Sep 1865
William T. Mitchell to Nancy H. Troxel 8 Sep 1871

"The History of Edgar Co., IL," Wm. LeBaron, Jr., 1879:
Abstracts:
   Bathsheba Mitchell b 18 Jan 1831 Washington Co., PA mar
15 Sep 1848 Thomas Carson b 15 May 1825 Washington Co.,
PA; lived there, then Tipton Co., IN, Vermilion Co., IL,
Edgar Co., IL, Marshall Co., IL, finally settling 1870 in
Ross Twp., Edgar Co., IL; 6 ch (CARSON) living Joel G.,
Oella J., Alvin J., John B., Clarence, Charles (p628).
   Elsie Mitchell b Fauquier Co., VA m Daniel M. Triplett b
24 June 1798 Frederick Co., VA; she d bef Nov 1847; 2 ch, 1
living Mary C. Triplett (p636).
   Elizabeth Mitchell b 23 Sep 1828 Washington Co., PA m
30 Oct 1851 John B. Galway b 31 Oct 1826 Washington Co.,
PA; to IL 1854; to Edgar Co. 1856; 2 ch (GALWAY) Roxana b
18 Mar 1853 (m John Kizar); James H. b 24 Dec 1856 (p 660).
   Jennie Mitchell d/o Rev. **R. A. Mitchell** m 12 Dec 1876
Charles Hite b 20 Jan 1851 Edgar Co., s/o John S. Hite, a
prominent pioneer; 1 son (HITE) Robert L. (pp 617-18).
   Mary Jane Mitchell of Ohio m Oct 1866 Mathias Chrisman b
31 Dec 1815 Fleming Co., KY; she d 16 Aug 1867 (pp 627-28).
   Rev. **R. A. Mitchell**, Kansas Twp., pastor of Presby. Ch.;
b 6 Apr 1819 Washington Co., TN; to Coles Co., IL with par.
when young. His father, **James A. Mitchell**, pioneer of
Coles Co., IL, settled 1833 where Charleston now stands;
James' wife living, age 79y. **Rev. Mitchell** educated at
Washington College, E. TN, at New Albany, IN Institute
(now Northwestern Theological Sem., Chicago); grad. 1848;
ordained 1856; has preached at Charleston since except 8
years in Kansas; in Mar 1849 m Anna E. Roberts of his

Miscellaneous Mitchell Data

(History abstracts of Edgar Co., <u>Illinois</u> con't)

native county (Washington Co., TN); has a family of 5
sons and 1 daughter, not named in biography (p620).

Rev. **Thomas W. Mitchell** was 3rd Rector of the Episcopal
Church, organized in 1860 (p328).

Taxpayers of Edgar Co., IL: **R.A. Mitchell**, farmer, P.O.
Conlogue, Grandview Twp.; **J. J. Mitchel**, laborer, Paris
Twp.; **John Mitchell**, blacksmith, Paris Twp.; **Dorcas
Mitchell**, farmer, P.O. Logan, Brouillett Twp.; **George D.
Mitchell**, farmer, P.O. Horace, Edgar Twp.; **James W.
Mitchell**, farmer, Paris Twp.; **Peter A. Mitchell**, farmer,
P.O. Paris, Edgar Twp.; **W. H. Mitchell**, farmer, P.O.
Logan, Brouillett Twp.

Edgar Co. Death Records:
Cinthia J. (Dares) Mitchell b1836 KY d1917 Paris, IL, d/o
    James & Lucinda (Baker) Dares of KY.
Espy Vinson Mitchell b1902 Elbridge Twp., Edgar Co., IL
    d1902, bur New Providence Cemetery.
Henry Mitchell b1888 Paris, Edgar Co., IL d1910.
Henry Steele Mitchell b1859 Coles Co., IL d1884 Kansas,
    Edgar Co., IL.
Isaac C. Mitchell b1850 IN d1887 Symmes Twp., Edgar Co.
James Wilson Mitchell b1827 Washington Co., PA d1880
    Paris, Edgar Co., IL.
Rev. John Mitchell b1821 England d1887 Dudley, IL.
John Mitchell b1844 Bentleyville, PA d1931 Ross Twp., Ed-
    gar Co., IL, s/o **John J. Mitchell** & Christina Faulkner;
    mar in NJ to Lucinda Thompson.
Lulu Maud Mitchell b1881 Paris, IL d1903.
Mary Eliza Mitchell b1861 Coles Co., IL d1878 Isabel, IL.
Mary J. Mitchell b1870 Coles Co., IL d1887.
Orlander Mitchell b1885 Paris, IL d1902.
Rachel (Hardy) Mitchell b1845 Cherry Point, Edgar Co., IL
    d1919 Metcalf, IL; mother's maiden name was Lowery.
Rev. Robert A. Mitchell b1819 Jonesboro, TN d1886 Kansas,
    IL; mar to Anna E. Roberts.
Roscoe Mitchell b1904 Paris, IL d1911.
Ruth Ann Mitchell b1908 d1908 Chrisman, IL.
Win C. Mitchell b1898 Chrisman, IL d1903.

Probate Records: Letters of Administration for **John
Mitchell** d 17 Sep 1931 at Chrisman, Edgar Co., IL; widow,

Miscellaneous Mitchell Data

(Probate Records Edgar Co., Illinois con't)

Rosella Mitchell; children Osa E. Bacon, Ora M. Thomas, Ersal M. Fath; administration granted to Osa E. Bacon on 1 Oct 1931, Edgar Co., IL.

Probate Records: Petition for settlement of estate of **Elizabeth Mitchell** without administration by **Joseph Mitchell** of Paris, IL, s/o Elizabeth Mitchell, dec'd on or about 28 Sep 1907, testate, in Edgar Co.; names survivors **Peter A. Mitchell** (husband) & children (**MITCHELL**) William V., Joseph L., & Peter E. E., and Mary F. BALLAH (nee Mitchell); dated 9 Feb 1909, Edgar Co., IL.

Edgar Co. Country Cemetery (off Rt. 36 near Rt. 1):
Albert C. Mitchell 24 Jan 1876-12 Jul 1966
Alexander C. Mitchell 21 Sep 1840-13 Dec 1926
Clara Lowry Mitchell 18 Jul 1882-24 Apr 1936
Hudson W. Mitchell 1874-1946
Ira P. Mitchell 1887-1949
Mary A. Mitchell 1880-1961
Rachel Hardy Mitchell 28 Dec 1845-7 Jul 1919
Selma L. Mitchell 1889-1964

EFFINGHAM COUNTY:

Marriages 1833-1877, pub. by the E.C.G.S., Effingham, IL:
Grooms:
David P. Mitchell to Sarah E. Mitchell 17 Nov 1867 B:98
David P. Mitchell to Mrs. Susan Warrsau 6 Oct 1875 B:101
H. B. Mitchell to Penelope J. Goddard 29 Apr 1858 B:96
James Mitchell to Susan N. Johnson 8 Jul 1869 B:98
John H. Mitchell to Marcy Tipsword 9 Sep 1859 B:96
Lucius W. Mitchell to Elner M. Writer 20 May 1874 B:100
Major Mitchell to Carrie J. Taylor __ __ B:101
Major Mitchell to Mary Clark 30 Nov 1868 B:98*
Mark Mitchell to Malissa Hicks 21 Jul 1867 B:98
William Mitchell to Louisa Walker 1 Jul 1849 A-1:100
William Mitchell to Margaret C. Wentz 4 May 1868 B:98
Brides:
Rebecca Michall to William Tolch 28 Apr 1856 A-2:40
Mahala Jane Mitchell to J. Bentz 6 Nov 1856 B:9
Emelia F. Mitchell to John W. Ford 29 Jan 1871 B:41
Martha Ann Mitchell to Thomas Guthrie 15 Mar 1865 B:49*

Miscellaneous Mitchell Data

(Bride's Marriages, Effingham Co., Illinois con't)

Hester Mitchell to Josiah Lowery 4 Feb 1849 A-1:98
Nancy Jane Mitchell to John T. Parks 23 Sep 1860 B:120
Mary Ann Mitchell to Martin V. Pontes 6 Oct 1867 B:121
Marion Mitchell to David K. Shouse 6 Sep 1862 B:145*
Mary J. Mitchell to Richard T. Worley 23 Jan 1877 B:180
Sarah E. Mitchell to David P. Mitchell 17 Nov 1867 B:98
(*These marriages performed by D. S. Mitchell, J.P.)

Marriages 1878-1882, pub. by E.C.G.S., Effingham, IL:
   Elizabeth Mitchell 19 b Jersey City, NJ d/o **Wm. Mitchell**
& Sarah Winslow, 1st, to Wm. H. Wright 31 b Effingham Co.
s/o H. H. Wright & Susan Selock, 2nd mar, 27 May 1878.
   George W. Mitchell 30 b Effingham Co. s/o **David S. Mit-
chell** & Mahala Parkhurst, 1st mar, to Mary E. Duvall 26 b
Belleville Co., OH d/o Upton Duvall & Mary Ann Roldans,
1st mar, 27 Feb 1880.
   James D. Mitchell 21 b Effingham Co. s/o **J. G. Mitchell**
& _____Clark, 1st mar, to Martha E. Smith 22 b Fulton Co.,
AR d/o C. J. Smith & _____Smith, 1st mar, 27 Oct 1878.
   Laura B. Mitchell 20 b AR d/o **Ignatious Mitchell** & Re-
becca York, 2nd mar, to John H. Moore 28 b Marion Co., IN
s/o Harvey B. Moore & Charlotte Said, 3rd mar, 6 May 1882.
   Mrs. **Mary A. (Mitchell)** Pontious 27 b Effingham Co. d/o
David S. Mitchell & Mahala Parkhurst, 2nd mar, to August
Stanke 26 b LaPorte Co., IN s/o Louis Stanke & Henrietta
Dolkin, 2nd mar, 10 Feb 1878.
   Sarah E. Mitchell 19 b Jersey City, NJ d/o **William Mit-
chell** & Sarah Winslow, 1st mar, to Charles J. Newbanks 22
b Teutopolis s/o Julius D. Newbanks & Elizabeth Kellim,
1st mar, 26 June 1879.
   William Mitchell 22 b Milwaukee, WI s/o **Wm. Mitchell** &
Susan McDonald, 1st mar, to Hannah Stalain 21 b VA d/o
Henry Stalain & Margaret Ryan, 1st mar, 20 Dec 1879.
   William Mitchell 50 b Scotland s/o **Wm. Mitchell** & Eliz-
abeth Thompson, 2nd mar, to Kate J. Goodell 30 b LaGrange,
IN d/o Wm S. Goodell & Catherine Herrick, 1st, 25 May 1882

Marriages 1883-1888, pub. by E.C.G.S., Effingham, IL:
   Carrie J. (Taylor) **Mitchell** of Effingham Co., 45 b TN
d/o James M. Taylor & Mildred McCammon, 3rd, to John J.
Pritchard of Coles Co., farmer, 41 b IN s/o John Pritchard
& Catharine Demmas, 2nd, 16 Apr 1887.

Miscellaneous Mitchell Data

(Marriages 1883-1888 Effingham Co., Illinois con't)

Frank S. Mitchell of Mason, harness maker, 23 b Greenville s/o **H. B. Mitchell** & N. J. Godard, 1st, to Fosest Blackman of Mason 20 d/o Samuel Blackman & Annie King, 1st, 7 Oct 1883 (J. A. Goddard, wit).

James J. Mitchell of LaSelle, IL, miner, 40 b Cornwall, Eng. s/o **George Mitchell** & Mary Thomas, 1st, to Alice A. Brady of Mattoon, IL, 32 b Mulberry Grove, IL d/o John Chandler (sic) & Sarah Anderson, 1st, 17 May 1883.

Lawrence McCallan Mitchell of Effingham, farmer, 25 b Effingham Co. s/o **J. Mitchell** & Susan Clark, 1st, to Sarah Johnson of Effingham Co., 28 d/o E. Johnson & Eliza Boyd, 1st, 10 Oct 1886.

Major H. Davis of Jackson Twp., farmer, 46 b TN s/o Henry W. Davis & **Jane Mitchell**, 2nd, to Mary J. (Read) Mesnard of Jackson Twp., 38 b Shelby Co., IL d/o A. J. Read & Sarah Douty, 2nd, 8 Aug 1887.

Margaret W. Mitchell of Effingham, 22 b Jersey City, NJ d/o **William Mitchell** & Sarah Winslow, 1st, to Alexander C. Phelon of Effingham, engineer, 37 b Vincennes, IN s/o Henry W. Phelon & Rachel Booth, 1st, 15 Jul 1886.

Mary Elizabeth (Huddleston) **Mitchell** of Effingham, 43 b TN d/o Joseph Huddleston & Isabelle Ferguson, 2nd, to Henry Cox of Effingham Co., farmer, 43 b NC s/o Henry Cox & P. Simmons, 3rd, 23 Mar 1888. (Note: No Mitchell-Huddleston marriage found in Effingham Co. records.)

History of Effingham Co., IL, ed. by W. H. Perrin, 1883:
George C. Mitchell b 14 Feb 1848 Turner, ME, went West at age 17; in Ottawa, IL just after the war; lvd Champaign, Springfield, Effingham, IL; mar 1874 Nannie E., d/o Col. J. J. Funkhouser of Effingham. (Note: This marriage is not in Effingham Co., IL marriage records.) (Vol. II:54)

Joshua G. Mitchell s/o **Daniel* S. Mitchell** b 27 Jan 1835 Smith Co., TN; with par to Johnson Co., IN 1837; to Effingham Co. 1840; m 19 Mar 1857 Susanna Clark d/o James D. Clark; Baptist since 1873. Ch **(i)** James D. b 13 Dec 1857; **(ii)** Lawrence M. b 12 Feb 1862; **(iii)** George A. b 22 Jan 1864; **(iv)** Izora B. b 16 Dec 1870; **(v)** Pinkney B. b 11 June 1872. Father, **David* S. Mitchell** b 11 Apr 1815 Smith Co., TN m 29 May 1833 Mahala Parkhurst. David S. d 23 Apr 1877 Jackson Twp., Effingham Co.; Mahala b 1811 Smith Co., TN d 15 Mar 1874 Jackson Twp., Effingham Co. (Vol. II:186-7)

Miscellaneous Mitchell Data

(Effingham Co., Illinois con't)

Wills & Estate Settlements 1836-1882, W. F. Sargent:

Book C:102 - Will of Jacob Goddard dated 12 May 1878 at
Mason, Effingham Co., IL names among ch his dau. **Penelope
J. Mitchell** (p36). (Note: Penelope J. Mitchell is same
as "Nettie" Mitchell, w/o H. B. Mitchell. See 1870 Census
Records & Marriage Records 1833-1877. Effingham Co., IL
Deaths list H. B. Mitchell d 2 Apr 1905 Mason, IL age 75y
8m 28d; b TN; bur 3 Apr 1905 Old Mason Cemetery. Penelope
J. Mitchell is bur in Union Cemetery, Mason Twp., b1839
d1926, her grst next to 3 Goddard stones.)

Probate Records (File Box 97): Estate of **Anna M. Mitchell**
dated 6 Apr 1904, administrix Mary E. Carter, mother; brothers & sisters, Arizona Forbes (wife of Joe); **Irvin Mitchell** of Oaktown, IN; Cassa (Cassie) Bishir of Melvin, IL;
Grover C. Mitchell of Dexter, IL; **Thomas M. Mitchell** of
Dexter, IL; **Etta D. (Estella) Mitchell** of Dexter, IL;
half-brothers William and John Deval of Dexter, IL. Final report filed 22 May 1904; fees paid to Fayette Co., IL
Circuit Clerk; city of Vandalia sued; final notices also
addressed to C. S. Miller & W. H. Smith of Dexter, IL;
George W. Parks & Charles S. Miller, sureties.

1850 Federal Census of Effingham Co., IL:

504/504 MITCHELL, Julia I. (male) 28 IL, Thusey M. 26 TN,
    Elizabeth 8 TN, Synthian Ann 5 mos. TN.
564/564 MITHEL, Magor 36 TN, Lefina 34 TN, Mahala 15 IN,
    John H. 13 IN, Mary Ann 12 IN, Sarah E. 10 TN, Marain
    (fem.) 8 IN, James H. 4 IL, Martha 1 IL.

1860 Federal Census of Effingham Co., IL:
(Key: 1st number = house number; H/H = in household of)

276 MITCHEL, Major 44 TN, Trifina 43 TN, Marian 16 IN,
    James H. 14 IL, Martha 12 IL, William 10 IL, Matilda 8
    TN, Jackson 4 IL, Richard 2 IL.
277 MITCHELL, John H. 22 IN, Mary 17 IL.
281 MITCHELL, J. G. 25 TN, Susanna 26 TN, David 3 IL.
731 MITCHELL, David 45 TN, Mahala 48 TN, Nancy 20 IN,
    David 18 IL, James 14 IL, George 10 IL, Mary 9 IL.

Miscellaneous Mitchell Data

(1860 Census of Effingham Co., <u>Illinois</u> con't)

996 MITCHELL, Wm. 4 IL, H/H of RAIBOURN, John 28 KY,
Manila 23 IL, Sarah F. 1 IL.

1870 Federal Census of Effingham Co., IL:
(Key: 1st number = house number; H/H = in household of)

Douglas Twp:
27 MITCHELL, Rachell 28 IN, Mary E. 5 mos. (Jan) IL, H/H
of SURRELLS, Jesse R. 67 VA, Mary 49 IN & ch b IL.
418 MITCHELL, David 28 IL, Lizzie 17 IN, Alice A. 1 IL,
H/H of WRIGHT, Henry H. 47 IL, Mary J. 34 IN & ch b IL.
Jackson Twp:
7 MITCHEL, Mark 24 TN, Jane 23 KY.
12 MITCHEL, William 22 IN, Mary 16 IN.
22 MITCHEL, James 23 TN, Susan 20 IN, H/H of CARPENTER,
I. P. (male) 27 OH, Jane 23 IL, James 25 OH, John 20 IL,
L. B. (male) 18 IL, L. V. (fem.) 15 TN.
28 MITCHEL, Major 55 TN, Mary 65 TN, B. (male) 12 IL,
PARKHIRST, W. (male) 69 VA, Mary J. 58 TN, James 11 TN,
William 8 TN, Mary 6 TN, D. M. (male) 3 IL, S. T. (fem.)
11 mos. IL, KINHARD, Mary 51 TN, Geo. 19 OH, Allen 14 OH.
60 MITCHEL, Willie 25 NC, Margaret 24 VA.
71 MICHEL, J. J. 35 TN, Susan 37 TN, David 12 IL, Lawrence
9 IL, George 5 IL, Loura 7 mos. (Nov) IL.
79 MITCHELL, George 27 Germany, Mary 20 IL, Eliza 1 IL.
Mason Twp:
55 MITCHEL, Hogeth (sic) 41 TN, Nettie 30 KY, Mark S. 11
IL, Mirtie 6 IL, Myra L. 3 IL, Samuel 1 IL.
210 MITCHEL, Wm. C. 48 VA, Rosella 17 IN, Emila 14 IN,
William 11 IL, David 8 IL.
Summit Twp:
84 MITCHELL, John 35 TN, Mary 30 IL, TIPSWORD, Anna 53 TN.
Teutopolis Twp:
104 MICHAEL, Joseph 13 MO (par. foreign born; student at
St. Joseph's College).

GREENE COUNTY:

History of Greene Co., IL, Donnelley, Gassette, & Loyd,
pub 1879 (Greene Co. Historical Society):
List of Early Settlers:
MITCHELL, N.L. (1835); A.K. (1835); J.G. (1838) p320.

Miscellaneous Mitchell Data

(History of Greene Co., Illinois con't)

Greene Co. Directory:
(Key: frm = farmer; frmh = farmhand; lab = laborer)
MITCHELL, A. B., frm, Sec 20, P.O. Whitehall; **Lafayette,** frm, Sec 16, P.O. Breese (Twp 12 NR 13W, p617). **MITCHELL, Andy K.,** frm, Sec 7; **James,** frm, Sec 6; **Newton,** frm, Sec 7; **Newton L.,** frm, Sec 6 (P.O. Greenfield, Twp 10 NR 10W, p687). **MITCHELL, Charles,** frm, Sec 8; **George,** frmh; **John,** renter, Sec 8; **George,** lab (P.O. Roodhouse, Twp 12 NR 11W pp 573 592). **MITCHELL, George,** frm, Sec 7, P.O. Carrollton (Twp 12 NR 11W, p712). **MITCHELL, J. C.,** frm, Sec 31, P.O. Greenfield (Twp 11 NR 10W, p624). **MITCHELL, J. G.,** frm, Sec 11, P.O. Murrayville, Morgan Co.; **Nancy,** wid of **Fielding,** Sec 17, P.O. Athensville (Twp 12 NR 10W, p607). **MITCHELL, JOHN,** frm, Sec 23, P.O. Wrightsville (Twp 11 NR 11W, p637).

Greene Co. Civil War Record:
Harvey Mitchell, pvt, Co. K, 154th Inf., enl 9 Feb 1865, mustered out 8 Sep 1865 as corp. (p462); **Newton L. Mitchell,** pvt, Co. F, 12th Cav., enl 7 Oct 1861; re-enl as vet 10 Nov 1863; transf to Co. F consolidated; mustered out 3 Apr 1865 as supply sgt. (p464-5); **Thomas J. Mitchell** (vet and recruit), Co. H, 6th Cav., enl 3 Feb 1865 deserted 26 Mar 1865 (p463); **William T. Mitchell** (recruit), Co. F., 12th Cav., enl 30 Dec 1863, d 26 Apr 1864 St. Louis (p465).

Roodhouse:
Roodhouse was founded in 1862 around the train depot when the Jacksonville branch of the Chicago & Alton Railroad was extended as far as Whitehall. In Apr 1866, John Roodhouse laid out the town - forty lots 66x130 feet & 75x150 feet. Additions since include Cobb & **Mitchell** (p320).

Marriages:
Harriet Mitchell to William T. Sorrells 24 Aug 1866.

HENDERSON COUNTY:

History of Henderson Co., IL:
(Newspapers) The "Oquawka Plaindealer" started 24 Jul 1852 by Mr. Dallam; 6 Mar 1855 Horace Bigelow bought half interest; 6 May 1856 Mr. Dallam sold to James H. Reed.

Miscellaneous Mitchell Data

(History abstracts Henderson Co., <u>Illinois</u> con't)

Reed & Bigelow sold concern 1 May 1857 to J. K. Magie and **David Mitchell.** (p896)
Henderson Co. officers - **Samuel Mitchell** elected Aug. 1847 as county recorder. (p900)

MERCER COUNTY:

<u>History of Mercer Co., IL</u>, Hill & Co., Chicago, 1882:
Keithsburg Twp: "Not long after his (James Garner) 1st election as magistrate he presided in a jury trial with C. M. Harris of Oquawka and **John Mitchell** of Monmouth as opposing attorneys. The former was a man of admirable physical resources...the latter would scarcely weigh a hundred pounds and...was disabled in the left arm from a wound received in the Mexican war. Harris stated the case to the jury and sat down. Mitchell arose and had proceeded but a little way...when Harris...said, 'That is a lie!' ...A few moments elapsed and again Harris interposed... 'That is another lie!' Mitchell turned...with gleaming eye and warned him not to repeat that insult or he would strike him...A minute or two more and Harris broke in: 'And that is an infernal lie!'...Mitchell delivered a stunning blow between his eyes which sent him over backward to the floor..."(p121)
Keithsburg Twp: List of tradesmen and mechanics; dates ca that of residence. **I. J. Mitchell** 1846-1865 (p135).
Duncan Twp: Sketch of George Vater, dec'd, who came to America with his brother...in 1865 bought **John Mitchel's** interest in 260 acres of land (p503).
Abington Twp: Sketch of Joseph Glancy b nr Harrisburg, PA 27 May 1794; to Wayne Co., IN 1820; married 4 times; by 3rd wife had 7 ch including Mrs. **I. J. Mitchell** (p515).
Mercer Twp: Rev. Thomas B. Turnbull b 27 Apr 1847 Warren Co., IL s/o David and **Nancy (Mitchell)** Turnbull; m 24 Apr 1873 Jean M. Horne of Monmouth, IL; 3 ch lvg (TURNBULL) Willie 6 yrs; David 4 yrs; Susie 8 mo; dau d age 7 (p617).
Mercer Twp: Milton S. Boise b 1827 Burgettstown, Washington Co., PA; came west 1854; settled Geneseo, Henry Co., IL; m 1846 **Rebecca Mitchell** of Allegheny Co., PA; two ch lvg (BOISE) Joseph 22; Horace 14 (p619).
Greene Twp: United Presby. Ch. (Twin Grove) organized 1855; ment. **John Mitchell, J. B. Mitchell** (p665).

Miscellaneous Mitchell Data

(History abstracts Mercer Co., <u>Illinois</u> con't)

Rivoli Twp: 1st Congregational Church, New Windsor, organized 1870...assisted by various pastors including **A. R. Mitchell**, pastor of the 1st Congregational Church at Viola, IL (p757).

The Soldier's Monument (roll of honor of county heroes who fell in defense of their country): **John P. Mitchell**, Co. A, Thirtieth Reg't. (p848)

Eleventh Illinois Cavalry, Co. B, 126th Reg't; original officers included **John B. Mitchell**, 1st Lt. (p858)

<u>1850 Federal Census of Mercer Co., IL:</u>
(Key: H/H = in household of)
126/126 MITCHELL, Elizabeth 29 OH, H/H of SHIELDS, David 31 NC, Mahala 22 OH (Twp. 13).
357/357 MITCHELL, Isaac 43 VA (Twp. 14).
13/13 MITCHELL, Isaac 20? VA, Susan B. 19 IN (Keithsburg).

<u>MORGAN COUNTY:</u>

Marriage Record Bk 2:166 - **John Nelson Mitchell** of Murrayville, farmer, age 29 next birthday, b Greene Co., IL s/o **Thomas W. Mitchell** & _____ Hubbell, 1st, to Sarah Elizabeth Sorrells of Murrayville, age 30 next birthday, b Greene Co., IL d/o William Sorrells & _____ Redmond, 1st, 6 Mar 1895; wit: Wm. Story, Mary S. Whitlock.

<u>PIATT COUNTY:</u>

<u>The Good Life in Piatt County</u>, ed. by J. B. Morgan 1968:
Sangamon Twp: Centerville Methodist Church organized 1867; purchased 1st parsonage 1870; 1st pastor to live in it was Rev. **J. G. Mitchell** (p171).

On 1st Piatt Co. Farm Bureau board of directors, organized in 1919, was **J. H. Mitchell** (p134).

Piatt Co. Supervisors Court held 1st meeting 28 May 1860; **Royal Mitchell** elected supervisor, Unity Twp. (p40)

Mackville (Unity Twp., nr Atwood) settled 1858; drugstore operated by **Dr. Mitchell** & Dr. Marshall (p110); 12 people met at Mackville School in 1860 to organize a Methodist Church; charter members included Mr. & Mrs. **T. J. Mitchell** (p156). Milmine community served in early days by Dr. **Thomas J. Mitchell**, formerly of Atwood (p209); 1st

Miscellaneous Mitchell Data

(History abstracts Piatt Co., <u>Illinois</u> con't)

doctor in what is now Unity Twp. was Dr. **Thomas J. Mitchell** who came to Mackville 1855...until 1871; to Milmine where he practiced for 5 years; later moved to Bement, IL where he remained until his death (p213).

ROCK ISLAND COUNTY:

The Past & Present of Rock Island Co., IL 1877, Kett & Co., Chicago (Key: Rep = Republican; Dem = Democrat; Cong = Congregationalist; Chris = Christian; M.E. = Methodist Episcopal; res = residence)

Mitchell & Lynde's Block ment. (pp 154 161 303) **Mitchell** & Parson's store ment. (pp 156 316)
Odd Fellows, Tema Rebecca Degree Lodge No. 65, Officers **J. E. Mitchell** N.G. (p206)
The M. E. Church was organized in 1836 with a membership of some 6 or 8 persons, among whom were Archibald Allen, Candace Allen, J. H. Lyford & wife, **Jno. Mitchell** & wife. The earliest meetings were held in a log cabin...(p214-15)
The 1st Church of the United Brethren in Christ, Village of Andalusia, earliest meetings held in the summer of 1863; the Sabbath-school maintained by this church had its origin in a Union Sabbath-school organized 1 May 1859 with teachers...**Miss M. J. Mitchell**...(p237)
A daily steam packet, "The Rockford," was commenced in 1864 between Andalusia, Rock Island, and Davenport; service discontinued at the close of the Civil War; in 1875 it was again established by Capt. **Samuel Mitchell** of Davenport, an experienced river captain, with his steamboat "The Lone Star"...(p240)
Rock Island County War Record: 12th IL Vol. Infantry, Co. D, Pvt. **Wm. Mitchell**, enlisted 23 Jul 1861, mustered out 10 Jul 1865; 19th IL Vol. Infantry, Co. H, Pvt. **R. B. Mitchell**, enlisted 10 June 1861, deserted 26 June 1861; 45th IL Vol. Infantry, Co. H, Pvt. **Abner Mitchell**, enlisted 23 Sep 1861, transferred to Invalid Corps 15 Sep 1863 (pp 246-48). See p148 of main text for further data.
Rock Island City & Twp: **George Mitchell**, foreman, res 24th St. betw 6th-7th Aves.; Dem; from NY (p296). **Henry Lee Mitchell**, Dry Goods, res corner of 23rd St. & 5th Ave; Rep.; Cong.; b 2 Aug 1833 York Co., ME; m 1861 Martha W.

Miscellaneous Mitchell Data

(History abstracts Rock Island Co., <u>Illinois</u> con't)

Bradbury; to this county 1873; one child. **H. B. Mitchell**, carpenter; Rep.; from VT. **P. L. Mitchell**, banker, res. corner of 2nd Ave. & 12th St.; Pres. of 1st Board of Water Commissioners; b Oct 1812 York Co., ME; to this county 1856; m Kate Hall of NH; 5 ch. **Philip Mitchell**, notary public, 2nd Ave.; b IL. (p296)

The Rock Island Glass Co., incorporated 1870, **P. L. Mitchell**, Treasurer; **H. L. Mitchell**, Secretary. (p149) **P. L. Mitchell**, Secretary-Treaurer of Chippiannock Cemetery management, organized 1855. (p173)

Moline City: **C. P. Mitchell & J. E. Mitchell** employed by Deere & Co. in wood department; both Rep. (p341) Moline Twp: **C. P. Mitchell**, farmer, Section 5. (p366)

Hampton Twp: **R. M. Mitchell**, Rapids City, millwright & merchant; b 20 June 1820 Greene Co., PA; to this county fall of 1854; m 18 Jul 1855 Julia A. McCarl b 13 Dec 1833 Ohio; 1 son and 2 daughters living; 1 daughter dec'd; Assessor 7 terms; Collector 5 years; Dem; Chris. (p446).

Hampton Twp: James Cozad, M.D., Andalusia, b 9 Jul 1836 Mercer, Mercer Co.,PA; to Lee Co., IA with par 1846; to Whiteside Co., IL 1851; to Andalusia, Rock Island Co. 1866; m **Martha Mitchell** of Fulton, Whiteside Co., IL, d/o **David Mitchell**, dec'd, who was 1st Co. Treasurer & Deacon of the Presbyterian Church; 4 ch (COZAD) James M., Louis E., Clara I, Letitia G. (p469)

<u>TAZEWELL COUNTY</u>:

<u>Greenwood Cemetery</u> (Little Mackinaw Twp):
James G. Mitchell d 16 Jul 1873 age 67y 7m 21d
Sophia Stears Mitchell w/o James G. d 3 Feb 1881, aged
    67y 11m 12d
Byron S. s/o Jas. & S. S. d 29 Aug 1863 at New Orleans, LA,
    aged 24y 9m 1d
Sophia P. w/o Ira C., d/o C. S. & M. Elliott, d 10 Jan
    1869, aged 21y 11m.

<u>County Deed Records</u>: 15 Apr 1837 **Samuel A. Mitchell** of the city & county of New Haven, CT, & wife Rhoda Ann, sold to Cyrus P. Smith land in Sections 9 & 10, Twp. 22; land originally purchased 25 Feb 1837 from Alpheus Fobes, Jr. Wit: **Caroline Mitchell** & Wm. A. Reynolds.

Miscellaneous Mitchell Data

(Deeds of Tazewell Co., Illinois con't)

10 Nov 1835 **Benjamin Mitchell** & wife **Martha C.** sold land
in Sect 2 Twp 20 to John Brownfield; on 3 Jul 1837 land in
Sect 19 Twp 20 to Elisa Haines; no wit to the deeds. (The
1840 census lists Martha with 1 m 10/15, 1 m 15/20, 1 m
20/30, 2 f 10/15, 1 f 15/20, 1 f 40/50.)
   5 Apr 1836 **James Mitchell** & wife **Nancy O.** sold land in
Sect 35 Twp 27 to Charles G. Parke, no wit; (1840 census
lists James with 1 m 5/10, 1 m 10/15, 1 m 15/20, 1 m 20/30,
1 m 40/50, 2 f un 5, 1 f 5/10, 1 f 30/40.)

WHITE COUNTY:

Marriages 1816-1844 (L.D.S. Film #848,656):
Jane Mitchell to Ezekiel Porter 31 May 1824
John Mitchell to Polly Tyner 1816
Mose Mitchell to Malinda Pierce 8 Oct 1839
William Mitchell to Polly Crowder 31 Oct 1827

1850 Federal Census of White Co., IL:
MITCHELL, Moses 40 TN, Malinda 39 TN, Mary 17 IL, Eliza-
beth A. 15 IL, Nancy L. 13 IL, Sarah L. 11 IL, Alex F. 7
IL, Margaret E. 4 IL.

INDIANA

DEARBORN COUNTY:

Dearborn Co., IN Obituaries 1820-1850, Chris McHenry,
   Lawrenceburg, IN 1983, p29 ("Western Commercial"):
Issue of 13 Jan 1849: Killed by a falling tree on the
   Aurora-Dillsboro turnpike 5th inst., **Mr. Mitchell.**
Issue of 20 Jan 1849: Tribute of Respect, Chosen Friends
   Lodge, to memory of **Joshua Mitchell,** deceased.
Issue of 27 Jan 1849: The body of **James Mitchell** landed at
   our wharf Thurs. last, from the steamer "Alhambra."
   Funeral preached by Rev. Robb. Odd Fellow.
Issue of 10 Feb 1849: Tribute of Respect, Chosen Friends
   Lodge; to memory of **James Mitchell,** who died 10 Jan at
   New Orleans, age 30.
Early Dearborn Co., IN Wills, Chris McHenry, comp., p21:
   Peter Mitchell was a witness to the will of Thomas Far-
ran, dated 12 Oct 1846, probated 31 May 1847.

-371-

Miscellaneous Mitchell Data

JOHNSON COUNTY, INDIANA:

A Historical Sketch of Johnson Co., IN, D. D. Banta, 1881:
"In 1825, Richard Hensly, a native of VA...who had mov-
ed to KY when quite a young man, and after a time to Jack-
son Co., IN...for a short time...came to Johnson Co...in
March, and was soon accompanied by Wm. Davenport and **Wm.
Mitchell**, his sons-in-law, and their families." (p40)
   The following persons were selected for grand jury at
Sept. term 1826...**Gavin Mitchell**... (p72)
   Nineveh Twp: In 1825...**Amos Mitchel**, from KY...moved
in (to the township)... (p114)
   Franklin Twp: "On the south and west sides and southwest corner of the township we find that **Thomas Mitchel**...
came in quite early, and then passing up the south side
are...**John D. Mitchel**...In the central and northern parts
were...**Thomas J. Mitchell**..."(after 1825) (p118)
   Hensley Twp: Richardson Hensley, b 10 Mar 1799 near
Fredericksburg, VA; moved with par to Fayette Co., KY; he
later moved to Mercer Co. were he m 1800 Elizabeth Cully;
to Jackson Co., IN for 1 year, then 1825 to Johnson Co.,
bringing with him sons-in-law Wm. Davenport, a North Car-
olinian, & **Wm. Mitchell**, a Virginian, & families. (p155)
   Union Twp: 1828 N.W. corner of twp. **John Mitchel** (p160)

1840 Federal Census of Johnson Co., IN:
(Key: m = male; f = female; un = under age.)

Benjamin Mitchell 2 m un 5; 1 m 30/40; 1 f 5/10; 1 f 20/30.
David S. Mitchell 1 m un 5; 1 m 5/10; 1 m 20/30; 1 f un 5;
   1 f 20/30.
Gavin Mitchell 1 m 5/10; 2 m 10/15; 1 m 50/60; 1 f 15/20.
James H. Mitchell 1 m un 5; 1 m 20/30; 1 f un 5; 1 f 20/30.
John Mitchell 1 m un 5; 1 m 5/10; 1 m 10/15; 1 m 15/20; 1 m
   20/30; 1 m 40/50; 1 f 15/20; 1 f 40/50.
John Mitchell 1 m un 5; 1 m 40/50; 1 f un 5; 1 f 15/20.
Mark Mitchell 1 m un 5; 1 m 10/15; 1 m 30/40; 1 f 30/40.
Thomas J. Mitchell 1 m un 5; 1 m 20/30; 1 f un 5; 1 f 30/40.

1850 Federal Census of Johnson Co., IN:
(Key: 1st number = house number; H/H = in household of)
Union Twp:
180 MITCHEL, Rebecca 38 VA, Margaret J. 14 IN, Thomas 12
   IN, Samuel D. 7 IN.

Miscellaneous Mitchell Data

(1850 Census of Johnson Co., Indiana con't)

White River Twp:
142 MITCHEL, Seth T. 37 ME, Mary E. 37 CT, Emerson 1 IN,
BRIGHT, Mary L. 13 IN, Septimus G. 9 IN.
Franklin Twp:
177 MITCHELL, Thomas J. 39 IN, Margaret 44 KY, Wm. H. 14
IN, Catherine 12 IN, Susan A. 10 IN, James B. 8 IN,
Thomas J. 7 IN, Sarah E. 5 IN.
263 MITCHELL, Abraham 19 IN, H/H of BYERS, Henry 26 KY.
505 MITCHEL, Juliet 26 KY, H/H of DEAN, Wm. 22 IN.
527 MITCHELL, John 24 IN, Margaret S. 27 IN, WATEN, John
J. 6 IN.
539 MITCHELL, Jefferson 24 KY, Elizabeth J. 24 IN. (In the
1860 C., family had Julia A. 7, Manerva F. 2, Mariah H.
5 mos., all b IN.)
Blue River Twp:
683 MITCHELL, William 36 OH, Hannah 32 OH, Rebecca M. 12
IN, Martha J. 8 IN, David G. 6 IN, James 1 IN.
Hensley Twp:
1074 MITCHELL, Gavin 64 PA, Jane 59 VA, ALLEN, Martha 18
IN. (1810 Adams Co., OH tax list has a Gavin Mitchell;
Johnson Co., IN Marriages - Gavin Mitchell to Jane Allen 10 Oct 1840).
1192 MITCHELL, Susannah 47 KY, Bloomfield 17 IN, Henry A.
15 IN, Woodford 12 IN, DEVENPORT, Sethanny 20 IN.
Nineveh Twp:
730 MITCHELL, James 36 KY, Elizabeth 37 TN, William 13 IN,
Hannah M. 10 IN, John 8 IN, Netty 2 IN.
736 MITCHELL, John D. 59 KY, Maria 55 VA, Noah 18 IN, Wilkins 15 IN, Stephen 12 IN, ABBETT, Nancy 20 IN.
927 MITCHELL, Peter A. 18 TN, Elizabeth 22 England.

1860 Federal Census of Johnson Co., IN:
(Key: 1st number = house number)
Franklin Twp:
766 MITCHELL, Wm. A. 22 IN, Laurinda 18 IN, Sarah E. 1 IN.
Edinburgh Twp:
283 MITCHELL, Wm. H. 48 OH, Sarah E. 24 IN, Rebecca M. 23
IN, Martha J. 18 IN, David G. 16 IN, Henry 8 IN, Hannah 8
IN, Houston? (male) 6 IN.
Nineveh Twp:
551 MITCHELL, John D. 71 KY, Mariah 65 VA, Stephen 21 IN,
PACE, Margaret (servant) 24 IN, CARTER, Phebe 14 IN.

Miscellaneous Mitchell Data

(1860 Census of Johnson Co., Indiana con't)

643 MITCHELL, Mark 52 TN, Cintha 51 TN, DAVIS, Matilda A.
16 (servant) TN.
644 MITCHELL, Peter A. 29 TN, Elizabeth 33 Eng., Wm. V. 6
IN, Joseph L. 2 IN.
645 MITCHELL, David A. 30 TN, Mary J. 23 KY, James W. 8 IN
Rice (male) 6 IN, Mark 2 IN. (David A. was also in the
1850 census, age 20 b TN, unmarried, living alone.)

Early Johnson Co. Landowners:

Mitchell, Amos & Nancy, Bk A Johnson Co., IN; **John** &
Mary, Bk C Brown Co., OH; **John L.**, Bk B, Shelby Co., IN;
Wm. H., Bk C, Johnson Co., IN.

Johnson Co. Land Records:
(Key: S. = section; Twp = township; R. = range)
Amos Mitchell S.28 R.4 23 May 1827 (twice).
David S. Mitchell S.28 Twp 11 R.3 21 Nov 1835.
David S. Mitchell S.29 Twp 11 R.3 17 Nov 1836.
Gavin Mitchell S.29 Blue River Twp 2 Aug 1837.
John Mitchell S.18 R.4 Nineveh Twp 18 Nov 1828.
John D. Mitchell S.1 R.4 Nineveh Twp. 30 Jul 1831.

ORANGE COUNTY:

Orange Co., IN Marriages 1816-1835, IN State Library:
James S. Mitchel to Margaret (Carr?) 10 June 1817.

PARKE COUNTY:

Indiana D.A.R. Roster of Revolutionary Ancestors:
   Mitchell, William b 20 Oct 1746 Essex Co.,VA d 8 Jul
1836 Parke Co., IN; m 5 Dec 1776 Chloe Nance b 22 Jan 1755
d 28 Jul 1842; enl. May 1778 as Pvt. in VA Troops; children
(i) Olivia m John Bullington; **(ii)** Frederick; **(iv)** Isaac
m Margaret McGaham; **(iv)** Elizabeth m1) John Lunsford; m2)
John Ellis; **(v)** Giles m Mary Moore; **(vi)** William m Mary
Logan; **(vii)** Robert m1) Margaret Adams; m2) Elizabeth
Miller; **(viii)** Mary m Levy Burton; **(ix)** Cloa m John Wesley
Nance; **(x)** James m Nancy Burton; **(xi)** Ann m Wesley Sparks.
(Their D.A.R. descendant is Clementine Mathis (Mathes),
No. 162677.)

Miscellaneous Mitchell Data

SWITZERLAND COUNTY, INDIANA:

Hoosier Genealogist, V.4 #4 July-Aug 1964:
(Switzerland Co. Marriages 1814-1830)
Alanson Mitchell to Tacy Jaques 27 Mar 1829
Elizabeth Mitchell to David Myers 3 Jan 1821
Elizabeth Mitchell to John Protsman 24 Oct 1820
George W. S. Mitchel to Maria Ann Sedam 13 Feb 1827
Joseph Mitchell to Polly Milligan 11 Mar 1824

WHITE COUNTY:

The History of White Co., IN, V.I, Lewis Pub. Co., 1915:

(Early settlers in White Co.)...Jackson Twp. received a
colony near what is now the town of Idaville. Composed of
...**William W. Mitchel**...These pioneers who came before
the county was organized usually settled in family groups
largely determined by their home states. (p61)
In 1837 and 1838 the poll lists show the following new
names...**William W. Mitchel, James T. Mitchel**...(pp 225-6)
"The late **George W. Mitchell** who claimed to be the first
native white child in Jackson Twp. was born Dec. 5, 1835
...a few years afterwards the family settled on the first
farm north of the present town of Idaville. His father,
William W. Mitchell, was a Kentuckian who moved to Madison
Co., OH where he married Miss Marie Phoebus. (Note: Madison Co., OH Marriages lists William Mitchell to Mariah
Phebus 15 Feb 1827, Bk A:108.) After the birth of a son
in 1828 the family located in Tippecanoe Co., IN 10 miles
north of Lafayette, and two daughters were born in that
locality before the family settled in Jackson Twp. during
1834. Most of Mr. Mitchell's life was spent on the old
farm except during the Civil War period, which he spent in
active service, but in 1890 he moved to Idaville, where he
died in 1913." (p480: George W. is also listed in the index on pp 14 154 227 477; also **John E. Mitchell** p179 and
Sallie Mitchell, teacher at Brookston Academy p132).

1840 Federal Census of White Co., IN (pp 439, 437):
(Key: m = male; f = female; un = under the age of)
James P. Mitchell 1 m 60/70, 1 f 60/70.
William W. Mitchell 2 m un 5, 1 m 10/15, 1 m 30/40, 1 f
5/10, 1 f 30/40.

Miscellaneous Mitchell Data

(White Co., <u>Indiana</u> con't)

<u>1850 Federal Census of White Co., IN</u> (130th District):
553 MITCHELL, William 47 KY, Maria 40 OH, Susana 16 IN,
George H. 14 IN, William S. 12 IN, James 9 IN, Barbary J.
4 IN, Franklin J. H. 1 IN.

<u>Early White Co., IN Marriages 1834-1906</u>, compiled by Mrs.
Cledith Scott, Mrs. Floyd Bixler, Mrs. Roberta Scott
Glick (L.D.S. Film #908,016):

Barbary G. Mitchell to William York 17 Nov 1862
Charles W. Mitchell to Lillie M. Eavly 30 Mar 1882
Franklin J. H. Mitchell to Christine V. Thomas 8 Nov 1877
George W. Mitchell to Ann E. Oates 11 Feb 1866
Grace Mitchell to David Garlinghouse 23 Feb 1839
Isham H. Mitchell to Rosalie Kenton 15 Sep 1868
James Mitchell to Mary E. Galloway 18 Nov 1868
John A. Mitchell to Malinda Holland 27 Sep 1875
John W. Mitchell to Margaret German 9 May 1849
John W. Mitchell to Amanda Oliver 13 Jan 1856
Lewis S. Mitchell to Ann Fogg 27 Dec 1881
Samuel W. Mitchell to Sarah Holland 27 Oct 1875
Susannah Mitchell to Joseph A. Fraser 6 Nov 1862
Thaddeus Mitchell to Dorcus E. Holder 24 Dec 1872

IOWA

List of Pensioners on the Roll Jan. 1, 1883," V.3, 1970:
<u>Blackhawk Co</u>: 173,787 **Chas. A. Mitchell**, LaPorte City,
chronic diarrhea, $14/mo., Feb 1881; #167,646 **David M.
Mitchell**, LaPorte City, nephritis & rheumatism, $6/mo,
Apr 1880. (pp657-58)
<u>Bremer Co</u>: #78,727 **Abner Mitchell**, Horton, gunshot wound
both hips, $12/mo., Sep 1880; #173,376 **Thos. W. Mitchell**
Plainfield, gunshot wound left ankle, $2/mo., Sep 1880.
(pp 661-62)
<u>Butler Co</u>: #9,293 **Caroline M. Mitchell**, Clarksville, wid.
$8/mo, June 1867. (p667)
<u>Clarke Co</u>: #6,730 **Susannah Mitchell**, Osceola, wid. $8/mo.
Nov 1867. (p678)
<u>Decatur Co</u>: #154,989 **John Mitchell**, Leon, injury to back,
$8/mo., Aug 1878; #15,541 **Geo. E. Mitchell**, Weldon, gun
shot wound left foot, $10/mo., Nov 1881. (pp 689-90)

Miscellaneous Mitchell Data

(Pensioner's Roll in <u>Iowa</u> con't)

<u>Floyd Co:</u> #37,449 **Catharine G. Mitchell**, Charles City, wid., $8/mo., May 1867. (p700)

<u>Hardin Co:</u> #112,166 **Boyd J. Mitchell**, Eldora, disease of lungs, $18/mo., Jul 1881. (p709)

<u>Harrison Co:</u> #55,971 **James Mitchell**, Logan, gunshot wound in thigh, $12/mo., Jul 1867. (p712)

<u>Lee Co:</u> #204,239 **Wm. Mitchell**, alias Teror, Fort Madison, gunshot wound right leg, $4/mo., Mar 1882; #183,074 **Michael W. Mitchell**, Warren, chronic rheumatism, heart disease & disease of abdominal viscera, $8/mo., Feb 1881. (pp 737 740)

<u>Lunn Co:</u> #181,035 **Mary Mitchell**, Central City, dependant mother, $8/mo., May 1878. (p742)

<u>Louisa Co:</u> #_____ **Henry H. Mitchell**, Wapello, exection 4" left humerus, $18/mo., Apr 1876. (p747)

<u>Lucas Co:</u> #6,375 **Eliza Mitchell**, Chariton, mother, $8/mo. Sep 1863. (p748)

<u>Madison Co:</u> #3,695 **William Mitchell**, Wells, wound left wrist joint, $8/mo., May 1878; #131,978 **Sarah J. Mitchell**, Winterset, wid., $8/mo., Jul 1868. (p751)

<u>Mahaska Co:</u> #48,213 **Geo. R. Mitchell**, Oskaloosa, gunshot wound right elbow, $12/mo., Aug 1877. (p754)

<u>Plymouth Co:</u> #_____ **Jay W. Mitchell**, LeMars, gunshot wound right side, chest, $2/mo., Jul 1879. (p775)

<u>Polk Co:</u> #33,446 **Milton Mitchell**, Des Moines, wound head, $2/mo., Mar 1882. (p777)

<u>Scott Co:</u> #92,133 **Chas. W. Mitchell**, Davenport, amputation left thigh & injury head, $24/mo., May 1882. (p787)

<u>Van Buren Co:</u> #7,083 **Angeline Mitchell**, Bonaparte, dependent wid., $8/mo., Aug 1876. (p797)

<u>Worth Co:</u> #93,071 **Joseph Mitchell**, Northwood, chronic opthalmia, $8/mo., Sep 1880. (p815)

KANSAS

<u>1855 Federal Census of Kansas Territory:</u>

<u>6th District</u> (Ft. Scott): **Charles Mitchell** 30; female 21; male & female child, all b MO (p6); **Cowan Mitchell** 40; wife 30; 5 male & 4 female children, all b MO (p15).

<u>3rd District</u> (Tecumseh, Topeka, Wabash Co.): **M. J. Mitchell** (male) 25, mechanic, b MO (p2).

Miscellaneous Mitchell Data

<u>16th District</u>: **D. H. Mitchell** (male) 21, farmer; Sarah A. age ?, both b MO (p44).

Lewis Mitchell m Nancy (McKibben) Walzer, half-sister of John S. McKibben, Sr. Lewis & Nancy lived in Belpre, Edwards Co., KS; son **John S. Mitchell** had a son **Charles Albert "Allie" Mitchell**. "Allie's" son, **Charles D.**, wife and 3 ch still live in that county. (Lillian Hooks, 1750 Prefumo Cnyn Rd., #56, San Luis Obispo, CA 93401: 1986.)

KENTUCKY

<u>Kentucky Pioneer Genealogy & Records</u>, V.1 #1 thru V.4 #4: Queries:
Need maiden name of Elizabeth, w/o **Charles C. Mitchell**, both b KY ca 1810-1814; to AL by 1835; to AR by 1860. (Mrs. V. C. Elms, R.R. #4, Kevil, KY 42053: 1979)

William Mitchell b 1779 MD m Mary Bruner; settled Derby, IN; son **Leonard** 1817-1882 m Mary Ellen Webb 1828-1865, d/o Fielding L. Webb & Elizabeth C. Gilliland of KY. (Mrs. V. B. Wimberley, 1466 Whitewater Rd., Memphis, TN 38117)

Mary Ellen Mitchell 1886-1951 Evansville, IN m Clarence Points 1884-1957, bur Grant Co., KY. (Janet K. Pease, 10310 W. 62nd Pl. #102, Arvada, CO 80004: 1981)

Robert Greenfield Mitchell b 12 Dec 1800 d 21 Feb 1883 m Eliza Boone Browning b 21 Aug 1805 d 29 Mar 1843; lvd Washington Co., KY; par from VA; believe Robert's father was **John Mitchell** & Eliza's was Francis Browning. (Martha M. Hazzard, P.O. Box 60689, Fairbanks, AK 99706)

Nancy Mitchell m Anderson Upwood in Barren Co., KY in 1813. (Billie L. McMullen, 805 E. Broadway, Ardmore, OK 73401: 1981)

Joseph B. Mitchell m May 1835 Elizabeth, d/o Stanislaus & Jinny (Blandford) Toon; **William C. Mitchell** m Jan 1826 Catherine Toon. (Leo Willett, 425 S. Lindbergh Blvd., St. Louis, MO 63131: 1981)

Wm. Washington Mitchell b 1780 NC m2) Polly Ross, d/o Mitchell & Mary (Hillhouse) Ross. (Norene Davis, 106 Grant, Russell, KS 67665: 1981)

Mary Mitchell m Wm. M. Johnson s/o Matthew Johnson (ca 1765-1824/30) of Hardin Co., KY & Perry Co., IN; **William Mitchell** (1777-1856) m Mary Bruner of Breckinridge Co.,

Miscellaneous Mitchell Data

(Queries - Kentucky - con't)

KY & Perry Co., IN, d/o George Leonard & Charlotte (Clay-comb) Bruner. (Elizabeth S. Moore, 703 Vender Lane, Pensacola, FL 32505: 1981)

Geo. Washington Goostree b 21 Feb 1847 Sumner Co., TN d 16 Dec 1925 KS s/o Watson Goostree bc 1792 NC, m **Martha Mitchell.** (Ray H. Garrison, 2625 Hawthorne Lane, Flossmoor, IL 60422: 1981)

Sarah, d/o Wm. & **Fanny (Mitchell)** Kendrick m 22 Nov 1810 Alexander Wilson, Bourbon Co., KY; all went to Brown Co., IL. (A. Maxim Coppage, 1356 Elderberry Dr., Concord, CA 94521: 1979)

Miscellaneous Data:

List of Letters remaining in P.O. at Lexington, KY on 4 Apr 1835 - Mrs. **Nancy Mitchell** (V.2 #3 p118)

"Mayfield Monitor," pub. in Graves Co., KY Oct 1885-Dec 1890 (abstr. by Mrs. Ray W. Higgins, Dallas, TX): 16 Jan 1889: Col. **B. F. Mitchell** was appointed Gen'l Passenger agent of this division of N.N. & M.V. Railroad. Col. Mitchell filled this position several yrs ago. (V.3 #2 p81)

13 Feb 1889 licensed to marry, **Maggie L. Mitchell** & B.F. Luther (V.3 #2 p87).

"Semi-Weekly South Kentuckian," Hopkinsville, KY 1887-1888, 14 Jan 1887: Mrs. **D. C. Mitchell** & children of San Antonio, TX visted Mrs. Mitchell's brother, Col. T. J. Morrow. (V.4 #1 p14)

19 Apr 1887 Mr. **Wm. Mitchell**, late of Georgetown, KY has opened a shoe store here (Hopkinsville, KY). (V.4 #2 p44)

29 Apr 1887 The 80th birth of Mrs. Cassie Allen, wid. of Newton Allen, was celebrated last Mon.; she has 5 living daus; her daus are...Mrs. **Jane Mitchell**...of this city. (Hopkinsville). (V.4 #2 p45)

27 Jan 1888 **Will Mitchell** & family will make their home in Paris, KY. (V.4 #4 p123)

BATH COUNTY:

1820 Federal Census of Bath Co., KY:
(Key: m = male; f = female; un = under the age of)
Arthur S. Mitchell (Bloomfield) 3 m un 10, 1 m 16/26, 1 m
    26/45, 1 f un 10, 1 f 26/45.
James Mitchell 1 m un 10, 1 m 26/45, 4 f un 10, 1 f 26/45.

Miscellaneous Mitchell Data

(1820 Census Bath Co., <u>Kentucky</u> con't)

John Mitchell 2 m 10/16, 1 m 16/26, 1 m over 45, 1 f 16/26,
   1 f over 45.
Marth Mitchell 1 m un 10, 1 m 16/18, 1 m 16/26, 1 f un 10,
   1 f 10/16, 1 f 26/45.
Robert Mitchell 2 m un 10, 1 m over 45, 3 f un 10, 2 f 26/45
   1 f over 45.
Samuel Mitchell 3 m un 10, 1 m 16/26, 2 f un 10, 1 f 16/26.
Samuel Mitchell 1 m un 10, 1 m 10/16, 1 m over 45, 1 f un
   10, 1 f 10/16, 1 f 16/26, 1 f over 45.

1830 Federal Census of Bath Co., KY:
(Key: m = male; f = female; un = under the age of)
Hiram Mitchell 1 m un 5, 1 m 20/30, 1 f un 5, 1 f 20/30.
James Mitchell 2 m un 5, 1 m 5/10, 1 m 10/15, 1 m 30/40,
   1 f un 5, 1 f 5/10, 2 f 10/15, 1 f 30/40.
James G. Mitchell 1 m un 5, 1 m 5/10, 1 m 10/15, 1 m 15/20,
   1 m 20/30, 1 m 40/50, 2 f un 5, 1 f 5/10, 1 f 15/20, 1 f
   20/30, 1 f 30/40.
Marthy Mitchell 1 m 15/20, 1 f 15/20, 1 f 50/60.
Robert Mitchell 1 m un 5, 1 m 5/10, 1 m 10/15, 1 m 15/20,
   1 m 50/60, 1 f 10/15, 1 f 40/50, 1 f 50/60, 1 f 80/90.
Samuel Mitchell 1 m 15/20, 1 m 60/70, 1 f 15/20, 1 f 40/50,
   1 f 60/70.

1840 Federal Census of Bath Co., KY:
(Key: m = male; f = female; un = under the age of)
Alex Mitchell 2 m un 5, 1 m 20/30, 1 f 20/30.
Alvin Mitchell 1 m un 5, 2 m 5/10, 1 m 30/40, 1 f un 5,
   1 f 20/30, 1 f 50/60.
James Mitchell 1 m 20/30, 2 f un 5, 1 f 20/30.
James Mitchell Jr. 1 m 20/30, 1 f 20/30.
James Mitchell Sr. 1 m 10/15, 1 m 15/20, 1 m 20/30, 1 m
   50/60, 3 f 15/20, 1 f 40/50.
John Mitchell 1 m 5/10, 1 m 10/15, 1 m 30/40, 1 f un 5,
   1 f 30/40.
Samuel Mitchell 2 m un 5, 1 m 5/10, 1 m 20/30, 1 m 70/80,
   1 f 20/30, 1 f 70/80.

Bath County Marriages (abstr. by Sandra Howell):
   Elizabeth Mitchell, age 21, b Hamilton Co., OH, res.
Hamilton Co., OH, to John H. Goodridge, age 33, b Albany,
York State, res. Hamilton Co., OH, 8 Apr 1852.

Miscellaneous Mitchell Data

BOURBON COUNTY, KENTUCKY:

Mitchel/Mitchell Marriages:
(Key: bm = bondsman; par = parent; sis = sister)
Abraham to Nancy Laughlin, John Laughlin bm 1 Feb 1831
Agness to David Ireland, Alexander Mitchell bm 5 Jul 1788
Alexander to Evaline Trendel 12 Aug 1830
Catherine to Noah Bevann, Jenny Mitchell sis 25 Nov 1818
David to Rosannah Porter Apr 1795
Elijah to Fidelia Hamilton, Rob't Hamilton bm 16 Apr 1816
Elizabeth to John Erwin, Sam'l Mitchell par 16 Sep 1794
Elizabeth to Wm. Phillips, Ann Mitchell bm 9 May 1815
James to Elizabeth Jones, Thos. Jones par 11 Jul 1815
James to Mary McConnel, Wm. McConnel par 9 Feb 1788
James G. to Separah Munford 14 Jan 1809
Jane to James Gayham, Mariah Briggs par 7 Nov 1809
Jesse to Sarah Purviance, Parson Purviance bm 7 Jan 1805
John to Milly Ladd, Ellison Ladd bm 4 Feb 1806
John to Mary Bugle 25 Dec 1833
Joseph to Nancy Smith 21 Oct 1830
Kesiah to Jos. Kirkpatrick, Alex Kirkpatrick bm 10Mar1791
Lillie to William Smith Dec 1795
Magory to Isaac Orchard, Isaac Orchard bm 21 Sep 1791
Martha to Elijah Kirkpatrick, Jos. Mitchell bm 23Feb1819
Martha to Malcolm McBride, Jas. H. Mitchell bm 21 Apr 1834
Martha to Benedict Marsh, Nicholas Marsh bm 25 Mar 1834
Patsy to Gavin Mathew 10 Feb 1828
Polly to Joseph K. Glenn, Sam'l Mitchell bm (no date)
Robina to Willoughby Sanford, W.B. Branahan bm 5 Jul 1817
Russel to Rebecca Sutton, Rowland Sutton bm 8 Dec 1826
Ruth B. to John Rankin, Wm. Mitchell bm 27 Apr 1830
Sarah to Thos. Hull, Jesse Mitchell bm 2 Jan 1805
Sarah to Parson Purviance, Elijah Purviance bm 25Sep1805
Sarah to John Welbarger 2 Sep 1818
Tilda to Robert Houston 15 May 1822
William to Nancy McCorkle 7 Mar 1798
William to Sara Wright 10 Aug 1797
William (bm for Alex Brown to Mary Duncan 6 Jul 1792)

FAYETTE COUNTY:

Tax List 1787: 17 May **Samuel Mitchell** 11 horses, mares, mules, colts; 22 cattle; 1 black over age 16; 17 May **Moses Mitchell** 4 horses, etc.; 11 cattle; 30 May **Thomas Mitchell**

Miscellaneous Mitchell Data

6 horses, etc.; 21 cattle; 13 June **Robert Mitchell** 2 white
males 16/21; 7 horses, etc.; 9 cattle; 12 Jul **Rosanna Mitchell** 2 white males 16/21, 5 horses, etc.; 17 cattle; 12
Jul **Jno Mitchell** 1 horse, etc; 3 cattle.

<u>Minute Book I</u> (abstr. by Sam McDowell):
26 Mar 1781:   Town of Lexington chose trustees...**David
Mitchell**...; lot granted to **Joseph Mitchell.**
20 Dec 1781: Distribution of Lots - to **David Mitchell**...to
William Mitchell (5 lots).
19 Mar 1782: Lot #66, out, lot & No. 70, in lot to **James
Mitchell, Jr.**; Lot #45, in lot changed with **Joseph Mitchell** for No. 59.
16 Mar 1782: Lexington choose as trustees...**Wm Mitchell.**
12 Dec 1782:   Chosen as trustee...**Wm Mitchell**...

<u>LINCOLN COUNTY:</u>
Tax List 1787: 27 June **Wm. Mitchel** 7 horses, mares, etc.

<u>MADISON COUNTY:</u>
Tax List 1787:   30 Jul **John Mitchell** 1 horse, mare, etc.

<u>MASON COUNTY:</u>

<u>Newspaper abstract</u> (dated 15 Feb 1900, name of paper not
   given; found at the Adams Co., OH Probate Clerk's.)
   "Maysville, KY, Apr. 19, 1812: Mr. Thomas Marshall and
Mr. **Charles Mitchell** met this day...in the State of Ohio,
where the gentlemen...exchanged a shot. Mr. Mitchell...
being quicker than Mr. Marshall, shot him in the hip...
(Signed) James A. Paxton, John Bickley."
   Charles Mitchell was promoted from Ensign to 1st Lt. of
Rifles and "served with distinction during the war, during which time he fought two duels, the first with a Lt.
named Bayless, the other with a Capt.; in both of these
encounters, he came off without a scratch, but inflicted
serious damage on both his opponents.   In 1810 while in
Cynthiana, KY, he got into a fight with a Dr. McMillen whom
he left for dead in the street and fled to Texas.   On his
way (on the gulf between New Orleans and Galveston) the
vessel was wrecked on an island and almost all on board
perished. Mitchell was washed ashore. Little is known of

Miscellaneous Mitchell Data

his life in Texas. Hearing that Dr. McMillen was not dead he returned to KY & soon got into trouble with a brother-in-law, a man named Masterson. They fought in a hotel in Ripley with knives. When it was over, Mitchell had only a few cuts, while Masterson was almost dead. The next fight he had was with a great big man by the name Stephen Lee, who quietly and quickly picked him up and threw him down a stairway. In his later years, Mitchell was sent to the legislature from Mason Co. and served 1 term. He died in June 1861 of heart disease. Upon his return from Texas, Col. Mitchell married a lady named Fowke by whom he had a number of children, one of whom, **Richard**, evidently a chip off the old block, got into trouble with a man in Ripley by the name of Tomlinson whom he killed on the spot...

Mason Co. Marriages:
Martha Mitchell to Charles Allen 14 Jan 1819

Probate Records Index (Mitchel/Mitchell):
George, Will Bk E:323; **Isaac**, Inventory Bk C:345; Acct., Bk C:360, Bk D:271; **Jane**, Will 1840-1847 Bk N:406; **John**, Will 1829-1831 Bk H:239; **John**, Inventory Bk H:338; **Richard**, Will 1853-1857 Bk 2:330; **Sarah**, Will 1823-1826 Bk F:220; **William**, Inventory Bk I:448 (1832-1834), Acct. Bk I:451; **William**, Will 1840-1847 Bk N:156.

McLEAN COUNTY:
Mitchell Births 1854 (abstr. by Sandra Howell):
1 June: Mary, d/o Rutherford & Jane (Cunningham) Mitchell (same listing for 1855).
31 May: Christina, d/o Whitlock & Christian (Mitchell) Edwards.

MONTGOMERY COUNTY:

1810 Federal Census of Montgomery Co., KY:
(Key: m = male; f = female; un = under the age of)
Alexander Mitchell 3 m un 10, 1 m 10/16, 2 m 16/26, 1 m 26/45, 1 f un 10, 1 f 10/16, 1 f 26/45.
John Mitchell 4 m un 10, 1 m 10/16, 1 m 16/26, 1 m 26/45, 1 f 10/16, 1 f 26/45.

Miscellaneous Mitchell Data

(1810 Census Montgomery Co., Kentucky con't)

Matthew Mitchell 1 m un 10, 1 m 26/45, 3 f un 10, 1 f 16/26
1 f 26/45.
Robert Mitchell 1 m un 10, 1 m 10/16, 1 m 16/26, 1 m 26/45,
1 f un 10, 2 f 16/26, 2 f 26/45, 1 f over 45.
Samuel Mitchell 3 m un 10, 1 m 16/26, 1 m over 45, 3 f un
10, 1 f 16/26, 1 f 26/45.

1820 Federal Census of Montgomery Co., KY:
(Key: m = male; f = female; un = under the age of)
Archibald Mitchell 1 m 26/45, 1 f un 10, 1 f 16/26.
James Mitchell 1 m 10/16, 1 m 26/45, 4 f un 10, 1 f 10/16,
1 f 26/45.
James Mitchell 2 m un 10, 1 m 26/45, 1 m over 45, 1 f un
10, 1 f 26/45.
William Mitchell 3 m un 10, 1 m 26/45, 1 f 16/26.

1830 Federal Census of Montgomery Co., KY:
(Key: m = male; f = female; un = under the age of)
James Mitchell 1 m 5/10, 1 m 40/50, 2 f 5/10, 1 f 10/15,
1 f 15/20, 1 f 40/50, 1 f 60/70.
James Mitchell 1 m un 5, 2 m 5/10, 2 m 10/15, 1 m 40/50,
1 f un 5, 1 f 5/10, 1 f 30/40.
John Mitchell 1 m un 5, 1 m 15/20, 2 f 20/30.
John Mitchell 2 m un 5, 1 m 30/40, 1 m 70/80, 3 f un 5,
1 f 30/40.
William Mitchell 1 m 5/10, 1 m 10/15, 1 m 15/20, 1 m 40/50,
1 f 5/10, 1 f 15/20.

1840 Federal Census of Montgomery Co., KY:
(Key: m = male; f = female; un = under the age of)
Elizabeth Mitchell 1 m 5/10, 2 m 10/15, 1 m 15/20, 1 f
15/20, 1 f 40/50.
John Mitchell 1 m un 5, 1 m 5/10, 1 m 10/15, 2 m 15/20, 1 m
40/50, 1 f un 5, 1 f 5/10, 1 f 10/15, 2 f 15/20, 1 f 40/50
John H. Mitchell 1 m un 5, 1 m 20/30, 1 f 20/30.
William Mitchell 1 m un 5, 1 m 5/10, 1 m 50/60, 2 f 5/10,
1 f 15/20, 1 f 20/30.

OHIO COUNTY:
Deaths:
Reuben Mitchell's infant d 20 Feb 1879.
Sarah W. Mitchell d 15 Jan 1879 (in Hartford).

Miscellaneous Mitchell Data

(Ohio Co., <u>Kentucky</u> con't)

1850 Federal Census of Ohio Co., KY:
(Key: 1st number = house number; H/H = in household of)
District #1:
319 MITCHELL, Jonathan 34 KY, Jenetta 26 KY, Almeda 4 KY,
    Amanda 6 KY, Judith 1 KY.
531 MITCHELL, Robert 67 PA, Judith 65 VA.
566 MITCHELL, Martin 27 KY, Susanna 24 KY, Elisabeth 6 KY,
    Ellen 5 KY, Sarah 1 KY.
625 MITCHELL, Thompson 37 KY, Martha 13 KY, Mary 11 KY.
631 MITCHELL, Joseph 3 KY, Anna 10 mos. KY, H/H of THOMAS,
    David of VA.
District #2:
454 MITCHELL, Jaberry 25 VA, Margaret 29 NC, William 9 TN,
    Mary J. 7 TN, Adaline 4 TN, Henry F. 3 KY, John C. 1mo KY
539 MITCHELL, Franklin 45 KY, Nancy 42 KY, Alpheus A. 19
    KY, Benjamin F. 17 KY, Ninean 13 KY, Martha 11 KY, Galen
    4 KY, Dulceruce? (female) 1 KY.

PENDLETON COUNTY:

1860 Federal Census of Pendleton Co., KY:
(Key: 1st number = house number; H/H = in household of)
1247 MITCHEL, Matthew 42 Eng., Jane 36 Eng., Matthew 17
    Eng., Jane 16 Eng., Robert 14 Eng., William 11 Eng.,
    Elizabeth 10 PA (Flower Creek P.O.)
1486 MITCHELL, George 70 MD, H/H of WEST, David 45 VA,
    Drusilla 42 VA & family (Molier? P.O.)

UNION COUNTY:

Marriage Bonds:
Absolom Pope Mitchell to Ann Eliz. Holeman 28 Feb 1839
Arramma A. Mitchell (wid), age 32, to W. B. Townsend,
    (widr), age 44 b MD - 20 June 1855.
John D. Mitchell to Pamelia Eddins 9 Aug 1834
Leroy S. Mitchell, age 33, to Sarah E. Hooper (wid), age
    29, 19 May 1854.
Peyton Mitchell to Betsy Briggs 3 Sep 1812

WOODFORD COUNTY:
1790 Tax List: 28 May **Thos. Mitchell** 1 tithe, 2 horses;
James Mitchell, 2 slaves over 12, 2 tithes, 2 horses.

Miscellaneous Mitchell Data

MAINE

Saco Valley Settlements & Families, G. T. Ridlon, Sr.,
(1984 reprint of 1895 edition), pp 1069-70:
(Key: C.E. = Cape Elizabeth; Ptld = Portland)
Records of **Isaac Mitchell,** Esq. of Limington indicate
this branch descended from **Jonathan Mitchell** b1624 Eng.,
came to Cambridge, MA, grad. Harvard College, ordained as
minister in 1650.
Robert Mitchell lvd C.E.; had sons **Dominicus²** & **Jona-
than²** of C.E., **Robert²** of Ptld. **Dominicus² Mitchell** b1744
C.E. m 1765 Ann Small; lvd Standish; ch **(i)** Elizabeth m
Wingate Frost; **(ii)** Daniel b1768 m Anna Small; **(iii)** Mary
m Abraham Parker; **(iv)** Dominicus m Apphia Whitney; **(v)**
Joshua m Hannah Myrick; **(vi)** Robert m Lydia Berry; **(vii)**
Isaac b1780 m1801 Martha Libby & had ch. Abner 1803; Lewis
1805; Isaac L. 1807; Harriet b1809 m ___ Small; Philemon
L. b1812 to Rock Island, IL; Anna b1815 d1818; Anna b1820;
Nancy m Winborn Adams; **(viii)** Anna m Wingate Frost; **(ix)**
Samuel m Margaret Berry; **(x)** Sarah m Joseph Davis.

History of Durham, ME, E. S. Stackpole, 1899, pp 222-224:
William Mitchell's mar intentions to Elizabeth Clark
recorded 21 Apr 1759 Old Falmouth; she was sister of Rev.
Ephraim Clark of Cape Elizabeth; ch b at Durham were:
(i) Peter² m 29 Nov 1802 Kezia Ring; sons James & Robert;
(ii) Thomas² - no record aft 1807; **(iii)** William² m1797
Avis Cushing; dc1836; ch John b1798 d1892 m1824 Lydia
Spaulding who d1893; 9 ch; William b1799 went to NY; Israel b/d1801; Silence m John Smith; Aaron b1805 d1895 m
1832 Susan Robinson d1892 age 85y d/o Rev. John of Lisbon;
6 ch; James m Anna Boston; Emaline m Carr Barker & d "out
West"; Betsey b1807 d1898 m1830 David Bowie; Clark m Ser-
ena Boston; 1 son; Mary unmar; **(iv)** Samuel² b1766 d1835
m1802 Betsey Dingley b1766 d1853; ch William b1803 d1823;
Eliza b1805 d1856 m Dea. Bangs; Isaiah b1809 d1823; Sally
b1811 m Sargent Whittum; Mary b1813 d1863; Samuel b1815
d1869 m1) Harriet Eveleth; m2)1858 Laura W. Jones; sons
George & Alvah lvd Boston, MA; Israel b1817 d1891 m1847
Eliza Fowler; ch James dy; Alonzo dy; Emma; Martha m ____
Lufkin; Susan b1822 d1897 unmar. (Portrait of Israel on
p224A of the above book.) **(v)** Richard² m1788 Eleanor Webster; ch Patience b1789 m1815 Jacob True; John b1792;
Christopher b1795 m Esther Penley; 9 ch; Lucinda b1797;

Miscellaneous Mitchell Data

Benjamin b1799 m Hannah Penley; James b1802; **(vi)** Robert[2]
m1793 Sally Dyer; ch Hannah b1794 m1814 Riggs Getchell;
Polly b1796 m1816 David Lincoln; David b1798; Jane b1800
m James Fowler; Francis b1803.

<u>Maine Wills 1640-1760</u>, W. M. Sargent (1972 reprint):
(Key: app = appraised; inv = inventoried; wit = witness-
ed; dtd = dated; prob = probated; est = estate;)
   Christopher & Joseph Mitchell app est of Edward Gaech
of Kittery 1717 (p195); will of **Christopher Mitchell** of
Kittery dtd 1739 prob 1743 ment wife **Sarah**, son **Samuel**,
daus **Mary** Brown, **Joanna** Blake, **Sarah** Partridge, **Elizabeth**
Leach, **Miriam** Phillips, **Susanna** Howard (pp 477-479).
Jacob Mitchell inv est of Josiah Plummer 1746 & John White
1747 N. Yarmouth (pp 536 599); **John Mitchell** app est of
John Walker in Arundel 1743 (p465); **Miriam Mitchell**, wife
of **Robert** ment as dau in will of Dominicus Jordan of Falmouth dtd 1746 (p643); **Noah Mitchell** a debtor to the est
of Phinehas Jones ca1743 (p483); **Richard Mitchell** app est
of John More of Yorke Co. 1713 (p169); **Robert Mitchell** of
Kittery, tavern keeper, will dtd 1730 prob 1731 ment sons
Roger, Robert; sons-in-law & daus Wm & **Mary** Kearswell,
Mannaren & **Sarah** Baile, Samuel & **Elizabeth** Grenough; wife
Sarah (pp 318-19); **Robert Mitchell** inv est of John Fernald
of Kittery ca1754 (p730); **Roger Mitchell** wit will of Roger Deering 1718 (p206); app est of John Walker in Kittery
1743 (p465); app est of Henry Barter of Kittery ca1747; &
app est of George Collings of Kittery 1747 (pp 545 563);
Sarah Mitchell wit will of Roger Deering of Kittery dtd
1717 prob 1718 & is named by him as dau (pp 205-6); **Sarah**
Mitchell of Kittery, will dtd 1734 prob 1735-6, wid of
Robert, dec'd, tavern keeper, ment sons **Robert & Roger**;
sons-in-law & daus Wm & **Mary** Kearswell, Mannarin & **Sarah**
Beal, Samuel & **Elizabeth** Greenough; father Roger Deering
dec'd; grsons James Kearswell, Robert Greenough, **Robert**
Mitchell (s/o Roger), grdau Sarah Kearswell (pp 372-74);
Solomon Mitchell app est of Benjamin Welch, Jr. 1759 &
Jacob Brown 1759, both in N. Yarmouth (pp 844 894).

<u>The Jordan Memorial</u>, Tristram Frost Jordan, comp., 1882:
Anjer Mitchell m Betsey Jordan b1799 Lisbon, d/o Robert &
Olive (Durgin) Jordan; lvd Dixfield; 6 ch (p427).

Miscellaneous Mitchell Data

(Abstracts from The Jordan Memorial in Maine con't)

Betsey Mitchell m 28 Oct 1813 (Scarsborough) Samuel Jordan b1787 s/o Stephen Jr. & Eliz. (Jordan) Jordan (p116)

Elizabeth A. Mitchell d/o **Joshua** & Polly W. (Jordan) **Mitchell,** m Seth Libby Jordan b1811 s/o Ignatius & Jane
(Johnson) Jordan (p204).

(Mrs) Jennie Mitchel of Chelsea, MA m as 2nd wife 5 Oct
1871 Franklin Jordan b1841 s/o Lawrence & Mary (Rice)
Jordan (p269).

Joshua Mitchel s/o **Jonathan** & Miriam (Jordan) **Mitchell** m
14 Oct 1814 Mrs. Polly W. (Jordan) Jordan wid of Ebenezer d/o Stephen Jr. & Elizabeth (Jordan) Jordan (p114).

Phebe Mitchell of Kittery m(int) 18 May 1741 Falmouth to
James Jordan b1716 s/o Jeremiah & Catharine (Randall)
Jordan (p403).

Robert Mitchel of Kittery m Miriam Jordan d/o Dominicus &
Joanna (Bray) Jordan; Robert lvd Falmouth; d1769 at age
59y; 5 ch (p145).

Wilson D. Mitchel of E. Corinth m 17 Dec 1866 Mary Pauline
Jordan b1844 d/o Samuel & **Betsey (Mitchell)** Jordan;
3 ch (p116).

The Libby Family in America 1602-1881, Chas T. Libby 1882:
Mitchel/Mitchell Marriages in Maine:

A. Mitchell (Capt) m Fannie Libby b1809 d/o Reuben & Martha (Farnsworth) Libby (p311-12).

Alfred Mitchell of Lewiston m Ann Libby b1831 d/o Capt.
John Cook & Nancy Gerrish (Libby) Libby pp 427-28).

Alonzo Mitchell m1850 Lydia Sherburne Libby b1825 d/o
Paul & Elizabeth (Sherburne) Libby (p225).

Benjamin Mitchell of Windham m1773 Sarah Libby d/o Matthew & Sarah (Hanscom) Libby (p82).

Benjamin Morse Mitchell m1875 Susan Jane Libby b1852 d/o
Dorville & Harriet A. (Cole) Libby (pp 448-49).

Betsey Mitchell d/o Jonathan & _____ (Lovett) Mitchell of
Cape Elizabeth m Luke Libby b1767 s/o Luke & Dorothy
(McKenney) Libby (pp 84 176).

Calvin H. Mitchell m1866 at Portland to Caroline M. Libby
(p541).

Charles Mitchell m Mary Libby b1835 d/o Richard & Lucy
(Libby) Libby (p316).

Christopher Mitchell m1715 Eleanor Larrabee d/o Thos. &
Elizabeth ( ) Larrabee of Scarborough (p41).

Miscellaneous Mitchell Data

(Abstracts from The Libby Family in _Maine_ con't)

Elizabeth J. Mitchell d/o Capt. **Joseph** & Hannah (Perry) **Mitchell** of Kittery m1848 Alfred Johnson Libby s/o Abraham & Betsey (Hill) Libby (p144).

Frances A. Mitchell m1857 Sewell Libby b1835 s/o Otis & Phebe (Smith) Libby (p317).

Harriet Mitchell m Jacob Sherburne of Atkinson; had dau Mary Sherburne who m1835 Thomas J. Libby (p119).

Isaac Mitchell Esq. of Limington m1801 Martha Libby d/o Philemon & Martha (Small) Libby (p67).

Jane W. Mitchell d/o **Joseph** & Jane (Webster) **Mitchell** m 1848 Daniel Libby b1807 s/o Dea. Jonathan & Hannah (Knox) Libby (p251).

John Mitchell of Yarmouth m Emeline Libby d/o Capt. Daniel & Hannah (Colley) Libby (p231).

John Mitchell m1843 Eliza Libby d/o Jonathan & Lydia (Larrabee) Libby (p338).

John Mitchell m bef 1848 Mary Libby b Mt. Prospect, Ire., d/o Thos. & Ann (McKue) Libby, arr. Boston 1848 (p539).

Jonathan Mitchell m1759 Keziah Libby b1738 d/o John & Keziah (Hubbard) Libby; had son **Richard Mitchell** whose grson was **Wm. H. Mitchell** (p51 88).

Joseph Mitchell m1881 Boston, MA Emma T. Libby b1862 d/o Daniel & Almira (Howard) Libby (p132).

Josiah Mitchell m1842 Sarah Libby b1808 d/o Dominicus & Dorothy (Small) Libby (p157).

Josiah Mitchell m1822 Betsey Libby b1804 d/o Enoch & Rebecca (Harmon) Libby (p158).

Lydia Mitchell, 2nd wife of Wm. Larrabee b1727 s/o Benjamin & Sarah (Johnson) Larrabee of Scarsborough (p41).

Lydia S. Mitchell d/o **James** & Mary C. (Roberts) **Mitchell** of Palmyra m1864 Calvin S. Libby b1840 s/o Isaac & Abigail S. (Hanscom) Libby (p390).

Mary Mitchell d/o **Richard** & Lydia (Remmick) **Mitchell** of Scarborough m Moses Libby b1796 s/o William & Mary (Fogg) Libby (p189 406) (Note: **Richard Mitchell** was s/o **Jonathan** & Keziah [Libby] **Mitchell**.)

Mary Mitchell m Bela True of Pownal; had dau Hannah L. True who m1839 David Tyler Libby (p446).

Rebecca Mitchell m Job Libby b1783 s/o Joseph & Jane (Cole) Libby (p148).

Robert Mitchell m1841 Mary M. Libby d/o David & Dorcas (McDonald) Libby (pp 356-57).

(Abstracts from The Libby Family in <u>Maine</u> con't)

Sarah Mitchell ment as d/o Mary (   ) Fogg-Libby, wid of
David Fogg, who m2)1810 Nehemiah Libby (p64).

Sarah Emory Mitchell d/o **Asa** & Mary (Sylvester) **Mitchell**
m1862 Edward Libby b1829 s/o Marrett & Mary (Libby)
Libby (pp 380-1).

Sarah J. Mitchell d/o **James** & Sally (Rackliff) **Mitchell** of
Unity m Allison Libby b1807 s/o Mark & Anna (Libby)
Libby (pp 169 383).

Susan Mitchell d/o **John** & Jane (   ) **Mitchell** of Harrington
m1) Josiah Libby s/o Josiah & Sarah (Holmes) Libby; m2)
Jesse Bateman; m3) Timothy Libby b1786 s/o Obadiah &
Mary (Hill) Libby (pp 148-49 543).

William Henry Mitchell m Mary Libby b1839 d/o William &
Ann H. (Harmon) Libby (p207).

William P. Mitchell of New Durham, NH m1824 Lydia Libby
b1803 d/o John & Sally (Langley) Libby (p237).

<u>Genealogical Dictionary of ME & NH</u>, Noyes, Libby & Davis,
(1979 reprint), pp 483-85:
Christopher Mitchell, Kittery, d1688; wid Sarah (Andrews); ch John; Christopher; Joanna m Joseph Flood; Sarah m ____ Pierce; Samuel; Robert; Richard; Joseph; Elizabeth m1) John Tinney, m2) Samuel Johnson; William. **Christopher Mitchell Jr.**, Kittery, m1) Mary Brackett & had dau
Mary m Charles Brown; m2) Sarah ____; ch Samuel b1694 m
Elizabeth, est adm 1756, 6+ ch; Joanna b1696/7 m Timothy
Blake & had son Christopher; Sarah b1699 m Jonathan Partridge; Elizabeth b1701/2 m Zachariah Leach; Benjamin
b1704; Miriam m Andrew Phillips; Susanna m Edward Howard.
(Capt) **John Mitchell** m Mrs. Sarah Gunnison who m bef 21
Mar 1664/5 Francis Morgan. **John Mitchell** s/o Christopher
Sr., d bef 1733, per son was Christopher Mitchell who
m1715 Eleanor Larrabee of Kittery. **Joseph Mitchell** s/o
Christopher Sr., est adm 1746; m Joanna Couch; ch Joseph
b1730; (Capt) Solomon b1706 m 1729/30 Mary Mitchell d/o
Richard, 9 ch; John b1708 d1799 m1735/6 Lydia Sewall who
d1770, 13 ch; Robert; Benjamin m1736 Mehitable Bradgon, 6
ch; Joshua; Samuel m1745 Martha Rackliff d/o Wm., & had
ch Joanna m Joseph Goodhue, Lydia m Wm. Couch Jr., Mary m
James Titcomb. **Matthew Mitchell**, Kittery, witness 1667,
soldier for Exeter 1676. **Paul Mitchell** of Sheviock, co.
Cornwall, Eng., lost in fishing disaster 1654. **Richard**

Miscellaneous Mitchell Data

Mitchell s/o Christopher Sr., Kittery, est adm 1756, m
Sarah Couch; ch John b1700; Sarah b1702 m Thos. Adams; Joanna b1704; Joseph m1726/7 Isabella Bragdon, his will
proved 1765, hers 1784, 8 ch; Richard m1)1736/7 Hulda
Weare d/o Peter; m2)1740 Sarah (Deering) Jones, will dtd
1784 proved 1786; William m1)1741 Sarah Weare d/o Peter;
m2)1756 Sarah Sellars; will dtd 1784 proved 1788, 6 ch;
Mary m Capt. Solomon Mitchell s/o Joseph; Temperance m Wm
Rackliff. **Robert Mitchell** s/o Christopher Sr., mariner,
tavern keeper, will proved 1731 names wife Sarah (Deering), her will proved 1735/6, ch Roger b1694 d1762 m1)1717
Sarah Cutts; m2)1720 Bridget (Bickford) Couch; m3)1726/7
Mary Gould, 10 ch; Robert b1697 d1698; Mary b1699 m Wm.
Carswell/Kearswell; Sarah b1702 m1720 Mannering Beale;
Elizabeth b1705 m1) Samuel Greenleaf; m2) Samuel Greenough; m3) Capt. Henry Kingsbury of Rowley; Robert b1710 d
1769 m Miriam Jordan. **Samuel Mitchell** s/o Christopher Sr.
per d by 1693 leaving wid Rachel of Newcastle (NH) & 3 ch;
found in Newcastle (NH) **Thomas Mitchell** m by 1721 Sarah
wid of Thos. Marshall; **David Mitchell** taxed 1726; **George
Mitchell** of Portsmouth had wife Sarah in 1743. **Thomas
Mitchell**, prob same as Thomas, mariner of Malden, MA who
m1655 Mary Moulton; he d at Malden 1709 age 81y 10m, 5 ch
including Thomas b1660; John b1664. **William Mitchell** s/o
Christopher Sr., killed by Indians at Scarborough 1724;
per m1) Honor____; m2) bef 1715 Elizabeth Tinney, ch Israel m1730 Mary Berry, d1749; Christopher m(int)1734 Deborah Mills; John; Elizabeth m(int)1736 Joseph Drisco; Job
b1720 m1743/4 Susannah Brown; William b1720 (twin) m1744
Hannah Berry; Mary unmar 1745; Relief b1724 m John Berry;
Mercy m James Marr. (Note: Gen. Dict. says that **Prudence**
Mitchell who m1) John Bradden, m2) Robert Tapley, & was
Prudence Spoor in 1726, may have been d/o William Mitchell
who m Honor_____, and not William s/o Christopher Mitchell, Sr. above.)

<u>Jordan Family Descendants</u>, Chas. M. Jordan, comp. (addi-
tional data relative to "The Jordan Memorial," other
than that already mentioned):
Carrie Mitchell m at Windham James Melville Jordan b 5
Aug 1860 Raymond d 30 Apr 1946 Gorham s/o James Monroe &
Mary (Smith) Jordan; 6 ch (p453).

(Abstracts from Jordan Family Descendants in Maine con't)

James Mitchell m Sarah Rackliff bpt 22 May 1782 Standish;
dau **Arabella Rackliff Mitchell** b 10 Apr 1802 Unity d 6
Sep 1878 Portland m1824 Joseph Woods b 18 Dec 1799 Unity
d 10 Jan 1878 Unity (p77).

Jonathan Mitchell s/o **Robert** & Miriam (Jordan) **Mitchell,**
b1736 d 1 May 1810 m 24 Feb 17__ Anna Lovett d/o Jonathan
& Mary (Woodbury) Lovett; dau **Elizabeth** b 8 Nov 1775 m1)
20 Aug 1796 Luke Libby; m2) 17 Jan 1801 Thos Murry (p65)

Joshua Mitchell m Ruth Dingley b1854; son **Charles Mitchell** b1881 (p194).

Lewis M. Mitchell b1868 d1948 m Susie M. Wheeler b 4 Sep
1868 d1930 d/o John N. & Mary Eliza (Jordan) Wheeler; ch
Leroy N. b1893 d1935; **Philip M.** b 1896 d1966; **Florence
M.** b1903 (p30).

(Capt) Seth Mitchell m 4 Apr 1770 Mary Scammon b1752 (p55)

MISSOURI

1850 Federal Census of Platte Co., MO:
(Key: 1st number = house number; H/H = in household of)
Marshall Twp:
2 MITCHELL, Henrietta 9 MO, H/H of GUTHRIE, Wm. A.
56 MITCHELL, Samuel R. 52 KY, Eliza 47 VA, William 23 KY,
David 21 KY, Henry 15 KY, George W. 12 IL, Martha 8 MO,
Eliza 5 MO.
79 MITCHELL, Madison 38 KY, Mary 28 KY, Mary 4 MO, Thomas 2
MO, Franklin 34 KY.
Weston Twp:
129 MITCHELL, John S. 20 KY, Benjamin W. 12 KY.
173 MITCHELL, Eliza 45 (wid) KY, OWENS, Laura 6 MO.
Green Twp:
40 MITCHELL, Robert B. 56 KY, Sarah 52 KY, Francis (male)
23 KY, George 19 KY, Nancy 18 KY, William 16 KY, China
Eliza? (female) 13 MO.

1870 Federal Census of Dade Co., MO:
(Key: 1st number = house number; H/H = in household of)
Centre Twp:
39 MITCHELL, James H. 40 TN, Charlotte A. 35 IN, Martha E.
14 MO, John E. 12 MO, James G. 10 MO, Andrew M. 8 MO,
Limen J. 3 MO.
4_? MITCHELL, James 74 NC, Martha 76 NC.

Miscellaneous Mitchell Data

(1870 Census of Dade Co., Missouri con't)

50 MITCHELL, Rachel 44 TN, William 19 IL, Mary 18 MO, Margaret 15 MO, Martha 13 MO, Anna 8 MO, RICHARDSON, John 19 (schoolteacher) MO.

52 MITCHELL, Moses 37 TN, Rebecca S. 26 MO, Cordelia E. 11 MO, Malinda A. 9 MO, James M. 5 MO, Fanny E. 3 MO, Malinda 67 TN.

59 MITCHELL, John A. 22? TN

62 MITCHELL, Richard 43 TN, Lucinda 43 TN, Layton L. 21 TN, Minerva E. 14 MO, Anna J. 8 MO.

89 MITCHELL, William 67 NC, Eleanor 66 NC, Mary E. 27 MS, David N. 32 MS.

99 MITCHELL, Thomas 19 TN, H/H of SHIPLEY, Liddance? 52 TN & family.

127 MITCHELL, James M.? 73 NC, Winnifred 63 TN, & black servants MITCHELL, Washington 32 MO, Eleanor 32 TN, Rebecca A. 18 MO, George 10 MO, Hattie 8 MO, Mary 5 MO, Lucy 3 mos. MO.

139 MITCHELL, John F. 35 MS, Mary T.? 28 AR, James M. 12 MO, Harriet E. 11 MO, Charles W. 6 MO, Luther? G. 4 MO, Anna M. 2 MO.

North Twp:

67 MITCHELL, Mary 22 TN, H/H of SHIPLEY, John 56 TN & fam.

74 MITCHELL, Dewitt C. 37 TN, Nancy 33 TN, Cordelia 15 TN, Monroe 14 MO, John 12 MO, Felix 9 MO, Martha 8 MO, Mary E. 4 MO, Ida Bell 2 MO.

Polk Twp:

10 MITCHELL, Matilda J. 39 TN, Marvel P. 18 TN, William H. 17 TN, Winnie R. 14 MO, Nancy J. 11 MO, Greenberry 10 MO.

18 MITCHELL, Preston 62 TN, Rachel 56 TN.

19 MITCHELL, Joel A. 27 TN, Frances 27 MO, John 3 MO, William 2 MO, Mary E. 4? mos. (May) MO.

20 MITCHELL, Wm. H. 32 TN, Elizabeth 34 KY, Zachariah 12 MO, Archie P. 10 MO, Nancy A. E. 7 MO, Mary C. 4 MO, Rachel E. 2 MO, Susan E. 4 mos. (March) MO.

Smith Twp:

36 MITCHELL, John 23 MO, Mary A. 17 MO.

South Twp:

81 MITCHELL, Sophia (black) 70 NC, H/H of RENFRO, Absalom.

Recommended: "Free or Inexpensive Research Aids," pub. by the St. Louis Gen. Soc., 1695 S. Brentwood Blvd., Suite 203, St. Louis, MO 63144 (for IL/MO research especially).

Miscellaneous Mitchell Data

NEW HAMPSHIRE

1820 Federal Census of Cheshire Co., NH:
(Key: m = male; f = female; un = under the age of)
Acworth Twp:
Bradley Mitchell 1 m un 10, 1 m 16/26, 2 m over 45, 1 f
  16/26, 1 f 26/45, 1 f over 45.
Jonathan Mitchell 1 m un 10, 1 m 10/16, 1 m 16/26, 1 m
  26/45, 2 f un 10, 1 f 16/26, 1 f 26/45.
Martha Mitchell 1 f over 45.
Thomas Mitchell 3 m un 10, 1 m 26/45, 1 f un 10, 1 f 26/45.
Claremont Twp:
Robert Mitchell 2 m un 10, 1 m 10/16, 1 m 16/26, 1 m 26/45,
  1 f 16/26.
William Mitchell 2 m un 10, 2 m 10/16, 1 m 16/26, 1 m over
  45, 1 f un 10, 3 f 10/16, 2 f 16/26, 2 f 26/45.
Lempster Twp:
James Mitchell 2 m un 10, 1 m 26/45, 2 f un 10, 2 f 26/45.
Nelson Twp:
Frederic A. Mitchell 2 m un 10, 1 m 26/45, 1 f 16/26, 1 f
  26/45.
Walpole Twp:
William Mitchell 2 m un 10, 1 m 26/45, 2 f un 10, 2 f 16/26
Wendell Twp:
Sarah Mitchell 1 m un 10, 2 f un 10, 1 f 26/45.

NEW JERSEY

Patents & Deeds & Other Early Records of New Jersey, ed.
  by Wm. Nelson, 1899:
  7 May 1683 **James Mitchell** of Northumberland, carpenter,
& family, indentured by Arent Sonmans of East NJ to work
in NJ for 3 years (p57); 1 May 1684 deed ment. land belonging to **Mary Mitchell**, widow (p58); 31 Mar 1684 **Marie Mitchell**, widow of Elizabeth Town, ment. in deed; 18 Aug 1687
ment. of **Marie Mitchell**, spinster (p103); 30 Dec 1687
will of **Mary**, widow of **James Mitchell** of Elizabeth Town,
names sons **John, Jacob, William, Nathaniel**; 12 Apr 1688
letters of administration granted to Andrew Hamptone,
tailor, executor of estate (p116); 31 Mar 1687/8, 12 May
1688, 21 Jul 1690 **Mary Mitchell's** land ment. in deed
records (pp 118 120 177). Oct 1684 **Mary Mitchell** indentured as servant for 4 years, brought to NJ by John Campbell (p65); 11 June 1686 **Richard Mitchell** ment. in deed;

Miscellaneous Mitchell Data

(Patents & Deeds in Early <u>New Jersey</u> con't)

1675 **Richard Mitchell** ment. as servant of Sir George & Phillip Carteret (p46); 22 Nov 1699 **Robert Mitchell** ment. on Committee of W. Jersey Society; same on 22 Feb 1698/9 (pp 298 305); 4 Mar 1691/2 Tripartite Indenture between Daniel Cox, Gov., & wife Rebecca; 3rd parties included **Robert Mitchell**, merchant; **Charles Mitchell**, merchant; **Francis Mitchell**, citizen & mercer, all of London (pp 316 317); 27 Feb 1700/1 & 7 June 1701 **Fran. Minschull**, mercer, and **Robert Mitchell**, merchant, of London. 31 Aug 1697 Certificate of Quietus Est issued to **Sarah Mitchell**, widow of Wm. Richardson of Elizabeth Town, as administrix of her husband's estate (p270).

<u>History of Elizabeth, N.J.</u>, Rev. Edwin F. Hatfield, 1868:
James Mitchell, early resident of the town, soon died; wife **Mary** was widow before 31 Mar 1684 when she bought Richard Beach's house-lot & improvements; she d early in 1688; Andrew Hampton adm. her estate; son, **Jacob**, admitted as Associate 1699-1700 & drew No. 107 of 100-acre lots on the Woodbridge line adjacent to Francis Barber & Benjamin Price. Jacob Mitchell was a tailor & married Mary, d/o Robert Morse, Jr. (p266); Richard Beach of New Haven, CT sold his house-lot #31 in Mar 1684 to **Mary**, widow of **James Mitchell**; house-lot of William Letts bounded by **Richard Mitchell** (p169).

<u>Family Group Sheet</u> (Ann Ingersoll, 849 Rio Dell Ave., Rio Dell, CA 95562: 1981)
James & Mary ( ) **Mitchell** of Scotland, to Elizabeth, NJ had son **Jacob² Mitchell** who m1) Mary (Morse) Broadwell, her will written 1724/5 Elizabeth, NJ (Ref: Dawes-Gates Genealogy, footnote, p543); he m2) Hannah Halstead b 1690 NJ d/o Timothy & Abigail (Carmen) Halstead.
Nathaniel³ Mitchell, s/o **Jacob** & Hannah (Halstead) **Mitchell**, was b 20 Jul 1728 NJ, d 2/8 Sep 1773 m 30 Aug 1752 Essex Co., NJ to Abigail Harris b 28 Mar 1731 Essex Co., NJ d 21 Mar 1822 Knox Co., OH d/o James Harris & ____ (Boleyn) Conkling. (18 Dec 1742 **Nathaniel Mitchell**, orphan, of age 14, guardian Jonathan Allen; **William Mitchell**, fellow bondsman.) Ch of **Nathaniel³ Mitchell** & Abigail Harris were **(i)** Hannah b 26 Aug 1753 NJ d 21 Sep 1828 Fredericktown, Knox Co., OH m 30 Nov 1768 Morris Co., NJ to John

(Mitchell Family Group Sheet - <u>New Jersey</u> - con't)

Young b 30 Nov 1750 Morris Co., NJ d 16 Feb 1826 Troy Twp., Richland Co., OH s/o Morgan & Elizabeth (Mills) Young; Quaker; Rev. soldier; 8 ch including son Aaron Young b 14 Nov 1788 Morris Co., NJ d 19 Apr 1856 m 17 Mar 1812 Wayne, Knox Co., OH to **Mary Mitchell**; **(ii)** Abigail b 5 Dec 1755 NJ m Benjamin Jackson; **(iii)** Elizabeth b 29 Jul 1758 NJ m John Kent; **(iv)** Mary b 11 Dec 1760 NJ d Warren Co., OH m Jonathan Whitaker; **(v)** Jacob b 8 June 1763 NJ d Charleston, S.C. m ____ Cobb; **(vi)** William b 14 Jul 1765 NJ d 13 Aug 1848 Knox Co., OH m 4 Nov 1789 Phebe Southard; **(vii)** Sarah b 2 Jan 1768 NJ d AR m Alexander Kirkpatrick; **(viii)** Nathaniel, Jr. b 23 Jan 1772 NJ; unmar. (Ref: "Our Young Family in America," Edward H. Hudson; "Some Descendants of Jonas Halstead," Laura Davis Shoptaugh.)

<u>New Jersey Marriage Records 1665-1800</u>, Wm. Nelson:
(Key: Bur = Burlington; Mon = Monmouth; Mid = Middlesex)
<u>MITCHEL/MITCHELL</u>:
Abraham, Bur, to Mary Piffets 29 Jan 1757
Daniel, Bur, to Anne Fort 27 Oct 1783
George, Bur, to Ann Croney, Bur, 2 Mar 1782
Isaac, Mon, to Byer Hallsteed, Mon, 14 June 1764
James, Mon, to Catharine Jonson, Mon, 25 Sep 1755
John, Mon, to Hannah Parker, Mon, 13 Apr 1762
John, Bucks, PA to Phebe Randall, Bucks, PA, 17 Oct 1763
John, Bucks, PA to Sarah Willett, Bucks, PA, 17 Jul 1776
Joseph, Mid, to Hannah Durham, Mid, 20 June 1753
Lewis, Mon, to Elizabeth Stevens, Mon, 6 May 1740
Richard, Mon, to Elizabeth Martsey, Mon, 17 Oct 1741
Richard, Mon, to Elisabeth Croxson, Mon, 23 Sep 1763
William, Cape May, to Elisabeth Townsend 21 Nov 1774
<u>Brides</u>:
Ann to John Nance, Staten Island, 28 June 1770
Catharine, Bur, to Jacob Cot, Bur, 23 Nov 1741
Catharine, Mon, to Elisha Johnston, Mon, 20 Nov 1759
Catherine, Mon, to Adam Brewer, Mon, 12 Jan 1742
Elizabeth to John Freestone, both of Bucks, PA 5 Jan 1769
Elizabeth, PA, to James Barbur, PA, 16 Sep 1728
Frances to Grover Stout, both of Amwell, 16 Mar 1775
Margaret to John Monroe, Bur, 9 Aug 1736
Margaret, Mon, to Thomas Ellison, Mon, 15 May 1764
Mary to Andrew Cole, Northampton, 29 Jul 1773

Miscellaneous Mitchell Data

(Marriages 1665-1800 in New Jersey con't)

Rachel, Mon, to Philip Denning, Mon, 29 ___ ___
Sarah to Joshua Wright, both of Bucks, PA, 26 Apr 1770
Lyon's Farm Baptist Church Book:
Nathaniel to Polly Marsh, both of Elizabeth, 3 Dec 1800
Middlesex Co. Clerk's Records 1795-1800:
James to Ruth Leamon 17 Nov 1799

Revolutionary Census of NJ, Kenn Stryker-Rodder, 1972:
MITCHEL/MITCHELL:
Edward, Reading, Hunterdon Co., 1778-1780
George, Town Ward, Elizabeth, Exxex Co., 1778-1780
George, Lebanon, Hunterdon Co., 1778-1780
Isaac, Shrewsbury, Monmouth Co., 1778-1780
Jacob (wid of) Town Ward, Elizabeth, Essex Co., 1778-1780
James, Shrewsbury, Monmouth Co., 1778-1780
John, Lebanon, Hunterdon Co., 1778-1780
John, Hanover, Morris Co., 1778-1780
John, Westfield Ward, Elizabeth, Essex Co., 1778-1780
John, Jr., Hanover, Morris Co., 1778-1780
Thomas, Hanover, Morris Co., 1778-1780
William, Shrewsbury, Monmouth Co., 1778-1780
William, Piscataway, Middlesex Co., 1778-1780

NEW YORK

History of Washington Co., NY, Everts & Ensign, 1878:
Salem Twp: Among the early settlers of the Camden Valley
...William Mitchell (p133); Salem District, 1st Town
meeting Apr 1787, appointed as one of the "Pathmasters"...
Isaac Michael (p137); Salem Presby. Church, signing a
call 27 Sep 1787 for a pastor...Isaac Mitchel (p157);
Granville Twp: Civil War - William Mitchell enlisted 21
Aug 1862 in the 123rd Reg't, Co. K. (p221).
Argyle Twp: So. Argyle, John Mitchell opened a store here
about 1824 (p243-44).
Dresden Twp: Principal of Marshall Seminary, established
1863, was Miss Fannie Mitchell ca 1878 (p295).
Fort Ann Twp (originally formed as Westfield): In 1795,
electors not possessed of freeholds, but renting tenements of the yearly value of forty shillings, and thereby
qualified to vote for assemblymen included James Mitchell
...Joseph Mitchell...James Mitchell...(p305)

-397-

Miscellaneous Mitchell Data

Fort Edward Twp: Fort Edward, present 1st Presbyterian Church was organized 17 Jan 1854...John Mitchell...ruling elder (p325).

Greenwich Twp: Civil War - Alexander Mitchell enlisted 6 Aug 1862 in Co. A, 123rd Reg't; died of disease at Chattanooga, TN 16 Aug 1864 (p357).

Hampton Twp: Hampton Town meeting 2 May 1786 appointed overseers of the poor...James Michel, Jr...(p364).

Whitehall Twp: May 1864 - fire destroyed a number of mills and factories, but "Mitchell's axe-helve factory was not destroyed." (p478)

1790 Federal Census of Washington Co., NY:
(Key: m = male; f = female; un = under the age of)
Isaac Michael 1 m over 16, 4 m un 16, 1 f (Salem Twp).
James Michael Jun. 1 m over 16, 3 m un 16, 3 f (Westfield).
James Mitchell 3 m over 16, 1 f (Westfield Twp).

Names & Sketches of Pioneer Settlers in Madison Co., NY, edited by Isabel Bracy:
   Joseph Mitchell settled in DeRuyter in 1807; juror in 1808; tavern keeper in 1810; built a cloth mill in 1814; had son Thomas and brothers Thomas & Benjamin.

History of Saratoga Co., NY, N.B. Sylvester:
   Joseph Mitchell was an early settler in Greenfield, NY (before 1795).

NORTH CAROLINA

North Carolina Marriages 1717-1868, from "Hunting For Bears, Inc., Box 278, Hammond, LA 70404:
MITCHEL/MITCHELL TO JONES:
Clary to William Jones 21 Dec 1866 Wake Co.
Issabella to Henry Jones 20 Jan 1853 Franklin Co.
Lucy to John Jones 18 Oct 1849 Wake Co.
Mary to John Jones 9 Mar 1867 Guilford Co.
Mary to Nathan Jones 20 Jul 1835 Person Co.
Nancey to William Jones 27 Nov 1802 Wilkes Co.
Penny to Richard Jones 11 Aug 1854 Northampton Co.
Sally Ann to Moses Jones 21 Nov 1844 Edgecombe Co.
Sarah to David Jones 3 June 1842 Cumberland Co.

(North Carolina con't)

<u>Cumberland Co., NC Abstracts of Wills 1754-1863</u>, by
  Mrs. Kate James Lepine & Mrs. Anna Sherman, 1984:
  Will of William Galespie Nov 1794; land on Cumberland
River to John Simpson Campbell, reserving 300 acres which
"I have already sold..." to **Irvan Mitchell** (p58).
  Will of William G. McDonald dated 8 Oct 1862, probated
Dec 1863, ment. dau. **Elizabeth Ann Mitchell** (p100).
  Will of **Nathan Mitchell** dated 17 Apr 1844, probated June
1844; wife Nancy, both houses & lots in Fayetteville; ex-
ecutor **William Mitchell** (p131).
  Will of Andrew Robertson of Fayetteville, proven by
oaths of...**Robert Mitchel**...on 7 Mar 179? (p148).

<u>Marriages of Granville Co., NC 1753-1868</u>, Brent H. Hol-
  comb, compiler, 1981:
<u>MITCHEL/MITCHELL (bonds to 1812)</u>:
Abraham to Messenier Davis 22 Dec 1769
Agness to Oliver Freeman 29 Aug 1801
Benjamin to Winny Anderson 19 Dec 1803
Charles to Jane Threft Critcher 16 Dec 1785
Charles to Mary Mitchel 19 Jul 1781
Charles to Nancy Wagstaff 15 Sep 1809 (John Mitchell bm)
Daniel to Mary Gregg 26 Nov 1763
David to Elizabeth Smith 20 Feb 1809
David to Polly Hackinyear 1 Jan 1804
Edmond to Mariah Bass 5 Jan 1795
Elijah to Salley Critcher 3 Mar 1779 (Chas. Mitchell wit)
Elisabeth to John Barnet 10 Dec 1781
Elisabeth to Samuel Denton 3 May 1798
Evan to Charsley Harriss 5 Nov 1798
Fanney to William Thornton 18 Jan 1781
Fanny to Richard Dolby 12 Nov 1807
Hannah to James Sanders (no date)
Isham to Sarah Hudpeth 13 Apr 1802 (Benj. Mitchel bm)
Jane to James Downey Jr. 4 Sep 1806
Jemiah Ann to Philip Sneed 9 Mar 1788
John to Phillis Williams 22 Dec 1777
John to Sarah Johnson 8 Nov 1798 (Evan Mitchell bm)
John to Jenney Minge Bullock 2 Feb 1799
Lucey to Benjamin Evans 1 Aug 1811
Major to Molley Wiggins 26 Dec 1778
Martha to Abraham Womack 31 Ma<u>h</u> 1763 (Jno. Mitchell bm)

Miscellaneous Mitchell Data

(Marriage bonds of Granville Co., <u>North Carolina</u> con't)

Martha to Solomon Walker 9 Aug 1779
Mary, d/o James Mitchell (consent of father) to John
   Bullock 12 Nov 1759
Mary to Charles Mitchel 19 Jul 1781
Mary Ann to Daniel Glover 18 Jan 1794
Michael to Lucy Bass 25 Apr 1805
Milley to Thomas Jeffreys 18 Sep 1792
Nancey to William Busbey 9 Dec 1803
Nancy to Thomas Mitchell 16 May 1798
Polley to Jethro Bass 3 Apr 1809
Rebecka to John Bugg 24 Dec 1788
Robert B. to Martha Burton 28 Nov 1800
Salley to Thos. Potter 1 Aug 1812
Sarah to Zachariah Sims 7 Sep 1801
Sealey to Thomas Wiggins 27 Dec 1802
Solomon to Mary Macvedr? 4 Dec 1797
Thomas to Nancy Mitchell 16 May 1798
Thomas to Liley Hawley 6 Jul 1811
William to Caty Rose 8 Oct 1792
William to Bytha Headspeth 11 Aug 1796
William to Rachel Harden 7 Dec 1800
Zachariah to Ja<u>in</u> Anderson 25 Aug 1795

<u>Granville Co., NC Research</u> (done at the NC State Archives,
   Raleigh, NC 1986):
11 Jan 1781 **Frances Mitchel** relinquished "unto my son
Major Mitchel" the adm. of her dec'd husband's estate. On
11 Feb 1781 **Major Mitchel**, John Cross & **Elijah Mitchel** of
Granville Co. gave bond in the adm. of the estate of **James
Mitchel**, dec'd. Granville Co. writs dtd Aug & Oct 1790
directed the High Sheriff to see that Major Mitchel answered in court a complaint of Frances Mitchel, widow of
James, dec'd; on 20 Oct 1790 Major Mitchel and Fredr. Wiggins of Granville Co. bound themselves to appear on the
1st Monday in Nov to answer the complaint. She charged
that 17 Nov 1785 Major Mitchel had promised her annually
and every year during her lifetime on Jan. 1st, certain
specified amounts of pork, indian corn, wheat, and brown
sugar, and that he had not. She asked damages. However,
Frances Mitchel apparently died before this case was presented, her adm. bond dated 2 Nov 1790 Granville Co., with
Charles Dodson, adm.; inventory brought to court May term

-400-

Miscellaneous Mitchell Data

(Research - Granville Co., North Carolina con't)

1791; estate sale 11 June 1791. At the estate sale, no Mitchel(1) names were among the purchasers.

22 Jan 1798 **Major Mitchel & James Mitchel** of Granville Co. signed a promisory note to Thomas Norman of the same county, payable before December of that year.

Major Mitchel died intestate in 1803, inventory dated 27 Oct, estate sale 3 Dec; purchasers included **John Mitchel**, William Busby, John Denton, **Molley Mitchel**, Samuel Denton, John Allison, Valentine White; Frederick Wiggins was adm.; final return dated 11 Jul 1808.

Will of **James Mitchell** dtd 1 Mar 1775, proved Feb 1779, names sons **Josiah, James, David, John, Abraham**; daughters **Jemima** Davenport, **Amey** Satterwhite, **Mary** Bullock; grandson **Randol Mitchell**; granddau. **Elizabeth Mitchell**. James had an extensive estate, sale in Feb 1779 totaled over 13,397 lbs. Purchasers at the sale included **Edwin, James, Major, Abraham, John, Elijah, Josiah, & David Mitchell**, and Michael Satterwhite. Scraps of paper in the estate file included notes that **John Mitchell**, son of James, was in Person Co., NC in 1797; **Josiah Mitchell**, son of James, had a daughter, **Elizabeth**, who was about age 18 at the death of her grandfather, James Mitchell; she married John Barnet. **Josiah Mitchell** was deceased before 1 May 1797. On 30 Nov 1778 **James Mitchell** "the elder" gave his grandson Michael Satterwhite the land on which he was then living which bordered that of **Josiah Mitchell** and James Taylor. Will of John Robinson dated 8 Apr 1773 left 50 acres of land and 1 negro to **James Mitchell**.

Gleanings from "Abstracts of the Wills & Estate Records of Granville Co., NC 1746-1808," by Zae Hargett Gwynn, 1973 ment. deed dtd 20 Jul 1778 in which Charles Gillam (Gilliam) gave a negro to grandson **James Mitchell**, son of **John Mitchell** & Martha his wife, wit. by **Jacob & Charles Mitchell** & John Smith; Charles Gillam's will dtd 4 Feb 1870, proved May 1784 names **John & Jacob Mitchell**, executors; ment. dau. **Martha Mitchell**, granddau. **Ann Mitchell**, grandsons **Charles, James, Joshua & Francis Mitchell**. On 8 Jan 1789 William Spears ment. dau. **Mary Mitchel**. In the will of **David Mitchel** dtd 4 Dec 1789, he ment. wife Hannah, sons **Elijah & Charles**; sons under age 21 **David, Thomas & John Mitchel**; daus. **Martha** Walker, **Susannah** Moore, **Elizabeth** Landers; **Hannah** Landers; **Milley Mitchel**.

Miscellaneous Mitchell Data

(Research - Granville Co., North Carolina con't)

Will of Thomas Wiggins dtd 11 May 1797, proved Feb 1799, ment. **"Molley Mitchell,** my daughter, all that bought of **Major Mitchell..."**
On 7 Aug 1803 **John Mitchell** of Sumner Co., TN appointed Hutching G. Burton his attorney in Granville Co. to sell his negroes and stock there; wit by **Robert B. Mitchell.** On the same date, Mary Burton of Sumner Co., TN appointed her son Hutching G. Burton of Granville Co. her attorney to sell her 6 negroes there, wit. by **Robert B. Mitchell.**
Granville Co. petition of Aug 1817 by James Downey & his wife Jenney widow of **Charles Mitchell** dec'd, names only child of Charles as **Anson Mitchell,** dec'd; children of **Elijah Mitchell** are named as **Thomas Mitchell,** William Pannell & wife **Martha, Susan** Moor(e), Thomas Jeffries & wife **Mildred, John Mitchell, Sally** Potter, **Nancy Mitchell, Solomon Mitchell, Fanny** James, & **Betsey Mitchell.** Children of **Hannah** Saunders named as Susanna Moor, James Berry & wife Polly, John Allen & wife Lethia, Nathaniel Saunders and wife Hariet, Grandison & David Saunders; children of **Betsey** Saunders named as Dudley Brown & Caney his wife, Romulus Saunders, Frances Saunders & Lethia his wife, and Franklin Saunders. Dudley Brown & wife, Francis Saunders & wife, and Franklin Saunders were all residents of Tennessee.
Aug 1818 **Robert Mitchell** & wife Hannah, formerly Hannah Russell, wid of John C. Russell, asked for her dower from the Russell estate.

State Census of NC 1784-1787, Mrs. A. K. Register 1983: MITCHEL/MITCHELL:
Bertie Co: Joseph; Chatham Co: George, William; Granville Co: John, Josiah, Jacob, Archibald, Charles, David (3), Elijah, Major; Halifax Co: John, Marthew (sic); Martin Co: Burwell (2), Isaac; Northampton Co: Jesse, John, William, William Jr., John; Onslow Co: B., G.; Surrey Co: Adam; Tyrell Co: Jane; Warren Co: James, Lydia, Nancy; Wilkes Co: William (2), Rachel, Nicholas.

NOTE: Joseph W. Watson, 406 Piedmont Ave., Rocky Mount, NC 27803 publishes the Zae Hargett Gwynn abstracts of Granville Co., NC records, plus others on early Edgecombe, Nash, Wayne & Franklin Cos.; brochure available.

OHIO

BROWN COUNTY:

Brown Co. Marriage Index to 1852:
Amos Mitchell to Matilda Pangburn Bk G p96
Boone Mitchell to Susan Power Bk D p88
George Mitchell to Abigail Hursh Bk C p50
George Mitchell to Louisa Winner Bk D p13
Ignatius Mitchell to Nancy Foulk Bk B p24
Isaac Mitchell to Sarah Cropper Bk E p4
James Mitchell to Sally R. Redman Bk D p98
James Mitchell to Sophia B. Hilligoss Bk G p196
James W. Mitchell to Katherine Tucker Bk G p153
John Mitchell to Holly Richey Bk C p11
Leonidas Mitchell to Sarah Allen Bk G p38
Thomas B. Mitchell to Jane Wiles Bk D p75

1840 Federal Census of Brown Co., OH:
Heads of Household:
Arthur Mitchell, Huntington Twp., p263, age 50/60.
George Mitchell, Pleasant Twp., p255, age 40/50.
George Mitchell, Union Twp., p309, age 30/40.
James Mitchell, Union Twp., p312, age 30/40.
James Mitchell, Union Twp., p312, age 50/60.
John Mitchell, Union Twp., p320, age 30/40.
Samuel Mitchell, Perry Twp., p334, age 40/50 (lvg alone).
Thomas Mitchell, Union Twp., p312, age 30/40.

Chancery Records (Vol. 3, 1829-1831):
 Heirs of Joseph Lewis dec'd vs. heirs of **Ignatious Mitchell** dec'd; Mitchell's heirs named as **Richard Mitchell, Charles Mitchell, Ignatious Mitchell,** Vachael & Mildred Masterson, Charles W. & Patsy Allen; refers to a deed made by Joseph Lewis 11 Jan 1825 for 44 acres with Ignatious Mitchell of Kentucky. (Note: Index to Transcribed Deeds of Adams Co., OH 1800-1818 include listings for **David, Ignatious, and John Mitchell.** Also refer to Mason Co., KY section of this chapter, newspaper article ment.**Charles Mitchell** who had a brother-in-law named Masterson.)
Vol. 5: 23 Feb 1841 Samuel Pangborn vs heirs of **Leonard F. Mitchell** dec'd; heirs are **John F. Mitchell** of MO; **Stanislaus Mitchell** of Mason Co., KY; minor children **Robert S. Mitchell** and **William Mitchell** of Brown Co., OH.

(Brown Co., Ohio con't)

Cemetery Records in Brown, Cuyahoga, Madison, Medina,
   Lorain, & Shelby Counties, OH (D.A.R.publication):
Hillman Methodist Cemetery, Pleasant Twp., Brown Co.:
A. W. Mitchell d 1872 aged ____
Abigail Mitchell (wife of George) b 1802 d 1878
George Mitchell b 1799 d 1883
Michael Mitchell b 1826 d 1899

CHAMPAIGN COUNTY:

Family Bible Records, V.II, Urbana, OH D.A.R. Chapter:
Mitchell Family Bible, published by Thomas Mason & George
Lane for the M. E. Church, James Collord, Printer 1840:
   (Rev) **John Thomas Mitchell** s/o (Rev) **Samuel Mitchell,**
m1835 Catherine Rice, at Mr. S. K. Levingley's nr Springfield, IL; she d 24 Feb 1863; he d 30 May 1863 "at 7 a.m.
on the steamer Itasca, Mississippi River nr Winona, WI,
while enroute with his two sons to Red Wing, MN to visit
his only surviving sister, Mrs. Bell." Ch of John T. &
Catherine (Rice) Mitchell: **(i)** Mary Ellen b 12 Aug 1837
Jacksonville, IL d 8 Aug 1862 Cincinnati, OH; **(ii)** Samuel
Charles b 19 Jan 1839 d 23 Jul 1839 Springfield, IL;
(iii) female b/d 22 May 1840 Springfield, IL; **(iv)** Catherine Arabella b 23 May 1841 d 10 Jan 1842 Chicago, IL; **(v)**
John Thomas b 30 June 1843 Mt. Morris, IL m 14 Aug 1866
Annie R. Hitt at Urbana, OH; had ch Nellie b 14 Aug 1868,
Sallie b 14 Nov 1869, both at Urbana, OH; **(vi)** Francis
Gridley b 24 Nov 1845 (see further); **(vii)** James William b
8 Apr 1847 Cincinnati, OH d 25 Jul 1853 Urbana, OH;
   Francis Gridley Mitchell s/o (Rev) **John T. Mitchell,** m
12 Aug 1869 Mary E. Davis at Malta, OH; he d 8/18 Sep 1931
at Urbana, OH; ch **(i)** Kate VanMeter b 26 June 1870 Catawba, OH; **(ii)** Walter Danna b 26 May 1822 (twin) Williamsburg, OH d 3 Dec 1881 Cincinnati, OH; **(iii)** Henry Davis b
26 May 1822 (twin) Williamsburg, OH m 11 Nov 1903 Iva
Glenn Higgens at home of Mrs. Wilbur Higgens, Chicago, IL,
by Rev. Frank G. Mitchell; **(iv)** Anna Laura b 24 Jul 1874
Greenfield, OH m 1 Jan 1906 Clement Hale Wright at Hartwell, OH, parsonage of Rev. Frank G. Mitchell; **(v)** Mary
Angie b 29 Mar 1877 Springfield, OH d 22 June 1927 at Indianapolis, IN; **(vi)** Frank Wylie b 14 Sep 1881 Ripley, OH.
(Also noted, Francis "Frank" G. Mitchell's granddau.,

Miscellaneous Mitchell Data

Eleanor Mitchell Wright b 23 June 1911 at Schofield Barracks, Hawaiian Terr., bpt 2 Oct 1913 by Rev. Frank G. Mitchell, d/o Clement H. & Anna L. [Mitchell] Wright.)

Champaign Co., OH Marriage Records (Probate Court):
MITCHEL/MITCHELL:

Angeline to Jesse Mitchel 5 Jul 1855 Bk E #6612
Bridget to John Carroll 9 Jul 1856 Bk F #6643
Celia to John Bray 6 Nov 1852 (lic issued) Bk E #5598
Cyrus to Sarah Pulling 5 Apr 1849 Bk D #4865
David to Arah Welgamuth 11 Mar 1863 Bk F #7915
Dixon to Electa Curryer 8 Mar 1849 Bk D #4842
Elias to Rebecca Sherwood 5 Feb 1844 Bk D #3924
Elisha to Elby Blue 25 Feb 1819 Bk A:1088 #935
Eliza A. to Levi Rathbun 12 May 1836 Bk C #2703
Elizabeth to Aaron Bell 9 May 1837 Bk C #2874
Elizabeth to John Hess 3 Aug 1849 Bk E #4938
Isaac to Polly Woodard 6 June 1850 Bk E #5106
Isaiah H. to Rachel Ellsworth 20 Apr 1843 Bk D #3791
Jane to Cyrus Taylor 16 Feb 1852 Bk E #5432
James to Elizabeth McDonald 10 Aug 1813 Bk A:1043 #308
James to Elizabeth Riddle 27 Feb 1806 Bk A:1043 #310
James to Elenor Rine 12 May 1838 Bk C #3059
James to Rebecca Pullins 3 Jan 1841 Bk D #3451
Jesse to Angeline Mitchell 5 Jul 1855 Bk E #6612
John to Mary Clark 9 Jul 1818 Bk A:1043 #838
John W. to Milly Miller 6 May 1833 Bk C #2277
Juliann to James Russel 6 Feb 1834 Bk C #2362
Lucy to John Moore 18 May 1854 Bk E #5952
Mahala to Edward Tribbett 28 Sep 1851 Bk E #5358
Mahlon to Rebecca Fleming 14 Dec 1854 Bk E #6094
Mariah to William Herd 18 Dec 1847 Bk D #4622
Mary to Elisha B. Hess 5 Feb 1835 Bk C #2505
Mary to John Chapman 13 Jul 1839 (lic issued) Bk C #3219
Mary B. to Ebenezer Huckins 15 May 1856 Bk F #6413
Minerva to George Dimsey 22 Jul 1836 Bk C #2736
Montgomery to Elizabeth Kenady 6 Apr 1837 Bk C #2859
Sarah to John Smail 20 May 1852 Bk E #5495
Samuel to Maria Mitchman 9 Feb 1838 Bk C #3005
Samuel to Sarah Black 31 Mar 1842 Bk D #3625
Thornton T. to Nancy Stephens 29 Jan 1850 Bk E #5037
(Note: Book G 1864-1865 - No Mitchell marriages.)

Miscellaneous Mitchell Data

(Champaign Co., Ohio con't)

1850 Federal Census of Champaign Co., OH:
(Key: 1st number = house number; H/H = in household of)
Goshen Twp:
198 MITCHELL, Samuel 40 VA, Sarah 30 OH, Jesse 7 OH, Peter
   G. 5 OH, Samuel N.? 1 OH.
Concord Twp:
121 MITCHEL, Sarah 13 OH, H/H of PULLENS, Wm. & family.
134 MITCHEL, Jesse 14 OH (black), H/H of BATES, David &
   family (black).
163 MITCHEL, James 29 OH, Rebecca 28 OH, Sarah J. 9 OH,
   Mary E. 7 OH, John P. 5 OH, Thomas L. 4 OH, Elias 1 OH.
164 MITCHEL, John 64 PA, Mary 57 VA, Edward 17 OH, John L.
   16 OH.
Union Twp:
238 MITCHEL, Mahala 20 PA, H/H McCLAIN, James & family.
Wayne Twp:
53 MITCHELL, Isaiah 26 OH, Rachel 26 OH, Isaiah 9 OH, Mary
   4 OH, John 1 OH.
64 MITCHELL, James 42 PA, Elizabeth 41 VA, Elizabeth Bell
   9 OH.
69 MITCHELL, Cyrus 23 OH, Sarah A. 19 OH.
83 MITCHELL, Elisha 65 R.I., Isabel 50 VA, Meriba 25 OH,
   Mahala 19 OH, Samuel 22 OH, Anne 16 OH, Elizabeth 10 OH.
Johnson Twp:
264 MITCHEL, Mahlon 29 OH, Rebecca 28 PA, Silas 7 OH, Daniel 6 OH, Thomas 9 mos. OH.
Urbana Twp:
60 MITCHELL, Sarah 21 Ire., H/H CRABILL, Henry & family.
66 MITCHELL, David, Margaret, Michael, John, all b Ire.
226 MITCHELL, Margaret 22 OH, Lorenzo 19 OH, County Poor-
   house, both insane.
Mad River Twp:
150 MITCHELL, Mittan? (male) 7 PA, H/H MITCHMAN?, Martin.
157 MITCHELL, Melinda 9 PA, H/H MITCHMAN?, J. A.

Tombstone Records of Champaign Co., OH Prior to 1900,
   Urbana, OH D.A.R. Chapter:
Edward Mitchell d 27 May 1874 aged 41y 8m 25d.
Elizabeth Mitchell w/o J. d 28 Mar 1862, 94th yr of age.
John Mitchell d 2 Sep 1852, 65th yr of age.
Mary Mitchell w/o J. d 8 Jul 1854 aged 57y.
Nancy Mitchell d/o J. & M. d 1 May 1812 age 17y.

-406-

Miscellaneous Mitchell Data

(Tombstone records of Champaign Co., Ohio con't)

Samuel Mitchell, consort of Mariah, d 4 Jan 1845, 57th yr.
Rosedale Cemetery:
Daniel Walter Mitchell 1873-1912
Lulu Fern Mitchell 1879-1925
Evergreen Cemetery:
Daniel Mitchell 1879-1925
Oakdale Cemetery:
Charles Mitchell 1843 - 2 May 1801
Col. J. T. Mitchell 30 June 1843 - 20 Jan 1896
Maple Grove Cemetery:
David T. Mitchell b 1882 d 25 May 1954

List of Pensioners on the Roll 1 Jan 1883, p43: Champaign
Co., #146,464 **John T. Mitchell,** Urbana, wound left
shoulder, $2/mo., June 1877.

1820 Federal Census of Champaign Co., OH:
(Key: m = male; f = female; un = under the age of)
Concord Twp:
James Mitchell 1 m 10/16, 1 m 26/45, 2 f 10/16, 1 f over 45
John Mitchell 1 m 26/45, 2 f un 10, 2 f 16/26
Samuel Mitchell 1 m 26/45, 1 f over 45
Mad River Twp:
Elisha Mitchell 1 m 26/45, 1 f un 10, 1 f 10/16, 1 f 16/26
William Mitchell 4 m un 10, 1 m 16/26, 1 m 26/45, 1 f 26/45
Urbana Twp:
Jesse Mitchell (free colored)
Wayne Twp:
James Mitchell 2 m un 10, 1 m 10/16, 1 m 16/18, 1 m 16/26,
   1 m 26/45, 1 f un 10, 1 f 10/16, 1 f 26/45

CLERMONT COUNTY:

Marriage Records 1800-1850, Clermont Co. Gen. Soc.:
MITCHEL/MITCHELL:
Barbara to Christopher Young 24 Mar 1822 Bk 2:33
Bridget to Stephen J. Sutton 31 Dec 1846 Bk 4:69
Catharine to Martin Miller 22 Apr 1813 Bk 1:37
Drussilla to Abraham Conrad 5 Jan 1826 Bk 2:137
Elizabeth to Charles Dickinson 24 June 1828 Bk 2:238
Elizabeth to Samuel Anderson 30 Jul 1837 Bk 3:109
Ellen to Benjamin Cord 26 Nov 1846 Bk 4:77

Miscellaneous Mitchell Data

(Marriages of Clermont Co., Ohio con't)

MITCHEL/MITCHELL:
George to Sally Hankins 10 Nov 1820 Bk 1:147
Henry to Elizabeth Corbin 23 Jan 1823 Bk 2:44
Jane to Jesse Cordery 28 June 1818 Bk 1:110
James to Martha Poe 26 June 1817 Bk 1:90
James to Sarah Conrad 20/30 Apr 1848 Bk 5:8
John to Sally Davis 25 Apr 1816 Bk 1:74
John to Elener Dimmitt 25 Feb 1823 Bk 2:48
John to Ruth Brown 24 Oct 1847 Bk 4:99
Kitty to James Garland 2 June 1825 Bk 2:125
Martha Ann to Franklin Dennis 23 Sep 1847 Bk 4:109
Mary to James Abernathy 6 Dec 1838 Bk 3:154
Mary to Jesse H. Parker 5 June 1845 Bk 4:15
Mordica to Catharine Eystone 15 Feb 1817 Bk 1:85
Nancy to John Burnet 14 Jan 1827 Bk 2:180
Nancy to Alfred B. Prindle 1 Jan 1846 Bk 4:37
Peggy to Jonathan Noble 4 Jan 1821 Bk 1:147
Rufus M. to Rebecca Jane Larkin 1 Dec 1841 Bk 3:272
Sarah to Charles Leverton 2 Nov 1848 Bk 5:43
Sarah Jane to Solomon J. Monjar 4 Mar 1847 Bk 4:83
Susan to James Ferguson (wid'r) 10 Sep 1849 Bk 5:97
William D. to Deborah Jordan 21 Apr 1826 Bk 2:151

FAIRFIELD COUNTY:

Pioneer Period & Pioneer People of Fairfield Co., OH, by
    C. M. L. Wiseman, 1901:

In 1831 **Matthew Mitchell** kept a school at Mt. Vernon,
OH (p87); Dr. **E. W. Mitchell** of Cincinnati, OH, only son
of Rev. **James Mitchell**, a M.E. minister, married Annie
Sophia Roe, d/o Thomas Roe of Zanesville, OH who married
1847 Cynthia Ann Tallman (p274).

GREENE COUNTY:

Marriages 1804-1820:
Eliza Mitchell to Adam Winter 12 Oct 1820
Margaret Mitchell to William McClure 20 Dec 1812
Margaret Mitchell to Josiah Espy 25 Oct 1815
Polley Mitchell to James Forgey 16 Mar 1809
Samuel C. Mitchell to Susanna Reed 28 Sep 1820

Miscellaneous Mitchell Data

MADISON COUNTY, OHIO:

Marriage Records (Book A 1810-1852; Book B 1858-1868):
MITCHEL/MITCHELL
Auburn to Louisa Spears 15 Jan 1829
Catharine Jane to Thomas J. Cook 9 Jul 1837
Daniel to Mariah Self 21 Mar 1861
David to Perlnia L. Jewett 18 Dec 1852
Drusilla Jane to William Brown 15 Oct 1846
Elizabeth to George Bell 10 May 1832
George to Peggy Bowls 6 Oct 1814
Hanson D. to Arvella Jones 3 Apr 1856
Hartwell to Mary Elizabeth Rouse 25 Nov 1867
James to Mrs. Matilda Baker 25 Jan 1842
John to Amanda Timmons 28 Oct 1852
John to Polly Ann Gibson 10 Jan 1866
Margaret to Robert Nellson 8 Oct 1812
Margaret to James Bowls 7 Mar 1814
Martha to Moses Hays 2 Nov 1814
Mary to William H. Drake 28 Nov 1865
Mary C. to George Brown 19 Oct 1862
Nelson to Amelia Donahue 29 Aug 1860
Sarah I. to E. M. Van Harlingen 9 Feb 1858
William to Mariah Phebus 15 Feb 1827
William B. to Caroline S. Thompson 2 Oct 1858

Probate Court - Wills:
Will Bk 1:6 dtd 20 Jul 1808 probated 16 Oct 1816, **Samuel Mitchell** of Franklin Co., Darby Twp., OH leaves to sons **David & Samuel, Jr.** 200 acres of land plus clothes, books; wife not ment by name; at her death, wife's property to be sold & proceeds divided between Jean Kirkpatrick & Elizabeth Taylor; half of Elizabeth's share to her sons Alexander & Samuel McCullough when they are of age; will wit by **Moses Mitchell, Samuel Mitchell,** John & Elizabeth Robinson; one of the associate judges when will was produced in court 1816 was **David Mitchell, Esq.** (See Union Co.)
Will Bk B:128 dtd 20 Sep 1856 probated 12 Oct 1856 **James Mitchell;** this will runs for pages, ment much property including land in Bates Co., MO, & large sums of cash; names ch **James & David** (twins who will be of age in a little over 4 years), **Oliver, Mary, George, Sarah, John;** names wife **Matilda,** sister **Ruhama Mitchell;** Wm. T. Davidson grdn of sons James & David; exrs Harvey Fellows, **Oliver Mitchell.**

Miscellaneous Mitchell Data

(Wills of Madison Co., Ohio con't)

Will Bk B:683 dtd 14 Dec 1870 probated 22 Apr 1871 **Matilda Mitchell** of Madison Co., names daus. Harriet Burnley & Mary Drake, w/o Wm. H. Drake; step-dau. **Sarah** Van Harlingin; step-son **Oliver Mitchell**; wit C. W. Finley & B. F. Clark.

Other Probate Records:
(Key: FB = file box; grdn = guardian; Dkt = docket)

Probate Court Docket A:
   Elizabeth Mitchell Heirs #451, grdn of; bond filed on 3 Apr 1839 (p67); **James Mitchell** Heirs #450, grdn of 14 May 1838; bond 17 Apr 1845 (p67); **Samuel Mitchell** Heirs #1534, Estate of, Bond 19 June 1815, Appraisal 13 Sep 1815, Account 19 Aug 1819 (p146).
Index to Decedents & Wards, Admistrators, Exectrs, Grdns:
   James Mitchell, et al, grdn James Mitchell appt (p247).
Index to File Boxs (No. 1, 1810-1890):
   #1402 **Clinton Mitchell; John Mitchell** appt grdn (FB A-433, Dkt C:140); #1395 **Harry & Oliver Mitchell, Cornelia Mitchell** appt grdn (FB A-425, Dkt B:163, C:216); #1403 **Ida B. Mitchell**, et al, **Daniel Mitchell** appt grdn (FB A-434, Dkt C-257); #1375 **James & David Mitchell**, minors, W. F. Davidson appt grdn (FB A-408, Dkt A-70); #1399 **Maggie & Ivy Mitchell, John Mitchell** appt grdn (FB A-433, Dkt C-140); #1387 **Mary J. Mitchell, Nelson Mitchell** appt grdn (FB A-420, Dkt B-66); **Nelson Mitchell**, insane (FB 990); **Newman Mitchell**, imbecile (FB A-2517, Dkt B-113).
Index to Administrators, Executors, Grdn's, Trustees:
   A. S. Mitchell as admr. Dora Betts Estate (Case#Aa2105, V.A:301); as assignee, Geo. R. Nicodemus, assigner (Case# 1480, V.5:23); as executor Elizabeth A. Dalay estate (Case#1539, V.2:127). **Charles T. Mitchell** grdn of **Helen J. Mitchell**, et al, minor (Case#1127, V.C:283). **David Mitchell** as admr. Jos. Gorrer estate (Case#Aa156); admr of Thomas Loyd estate (Case#Aa1433); as grdn of **Ida Mitchell**, et all, minor (Case#Aa434, V.A:256). **James Mitchell** as admr. Geo. Kilen estate (Case#Aa1372, V.A:139); as grdn of **Jno. Mitchell**, et al, minor (Case#Aa451, V.A:67); as grdn of **Jas. Mitchell**, et al, minor (Case#Aa454, V.A:67). **John Mitchell** as grdn James Harper, imbecile (Case# Aa300, V.B:56); as grdn Mary & Jas. Harper, minors (Case#

Miscellaneous Mitchell Data

(Probate Records of Madison Co., Ohio con't)

Aa306, V.A:217/218); as grdn of Josephine Harvey, minor
(Case#Aa322, V.A:323); as adm. E. T. Lemsor? estate (Case
#Aa1939, V.B:114 & 176); as admr of **Oliver Mitchell** estate
(Case#Aa1520, V.B:123). **Joseph Mitchell** as grdn of New-
berry Sabin, et al, minors (Case#Aa591, V.A:79).
Index to Files - Book 1:
   John B. & Thos. Mitchell, minors, #357 V.2:23 **Benj. F.
Mitchell grdn; Maggie M. Mitchell** estate? V.2:40, B. F.
Clark, trustee. **Nelson Mitchell** #990 V.1:206. **Rose Mit-
chell**, will, #3198, V.3:75. **Maggie May Mitchell**, trust,
#449, V.6:13, E. W. Ruggins, trustee. **Thaddeus A. Mitch-
ell**, estate, #350, V.7:124, **David Mitchell**, admr.
Final Record of Accounts:
   13 Oct 1856 **James Mitchell** estate; widow **Matilda**; Bk A
pp 204 & 211; heirs Bk A p250.
Inventory Record:
   15 Nov 1815 **Samuel Mitchell** Bk A pp 76 & 93.
(NOTE: Will Books 2 and 3 (or A?) are missing; not in the
probate office or the attic. All will books are in the
attic for years prior to early 1900's except Book 1 and
Book B which are in the probate office. Inventory Record
Books B & C are missing totally.)

Recorder's Office:

   Transactions in Grantee/Grantor Index 1 are numerous &
too lengthy to print in full. Names appearing in alpha
order are: MITCHEL/MITCHELL, Andrew, B. F., David, David
Jr., Daniel, George H., James, John, Joseph, Joshua,
Maria, McGill, Moses, Oliver and Phillip.

List of Pensioners on the Roll Jan. 1, 1883, V.II:
   #120,069 **Andrew Mitchell**, Sterling, Madison Co., chronic diarrhea, $10/mo., Apr 1880 (p203).

Tombstone Inscriptions (Madison Co., OH D.A.R. pub.):

McClimans Cemetery:
Allen Mitchell s/o John & Katherine d 19 May 1876, 3m 19d.
Ivan Mitchell s/o John & Katherine d Oct 1878 in infancy.
Lydia Katherine McClimans Mitchell, 1st w/o John Mitchell
   d 15 Sep 1878 aged 36y 1m 15d.

Miscellaneous Mitchell Data

UNION COUNTY, OHIO:

History of Union Co., OH, W. H. Beers, 1883, V.II, p274:
Judge **David Mitchell** of Darby Twp., purchased 600 acres on Sugar Run at an early date (Survey #5); divided it into 3 portions, on each of which one of his sons, **George, David Jr., and Jesse,** settled.

George Mitchell s/o David above, m Margaret Boles 6 Oct 1814; d of pneumonia soon after settling at Jerome; had ch **(i)** David **(ii)** James F. **(iii)** Martha E. m Dixon Robinson.

David Mitchell Jr. s/o David above, lived on the tract adjoining his father in 1816; years later he moved to Darby Plains, then Columbus, then St. Louis, MO, but returned to OH and lived with one of his children at Hilliard; had ch **(i)** David A., dec'd; **(ii)** Joseph H., of CA; **(iii)** Zenus M., in the "West"; **(iv)** Belinda m ___ Cushman; res. CA; **(v)** Hasson Shaw of St. Louis; **(vi)** Dixon A. of CA; **(vii)** Samantha; **(viii)** Maria L. m ___ Welch; **(ix)** Delmore.

Jesse Mitchell s/o David, Sr. above, was the 1st white child born in what is now Union Co., on 4 Nov 1799, a few weeks after his par settled in Darby Twp. He m Dec 1823 Elizabeth Robinson d/o Rev. James Robinson, then of Union Twp. Jesse d 13 May 1881; wife survives (1883) & resides with dau Amanda in Plain City; 13 ch; named are **(i)** Maria m A. H. Campbell; **(ii)** Martha E. d unmar; **(iii)** Lucinda m Levi Hall, a M.E. minister; of Minneapolis; **(iv)** James "on the home place"; **(v)** David died young; **(vi)** George W. d in service, St. Louis Hospital; **(vii)** Electa died young; **(viii)** Hester, wid of Z. H. McCullough, Franklin Co.

OHIO - GENERAL:

The Official Roster of the Soldiers of the American Revolution Buried in the State of Ohio, V. I-II, Trumbull Co., OH chapter of the O.G.S. reprint 1973:
(Key: appl = application; enl = enlisted; pens = pension)

AMASA MITCHELL, Hamilton Co., fifer MA Cont'l; enl 1779 West Point, NY; b1752; wife lvg 1839; ch John 19, Lucy 17, James 14, Harvey 10, Eliza 6; to IN 1839; pens appl Kanawha Co., VA 1821; Hamilton Co., OH 1823; to Madison Co., IN 1839; ref: MA S-36699 (V.II:250).

DAVID MITCHELL, Trumbull Co., pvt NC militia; pens 1833 Trumbull Co.; rept from pens bur. "not found" (V.II:250).

Miscellaneous Mitchell Data

DAVID MITCHEL, Scioto Co., pvt PA militia; enl 1776; for further info, Joseph Spencer Chapter (V.I:258).

DAVID MITCHELL, Greene Co., enl 1776 Lancaster Co., PA; b1737 Scotland; m **Margaret Mitchell**; d1817 Cedarville, OH; ref: Nat'l #57,707, V.58:242 DAR Lineage (V.I:259).

ELIJAH MITCHELL, Preble Co., pvt; enl 1779 Mecklenburg Co., NC; b 6 Mar 1761 VA d 1 Aug 1847; from Preble Co. to Huntington Co., IN by 1845; ref: S-2838 NC (V.II:250).

JAMES MITCHELL (no county given); Cont'l Regt; only 6 mos.; pens refused; ref: Doc 31 1-6-1831 (V.II:250).

JOSEPH MITCHELL (no county given); served in Reg't not on Cont'l Estab so was refused a pens; ref: Doc 31 1-6-1831 (V.II:250).

NATHANIEL MITCHELL, Washington Co., pvt PA Line 3 yrs; enl 1776 8th PA Regt; b1750; m 27 Dec 1782 Nancy _____; his youngest ch age 22; one grson abt 6 yrs old lvg with him in 1820; d 20 May 1836; pens 1818 Washington Co., OH; widow's pens 1839 & 1843 there; ref: W-38350 (V.II:250-51).

PHILIP MITCHELL, Hamilton Co., b PA; d1832; S.A.R., Cincinnati Chapt. (V.I:259).

ROBERT MITCHELL, Belmont Co., age 80 in 1820; pvt; pens 1818; in VA Regt 2 yrs; pens to widow Eve 1844, sent to Carroll or Pennington St., Clairsville, OH; transfered to Ohio Co., VA 1826; m Eve _____ Jul 1773 Winchester, VA by Rev. **Mr. Mitchell**, a Lutheran; dau **Mary** Bramball, age 55 in 1839; other ch; d June 1827; enl in Winchester, VA in 1774/5; ref: W-7459 (V.II:251).

SAMUEL MITCHELL, Miami Co., enl age 16 in VA; b 15 Mar 1759 King George Co., VA; 1 report says he m a sister of Daniel Boone; 2 others say he m 1780 Malinda Cecil; d 25 Apr 1840 Miami Co.; ref: Pens Bur. U.S. & Vol. 56, Nat'l No. 55,279 DAR Lineage (V.I:259).

. SAMUEL MITCHELL, Union Co., buried Woods Cemetery in Unionville (V.I:259).

SAMUEL MITCHELL, Preble Co., pvt/sgt PA; enl 1776 PA; b Apr 1751 Derry Co., Ire; to America 1772; lvd Cumberland Co., PA; m 1781 & lvd York Co., PA, Washington Co., PA, and Ohio Co., VA; to Preble Co., OH 1814; 2 ch; pens appl 1832 Greene Co., OH; ref: S-2837 PA (V.II:251).

WILLIAM MITCHELL, Miami Co; PA militia; m Martha Patterson; on pens roll Miami Co. 1831, age 78; ref: Nat'l No. 13,697, DAR Lineage V.14:260 (V.I:259).

Miscellaneous Mitchell Data

PENNSYLVANIA

The John Mitchell Family Association, 7209 14th Ave.,
Takoma Park, MD 20912 (1984):
This family association is concerned with the ancestry
& descendants of **John Mitchell**, granted land in Drumore
Twp., Lancaster Co. (now York), PA 1738; will dtd 27 Oct
1767, proved 18 Nov 1767; wife **Mary** d bef 18 Nov 1767;
known ch **(i)** George² (see further); **(ii)** Thomas, d bef
1767 leaving son John; **(iii)** Jenny m (Col.) Thomas Porter;
(iv) Mary m Robert Luckey; **(v)** Isabel m Alexr. McLaughlin.

  George² Mitchell s/o John, will dtd Dec 1815, proved Apr
1816; m Elizabeth Porter d/o John & Rebecca (   ) Porter;
she d ca 1825/28; ch were: **(i)** Mary m (Maj.) **Joseph Mitchell**; she d 1803; he d 1814; dau Elizabeth* m James Clark;
sons George, David, Joseph & (Rev.) Benjamin Mitchell;
ch settled York Co., PA except Benjamin who "followed his
6 uncles to Belmont Co., OH"; **(ii)** Rebecca; **(iii)** Isabel
per m ____ Rice; **(iv)** Elizabeth m ____ Thaker/Theaker;
(v) Violet m Wm. Whiteside; and 6 sons incl **John³** b 26
Mar 1760 d 30 Oct 1814 m Jannet Clark b 21 Oct 1761 d 30
Oct 1820 d/o James & Isabella (Breckenridge) Clark; **Thom-
as³** b1762 m Nancy Clark, sis of Jannet; **Robert³** (youngest)
who was a doctor; early settler of Zanesville, OH; State
Legislator; U.S. Congressman; Brigadier Gen'l (OH Militia); supposedly father of 13 ch; d 1848 at Zanesville.

  According to Margaret (Jones) Harp, 4025 Toledo Rd.,
Bartlesville, OK 74006: Elizabeth* (Mitchell) Clark had
dau. Jane Clark (1821-1897) who m **Joseph A. Gardner Mitchell** (1819-1896), s/o **George Mitchell** (1794-1822) & Margaret Clark (d/o Col. Matthew Clark); George (1794-1822)
was brother of Elizabeth (Mitchell) Clark, uncle of Jane
Clark; Joseph A. Gardner Mitchell had a son **John Joseph
Mitchell** (1858-1909) who m **Annie Ellen Mitchell,** a 3rd &
unrelated line.

The Susquehannah Co. Papers, V.I-II, Univ. of TX Library:

  Relinquishment of CT Claim (title) for 950 acres near
Sugar Creek (general location, Luzerne Co., PA before its
division into Bradford & other counties), made by **Reuben
Mitchell** 22 June 1801. (1800 Federal Census of Luzerne
Co., PA p420 shows Reuben with 2 m un 10, 2 m 10/16, 2 m
16/26, 1 m over 45, 2 f un 10, 1 f 10/16, 1 f over 45.)

(Pennsylvania con't)

Genealogical & Personal History of Northern PA, V.II,
John W. Jordan, editor, 1913, p558:
Richard Mitchell (Nathaniel, Jacob, James, Matthew) was
b 5 Jul 1769 Orange, NJ d 11 Mar 1847 Tioga Co., PA; one of
the early settlers of Chemung Co., NY, locating in the
town of Southport 1791 with brothers Thomas & Robert; a
year later, Richard & Thomas came up the Tioga River in a
canoe, settling 27 Aug 1793 at what has since been known
as Mitchell Creek; Richard cleared & improved a farm on
Tioga River which he cultivated until his death.

1800 Federal Census of Lycoming Co., PA:
(Key: m = male; f = female; un = under the age of)
John Mitchell 1 m over 45, 1 f un 10, 1 f 16/26, 1 f over
45 (p534).
Richard Mitchell 2 m un 10, 1 m 26/45, 1 f un 10, 1 f
16/26, 1 f 26/45 (p548).
Robert Mitchell 1 m un 10, 1 m 16/26, 1 f 10/16 (p548).
Thomas Mitchell 2 m un 10, 1 m 26/45, 1 f un 10, 1 f
16/26 (p548).
William Mitchell 1 m over 45, 1 f un 10, 1 f 16/26, 1 f
over 45 (p562).

Family Group Sheet (Ruth Ann Neal, 118 Town Rd., Mahaffey,
PA 15757):
Robert Mitchell b 18 Jul 1779 VT d 18 Mar 1860 PA m Abi-
gail Ives b 1778 CT d 25 Sep 1856 PA; Robert to PA ca 1800;
Ch were: (i) John m Elizabeth Hartsock; (ii) Ruth m Olney
Albee or Seeley; (iii) Nancy m Seth Albee; (iv) Lavina m
Jonathan Roe; (v) Abigail m William Butler; (vi) Phebe m
_____ Baker; m2) _____ Walton; (vii) Thaddeus m Amelia Town-
er; (viii) Lucy m Alonzo Phelps; (ix) Rosina m George
Mitchell; (x) Lydia m _____ Hartsock; (xi) Cynthia* m Amos
Mudge; (xii) Matilda m Sam Hartsock. (In response to a
query in Yankee Magazine, Mrs. Neal received data that
Robert Mitchell came to Mitchell's Creek about 1796, his
brothers, Thomas & Richard, having settled there in 1792;
ref: History of Tioga Co., PA.)

*(xi) Cynthia Mitchell was b 25 Mar 1801 Tioga Co., PA d
16 Nov 1850 La Grange, IN; m 24 Jul 1823 Amos Mudge, s/o
Joshua & Fransy Mudge, b 6 Oct 1799 Otsego Co., NY (Data

Miscellaneous Mitchell Data

(Pennsylvania con't)

from The Connecticut Nutmegger, V.20:3, Dec 1987, query
of Ellen L. Jacobus, 511 Jefferson St., Elmira, NY 14904)

John Mitchell of Scotch ancestry, settled in Dauphin
Co., PA (then Chester Co.) on the NJ border, prior to 1724
(source unknown).

TENNESSEE

Tennessee Marriage Records (dates of license):
MITCHEL/MITCHELL:
Bedford Co.:
Adaline to John A. Strawn 31 Aug 1863
E. F. to F. J. Davis (no dates)
Coffee Co.:
David to Sarah Ann Walker 15 June 1858
Davidson Co.:
Abijah D. to Sarah Forehand 4 June 1844
Abram H. to Tennessee C. Pritchett 14 June 1841
William to Sarah Foster 12 Aug 1840
Dickson Co.:
W. D. to Martha E. Darrow 26 Oct 1848
William M. to Surrena Speights 24 Jan 1840
Franklin Co.:
D. W. to Martha C. Banks 10 May 1856
George W. to Marthy A. Day 25 Dec 1850
Isaac R. to Nancy M. Cobble 17 Jan 1857
Joseph to Elizabeth Banks 24 Nov 1857
Newton J. to Mary J. Sexton 24 Mar 1858
Solomon to Nemma Kennedy 9 Sep 1868
William to Matilda Edwards 24 Dec 1851
William to Arrenia Smith 10 Jan 1856
William M. to Fedella T. Matthews 11 June 1844
William P. to Lidda Banks 18 Feb 1856
Giles Co.:
Henry T. to Nancy B. Kimbrough 3 Feb 1860
James O. to Mary F. Angus 14 Aug 1856
Greene Co.:
Martha to William Logan (no dates)
Knox Co.:
Charles to Nancy McPherrin 18 Oct 1823
Henry T. to Rebecka Meek 16 Dec 1823

-416-

(Marriages in Tennessee con't)

MITCHEL/MITCHELL (Knox Co. con't):
Jesse to Rachel Gentry 6 Mar 1820
Mordecai to Nancy Casteel 6 June 1798
Payton to Catherine Davis 4 Jul 1836
Thomas M. to Rossanna Smith 6 Apr 1837
Lawrence Co.:
John A. to Malinda A. Warren 2 Aug 1866
Maury Co.:
Mahala to Abijah Rhedding (no dates)
Mary to William Fly (no dates)
Mary to Ephraim McCrackin (no dates)
Thomas to Betsey Evans 18 Dec 1810
Meigs Co.:
David to Katherine Smith 6 Apr 1846
Montgomery Co.:
C. T. to Malvira Blaine 23 Nov 1850
Robertson Co.:
B. D. to Jane R. Collins 24 Apr 1859
C. M. to Mary Head 16 Jul 1859
Samuel F. to Mary E. Limebaugh 14 Apr 1841
Rutherford Co.:
Charles C. to Ann Bevirt 11 Jul 1833
David to Margaret V. Peebles 1 Jan 1829
Ebenezer to Nancy Currin 16 Dec 1833
James to Mary Maxey 30 Jan 1833
James C. to Fanny A. Bedford 3 Jan 1821
John to Ann Burnett 12 Dec 1835
Stephen to Nancy Finley 28 Oct 1829
Thomas C. to Susanna Robinson 13 Nov 1823
Thomas R. to Nancy Pullam 7 Oct 1837
William to Miss ____ Burnett 22 Jan 1824
Stewart Co.:
Willis to Mary Jane McCormack 17 Jul 1843
M. F. to Martha Taylor 27 Dec 1838
Sumner Co.:
Addison to Mary Ann Hodge 25 Oct 1836
David to Elizabeth Clary 1 Jan 1808
James to Sally Donoho 17 Nov 1821
John to Sally Gardner 3 Oct 1806
John to Fanny Busby 23 Jul 1808
John to Susan Hunt 17 Oct 1830
John to Cinthia Langford 1 Oct 1831

Miscellaneous Mitchell Data

(MITCHEL/MITCHELL Marriages in Tennessee con't)

Major to Catharin Roney 22 Sep 1846
Major to Sallie Armstrong 13 Aug 1869
Pleasant to Sarah Hunt 17 Dec 1833
Robert to Nancy Latimer 5 Jul 1809
Van Buren Co.:
David L. to Elisabeth A. Wheeler 14 Feb 1855
Ichabod to Clerinda Steakly 17 Feb 1852
James to Elizabeth Mooneyham 13 Aug 1859
Joseph G. to Susannah Parker 21 Mar 1841
Mark to Samantha Clark 8 Jan 1859
Martain to Anjeline Moore 15 Feb 1853
Oliver L. to Polly Martain 29 Apr 1847
William to Louseyann Martain 18 Dec 1856
Wilson Co.:
Allen to Patsey Glasgow 13 Sep 1821
George to Judith Flood 1 June 1816
Henry to Nancy Graves 22 Dec 1819
Henry to Henrietta Jackson 20 Nov 1827
Henry to Elizabeth Craig 27 Jul 1833
James to Eliza Reese 12 Dec 1821
John to Elizabeth Crocker 31 Oct 1827
Jones to Susan Owen 29 Sep 1818
Moses to Elenor Hodge 24 Feb 1817
Robert to Agey Moore 28 Jul 1812
Sion H. to Elizabeth Cook 22 Feb 1817
Tayswell to Sally Stuart 17 Dec 1816 (Jones Mitchell bm)

Roster of Soldiers & Patriots of the American Revolution
Buried in TN, Lucy Womack Bates , compiler, DAR, 1974:

ADAM MITCHELL bc 1742 d 1802 Washington Co.; m1) **Jennett
Mitchell**; m2) Elizabeth McMahan; will proved 3 Apr 1802
(Bk 1:59); ch Margaret; Robert; William; Adam; Samuel;
David; James; Hezekiah; Abby; Rebecca; Jenny.
EDWARD MITCHELL, officer in Rev. War (Ref: "History of
Wilson Co., TN).
JAMES MITCHELL b 20 Dec 1765 Orange Co., NC d 11 Nov
1843 Maury Co., TN; enl Orange Co., NC; 1832 pens list age
69; 1840 census Maury Co.; m 29 Nov 1789 Mary Craig b 9 Mar
1771 Orange Co., NC d 7 Nov 1844 Maury Co., TN; ch were
(i) Mary b 21 Nov 1790 m Alexander Pickard; **(ii)** David b
15 Mar 1792 m Martha Leeper; **(iii)** Eleanor b 21 Nov 1793;

Miscellaneous Mitchell Data

(iv) Andrew b 29 June 1795; **(v)** James b 27 June 1797 m
Winnifred H. Ridley; **(vi)** Elizabeth b 20 Mar 1799 m William Neely; **(vii)** John b 11 Mar 1801 m Letty Stockard;
(viii) Isabella b 21 June 1806 m Anthony H. Buckner; **(ix)**
Samuel b 10 May 1808 m Mary D. Biffle; **(x)** Robert b 10 May
1808; **(xi)** Thomas b 22 Mar 1810 m1) Elizabeth Durham m2)
Sally Peyton; **(xii)** Susan b 21 Nov 1812 m Nat Brown Erwin;
(xiii) George b 3 May 1815 m Eliza Jane Isom;

JAMES MITCHELL, JR. b 17 Nov 1754 Bedford Co., VA d 18
May 1835 Robertson Co., TN; m Elizabeth Broomfield b1750
d1837; ch **(i)** Robert B. b1798 d1862 m1835 Margaret Linebaugh; **(ii)** Findley b1802 d1895 m Elizabeth Linebaugh.

JAMES MITCHELL d Calhoun, McMinn Co., TN;

JOHN MITCHELL bc 1758; NC militia; age 74 on 1832 pens
list, Maury Co., TN.

MARK MITCHELL bc 1737; VA troops; age 81 on 1818 pens
list, Warren Co., TN.

SOLOMON MITCHELL b1769 Dorchester Co., MD d aft 1834
Sumner Co., TN; enl MD 1777; re-enl. 1781 Guilford Co.,
NC; age 73 on 1832 pens list, Sumner Co., TN.

SOLOMON MITCHELL b 6 June 1760 Granville Co., NC d 27
Jan 1839 Hawkins Co., TN; service in SC; age 74 on 1832
pens list Hawkins Co., TN; m Apr 1787 Abbeville District,
SC to Nancy Broughton/Broton b 10 Apr 1767 d 22 Jul 1849;
ch **(1)** Stephen died young; **(ii)** Rebecca b 26 Nov 1790 m
_____ Cloud; **(iii)** Lewis b 25 Nov 1792 m Nancy Daff; **(iv)**
Greenberry b 28 Dec 1796 m Elizabeth Wilborn; **(v)** Jesse b
16 May 1798; **(vi)** Polly bc1799 m George Rogers; **(vii)** Robert b 16 June 1801; **(viii)** Morris b 7 Jul 1803 m _____ Mills;
(ix) Nancy b 29 Oct 1804 m_____ Duff; **(x)** Richard b 18 Jul
1806 d 1839 m Elizabeth Davis b 26 Apr 1812 d 27 Nov 1890;
(xi) Elizabeth b 6 Oct 1810 m John Allen; **(xii)** John b 11
Mar 1788 (sic) d 3 Aug 1855.

WILLIAM MITCHELL b1763 NC d 27 Jan 1850 Rutherford Co.,
TN; NC troops; age 73 on 1832 pens list; 1840 census Rutherford Co.; m1790 Elizabeth Curry b 3 Jul 1773 d 7 Apr
1828; ch **(i)** John; **(ii)** Mary m Daniel William McMurry;
(iii) Eliza d age 5y; **(iv)** James C. m Fannie Bedford; **(v)**
Sarah b 3 Jul 1799 m Samuel Hodge; **(vi)** William b 8 Nov
1801 m Mary Ledbetter; **(vii)** David b 24 Nov 1803 m Margaret Paplock; **(viii)** Charicle b1806; **(ix)** Nealine d unmar;
(x) Parthenien b 23 Jan 1809 m Robert P. Steaford; **(xi)**

Miscellaneous Mitchell Data

Addison b Oct 1811 m Mary Ann Hodge; **(xii)** Calvin Gorrell b 3 Sep 1814 m1) Sadie Gannaway; m2) Olivia Gannaway.

<u>NC Land Grants in TN 1778-1791</u>, Betty Cartwright & Lillian Gardener, 1958:
MITCHELL, Andrew, Greene Co. 1787; David, Jr., Davidson Co., 1783; James, Washington Co. 1783; Joab, Sullivan Co. 1782; Joseph, Davidson Co. 1786; Mark, Sullivan Co. 1782; Mark, Greene Co. 1788; Richard, Hawkins Co. 1790, Thomas, Washington Co. 1782, 1783; William, Davidson Co. 1783, 1787. (Note: Washington Co. covered all of TN & parts of present NC counties when it was formed 1777; from Washington came Davidson & Greene Cos. 1783, Sullivan Co. 1779. Hawkins was formed from Sullivan Co. in 1786.)

MACON COUNTY:

<u>1850 Federal Census of Macon Co., TN</u>:
(Key: 1st number = house number)
135 MITCHEL, Bluford 28 KY, Louisa 21 TN, William 6 TN, Austin 1 TN.
159 MITCHEL, Henry 25 TN, Mary 18 TN, Sarah 3 TN.
162 MITCHEL, John 28 TN, Minney 50 TN, Bartly 18 TN, RUSSEL, Rebecca 13.
390 MITCHEL, Hampton 29 TN, Jane 26 TN, Polly A. 6 TN, William A. 5 TN, Frances 3 TN, Amanda 1 TN, Henry S. 5 mos. TN.
430 MITCHEL, Stanford 40 TN, Catharine 29 TN, Sarah J. 13 TN, Emeline 9 TN, John 8 TN, Henry 6 TN, Marcus 5 TN, William 3 TN, James 8 mos. TN.

RUTHERFORD COUNTY:

<u>1850 Federal Census of Rutherford Co., TN</u>:
(Key: 1st number = house number)
75 MITCHEL, James M. 44 VA, Elizabeth 32 (unknown), Joseph L. 15, James M. 13, Robert M. 12, Sarah H. 9, Elizabeth 8, Catharine P. 6, Jacob D. 3.
131 MITHCEL, Stephen 32 TN, Hannah 33 TN, Robert 8 TN, Paines 3 TN, Mary 1 TN, Mary M. 13, ROLPH, Jane 69.
321 MITCHELL, Addison 37 NC, Mary A. 32 TN, William 9 TN, Samuel H. 7 TN, Azariah 44.

Miscellaneous Mitchell Data

(1850 Census of Rutherford Co., Tennessee con't)

323 MITCHELL, Calvin G. 35 NC, Sarah E. 28 TN, Malinia 44.
528 MITCHEL, David 46 NC, Margaret 41 NC, Sarah 6,
WADE, Mary 75.
1458 MITCHEL, Mary 45 TN, Adney 14, Mary 12, ASHFORD, Le-
vinish 19, EDWARD, Alsa 17, Alva 14, HILL, Wm. 19.

SMITH COUNTY:

Smith Co. Marriages (none before 1838):
MITCHEL/MITCHELL
Amanda (col.) to Edward Stewart (col.) 26 Mar 1868
Elizabeth to William Hill 4 Mar 1856
Ellen Y. (col.) to James Valentine (col.) 27 Dec 1866
Frances to Edmond Green 10 Aug 1863
Hampton P. to Mary A. Knight 13 June 1861
Henry A. to Elizaan Porter 18 Oct 1859
Leroy E. to Elizabeth Watkins Howard 1 Nov 1836 (grst)
Martha J. to William Ballard 5? Jul 1866
Martha Jane to William Ballard 3? Jul 1866
Massellor (col.) to Americus Valentine (col.) 29 Dec 1870
Mary M. to John H. Fite 27 Dec 1866
Matilda to John C. (V)oluntine 24 Dec 1868
Milbury to William Valentine 29 Mar 1866
Nancy to Henry Dickerson 26 Oct 1848
Nancy to Jo. Ballard 25 Dec 1873
Roena E. to Edward M. Hicks 31 Oct 1848
Sarah to Rufus Smith lic issued 17 Nov 1880 (no return)
S. M. to W. W. Reed 31 Aug 1879
Susan (col.) to William Jennper?(col.) 26 Apr 1868
Winnie (col.) to John Jumper (col.) 30 Dec 1869
Wooda to Mary Green 19 Dec 1880

Smith Co., TN Deed Records (TN Nat'l Archives research):

ALLEN MITCHELL & Patcy his wife, Grantors; Jos. Somer-
sett, Grantee 30 Jan 1823 (land in Smith Co., part of
tract of William Glasgow, dec'd) Bk H:347.
DAVID MITCHELL, Grantor; Charles Muridrine, Grantee,
23 Dec 1812 Bk D:351; David, Grantee, Peter Turney dec'd,
Grantor 25 May 1818 Bk F:419; David, Grntee; Elisha Brockett, Grantor 23 Feb 1819 Bk G:76; David, Grantee, Elisha
Brockett, Grantor 23 Feb 1819 Bk G:93; David, Grantor; Wm.

Miscellaneous Mitchell Data

(Deeds of Smith Co., Tennessee con't)

Gregory, Grantee 23 Dec 1821 Bk H:82; David, Grantor; Wm.
Wakefield, Grantee 19 Feb 1824 Bk H:424.

DAVID S. MITCHELL of Johnson Co., IN, land on Peyton's
Creek, to George Boston 26 Oct 1836 Bk O:331 (signed by
David Parkhurst, agent); David S. of IN, land on Peyton's
Creek to Smith Gregory 2 Oct 1836 Bk P:40 (signed by David
Parkhurst, agent).

FREDERICK MITCHELL, Grantee; Noble Osburne, Grantor,
11 Feb 1808 Bk C:81; Frederick, Grantee; Patrick Donoho,
Grantor, 23 Feb 1809 Bk C:193; Frederick, Grantor; Robert
Moore, Grantee, 16 Dec 1809 Bk C:307; Fredrick, Grantor,
Richard Womack, Grantee 15 Dec 1809.

JOHN MITCHELL, Grantor; John Reeves, Grantee, 27 Aug
1838 Bk O:365-66 (Smith Co. land next to land of **Wm. N.
Mitchell**); John, Grantor; John Reeves, Grantee, 13 Oct
1839 Bk P:388 (part of 640 acres entered for Samuel Barton
by N.C. Warrent for Rev. War service by Wm. Reins).

LEROY E. MITCHELL, Grantee; Lemuel Tillston, Grantor,
Bk R:135 (land in Carthage, TN); Leroy E., purchase of a
negro boy named Solomon from And. G. Pickett & Jer. Jame-
son Bk R:370.

MARTHA MITCHELL, widow of Frederick N. Mitchell dec'd,
relinquishment of administration 18 Dec 1844 Bk R:353.
(Note: 1850 Smith Co., TN shows Martha 69 VA in H/H 1118
of James H. Vaughn & family.)

WINNEY MITCHELL conveyed to son Robert J. F. Mitchell in
return for her lifetime support as well as for her dau.
Elizabeth as long as she may live single & unmarried, land
in Civil District #16 of Smith Co. 6 Oct 1851 Bk U:332.

Smith Co. Minute Book 1808-1811: (TN Nat'l Archives):
1808 p73: **David Mitchel** on a jury; 1809 p73 Dec 13: law
suit in Gallatin - if the majority can't agree, to meet at
the house of **John Mitchell**...

Smith Co., TN Court Minutes (Historical Soc. research):
Nov 1830: Sam'l D. McMurry & **Polly Mitchell** appointed
administrators of **Allen Mitchell** dec'd; John McMurry &
Able Gregory, securities (p41); Feb 1831: Co. commissioners appointed to lay off & set apart 1 years provisions for
the widow & family of **Allen Mitchell** dec'd; Nov 1832 Commissioners appointed to settle with admistrators of **Allen**

Miscellaneous Mitchell Data

Mitchell dec'd; May 1833: settlement of estate rendered into court & accepted; Feb 1833: Pettis Gregory appointed guardian to **Major & Hampton Mitchell**; John Hyson appointed guardian to **Stanford Mitchell** (Will Bk12:61).

<u>Chancery Court Minutes</u> 1831: **David Mitchell, Sr.** died intestate leaving ch **David Mitchell, Jr., Margaret** Brawner w/o Meredith, **Nancy** Bird w/o Mirus, **Polly** Dale w/o George; widow named as Nancy; adm. of estate Joshua Goad; Nov 1832: Nancy, wid of David Mitchell Sr. made a deed of trust to Joshua Goad, Adm.; May 1833: final settlement of estate. **David Mitchell** of Smith Co., TN was named executor of James Dobbins' estate, will of 1830 Jackson Co., TN in which Dobbins calls David Mitchell his step-brother.

<u>1820 Federal Census of Smith Co., TN</u>:
(Key: m = male; f = female; un = under the age of)
1269 Char<u>ly</u> Mitchel 1 m 16/26, 1 f 26/45
1354 Davi<u>s</u> Mitchell 1 m un 10, 1 m over 45, 2 f 10/16, 1 f over 45.
1381 Alli<u>n</u> Mitchell 3 m un 10, 1 m 10/16, 1 m 26/45, 1 f un 10, 1 <u>f</u> 10/16, 1 f 16/26, 1 f 26/45.

<u>1830 Federal Census of Smith Co., TN</u>:
(Key: m = male; f = female; un = under the age of)
266 David Mitchell 1 m 15/20, 1 m 30/40, 1 m 40/50, 1 m 50/60, 1 f 10/15, 1 f 50/60
303 Mark Mitchell 1 m un 5, 1 m 20/30, 1 f un 5, 1 f 20/30
1297 Allen Mitchell 1 m 5/10, 1 m 10/15, 2 m 15/20, 1 m 20/30, 1 m 50/60, 1 f 50/60
1809 Nelson Mitchell 1 m un 5, 1 m 20/30, 2 f un 5, 1 f 20/30
2236 John Mitchell 1 m 10/15, 1 m 15/20, 1 m 20/30, 1 m 40/50, 1 f 15/20, 1 f 30/40
2237 William Mitchell 1 m 20/30, 2 f un 5, 1 f 15/20, 2 f 20/30.

<u>1840 Federal Census of Smith Co., TN</u>:
(Key: m = male; f = female; un = under the age of)
221 Leroy E. Mitchell 1 m 20/30, 1 f 20/30
287 Major Mitchell 1 m un 5, 1 m 20/30, 1 f un 5, 1 f 5/10, 1 f 20/30
287 Stanford Mitchell 1 m 20/30, 1 f 15/20

(Census Records of Smith Co., <u>Tennessee</u> con't)

<u>1850 Federal Census of Smith Co., TN:</u>
(Key: 1st number = house number)
219 MITCHELL, Winney 66 NC, Robert 29 TN, Jane 27, Milbry
    3, Monticellus 1, Amanda E. 6 mos, Elizabeth 26 (black
    family per census record).
342 MITCHELL, Joseph 37 TN, Silvana 38 NC, William C. 17,
    Thomas J. 15, Martha A. 13, Sina O. 11, Chesley S. 9,
    Balcum (male) 7, Samuel 5, James W. 4, Joseph B. 1 (ch
    all b TN), PRESLY, Rebecca 75 NC.

<u>Smith Co., Tn Cemetery Records:</u>
<u>Old Carthage Cemetery</u> (Third Ave.):
Bettie W. Mitchell 23 Mar 1844 - 29 Nov 1863
Elizabeth Mitchell 26 Dec 1816 - 30 Apr 1846
Leroy E. Mitchell 26 Aug 1811 - 5 Aug 1863
Lucy B. Mitchell 27 Nov 1837 - 4 Jul 1858
<u>Tilman Dixon Cemetery</u> (Dixon Springs, TN):
C. P. Mitchell 14 Jan 1807 - 16 Jul 1838
Martha Mitchell 16 Sep 1781 - 7 Sep 1854
(Note: This crypt is now destroyed.)

SUMNER COUNTY:

<u>Sumner Co., TN Will Abstracts 1788-1882</u>, Shirley Wilson:
  JOHN MITCHELL will dtd 4 Nov 1853, probated 1865; wife
Frances; ch Major W. Mitchell, James Mitchell, John Mit-
chell, Nancy Sadler, Mary Strother, ch of dau. Elizabeth
Dempsey, dau. Patsy Dempsey, daus. Sallie & Caroline Mit-
chell; exr. Major W. & James Mitchell (Bk 3:375).
  NANCY MITCHELL will dtd 4 Feb 1832, probated May 1832;
sons Silas Polk, Hiram Mitchell, Lucilla Polk; daus Jane
Williams, Amelia Brashaer, Athena Moore; exr. Hiram Mit-
chell & Lucilla Polk (Bk ?:256).
  WILEY MITCHELL will dtd 29 Aug 1819; life estate to par
Soloman & Elizabeth Mitchell; then half to ch of John &
Elizabeth Moore; half to ch of John & Sarah Herman; exr.
Silas Polk (Bk ?:104).

<u>1850 Federal Census of Sumner Co., TN:</u>
(Key: 1st number = house number)
28 MITCHELL, James 33 VA, Louisa J. 27 VA, Elizabeth 9,
    Samuel 7, Mary 5, William 3, Martha 1, CELMONS, Joel 20.

Miscellaneous Mitchell Data

(1850 Census of Sumner Co., Tennessee con't)

151 MITCHELL, James 33 TN, Lucy M. 21 TN, Charles W. 6 mos
TN, Nancy 2 TN, Jane 1 TN, HUNT, John 16.
152 MITCHELL, John 36 VA, Mary W. 30 VA, William 7, Major
W. 5, Caroline 3.
160 MITCHELL, Majah W. 30 TN, Catharine 22 TN, Mary 4 TN,
Johnetta 2 TN.
274 MITCHELL, John 65 NC, Francis (female) 54 NC, Sarah 20
TN, Caroline 19 TN, COLEMAN, Hardy 48.

WHITE COUNTY:

1840 Federal Census of White Co., TN (TN Nat'l Archives):
(Key: m = male; f = female; un = under the age of)
Allen L. Mitchell 1 m 5/10, 1 m 10/15, 1 m 40/50, 1 m 50/60
2 f un 5, 2 f 5/10, 1 f 10/15, 1 f 15/20, 2 f 30/40, 1 f
60/70, 1 f 90/100, 1 f slave 10/24
James C. Mitchell 1 m un 5, 1 m 5/10, 3 m 15/20, 1 m 40/50,
1 f un 5, 1 f 5/10, 1 f 10/15, 1 f 15/20, 1 f 30/40
John Mitchell 1 m 5/10, 1 m 10/15, 1 m 20/30, 1 m 40/50,
2 f un 5, 1 f 10/15, 1 f 15/20, 1 f 20/30, 1 f 30/40

VERMONT

MITCHEL/MITCHELL VITAL STATISTICS (from Montpelier):
(Key: res = residence; bur = buried; s/o = son of)
James b Ire., potter, d 2 Jul 1859 age 43y at Middlebury;
bur Central Cemetery; s/o **Daniel Mitchell.**
James, res Irasburg m there 1 Jan 1845 Elizabeth Sargent.
James d 5 Nov 1834 age 25y at Williston; bur Old Cemetery.
James, res Peterborough, NH, m 7 Apr 1814 Sally Joy at
Marlboro.
James, res Bath, NY, m 31 Jan 1802 Anna Ring at Hardwick.
James, res Lempster, NH, m 18 Sep 1832 Mrs. Polly Grout at
Weathersfield; he d 18 Feb 1862 age 76y, bur Weathers-
field Burying Grounds.
James b 3 Apr 1867 Vergennes, s/o **Patrick & Margaret/Mag-
gie Mitchell,** both b Ire.
James B. d 3 Apr 1854 age 4m at Glover, bur West Glover,
s/o **William & Susanna Mitchell.**
James Edward s/o **James Mitchell** b 28 Mar 1854 Springfield.
James H. d 9 Jul 1866 age 30y at Burlington; bur Elmwood
Cemetery, s/o **James & Sarah Mitchell.**

Miscellaneous Mitchell Data

(Vital Statistics in Vermont con't)

MITCHEL/MITCHELL:

James W. s/o **James & Jane Mitchell** d 11 Jan 1857 age 3m 16d
at Bennington; bur Village Cemetery.
John m 30 Dec 1813 Miriam Grover at Stamford.
John, Jr. b 18 Apr 1784 at Georgia, VT, s/o **John Mitchell.**
John, res. Isle La Mott, m Nov 1854 Catherine Gooddess at
Isle La Mott.
John, res Ackworth, NH, m 15 Mar 1818 Sally Wallace at
Berlin.
John, res Rockingham, m 7 Jan 1823 Lucretia Mason at
Rockingham.
John, b Canada, d 18 June 1869 age 63y at Milton; married.
John d 15 Apr 1867 age 87y 7m 18d at Coventry; widowed; bur
Village Cemetery; s/o **John & Mary** (Lines) **Mitchell.**
John d 6 Dec 1838 age 67y at Sharon; wife, Martha.
John d 22 Nov 1843 age 2m at Glover; bur at Glover.
John b1804 d 10 Jan 1833 at St. Albans; bur St. Albans.
John b 8 Aug 1863 at Burlington, s/o **Jonathan** b Canada;
spouse listed as L____ .
John b & res Alburg, m1) 21 Oct 1867, age 21, Sophia Babba
at Alburg; s/o **Orrin & Adaline Mitchell.**
John b 17 Aug 1868 Ferrisburg, s/o **Patrick & Margaret/Mag-
gie Mitchell**, both b Ire.
John b 3 Nov 1869 Burlington, s/o **Zeb & Annie** (Blair) **Mit-
chell** (Zeb b Brandon; Annie b Burlington).
John C. d 25 Aug 1823 age 28y at Williston; bur Old Cem.
John E., res Walpole, NY, m 29 Dec 1857 Nancy O'Brien at
Westminster.
John M. d 5 Feb 1865 age 13y at Middlebury; bur Central
Cemetery; s/o **James & Betsey Mitchell.**
John N. d 22 Nov 1841 age 21y at St. Albans; bur St. Albans
Point; s/o **Samuel & Nancy Mitchell.**
John R. b 20 June 1787 Chester, s/o **Thomas & Lucy Mitchell.**
Michael, Burlington m 4 Nov 1816 Sally Telmiter at Essex.
Robert b Scotland s/o **James & Margaret Mitchell**, age 38,
m2) 31 Dec 1867 Julia A. Wilkins at Glover.
Robert, Jr. b Palmer, MA, res Lyndon, d 29 Jul 1860 age 77y
5m 15d at Sheldon; wife Susanna; he was s/o **Robert &
Sarah Mitchell** (Sarah b Scotland).
Thomas b 8 Mar 1785 Chester, s/o **Thomas & Lucy Mitchell.**
Thomas J., res Sheffield, s/o **Solomon & Hannah Mitchell**,
age 27, m 3 Mar 1870 Persis Allard at Wheelock.

Miscellaneous Mitchell Data

(Vermont con't)

1790 Federal Census of Vermont:
(Key: m/f = male/female; ov = over age; un = under age)
Chittenden Co:
George Mitchell 1 m ov 16 (Huntsburgh Twp)
John Mitchell 1 m ov 16, 2 m un 16, 3 f (Smithfield Twp)
Rutland Co.:
Ichabod Mitchell 2 m ov 16, 2 m un 16, 6 f (Fair Haven)
Windham Co:
Joshua Mitchell 1 m ov 16, 1 m un 16, 2 f (Townsend Twp)
William Mitchell 1 m ov 16 2 f (Townsend Twp)
Windsor Co:
Thomas Mitchell 1 m ov 16, 4 m un 16, 1 f (Chester Twp)

VIRGINIA

Pittsylvania Co., VA Marriages 1767-1805, Catherine Lind-
  say Knorr, compiler:
MITCHEL/MITCHELL:
Ann to Thomas Lovelace ___ 1799
Daniel to Sarah Bradley 11 Feb 1790
Elizabeth, d/o Sarah, to Hugh Reynolds 21 Sep 1801
Elizabeth to Burdet Roach ___ 1795
Frederick to Patsy Perkins, d/o Mary, 18 Nov 1799
Isaac to Anna Perkins, d/o Mary, 7 Dec 1801
Jane, d/o Sarah, to Richard Parris 26 Feb 1805
James to Agitha Dalton, d/o Robert, 25 Nov 1768
James to Sarah Waren Hubbard 28 ___ 1779
James to Winifred Lockett 29 Sep 1790
John to Anne Atkins, surety Edw. Atkins, 15 Oct 1804
Lucy to Robert Gilmore 18 Jan 1785
Polley to James Loveland, sur Wm. G. Mitchell, 19 Jan 1802
Richard to Susanna Richardson, surety George Mitchell,
  15 Feb 1794

Pittsylvania Co., VA Tax Lists 1782 & 1785:
(Key: wh = whites; bl = blacks; dw = dwelling; bldg =
other buildings)
Henry Mitchell 10 wh (1782); 10 wh, 1 dw, 2 bldg (1785)
James Mitchell 6 wh 2 bl (1782); James 6 wh (1782); James
  8 wh 1 dw 6 bldg (1785); James 8 wh 1 dw 2 bldg (1785);
  James 7 wh 6 bldg (1785).
Michael Mitchell 2 wh 1 dw

Miscellaneous Mitchell Data

William Mitchell 3 wh (1782); William 5 wh (1782); William 6 wh 2 bldg (1785).

MISCELLANEOUS

Hubbards History & Genealogy, Leslie S. Hubbard, 1974:
James M. Hubbard, M.D. b1853 near Houston, Texas Co., MO, s/o John H. & **Louisa C. (Mitchell)** Hubbard; John H. was b Randolph Co., MO; Louisa (Mitchell), b TN, was d/o **Spencer M. Mitchell,** one of the 1st settlers of Texas Co., MO and 1st sheriff of that county (p132).
Roswell Hubbard b1780 s/o Moses & Mabel (Hopkins) Hubbard, m1) **Sarah Mitchell;** lvd Northampton, MA (p160).
William Hubbard b1781 s/o Edmund & Margaret (Gaylord) Hubbard m1) Mercy Holbrook; m2) Sarah Holbrook; had ch William b1808 m **Laura Mitchell;** Samuel b1812 m **Venetta Mitchell;** Andalusia b1816 m **Newell Mitchell** (p160).

The Calvin Families, by Claude W. Calvin, 1945:
John Franklin Calvin b1867 Edgar Co., IL s/o Raleigh Bell Calvin II & Livonia H. Long, m1889 **Minnie Belle Mitchell** b1867; 7 ch (pp 285, 296).
Nancy Calvin d/o James Calvin & Susannah Puckett of Christian Co., KY m 7 May 1807 **Edward Mitchell** (p363).

For King Or Country, pub by Orange Co., CA Gen. Soc., Box 1587, Orange, CA 92668 (contributions of members):
Elizabeth Banta b 10 Sep 1789 Saratoga Co., NY d/o Hendrich & Engeltje (Schermerhorn) Banta, m **Hugh Mitchell** (V.I:13 Edgar R. Barton).
Elizabeth Rogers d/o Thomas Rogers & Penelope Chancellor (m1810 Orange Co., VA) m **Robert Mitchell** per in Jackson Co., MO where her par moved ca1840 (V.I:45 Caroline Vosskuhler).
William Norwood Branch b1886 Warren Co., NC m1) Icy Maud Amelia Christian b1891 Logan Co., WVA, d/o **Emma Lodosky Mitchell** & Albert L. Christian (p37 Agnes Pearlman)
Patterson Christian b1828 s/o James Pine & Anne (Moore) Christian of Logan Co., WVA m1) ca1848 **Mary Ann Mitchell;** Paren C. Christian b1833, bro of Patterson, m1854 **Isabel J. "Ibbie" Mitchell,** d/o **Jordan D. Mitchell** & Isabel J. Gore (V.I:55 Agnes Pearlman).

Miscellaneous Mitchell Data

(Abstracts from <u>For King Or Country</u> con't)

Albert Leander Christian b1865 Boone Co., WVA m1886 Logan Co., WVA his 1st cous **Emma Lodosky Mitchell** b1870 in Boone Co., WVA, d/o **Micajah G. Mitchell** & Clarinda White (V.1:56 Agnes Pearlman).
NOTE: The preceeding Mitchells are traced back in V.II pp 183-86 to **Archelaus Mitchell, Sr.** who d1799 Amherst Co., VA, leaving wid Hannah & ch: **(i)** Archelaus Jr. m1791 Spicey Goodwin; **(ii)** John; **(iii)** Patsy m1792 John B. Trent s/o Henry; **(iv)** Thomas m1792 Eady Trent d/o Henry; **(v)** Bowling m1805 Nancy White d/o Arthur; **(vi)** Stella m 1802 William Jones. Also refer to p110 (Goodwin), p274 (White), and p280 (Branch).

Margie E. Collins d/o Wm. Bryan Collins & Martha Ann Juvinall (m1856 Monroe Co., IN) m **Andrew Mitchell** and had ch Dora; Frank; Normal; Otto; Oscar; Fina; Stella; Orvall; Orlie, Ninette (V.I:69 Mary Van Manen).

John Eubank d1832 s/o James Eubank & Peggy Lewis of Henrico Co., VA, m **Sally Mitchell** (V.I:111 Esther T. Bohanon)

James Madison Nicholls b1818 s/o James Nicholls & Margaret Randolph of Muehlenberg Co., KY, m2) **Margaret Mitchell** (V.I:212 Caroline Vosskuhler).

John Burnham m1816 Isabella Malcolm of Newcastle (NH) b1795 d/o Allen Malcolm, Jr. & **Hannah Mitchell** (V.II:26 Dr. Ephraim Burnham Dunton).

Elizabeth Bye b1705 d/o John Bye & Sarah Pearson (Quakers of PA) m2)1730 **George Mitchell** of Wrightsville; had ch (V.II:34 Frances M. LeBlanc).

Judith Prewitt bc1751 VA d Shelby Co., KY, d/o Michael Prewitt & Elizabeth Simpkins, mc1770 **Daniel Mitchell**, Bedford Co., VA (V.II:217 Doris E. Dean & Ralph H. Dean).

Lulu Belle Rutherford b1871 d1944 d/o Isaiah A. Rutherford & Evelyn Gertrude Ellis (m1868 Bradford, OH) m1890 **Mr. Mitchell** in MO; had sons Donald b1894; Lynn b1896 (V.II:241 Doris Palmer Buys).

<u>Mitchell Family Record</u>, by J. Montgomery Seaver, p32, lists the first names of 789 Mitchells who served in the American Revolution from the respective colonies. (Copy at the CT State Library, Hartford, CT)
Connecticut: Amasa, Asahel Jr., David (4), George, Ishabod, James, John (6), John Jr., John B.(3), Joseph (2) Matthew, Oliver, Rueben, Samuel (4) Simeon, Thomas (2),

Miscellaneous Mitchell Data

(Mitchells in the American Revolution con't)

William (11), Zephaniah (3); **Delaware:** George (2), Isaac, James (7), John (13), Joseph (7), Nathaniel (7), William; **Georgia:** Charles, David, Eleanor, Francis (2), George B., Henry (5), John (5), Reuben (2), Robert (7), Sarah, Thomas (7), William (20); **Maryland:** Aaron (7), Andrew, Charles, Conrad, Edward, Francis (5), Henry, Ignatius, Isaac (3), James (2), John (18), Levin, Miles, Nathan, Nathaniel; Richard (6), Robert (9), Thomas, William (7); **Massachusetts:** Abiel, Abner, Amos, Bela, Benjamin (3), Benjamin Jr., Bradford, Bradley, Caleb, Cuff, David (5), Day, Dominicus, Dummer, Ebenezer (2), Edward (4), Eliphay, Elisha (2), Francis (2), George, Gregory, Harvey, Henry, Harton, Hugh (2), Isaac, Jacob, James (8), James Jr., James Mills, Jeremiah, Jesse, Job (3), John (17), Jonathan (2), Joseph (3), Joshua (2), Josiah, Jotham, Nathan (2), Nathaniel, Peter, Reuben, Richard, Robert (4), Rothens, Samuel (5), Samuel Jr., Seth, Stephen (3), Thomas (7), Timothy, William (8); **New Hampshire:** Benjamin (2), Caleb, Charles (4), David, Francis (4), George (2), Hugh, Isaac (12), James (5), John (30), John W., John Jr., Joseph (2), Joshua (2), Josiah, Michael, Philip, Robert (10), Samuel (15), Samuel, Jr., Thomas (8), William (7); **New Jersey:** Benjamin, Edward (2), George, Jacob, James, John (7), Joseph, Martin (2), Reuben, Richard, Thomas (2), William (2); **Pennsylvania:** Abraham (3), Alexander (8), Andrew (6), Charles (2), David (14), Edward, Ezekiel (2), Francis (2), George (5), Henry (5), James (28), Jesse (3), John 57), Joseph (18), Joshua, Mathew (2), Matthew, Michael (4), Nathaniel (5), Nicholas, Paul, Peter, Philip, Richard, Robert (21), Ross (4), Samuel (24), Simon, Thomas (22), William (22); **Rhode Island:** Elisha (4), Thomas (12); **Vermont:** Beriah, William; **Virginia:** Archelaus (2), Archibald, David, Edmund, Frederick, George, Henry (3), James (2), Jesse, John (7), Joseph (4), Mark, Nathaniel, Oliver, Peter (2), Ralph, Reaps, Reps, Richar (2), Rober (6), Ross, Samuel (2), Stephen (3), Thomas (4), William (8), Wyatt.

QUERY LETTERS

Annie Arcilia Mitchell b 7 Mar 1860 Cass Co., TX, youngest of 2 full sisters & 2 full brothers; m 8 Aug 1886 to

Miscellaneous Mitchell Data

(Query Letters con't)

Thomas Edward Loer in McClennan Co., TX; d 4 Feb 1904 in
Bosque Co., TX; prob bur Harris Creek Cem. where her bro
Jerome is bur; her dau Esther (Loer) White b Mar 1894 TX
wrote that her mother had brother "Rome" Mitchell, sisters Fannie Crain and Maria Watson, half-brother Frank,
half-sisters Mandy & Dicie; her mother's parents left TX
for Mexico with a group in a covered wagon train; the parents d there; her mother returned to McClennan Co., TX
where her brother & sisters lived; names of Annie Arcilia
Mitchell's parents unknown. (Joyce E. Jones, 956 Windy
Meadow Dr., Plano, TX 750123 - 1980)

Houston Mitchell m Isabel Whorton in Edinburg, Scotland
& came to U.S. ca1784; he was killed in the War of 1812; ch
(i) Gavin b1795 OH m 31 Mar 1812 Rebecca Collier Highland
Co., OH; ca 1821 to Edinburgh, IN; Rebecca d1839 & Gavin
m2) Jane Allen, wid; Gavin d at age 82y; **(ii)** Isabella m
17 Aug 1809 John Henderson (prob in KY); **(iii)** John b 24
Jan 1780 PA; d 12 Dec 1854 Johnson Co., IN. (Ray Banta,
8805 Madison Ave. #308-B, Indianapolis, IN 46227 - 1981)

Isaac A. Mitchell bc 1782 PA m Sarah _____ b PA; lvd Ripley, Brown Co., OH (census, wife, 2 sons, 4 dau); purchased land 1835 at Hennepin, Putman Co., IL; 1850 lvg in Ripley, Brown Co., OH, age 68; will there (not dtd); Isaac in
77th year & "very sick;" son **Thomas B. Mitchell**, Russell-
ville, exec; life interest to wife Sarah; at her death,
property to be sold & proceeds to go to ch & ch of dec'd
ch; dau **Margaret Mitchell** b 1816 PA m 1 Oct 1835 Moses
Slayton Short at Hennepin, IL (Isaac gave consent); 1900
census San Luis Obispo Co., CA lists Margaret Short, age
84, widow, b Feb 1816 PA, par both b PA. (Barbara Hubbard,
13569 Wichita Dr., Magalia, CA 95954 - 1982)

James A. Mitchell m 17 Oct 1850 Mary Jane Skidmore in
Brown Co., IN; his sister **Lucinda Mitchell** b 1829/30 in
Franklin Co., IN m 17 Dec 1846 William Skidmore in Brown
Co., IN; 8 ch (Skidmore) b in Brown & Johnson Cos., IN;
1868 to Piatt Co., IL where Lucinda d 1886/87; father b NC
& mother b KY (census); it is "known" that Lucinda was a
half-breed Indian. (Timothy M. Blomquist, 21 Electra
Dr., Hot Springs, AR 71913 - 1983)

James Coffield Mitchell b 10 Mar 1786 Augusta Co., VA
s/o **James Mitchell** & Mary Coffield; d 7 Aug 1843 MS; as a
young man moved to present day Sevier Co., TN; m there on

(Query Letters con't)

7 May 1807 Margaret Lewis b1790 dc1836; James C. was the
Solicitor Gen'l of 2nd District of TN 1813-1817; member
of U.S. Congress from TN 1825-1829; judge of 11th Circuit
1830-1836; moved to Hinds Co., MS ca 1837 & was unsuccessful candidate for Governor on the Whig ticket; was a member of the MS House of Representatives when he died 1843.
(Mrs. Margaret Leary, 6401 Winston Drive, Bethesda, MD
10817 - 1986)

James Franklin Mitchell b Aug 1813 TN m1) Catherin ____
bc 1811 TN; m2) Eva ____ bc 1817 VA; m3/4?) 14 Jan 1891
Mary Ann Couch; d aft 1905 Boone Co., AR; per a grdau.,
James Franklin's father was **Mark Mitchell,** & Mark's father was **Wilain Mitchell;** both were b & raised in London, and
"lived under the sound of Big Ben." Mark came to America
as a stowaway; landed near Philadelphia, PA at the start
of the Rev. War; joined & served all thru the war; wounded
in neck & shoulder. Children of James Franklin Mitchell
by 1st mar: **(i)** Susan bc1835 TN; **(ii)** William bc1837 TN;
(iii) Jane bc1839 AR m ____ Dunnaway; **(iv)** Nancy bc1843
AR; **(v)** Malinda bc1844 AR; **(vi)** Catherin bc1846 AR; **(vii)**
Mark Lafayette bc1848 AR m Polly Dawes (Doss?); both dc
1876 Boone Co., AR. Ch by 2nd mar: **(viii)** Matilda E. bc
1856 AR m 1 Jan 1878 James W. Slape; **(ix)** Isaac Jasper bc
1858 AR; **(x)** Mary bc 1864 AR m 7 May 1881 Leroy Ussery in
Boone Co., AR. (John D. Denny, 1455 E. 52nd Place, Tulsa,
OK 74105 - 1986)

John Mitchell b1744 Londonderry, NH, settled 1767 at
Bridgewater, NY nr Bristol where he d 19 Mar 1816; m 2 Dec
1767 Lydia Johnson of Hampstead, NY, b 1744/47 d 8 Nov
1827; ch: **(i)** John b 19 Oct 1768; **(ii)** Charles b 3 Nov 1770
m Margaret Morse; **(iii)** Sarah b 15 Oct 1772; **(iv)** Betsey b
8 Mar 1775; **(v)** Robert b 8 Apr 1777 m Abigail Morse;
(vi) Anna b 26 May 1779 m Jacob Barnard; **(vii)** Molly b 8
May 1781; **(viii)** Ruth b 22 May 1785; **(ix)** M___bal b 12 Oct
1788 m Rebecca Nutting. (D.A.R. papers of Lora Edith
Brown Courser, Bath, ME, 1917, Nat'l #107290)

John Mitchell m Nancy Edgar; blacksmith in early Harri-
son Co., OH; ch: **(i)** Permilla b 27 Dec 1832 PA d 1925 m
Thomas Irons; **(ii)** John, sharpshooter in Civil War; on
march to the sea with Sherman; d just short of age 100y in
Mahomet, IL, last Union soldier to die in IL. (Evelyn
Thomas, 419 Harding St., Medina, OH 44256 - 1983)

Miscellaneous Mitchell Data

(Query Letters con't)

John Mitchell m Agnes Vye, d/o Harry; son **John** m Evelyn Weeks & had dau. **Mary Mitchell** b 4 Dec 1576, bur 20 Sep 1648, m 10 Oct 1602 Rawkey Dolbere. (Wilma Lea, 1460 Cherry Garden Lane, San Jose, CA 95125; ref: "Computerized Surname Index.")

John Mitchell b 11 Dec 1803 NY (per Chemung Co.); d 25 Nov 1876, bur Mitchell's Corners Cemetery, Erin, Chemung Co., NY; m Caroline ____ b 11 Feb 1808 (PA or NY) d 3 May 1880; ch: **(i)** Anna Eliza b 14 Aug 1832 PA d 3 Apr 1919 Chemung Co., NY m1) Rulandus B. Warren; m2) Amasa Herrington; **(ii)** Adeline bc 1835 PA; **(iii)** Calista C. "Kitty" bc 1840 PA m1) Stoddard Maxwell; m2) Fred A. Phillips; **(iv)** Stella b 2 Jan 1842 NY d 14 Jan 1895 unmar; **(v)** John Cresswell b 1845 NY d 1929 Elmira Heights, NY m Mary Emily Pierce; **(vi)** James R. bc1848 d1929 m Malona ____. (Shirley Tuthill, 929 W. Clinton St., Elmira, NY 14905 - 1983)

Mary Mitchell d/o **Nathaniel** (Rev. War soldier) m John Sharp bc1771 PA; to Washington Co., OH ca1800; made an improvement on east side of Little Muskingum river nr Newport Twp line; associate judge of common pleas; commissioned judge of superior court a few days bef he d 1823; wife & 10 ch survived him. A John Sharp & a **John Mitchell** bought land together in Marietta, Washington Co., OH patent dtd 12 Jul 1811; a Mary Sharp, w/o John, d 17 June 1821 aged 38y. Ref: "History of Washington Co., OH," H.Z. Williams, 1881, p657; D.A.R. Cemetery Rec., Beach Grove Presby. Church Yard inscriptions. (Lillian Hooks, 1750 Prefumo Cnyn Rd., #56, San Luis Obispo, CA 93401 - 1986)

Mary Mitchell b 19 Jul 1801 St. Glivias, Cornwall, Eng., per d/o **James & Anne**; m 16 Mar 1825 Richard Hocking; she d 6 May 1833 Eng; Richard m2) 22 May 1835 **Eliza Mitchell** sister of Mary; to Morgan Co., IL bef 1841; Richard Hocking d 1879; Eliza bur next to him under name of Burridge; Mary's ch (HOCKING): **(i)** Charles Mitchell b 17 Jan 1826 Eng. m 10 Oct 1852 Martha Fletcher; Eliza's ch (HOCKING): **(ii)** Richard Edmund b 23 Apr 1836; **(iii)** Joseph James b 27 Sep 1837; **(iv)** Eliza Jane b 2 Aug 1840 d 27 Oct 1841; **(v)** Frederick George b 10 Feb 1844; **(vi)** George b 28 Sep 1858. (Carol H. Western, 403 E. Colegrove St., Assumption, IL 62510 - 1987)

Robert Mitchell b Londonderry, Ire. in late 1600's, m Mary Tunnis of Edinburgh, Scotland; to Lancaster, PA, and

Miscellaneous Mitchell Data

(Query Letters con't)

Bedford Co., VA; 13 ch. Not proved, but per a grson was **Robert Mitchell** m Sarah Shipley (the Shipley family came to America from Eng. ca1750, settling in Lunenburg Co., VA); Robert & Sarah lvd NC; left 1789 by horseback for KY; they were attacked by Indians, wife Sarah slain, dau. **Sarah** carried off; a son **Daniel** settled in Washington Co., KY; after the Wayne treaty, his sister Sarah was returned & lived with him and her uncle & aunt, Richard & Lucy (Shipley) Berry; the Berry's also took in another niece Nancy Hanks, d/o Sarah (Shipley) Mitchell's sister, Nancy; **Robert Mitchell** drowned in Dix River nr present day Dix River dam in KY while on a trip East; ch of Robert & Sarah (Shipley) Mitchell: **(i)** John b1771 m1798 Judy Bass b1774; lvd & d Green Co., KY; slaveholder; 8 ch incl Josiah & John Bass Mitchell. **John Bass Mitchell** b1807 m 8 Jan 1835 Elizabeth P. Edwards; she d KY; he d MO; had son **James Daniel Mitchell** b 8 Mar 1844 Green Co., KY m 8 Dec 1864 Edie A. Shofner b 12 May 1844; to Sangamon Co., IL 1883 with 7 ch; James D. d 19 Dec 1924; Edie A. d 18 Oct 1915; both bur Pleasant Plains Cem., Sangamon Co., IL. (Lester G. Pennick, Franklin, IL - 1987)

Samuel Mitchell bc 1785 PA m Hope Bishop bc1786 Culpeper Co., VA, d/o Josiah & Susanna (Inskeep) Bishop of VA & Zane Twp., Logan Co., OH; Samuel to Union Co., OH by 1816; sold land on west side of Darby River & went to Clinton Co., IN 1830; will dtd 1858 Frankfort, IN, names only two daus. (Marguerite N. Lambert, 1200 Earhart Rd., #419, Ann Arbor, MI 48105 - 1986).

Solomon Mitchell b1791/93 CT m Mary/Mariah Bradley; in service War of 1812; ch: **(i)** H. B.; **(ii)** Francis Leroy b 1829 Syracuse, NY; **(iii)** Eber Murray b1836; **(iv)** Calista. (Pauline Nichols, P.O. Box 21, Gibbon, NE 68840 - 1982)

Thomas Mitchell m1) Susannah_____; m2) Ann_____; patented land 1710 Baltimore Co., MD; ch by 1st mar: **(i)** Susannah; **(ii)** Richard b 26 Aug 1710. Ch by 2nd mar: **(iii)** Hannah b Easter Monday 1716 m John Johnson; **(iv)** Thomas b Feb 1719 m Hannah Osborn; **(v)** Kent b Jan 1724 m Hannah Barnes; **(vi)** Edward b 21 Apr 1727 m Rachel_____; **(vii)** William b 10 Aug 1730 m Sarah Osborn. (Esther G. Hannon, 407 East Cherry, Normal, IL 61761 - 1980)

William Mitchell bc1802 ME m Lydia Prosser bc1809 NY; in Northville Twp., LaSalle Co., IL in 1850 census; ch per

Miscellaneous Mitchell Data

(Query Letters con't)

census: **(i)** Samuel 18 NY; **(ii)** George 16 OH; **(iii)** Luther
E. 12 OH (b 18 Aug 1838 Huron Co., OH m 24 Dec 1855 Sarah M.
Smith, Ottawa, IL); **(iv)** Zachariah 7 IL; **(v)** Susannah 5
IL; also lvg with the family was Susannah Mitchell, age
60 ME. (Juanita M. Koskan, Rt. 1, Wood, SD 57585 - 1986)
   William C. Mitchell m Diana Baxter; ch born betw 1850-
1864: **(i)** Olney; **(ii)** Melvin; **(iii)** Eliza; **(iv)** Anna.
(Mary Baxter Harrell, 1408 Pineland Dr., Bainbridge, GA
31717 - 1987)

BIBLIOGRAPHY

(A listing of main sources used or consulted:)

Abbot, Susan Woodruff, comp., "Families of Early Milford, CT," Genealogical Publishing Co., 1979.
"American Heritage Civil War Chronology," American Heritage Pub. Co., Inc., New York, 1960.
Andrews, Charles M., "Our Earliest Colonial Settlements," Cornell University Press, Ithaca, NY 1933.

Bailey, Frederic W., "Early Connecticut Marriages," Genealogical Publishing Co., (1966 reprint).
Baker, C. Alice & Coleman, Emma L., "Epitaphs in the Old Burying Ground at Deerfield," 1924.
Baldwin, Rev. Elijah C., "Branford Annals" (in "Papers of the New Haven Colony Historical Society," Vol. III, New Haven, 1882).
Baldwin, Leland D. & Erickson, Erling A., "The American Quest," Vol. I, 1973.
Barbour, Lucius Barnes, "Families of Early Hartford, CT," Genealogical Publishing Co. (1982 reprint).
Bassett, T. D. Seymour, ed. & comp., "Outsiders Inside Vermont," Brattleboro, VT.
Bateman, Newton, ed., "History of Tazewell Co., IL, 1905.
Bateman, Newton & Selby, Paul, eds., "History of Effingham Co., IL," 1910.
Beers, F. W., "Atlas of Franklin Co., MA," 1871.
Beers, W. H., "History of Champaign Co., OH," 1881.
Beers, W. H., "History of Madison Co., OH," 1883.
Beers, W. H., "History of Union Co., OH," 1883.
Bent, Frank R., ed., "History of the Town of Essex," pub. by the Town of Essex, Chittenden Co., VT, 1963.
"Biographical Record of Clark Co., OH," S.J. Clarke Publishing Co., NY, 1902.
Bond, Henry, "Genealogies & History of Watertown, MA," 2nd edition, N.E.H.G.S., Boston, MA (reprint 1978/81).

Bibliography

Bowman, Fred Q., "Landholders of Northeastern New York,"
Genealogical Publishing Co., 1983.

Boyer, Carl III, "Ship Passenger Lists, National & New
England (1600-1825)," 1977.

Brainard, Lucy Abigail, "The Genealogy of the Brainerd-
Brainard Family in America 1649-1908," Vol. II, Part V,
(line of Caleb^2 Brainerd), 1908.

Bryan, Chester E., "History of Madison Co., OH," 1915.

Calvin, Claude W., "The Calvin Families," Edward Bros.,
Ann Arbor, MI, 1945.

Catton, Bruce, "Grant Takes Command," Little, Brown &
Co., 1968.

Catton, Bruce, "This Hallowed Ground," Doubleday & Co.,
Garden City, NY, 1955/56.

Chapman Bros., "History of Tazewell Co., IL," 1879.

Chapman Bros., "Portrait & Biographical Album of Rock
Island Co., IL," 1885.

Chapman Bros., "Portrait & Biographical Album of Vermilion & Edgar Cos., IL," 1889.

Chidsey, Donald Barr, "The War in the North," Crown Publishing Co., NY.

Clemens, William Montgomery, "American Marriage Records
Before 1699," (1977 reprint).

Crary, Catherine S., "The Price of Loyalty," McGraw-Hill
Book Co., 1973.

Cutter, William R., "Genealogical & Family History of
Central New York," 1912 (3 Vols).

Davis, Charles H. S., "History of Wallingford, CT," 1870.

Earle, Alice Morse, "Home and Child Life in Colonial Days"
(edited by Shirley Glubok), The MacMillan Co., 1969.

Earle, Alice Morse, "Stagecoach and Tavern Days," 1900
edition reissued 1969 by Benjamin Blom, IN, NY.

Evans, Elizabeth, "Weathering the Storm" (Women of the
American Revolution), Charles Scribner's Sons, NY.

Everts & Ensign, "History of Washington Co., NY," 1878
(reprint 1979 Heart of the Lakes Pub. Co., NY).

Everts, Louis H., "History of the Connecticut Valley in
Massachusetts," J. B. Lippincott & Co., 1879 (2 Vols).

Feldhake, Hilda Engbring, "Effingham Co., Illinois, Past
and Present," 1968.

Bibliography

Fisher, Sydney George, "Men, Women & Manners in Colonial Times," Vol. I, 1969 (reprint of 1897 edition).

Foote, Shelby, "The Civil War," Random House, NY, 1963.

French, Allen, "The First Year of the American Revolution," Houghton Mifflin Co., 1934.

Garraty, John A., "The American Nation," Vol. I, Harper & Row, 3rd edition, 1966.

Gillespie, C. Bancroft & Curtis, George Munson, "A Century of Meriden, CT," 1906.

"Great Battles of the Civil War," by the editors of Civil War Times Illustrated," introduced by William C. Davis, Gallery Books, NY.

Halley, William, "The Rights of the People Under the Laws of the State" (Illinois), Peoria, IL, 1881.

Hemenway, Abby Maria, ed., "Vermont Historical Gazateer," Vols. 1/3/4 ("History of Montpelier," D. P. Thompson).

Hesseltine, William B., ed., "Civil War Prisons," Kent State University Press.

Hill, Don Gleason, ed., "Dedham Records" (MA), Church and Cemetery 1638-1846, (1888).

"History & Proceedings of the Pocumtuck Valley Memorial Association 1870-1879," Vol. I, Deerfield, MA, 1890 (from "Ensign John Sheldon," by C. Alice Baker).

Holch, Lillian Hubbard, comp. & ed., "Sizer Genealogy," 1941, Brooklyn, NY.

Holmes, Frank R., comp., "Directory of the Ancestral Heads of New England Families, 1620-1700," 1964.

Hopp, Clara Lue, "Nettie Jane (Mitchell) Redman, Her Ancestors and Descendants," privately printed 1963.

"Hoult Record," published 1907.

Howe, Gilman Bigelow, "The Bigelow Family of America," published 1890.

Howe, Henry, "Historical Collections of Ohio," Vol. I.

Howes, Frederick G. & Shepard, Rev. Dr. Thomas, "History of the Town of Ashfield, Franklin Co., MA, 1742-1910."

Hurlbut, Henry H., "The Hurlbut Genealogy," 1888.

Jacobus, Donald Lines, "Families of Ancient New Haven" (CT), 1932.

James, Alma Lewis, ed., "The Ancestry & Posterity of Obil Beach," Blade Pub. Co., Fairbury, IL.

Jellison, Charles A., "Ethan Allen," 1969.

Bibliography

Johnston, Gen. Joseph E., C.S.A., "Narrative of Military
    Operations Directed, during the Late War Between the
    States, Indiana University Press, Bloomington, 1959.
Judd, Sylvester, "History of Hadley, MA," New Hampshire
    Pub. Co., reprint 1976 of 1905 edition.

Kellogg, Lucy M., "History of the Town of Bernardston,
    Franklin Co., MA, 1736-1900," published 1902.
Kaynor, Fay C., "Deerfield Probate Inventories and Ac-
    counts 1747-1800," published 1975.

LeBaron, Wm. Jr. & Co., "The History of Edgar Co., IL,"
    Chicago, 1879 (reprinted 1968 Unigraphic, Inc., IN).
"List of Pensioners on the Roll, Jan 1, 1883," Vol. III,
    (Edgar Co., IL), Genealogical Pub. Co., 1970.
Lock, John Goodwin, "A Genealogical & Historical Record
    of William Lock of Woburn," published 1853.

Manwaring, Chas. W., "Early Connecticut Probate Records,"
    Hartford District, 3 Vols.
Marrs, Mabel, "Marrs Family," Mennonite Press, 1977.
Melvoin, Richard I., "Communalism in Frontier Deerfield"
    (in "Early Settlement in the Connecticut Valley," A
    Colloquium at Historic Deerfield," 1984).
Miller, Rachel H. & Hannah, Pauline, comp., "Hannah Fam-
    ily Record 1747-1986," privately printed 1987.
"Minutes of the Methodist Conference Annually Held in
    America" (extracts), 1773-1813, Hitt & Ware, 1813.
Mitchell, J. Calvin, "Excerpts from the Crater of Gold,"
    Crater of Gold Pub. Co., Hammond, IN, 1918.
Mitchell, Lt. Col. Joseph B., "Decisive Battles of the
    Civil War, G. P. Putnam's Sons, New York, 1955.
Moore, Frank, "The Diary of the American Revolution,"
    edited by John Anthony Scott, 1967.
Morton, Doris Begor, "Philip Skene of Skenesborough,"
    Granville, NY, 1959.

Nelson, William, ed., "Documents Relating to the Colonial
    History of the State of New Jersey," Vol. XXI, 1664-
    1703, The Press Printing & Pub. Co., 1899.
"New Haven Historical Society Ancient Records Series,"
    Vols. I & II.
Nye, Mary Greene, "State Papers of Vermont," Vol. V,
    Petitions for Grants of Lands 1778-1811, pub. 1939.

Bibliography

O'Connor, Hyla, "The Early American Cookbook," Prentice-Hall, Inc., Englewood Cliffs, NJ, 1974.

"The Official Roster of the Soldiers of the American Revolution buried in the State of Ohio," D.A.R. publication (reprint 1973 by the Trumbull Co., Chapt. OGS).

"Ohio Source Records," pubished by the Ohio Genealogical Society, 1986 ("Other Ohio Records," contributed by Blanche Collins).

Partridge, Charles A., ed., "History of the Ninety-Sixth Regiment Illinois Volunteer Infantry, 1862-1865," Chapter XXXIV (Libbey Prison), 1887.

Pease, Theodore Calvin, "The Story of Illinois."

"Pekin, IL 1824-1974 Sesquicentennial: A History Book."

Perrin, William Henry, ed., "History of Effingham Co., IL," 1883 (1972 reprint, Unigraphic, Evansville, IN).

Pettengill, Samuel B., "The Yankee Pioneer," Charles E. Tuttle Co., Rutland, VT.

Pollock, W.D. & Schultz, R.G., "Gold Mining Areas & Trails & Roads of WHOA Navigation in Early Siskiyou Co." (Siskiyou Co. Museum, Yreka, CA), Mar 1957.

"Portrait & Biographical Album of Henry Co., IA," Acme Publishing Co., 1883.

"Portrait & Biographical Record of Macon Co., IL," Lake Publishing Co., 1893.

Randall, Ruth Palmer, "Mary Lincoln," Little, Brown & Co., 1953, pp 149-50.

Reece, Brig. Gen. J.N. (revised by), "Report of the Adjutant General of the State of Illinois," Vol. II, 1861-1866, Phillips Bros., Springfield, IL, 1900.

Roberts, George S., "Historic Towns of the Connecticut River Valley," Robson & Adee, Publishers, 1906.

Sandburg, Carl, "Abraham Lincoln, The War Years," Harcourt, Brace & Co., NY, 4 Vols., 1939.

Savage, James, "Genealogical Dictionary of the First Settlers of New England," Genealogical Pub. Co., 1965.

Schwarz, Jeanne M., "History of Galway, NY."

Seaver, J. Montgomery, "Mitchell Family Records" (at the Connecticut State Library, Hartford).

Sheldon, George, "History of Deerfield, MA," New Hampshire Publishing Co. (1972 reprint), 2 Vols.

Smith, E.C., "The Story of Our Names," Harper Bros., NY.

Bibliography

Smith, John Montague, "History of Sunderland, MA," E.A. Hall & Co., 1899.

Stiles, Henry R., "The History of Ancient Wethersfield, CT," Vol. II, The Grafton Press, NY, 1904.

Stiles, Henry R., "The History of Ancient Windsor, CT," Vol. II, 1859.

Sylvester, N.B., "History of Saratoga Co., NY," 1878.

Tepper, Michael, ed., "Passengers to America," Genealogical Publishing Co., 1977.

Tepper, Michael, ed., "New World Emigrants," Genealogical Publishing Co., 1980 (Vol. I).

Thompson, Francis M., "History of Greenfield, MA," 1904.

Thompson, Col. William, ed., "Reminiscences of a Pioneer," Chapt. III, Alturas, CA Plaindealer, 1912.

Torrey, Clarence Almon, "New England Marriages Prior to 1700," Genealogical Pub. Co. (reprint 1986).

Tuttle, Alva M., "Tuttle-Tuthill Lines in America," pub. by the compiler, Columbus, OH, 1968.

Vance, Brig. Gen. J.W. (revised by), "Report of the Adjutant General of the State of Illinois," Vol. III, 1861-1866, published in 1866.

Van Sellar, H., ed., "History of Edgar Co., IL," 1905.

Virkus, Frederick Adams, "Immigrant Ancestors," reprint 1980, Genealogical Publishing Co.

Waters, M. & Milliken, M., "Western Christian Advocate & Journal, obits. & mss. abstracts for Carolyn Scott Harrison, D.A.R. (Ref: DePauw University & Indiana State Library).

Wheeler, Richard, "The Siege of Vicksburg," Thomas Y. Crowell Co., NY, 1978.

Wiley, Bell Irwin, "The Life of Billy Yank," The Bobs-Merrill Co., Inc., 1952.

Magazines, Newspapers, Quarterlies

"Altamont Telegram," Altamont, Effingham Co., IL.

"Baptist Register Magazine," Oneida Co., NY.

"Branches & Twigs," Genealogical Society of VT, Vol. 4, No. 3 (Fall, 1975), p 122 (list of tenants of Philip Skene of Skenesborough, NY).

"Clinton Courier," Clinton, Oneida Co., NY.

Bibliography

Cott, Nancy F., "Divorce & the Changing Status of Women in Eighteenth Century Massachusetts" (William and Mary Quarterly, 3rd Series, V.33:4, Oct 1976, p 602).

Cuneo, Ernest, "Our Unshakeable Faith in America" (from American Legion Magazine, Feb 1987).

"Effingham Democrat," Effingham, Effingham Co., IL.

"Greenfield Gazette & Courier," Greenfield, MA.

"The Hoosier Genealogist," Sep 1978 issue (Jennings Co., IN Marriage Records 1818-1837).

"The Hoosier Journal of Ancestry" (special Jennings Co., IN issue).

"Journal Review," Crawfordsville, IN.

"Newman Independent," Newman, Douglas Co., IL.

"Paris Daily News," Paris, Edgar Co., IL.

"Paris Gazette," Paris, Edgar Co., IL.

"Piatt Co. Republican," Monticello, Piatt Co., IL.

"Rapid City Journal," Rapid City, Pennington Co., SD.

"Utica Observer," Utica, Oneida Co., NY.

Primary Sources

Connecticut:

Holbrook, Jay Mack, "Connecticut 1670 Census," Holbrook Research Institute, Oxford, MA, 1977.

Probate records of Hartford District (Wethersfield); Wallingford District (Wallingford & Meriden); New Haven District (Wallingford).

Vital Records (births, deaths, marriages) of Durham, Farmington, Guilford, Middleton, Wallingford.

Wallingford, CT Land Records, Vols. I & II.

Illinois:

Clay Co. Deeds, Clerk/Recorder's Office, Louisville.

Douglas Co., Newman City Cemetery (grst readings).

Edgar Co. Deeds, Probate records; grst readings Edgar, Franklin, Wynn cem; 1860 Mortality Schedule (Film 31-88, IL State Arch.); Bible records (in possession of Catherine M. Savoye & Chandler E. Mitchell); Shutt, Philip R., "Edgar Co., IL Marriage Returns," 1823-1869," copied Oct 1964.

Effingham Co. Deeds, Probate records; grst readings Old Turner, Little Prairie Baptist Church cem; "Effingham Co., IL Marriages" 1833-1877, 1878-1882, 1883-1888, pub. of the Effingham Co. Genealogical Society,

Bibliography

Effingham, 1987 & 1986; birth and death records.

Macon Co.: "Cemetery Inscriptions of Macon Co., IL,"
Vol. IV, Brown Cemetery, Macon Co. Historical Society, Decatur, IL.

Piatt Co. birth, death, marriage records.

Pike Co. Probate records.

Tazewell Co. grst readings Hirstein Cem.; probate re-
cords; deed records; research of Loree Bergerhouse,
Corrs. Sec'y, Tazewell Co. Genealogical Soc., P.O.
Box 312, Pekin, IL 61554.

Indiana:

Johnson Co. Marriage records.

Miami Co. Marriage records.

Iowa:

Henry Co. Probate, Marriage, Death records.

Jackson, Ronald Vern, "Iowa Census Records 1841-1849."

Massachusetts:

Franklin Co. Probate records.

Hampshire Co. - Ashfield: Proprietor's Book 1736-1803;
Town Records; tax lists; voters lists. Deerfield:
tax lists; 1st Congregational Church records 1733-
1762. Probate records; records of the Inferior Court
of Common Pleas; records of the Court of General Sessions of the Peace; research of Wendall B. Cook, Conway, MA (deceased).

Massachusetts Council Records, Vol. VI, pp 305 & 621,
Massachusetts State Archives, Boston.

Vital Records (births, deaths, marriages) to 1850 of
Ashfield, Bernardston, Charlemont, Conway, Deer-
field, Greenfield, Monson, Montague, Shelburne, and
West Springfield.

Worcester Co. Probate Records (Westborough).

Michigan:

Van Buren Co. grst reading Porter Cem.

New York:

Lewis Co. Deed and Probate records.

Oneida Co. Deeds, Probate records; "Cemetery Records in
the Town of Kirkland...", Vol. I (D.A.R. pub.); "Old
Clinton Burying Ground," Vol. 7 (D.A.R. pub., taken

from a booklet published at Clinton by J.B. & H.B.
Sykes, 1896); "Remsen-Steuben Cemetery Lists," Remsen-Steuben Historical Soc., Remsen, NY, Jul 1983;
tax lists; church records (Baptist); research of Vivian Brecknell, Coates Rd., Holland Patent, NY 13354.
Washington Co.: Records from the first town book of
Whitehall (formerly Skenesborough) on negative film
in possession of Doris Morton, Town Historian, Whitehall; "Whitehall Papers," Vol. XXI:102, Vol. XV:319
(Albany, NY State Library).

Ohio:
Brown Co. Deeds; "Early Ohio Tax Records," Esther W.
Powell (Brown Co. listing); research of Pat Donald-
son, P.O. Box 43, Georgetown, OH 45121.
Champaign Co. Probate Records; "Tombstone Records of
Champaign Co., OH," (prior to 1900), Urbana Chapter,
D.A.R., Vol. IV (Maple Grove); "Champaign Co., OH
Marriage Records," Probate Court, Urbana, OH (on film
at OH State Arch., Columbus); Nixon, Caroline R. &
Bolton, Emma Nixon, comp., "Burial Places of Cham-
paign Co., OH"; "Early Ohio Tax Records," Esther W.
Powell (Champaign Co. listing); family bible records
in possession of Jean M. Jackson, Zionsville, IN.
Clermont Co.: "Marriage Records of Clermont Co., OH
1800-1850," Clermont Co. Genealogical Soc., 1978.
Madison Co. Deeds, Probate records; "Caldwell's Atlas
of Madison Co., OH," pub. by J.A. Caldwell, Condit,
OH, 1875; "Marriage Records of Madison Co., OH," as
copied by Mrs. Ralph Oral Whittaker, D.A.R. publication, 1944; family bible records in possession of
Jean M. Jackson, Zionsville, IN.

South Dakota:
Pennington Co. Deeds, Probate records; tax lists; death
records; cemetery records (Rapid City); research of
Audrey Balcom, Rt. 8, Box 56, Rapid City, SD 57701.

Vermont:
Chittenden Co., Dept. of Vital Records (freeman's oaths
in Essex).

Washington:
Garfield Co. marriage records.

Bibliography

General - death records from the Vital Records Division
of the Dept. of Social & Health Services, Olympia.

Miscellaneous:

"D.A.R. Patriot Index," published 1967.
Family data supplied by descendants.
Federal Census Records of the United States (microfilm)
for the years 1790 through 1900 for CT, MA, VT, NY,
PA, OH, IL, IA, WI, MO, NE, IN, WA, OK.
National Archives, Washington, D.C., Revolutionary War
pension, bounty land, military papers.
National Archives, Washington, D.C., Civil War pension
and military papers.

INDEX

The index covers the main text except the allied lines chapter which is in alphabetical order. Not indexed are authors or persons appearing in book titles, persons with unknown surnames, or historical personages. Parents' names are not re-indexed where they appear in their children's paragraphs. No distinction is made in the index between Jr. and Sr. Titles such as Rev., Capt., etc. are not used unless a given name is unknown. Married females are indexed under maiden and married names when both are known. A name may appear more than once on the same page. Numbers in **boldface** indicate pages where persons appear in their own paragraph. Hyphenated numbers such as 117-22 means that name appears on all pages between and including those numbers.

BRAWNER Margaret 423 Meredith 423
BRAY Celia 405 Joanna 388 John 405
BRECKINRIDGE Isabella 414
BREWER Adam 396 Catherine 396 Raymond R. 253 Samuel 46
BRICKER Mary Camilla 279
BRIGHT Mary L. 373 Septimus G. 373
BRIGGS Betsey 385 Mariah 381
BRITTIN Sarah 133
BROADWELL Mary 395
BROCK Elden James 266 Helen 266 Jane Ann 266 Stephen Edward 266
BROCKETT Elisha 421
BRODIN Betty 293 Catherine Tena 293 Peter 293
BROOKS Anne 64 Barnabas 64 Ebenezer 23
BROOMFIELD Elizabeth 419
BROTON/BROUGHTON Esther 57 Nancy 419 Wait 57
BROUN Deborah P. 353 Theodore M. 353
BROWN Alex 381 Caney 402 Charles 390 Drusilla Jane 409 Dudley 402 Electa M. 353 Emma 185 Etta 134 George 409 George M. 180 Harriet 115-6 351 Jacob 387 James 196 Jane 196 Jennett 226 Mary 381 387 390 Mary Ann 196 Mary C. 409 Maude 196 Myrtle 196 Nancy 354 Nella 196 Ruth 408 Susannah 391 Walter 196 William 196 409
BROWNFIELD John 371
BROWNING Eliza Boone 378 Francis 378
BRUNER Charlotte 379 George Leonard 379 Mary 378
BRZYCKI Sarah Theresa 326
BUCEK Sally 69 Schuyler 69
BUCK Daniel 350 Julia 350
BUCKINGHAM D. P. 201
BUCKNER Anthony H. 419 Isabella 419
BUELL Lydia 29
BUGBEE Hannah 58 Jotham 58
BUGG John 400 Rebecka 400

BUGLE Mary 381
BULL ___ (Capt.) 349
BULLINGTON John 374 Olivia 374
BULLOCK Jenny Minge 399 John 400 Mary 400-1
BURCH Diantha G. 189 Obed Leroy 189-90
BURNET(T) ___ (Miss) 417 Ann 417 John 408 Nancy 408
BURNHAM Isabella 429 John 429 John H. 139
BURNLEY Harriet 410
BURNSIDE Lovena 182 Mary Ann 196 William 182
BURRIDGE Eliza 433
BURSHUR Janean Kay 296 Stephen Anthony 296
BURT Ithmar 35 Jennie 138 J. Francis 137-8 Sarah Jane 138
BURTON A. G. 155 Hutching G. 402 Levy 374 Martha 400 Mary 374 402 Nancy 374
BUSB(E)Y Fanny 417 Nancey 400 William 400-1
BUSH Catherine Elizabeth 232
BUSHELL Rebecca 354
BUSHUE Irene Josephine 333
BUTKOVICH Mary Elizabeth 317
BUTLER Abigail 415 William 415
BYE Elizabeth 429 John 429 Sarah 429
BYERS Henry 373
CALHOUN Clark 210 Lulu B. 210 J. R. 210
CALHUS James 349
CALVERT Harriet Elizabeth 312
CALVIN David 121 172 Elizabeth 119 124 Ensign 156 Harriet Jane 172 Hiram 156 James 119 156 428 James W. 173 Jane 172 John Franklin 428 Livonia H. 428 Luther 122 172 Minnie Belle 428 Nancy 119 162 428 Raleigh Bell 428 Samuel 120 Susannah 428
CALWELL Ruth 104
CAMPBELL A. H. 412 Benjamin W. 331 Bessie L. 331 James B. 147 John 394 John Simpson 399 Maria 412 Mary Louise 335 Ocie Louise 329 Phebe A. 354

Index

CULLY Elizabeth 372
CUMINS Asa 116 Charlotte 115-16
Fidelia 116 James M. 116
CUMMING(S) Christopher Allen
316 Elizabeth Anne 316 Glenna
Dee 304 Henry Boone 315-16
James 304 Katherine Elizabeth
316 Mary Anne 316 Oswill McGee
316
CUNDIFF Jane 355
CUNNINGHAM Jane 383
CURL William 96
CURRIN Nancy 417
CURRY Elizabeth 419 James 120
Lucinda 120 Phebe 120 Robert
120
CURRYER Electa 405
CURTIS Stella E. 194
CUSHING Avis 386
CUSHMAN Belinda 412
CUSIK Candi Lee 335 Carrie Ann
335 Connie Louise 335 Jerry Lee
335 Mary Louise 335 Rebecca
Ann 335
CUTTS Sarah 391
DAFF Nancy 419
DAILEY Olive E. 264 Stewart 264
DAIRS Cynthia J. 359
DALAY Elizabeth A. 410
DALE George 423 Polly 423
DALLAM ___ (Mr.) 366
DALTON Agitha 427 Ida B.
179 Robert 427
DANBURY Amelia 209
DANIEL Aereatla F. 359
DARBY James A. 179 Olive O. 179
DARELY ___ (family) 352
DARES Cynthia S. 360 James 360
Lucinda 360
DARROW Martha E. 416
DAVENPORT Jemima 401 John 5
William 372
DAVIDSON Hannah 358 Jane 236
J. R. 234 Lizzie Belle 236
Robert 236 W. F. 410 Wm. T. 409
DAVIES(S) J. H. 89 Wm. 349
DAVIS Anthony Dwayne 309 Betty
Alleen 315 Catherine 417
Elizabeth 30 59 419 F. J. 416
Henry W. 363 Jane 263 Joseph

386 Major 261 Major H. 363
Margaret E. 261 Martha Jane
261 Mary 404 Matilda A. 374
Messenier 399 Nancy Leigh 309
Philip 355 Roxanna 354 Sally
408 Sarah 386 Walter 354
DAVISON Daniel D. 138 Margaret
A. 138
DAWES Polly 432
DAY Marthy A. 416
DEAN(E) ___ (Dr.) 117 Wm. 373
DEERING Roger 387 Sarah 391
DELASHMUT Rachel 194
DELAY Coleman 356
DE MAR Anita 304 Corinne 304
Donald 304 Frank Lawrence 304
Lorna Lucile 304 Michael 304
Zane 304
DEMING Olive 79
DEMMAS Catharine 362
DEMORAT Bette Louise 308 For-
rest Clarence 308 Gladys L. 308
DEMPSEY Elizabeth 424 Patsy 424
DEMSTER John 348
DENIO Aaron 27
DENNING Philip 397 Rachel 397
DENNIS Franklin 408 James
120 Martha Ann 408
DENNISON Dorothy 28 James 28
Lydia 28
DENT Vincent 348
DENTON Elisabeth 399 John 401
Samuel 399 401
DENVER Lydia Elizabeth 131
DESPANE Mary 355
DEVAL John 364 William 364
DEVENPORT Sethanny 373
DICKERSON Georgeanna 266
Henry 421 Nancy 421
DICKENSON/DICKINSON Charles
407 Elizabeth 76 407 Gideon 61
John 6 Lydia 104 Mary 6
DICKEY Hamilton 159 Mary 159
Rhonda G. 331
DICKMAN Fred 242 John 241-2
DICKSON Missouri 354
DIEL Zelda B. 321
DIMMIT Elener 408
DIMSEY George 405 Minerva 405
DINGLEY Betsey 386 Ruth 392

Index

Index

Index

Index

Index

Index

Index

Index

www.ingramcontent.com/pod-product-compliance
Lightning Source LLC
Chambersburg PA
CBHW070239290326
41929CB00046B/1887